Economic Analysis of Law in European Legal Scholarship

Volume 13

Series Editor

Klaus Mathis, Faculty of Law, University of Lucerne, Lucerne, Switzerland

Editorial Board Members

Pierluigi Chiassoni, University of Genova, Genova, Italy

Péter Cserne, University of Hull, Hull, UK

Bruno Deffains, University of Paris II - Sorbonne Universities, Paris, France

Thomas Eger, University of Hamburg, Hamburg, Germany

Mariusz J. Golecki, University of Łódź, Łódź, Poland

Andreas Heinemann, University of Zurich, Zurich, Switzerland

Régis Lanneau, University of Paris Nanterre and Sciences Po Paris, Paris, France

Aurélien Portuese, De Montfort University Leicester, Leicester, UK

Kai Purnhagen, University of Wageningen and Erasmus University Rotterdam, Wageningen, The Netherlands

Lucia A. Reisch, Copenhagen Business School, Copenhagen, Denmark

Anne-Lise Sibony, University of Louvain, Louvain-la-Neuve, Belgium

Endre Stavang, University of Oslo, Oslo, Norway

The purpose of the book series "Economic Analysis of Law in European Legal Scholarship" is to publish high quality volumes in the growing field of law and economics research in Europe, from a comprehensive theoretical and practical vantage point. In particular, the series will place great emphasis on foundational and theoretical aspects of economic analysis of law and on interdisciplinary approaches in European Legal Scholarship. Following Nobel laureate Ronald Coase's famous essay "The Problem of Social Cost" (1960) fifty years ago law and economics has become the lingua franca of American jurisprudence. In recent decades, law and economics has also gained widespread popularity in Europe and its influence on Legal Scholarship is growing significantly.

Therefore, the economic analysis of law in European Legal Scholarship academic book series illustrates how law and economics is developing in Europe and what opportunities and problems – both in general and in specific legal fields – are associated with this approach within the legal traditions of European countries. Rather than further exploring economic analysis as such, the main focus of this series lies on the implementation of economic methods in legislation and legal adjudication from a European perspective. It takes into account the particular challenges the European legal systems face. Volumes will address law and economics research in Europe from a critical and comparative viewpoint. The studies in this series are strong and bold narratives of the development of economic analysis of law in European Legal Scholarship. Some are suitable for a very broad readership.

Contributions in this series primarily come from scholars in Europe. The purpose is to provide the next generation of European lawyers with the models and skills needed to understand and improve the economic analysis of law in their own legal field. The series includes monographs focusing on specific topics as well as collections of essays covering specific themes.

More information about this series at https://link.springer.com/bookseries/11927

Klaus Mathis • Avishalom Tor
Editors

Law and Economics of the Coronavirus Crisis

 Springer

Editors
Klaus Mathis
Faculty of Law
University of Lucerne
Lucerne, Switzerland

Avishalom Tor
The School of Law
University of Notre Dame
Notre Dame, IN, USA

ISSN 2512-1294   ISSN 2512-1308 (electronic)
Economic Analysis of Law in European Legal Scholarship
ISBN 978-3-030-95875-6   ISBN 978-3-030-95876-3 (eBook)
https://doi.org/10.1007/978-3-030-95876-3

© The Editor(s) (if applicable) and The Author(s), under exclusive license to Springer Nature Switzerland AG 2022

This work is subject to copyright. All rights are solely and exclusively licensed by the Publisher, whether the whole or part of the material is concerned, specifically the rights of translation, reprinting, reuse of illustrations, recitation, broadcasting, reproduction on microfilms or in any other physical way, and transmission or information storage and retrieval, electronic adaptation, computer software, or by similar or dissimilar methodology now known or hereafter developed.

The use of general descriptive names, registered names, trademarks, service marks, etc. in this publication does not imply, even in the absence of a specific statement, that such names are exempt from the relevant protective laws and regulations and therefore free for general use.

The publisher, the authors and the editors are safe to assume that the advice and information in this book are believed to be true and accurate at the date of publication. Neither the publisher nor the authors or the editors give a warranty, expressed or implied, with respect to the material contained herein or for any errors or omissions that may have been made. The publisher remains neutral with regard to jurisdictional claims in published maps and institutional affiliations.

This Springer imprint is published by the registered company Springer Nature Switzerland AG
The registered company address is: Gewerbestrasse 11, 6330 Cham, Switzerland

Preface

This edited volume "Law and Economics of the Coronavirus Crisis" is a collection of papers, which were due to be presented at the annual Law and Economics Conference in Lucerne on the 16th and 17th of April 2021, co-organised by the University of Lucerne, Institute for Economy and Regulation, and the Notre Dame Research Program on Law and Market Behaviour (ND LAMB). Unfortunately, due to the global COVID-19 pandemic, the conference could not take place. Irrespective of these unfortunate circumstances, the editors and authors have created and edited a volume on the current issues associated with the economic analysis of the Coronavirus Crisis.

The main focus of this volume lies in presenting European legal scholars' perspectives on the issues surrounding the Law and Economics of the Coronavirus Crisis. These are complemented by insights from distinguished scholars from the USA, Israel, and Australia in order to foster the international dialogue among the different legal cultures. The thematic scope of this volume spans both the theoretical foundations and specific practical applications of the Law and Economics of the Coronavirus Crisis.

The authors examine the Law and Economics of the Coronavirus Crisis from behavioural economics, regulatory, technological, and various other perspectives. They do not only deal with the Law and Economics of the immediate impacts of and responses to the Coronavirus Crisis, but also highlight opportunities and propose new approaches that open up future possibilities because of the scholarly analysis of the current crisis.

On the one hand, already existing problems from different areas are placed in the current context of the Coronavirus Crisis and critically examined with a Law and Economics approach. On the other hand, new and unforeseeable challenges that have arisen as a result of the Coronavirus Crisis are addressed from a Law and Economics point of view.

We take this opportunity to thank all those who have contributed to the successful completion of this volume. Therefore, we would like to thank Lyanne Elsener, BLaw and Philipp Gisler for their reviewing and diligent proofreading. We are also grateful to Kay Stoll and Anja Trautmann at Springer International Publishing for overseeing the publishing process.

Lucerne, Switzerland Klaus Mathis
Notre Dame, IN, USA Avishalom Tor
October 2021

Contents

Part I Immediate Impact and Responses

Law, Economics, and Compliance in the Times of COVID-19:
A Behavioural Perspective................................... 3
Doron Teichman

Fake News in Times of Pandemic and Beyond: Enquiry into
the Rationales for Regulating Information Platforms............... 31
Mira Burri

A Behavioural Economics Approach to the Covidian Crisis.......... 59
Rute Saraiva

Contracts and the Coronavirus Crisis: Emergency Policy Responses
Between Preservation and Disruption........................... 105
Valentin Jentsch

The Giant Awakens.. 123
Behrang Kianzad

Balancing Lives and Livelihoods.............................. 177
Jean-Claude Misenga

Business Interruption Insurance and Covid-19: Between Embracing
Risk and Spreading Loss.................................... 215
Piotr Tereszkiewicz

Remote Teaching and Remote Exams Due to COVID-19: Some
Evidence from Teaching Law and Economics..................... 237
Ido Baum, Jarosław Bełdowski, and Łukasz Dąbroś

Part II Future Possibilities

Access and Development Rights in Pandemic Crises................ 251
Rolf H. Weber

COVID-19 and the Issue of Affordable Access to Innovative Health Technologies: An Analysis of Compulsory Licensing of Patents as a Policy Option 265
Muhammad Zaheer Abbas

Financial (In)Stability and the UN's Agenda 2030 on Sustainable Development in the Face of the Coronavirus Crisis 295
Giulio Peroni

Innovative Foods with Transparent Labels That Will Have the Next Pandemic for Breakfast 315
Danny Friedmann

The Coming of Age of Open Data 371
John M. Yun

Index 403

Part I
Immediate Impact and Responses

Law, Economics, and Compliance in the Times of COVID-19: A Behavioural Perspective

Doron Teichman

Abstract This Article explores which tools the legal system should use to promote pro-social behaviour in the face of the COVID-19 pandemic. More specifically, the Article compares nudges (i.e., choice-preserving, behaviourally informed tools that encourage people to behave as desired) and mandates (i.e., obligations backed by sanctions that dictate to people how they must behave), and it argues that mandates rather than nudges should serve in most cases as the primary legal tool used to promote risk reduction during a pandemic. The Article nonetheless highlights the role nudges can play as complements to mandates, and surveys numerous nudges that were used by regulators around the world.

1 Introduction

In December 2019, a novel coronavirus (SARS-CoV-2) causing an acute respiratory syndrome (COVID-19) appeared in the Chinese province of Wuhan.[1] The virus quickly spread across the world, triggering an unprecedented global public-health crisis. At the time of writing of this chapter, the global death toll of the pandemic has surpassed three million lives.[2]

Since the outset of the pandemic, policymakers around the world have recognized that as long as a treatment or vaccine for COVID-19 is not widely available, the main policy goal is to slow the rate of transmission of the virus by changing human behaviour. That means promoting social distancing, minimizing face-to-face interactions, and when these occur, using precautions such as face masks. Applying an economic framework to this goal suggests that the law should incentivize desirable behaviour through positive and negative payoffs. This chapter shifts the focus away

---

[1] Zhou et al. (2020), p. 270.
[2] See Abraham and Mann (2021).

D. Teichman (✉)
Hebrew University of Jerusalem, Jerusalem, Israel
e-mail: doron.teichman@mail.huji.ac.il

from incentives, and highlights the contributions of the behavioural analysis of the law to achieving this policy goal.[3]

Needless to say, this proposed focus on the role of behavioural insights does not suggest that the basic tenets of traditional models of deterrence and compliance should be ignored. The Israeli experience appears to suggest that in communities where the police refrained from enforcing public-health rules, wide violations were prevalent, and consequently, transmission rates were extremely high.[4] Effective enforcement of mandates clearly plays a key role in compliance decisions. Nonetheless, as this chapter will show, behavioural insights can also help policymakers who wish to bolster compliance. Simple interventions in the decision-making environment may make compliance easier, and prove to be an effective complement to enforcement efforts.

The chapter unfolds as follows: after this brief introduction, Sect. 2 examines the proper role of nudges within the legal response to the COVID-19 pandemic. As the analysis will demonstrate, nudges can play a constructive role within this response, but their choice-preserving nature makes them inadequate in regulating human behaviour during an infectious and deadly pandemic. Section 3 highlights concrete examples of nudges that have been used during the pandemic, and shows how insights from behavioural economics can guide both public messaging regarding the required behaviour, and the design of the decision-making environment. Section 4 turns from the individual to the community, by analyzing the effect of social norms on individual decision-making, and examining how the law can harness such norms to bolster compliance. Finally, Sect 5 shows how people's tendency to interpret reality to suit their self-interest and their cultural priors may hinder compliance with legal rules. It then reviews findings from the area of behavioural ethics, and demonstrates their applicability in the context of the pandemic.

2 Choosing the Means to Promote the Goal: Nudges v. Mandates

This section presents a general theoretical framework that defines the desirable role of behaviourally informed modes of regulation—commonly referred to as *nudges*—within the regulatory response to the pandemic.[5] It will do so while comparing nudges to the main alternative tool that regulators might opt for—namely, *mandates* that are backed by sanctions.[6]

---

[3] For previous contributions, see Teichman and Underhill (2021); Bonell et al. (2020); Van Bavel et al. (2020); Lunn et al. (2020a); Soofi et al. (2020).

[4] See Yoffie (2021).

[5] The term nudge was popularized by Thaler and Sunstein (2009).

[6] Policymakers could also use positive incentives (such as rewards, and subsidies) to encourage desired behaviour. For example, policymakers seeking to encourage the use of face masks might

Broadly defined, nudges are "low-cost, choice-preserving, behaviourally informed approaches to regulatory problems."[7] They do not "significantly chang[e] economic incentives", but rather affect behaviour without modifying prices, fines, or subsidies.[8] A key aspect of nudges is that they preserve individual liberty[9]—that is, they seek to guide and help people make their decisions, but do not remove any options from the choice set.

As research has demonstrated, regulators can often change people's decisions through nudges. Examples of such policies include defaults that steer people toward the desired choice;[10] decision menus that control the order in which options are presented;[11] sensory cues (such as pictures or ambiance) that prime people to choose certain options;[12] and smart disclosures that help people make decisions that best serve their long-term interests.[13] Over the past few decades, nudges have had a profound impact on public policy around the world, and various countries have even created special "Nudge Units" with the specific task of promoting the use of behaviourally informed regulation.[14]

Numerous jurisdictions have examined the possibility of placing nudges at the forefront of their regulatory response to the pandemic. Such regulation would focus on providing people with clear and simple information that can help foster social distancing, while retaining individual choice. Governments following this approach published recommendations to stay at home or self-isolate, sought to inculcate hand-washing habits, and issued advice regarding social (and even sexual) interactions.[15] Salient examples include Sweden (throughout the pandemic), and the United Kingdom (briefly, at the outset of the crisis).[16]

---

provide them free of charge. However, this tool seems ill-suited for dealing with a pandemic, given the likely costs of rewarding everyone who takes part in routine activities. On the role of positive incentives, see Galle (2012); De Geest and Dari-Mattiacci (2013).

[7] See Sunstein (2014), p. 719.

[8] Thaler and Sunstein (2009), p. 6.

[9] Thaler and Sunstein (2009), p. 5.

[10] See, e.g., Johnson and Goldstein (2003).

[11] See, e.g., Bucher et al. (2016).

[12] See, e.g., Wilson et al. (2016), pp. 51–52.

[13] See, e.g., Newell and Siikamäki (2014).

[14] For an overview, see Zamir and Teichman (2018), pp. 177–185.

[15] See e.g., Hutton, Bloomberg, 11 March 2020 (hand washing); Secretary of State, Health and Social Care (2020) Controlling the Spread of COVID-19: Health Secretary's Statement to Parliament. https://www.gov.uk/government/speeches/controlling-the-spread-of-covid-19-health-secretarys-statement-to-parliament (social interactions and travel) (last access 11 September 2021); Public Health Agency of Sweden (2020) Public Gatherings. https://www.folkhalsomyndigheten.se/the-public-health-agency-of-sweden/communicable-disease-control/covid-19/public-gatherings/ (public gatherings including weddings and graduation parties) (last access 11 September 2021); Buffy, The Guardian, 15 May 2020 (sexual interactions).

[16] See Pierre (2020) (describing Swedish policies); Sibony (2020) (examining the early British response).

While countries adopted a wide range of legal responses to the pandemic, most developed economies relied primarily on mandates, rather than on nudges:[17] they shut down significant sectors of their economies, and limited public gatherings. In addition, broad travel restrictions were implemented—including curfews, and rules restricting people's movement from their homes to certain limited purposes. International travel was curtailed to an even greater degree, and many countries chose to close their borders entirely. Individuals infected by the virus were placed in isolation, and those who were exposed to it were required to enter quarantine. These mandates were backed by significant penalties, and vigorously enforced.[18]

There are several reasons why nudges could not serve as the backbone of the legal response to the pandemic. One problem is the lack of relevant knowledge necessary to craft effective nudges. The situation faced by regulators in late 2019 and early 2020 was unprecedented, and the ability to extrapolate policies from existing research was extremely limited. Policymakers who sought to make people wear face masks in public, or to avoid large gatherings, simply did not know which nudge could achieve this goal. Mandates, on the other hand, require less information from the policymakers' viewpoint, who only need to specify the behaviour that is required or prohibited and implement an enforcement strategy.

However, even if behavioural scientists had provided policymakers with timely proposals for concrete nudges, it is unlikely that these interventions would have sufficed as the primary response to the pandemic. The key issue in this regard is the *effect size* associated with most nudges. While nudges may be able to change the behaviour of some of the population enough to create a statistically significant effect when examined experimentally, the scope of the behavioural change is often quite modest—either because they cause a large change among only a small subset of the population, or because they bring about an infinitesimal change among a very large group of people.

A recent systematic review of 100 studies and 317 effect sizes showed that nudges have a median relative effect size of 21%[19]—which is typically thought to be small.[20] This figure probably overstates the actual number, given a well-known publication bias in academic journals in favor of studies in which a given effect is documented.[21] A study into the effect size of nudges implemented in the field by various "Nudge Units" documented an average effect size of only 1.4%.[22] Moreover, the most effective nudge that pushes the median upward is the *default effect*[23]—which does not appear to be relevant to the COVID-19 context. While the modest effect size of many nudges may not undermine their efficacy, given the

---

[17] For an overview of the common measures used, see Hale et al. (2020).
[18] See White and Fradella (2020).
[19] See Hummel and Maedche (2019), pp. 48, 53.
[20] Cohen (1988), p. 25.
[21] See Hummel and Maedche (2019), p. 54.
[22] See DellaVigna and Linos (2020), pp. 2–3.
[23] See DellaVigna and Linos (2020), pp. 54–55.

low costs that many of them entail, it does suggest that nudges are insufficient, in and of themselves, to bring about a broad shift in behaviour in the context of a deadly pandemic.[24]

Finally, there is a more fundamental reason to believe that, however expertly behavioural scientists design nudges, such interventions are unlikely to suffice as the main regulatory response to a deadly infectious disease. In a pandemic, individual choices entail significant *negative externalities*—namely, individuals carrying the virus pose a risk not only to themselves, but also to those whom they might infect, and other people who are consequently infected further downstream. Furthermore, when the healthcare system reaches capacity, every additional sick patient reduces the level of care received by other patients (and in extreme situations, may result in scarcity, and denials of care). One study estimated the social cost associated with each additional COVID-19 infection to be possibly as high as $576,000—whereas the private cost internalized by decision-makers is only $80,000.[25]

Choice-preserving regulation may be useful in instances where the regulator wishes to help people make choices that are in their own best interests. In areas such as dieting, saving for retirement, or choosing financial products, a nudge may improve the choices that people make, thereby making it more likely to be adopted. The response to an infectious disease, however, is a *collective action* problem: many people may decide that it is in their best interest to ignore that nudge—creating negative externalities that, in this case, may prove fatal. Consequently, the likelihood that such nudges will prevail over time—certainly within the population as a whole—is low. Even Cass Sunstein—a devout proponent of nudges—acknowledges that in cases involving negative externalities "choice-preserving approaches might well prove inadequate."[26]

While mandates, rather than nudges, should probably be the primary legal tool used in the face of a major pandemic, nudges can still make useful contributions to the legal response to COVID-19. At times, nudges might *substitute* mandates. Policymakers may opt to use a nudge even though welfare could be enhanced by using mandates because there are constraints that limit their ability to put an effective mandate in place. This may arise, for example, in situations when constitutional rules prohibit certain types of legislation. Substitution may also occur due to political constraints, even when policymakers are legally allowed to enact mandates: for example, if a given mandate generates significant opposition, a nudge may be a useful compromise, which may be better than doing nothing.[27] It should be noted, however, that the availability of nudges on the political menu may undermine policymakers' ability or motivation to promote the first-best necessary regulation (i.e., mandates).[28] In such cases, low-cost and choice-preserving nudges may end up

---

[24] See Bubb and Pildes (2014), pp. 1597–1598.

[25] See Bethune and Korinek (2020), p. 33.

[26] See Sunstein (2017), p. 7.

[27] See Sunstein (2017), p. 19.

[28] See Hagmann et al. (2019), p. 488.

substituting much needed and more effective mandates, simply because they are an easier option, politically speaking.[29]

In the context of COVID-19, nudges have occasionally functioned as a substitute for mandates in situations where legislatures were constrained. In Japan, for example, much of the country's response to the pandemic was driven by strict constitutional restrictions, that limited the government's ability to enact key mandates—such as business closures, or shelter-in-place orders.[30] Consequently, the Japanese government put in place a framework of soft regulation, based on nudges and requests.[31] The regulation of places of worship is another case in point: while religious institutions pose a significant transmission risk,[32] they also play a critical role in the lives of many communities. In the United States, for example, the Supreme Court has struck down numerous limitations imposed by states on religious gatherings.[33] In such situations, guidelines and nudges may serve as a useful substitute for mandates, thereby helping to lower the risk of transmission.[34] Finally, the issue of vaccination appears to be particularly well suited for the use of nudges: countries that respect individual autonomy over medical procedures might be reluctant to mandate vaccination. In these circumstances, nudging may be one of the few tools available to policymakers.

Alternatively, nudges may serve as *complements* to a regulatory regime that is based on mandates. The traditional rational-choice model predicts that punishing violators creates specific and general deterrence, which reduces the level of undesirable activity. Based on this model, sanctions and enforcement efforts geared toward detecting violations are the key tools that policymakers have at their disposal.[35] However, a rich body of behavioural research suggests that peoples' decisions on whether or not to obey the law are governed by a wide range of additional factors[36]—such as social norms, subjective perceptions of probabilities, and the fairness of the legal system.[37] Building on this body of research, behavioural scientists can guide policymakers to the tools that may enhance compliance.

In the context of COVID-19, many public-health mandates imposed by regulators are self-enforcing or very simple to enforce: when countries close their borders, public schools, or other governmental services, non-compliance is generally not an option. Similarly, enforcing a lockdown of major business is relatively

---

[29] See Zamir and Teichman (2018), p. 177.

[30] See Cato et al. (2020), p. 2.

[31] See Cato et al. (2020), p. 2.

[32] See Quadri (2020).

[33] See, e.g., Robinson v. Murphy, 141 S. Ct. 972, 972 (2020) (suspending a capacity limit on houses of worship in New Jersey).

[34] See Villa, Pew Research Center, 27 April 2020.

[35] See Becker (1968), p. 169; For a later review, see Shavell (2004), pp. 473–530.

[36] For an overview of the literature, see Zamir and Teichman (2018), pp. 433–455.

[37] See, e.g., Nolan et al. (2008) (social norms); Guttel and Harel (2008) (probability estimates); Nadler (2005) (fairness of the law).

straightforward—since deviations are easily detected, and sanctions can be swiftly applied. This has been borne out by the aggressive measures taken by governments to quickly shut down the occasional rogue private school that opens,[38] or the defiant restaurant that has decided to open for in-house dining.[39]

Other public-health rules, however, are harder to enforce. Mandates concerning behaviours such as wearing face masks in public are much more difficult to implement. When limitations apply to behaviour within the home (such as limiting the number of house guests), enforcement may be possible only in cases of exceptionally flagrant violations. And some very important forms of behaviour, such as hand-washing, simply cannot be regulated by the state. To help bolster voluntary compliance in such settings, policymakers may wish to make use of insights from behavioural economics to complement mandates.

3 Nudges: Behaviourally Informed Messaging, and Choice Architecture

This section reviews several prominent examples of nudges during the pandemic, in two contexts. One is public messaging that may boost compliance, and the other is interventions in the decision-making environment that make compliance easier. In both these contexts, the policies in question did not limit people's choice set in any meaningful way, nor did they change the incentive structure that people faced.

3.1 Behaviourally Informed Messaging

Public messaging is one way of promoting compliance using psychological mechanisms, rather than incentives. Behavioural insights can help policymakers communicate their message more effectively. Just as firms competing in the marketplace, or rival political candidates running for office, use psychological insights when designing their messages, regulators can, and should, do the same in times of a pandemic. Fields such as marketing, communications, and organizational behaviour have made great strides in this area.

Since human attention is a scarce resource, policymakers face a challenge if they want their messages to be noticed, understood, and elicit the desired response. At the broadest level, much as in other contexts of mass communication, effective messages must be "concrete, straightforward, simple, meaningful, timely, and salient."[40]

---

[38] See Kenton, Daily Mail, 19 May 2020.
[39] See Evans, Desert News, 17 May 2020.
[40] Sunstein (2014), p. 729. See also, Kahneman (2013), p. 63.

This very general framework has been successfully applied in areas such as energy efficiency and preventive health care.[41]

Numerous leaders have used behaviourally informed messaging during the pandemic. In New York State, for example, the message: "*Stay Home. Stop the Spread. Save Lives*" was used consistently during the early stages of the pandemic.[42] In the United Kingdom, a similar message that included a reference to the nationally cherished institution of the national health service—"*Stay Home, Protect the NHS, Save Lives*"—was the centerpiece of governmental communications, and has been described as "one of the most successful communications in modern political history."[43] These messages are simple and short, and convey in concrete terms what is required of people (i.e., stay home), and why it is required (namely, to support health care workers, and save lives). Furthermore, this simple wording was often coupled with a visual design that was geared to make it more vivid—which likely bolstered the impact of the message.[44] In the United Kingdom, for example, the message was blazoned on the front of the Prime Minister's podium during his press briefings, and the eye-catching design included a yellow background, black lettering, and red arrows.[45] According to one public-relations expert, this visual design "helped to drive the message home and create a sense of urgency."[46]

Behavioural insights may also offer guidance about how the nuanced content of governmental messages is aimed at boosting compliance. A key example from the COVID-19 response is whether to emphasize people's self-interest, or societal interests, when trying to promote compliance with self-distancing rules. From a rational-choice perspective, people are expected to care foremost about themselves rather than about others. Thus, the most effective message should focus on the benefits associated with not catching the virus, rather than the benefits of not spreading it to others. A large body of behavioural studies, however, has demonstrated that people's behaviour is influenced by pro-social motivations.[47] People cooperate with others voluntarily in non-cooperative games such as Prisoner's Dilemma;[48] they choose to share resources with others in an egalitarian fashion;[49] and they are willing to forgo income to punish people who deviate from such pro-social norms.[50] This body of work suggests that using pro-social messaging may be an effective way of promoting compliance with COVID-19 restrictions—

---

[41] See, e.g., Schubert (2017), p. 332 (on the matter of eco-labeling); Blumenthal-Barby and Burroughs (2012), p. 4 (on salience in the context of health care).

[42] See Gallo (2020).

[43] See Hope and Dixon, The Telegraph, 1 May 2020.

[44] See Zamir and Teichman (2018), pp. 34–36.

[45] See Hope and Dixon, The Telegraph, 1 May 2020.

[46] See Hope and Dixon, The Telegraph, 1 May 2020.

[47] For a review, see Gächter (2014).

[48] See, e.g., Van den Assem et al. (2012).

[49] See Engel (2011).

[50] See Fehr and Gächter (2002).

particularly among the younger population, who face a significantly lower personal risk in the case of illness.[51]

Preliminary studies have confirmed the effectiveness of pro-social messaging in promoting precautions against COVID-19.[52] One such study found that in the early stages of the pandemic, a public-service announcement focusing on public (i.e., other-regarding) benefits was more effective than a message focused on personal benefits—and no less effective than a message focusing on both.[53] A second, identical, experiment conducted at a later stage of the pandemic showed that the different messages had similar effects—but still suggested that the perceived threat of COVID-19 to the public was more successful at predicting preventive behaviour than perceived threats to the individual decision-maker.[54] Governments around the world took note of these insights, and used messages such as *"Do It for Them"* and *"We Must Keep On Protecting Each Other."*[55]

Another psychological dimension that may help bolster compliance with public-health regulation is the *identifiability* of the victims. A wide body of psychological literature shows that people value the life of an identifiable person more than that of an unidentifiable, statistical individual.[56] Experimental studies have shown that merely adding a picture and a name to a message can significantly enhance people's willingness to respond in a prosocial manner.[57] This is why people agree to spend tremendous amounts of money to save an identifiable person in peril, but fail to invest in preventive measures that would save many more (unknown) lives.[58] Charities routinely construct their messaging based on this insight, and focus their fundraising campaign on an individual story, rather than on the broader picture.[59]

These findings suggest that humanizing the messages calling for public-health precautions may increase peoples' willingness to comply. Thus, the effectiveness of messages about protecting healthcare workers, or saving the lives of at-risk populations, can be bolstered by incorporating names and pictures of individual members of those groups. One preliminary study conducted in Ireland found that when experimenters led subjects to think of specific individuals as potential victims of a coronavirus infection, subjects were more willing to adopt some types of

---

[51] See Bonell et al. (2020).

[52] See, e.g., Pfattheicher et al. (2020); Gouin et al. (2020).

[53] See Jordan et al. (2020), pp. 3–11.

[54] See Jordan et al. (2020), pp. 12–17.

[55] See New York City Twitter Account, Feb 4, 2020; https://twitter.com/nycgov/status/135717404 8132849668 ("Do it for Them") (last access 22 September 2021); Milton Keynes Council Twitter Account, Oct. 17, 2020; https://twitter.com/mkcouncil/status/13173599927623622657 ("We Must Keep On Protecting Each Other") (last access 20 September 2021).

[56] For an overview, see Lewinsohn-Zamir et al. (2017), pp. 509–519.

[57] See, e.g., Kogut and Ritov (2005), p. 109.

[58] See Jenni and Loewenstein (1997), p. 235.

[59] See Lewinsohn-Zamir et al. (2017), p. 537.

precautions.[60] Following this insight, public-health agencies in the United Kingdom published posters including close-up facial pictures of COVID-19 patients identified by name, with a message such as *"Look Her in the Eyes and Tell Her You Never Bend the Rules."*[61]

Beyond simply naming individuals, *narrative framing* approaches—i.e., telling stories with identifiable characters to illustrate important information—function by eliciting the feeling of relationships with characters, reducing negative cognitive reactions by eliciting a "pleasurable mental state," and increasing the realism of information.[62] These mechanisms suggest that more detailed individual stories, with real or relatable characters, may be effective at communicating COVID-19 public-health information. Narrative approaches may also reduce culturally polarized responses among listeners.[63]

Finally, policymakers in later stages of the pandemic may adopt messages that capitalize on the *sunk costs effect*—a phenomenon that stems from *loss aversion*.[64] The sunk costs effect occurs when people who have made past investments in a project are biased toward investing more (even if the project is no longer worthwhile).[65] The larger the sacrifices that people believe that they have made, the stronger this effect becomes.

Large-scale lockdowns entail enormous costs, and policymakers may choose to emphasize these costs when further costly measures are needed. More specifically, arguments that invoke the public's fear of losing or wasting the progress they have made during the lockdown may prove persuasive. In fact, paradoxically, the *costlier* lockdowns have been, the *more persuasive* sunk-costs arguments are likely to be in maintaining them over a long period of time. It is for this reason that leaders across the globe have echoed the message that "[t]he sacrifices made to protect people during the coronavirus pandemic must not be squandered" when advocating for further preventive measures.[66]

3.2 Choice Architecture

Aside from informing messaging, behavioural research may also be instrumental in the design of the decision-making environment to promote compliance. *Choice architecture* studies have demonstrated that subtle changes in the decision-making

---

[60] See Lunn et al. (2020b).

[61] See Magee (2021).

[62] See Harrington et al. (2015), p. 386.

[63] See Kahan et al. (2011), p. 170.

[64] For an overview of the findings, see Zamir and Teichman (2018), pp. 56–57.

[65] Arkes and Blumer (1985).

[66] France-Presse (2020); See also, Hagemann (2020), (quoting Scotland's first minister, Nicola Sturgeon); Chaffin (2020) (quoting New York Governor Andrew Cuomo).

environment can significantly sway subjects' decisions. Thus, the order in which different kinds of food are presented in cafeterias, the layout of forms, and the design of highways, have all been guided by behavioural insights with a view to bringing about desirable outcomes.[67]

Similarly, policymakers can use choice-architecture nudges to facilitate compliance with COVID-19 rules. One example of such a nudge is floor markings that indicate to people where they should stand in a crowded area, to maintain proper social distance. Numerous regulators have mandated such markings as part of the safety measures required of businesses that are open to the public (such as drugstores and supermarkets).[68] Others have used similar methods to promote social distancing in public parks. In response to growing evidence of social distancing non-compliance in popular public parks, New York and San Francisco began drawing circles on the grass, to mark boundaries between park-goers.[69] This method has even been used to facilitate safe demonstrations during the pandemic. In Tel Aviv, the city marked its entire central square—which is often used for large demonstrations—with markers indicating where people may stand while maintaining social distance (with the words *"Protecting Democracy – Protecting Health"* on each one).[70] This allowed for demonstrations with thousands of people to proceed safely during the pandemic.[71]

From a behavioural perspective, incorporating social distancing into the physical landscape has two major advantages. The first, and perhaps most obvious, is that it makes compliance easier for those who already wish to obey the law: the markings function as a simple instruction that all people can follow. This matters, since studies have indicated that ease of compliance is a key factor in compliance decisions.[72]

Space markers can also bolster the informal enforcement of social-distancing norms by peers. Someone sitting in the park may feel uncomfortable confronting someone else who sits down next to them—but once a circle is drawn on the ground, it marks a notional territory, and whoever is in the circle first may view themselves as its "possessor." A broad body of game-theoretical literature, supported by experimental studies, has demonstrated that possession plays a central role in people's willingness to confront others with regard to protecting assets (and in the tendency of

---

[67] See Thaler et al. (2013), pp. 433–434.

[68] See, e.g., Roy Cooper, State of North Carolina (2020) Executive Order No. 131 §1(B). https://files.nc.gov/governor/documents/files/EO131-Retail-Long-Term-Care-Unemployment-Insurance.pdf (last accessed 09 April 2020); State of Michigan, The Office of Governor Gretchen Witmer (2020) Executive Order No. 2020–114 § 8(f). https://www.michigan.gov/whitmer/0,9309,7-387-90499_90705-531123%2D%2D,00.html (last access 05 June 2021).

[69] See Wigglesworth (2020); Whiteman (2020).

[70] A description of the initiative, along with the process-relevant legal procedures, was publicized on the city's website, see Digitel (2020).

[71] See Serhan (2020).

[72] See Kooistra et al. (2020).

non-possessors to avoid such confrontations).[73] Thus, creating areas of possession within the public space may encourage private enforcement of social distancing, which in turn will reinforce the social norm.

Behavioural insights can also be used to increase compliance among businesses. As various sectors of the economy reopen (or, in the case of essential businesses, remain open), they are often subject to new regulations, that minimize the risk of transmission. Consequently, business owners may find themselves facing a host of intricate new rules on issues such as the distance between tables at restaurants; the installation of protective equipment at cash registers; cleaning protocols; maximal capacity; and employee screening.[74] Even for business owners with the best intentions, adhering to these new regulations can pose a serious challenge.

One measure from the choice-architecture toolkit that can help boost business compliance with COVID-19 regulations is checklists.[75] Mostly studied in the context of medical decisions, checklists have been shown to be an effective tool that help decision-makers.[76] By breaking down a complex decision into smaller, simpler steps, and by reminding decision-makers of the steps they are required to take, checklists can improve the quality of decisions.[77] Checklists that enumerate all the measures that a business must adopt (either daily, or upon reopening, depending on the context), can help business owners deal with an unfamiliar and complex situation.[78] In California, for example, regulators have published numerous industry-specific checklists that are geared to easing compliance.[79]

The measures reviewed in this subsection are not meant to be an exhaustive list of the behaviourally informed interventions that can support the regulatory response to a pandemic. Rather, they merely illustrate the constructive role that behavioural science can play in designing a regulatory environment that fosters compliance. Numerous further measures—ranging from putting up posters with stern-looking

---

[73] See, e.g., Krier and Serkin (2015), pp. 150–152 (reviewing the game-theoretical literature); DeScioli and Wilson (2011) (experimental findings on human protection of territory).

[74] See, e.g., Ned Lamont, State of Connecticut (2020) Reopen Connecticut: Safer. Stronger. Together. https://portal.ct.gov/-/media/DECD/Covid_Business_Recovery-Phase-2/0617CTReopens_IndoorDining__C4_V1.pdf (last access 06 June 2020) (review of rules applying to restaurants in Connecticut); State of California, Department of Industrial Relations (2020) COVID-19 Industry Guidance: Retail. https://files.covid19.ca.gov/pdf/guidance-retail.pdf (last access 02 July 2020) (review of rules applying to retail in California).

[75] See Thaler et al. (2013), p. 433.

[76] For recent systematic reviews and meta analyses, see Lau and Chamberlain (2016); Gillespie et al. (2014).

[77] See Thaler et al. (2013), p. 433.

[78] Of course, checklists come with problems of their own. For example, they can lead to technocratic compliance that does not truly aim at reducing risk. See Ho et al. (2018), p. 243.

[79] See, for example, State of California, Department of Industrial Relations (2020) COVID-19 General Checklist for Construction Employers. https://files.covid19.ca.gov/pdf/checklist-construction.pdf (last access 02 July 2020); State of California, Department of Industrial Relations (2020) Cal/OSHA COVID-19 General Checklist for Day Camps, https://files.covid19.ca.gov/pdf/checklist-daycamps%2D%2Den.pdf (last access 17 July 2020).

middle-aged male eyes where people are expected to wash their hands to highlighting the explanations for various regulations—can positively affect peoples' choices, and induce them to behave more cautiously.[80]

4 Harnessing Social Norms

So far, the analysis has focused on individual decision-making. Another aspect of human decision-making that may bolster compliance is that of *social norms*. A large body of research has shown that people's behaviour is unconsciously but strongly influenced by what they believe others are doing—even more so than by other factors, such as their own opinion about the desirability of a given behaviour.[81] For example, people tend to contribute more to charity,[82] conserve energy,[83] and pay taxes,[84] because of the social factors at play, rather than due to material factors (e.g., fines).[85]

A key finding in the social-norms literature is that people are *conditional cooperators*.[86] That is to say, people are willing to engage in costly prosocial behaviour if they know that other members of the community are reciprocating. This insight has highlighted two dimensions that affect social interventions. First, behaviour should be *observable*—so that people know that others are cooperating, so they themselves may sanction those who do not.[87] For example, listing the names of those who contribute to the public good (rather than listing anonymous ID numbers) has been shown to promote cooperation.[88] Second, providing people with information about a given compliance norm will boost their willingness to comply.[89] For instance, hotel guests were 9% more likely to reuse their towel if told "*Almost 75% of guests who are asked to participate in our new resource savings program do help by using their towels more than once*" as opposed to the generic message, "*Help Save the Environment.*"[90]

---

[80] See King et al. (2016) (experiment with a stern-eye image). Judah et al. (2009 (experiment using various messages in a public restroom).
[81] See, e.g., Nolan et al. (2008); Goldstein et al. (2008).
[82] See, e.g., Frey and Meier (2004).
[83] See, e.g., Ayres et al. (2013).
[84] See, e.g., Frey and Torgler (2007).
[85] See Kraft-Todd et al. (2015), p. 98.
[86] For a notable early contribution, see Fischbacher et al. (2001). For a later review, see Thöni and Volk (2018).
[87] See Kraft-Todd et al. (2015), p. 98.
[88] See Yoeli et al. (2013).
[89] See Kraft-Todd et al. (2015), p. 98.
[90] See Goldstein et al. (2008), pp. 473–475.

Social norms can also play a role in promoting compliance with COVID-19 precautions.[91] Preliminary empirical findings from several countries suggest that perceived compliance by others corresponds with greater self-reported compliance with COVID-19 prevention rules.[92] These studies further show that the traditional factors of deterrence theory—the probability of detection and the sanction if caught—may not play a significant role in people's compliance decisions.[93] These findings suggest that policymakers should convey the message that compliance with precautions is already widespread.[94] This message can be conveyed by disseminating images of compliance (such as social distancing at a local grocery store) and data (such as public transportation statistics) that demonstrate conformity with the norm.[95] Conversely, when facing flagrant violations of the rules, policymakers should attempt to contain these violations quietly,[96] rather than expressing their outrage on social media, as some have done.[97] In Japan, for example, an initiative to shame *pachinko parlors* (shops that offer a form of gambling that is a mixture of pinball and slots, and tend to draw large crowds), which remained open despite a non-binding call to close, proved to be counterproductive, because it gave publicity to the violators, and attracted more consumers to them.[98]

Social norms and conditional cooperation can also guide the strategic decision as to whether or not to lock down the economy. The pandemic has required radical changes in multiple behaviours—including washing hands, maintaining distance from others, and wearing face masks. Policymakers' goal was not to achieve this change in slow incremental steps, but to bring it about swiftly and immediately. To that end, the lockdown itself, with its attendant imagery, may have facilitated a quick shift in norms. The sight of famous landmarks such as Times Square, the Trevi Fountain, the Eiffel Tower, and the Great Wall of China standing empty of crowds, projects a powerful message that business is not as usual. This, in turn, could help facilitate a speedy shift in social norms, by vividly (and saliently) illustrating that the vast majority of the public is adhering to a new set of pandemic-related rules. The Dutch Prime Minster explicitly made this point when, in March 2020, he stated that:

---

[91] See Van Bavel et al. (2020), p. 463.

[92] See Van Rooij et al. (2020); Kuiper et al. (2020); Bogg and Milad (2020). But see, Kooistra et al. (2020) (finding no association between compliance with COVID-19 related measures in the United Kingdom and perceived social norms).

[93] See Van Rooij et al. (2020), p. 26; Kuiper et al. (2020), p. 25; Kooistra et al. (2020), p. 25.

[94] This may be less effective, however, in subgroups with countervailing norms (such as norms against mask-wearing), in situations where actual compliance is low, or where people already believe that overall compliance is high. See, e.g., Thombs and Hamilton (2002); Carter and Kahnweiler (2010).

[95] See Bonell et al. (2020), p. 617.

[96] See Bonell et al. (2020), p. 617.

[97] New York's Mayor, De Blasio, offered some vivid examples of such reactions. See Stack, N.Y. Times, 28 April 2020.

[98] See Sposato (2020).

[m]ost of us comply with the measures, almost all do so ... [W]hen you see the empty streets, the empty offices, the empty highways, the empty train platforms, I think the message has landed with many people in the country, and many comply with the measures.[99]

Finally, leaders (both political and social) can play a key role in fostering (or, regretfully, in some cases, undermining) cooperative norms. Social norms scholarship often alludes to *norm entrepreneurs*[100]—individuals who function as social focal points, and are therefore capable of powerfully shifting social norms.[101] More specifically, they can do so by: "(a) signalling their own commitment to change, (b) creating coalitions, (c) making defiance of the norms seem or be less [or more] costly, and (d) making compliance with new norms seem or be more [or less] beneficial."[102]

In recent years, behavioural economists have developed this concept, and empirically documented how leadership can raise the level of cooperation in public-good games.[103] The paradigmatic design of such studies requires designated leaders to contribute to the public good before other players in the game—thereby leading by example.[104] In one such study, conducted in rural Bolivia, local leaders exerted a significant influence over voluntary contributions to a public resource, even without the ability to monitor, sanction, or coerce.[105] More concretely, the mere addition of an elected leader to the group increased total contributions by approximately 20%.[106] Apparently, by setting a positive example, leaders can reassure members of the community that others will cooperate, thereby facilitating conditional cooperation.

In the COVID-19 context, several high-ranking leaders have conspicuously violated social distancing norms. In the United States, President Trump repeatedly refused to wear a face mask,[107] and Vice President Pence similarly visited patients, and was photographed with campaign staff, without one.[108] In Israel, Prime Minister Netanyahu violated public-health directives, and hosted his son at his home.[109] In the United Kingdom, Professor Ferguson—one of the nation's leading

---

[99] See Kuiper (2020), pp. 6–7.

[100] For an overview, see Pozen (2008), pp. 305–310.

[101] See Sunstein (1996), p. 929.

[102] See Sunstein (1996), p. 929.

[103] See, e.g., Jack and Recalde (2015) (field experiment); Simon Gachter et al. (2012) (lab study).

[104] See Eichenseer (2019).

[105] See Jack and Recalde (2015), p. 92.

[106] See Jack and Recalde (2015), p. 92. For a meta analysis, see Eichenseer (2019).

[107] See Krisher and Eggert (2020). In fact, President Trump went beyond mere non-compliance, by seemingly encouraging defiance in some of his messages on social media. See Shear and Mervosh (2020).

[108] Klar (2020).

[109] See Breiner (2020).

epidemiologists, who had taken part in crafting the nation's COVID-19 policies—was caught violating the lockdown to meet with his lover.[110] The list goes on.[111]

The behavioural findings on social norms and conditional cooperation suggest that such behaviour may undermine compliance with COVID-19 related regulations. One study in Brazil, for example, estimates that President Jair Bolsonaro's participation at a demonstration against public-health regulations in March 2020 brought about a decrease in social distancing, and a rise in COVID-19 cases, in municipalities where he had a big following.[112] Given the seemingly diminished impact of deterrence considerations on people's pandemic-preventive behaviour, social norms may be acutely important for compliance. Global leaders should realize that with great power comes great responsibility to lead by example—and to adhere to the new norms.[113]

5 Behavioural Ethics: Addressing Motivated Reasoning and Partisanship

Research on compliance suggests that when people contemplate whether or not to obey the law, they often engage in *motivated reasoning*.[114] That is to say, they do not frame their decision as a rational cost-benefit analysis, that weighs their own self-interest against the cost of a potential sanction. Rather, they perceive the decision in a self-serving manner, and attempt to justify to themselves why they decided to behave selfishly and violate the norm.

Motivated reasoning is driven by a host of underlying mechanisms, some of which are subconscious.[115] *Biased assimilation* is the process by which people tend to believe new information that validates their prior beliefs, and to dismiss new information that challenges their priors.[116] This is one reason why people tend to grow more polarized, not less so, after reading balanced information about a topic.[117] *Confirmation bias* is a similar process, whereby people tend to seek out and process new information in ways that are favorable to their own prior beliefs.[118]

---

[110] See Cowburn (2021).

[111] See O'Grady (2020).

[112] See Mariani et al. (2020).

[113] See van Bavel et al. (2020), p. 466 (arguing that, in the context of COVID-19, leaders' "exemplary behaviour and sacrifice could help promote prosocial behaviour and cooperation").

[114] For an overview of the behavioural findings, see Zamir and Teichman (2018), pp. 58–76.

[115] Kahan (2011), p. 1.

[116] In a foundational study of biased assimilation, people with strong prior beliefs in favor or against the death penalty rated research as more convincing when it confirmed their beliefs about deterrence. Lord et al. (1979).

[117] Lord et al. (1979).

[118] See Nickerson (1998).

The credibility heuristic also shapes information-processing: people tend to accept or dismiss experts based on their perception of whether the expert is part of their ingroup, or an outgroup.[119] Similarly, people tend to overestimate the likelihood of scientific consensus on their own position[120] and to overestimate the likelihood that others agree with them (i.e., the *false consensus effect*).[121]

A specific aspect of motivated reasoning that has been shown to play a role in numerous contexts, some of which are highly related to the pandemic, is *cultural cognition*. Cultural cognition models of risk perception suggest that people's beliefs about what is threatening or non-threatening depend, in part, on their cultural priors—specifically, whether they are more hierarchical or egalitarian, and more individualistic or solidaristic.[122] Although cultural orientation is not a perfect match for conservative vs. liberal political affiliation, research has shown that conservatives are more likely to endorse hierarchical and individualistic values, while liberals are more likely to endorse egalitarian and solidaristic ones.[123] Hierarchical and individualistic individuals tend to be less concerned about environmental and technological risks (such as climate change), and more concerned about risks to individual autonomy, or social roles (such as gun control).[124] Egalitarian and solidaristic individuals, on the other hand, tend to worry more about threats to the environment and the collective (such as the human papilloma virus), and less about relinquishing individual autonomy to benefit the group (such as mandatory vaccination).[125]

In the context of COVID-19, preliminary evidence suggests that motivated reasoning plays a significant role in people's compliance decisions. Anecdotal examples show that people routinely justify violations by interpreting the situation in self-serving fashion. For instance, people often presume that their activity poses less of a risk than that of others, and therefore it is less necessary for them to comply with regulations.[126] More methodical studies have documented the key role of cultural cognition in compliance decisions in the United States. In particular, individuals who are comparatively hierarchical and individualistic tend to perceive the virus as less dangerous, and tend to comply less with public-health regulations.[127]

Behavioural research can help policymakers address motivated reasoning. One aspect of specific importance is the degree of ambiguity generated by legal rules.

---

[119] Pornpitakpan (2004).

[120] Kahan et al. (2011).

[121] Ross et al. (1977).

[122] Kahan and Braman (2006).

[123] Wildavsky and Dake (1990). Notably, however, these cultural values are more predictive of risk perception than party identity alone—and also more predictive than gender or race. See Michaud et al. (2009).

[124] Kahan and Braman (2006).

[125] Kahan and Braman (2006), pp. 158–159; Kahan et al. (2010a).

[126] For example, in Israel participants in religious services and in demonstrations routinely compared themselves with each other to justify their choices. See Teichman and Zamir (2021).

[127] For an overview of the findings, see Teichman and Underhill (2021), pp. 222–230.

Existing research has shown that people tend to use legal ambiguity, and interpret the law in a self-serving manner.[128] This, in turn, enables them to justify in their own eyes decisions that promote their own interests.

At first glance, there was very little ambiguity about the public-health rules that were put in place in response to the pandemic: governments around the world followed the behavioural prescription, and enacted highly detailed rules that specified precisely on matters such as the number of people allowed to gather, the distance from home one is permitted to travel, etc.[129] However, even such highly specific rules might generate ambiguity that can foster motivated reasoning, given the complexity of an intricate web of finely tuned rules. In Israel, for example, the rules governing places of worship during the High Holidays were based on a convoluted formula based on the square footage of the venue, the number of entrances, and its location in the country. That last point alone—rules that varied from region to the next, based on epidemiological criteria—while potentially sound from a public-health perspective, generated tremendous legal complexity: once people are subject to different rules at the places where they live, work, and recreate, confusion is likely to ensue, and self-serving deduction is quite likely.

Aside from the structure of legal rules, specially crafted *ethical nudges* can also help public-health regulators deal with motivated reasoning. Such nudges can clarify the choice faced by the decision-maker, and render the decision to violate the norm more explicit and salient. This, in turn, may hinder people's ability to interpret their behaviour in a self-serving manner.

A case in point is that of *compliance pledges*. Research in behavioural ethics has demonstrated that oaths and pledges tend to reduce people's tendency to cheat.[130] Recently, Pe'er and Feldman extended this finding to a regulatory setting involving mandates.[131] More specifically, they found that pledges can complement fines: while fines and pledges were found to reduce cheating individually, together they reduced cheating even more.[132] Thus, adding a personal declaration in which the business owner declares they are complying with the rules required for opening, may be a simple and cost-effective method of promoting compliance.[133]

Declarations may also help discourage people from engaging in social interactions when they suspect that they have contracted the virus. When people only suspect that they are infected, they might interpret their condition as one that allows them to continue with their planned activities. Requiring them to actively declare

---

[128] See Feldman and Teichman (2009).

[129] See Teichman and Underhill (2021), p. 231.

[130] See, e.g., Beck et al. (2018), p. 476; Jacquemet et al. (2019), p. 432.

[131] See Pe'er and Feldman (2020).

[132] Pe'er and Feldman (2020), pp. 12–13.

[133] For examples of mandatory self-certification programs, see Connecticut's Official State Website (2020) Self-Certify Your Business. https://service.ct.gov/recovery/s/?language=en_US (last access 22 July 2020); Municipality of Jerusalem (2020) The Purple Badge for Business – Guidelines for Routine During Corona. https://www.jerusalem.muni.il/he/newsandarticles/businessmessages/online-affidavit/ (last access 09 July 2020).

that they do not have any COVID-19 symptoms may mitigate this tendency, as it minimizes the moral ambiguity of the situation. Furthermore, such a declaration renders an act that could be perceived as a mere omission (i.e., not reporting symptoms), to the commission of actively lying—and studies suggest that people feel a greater sense of responsibility in cases involving commissions.[134] Examples of such declarations can be found in many contexts. At universities, for instance, members of the community are asked to declare their health status (i.e., lack of COVID-19 symptoms) daily before entering the campus,[135] while at daycare centers and schools, parents are required to declare the health status of their children.[136]

Finally, research on cultural cognition has yielded insights that can further guide public messaging. One strategy is to increase the public's exposure not just to information in general, but to information from *speakers* who are perceived to share the listeners' values. When people see their *disfavored* arguments expressed by someone who shares their values, and their *favored* arguments expressed by someone who does not share their values, they exhibit far less group polarization in their responses.[137] Kahan and colleagues have referred to this phenomenon as a *genuinely pluralistic-argument environment.*[138] Although speakers with such mismatched views may be difficult to identify, research suggests that they may be effective conduits for information in a culturally polarized environment.[139]

Studies conducted in the COVID-19 context bear out this insight. One striking example comes from US cable news. Early in the pandemic, Fox News host Sean Hannity tended to downplay the threat, while host Tucker Carlson (also on Fox News) described it as serious, and lethal.[140] Subsequent analyses showed that Hannity's viewers were slower to adopt precautionary measures than Carlson's viewers, and that this likely produced differential disease transmission rates (and, likely, death rates) among viewers: viewing Hannity was associated with 32% more COVID-19 cases by March 14, 2020, and 23% more COVID-19 deaths by March 28, 2020.[141] Similarly, an analysis of US governors' messaging on social media found that stay-at-home cues from Republican governors (a policy unpopular among national Republican leaders) were significantly more effective than cues from Democratic governors—largely because of an "especially responsive" effect in

---

[134] Emma Levine et al. (2018).

[135] See e.g., Resource Guide for the Columbia Community (2021).

[136] See State of Israel, Ministry of Education (2020) Digital Health Declaration. https://parents.education.gov.il/prhnet/gov-education/corona/daily-health-statement (last access 11 September 2021).

[137] Kahan et al. (2010b), p. 511.

[138] Kahan et al. (2010b), p. 513.

[139] Kahan et al. (2010b), p. 512.

[140] Bursztyn et al. (2020).

[141] Bursztyn et al. (2020), Other studies have documented the independent impact of watching Fox News on people's behaviour. See Simonov et al. (2020); Ash et al. (2020).

Democratic-leaning counties.[142] By the same token, as the public's perception of Anthony Fauci shifted to align him with more Democratic-linked values, he became a less effective source of information for conservative communities.[143]

Another strategy that may make people more responsive to unwelcome information is the use of arguments that affirm, or align, with people's cultural identities.[144] For example, the long-running *"Don't Mess with Texas"* campaign for reducing litter was successful, because it presented non-littering as congruent with Texans' well-known pride in their state (and reinforced through social norms messages featuring images of popular cultural figures).[145] Some COVID-19 response efforts have harnessed similar messaging—such as the *#MaskUpHoosiers* advertising and social campaign in Indiana, which also appeals to state membership and pride.[146] But when policymakers seek to persuade people who particularly value *individualism*, which is associated with lower risk perceptions of COVID-19,[147] arguments that emphasize the protection of self and one's own family—such as arguing that your own family members will ultimately benefit from a costly policy of school closures—may be more effective than arguments emphasizing the protection of others.[148] Messaging campaigns can combine these with images that have cultural resonance. Thus, the Oregon mask PSA contains language such as *"A Mask Should Not Be a Sign of Weakness"* and displays the words *"A Barrier to Protect You"*, with images of a mask in a camouflage pattern.[149]

6 Conclusion

This chapter reviewed the potential contribution of behavioural economics to promoting public health during the COVID-19 pandemic. The analysis showed that given the practical limitations of behavioural interventions on the one hand, and the

---

[142] Grossman et al. (2020), The authors, however, also suggested that there may have been "backlash effects" in the most conservative Republican counties, where stay-at-home tweets from Republican governors may have produced "either indifference or outright hostility" for contradictory national-level party messaging (p. 15).

[143] For media polls suggesting this, see Khanna and Backus (2020); Sanger-Katz (2020).

[144] Kahan et al. (2011), p. 169; See also Cohen et al. (2007); Kahan et al. (2010a), p. 135.

[145] Thaler and Sunstein (2009), p. 60.

[146] State of Indiana (2020) We Need You to #MaskUpHoosiers. https://www.coronavirus.in.gov/maskuphoosiers/ (last access 23 July 2020).

[147] See Dryhurst et al. (2020), This recommendation is at odds with the earlier discussion of pro-social messaging. See supra notes 47–55, and accompanying text. But one size need not fit all: campaigns can be tailored differently for different groups.

[148] These messages may also be effective among communitarians in times of crisis. See Leder (2020).

[149] Governor Kate Brown (2020) PSA: A Mask is Just a Mask. https://www.youtube.com/watch?v=tWpnX-fEq2U (last access 02 July 2020).

presence of massive negative externalities on the other, choice-preserving nudges cannot serve as the primary legal response to the pandemic. Nonetheless, behavioural informed regulatory interventions can be incorporated into the legal response to the pandemic, and can help boost compliance with legal mandates cheaply and effectively.

Future research should continue to explore the role of behaviourally informed regulation. In the context of COVID-19, this could include empirically examining the efficacy of the numerous measures reviewed in this chapter. One particular topic that is expected to draw significant attention is that of vaccination decisions: with the emergence of effective vaccines for the virus, countries will face the challenge of convincing most of the population to vaccinate. A significant body of behavioural work has already outlined various interventions that may help governments in this regard[150]—however, this will need to be examined in the specific context of COVID-19 vaccines, with their distinctive characteristics.

More generally, the framework presented in this chapter regarding the proper role of behaviourally informed regulation can be applied to other areas as well. Key examples are climate change, and sustainability. Much as in the case of COVID-19, individual choices in these settings also entail significant negative externalities. Consequently, while nudges such as electricity bills that incorporate comparisons with one's neighbors' consumption may reduce the negative externalities that people generate, "they are unlikely to make much of a dent in the problem of global warming."[151] Thus, there is a growing understanding among behavioural scientists and legal scholars alike that traditional regulatory tools—in particular, emissions taxes, and fuel-efficiency mandates—are necessary to change behaviour.[152]

Dealing with a pandemic requires the legal system to use all the tools at its disposal in a prudent fashion. Behaviourally informed regulation—and nudges in particular—is certainly one important tool that should be incorporated into this effort and used, whilst recognizing both its great potential and its inherent limitations.

References

Abraham R, Mann A (2021) Global COVID-19 Death Toll Surpasses 3 Million Amid New Infections Resurgence. Reuters, 6 April 2021. https://www.reuters.com/article/us-health-coronavirus-global-casualties-idUSKBN2BT0V9 (last access 11 September 2021)

Arkes HR, Blumer C (1985) The psychology of sunk cost. Organ Behav Hum Decis Process 35: 124–140. https://doi.org/10.1016/0749-5978(85)90049-4. (last access 22 September 2021)

Ash E et al (2020) The Effect of Fox News on Health Behavior During COVID-19. SSRN Electronic Journal. https://doi.org/10.2139/ssrn.3636762 (last access 22 September 2021)

---

[150] See, e.g., Chen and Stevens (2017); Buttenheim and Asch (2013); Cappelen (2010).

[151] See Loewenstein and Chater (2017), p. 44.

[152] See Bubb and Pildes (2014), pp. 1673–1677; Loewenstein and Chater (2017), p. 45.

Ayres I et al (2013) Evidence from two large field experiments that peer comparison feedback can reduce residential energy usage. J Law Econ Organ 29:992–1022. https://doi.org/10.3386/w15386. (last access 22 September 2021)

Beck T et al (2018) Can honesty oaths, peer interaction, or monitoring mitigate lying? J Bus Ethics 163:467–484. https://doi.org/10.1007/s10551-018-4030-z. (last access 22 September 2021)

Becker GS (1968) Crime and punishment: an economic approach. J Polit Econ 76:219–221. https://doi.org/10.1086/259394. (last access 22 September 2021)

Bethune ZA, Korinek A (2020) Covid-19 Infection Externalities: Trading Off Lives vs. Livelihoods. NBER Working Paper No. 27009. https://doi.org/10.3386/w27009. (last access 22 September 2021)

Blumenthal-Barby JS, Burroughs H (2012) Seeking better health care outcomes: the ethics of using the "Nudge". Am J Bioeth 12:1–10. https://doi.org/10.1080/15265161.2011.634481. (last access 22 September 2021)

Bogg T and Milad E (2020) Slowing the spread of COVID-19: demographic, personality, and social cognition predictors of guideline adherence in a representative U.S. Sample. PsyArXiv Preprints. https://doi.org/10.31234/osf.io/yc2gq. (last access 22 September 2021)

Bonell C et al (2020) Harnessing behavioural science in public health campaigns to maintain "social distancing" in response to the COVID-19 pandemic: key principles. J Epidemiol Commun Health 74:617–619. https://doi.org/10.1136/jech-2020-214290. (last access 22 September 2021)

Breiner J (2020) Netanyahu Violated Coronavirus Regulations by Meeting Son While Quarantined, Haaretz, 9 April 2020. https://www.haaretz.com/israel-news/.premium-netanyahu-denies-violating-coronavirus-regulations-when-photographed-with-son-1.8754841 (last access 11 September 2021)

Bubb R, Pildes RH (2014) How behavioral economics trims its sails and why. Harv Law Rev 127:1593–1678

Bucher T et al (2016) Nudging consumers towards healthier choices: a systemic review of positional influences on food choice. Br J Nutr 115:2252–2263. https://doi.org/10.1017/S0007114516001653. (last access 22 September 2021)

Buffy D (2020) Dutch official advice to single people: find a sex buddy for lockdown. The Guardian, 15 May 2020. https://www.theguardian.com/world/2020/may/15/dutch-official-advice-to-single-people-find-a-sex-buddy-for-lockdown-coronavirus (last access 11 September 2021)

Bursztyn L et al (2020) Misinformation during a pandemic. NBER Working Paper No. 27417. https://doi.org/10.3386/w27417 (last access 22 September 2021)

Buttenheim AM, Asch DA (2013) Making vaccine refusal less of a free ride. Hum Vaccines Immunother 9:2674–2675. https://doi.org/10.4161/hv.26676. (last access 11 September 2021)

Cappelen A (2010) Demand for childhood vaccination – insights from behavioral economics. Forum Dev Stud 37:349–364. https://doi.org/10.1080/08039410.2010.507778. (last access 11 September 2021)

Carter CA, Kahnweiler WM (2010) The efficacy of the social norms approach to substance abuse prevention applied to fraternity men. J Am College Health 49:66–71. https://doi.org/10.1080/07448480009596286

Cato S et al (2020) The effect of soft government Directives about COVID-19 on social beliefs in Japan. SSRN Electronic Journal. https://doi.org/10.2139/ssrn.3577448. (last access 11 September 2021)

Chaffin J (2020) New York poised to being reopening as new virus cases fall. Financial Times, 11 May 2020. https://www.ft.com/content/f8d44024-ea4d-4d9a-ae21-80b9bb3e6db5 (last access 11 September 2021)

Chen F, Stevens R (2017) Applying lessons from behavioral economics to increase vaccination rates. Health Promot Int 32:1067–1073. https://doi.org/10.1093/heapro/daw031. (Last access 11 September 2021)

Cohen GL et al (2007) Bridging the partisan divide: self-affirmation reduces ideological closed-mindedness and inflexibility in negotiation. J Personal Soc Psychol 93:415–430. https://doi.org/10.1037/0022-3514.93.3.415. (last access 11 September 2021)

Cohen J (1988) Statistical power analysis for the behavioral sciences. Lawrence Erlbaum Associates Publishers

Cowburn A (2021) Neil Ferguson: Government Coronavirus Adviser Quits After Home Visits from Married Lover. Independent, 5 May 2020. https://www.independent.co.uk/news/uk/politics/neil-ferguson-resigns-coronavirus-antonia-staats-social-distancing-government-a9500581.html (last access 11 September 2021)

De Geest G, Dari-Mattiacci G (2013) The rise of carrots and the decline of sticks. Univ Chic Law Rev 80:341–392. https://doi.org/10.2307/41825878. (last access 11 September 2021)

DellaVigna S, Linos E (2020) RCTs to Scale: Comprehensive Evidence from Two Nudge Units. NBER Working Paper No. 27594. https://doi.org/10.3386/w27594. (last access 11 September 2021)

DeScioli P, Wilson BJ (2011) The Territorial Foundations of Human Property. Evol Hum Behav 32:297–304. https://doi.org/10.1016/j.evolhumbehav.2010.10.003. (last access 11 September 2021)

Digitel (2020) Preserving Democracy–Preserving Health. https://www.tel-aviv.gov.il/Pages/MainItemPage.aspx?WebID=3af57d92-807c-43c5-8d5f-6fd455eb2776&ListID=81e17809-311d-4bba-9bf1-2363bb9debcd&ItemId=1017 (last access 17 July 2020)

Dryhurst S et al (2020) Risk perceptions of COVID-19 around the world. J Risk Res 23:994–1006. https://doi.org/10.1080/13669877.2020.1758193. (last access 11 September 2021)

Eichenseer M (2019) Leading by example in public good games: what do we know?. SSRN Electronic Journal. https://doi.org/10.2139/ssrn.3441638. (last access 11 September 2021)

Engel C (2011) Dictator games: a meta study. Exp Econ 14:583–610. https://doi.org/10.1007/s10683-011-9283-7

Evans E (2020) Defying Lockdown Orders: Here's why these Business Owners Decided to Break the Rules and Open Up. Desert News, 17 May 2020. https://www.deseret.com/indepth/2020/5/17/21256650/coronavirus-covid-19-lockdown-orders-california-pennsylvania-business-owners-reopen-restaurants (last access 11 September 2021)

Fehr E, Gächter S (2002) Altruistic Punishment in Humans. Nat 415:137–140. https://doi.org/10.1038/415137a. (last access 22 September 2021)

Feldman Y, Teichman D (2009) Are all legal probabilities created equal? New York Univ Law Rev 84:980–1022

Fischbacher U et al (2001) Are people conditionally cooperative? Evidence from a public goods experiment. Econ Lett 71:397–404. https://doi.org/10.1016/s0165-1765(01)00394-9. (last access 22 September 2021)

France-Presse A (2020) Don't Squander Sacrifices of 2020: WHO Chief. Hindustan Times, 26 December 2020. https://www.hindustantimes.com/world-news/don-t-squander-sacrifices-of-2020-who-chief/story-hcUcUPtvXvLiml7vHRTL1O.html (last access 11 September 2021)

Frey BS, Meier S (2004) Social comparisons and pro-social behavior: testing "conditional cooperation" in a field experiment. Am Econ Rev 94:1717–1722. https://doi.org/10.1257/0002828043052187. (last access 22 September 2021)

Frey BS, Torgler B (2007) Tax morale and conditional cooperation. J Comp Econ 35:136–159. https://doi.org/10.1016/j.jce.2006.10.006. (last access 22 September 2021)

Gächter S (2014) Prosocial motivation and the maintenance of social order. In: Zamir E, Teichman D (eds) The Oxford handbook of behavioral economics and the law. Oxford University Press, pp 28–60. https://doi.org/10.1093/oxfordhb/9780199945474.013.0002. (last access 11 September 2021)

Gächter S et al (2012) Who makes a good leader? Cooperativeness, optimism, and leading-by-example. Econ Inq 50:953–967. https://doi.org/10.1111/j.1465-7295.2010.00295.x. (last access 11 September 2021)

Galle B (2012) Tragedy of the carrots. Stanf Law Rev 64:797–850

Gallo C (2020) Finding the right words in a crisis. HBR. https://hbr.org/2020/04/finding-the-right-words-in-a-crisis (last access 17 April 2020)

Gillespie BM et al (2014) Effect of using a safety checklist on patient complications after surgery—systematic review and meta-analysis. Anesthesiol 120:1380–1389. https://doi.org/10.1097/aln.0000000000000232. (last access 22 September 2021)

Goldstein N et al (2008) A room with a viewpoint: using social norms to motivate environmental conservation in hotels. J Consum Res 35:472–482. https://doi.org/10.1086/586910. (last access 22 September 2021)

Gouin JP et al (2020) Social, cognitive, and emotional predictors of adherence to physical distancing during the COVID-19 Pandemic. SSRN Electronic Journal. https://doi.org/10.2139/ssrn.3594640. (last access 22 September 2021)

Grossman G et al (2020) Political partisanship influences behavioral responses to governors' recommendations for COVID-19 prevention in the United States. PNAS 117:24144–24153. https://doi.org/10.1073/pnas.2007835117. (last access 22 September 2021)

Guttel E, Harel A (2008) Uncertainty Revisited: legal prediction and legal postdiction. Mich Law Rev 107:467–499

Hagemann H (2020) Boris Johnson Outlines Plan to Ease Coronavirus Restrictions in England. NPR, 29 May 2020. https://www.npr.org/sections/coronavirus-live-updates/2020/05/10/853538566/boris-johnson-outlines-plan-to-ease-coronavirus-restrictions-in-u-k (last access 11 September 2021)

Hagmann D et al (2019) Nudging out support for a carbon tax. Nat Clim Change 9:484–489. https://doi.org/10.1038/s41558-019-0474-0. (last access 22 September 2021)

Hale T et al (2020) Variation in Government Responses to COVID-19. BSG Working Paper Series. https://www.bsg.ox.ac.uk/sites/default/files/2020-09/BSG-WP-2020-032-v7.0.pdf (last access 11 September 2021)

Harrington NG et al (2015) Message design approaches to health risk behavior prevention. In: Scheier LM (ed) Handbook of adolescent drug use prevention research. American Psychological Association, pp 381–396

Ho DE et al (2018) Do checklists make a difference? A natural experiment from food safety enforcement. J Empir Leg Stud 15:242–277

Hope C, Dixon H (2020) The Story Behind "Stay Home, Protect the NHS, Save Lives" – the Slogan that was "Too Successful". The Telegraph, 1 May 2020. https://www.telegraph.co.uk/politics/2020/05/01/story-behind-stay-home-protect-nhs-save-lives/ (last access 11 September 2021)

Hummel D, Maedche A (2019) How effective is nudging? A quantitative review on the effect sizes and limits of empirical nudging studies. J Behav Exp Econ 80:47–58. https://doi.org/10.1016/j.socec.2019.03.005. (last access 22 September 2021)

Hutton R (2020) Keep Calm and Wash Your Hands: Britain's Strategy to Beat Virus. Bloomberg, 11 March 2020. https://www.bloomberg.com/news/articles/2020-03-11/keep-calm-and-wash-your-hands-britain-s-strategy-to-beat-virus (last access 11 September 2021)

Jack BK, Recalde MP (2015) Leadership and the voluntary provision of public goods: field evidence from Bolivia. J Public Econ 122:80–93. https://doi.org/10.1016/j.jpubeco.2014.10.003. (last access 22 September 2021)

Jacquemet N et al (2019) Truth telling under oath. Manage Sci 65:426–438. https://doi.org/10.1287/mnsc.2017.2892

Jenni KE, Loewenstein G (1997) Explaining the "Identifiable Victim Effect". J Risk Uncertainty 14:235–257. https://doi.org/10.1023/A:1007740225484. (last access 22 September 2021)

Johnson EJ, Goldstein D (2003) Do defaults save lives? Sci 302:1338–1339. https://doi.org/10.1126/science.1091721. (last access 22 September 2021)

Jordan J et al (2020) Don't get it or don't spread it? Comparing self-interested versus prosocially framed COVID-19 prevention messaging. PsyArXiv Preprints. https://doi.org/10.31234/osf.io/yuq7x. (last access 22 September 2021)

Judah G et al (2009) Experimental pretesting of hand-washing interventions in a natural setting. Am J Public Health 99:405–411. https://doi.org/10.2105/ajph.2009.164160. (last access 22 September 2021)

Kahan DM (2011) Foreword: neutral principles, motivated cognition, and some problems for constitutional law. Harv Law Rev 125:1–77

Kahan DM, Braman D (2006) Cultural cognition and public policy. Yale Law Policy Rev 24:149–172

Kahan DM et al (2010a) Cultural cognition and public policy: the case of outpatient commitment laws. Law Hum Behav 34:118–140. https://doi.org/10.1007/s10979-008-9174-4. (last access 22 September 2021)

Kahan DM et al (2010b) Who fears the HPV vaccine, who doesn't, and why? An experimental study of the mechanisms of cultural cognition. Law Hum Behav 34:501–516. https://doi.org/10.1007/s10979-009-9201-0. (last access 22 September 2021)

Kahan DM et al (2011) Cultural cognition of scientific consensus. J Risk Res 14:147–174. https://doi.org/10.1080/13669877.2010.511246. (last access 22 September 2021)

Kahneman D (2013) Thinking, fast and slow. Farrar, Straus and Giroux

Kenton L (2020) Cops shut down illicit orthodox Brooklyn Yeshiva school where more than 100 children without masks were taking classes while the rest of the city is on Lockdown. Daily Mail, 19 May 2020. https://www.dailymail.co.uk/news/article-8336051/NYPD-cops-60-children-taking-classes-Brooklyn-Orthodox-school-despite-coronavirus-lockdown.html (last access 11 September 2021)

Khanna K, Backus F (2020) Trump's marks for handling COVID-19 outbreak decline. CBS News, 14 May 2020. https://www.cbsnews.com/news/coronavirus-donald-trump-marks-handling-covid-outbreak-decline-cbs-news-poll-today-2020-05-14/ (last access 11 September 2021)

King D et al (2016) "Priming" hand hygiene compliance in clinical environments. Health Psychol 35:96–101. https://doi.org/10.1037/hea0000239. (last access 22 September 2021)

Klar R (2020) Pence posts, deletes photo of trump campaign staff without face masks, not social distancing. The Hill, 11 June 2020. https://thehill.com/homenews/administration/502225-pence-posts-deletes-photo-trump-campaign-staff-without-face-masks-not (last access 11 September 2021)

Kogut T, Ritov I (2005) The singularity effect of identified victims in separate and joint evaluations. Organ Behav Hum Decis Process 97:106–116. https://doi.org/10.1016/j.obhdp.2005.02.003. (last access 22 September 2021)

Kooistra EB et al (2020) Mitigating COVID-19 in a nationally representative UK sample: personal abilities and obligation to obey the law shape compliance with mitigation measures. SSRN Electronic Journal. https://doi.org/10.2139/ssrn.3598221. (last access 22 September 2021)

Kraft-Todd GT et al (2015) Promoting cooperation in the field. Behav Sci 3:96–101. https://doi.org/10.1016/j.cobeha.2015.02.006. (last access 22 September 2021)

Krier J, Serkin C (2015) The possession heuristic. In: Chang Y (ed) Law and economics of possession. Cambridge University Press, pp 149–174. https://doi.org/10.1017/CBO9781316017814.007. (last access 22 September 2021)

Krisher T, Eggert D (2020) Trump could violate ford face mask requirement on plant tour. Associated Press, 19 May 2020. https://apnews.com/9ca93f81c2aa227184247b4e19c46e86 (last access 11 September 2021)

Kuiper ME et al (2020) The intelligent lockdown: compliance with COVID-19 mitigation measures in the Netherlands. SSRN Electronic Journal. https://doi.org/10.2139/ssrn.3598215. (last access 22 September 2021)

Lau CSM, Chamberlain RS (2016) The World Health Organization surgical safety checklist improves post-operative outcomes: a meta-analysis and systematic review. Surg Sci 7:206–217. https://doi.org/10.4236/ss.2016.7402. (last access 22 September 2021)

Leder J (2020) Even prosocially oriented individuals save themselves first. PsyArXiv Preprints. https://doi.org/10.31234/osf.io/nugcr. (last access 22 September 2021)

Levine E et al (2018) The surprising costs of silence: asymmetric preferences for prosocial lies of commission and omission. J Personal Soc Psychol 114:29–51. https://doi.org/10.1037/pspa0000101. (last access 22 September 2021)

Lewinsohn-Zamir D et al (2017) Law and identifiability. Ind Law Rev 92:505–557

Loewenstein G, Chater N (2017) Putting nudges in perspective. Behav Public Policy 1:26–53. https://doi.org/10.1017/bpp.2016.7. (last access 22 September 2021)

Lord CG et al (1979) Biased assimilation and attitude polarization: the effects of prior theories on subsequently considered evidence. J Personal Soc Psychol 37:2098–2109. https://doi.org/10.1037/0022-3514.37.11.2098. (last access 22 September 2021)

Lunn PD et al (2020a) Motivating social distancing during the Covid-19 pandemic: an online experiment. Soc Sci Med 265:113478. https://doi.org/10.1016/j.socscimed.2020.113478. (last access 22 September 2021)

Lunn PD et al (2020b) Using behavioural science to help fight the coronavirus: a rapid narrative review. J Behav Public Admin 3:1–15. https://doi.org/10.30636/jbpa.31.147. (last access 22 September 2021)

Magee K (2021) Will the government's new emotive covid ad make people obey the rules?, Campaign, 27 January 2021. https://www.campaignlive.co.uk/article/will-governments-new-emotive-covid-ad-people-obey-rules/1705634 (last access 11 September 2021)

Mariani LA et al (2020) Words can hurt: how political communication can change the pace of an epidemic. Covid Econ 12:104–137

Michaud KEH et al (2009) The relationship between cultural values and political ideology, and the role of political knowledge. Polit Psychol 30:27–40. https://doi.org/10.1111/j.1467-9221.2008.00679.x. (last access 22 September 2021)

Nadler J (2005) Flouting the law. Tax Law Rev 83:1398–1441

Newell RG, Siikamäki JV (2014) Nudging energy efficiency behavior: the role of information labels. J Assoc Environ Resour Econ 1:555–598. https://doi.org/10.1086/679281. (last access 22 September 2021)

Nickerson RS (1998) Confirmation bias: a ubiquitous phenomenon in many guises. Rev Gen Psychol 2:175–220. https://doi.org/10.1037/1089-2680.2.2.175. (last access 22 September 2021)

Nolan JM et al (2008) Normative social influence is underdetected. Personal Soc Psychol Bull 34:913–923. https://doi.org/10.1177/0146167208316691. (last access 22 September 2021)

O'Grady S (2020) Top officials around the world keep getting caught breaking lockdown rules. Washington Post, 26 May 2020. https://www.washingtonpost.com/world/2020/05/06/top-officials-around-world-keep-getting-caught-breaking-lockdown-rules/ (last access 11 September 2021)

Pe'er E, Feldman Y (2020) Honesty pledges for the behaviorally-based regulation of dishonesty. SSRN Electronic Journal. https://doi.org/10.31234/osf.io/pr78t. (last access 22 September 2021)

Pfattheicher S et al (2020) The emotional path to action: empathy promotes physical distancing and wearing of face masks during the COVID-19 pandemic. Psychol Sci 31:1363–1373. https://doi.org/10.1177/0956797620964422. (last access 22 September 2021)

Pierre J (2020) Nudges against pandemics: Sweden's COVID-19 containment strategy in perspective. Policy Soc 39:478–493. https://doi.org/10.1080/14494035.2020.1783787. (last access 22 September 2021)

Pornpitakpan C (2004) The persuasiveness of source credibility: a critical review of five decades' evidence. J Appl Soc Psychol 34:243–281. https://doi.org/10.1111/j.1559-1816.2004.tb02547.x. (last access 22 September 2021)

Pozen DE (2008) We are all entrepreneurs now. Wake For Law Rev 43:283–340

Quadri SA (2020) COVID-19 and religious congregations: implications for spread of novel pathogens. Int J Infect Dis 96:219–221. https://doi.org/10.1016/j.ijid.2020.05.007. (last access 22 September 2021)

Richard H. Thaler, Cass R. Sunstein (2009) Nudge: improving decisions about health, wealth, and happiness

Ross L et al (1977) The "False Consensus Effect": an egocentric bias in social perception and attribution biases. J Exp Soc Psychol 13:279–301. https://doi.org/10.1016/0022-1031(77)90049-x. (last access 22 September 2021)

Sanger-Katz M (2020) On coronavirus, Americans still trust the experts. N.Y. Times, 27 June 2020. https://www.nytimes.com/2020/06/27/upshot/coronavirus-americans-trust-experts.html (last access 11 September 2021)

Schubert C (2017) Green nudges: do they work? Are they ethical? Ecol Econ 132:329–342. https://doi.org/10.1016/j.ecolecon.2016.11.009. (last access 22 September 2021)

Serhan Y (2020) Israel shows us the future of protest. The Atlantic, 23 April 2020. https://www.theatlantic.com/international/archive/2020/04/protest-demonstration-pandemic-coronavirus-covid19/610381/ (last access 11 September 2021)

Shavell S (2004) Foundations of economic analysis of law. The Belknap Press of Harvard University Press

Shear MD, Mervosh S (2020) Trump encourages protest against governors who have imposed virus restrictions. New York Times, 17 April 2020. https://www.nytimes.com/2020/04/17/us/politics/trump-coronavirus-governors.html (last access 11 September 2021)

Sibony AL (2020) The UK COVID-19 response: a behavioural Irony? Eur J Risk Regul 11:350–357. https://doi.org/10.1017/err.2020.22. (last access 22 September 2021)

Simonov A et al (2020) The persuasive effect of fox news: non-compliance with social distancing during the COVID-19 pandemic. NBER Working Paper No. 27237. https://doi.org/10.3386/w27237. (last access 22 September 2021)

Soofi M et al (2020) Using insights from behavioral economics to mitigate the spread of COVID-19. Appl Health Econ Health Policy 18:345–350. https://doi.org/10.1007/s40258-020-00595-4. (last access 22 September 2021)

Sposato W (2020) Japan's halfhearted coronavirus measures are working anyway. Foreign Policy, 14 May 2020. https://foreignpolicy.com/2020/05/14/japan-coronavirus-pandemic-lockdown-testing/ (last access 11 September 2021)

Stack L (2020) De Blasio breaks up Rabbi's funeral and lashes out over virus distancing. N.Y. Times, 28 April 2020. https://www.nytimes.com/2020/04/28/nyregion/hasidic-funeral-coronavirus-de-blasio.html (last access 11 September 2021)

Sunstein CR (1996) Social norms and social roles. Columbia Law Rev 96:903–968. https://doi.org/10.2307/1123430. (last access 22 September 2021)

Sunstein CR (2014) Nudges.Gov: behaviorally informed regulation. In: Zamir E, Teichman D (eds) The Oxford handbook of behavioral economics and the law. Oxford University Press, pp 719–747. https://doi.org/10.1093/oxfordhb/9780199945474.013.0028. (last access 22 September 2021)

Sunstein CR (2017) Nudges that fail. J Behav Public Policy 1:4–25. https://doi.org/10.1017/bpp.2016.3

Symptom Self-Checking (2021) Resource Guide for the Columbia Community. https://covid19.columbia.edu/content/symptom-self-checking (last access 11 September 2021)

Teichman D, Underhill K (2021) Infected by bias: behavioral science and the legal response to COVID-19. Am J Law Med 47:205–248

Thaler RH et al (2013) Choice architecture. In: Shafir E (ed) The behavioral foundations of public policy. Princeton University Press, pp 428–439. https://doi.org/10.2307/j.ctv550cbm.31. (last access 22 September 2021)

Thombs DL, Hamilton MJ (2002) Effects of a social norm feedback campaign on the drinking norms and behavior of division I student-athletes. J Drug Educ 32:227–244. https://doi.org/10.2190/2uyu-6x9m-rj65-3yyh. (last access 22 September 2021)

Thöni C, Volk S (2018) Conditional cooperation: review and refinement. Econ Lett 171:37–40. https://doi.org/10.1016/j.econlet.2018.06.022. (last access 22 September 2021)

van Bavel JJ et al (2020) Using social and behavioural science to support COVID-19 pandemic response. Nat Hum Behav 4:460–471. https://doi.org/10.1038/s41562-020-0884-z. (last access 22 September 2021)

van den Assem MJ et al (2012) Split or steal? Cooperative behavior when the stakes are large. Manag Sci 58:2–20. https://doi.org/10.1287/mnsc.1110.1413. (last access 22 September 2021)

van Rooij B et al (2020) Compliance with COVID-19 Mitigation Measures in the United States. SSRN Electronic Journal. https://doi.org/10.2139/ssrn.3582626. (last access 22 September 2021)

Villa V (2020) Most states have religious exemptions to COVID-19 social distancing rules. Pew Research Center, 27 April 2020, https://www.pewresearch.org/fact-tank/2020/04/27/most-states-have-religious-exemptions-to-covid-19-social-distancing-rules/ (last access 11 September 2021)

White MD, Fradella HF (2020) Policing a pandemic: stay-at-home orders and what they mean for the police. Am J Crim Justice 45:702–717. https://doi.org/10.1007/s12103-020-09538-0. (last access 22 September 2021)

Whiteman H (2020) Domino Park Circles Keep New York City Sunbathers in Check. CNN, 19 May 2020. https://www.cnn.com/style/article/domino-park-new-york-city-circles-sociaL-distancing/index.html#:~:text=But%20the%20large%2C%20painted%20-circles,200%2C000%20cases%20of%20Covid%2D19 (last access 11 September 2021)

Wigglesworth A (2020) Social distancing circles drawn on grass at San Francisco Parks. L.A. Times, 22 May 2020. https://www.latimes.com/california/story/2020-05-22/social-distancing-circles-drawn-on-grass-at-san-francisco-parks (last access 11 September 2021)

Wildavsky A, Dake K (1990) Theories of risk perception: who fears what and why? Daedalus 119: 41–60

Wilson AL et al (2016) nudging healthier food and beverage choices through salience and priming. Evidence from a systematic review. Food Q Pref 51:47–64. https://doi.org/10.1016/j.foodqual.2016.02.009. (last access 22 September 2021)

Yoeli E et al (2013) Powering up with indirect reciprocity in a large field experiment. PNAS 110: 10424–10429. https://doi.org/10.1073/pnas.1301210110. (last access 22 September 2021)

Yoffie EH (2021) Israel must deal with its ultra-orthodox insurrection. Right Now, Haaretz, 1 February 2021. https://www.haaretz.com/israel-news/.premium-israel-must-deal-with-its-ultra-orthodox-insurrection-right-now-1.9500059 (last access 11 September 2021)

Zamir E, Teichman D (2018) Behavioral law and economics. Oxford University Press

Zhou P et al (2020) A pneumonia outbreak associated with a new coronavirus of probable bat origin. Nat 579:270–273. https://doi.org/10.1038/s41586-020-2012-7. (last access 22 September 2021)

Fake News in Times of Pandemic and Beyond: Enquiry into the Rationales for Regulating Information Platforms

Mira Burri

Abstract The COVID-19 pandemic threw our societies in dire times with deep effects on all societal sectors and on our lives. The pandemic was accompanied by another phenomenon also associated with grave consequences—that of the "infodemic". Fake news about the cause, prevention, impact and potential cures for the coronavirus spread on social platforms and other media outlets, and continue to do so. The chapter takes this infodemic as a starting point to exploring the broader phenomenon of online misinformation. The legal analysis in this context focuses on the rationales for regulating Internet platforms as critical information intermediaries in a global networked media space. As Internet platforms do not fall under the category of media companies, they are currently not regulated in most countries. Yet, the pressure to regulate them, also in light of other negative phenomena, such as hate speech proliferation, political disinformation and targeting, has grown in recent years. The regulatory approaches differ, however, across jurisdictions and encompass measures that range from mere self-regulatory codes to more binding interventions. Starting with some insights into the existing technological means for mediating speech online, the power of platforms, and more specifically their influence on the conditions of freedom of expression, the chapter discusses in particular the regulatory initiatives with regard to information platforms in the United States and in the European Union, as embedded in different traditions of free speech protection. The chapter offers an appraisal of the divergent US and EU approaches and contemplates the adequate design of regulatory intervention in the area of online speech in times of infodemic and beyond it.

M. Burri (✉)
University of Lucerne, Lucerne, Switzerland
e-mail: mira.burri@unilu.ch

1 Introduction: The Changing Landscape of Fake News

The COVID-19 pandemic has had disastrous effects on human health and well-being as well as on the economy and other areas of societal life. One factor that played into this global crisis has been the lack of trustworthy and reliable information sources and the simultaneous inflow of misinformation that fed into unfortunate individual choices, shared conspiracy theories[1] (such as myths about 5G installations spreading COVID-19 or a particular ethnic or religious group being at the virus' origin) and patterns of group resistance.[2] The novelty of the COVID virus and the related gaps in knowledge created an almost ideal breeding ground for false or misleading narratives to spread.[3] Pursuant to the World Health Organization (WHO), such an infodemic creates confusion and distrust, and ultimately undermines an effective public health response.[4] There are numerous studies that show how exponentially this infodemic has spread on different social platforms and how real its implications have been.[5]

Admittedly, fake news, including ones about the origins and spread of diseases, are not new: "[m]isinformation, disinformation and propaganda have been features of human communication since at least the Roman times",[6] and over the ages, they have only been facilitated by technological advances starting with the invention of the printing press and now being immensely expedited by the Internet as a global communication platform.[7] While there are different narratives and timelines on the beginnings and the evolution of fake news as a societal phenomenon,[8] for the purpose of this chapter's discussion, it is critical to highlight what is specific about the nature of contemporary fake news: "[t]here are three unique parts to modern fake news that make it different from older varieties of intentionally exaggerated or false

---

[1] On the origins and the reason for distribution of conspiracy theories, see e.g. Sunstein and Vermeule (2009).

[2] For an overview of the different misinformation threats, see e.g. European Commission and the High Representative of the Union for Foreign Affairs and Security Policy (2020); See also Brennen et al. (2020); Baines and Elliott (2020); Enders (2020).

[3] See European Commission and the High Representative of the Union for Foreign Affairs and Security Policy (2020).

[4] WHO stated that "infodemics are an excessive amount of information about a problem, which makes it difficult to identify a solution. They can spread misinformation, disinformation and rumours during a health emergency. Infodemics can hamper an effective public health response and create confusion and distrust among people." See WHO (2020); see also WHO et al. (2020).

[5] See e.g. Knuutila et al. (2020); Brennen et al. (2020); Center for Countering Digital Hate (2020); Nielsen et al. (2020).

[6] Posetti and Matthews (2020), at 1; for understanding the different types of fake news, making a difference between disinformation, misinformation and malinformation, see Wardle (2019); For a slightly different classification, see Tandoc et al. (2018).

[7] See e.g. Ireton and Posetti (2018) and the next section.

[8] See e.g. Posetti and Matthews (2020); Soll (2016); Wendling (2018); Merriam-Webster (2021); Poole (2019).

reporting: the who, the what, and the how."[9] With regard to the "who", what is peculiar is that today's fake news are not produced by classic media outlets, although they may be taken up by them.[10] The origins of misinformation rather lead back to governments driven by ideological interests or tech-savvy individuals looking for a certain reward. With regard to the "what" of fake news, it is not only the content that may be distorted but also the source. Deep fake technology has only facilitated the production of pieces of content that appear to be entirely truthful and authentic.[11] Finally, the "how" is quite different, as online platforms are key in the distribution of fake news and their seamless embeddedness in communication processes. Social media tend to be "source-agnostic", as they collect and present news stories from a variety of outlets, regardless of the quality and reliability of the original source. Also, because news stories often reach the users through a certain circle of friends or people they follow, there is a sort of endorsement of the story. Finally, and critically, through the inherent functionality of social platforms' algorithms, the popularity of fake news can be significantly enhanced and their outreach magnified.[12]

The infodemic and the fake news phenomenon, in general, have become well acknowledged by policy-makers and legislators around the world and have spurred a number of initiatives that try to address them,[13] which have been linked to larger projects of regulating platforms that relate to other negative phenomena, such as hate speech proliferation or extreme opinion building. The following section explores these initiatives and the surrounding debates by first providing a look into the changing role of platforms in the new digital media space and the associated dangers for individual free speech, as well as for a healthy public discourse as a fundament of a democratic society.

2 Regulating Online Platforms

2.1 *Understanding Platforms as Information Intermediaries*

The Internet has enabled instantaneous sharing of information and communication among millions of people, with a relatively low threshold for participation and seemingly no barriers.[14] Many have hoped that this digital space would, even without the need for state intervention, create the conditions necessary for individual freedom of speech, both in its active and passive dimensions, for a sustainable public

---

[9] Center for Information Technology and Society (2019).
[10] Ibid.
[11] Ibid.; see also Chesney and Citron (2019).
[12] Center for Information Technology and Society (2019).
[13] For updated information on the initiatives around the world, see e.g. https://infogram.com/covid-1 9-fake-news-regulation-passed-during-covid-19-1h8n6md5q9kj6xo (last access 23 February 2022)
[14] See e.g. Benkler (2006); Whitt (2013).

discourse and content diversity to flourish.[15] Sadly, this brave new world of the "marketplace of ideas"[16] has not materialized so far; instead, the digital space has brought discrete new challenges with it, some of which may call for a deliberate action.

A distinct new phenomenon that has captured the attention of both scholars[17] and policy-makers[18] in this debate is the critical role played by platforms.[19] Platforms like social networking sites, search engines and other types of aggregators, often driven by algorithms, have turned into gatekeepers that command substantial powers in contemporary media environments. They have become content curators and profoundly changed the processes of cultural production, distribution, the conditions for access to content, its use and re-use—in many aspects effectively replacing the role of traditional media as a "general interest intermediary"[20] but without any public or other regulatory mandate.[21] The implications of this transformation are multiple, many of them are critical for the design of the law. Some domains, such as copyright law, have been substantially adjusted to this new environment in the last couple of decades, whereby intermediaries have become key enforcers of copyright law and subject to specific types of liability.[22] Other areas, such as antitrust law,[23] have been much slower in this adaptation. The same is true for media law, which has traditionally been entrusted with key functions to ensure conditions for opinion formation, public debate, political and cultural engagement, and social cohesion,[24] as discussed in more detail below.

One key implication of the new digital media space that complicates conventional conditions of free speech, as well as the initiatives to regulate it, is the shift from the standard dualist model of state versus speakers-publishers towards a pluralistic model with complex relations along a tringle of actors, where both the audience and the state become highly dependent on platforms.[25] It has been argued that in such a configuration, nation states tend to create different liability regimes for digital companies that may trigger collateral censorship and prior restraint.[26] Social media

---

[15] See e.g. Benkler (2006); Lessig (2009).

[16] For a clarification of the term, see below.

[17] See e.g. Balkin (2012); Cohen (2018); Lobel (2016).

[18] See e.g. European Commission (2016); UK House of Commons (2019).

[19] The focus here is placed not upon the physical intermediaries, such as network operators or Internet service suppliers (although these matter too: see e.g. Benkler (2006); DeNardis (2009); Frishmann (2012) but upon those gatekeepers existing at the applications and the content levels—the so-called "choice intermediaries" or "new editors". See Helberger (2011); Miel and Farris (2008).

[20] Sunstein (2007).

[21] Napoli (2012, 2015).

[22] See e.g. Sag (2018); Spindler (2020); Frosio (2020); Burri and Zihlmann (2021).

[23] See e.g. Ezrachi and Stucke (2016); for a brief overview of the issues, see Burri (2019a).

[24] See e.g. Burri (2015).

[25] Balkin (2012); also Balkin (2018).

[26] Balkin (2012).

companies, in their own right, create sophisticated systems of private governance that govern end users arbitrarily and without due process and transparency. At the same time, users are vulnerable to digital surveillance and manipulation, and the intensified datafication of the digital economy only exacerbates this vulnerability.[27] A second fundamental shift in the new media environment has been epitomized by the enhanced editorial functions of digital platforms as "choice intermediaries" that control the choices for content, communication and engagement we make and the possibility for choices we see.[28] A number of issues can be noted in this context: the first relates to the critical role of technology, of algorithms, as automated filters,[29] aggregators and even content producers.[30] Another important feature that explains the motivation in selecting a particular algorithm design or making a governance decision as to the availability and prominence of content[31] relates to the nature of multi-sided markets inherent to most digital platforms, where they give users free access to certain services on one side of the platform, while also selling the information collected to advertisers and other companies.[32] This model incentivizes the battle for the attention of the many but also for tailored offerings; it makes data collection and data use more intrusive, which bears upon competition and data protection[33] but is yet to be seriously considered in the domain of media law—despite the fact that it deeply impacts information flows and the conditions of free speech.[34]

Thinking about the societal functions of the media in the context of this chapter's discussion, it can also be that this complex platform-mediated environment engenders certain risks for the animated public sphere and for a vibrant and diverse culture. First, the possible interferences with users' individual autonomy and freedom of choice need to be acknowledged. As Latzer et al. argue, while filtering reduces search and information costs and facilitates social orientation, it can be "compromised by the production of social risks, amongst others, threats to basic rights and liberties as well as impacts on the mediation of realities and people's future development".[35] The second worry relates to the impact of tailored consumption on the engagement of the user in political, social and cultural debates. The personalization of the media diet, as based on a distinct profile or previous experience, "promotes content that is geographically close as well as socially and conceptually familiar";[36] it reflects each individual's interests and biases and provides no

---

[27] Balkin (2012, 2018); Klonick (2018).
[28] See Helberger (2011); Miel and Farris (2008).
[29] For a taxonomy of the different algorithmic filters, see Bozdag (2013).
[30] Napoli (2014), pp. 33–38; Also Saurwein et al. (2015); Helberger et al. (2015); Burri (2019b).
[31] Klonick (2018).
[32] See e.g. Bamberger and Lobel (2018); Burri (2019a).
[33] Burri (2019a); European Data Protection Supervisor (EDPS) (2014); Pollicino (2021).
[34] Cohen (2018); Kreiss and Mcgregor (2017); Benkler et al. (2018).
[35] Latzer et al. (2014), at pp. 29–30.
[36] Hoffman et al. (2015), at p. 1365.

information to disrupt preconceptions or prejudices.[37] Hoffman et al. further argue that social media only exacerbate this effect by combining two dimensions of "homophily"—similarity of peers and of content.[38] While these situations have been labelled differently—as "cyber-ghettos",[39] "filter bubbles"[40] or "echo chambers"[41]—they all point to a fragmentation of the public discourse, possible polarization of views and augmentation of the impact of unwanted content, such as fake news.[42] From the perspective of media law and policy, one should also acknowledge that in most media policy toolkits, the underlying causal link between diversity in supply and diversity in consumption may be destroyed.[43] Local and national identities and debates, as well as cultural diversity, may be endangered, as local, regional and national content and quality journalism, especially in the domains of news and current affairs, are marginalized online and rendered hard to "discover".[44]

A final element that complicates the conditions of free speech in the era of platforms is their staggering power—vis-à-vis the states (both domestic and foreign regulators), vis-à-vis other companies on the same or adjacent markets and ultimately vis-à-vis the users. Indeed, it has been argued that platforms have become the "new governors"[45] or the "emergent transnational sovereigns" of the digital space.[46] Yet, and as mentioned earlier, this power is often unchecked, and platforms moderate speech practice and cultural communication and engagement with any accountability—neither to their users nor to state agencies.[47] Against this backdrop of the new digital space and its increasing platformization, the next sections explore the initiatives that have been developed in the past few years to regulate platforms in diverse ways, with a specific focus laid upon the diverging approaches of the United States (US) and the European Union (EU) in this context.

---

[37] Hoffman et al. (2015); Sunstein (2007).

[38] Hoffman et al. (2015), at p. 1365.

[39] Dahlgren (2005).

[40] Pariser (2011).

[41] Sunstein (2001, 2007, 2009).

[42] Filter bubbles, together with "information cascades" and the human attraction to negative and novel information have been said to fuel the distribution and virality of fake news. For a careful analysis of these phenomena of online communication, see Chesney and Citron (2019), in particular pp. 1765–1768.

[43] Goodman Ellen (2004); Helberger (2012); Napoli (2012); Napoli et al. (2018).

[44] Napoli et al. (2018); Burri (2019b); McKelvey and Hunt (2019).

[45] Balkin (2012); Klonick (2018).

[46] Cohen (2018).

[47] Balkin (2018); see also Kaye (2019).

2.2 Regulatory Initiatives Addressing the Platformization of the Media Space and Online Misinformation

2.2.1 Introduction

The developments around platformization of the communication environment and the risks brought with it do not occur in a regulatory vacuum. They are embedded in long-standing traditions of international human rights protection,[48] as well as in domestic constitutional traditions and sophisticated frameworks of secondary legislation and judicial precedent.[49] This has been clearly recognized with regard to fake news, as several key international and regional human rights bodies, confirmed the applicability of existing frameworks in that: "States may only impose restrictions on the right to freedom of expression in accordance with the test for such restrictions under international law, namely that they be provided for by law, serve one of the legitimate interests recognised under international law, and be necessary and proportionate to protect that interest"[50] and that "[g]eneral prohibitions on the dissemination of information based on vague and ambiguous ideas, including "false news" or "non-objective information", are incompatible with international standards for restrictions on freedom of expression [...] and should be abolished".[51]

Yet, it should also be noted that free speech law has not been harmonized sufficiently at the international level, and we have, at times, profoundly different regimes in different countries. As platforms act as global players across jurisdictions and considering the borderless nature of the Internet,[52] the legal design that should appropriately safeguard fundamental rights and values within the sovereign state is only made more difficult.[53] In addition, most, if not all, of the platforms are

---

[48] See e.g. De Schutter (2014).

[49] See e.g. Farber (2019); Feldman and Sullivan (2019); Keller (2011); Oster (2017); Pollicino (2021).

[50] The United Nations (UN) Special Rapporteur on Freedom of Opinion and Expression, the Organization for Security and Co-operation in Europe (OSCE) Representative on Freedom of the Media, the Organization of American States (OAS) Special Rapporteur on Freedom of Expression and the African Commission on Human and Peoples' Rights (ACHPR) Special Rapporteur on Freedom of Expression and Access to Information, Joint Declaration on Freedom of Expression and "Fake News", Disinformation and Propaganda, FOM.GAL/3/17, 3 March 2017, at 1. General Principles, para. (a).

[51] Ibid., at 2. Standards on Disinformation and Propaganda, para. (a).

[52] See e.g. Eichensehr (2015); Daskal (2016); Eichensehr (2017).

[53] See e.g. the Yahoo! case as one of the first on free speech violation and online jurisdiction. There the US court when faced with the recognition and implementation of the French court order under the "comity of nations" doctrine stated that: "Absent a body of law that establishes international standards with respect to speech on the Internet and an appropriate treaty or legislation addressing enforcement of such standards to speech originating within the United States, the principle of comity is outweighed by the Court's obligation to uphold the First Amendment." (see Yahoo! II, 169 F. Supp. 2d, at 1193). For more on the case, see Goldsmith and Wu (2001), at pp. 49–64; Greenberg (2003).

American and as such tend to govern, both by technological means and human intervention, reflecting the First Amendment principle, social and corporate responsibility and the liability exceptions under US law.[54] In the following sections, we briefly trace the differences in the US and EU standards of free speech protection and subsequently expound on the initiatives undertaken to regulate free speech on platforms, and fake news in particular, in these major jurisdictions. While the initiatives to fight misinformation can be put into different categories covering a great variety of responses, such as (i) identification responses (including monitoring, fact-checking and investigative responses); (ii) ecosystem responses aimed at producers and distributors (including legislative and policy responses, counter-disinformation campaigns and electoral-specific responses); (iii) responses within production and distribution (including curatorial, technical, demonetization and advertising-linked responses); and (iv) responses aimed at target audiences (including normative ethical and educational responses; empowerment and credibility labelling responses),[55] the focus of this chapter is solely on the legislative responses with regard to platforms. It should also be noted that the chapter's enquiry is by no means comprehensive but is merely illustrative, as there is a flurry of initiatives around the world with currently around 28 countries having passed legislation related to disinformation, either through new laws or by updating existing regulations in the areas of media, electoral, cybersecurity or criminal law.[56]

2.2.2 Developments in the United States

To begin with, it is fair to note that there have not been any major regulatory projects in the United States that seek to address online misinformation. And the developments that we have seen in the past years with regard to online platforms have been in the field of self-regulation, with major companies like Facebook or Twitter designing a palette of measures for their platforms to tackle misinformation in particular and bad speech in general.[57] This is not surprising, as the protection of free speech in the United States is in many ways specific when compared with other countries and awarded a higher value.[58] For starters, the First Amendment to the US Constitution clearly states that "Congress shall make no law [...] abridging the freedom of speech". Whereas there have been some restrictions on free speech, as later discussed, these are fairly limited in scope, and the doctrine of "the marketplace of ideas" as endorsed by Justice Oliver Wendell Holmes,[59] which sees free speech as

---

[54] See Klonick (2018); see also Chander (2014).
[55] See Bontcheva and Posetti (2020), in particular pp. 36–40.
[56] Boncheva and Posetti (2020), ibid., at p. 108; see also Bayer et al. (2019); Roudik et al. (2019).
[57] See e.g. Nunziato (2019); Klonick (2020).
[58] See e.g. Haupt (2005) (also providing an overview of the comparative literature); Tourkochoriti (2016).
[59] Abrams v. United States, 250 U.S. 616 (1919) (dissenting opinion Holmes).

an open marketplace where ideas compete against each another for acceptance by the public, has been sustained. The Internet has not been seen to change the nature of the First Amendment's application, as confirmed by the very first Internet-related case by the US Supreme Court in *Reno v. ACLU*,[60] where the Court pointed out that "the content on the Internet is as diverse as human thought" and established "no basis for qualifying the level of First Amendment scrutiny that should be applied to this medium".[61]

For the legal test in defining the scope of the First Amendment, as developed over the years, courts need to determine (i) whether the law regulates a category of speech that is unprotected under the First Amendment or granted lesser than full protection, which gives the government certain regulatory authority, and (ii) whether the law is a content-based restriction, which is then presumed invalid under strict scrutiny, or a content-neutral restriction, which is subject to intermediate scrutiny, a less speech-protective test.[62] The content-based restriction never passes the test, as "... the government has no power to restrict expression because of its message, its ideas, its subject matter, or its content"[63] and the state may not prohibit the expression of an idea "simply because society finds the idea itself offensive or disagreeable".[64] In the application of strict scrutiny, a law can "survive" only when it is narrowly tailored to promote a compelling government interest.[65] Restrictions on speech that have been upheld so far relate to a limited number of situations, such as obscenity, child pornography, fraud, treason, incitement to crime, fighting words, true threats, and speech presenting some grave and imminent threat the government has the power to prevent,[66] whereby there must be a realistic, factual assessment of harm.[67] The test with regard to defamation and libel is also hard to pass since *New York Times Co. v. Sullivan*, where the Court found that a public official seeking to recover damages for a defamatory falsehood relating to his official conduct must prove that the statement was made with "actual malice"—that is, with the knowledge that it was false or with reckless disregard of whether it was false or not.[68]

---

[60] 521 U.S. 844 (1996).

[61] Ibid., at para. 885. In the more recent case of Packingham v. North Carolina, 137 S. Ct. 1730 (2017), the Supreme Court compared social media platforms to a town square and recognized their function as a forum to exchange ideas and viewpoints.

[62] Tompros et al. (2020), at pp. 88–89.

[63] Police Dep't of Chi. v. Mosley, 408 U.S. 92, 95 (1972).

[64] United States v. Eichman, 110 S. Ct. 2404, 2410 (1990).

[65] Tompros et al. (2020), at p. 90, referring to Burson v. Freeman, 504 U.S. 191, 199 (1992).

[66] See e.g. United States v. Alvarez, 567 U.S. 709, 717 (2012). A regulation of unprotected speech may still violate the First Amendment with regard to content discrimination if it includes distinctions among subcategories of speech that cannot be justified. See e.g. R.A.V. v. City of St. Paul, 505 U.S. 377 (1992).

[67] United States v. Williams, 553 U.S. 285, 322 (dissenting opinion Souter).

[68] New York Times Co. v. Sullivan, 376 U.S. 254 (1964), at 279–280. The decision in Gertz extended the NY Times standard of "reckless disregard" from public officials to public figures and

Since the 2012 Supreme Court decision in *United States v. Alvarez*,[69] it has also become clear that false statements fall within the scope of the First Amendment. In *Alvarez*, the Court found the 2005 Stolen Valor Act, which criminalized a falsely claimed receipt of military decorations or medals, unconstitutional, and the majority highlighted that punishing false speech would deter an open and vigorous expression of views[70] and that less restrictive measures, such as counter-speech, could promote the state's legitimate interests.[71] This said, some US states do have false reporting statutes for very specific situations imposing criminal liability for false speech related to emergencies or natural catastrophes, with New York's false reporting statute[72] being the most far-reaching in this regard, as it does not require knowledge or intent with respect to the ensuing public alarm or inconvenience.[73] Next to this robust protection of free speech granted in the United States, which very often is given primacy over other rights, such as privacy,[74] the US Speech Act bans enforcement of judgements that would violate the free speech safeguards under the First Amendment and other domestic statutes,[75] and so insulates American companies from liability.

In the context of online platforms, US law grants an almost perfect safe harbour from liability through Section 230(c)(1) of the Communications Decency Act (CDA),[76] which states that: "No provider or user of an interactive computer service shall be treated as the publisher or speaker of any information provided by another information content provider". Section 230 gives important substantive and procedural advantages that only enhance the safeguards of the First Amendment.[77] These

---

defined these as the persons who, due to their notoriety, achievements, or the rigour of their success, seek the attention of the public. See Gertz v. Robert Welch, Inc., 418 U.S. 323, 350 (1974).

[69] 567 U.S. 709 (2012). For a fully analysis of the case, see Tompros et al. (2020), at pp. 93–97.

[70] Ibid., at 718.

[71] Ibid., at 710, 726.

[72] N.Y. Penal Law §240.50 reads: "A person is guilty of falsely reporting an incident in the third degree when, knowing the information reported, conveyed or circulated to be false or baseless, he or she [...] [i]nitiates or circulates a false report or warning of an alleged occurrence or impending occurrence of a crime, catastrophe or emergency under circumstances in which it is not unlikely that public alarm or inconvenience will result." Falsely reporting an incident in the third degree is a class A misdemeanor and punishable by up to 1 year's imprisonment and a fine of USD 1'000. The statute permits in addition entities providing emergency services to seek restitution for "the amount of funds reasonably expended for the purpose of responding" to false reports.

[73] For a fully-fledged analysis of the law, as well as its possible unconstitutionality post-Alvarez, see Tompros et al. (2020).

[74] See e.g. Tourkochoriti (2016); Burri (2021).

[75] Securing the Protection off Our Enduring and Established Constitutional Heritage Act (SPEECH Act), 124 Stat. 2380 (2010). See Goldman (2020).

[76] Communications Decency Act of 1996, (CDA), Pub. L. No. 104-104 (Tit. V), 110 Stat. 133 (8 February1996), codified at 47 U.S.C. §§223, 230. For a detailed analysis, see Brannon and Holmes (2021).

[77] Goldman (2020); see also Goldman (2019); Bone (2021).

famous "twenty-six words that created the Internet"[78] have been critical in the evolution of online platforms, as well as in their positioning as "new governors" of the online media space.[79] Especially important in the latter context is that Section 230 enables the intermediary to make a decision in good faith to block or remove content that the intermediary considers "to be obscene, lewd, lascivious, filthy, excessively violent, harassing, or otherwise objectionable, *whether or not such material is constitutionally protected*".[80] Platforms thus have a critical toolkit for content moderation and have used this at times aggressively—for instance, by permanently suspending the Twitter account of President Trump (@realDonaldTrump) on 8 January 2021. Section 230 is, in this sense, a unique type of platforms' immunity[81] that, next to the strong protection granted under the US Constitution's First Amendment, shields platforms. In recent years through the channel of free trade agreements, the US has tried to diffuse this unique arrangement, for instance by inserting a similar rule on "interactive computer services" in the updated North American Free Trade Agreement (NAFTA, now called United States Mexico Canada Agreement, USMCA) with Canada and Mexico.[82] Section 230 has not been left without criticism, though, and there have been a number of attempts to constrain its broadly defined immunity, especially in consideration of the changed media environment and the critical role of platforms in it.[83] One attempt that has been successful was the adoption of the 2017 FOSTA[84] to fight online sex trafficking. But there are also other projects in the pipeline aiming at an amendment of Section 230 and addressing the power of Big Tech, such as the "Ending Support for Internet Censorship Act",[85] the "Biased Algorithm Deterrence Act",[86] and the "Algorithmic Accountability Act".[87] The laws particularly seek to calibrate the content moderation power of platforms,[88] but their fate is still uncertain. In scholarly debates, there have also been initiatives to use common law doctrines for guidance—in particular, the fiduciary duty-based relationships, such as those between doctors

---

[78] Kloseff (2019).

[79] Klonick (2018).

[80] 47 U.S.C. §230(c)(2)(A) (emphasis added).

[81] Goldman (2020).

[82] See e.g. Burri (2022).

[83] See e.g. Goldman (2019); On the constitutionality of possible Section 230 amendments, see e.g. Brannon and Holmes (2021); see also Citron and Wittes (2017) (arguing that platforms should enjoy immunity from liability if they could show that their response to unlawful uses of their services was reasonable).

[84] Allow States and Victims to Fight Online Sex Trafficking Act of 2017, H.R.1865 (115th Cong. 2017–18).

[85] Ending Support for Internet Censorship Act, S. 1914, 116th Cong. (2019).

[86] Biased Algorithm Deterrence Act of 2019, H.R. 492, 116th Cong. (2019).

[87] Algorithmic Accountability Act, S. 1108, 116th Cong. (2019).

[88] For details on and analysis of the legislative proposals, see Bone (2021).

and their patients; lawyers and their clients, and to create new types of obligations for platforms as information fiduciaries[89] in this frame.

2.2.3 Developments in the European Union

Remarks on the General Framework for the Protection of Freedom of Expression

The developments in Europe with regard to the regulation of platforms have occurred in multiple areas of law and in the broader policy context starting around 2015.[90] While free speech is robustly protected in Europe, the protection does differ from that awarded in the United States and the constitutional balance is differently struck. Importantly in this context, although the right to freedom of expression does not have a direct horizontal application,[91] there is a positive duty of the state to protect it and act as the "ultimate guarantor" of media pluralism.[92] The fundamental right of freedom of expression, both its active and passive dimensions, is enshrined in Article 10 of the European Convention of Human Rights (ECHR),[93] and the ambit of the protection is wide. The right covers both the content and the form of communication, and applies to any means of dissemination or reception of communication.[94] Much in light of the US Supreme Court's judgements, the European Court of Human Rights (ECtHR) has held that freedom of expression is protected not only for information and ideas that are favourably accepted, inoffensive or indifferent but also for such that "offend, shock or disturb the State or any sector of the population".[95] Yet, in contrast to the US stance and because of their historical experience, Europeans have not shared the concept of the marketplace of ideas, and different tests have been developed to strike a balance in clashes between different rights, as well as to protect key societal values, such as equality, anti-discrimination and democracy, which may ultimately lead to constraining freedom of expression.[96] For instance, the ECtHR has permitted in this context that harmful effects on social

---

[89] The IF model maintains that platforms should be required to abide by fiduciary duties of care, loyalty and confidentiality with regard to their end users. For a discussion, see Balkin (2016, 2018); Balkin and Zittrain (2016); Khan and Pozen (2019); Whitt (2019); Haupt (2020).

[90] See e.g. De Gregorio (2020); Bloch-Wehba (2019).

[91] Dink v Turkey [2010] ECtHR 2668/07, 6102/08, 30079/08, 7072/09 and 7124/09.

[92] Informationsverein Lentia and Others v Austria [1993] ECtHR 13914/88; 15041/89; 15717/89; 15779/89; 17207/90.

[93] European Convention on Human Rights, 4 November 1950, 213 U.N.T.S. 221; see also Article 11 (Freedom of Expression and Information) of the Charter of Fundamental Rights of the European Union (CFREU), OJ C [2012] 326/393, 26 October 2012.

[94] See e.g. Autronic AG v Switzerland [1990] ECtHR 12726/87; Schweizerische Radio- und Fernsehgesellschaft SRG v Switzerland [2012] ECtHR 34124/06.

[95] Handyside v. United Kingdom [1976] ECtHR 5493/72, at para. 49.

[96] For details, see Oster (2017), at Chapter 3; Pollicino (2021).

peace and political stability do justify an interference with freedom of expression.[97] Amongst others, denial of the Holocaust[98] or incitement to hatred or racial discrimination[99] have been held as not protected under Article 10 ECHR. In recent years and because of the critical importance of personal data in the contemporary data-driven society,[100] privacy protection has been given in many cases primacy over the right to freedom of expression. This has been clearly illustrated by the stance of the European Court of Justice (CJEU) in the *Google Spain* case,[101] which famously coined the "right to be forgotten".[102] The Court held that an individual has the right to object to a search engine's linking to personal information and that the evaluation of such an objection calls for a balancing of rights and interests, in the context of which account must be taken of the significance of the data subject's rights arising from Articles 7 and 8 of the Charter of Fundamental Rights of the European Union.[103] Effectively, the right to be forgotten, which is now also enshrined under the General Data Protection Regulation (GDPR),[104] trumps, under certain circumstances,[105] the economic freedom of search engines, their freedom of expression, and constrains the passive dimension of the freedom of expression, as it makes information unavailable for the public. Importantly for this chapter's discussion, the truthfulness of a statement plays an important role when balancing conflicting

---

[97] See e.g. Perinçek v. Switzerland [2015] ECtHR 27510/08.

[98] See e.g. Lehideux and Isorni v. France [1998] ECtHR 55/1997/839/1045; Garaudy v. France [2003] ECtHR 65831/01; Witzsch v. Germany [2005] ECtHR 7485/03.

[99] See e.g. Pavel Ivanov v. Russia [2004] ECtHR 35222/04; Aksu v. Turkey [2012] ECtHR 4149/04 and 41029/04.

[100] See e.g. Mayer-Schönberger and Cukier (2013); van der Sloot et al. (2016); Burri (2021).

[101] Case C-131/12, Google Spain SL and Google Inc. v. Agencia Española de Protección de Datos (AEPD) and Mario Costeja González, Judgment of the Court (Grand Chamber) of 13 May 2014, ECR [2014] 317 [hereinafter Google Spain].

[102] See e.g. Wechsler (2015); Hoffman et al. (2016).

[103] *Google Spain*, at para. 74, referring to Joined Cases C-468/10 and C-469/10, Asociación Nacional de Establecimientos Financieros de Crédito (ASNEF) and Federación de Comercio Electrónico y Marketing Directo (FECEMD) v. Administración del Estado, Judgment of 24 November 2011, ECR I-12181, at paras 38, 40.

[104] Directive 2016/680 of the European Parliament and of the Council of April 27, 2016, on the protection of natural persons with regard to the processing of personal data by competent authorities for the purposes of the prevention, investigation, detection, or prosecution of criminal offences or the execution of criminal penalties, and on the free movement of such data, and repealing Council Framework Decision 2008/977/JHA, OJ L [2016] 119/89. [hereinafter GDPR].

[105] Google Spain, at para. 88. There is a qualification in para. 99: "As the data subject may, in the light of his fundamental rights under Articles 7 and 8 of the Charter, request that the information in question no longer be made available to the general public on account of its inclusion in such a list of results, those rights override, as a rule, not only the economic interest of the operator of the search engine but also the interest of the general public in having access to that information upon a search relating to the data subject's name. However, that would not be the case if it appeared, for particular reasons, such as the role played by the data subject in public life, that the interference with his fundamental rights is justified by the preponderant interest of the general public in having, on account of its inclusion in the list of results, access to the information in question."

interests, such as, for instance, hate speech or privacy protection.[106] The Court has also stressed that, while Article 10 affords journalists wide protection, it is not unlimited but "subject to the proviso that they are acting in good faith and on an accurate factual basis and provide "reliable and precise" information in accordance with the ethics of journalism",[107] which is to be judged depending on the situation and the technical means used.[108]

The Court has repeatedly emphasized the importance of the Internet for the exercise of freedom of expression, since it provides "essential tools for participation in activities and discussions concerning political issues and issues of general interest".[109] Although the Court has not yet had the opportunity to squarely address the duties and responsibilities of social media platforms under Article 10 ECHR,[110] it has tackled cases with regard to automated content moderation.[111] The Court found, in particular, in *Delfi* that a news organization can be held responsible for users' comments if it fails to identify and remove infringing ones, despite the filtering system that the organization had in place.[112] The Court has, however, somewhat moved away from this strict liability for unfiltered comments in *MTE v. Hungary*, where it found that "this amounts to requiring excessive and impracticable forethought capable of undermining freedom of the right to impart information on the Internet".[113]

In consideration of the global nature of the Internet, the extraterritorial effect of European precedents appears critical. In the landmark follow-up case to *Google Spain*, *Google v. CNIL*,[114] which discussed whether the right to be forgotten should have a global reach, the CJEU was cautious and stated that the effect should be limited to the European Union, while using geo-blocking technology in making sure that the right to de-referencing is properly safeguarded.[115] The protection of freedom

---

[106] Oster (2017), at p. 18 and Chapter 3.

[107] Bladet Tromsø and Stensaas v Norway [1999] ECtHR 21980/93, at para. 65.

[108] Stoll v Switzerland [2007] ECtHR 69698/01.

[109] Ahmet Yildirim v Turkey [2012] ECtHR 3111/10, at para. 54.

[110] See Helberger et al. (2020).

[111] See ibid.

[112] Delfi v Estonia [2015] ECtHR 64569/09.

[113] MTE v Hungary [2016] ECtHR 22947/13, at para. 82.

[114] C-507/17, Google v. Commission nationale de l'informatique et des libertés (CNIL), Judgment of 24 September 2019, ECLI:EU:C:2019:772. For a great summary of the case and references to the primary sources, see Columbia Global Freedom of Expression, https://globalfreedomofexpression.columbia.edu/cases/google-llc-v-national-commission-on-informatics-and-liberty-cnil/ (last access 23 February 2022).

[115] Ibid., at para. 74: "... the operator is not required to carry out that de-referencing on all versions of its search engine, but on the versions of that search engine corresponding to all the Member States, using, where necessary, measures which, while meeting the legal requirements, effectively prevent or, at the very least, seriously discourage an internet user conducting a search from one of the Member States on the basis of a data subject's name from gaining access via the list of results displayed following that search, to the links which are the subject of that request."

of expression did play a key role in the Court's decision, as well as the consideration of the different free speech standards around the world,[116] and that Google, if made to comply with a global obligation to de-reference, would effectively be faced with an infringement of the First Amendment in the US. Indeed, as noted earlier, both the First Amendment and Section 230 immunize search engines for their indexing decisions,[117] and operators cannot be legally compelled to implement a right to be forgotten in the United States.[118] Yet, in a later case concerning defamation of an Austrian politician on Facebook, the CJEU found differently.[119] First and importantly, the Court held that national Courts could order platforms to take down both a specific piece of content and identical content, as well as *equivalent* content (that is, content which conveys the same message, albeit slightly differently worded), as a type of a continued obligation for the platforms. The Court's argument for this extension of the duty was that otherwise, it would be too easy to circumvent an order. However, the Court was careful to delimit the obligation on platforms, by stating that the equivalent information had to be identified in the order, such that the hosting provider did not have to carry out an independent assessment of what constitutes equivalent content. The Court found in addition that such an order was not excessive, since hosting platforms have automated search tools and technologies, and there is no general monitoring obligation involved, which will be contrary to Article 15 of the 2000 E-Commerce Directive[120] that regulates providers' liability for third party content.[121] Second, and critically for the extraterritorial impact of the judgment, the Court found that the E-Commerce Directive does not preclude orders from

---

[116] See ibid., at para. 27; see also Opinion of Advocate General Szpunar delivered on 10 January 2019, ECLI:EU:C:2019:15.

[117] Goldman (2019), referring to Search King, Inc. v. Google Technology, Inc., 2003 WL 21464568 (W.D. Okla. 2003); Langdon v. Google, Inc., 474 F. Supp. 2d 622 (D. Del. 2007); Zhang v. Baidu. com, Inc., 10 F. Supp. 3d 433 (S.D.N.Y. 2014); Google, Inc. v. Hood, 96 F. Supp. 3d 584 (S.D. Miss. 2015); e-ventures Worldwide v. Google, Inc., 2017 WL 2210029 (M.D. Fla. 2017); Martin v. Hearst Corporation, 777 F.3d 546 (2d Cir. 2015).

[118] Goldman (2019), referring to Maughan v. Google Technology, Inc., 143 Cal. App. 4th 1242 (Cal. App. Ct. 2006); Murawski v. Pataki, 514 F. Supp. 2d 577 (S.D.N.Y. 2007); Shah v. MyLife. Com, Inc., 2012 WL 4863696 (D. Or. 2012); Merritt v. Lexis Nexis, 2012 WL 6725882 (E.D. Mich. 2012); Nieman v. Versuslaw, Inc., 2012 WL 3201931 (C.D. Ill. 2012); Getachew v. Google, Inc., 491 Fed. Appx. 923 (10th Cir. 2012); Mmubango v. Google, Inc., 2013 WL 664231 (E.D. Pa. 2013); O'Kroley v. Fastcase Inc., 831 F.3d 352 (6th Cir. 2016); Fakhrian v. Google Inc., 2016 WL 1650705 (Cal. App. Ct. 2016); Despot v. Baltimore Life Insurance Co., 2016 WL 4148085 (W.D. Pa. 2016); Manchanda v. Google, Inc., 2016 WL 6806250 (S.D.N.Y. 2016).

[119] Case C-18/18 Eva Glawischnig-Piesczek v Facebook Ireland Limited, Judgment of 3 October 2019, ECLI:EU:C:2019:821. For a great summary of the case and references to the primary sources, see Columbia Global Freedom of Expression, https://globalfreedomofexpression.columbia.edu/cases/glawischnig-piesczek-v-facebook-ireland-limited/; For a critique of the case, see Keller (2019).

[120] Directive 2000/31/EC of the European Parliament and of the Council of 8 June 2000 on certain legal aspects of information society services, in particular electronic commerce, in the Internal Market (Directive on electronic commerce), OJ L [2000] 178/1.

[121] See in particular Article 14 E-Commerce Directive.

producing worldwide effects, provided that it is consistent with international law, which is for the Member States to assess. In the first follow-up case after *Glawischnig/Facebook*,[122] the Austrian Supreme Court confirmed and clarified some aspects of the CJEU decision and made it clear that when evaluating the removal of "information with an equivalent meaning", the balance of interests must not depend on the availability of automated search tools but requires that it can be determined at first glance by a layperson. The Austrian Court also confirmed the possibility of worldwide relief against the infringement of personal rights; noted though that there must be a specific plaintiff's request for this.[123]

Even from this relatively short analysis of the protection of free speech in the United States and in the European Union, it becomes readily evident that the constitutional balances are quite differently struck and the possibilities, indeed the duties, that EU states have to regulate platforms in order to protect vital societal interest are multiple and may lead to certain constraints on freedom of expression, both in its active and passive dimensions. The EU and its Member States also have secondary legislation in place that addresses platforms more squarely. The next section offers a glimpse into these regulatory initiatives.

Specific Initiatives Regulating Platforms

The EU framework on platform regulation has evolved over the years and includes different pieces of legislation, some of them predating the predicament of online misinformation. The starting point is the above-mentioned and now relatively dated 2000 E-Commerce Directive, which horizontally regulates the liability of Internet service providers for all types of infringement (excluding tax and data protection, audiovisual services and gambling). The E-Commerce Directive specifies in particular the "notice and takedown" regime depending on the different types of interaction between the platform and the content,[124] while prohibiting general monitoring obligations as a guarantee for fundamental rights protection.[125] The E-Commerce

---

[122] Austrian Supreme Court, ORF/Facebook, Judgment 4Ob36/20b of 30 March 2020.

[123] There was not such a request involved in the case at issue.

[124] Articles 12–14 E-Commerce Directive.

[125] Article 15 E-Commerce Directive. In Scarlet v SABAM (Case C-70/10, Scarlet Extended SA v Société belge des auteurs, compositeurs et éditeurs SCRL (SABAM), ECLI:EU:C:2011:771), the Belgian collecting society SABAM applied for a permanent order requiring a network access provider to monitor and block peer-to-peer transmission of music files from SABAM's catalogue. The CJEU decided that a broad order of the type requested would go both against the prohibition of general monitoring obligations of the E-Commerce Directive and the fundamental rights of Internet users to the protection of their personal data and freedom of expression guaranteed under the EU Charter of Fundamental Rights. See also Case C-360/10, Belgische Vereniging van Auteurs, Componisten en Uitgevers CVBA (SABAM) v Netlog NV, ECLI:EU:C:2012:85. Specific monitoring obligations have been however found not in violation of Article 15 E-Commerce Directive (see De Streel et al. (2021)).

Directive also includes specific norms on co- and self-regulatory measures[126] and a duty to cooperate with competent authorities.[127] In 2018 the European Commission provided more specific guidance with the Recommendation to fight illegal content online,[128] which set out the general principles for all types of illegal content online and recommended stricter moderation for terrorist content. In particular, the Recommendation addressed the "notice and takedown" procedures and specified that they must (i) be effective, precise and adequately substantiated; (ii) respect the rights of content providers with possibilities of counter-notices and out-of-court dispute settlement and (iii) be transparent.[129] With regard to the proactive measures that operators should adopt, the Recommendation encouraged appropriate, proportionate and specific measures, which may use automated means but with safeguards in place, in particular human oversight and verification.[130] The Recommendation also encouraged closer cooperation with national judicial and administrative authorities as well as with trusted flaggers with the necessary expertise and determined on a clear and objective basis; it fostered cooperation among hosting providers, in particular smaller ones that may have less capacity to tackle illegal content.[131]

In addition to the intermediaries' liability regulation, the EU has had since 1989 an instrument to regulate media services,[132] whose scope of application has been extended to cover online content services as well over the years and in light of technological developments. The most recent revision of the Audiovisual Media Service Directive (AVMSD)[133] of 2018 also applies to the so-called video-sharing platforms (VSPs), which in essence address user-generated content platforms.[134]

---

[126] Article 16 E-Commerce Directive.

[127] Article 15(2) E-Commerce Directive.

[128] European Commission (2018); see also European Commission (2017).

[129] European Commission (2018), ibid., at points 5–17.

[130] European Commission (2018), ibid., at points 16–21.

[131] European Commission (2018), at points 22–28. For an evaluation of the rules, see de Streel et al. (2021), at pp. 22–23.

[132] Council Directive 89/552/EEC of 3 October 1989 on the coordination of certain provisions laid down by law, regulation or administrative action in Member States concerning the pursuit of television broadcasting activities, OJ L [1989] 298/23.

[133] Directive 2010/13 of the European Parliament and of the Council of 10 March 2010 on the coordination of certain provisions laid down by law, regulation or administrative action in Member States concerning the provision of audio-visual media services (Audio-Visual Media Services Directive), OJ L [2010] 95/1, as amended by Directive 2018/1808, OJ L [2018] 303/69 [hereinafter AVMSD].

[134] Article 1(1aa) AVMSD defines the "video-sharing platform service" as "a service as defined by Articles 56 and 57 TFEU, where the principal purpose of the service or of a dissociable section thereof or an essential functionality of the service is devoted to providing programmes, user-generated videos, or both, to the general public, for which the video-sharing platform provider does not have editorial responsibility, in order to inform, entertain or educate, by means of electronic communications networks [...] and the organisation of which is determined by the video-sharing platform provider, including by automatic means or algorithms in particular by displaying, tagging and sequencing."; see also European Commission (2020).

VSPs face lighter duties and responsibilities than broadcasting channels and platforms with editorial responsibility (such as Netflix, for instance) but must take appropriate measures to protect the general public from certain types of online content, in particular racism and xenophobia, as well as hate speech based upon the illegal grounds as laid down in the EU Charter of Fundamental Rights (sex, race, colour, ethnic or social origin, genetic features, language, religion or belief, political or any other opinion, membership of a national minority, property, birth, disability, age or sexual orientation).[135] VSPs must also protect minors from content, which may impair their physical, mental or moral development.[136] The AVMSD notes that the measures must be "appropriate" in the light of the nature of the content, the potential harm, the characteristics of the category of persons to be protected, the rights and legitimate interests at stake, as well as "practicable and proportionate", taking into account the size of the VSP and the nature of the provided service.[137] In addition to the AVMSD, platforms bear certain distinct duties with regard to fighting terrorist content online under the Counter-Terrorism Directive[138] and the Directive against Child Sexual Abuse.[139]

With regard to platforms, the EU has also adopted a number of more recent measures of self- and co-regulatory nature. Noteworthy in the context of this chapter's discussion is first, the 2016 Code of Conduct on Countering Illegal Hate Speech Online[140] and second, the 2018 Code of Practice on Disinformation.[141] Under the Illegal Hate Speech Code, platforms have made amongst others the following commitments: (i) to draw users' attention to the types of content not allowed by their Community Standards/Guidelines and specify that they prohibit the promotion of incitement to violence and hateful behaviour; (ii) to put in place clear, effective and speedy processes to review notifications of illegal hate speech

---

[135] Article 28b (1b) and (1c) AVMSD.

[136] Article 28b (1a) AVMSD.

[137] Article 28b (3) AVMSD. The AVMSD lists certain appropriate measures, such as transparent and user-friendly mechanisms to report and flag the content and easy- to-use and effective procedures for the handling and resolution of users' complaints.

[138] Directive 2017/541 of the European Parliament and of the Council of 15 March 2017 on combating terrorism and replacing Council Framework Decision 2002/475/JHA and amending Council Decision 2005/671/JHA, OJ L [2017] 88/6.

[139] Directive 2011/93/EU of the European Parliament and of the Council of 13 December 2011 on combating the sexual abuse and sexual exploitation of children and child pornography, and replacing Council Framework Decision 2004/68/JHA, OJ L [2011] 335/1. For an analysis of both documents, see e.g. de Streel et al. (2021), at pp. 25–29.

[140] The Code was signed in 2016 by Facebook, Microsoft, Twitter and YouTube. Google+, Instagram, Dailymotion and Snapchat and Jeuxvideo.com joined subsequently. The Code's text is available at: https://ec.europa.eu/info/policies/justice-and-fundamental-rights/combatting-discrimination/racism-and-xenophobia/eu-code-conduct-countering-illegal-hate-speech-online_en (last access 23 February 2022)

[141] The Code was signed by Facebook, Google and Twitter, Mozilla, as well as by advertisers and parts of the advertising industry in October 2018; Microsoft joined in May 2019, while TikTok became a signatory in June 2020. Code's text is available at: https://digital-strategy.ec.europa.eu/en/policies/code-practice-disinformation (last access 23 February 2022)

and remove illegal content; (iii) to encourage the reporting of illegal hate speech by experts, including through partnerships with civil society organizations; (iv) to strengthen communication and cooperation between the online platforms and the national authorities, in particular with regard to procedures for submitting notifications. The Code of Practice on Disinformation involves similar obligations with regard to transparency, due processes and cooperation. It seeks, in particular, to ensure the credibility of information and improve content moderation practices, for instance, by closing false accounts; removing bots; investing in technologies that help users make informed decisions when receiving false information (e.g. through reliability indicators/trust markers); prioritizing relevant and authentic information; facilitating the finding of alternative content on issues of general interest; improving transparency of political and issue-based advertising; empowering the research community, fact-checkers and other relevant stakeholders (e.g. with better access to data).[142] In May 2021, very much in light of the Covid-19 infodemic, the European Commission presented a new Guidance to strengthen the Code of Practice on Disinformation,[143] which aims to address gaps and shortcomings[144] and create a more transparent, safe and trustworthy online environment. The Guidance also aims at evolving the existing Code of Practice towards a co-regulatory instrument foreseen under the Digital Services Act (DSA),[145] which would increase the bindingness of the rules and the level of scrutiny by the European Commission. Building upon the newly announced European Democracy Action Plan (EDAP),[146] the DSA, which would replace the 2000 E-Commerce Directive, introduces wide-ranging transparency measures around content moderation and advertising, and proposes binding and enforceable legal obligations, in particular for very large online platforms,[147] to assess and address systemic risks for fundamental rights or presented by the intentional manipulation of their services. When adopted, the DSA would create a new basis for the regulation of platforms and substantially increase their duties and

---

[142] The Code includes also an annex identifying best practices that signatories will apply to implement the Code's commitments. For all documents, see https://ec.europa.eu/digital-single-market/en/news/code-practice-disinformation (last access 23 February 2022)

[143] European Commission (2021).

[144] The Commission's Assessment of the Code of Practice in 2020 revealed in particular include inconsistent and incomplete application of the Code across platforms and Member States, limitations intrinsic to the self- regulatory nature of the Code, as well as gaps in the coverage of the Code's commitments. The assessment also highlighted the lack of an appropriate monitoring mechanism, including key performance indicators, lack of commitments on access to platforms' data for research on disinformation and limited participation from stakeholders, in particular from the advertising sector. See European Commission (2020a, 2021).

[145] European Commission (2020b).

[146] European Commission (2020c).

[147] The DSA defines very large platforms in Article 25 as online platforms which provide their services to a number of average monthly active recipients of the service in the EU corresponding to 10% of the EU's population.

responsibilities, also with regard to fighting misinformation online.[148] The DSA would also harmonize the rules across different EU Member States' jurisdictions in this context, which have so far developed independently.[149]

One EU Member State's law that has been particularly controversial in policy and academic circles on both sides of the Atlantic[150] has been Germany's Network Enforcement Act (Netzwerkdurchsetzungsgesetz, NetzDG) enacted in 2017 and also known as the "Facebook Act".[151] While the NetzDG does not criminalize new activities, it seeks to enable better enforcement of the German Criminal Code online. For this purpose, the NetzDG enumerates discrete criminal code provisions whose violation it sanctions in the digital space. These include, amongst others, dissemination of propaganda material or use of symbols of unconstitutional organizations; encouragement of the commission of a serious violent offence endangering the state; commission of treasonous forgery; public incitement to crime; incitement to hatred, and defamation.[152] The NetzDG is limited in its scope and only applicable to social media networks that have two million or more registered users in Germany. Social media networks are defined as "telemedia service providers that operate online platforms with the intent to make a profit and on which users can share content with other users or make that content publicly available".[153] The NetzDG requires social media networks to remove "manifestly illegal" content within 24 h after the content is flagged; other illegal content must be removed within 7 days after receiving a notification.[154] The social media platforms are also obliged to offer their users an easy and transparent complaint mechanism that is constantly available; the decisions taken with regard to the complaint and the reasoning behind accepting or rejecting it must, without delay, be communicated to both the complainant and the affected user.[155] In addition, the NetzDG includes reporting requirements for platforms that receive more than 100 complaints of unlawful

---

[148] For an overview of the new obligations depending on the type of platform, see https://ec.europa.eu/info/strategy/priorities-2019-2024/europe-fit-digital-age/digital-services-act-ensuring-safe-and-accountable-online-environment_en (last access 23 February 2022)

[149] For an overview of the different initiatives, see e.g. de Streel et al. (2021); Roudik et al. (2019).

[150] See e.g. Kaye (2017); Haupt (2021); see also Zurth (2021); Tworek and Leerssen (2019); Citron (2018).

[151] Gesetz zur Verbesserung der Rechtsdurchsetzung in sozialen Netzwerken [NetzDG] [Network Enforcement Act], 01 September 2017 [BGBL I] at 3352. The law entered into force on 1 January 2018.

[152] § 1(3) NetzDG, referring to §§ 86, 86a, 89a, 91, 100a, 111, 126, 129 bis 129b, 130, 131, 140, 166, 184b, 185 bis 187, 201a, 241 and 269 of the German Criminal Code.

[153] § 1(1) NetzDG. Platforms that post original journalistic content, email or messaging services are not covered.

[154] The deadline may be extended if additional facts are necessary to determine the truthfulness of the information or if the social network hires an outside agency to perform the vetting process.

[155] § 3 paras 1 and 2 NetzDG.

postings per calendar year.[156] A social media network that intentionally or negligently violates its duties under the NetzDG may be fined up to EUR 50 million.[157]

Despite being highly controversial, in particular as to its constitutionality,[158] and as to creating real concerns for freedom of speech because of the outsourcing of legal enforcement to private entities and the possibilities for over-blocking,[159] there have been efforts to update the NetzDG. The revision projects have been in line with other legislative initiates in Germany introduced by the national implementation of the AVMSD and the new law against right-wing extremism and hate crimes.[160] The updated NetzDG[161] was adopted in June 2021. It now also covers VSPs,[162] as well as includes a number of new rules with regard to the simplification of the reporting channels for the complaint procedure and additional information obligations for the half-yearly transparency reports of the platform operators (for instance, with regard to the so-called "put backs"). In light of the over-blocking concerns, the amendment of the NetzDG provides that users may request a review of the platform provider's decision to remove or retain reported content and have a right to have the content restored.[163]

---

[156] § 2 paras 1 and 2 NetzDG. The report has to be published in German in the Federal Gazette and on the website of the social media network one month after the end of each half-year period. The report must be easily identifiable, immediately accessible, and permanently available. It must include information on the general efforts to prevent illegal actions on the platform, a description of the complaint procedure, the number of complaints received, the number and qualifications of employees who are handling the complaints, the network's association memberships, the number of times an external party has been used to decide the illegality of the content, the number of complaints that led to the content being deleted, the time it took to delete the content, and measures that were taken to inform the complainant and the member who posted the deleted content.

[157] § 4 NetzDG, in conjunction with Gesetz über Ordnungswidrigkeiten [OWiG] [Act on Regulatory Offenses], 19 February 1987 [BGBL. I] at 602, as amended, § 30(2). The fine is rendered by the Department of Justice upon a Court decision. The decision of the Court is final and binding on the Department of Justice.

[158] See e.g. Haupt (2021); also Guggenberger (2017); Nolte (2017).

[159] See e.g. Zurth (2021); see also the refences listed in note 150 above.

[160] Gesetz zur Bekämpfung des Rechtsextremismus und der Hasskriminalität, 30 March 2021 [BGBl. I], at 441.

[161] Gesetz zur Änderung des Netzwerkdurchsetzungsgesetzes, 3 June 2021 [BGBL I] at 1436.

[162] § 3d amended NetzDG.

[163] For overview of the changes, see https://www.bmjv.de/SharedDocs/Gesetzgebungsverfahren/DE/NetzDGAendG.html (last access 23 February 2022) (in German).

3 Appraisal of the Emergent Regulatory Framework for Platforms

The Covid-19 crisis has recently and painfully revealed the perils of online disinformation, and spurred a flurry of initiatives around the world to curb this negative phenomenon and regulate information platforms to this effect. As Goldsmith and Keane Woods have pointed out, hopefully sometime in the near future, this grave period for global societies will be over, but "when the crisis is gone, there is no unregulated 'normal' to return to",[164] as the general trend towards the regulation of digital speech will not abate.[165] This chapter has offered some insights into the emergent regulatory framework for information platforms and revealed the different approaches across jurisdictions with a distinct focus on the United States and the European Union. It became evident that the different constitutional traditions and understandings of the role of the State in the protection of fundamental rights have led to the emergence of very different regulatory environments. Both come with certain pros and cons and raise questions as to the proper balance between freedom of speech and the protection of other vital public interests and individual rights. One should acknowledge in this context in particular that social media platforms, despite their essential role in contemporary communicative processes, are still relatively young, and the risk of over-regulation and unintended consequences is real.[166] In the EU context, while the regulatory efforts are properly based on the international and constitutional frameworks, it remains critical that there are sufficient substantive and procedural safeguards in place that take the different interests involved into account and recognize that with digital speech, we do face a "problem of many hands", where there is a corresponding need to conceptualize a framework with participation of and different responsibilities for all stakeholders—platforms, users, civil society and governments.[167] Otherwise, many of the already recognized dangers associated with speech regulation in undemocratic societies may occur,[168] and digital innovation may be seriously hindered. As for the United States, it remains uncertain whether and in what form platform liability would be reformed against the backdrop of the high standards of protection of the First Amendment, and to what extent platforms themselves would use their leeway and more aggressively moderate content. At this point in time, we do have "geographically-segmented speech",[169] and regulators would need to make sure that this situation is not exacerbated, either

---

[164] Goldsmith and Woods (2020).

[165] Ibid.

[166] See e.g. Bhagwat (2021).

[167] Helberger et al. (2017), at p. 2; see also Finck (2018) (arguing for a co-regulatory model of platform regulation); Saurwein and Spencer-Smith (2020) (mapping the different governance approaches).

[168] See e.g. with regard to Russia, Moyakinea and Tabachnik (2021); for a discussion of other cases, see Roudik et al. (2019).

[169] Daskal (2019), at p. 1605.

by means of geographic filtering and geo-blocking or by agreeing upon new baselines of transparency and accountability, and enhanced cooperation between governments and tech companies.[170]

References

Baines D, Elliott RJR (2020) Defining misinformation, disinformation and malinformation: an urgent need for clarity during the COVID-19 infodemic. University of Birmingham Department of Economics Discussion Papers 20-06
Balkin JM (2012) Free speech is a triangle. Columbia Law Rev 118:2011–2055
Balkin JM (2016) Information fiduciaries and the first amendment. Univ California Davis Law Rev 49:1183–1234
Balkin JM (2018) Free speech in the algorithmic society: big data, private governance, and new school speech regulation. Univ California Davis Law Rev 51:1149–1210
Balkin JM, Zittrain J (2016) A grand bargain to make tech companies trustworthy. The Atlantic, 3 October 2016
Bamberger KA, Lobel O (2018) Platform market power. Berkeley Technol Law J 32:1052–1092
Bayer J et al (2019) Disinformation and propaganda – impact on the functioning of the rule of law in the EU and its Member States, study for the European Parliament. European Parliament, Brussels
Benkler Y (2006) The wealth of networks: how social production transforms markets and freedom. Yale University Press, New Haven
Benkler Y et al (2018) Network propaganda: manipulation, disinformation, and radicalization in American politics. Oxford University Press, Oxford
Bhagwat A (2021) The law of Facebook. Univ California Davis Law Rev 54:2353–2403
Bloch-Wehba H (2019) Global platform governance: private power in the shadow of the state. SMU Law Rev 73:27–80
Bone T (2021) How content moderation may expose social media companies to greater defamation liability. Wash Univ Law Rev 98:937–963
Bontcheva K, Posetti J (eds) (2020) Balancing act: countering digital disinformation while respecting freedom of expression, Broadband Commission research report on "Freedom of expression and addressing disinformation on the internet". ITU/UNESCO, Geneva/Paris
Bozdag E (2013) Bias in algorithmic filtering and personalization. Ethics Inf Technol 15:209–227
Brannon VC, Holmes EN (2021) Section 230: An Overview. Congressional Research Service Report R46751, 7 April 2021
Brennen JS et al (2020) Types, sources, and claims of COVID-19 misinformation. Reuters Institute for the Study of Journalism, Oxford
Burri M (2015) Public service broadcasting 3.0: legal design for the digital present. Routledge, London
Burri M (2019a) Understanding the implications of big data and big data analytics for competition law: an attempt for a primer. In: Mathis K, Tor A (eds) New developments in competition behavioural law and economics. Springer, Berlin, pp 241–263
Burri M (2019b) Discoverability of Local, National and Regional Content Online, A Thought Leadership Paper written for the Canadian Commission for UNESCO and Canadian Heritage, 7 February 2019
Burri M (2021) Interfacing privacy and trade. Case West J Int Law 53:35–88

---

[170] Ibid.

Burri M (2021) Approaches to digital trade and data flow regulation across jurisdictions: implications for the future ASEAN-EU agreement. Legal Issu Econ Integr 49(2022)

Burri M, Zihlmann Z (2021) Intermediaries' liability in light of the recent EU copyright reform. Indian J Intell Prop Law 11

Center for Countering Digital Hate (2020) Malgorithm: How Instagram's Algorithm Publishes Misinformation and Hate to Millions during a Pandemic. Center for Countering Digital Hate, London

Center for Information Technology and Society – UC Santa Barbara (2019) A Brief History of Fake News. Center for Information Technology and Society, Santa Barbara

Chander A (2014) How law made Silicon Valley. Emory Law J 63:639–694

Chesney B, Citron DK (2019) Deep fakes: a looming challenge for privacy, democracy, and National Security. Calif Law Rev 107:1753–1820

Citron DK (2018) Extremist speech, compelled conformity, and censorship creep. Notre Dame Law Rev 93:1035–1072

Citron DK, Wittes B (2017) The internet will not break: denying bad samaritans § 230 immunity. Fordham Law Rev 86:401–423

Cohen JE (2018) Law for the platform economy. Univ California Davis Law Rev 51:133–204

Dahlgren (2005) The internet, public spheres, and political communication. Polit Commun 22:147–162

Daskal J (2016) The un-territoriality of data. Yale Law J 125:326–398

Daskal J (2019) Speech across Borders. Va Law Rev 105:1605–1666

de Gregorio G (2020) Democratising online content moderation: a constitutional framework. Comput Law Secur Rev 36. https://doi.org/10.1016/j.clsr.2019.105374 (last access 23 February 2022)

de Schutter O (2014) International human rights law, 2nd edn. Cambridge University Press, Cambridge

de Streel A, Kuczerawy A, Ledger M (2021) Online platforms and services. In: Garzaniti L et al (eds) Electronic communications, audiovisual services and the internet. Sweet and Maxwell, London, pp 125–157

DeNardis L (2009) Protocol politics: the globalization of internet governance. MIT Press, Cambridge

Eichensehr KE (2015) The cyber-law of nations. Georgetown Law J 103:317–380

Eichensehr KE (2017) Data extraterritoriality. Texas Law Rev 95:145–160

Enders AM (2020) The Different Forms of COVID-19 Misinformation and Their Consequences, The Harvard Kennedy School (HKS) Misinformation Review

European Commission (2016) Online platforms and the digital single market, COM (2016) 288 final, 25 May 2016

European Commission (2017) Tackling Illegal Content Online. Towards an Enhanced Responsibility for Online Platforms, COM (2017) 555 final, 28 September 2017

European Commission (2018) Recommendation 2018/334 of 1 March 2018 on measures to effectively tackle illegal content online, OJ L [2018] 63/50

European Commission (2020a) Guidelines on the practical application of the essential functionality criterion of the definition of a "video-sharing platform service" under the Audiovisual Media Services Directive, OJ C [2020] 223/3, 7 July 2020

European Commission (2020b) Assessment of the Code of Practice on Disinformation: Achievements and Areas for Further Improvement, SWD (2020)180, 10 September 2020

European Commission (2020c) Proposal for a Regulation of the European Parliament and the Council on a Single Market for Digital Services (Digital Services Act) and amending Directive 2000/31/EC, COM (2020) 825 final, 15 December 2020

European Commission (2020d) Communication on the European Democracy Action Plan, COM (2020) 790 final, 3 December 2020

European Commission (2021) Guidance on Strengthening the Code of Practice on Disinformation Brussels, COM (2021) 262 final, 26 May 2021

European Commission and the High Representative of the Union for Foreign Affairs and Security Policy (2020) Tackling COVID-19 Disinformation: Getting the Facts Right, JOIN (2020) 8 final, 10 June 2020

European Data Protection Supervisor (EDPS) (2014) Privacy and competitiveness in the age of big data

Ezrachi A, Stucke ME (2016) Virtual competition: the promise and perils of the algorithm-driven economy. Harvard University Press, Cambridge

Farber DA (2019) The first amendment: concepts and insights. Foundation Press, St. Paul, MN

Feldman NR, Sullivan KM (2019) First amendment law, 7th edn. West Academic, St. Paul, MN

Finck (2018) Digital co-regulation: designing a supranational legal framework for the platform economy. Eur Law Rev 43:47–68

Frishmann BM (2012) Infrastructure: the social value of shared resources. Oxford University Press, Oxford

Frosio G (ed) (2020) Oxford handbook of online intermediary liability. Oxford University Press, Oxford

Goldman E (2019) Why section 230 is better than the first amendment. Notre Dame Law Rev Reflect 95:33–46

Goldman E (2020) An overview of the United States' Section 230 internet immunity. In: Frosio G (ed) The Oxford handbook of online intermediary liability. Oxford University Press, Oxford, pp 155–171

Goldsmith J, Woods AK (2020) Internet Speech Will Never Go Back to Normal. The Atlantic, 26 April 2020

Goldsmith J, Wu T (2001) Who controls the internet? Illusions of a borderless world. Oxford University Press, Oxford, p 2001

Goodman Ellen P (2004) Media policy out of the box: content abundance, attention scarcity, and the failures of digital markets. Berkeley Technol Law J 19:1389–1472

Greenberg MH (2003) A return to Lilliput: the LICRA v. yahoo – case and the regulation of online content in the world market. Berkeley Technol Law Rev 18:1191–1258

Guggenberger N (2017) Das Netzwerkdurchsetzungsgesetz – schön gedacht, schlecht gemacht. Zeitschrift für Rechtspolitik 2017:98–101

Haupt CE (2005) Regulating hate speech: damned if you do and damned if you don't – lessons learned from comparing the German and U.S. approaches. Boston Univ Int Law J 23:300–335

Haupt CE (2020) Platforms as trustees: information fiduciaries and the value of analogy. Harv Law Rev Forum 134:34–41

Haupt CE (2021) Regulating speech online: free speech values in constitutional frames. Wash Univ Law Rev 99:751–786

Helberger N (2011) Diversity by design. J Inf Policy 1:441–469

Helberger N (2012) Exposure diversity as a policy goal. J Media Law 4:65–92

Helberger N, Kleinen-von Königlöw K, van der Noll R (2015) Regulating the new information intermediaries as gatekeepers of information diversity. Info 6:50–71

Helberger N, Pierson J, Poell T (2017) Governing online platforms: from contested to cooperative responsibility. Inf Soc. https://doi.org/10.1080/01972243.2017.1391913 (last access 23 February 2022)

Helberger N et al (2020) A freedom of expression perspective on AI in the media – with a special focus on editorial decision making on social media platforms and in the news media. Eur J Law Technol 11

Hoffman CP et al (2015) Diversity by choice: applying a social cognitive perspective to the role of public service media in the digital age. Int J Commun 9:1360–1381

Hoffman D, Bruening P, Carter S (2016) The right to obscurity: how we can implement the Google Spain decision. North Carolina J Law Technol 17:437–481

Ireton C, Posetti J (eds) (2018) Journalism, "Fake News" and disinformation. UNESCO, Paris

Kaye D (2017) How Europe's New Internet Laws Threaten Freedom of Expression Recent Regulations Risk Censoring Legitimate Content, Foreign Affairs, 18 December 2017

Kaye D (2019) Speech policy: the struggle to govern the internet. Columbia Global Reports, New York

Keller D (2019) Dolphins in the net: internet content filters and the advocate General's Glawischnig-Piesczek v. Facebook Ireland Opinion, Stanford Center for Internet and Society, 4 September 2019

Keller P (2011) European and international media law: liberal democracy, trade, and the new media. Oxford University Press, Oxford

Khan LM, Pozen DE (2019) A skeptical view of information fiduciaries. Harv Law Rev 133:497–541

Klonick K (2018) The new governors: the people, rules, and processes governing online speech. Harv Law Rev 131:1598–1670

Klonick K (2020) The Facebook oversight board: creating an independent institution to adjudicate online free expression. Yale Law J 129:2418–2299

Kloseff J (2019) The twenty-six words that created the internet. Cornell University Press, Ithaca

Knuutila A et al (2020) Covid-related misinformation on YouTube: the spread of misinformation videos on social media and the effectiveness of platform policies. Oxford Internet Institute, COMPROP Data Memo

Kreiss D, Mcgregor SC (2017) Technology firms shape political communication: the work of Microsoft, Facebook, Twitter, and Google with campaigns during the 2016 US presidential cycle. Polit Commun:1–23

Latzer M et al (2014) The economics of algorithmic selection on the internet. Media Change and Innovation Working Paper, pp 29–30

Lessig L (2009) Remix: making art and commerce thrive in the hybrid economy. Penguin, New York

Lobel O (2016) The law of the platform. Minnesota Law Rev 101:87–166

Mayer-Schönberger V, Cukier K (2013) Big data: a revolution that will transform how we live, work, and think. Eamon Dolan/Houghton Mifflin Harcourt, New York

McKelvey F, Hunt R (2019) Discoverability: toward a definition of content discovery through platforms. Social Media + Society, January/March, pp 1–15

Merriam-Webster (2021) The real story of "Fake News". Available at: https://www.merriam-webster.com/words-at-play/the-realstory-of-fake-news (last access 23 February 2022)

Miel P, Farris R (2008) News and information as digital media come of age. The Berkman Center for Internet and Society, Cambridge

Moyakinea E, Tabachnik A (2021) Struggling to strike the right balance between interests at stake: the "Yarovaya", "Fake news" and "Disrespect" laws as examples of Ill-conceived legislation in the age of modern technology. Comput Law Secur Rev 40, https://doi.org/10.1016/j.clsr.2020.105512 (last access 23 February 2022)

Napoli PM (2012) Persistent and emergent diversity policy concerns in an evolving media environment. In: Pager SA, Candeub A (eds) Transnational culture in the internet age. Edward Elgar, Cheltenham, pp 165–181

Napoli PM (2014) On automation in media industries: integrating algorithmic media production into media industries scholarship. Media Ind J 1:33–38

Napoli PM (2015) Social media and the public interest: governance of news platforms in the realm of individual and algorithmic gatekeepers. Telecommun Policy 39:751–760

Napoli PM et al (2018) Assessing local journalism: news deserts, journalism divides, and the determinants of the robustness of local news. News Measures Research Project, New Brunswick

Nielsen RK et al (2020) Communications in the coronavirus crisis: lessons for the second wave. Reuters Institute for the Study of Journalism, Oxford

Nolte G (2017) Hate-Speech, Fake-News, das Netzwerkdurchsetzungsgesetz und Vielfaltsicherung durch Suchmaschinen. Zeitschrift für Urheber- und Medienrecht 61:552–565

Nunziato DC (2019) The marketplace of ideas online. Notre Dame Law Rev 94:1519–1583

Oster J (2017) European and international media law. Cambridge University Press, Cambridge

Pariser E (2011) The filter bubble: what the internet is hiding from you. Viking, New York

Pollicino O (2021) Judicial protection of fundamental rights on the internet. Hart, Oxford
Poole S (2019) Before trump: the real history of fake news. The Guardian, 22 November 2019. Available at: https://www.theguardian.com/books/2019/nov/22/factitious-taradiddle-dictionary-real-history-fake-news (last access 23 February 2022)
Posetti J, Matthews A (2020) A short guide to the history of "fake news" and disinformation. International Center for Journalists, Washington
Roudik P et al (2019) Initiatives to counter fake news in selected countries: Argentina, Brazil, Canada, China, Egypt, France, Germany, Israel, Japan, Kenya, Malaysia, Nicaragua, Russia, Sweden, United Kingdom. The Law Library of Congress, Washington, DC
Sag M (2018) Internet safe harbors and the transformation of copyright law. Notre Dame Law Rev 93:499–564
Saurwein F, Spencer-Smith C (2020) Combating disinformation on social media: multilevel governance and distributed accountability in Europe. Digit Journal 8:820–841
Saurwein F et al (2015) Governance of algorithms: options and limitations. Info 17:35–49
Soll J (2016) The long and brutal history of fake news. POLITICO Magazine, 18 December 2016. Available at: http://politi.co/2FaV5W9 (last access 23 February 2022)
Spindler G (2020) Copyright law and internet intermediaries liability. In: Tatiana-Eleni Synodinou et al (eds) EU internet law in the digital era. Springer, Berlin, pp 3–25
Sunstein CR (2001) Echo chambers: bush v. Gore impeachment, and beyond. Princeton University Press, Princeton
Sunstein CR (2007). Republic.com 2.0. Princeton University Press, Princeton
Sunstein CR (2009) Going to extremes: how like minds unite and divide. Oxford University Press, Oxford
Sunstein CR, Vermeule A (2009) Consipiracy theories: causes and cures. J Polit Philos 17:202–227
Tandoc EC Jr, Lim ZW, Ling R (2018) Defining "Fake News". Digit Journal 6:137–153
Tompros LW et al (2020) The constitutionality of criminalizing false speech made on social networking sites in a post-Alvarez, social media-obsessed world'. Harv J Law Technol 31: 66–109
Tourkochoriti I (2016) Speech, privacy and dignity in France and in the U.S.A.: a comparative analysis, Loyola L.A. Int Comp Law Rev 38:101–182
Tworek H, Leerssen P (2019) An Analysis of Germany's NetzDG Law. Transatlantic High Level Working Group on Content Moderation Online and Freedom of Expression
UK House of Commons (2019) Disinformation and "fake news": final report of the digital. Culture, Media and Sport Committee
United Nations (UN) Special Rapporteur on Freedom of Opinion and Expression, the Organization for Security and Co-operation in Europe (OSCE) Representative on Freedom of the Media, the Organization of American States (OAS) Special Rapporteur on Freedom of Expression and the African Commission on Human and Peoples' Rights (ACHPR) Special Rapporteur on Freedom of Expression and Access to Information (2017) Joint Declaration on Freedom of Expression and "Fake News", Disinformation and Propaganda, FOM.GAL/3/17, 3 March 2017
van der Sloot B, Broeders D, Schrijvers E (eds) (2016) Exploring the boundaries of big data. Amsterdam University Press, Amsterdam
Wardle C (2019) Understanding information disorder. First Draft, London
Wechsler S (2015) The right to remember: the European convention on human rights and the right to be forgotten. Columbia J Law Soc Probl 49:135–165
Wendling M (2018) The (almost) complete history of "fake news". BBC News, 22 January 2018. Available at: https://www.bbc.co.uk/news/blogs-trending-42724320 (last access 23 February 2022)
Whitt RS (2013) A deference to protocol: fashioning a three-dimensional public policy framework for the internet age. Cardozo Arts Entertain Law J 31:689–768

Whitt RS (2019) Old school goes online: exploring fiduciary obligations of loyalty and care in the digital platforms era. Santa Clara High Technol Law Rev 36:75–131

WHO (2020) Coronavirus disease 2019 (COVID-19). Situation Report 45, 5 March 2020. Available at: https://www.who.int/docs/default-source/coronaviruse/situation-reports/20200305-sitrep-45-covid-19.pdf?sfvrsn=ed2ba78b_4 (last access 23 February 2022)

WHO et al (2020) Managing the COVID-19 infodemic: promoting healthy behaviours and mitigating the harm from misinformation and disinformation. Joint Statement by WHO, UN, UNICEF, UNDP, UNESCO, UNAIDS, ITU, UN Global Pulse, and IFRC, 23 September 2020. Available at: https://www.who.int/news/item/23-09-2020-managing-the-covid-19-infodemic-promoting-healthy-behaviours-and-mitigating-the-harm-from-misinformation-and-disinformation (last access 23 February 2022)

Zurth P (2021) The German NetzDG as role model or cautionary tale? Implications for the debate on social media liability, Fordham intellectual property. Media Entertain Law J 31:1084–1153

A Behavioural Economics Approach to the Covidian Crisis

Rute Saraiva

Abstract This study intends to answer three questions building on Behavioural Economics insights, namely: 1. why there was no preventative response to the pandemic, looking mainly into bounded motivation, scientific overconfidence, and lack of saliency; 2. how governments and their citizens reacted and why, focusing on fear, loss, and uncertainty aversions and risk communication (especially from social media) but also on the precautionary and proportionality principle and the way they were (wrongly and inefficiently) used in public health policies; 3. and how to align individual behaviours with the guidelines and rules from health authorities, mainly handwashing, masks and social distancing, based on the existing literature, looking at possible nudges to help with compliance.

1 Introduction

In the last year, the covidian pandemic has been scrutinized by scientists from all fields, especially from the health sector, with a fervour to find answers to reduce losses and allow a faster and more adequate overcoming of the crisis.

As this asks for a collective but also individual, public but also private response in behaviour changes, it seems appropriate to address this problem with the tools and knowledge of Behavioural Sciences and Behavioural Economics in particular, since, more so than a normative approach, they attempt to understand how individuals (and organizations) really behave and what may condition their actions and omissions. Thus, instead of starting from models of politicians and citizens with full rationality and motivation, who pursue their self-interest and the maximization of the expected utility, we look at flesh and blood people, with emotions, cognitive, volitional, and self-interest limitations, presenting, in certain contexts, predictable and systematic errors and biases.

R. Saraiva (✉)
University of Lisbon Law School, Lisbon, Portugal
e-mail: rutesaraiva@fd.ul.pt

© The Author(s), under exclusive license to Springer Nature Switzerland AG 2022
K. Mathis, A. Tor (eds.), *Law and Economics of the Coronavirus Crisis*, Economic Analysis of Law in European Legal Scholarship 13,
https://doi.org/10.1007/978-3-030-95876-3_3

With this approach, we hope to be able to bring new light to three major issues, even at the risk of the text, through the illustrations used, becoming somewhat dated[1]:

(i) why were we not prepared for the pandemic?
(ii) how did States and their citizens react to the threat and why?
(iii) how can the teachings of Behavioural Economics help to sustain adherence to the main public health rules/guidelines and measures?

2 Why Can We Not Learn from History?

Contrary to what is read and heard in the media and in political and governmental statements, the SARS-Cov-2[2] pandemic is neither a novelty nor an event without historical parallel. In fact, so much so that comparisons with the Spanish flu and the bubonic plague are transversal from technicians to bench commentators. This coronavirus may be new and involve unknown, ambivalent, uncertain, and risky aspects,[3] but it also has perfectly identifiable characteristics. Nonetheless, the pandemic phenomenon, in itself, is not an originality, knowing its recurrent incidence with cycles of about 80 years for more serious health situations or three times a century for influenza variations, similar to what happens with other "natural" disasters, such as earthquakes, floods, and droughts, in which it is possible to make frequency forecasts.[4] Furthermore, it is known that there are three to four zoonotic phenomena per year.[5] If it is true that transmission lines today are more complex than in the past, whether due to the overexploitation of forests (with possible zoonoses) or to the flexibility and expansion of human mobility, the question is not so much whether a pandemic will occur, but exactly when will it happen.[6]

The real novelty is reflected in the global and transversal response to the threat with very restrictive measures of confinement[7] and physical distancing (that most stubbornly call social distancing) and an unprecedented paralysis of cross-border and

---

[1] For all intents and purposes, after an analysis of advantages and disadvantages, in academic terms, in using as references, in some cases, newspaper articles, we decided in favour when necessary, in view of the novelty of the theme, for a hand, and, on the other hand, because of the role that the media plays in framing the narrative around the pandemic.

[2] Despite the scientific difference between coronavirus, SARS-CoV-2 and Covid-19, for reasons of convenience, they will, as a rule, be used as synonyms.

[3] On the differences between risk, uncertainty, ambivalence, ignorance, see Saraiva (2009), pp. 145 et seq.

[4] Mato (2018).

[5] WWF (2020).

[6] Saunders-Hasting and Krewski (2016).

[7] Although technically they do not have exactly the same meaning, expressions such as confinement, quarantine, seclusion, self-isolation, isolation, lockdown will be used as synonyms. As a rule,

internal mobility and "non-essential" economic activity. Not that in the past, quarantine or distancing solutions were not promoted. The difference lies in its non-systematic and worldwide character, that is, in the "pandemic" and "contagious" dimension of lockdown policies, suspension and restriction of rights, freedoms, and guarantees in the name of public health, in a true phenomenon of global herd effect.

The question that arises,[8] considering there have been several mediatic (e.g., Bill Gates or Barack Obama) and scientific warnings in recent years,[9] is to understand why we have not learned from the past and did not change behaviours and built public policies that sustainably prevented and mitigated the risk of a pandemic and the consequent impact on health, society, and the economy.[10]

Now, the problem does not seem to arise from a lack of information, scientific knowledge, or access to data, as they currently exist just a click away. It also cannot be due to a total memory failure, since the aforementioned warnings, regular vaccination campaigns, blockbusters which exploit fear, or recurrent news about outbreaks and epidemics involving, in addition to the "traditional" influenza, poultry, and swine flu, MERS, SARS, Ebola, Zika or even AIDS are frequent reminders. Moreover, and looking at a shorter time period, data on the new coronavirus began to arrive from China in late 2019, with alerts in February about a possible pandemic.

Various cognitive, emotional, and volitional limitations and distortions may help to understand this phenomenon.

The first question that arises is one of availability heuristic. It is associated with a problem of salience, especially in view of the high number of daily requests that fall on citizens and governments.[11] Indeed, it is difficult to keep an eye on probable pandemics when you are faced with dozens of pieces of news every day, warning, depending on fashions and circumstantial elements, about climate change, new capital injections into banks, domestic violence, bullying, rising populism and extremism, elections, public debt or over-indebtedness of families, forest fires, among so many needs that have to be met. Not only are resources scarce to satisfy them optimally and effectively, but the capacity for attention, public and private, is also constrained. Maintaining the level of alertness and motivation requires continuous feedback that fosters and sustains salience, which is still a Herculean task in a scenario of scarcity and limited rationality.[12] This is all the more true when the latest epidemics and/or pandemics have developed outside the traditional scientific and political-international power centres, being concentrated in Asia, especially in

---

except when necessary, no distinction will be made between mandatory confinements or "civic" duties of confinement.

[8] See in this regard, Saraiva (2013); Meyer (2010), pp. 120 et seq.

[9] For all, stressing the need to strengthen national health systems and the economic impacts of a pandemic, International Working Group on Financing Preparedness (2017).

[10] There are of course other impacts, for example political (including in terms of strengthening and eroding democracy, authoritarianism or populism), cultural and environmental.

[11] Gertner (2009).

[12] Ester and Mandemaker (1994), p. 61.

China, the Arabian peninsula, Africa or South America. As they are perceived as distant phenomena (geographically and culturally) and reaching populations with which there is weak or no identification, including physical and emotional, the availability aroused by an affective heuristic is removed. In addition, the invisible nature of the coronavirus or for any other epidemic/pandemic responsible organism reduces the perception of the potential seriousness of the threat.

Secondly, the issue of treatment of the pandemic, its prediction, mitigation, management, and combat/eradication is primarily scientific, which brought epidemiologists, virologists, and mathematicians to the stage lights and transformed political and social discourse into a scientific pseudo-language around more or less flattened curves, exponential growth, lethality rates or indicators such as the now famous Rt. This scientific "stronghold" in which the study and debate about pandemics have lived does not necessarily fit with its treatment and understanding by the political sphere and public institutions and by the lay citizen. There are several reasons that can be pointed out for this divorce, which we will try to summarize here, but without intending to exhaust them (or develop them).

On the one hand, and as has just been pointed out, the technicality and hermeticism of the language used by scientists are difficult to grasp by laypeople (including government officials and administration),[13] which makes it difficult to pass, and consequently, weakens the salience and retention of the message. In fact, the scientific hyper-specialization that has been witnessed, each branch with its jargon, hinders efforts of trans-, multi-, and interdisciplinary research and approaches, generating and sometimes aggravating misunderstandings. Just remember that the technical terms of uncertainty, risk, or danger are cut differently in Economics, Engineering, or Health Sciences. But in addition to deaf dialogues between scientists from different fields and between them and the policy maker and/or citizens, there are (natural) divergences even within the same field of knowledge. An example for this is the recent phenomenon, which has been impressing the most unwary in matters of science (including Heads of Government[14]), of the multiplication of studies on SARS-CoV-2 and Covid-19, with very dissimilar and even contradictory

---

[13] For instance, in Portugal, the sovereign organs meet regularly with some pre-designated specialists in the so-called Infarmed Meetings, where red lines for levels of lockdown were recommended. The Government transformed them in a risk matrix, presented in a public conference about the plan for the deconfinement. Its methodology was heavily criticized by the same specialists that advised the Government for not perceiving their recommendations and was changed twice a few days later, including in its legal prevision in Resolution of the Council of Ministers n. 19/2021, 13th March, where not only did it include new parameters but also opened the criteria (and political margin for lockdown/deconfinement) with a strategic "namely". For example, although not expressly foreseen (even though with a current ongoing vaccination plan), the level of immunization of the population, in general, and of the risk groups, in particular, should be a fundamental criterion, along the now provided R(t) and cases incidence.

[14] For example, the Portuguese Prime-Minister, with the divergence of opinions of the specialists at the Infarmed Meetings, not only stressed out several times the difficulty to decide according to these disagreements (namely on closing or opening schools) but even asked these scientific advisors to search for some unanimity on their findings and suggestions for action.

results, whether on their origin (natural or artificial) and animal transmission, their transmissibility through air or contact with "infected" surfaces or sexual fluids, even on their seasonality, second or more waves, individual immunity or the (level of) group immunity, new variants, the role of asymptomatic or children or the use of masks (and which types). The scientific debate and lack of unanimity are inherent and necessary characteristics of the very dynamics of the scientific process, which is poorly understood by laypeople and policy makers who like certainties and have a high aversion to risk and risk cascades. Furthermore, in this case, this disparity of opinions and results is aggravated by the speed and turbo-science of the moment, in which the pressure to produce studies and publish is strongly felt,[15] both for "altruistic" reasons—wanting to collaborate and contribute to a better knowledge of the pandemic and help in finding answers –, as for reasons of notoriety, either for the affirmation of egos or obtaining and to guarantee more funding for research.[16] In this context of haste, errors, including methodological, formal, and substantive, tend to multiply and worsen entropy, for example, by skipping confirmation steps such as peer review, which, while not being an absolute assurance of quality, help to reduce errors and distortions. Remember the significant number of retractions that have been seen or the fact that many initial studies have been based on Chinese data, whose reliability, for political reasons, raises some suspicion. In short, the amount of information available and its heterogeneity shuffle and skew policy makers and citizens/economic agents, who, depending on the circumstances, either ignore or devalue it, or, in a phenomenon of confirmation bias, make a cherry-picking of research and results that confirm their beliefs (or masked interests)[17] and justify their attitudes and behaviours, including about risk,[18] or further enhance the phenomena of conspiracy theories and fake news (e.g., military origin of the virus, unauthorized contagion experience, connection to 5G networks), which dangerously erode trust in science, information, communication, and institutions.[19]

---

[15] Vos (2021), Table 2.1., p. 10.

[16] On issues of agency theory and capture by interests, as well as other limitations associated with the scientific production process, see Saraiva (2009), pp. 43 et seq. In short: part of the knowledge, especially technical and scientific, "is in the hands of a small number of experts whose interests do not always coincide with those of their constituents (e.g., public institutions or citizens) and whose gap can be covered with informational advantage they have. Think, for example, of poorly done or plagiarized studies, minimizing or with bombastic results, with the aim of enabling rents and then later excused, when eventually challenged, with the existence of 'unexpected' and 'incalculable' facts." Saraiva (2013).

[17] In the case of policy makers and of the Administration, agency problems also arise, in addition to public choice and failure to intervene. Moreover, the increasingly pointed cognitive (and even volitional and emotional) limitations of organizations and, in particular, of public institutions, in line with the new Behavioural Public Economics.

[18] For example, focusing and anchoring their behaviours on extremely rare cases of healthy children's death or of deadly thromboembolic reactions to some vaccines, completely perverting the objective probabilities and therefore rational judgements and decisions.

[19] van Bavel et al. (2020), p. 464. This explosion of fake news and conspiracy theories around covid and its partial success result, namely, from confirmation bias, information overload,

On the other hand, the scientific method of trial-error is hardly compatible with the problem of "natural"[20] and, here, pandemic disasters. Empirical experiments, even laboratory ones, with (corona)viruses raise major security and ethical problems, which, incidentally, feed fear and Hollywood conspiracy theories. Indeed, the manipulation of pathogens, for their understanding and to discover ways to control or annihilate them, can, if improperly done, constitute a danger (even greater than that of the virus) and trigger the fury of the elements. Basically, the famous argument of avoiding playing or replacing God is at stake. Furthermore, purposely infecting the population or experimenting with medication and vaccines (with potential adverse side effects) to assess the spread, symptoms, the response of the immune system, the evolution of the disease and/or cure require ethical precautions (and the preservation of fundamental rights), which include, but are not limited to, prior informed and free consent (including of high emotional pressure associated with fear).[21]

In short, one of the explanations for not learning and maintaining the alert level may be the lack of understanding of scientific dynamics and discourse by political decision-makers and real citizens/economic agents (as opposed to perfectly rational cyborgs assumed in the models of the blackboard Economics).

A third reason, in line with this, may be the consequent recourse to precarious mental models, often dangerous in scenarios of uncertainty and risk, through a primitive and mythical practice of use of unfounded and almost incomprehensible superstitions and beliefs in this era of knowledge. As an example, there are many speeches about the divine punishment that this plague represents, or prayer sessions to end the pandemic, namely with the city hall of the town of Ladário, in the state of Mato Grosso do Sul, decreeing a period of 21 days of fasting and prayer to ask for divine intercession in the fight against Covid, or even children sacrifices in Bragança, also in Brazil, or with the advice of several African governments to buy mugwort tea and to force children or workers to take it, in order to return to classes and jobs.[22] Another variation of these beliefs is to trust that if a wave of contagion

---

(over)confidence in others and in-group phenomenon, (un)adaptative cognitive capacity and predisposition to accept symbolic information as real (acceptance bias), and difficulty to defy them as soon as they integrate our memory, enhanced by repetition (saliency) and the focus on emotions, cognitive myopia, representativeness and the need for some pattern and control over uncertainty, proportionality bias (e.g., big events need big explanations) or even personal traits as emotional vulnerability. Forgas and Baumeister (2019); Myers (2019); Douglas et al. (2019); Taylor (2019) pp. 23–49, 63–69; Basol et al. (2020). Furthermore, there seems to be a higher probability in sharing fake information than true facts. Vosoughi et al. (2018).

[20] It is important to stress the difficulty, in an anthropogenized world, of distinguishing the natural from the unnatural, both in terms of the origin of the disaster and in terms of its impacts.

[21] The ongoing "telenovela" around the side effects of AstraZeneca and Janssen vaccines is a good example of this emotional distress that feeds conspiracy theories and anti-vaccine movements. The normal procedure of drug-evaluation, especially with its massive administration, is now happening in real time under the inflated lights of media.

[22] Decree n.°5.194/2020/PML of the Municipality of Ladário https://www.bibliatodo.com/En/christian-news/brazilian-mayor-declares-21-days-of-fasting-and-prayer-to-fight-the-coronavirus/

has already been suffered, it will not be repeated, when, in fact, the probability of the location being reached is independent of former impacts. Strictly speaking, in the case of pandemics, it is, on the contrary, empirically observed that the new waves start to break in the first places affected and are usually stronger.[23] As for fake news and conspiracy theories, the need for control and patterns and the strong aversion to uncertainty help, *inter alia*, to explain this phenomenon.

A fourth reason, no less important, and even paradoxical, is the moral risk enhanced by more access to information, increased knowledge, and scientific and technological development, fostering overoptimism and overconfidence associated with the feeling of control over virological forces. Knowledge enhances the belief that it is possible to predict, mitigate, manage, combat, eliminate, and overcome SARS-CoV-2 and the pandemic, giving a feeling of greater security and invulnerability, even increasing the distortion of the illusion of control that, in the covidian crisis, translates, on the one hand, into blind faith in a full proof vaccine (and its rapid development and availability) or, for some, medication such as hydroxychloroquine and, on the other hand, into the belief in the total eradication of the coronavirus (even when its transmission is already communitarian and global, progressing gradually towards an endemic state). In this sense, we understand the warnings of various health authorities against the (moral) risk linked to the (false) sense of security that the masks or vaccines can give, thus feeding risk behaviours and decreasing zeal, such as reducing hand hygiene or respiratory etiquette, physical distancing and attendance of very crowded spaces, or even sloppiness in the use of the protection equipment itself (not washed or disposed of properly or misplaced). In addition, surviving infections and, collectively, the pandemic (e.g., no saturation of the health system, "controlled" number of critically ill patients and deaths, but also, in the perspective of policy makers, the maintenance or strengthening of confidence in its actions—regardless of their suitability) also reinforces dangerous optimism, illusions of invulnerability[24] and future actions.[25]

(last access 09 September 2021); https://www.cmjornal.pt/mundo/detalhe/ritual%2D%2Dcriancas-penduradas-em-cruzes-para-acabar-com-a-pandemia-salvas-pela-policia-no-brasil (last access 09 September 2021), (Bragança, Brazil); https://time.com/5840148/coronavirus-cure-covid-organic-madagascar/ (last access 09 September 2021).

[23] For instance, this might help explain, the narrative of surprise of the Portuguese Government when faced with a big second wave (and then third wave), signalling that no one expected it, at least so soon or so strong. The narrative was however dismantled by recalling former Government declarations and documents, including a Fall/Winter health plan.

[24] Sousa Mendes (2000), p. 71.

[25] The narrative of the Portuguese miracle during the first wave might have enhanced some overconfidence and overoptimism by the citizens and Government authorities, inducing risk, and might contributed to major second/third waves. It should be noted, however, that this distortion contrasts with the worsening of risk aversion also seen in the aftermath of experiencing a natural catastrophe, from the perspective of the availability heuristic, and there is still a lack of studies to ascertain its interactions, prevalence and conditions. Regarding this worsening of risk aversion, Cameron and Shah (2011).

In short, as written elsewhere, if "more or less (in)conscious and (re)active ignorance to which no economic agent is immune in high-risk scenarios promotes disaster",[26] excess information also hinders, due, paradoxically, to the difficulty of choosing in a context of abundance, or to the "arrogance" and increased levels of negligence it produces. In other words, in the end, in one way or another, there is no guarantee that we will always learn from the past (and from mistakes).

Finally, it is essential to underline the role of the adaptability and resilience demonstrated empirically by the human being.[27] If he/she is able to live in the most extreme climates, geographical conditions, or socio-political and economic contexts, such as wars, or to adapt to changes in his/her conditions and abilities (e.g., blindness due to illness or amputation following an accident), sometimes due to the power of positive illusions,[28] then he/she reveals that he/she has become accustomed to living with various pathogenic elements (such as coronavirus and viruses) that circulate in a more or less endemic way in different societies. Physical proof of the same adaptation also includes, in many cases, the evolution and suitability of the immune systems, including via vaccination, which helps to explain individual and/or collective immunities, but also demographic differences that are behind disasters such as epidemics/pandemics in Central America, brought by the conquerors, and that annihilated civilizations that were not immunized. In the same way that it would be possible to consider adapting and getting used to daily and "free" coexistence with the virus, at the individual, collective, and institutional level, it would also be possible to consider resilience to live more or less confined and restricted or to learn to live a "new (softer and less intrusive) normality" with the use of a mask, frequent hand hygiene or physical distancing.

However, assuming that this adaptation happens, it can raise, once again, moral hazard problems, potentiating systematic bias and consequent losses. Furthermore, the adaptation and the creation of a habit (sometimes with the introduction of new social norms in both the descriptive and normative plan) can crystalize pernicious errors, biases, inefficiencies, and path dependencies. Rephrasing the old Portuguese adage that "the habit makes the monk", the "habit makes the moron", since automatisms are activated (system 1) and the deliberative and reflective system (system 2) is turned off, even for monitoring purposes (and correction) of the adequacy of the behaviour to the concrete circumstances, thus reducing attention and care.

Perhaps, however, this tendency towards adaptation is not so clear and real, even within the behavioural sciences. After all, here too, scientists disagree with each other, with studies for all tastes, especially if, in a policy of "confirmation bias", their basic and methodological conditions are forgotten, and abusive extrapolations (especially normative) are made. This is all the more true in a scientific field not only under construction, still in its puberty, and without a unified theory (assuming it is necessary), which is often attacked for methodological issues [e.g., variables

---

[26] Saraiva (2013).

[27] Ariely (2011), pp. 144 et seq.

[28] Taylor and Armor (1996).

defined in the models, type of data collection (revealed or declared preferences, sample size), type of participants (e.g., diversity limitations for focusing on WASP), "fabricated" laboratory environment] and because it is apparently a collection of anomalies that occur under very particular conditions.

The question is all the more pressing here for two reasons.

The first, insurmountable, is that these pages are built on the back of the insights of Behavioural Economics and, therefore, even if one tries to develop a debiasing effort, especially in relation to a confirmation bias or normative extrapolation, the risk is always present of contaminating our present reflections.

The second is the assumed use, in at least two countries (United Kingdom and Sweden), during the current covidian crisis, of public health policy models based on behavioural sciences. It is not our purpose here, even due to the absence, incompleteness, and/or not total reliability of the data collected, to make any value judgment on the strategy of each country,[29] although, in a transparent manner, we assume, within the principle of proportionality, a preference for softer solutions, when more effective and efficient than hard solutions, and, *in dubio*, less intrusive measures are preferred by default.

Now, in the British case, the Government used, in a first phase, the insights of the famous Behavioural Unit Team, which proposed less interfering actions, at least at the beginning, such as information campaigns and hygiene education ("keep calm and wash your hands"), and the focus on group immunization, in order to avoid "behavioural fatigue" resulting from restrictive measures, including various impositions and prohibitions and a hard confinement, which should only be applied at the peak of the pandemic. In other words, in order to ensure, in behavioural terms, greater effectiveness, a policy of precision is adopted for the most invasive solutions, avoiding that, until its true need and adequacy, there is a phenomenon of saturation and consequent behavioural relaxation, either by an adaptation that generates moral risk, or by an increase of more violent emotions (such as despair and anger) that incite attitudes of defiance and disorder. Some empirical data seem to support this thesis, although it is difficult (especially at this early stage) to establish causal links, with some scientists establishing at least hypothetical correlations between outbreaks of violence in Germany and lockdown policies[30] (but that are verified in several countries like the Netherlands, France, Italy, Spain, the United States, or Senegal

---

[29] There is no international harmonization neither in the number and type of tests used, nor in the criterion for defining death by Covid, with some States, including Portugal or Spain, changing the methodology during the reaction to the pandemic. Furthermore, since this pandemic is described as a marathon and not a sprint, with the possibility of new contagious waves, and with large sections of the population not tested, it will only be possible in the end, with the necessary and adequate cooling, to draw conclusions, both on the danger of SARS-CoV-2 and Covid-19, as well as on the appropriateness of the measures taken, in a broad analysis of costs and benefits (including global health—i.e. not only Covid –; economy, finance, social, environment, culture, politics/democracy).

[30] https://www.publico.pt/2020/06/22/mundo/noticia/violencia-motins-estugarda-origem-restricoes-covid19-especulam-especialistas-1921515 (last access 09 September 2021).

with Portugal, for example, observing a spike in violent crime in the early stages of relaxation after the first confinement).

At the opposite pole, a group of six hundred behavioural scientists wrote an open letter[31] to the British Prime Minister questioning, from the point of view of scientific scrutiny, the theory of "behavioural fatigue" and, consequently, the chosen libertarian approach, demanding the use of tougher instruments. One of the arguments behind the letter's motivation is the idea of an elastic capacity for human adaptation, especially in situations of danger. Additionally, in their opinion, there is no conclusive evidence that there may be fatigue associated with physical distancing (with very few studies on the subject due to its empirical rarity) or other measures and that it may pervert those that have been adopted, especially in a context of pandemic threat that they classify as high risk (i.e., health, both individual—for some groups-, and public). In fact, the gravity and novelty of the situation is, for this group of experts, in itself a factor in questioning the soft policy based on putative tiredness. On the one hand, there may be more motivation for the sustainability of behaviours and the acceptance of harsh measures in the face of danger, and, on the other hand, the research carried out and published does not encompass this type of extreme situation. Even so, they recognize that the known studies, namely on the prolongation of protection measures during past scourges, such as H1N1, seem to indicate that their compliance, and therefore the maintenance of behaviours, tends to decrease throughout an epidemic.[32] However, it is not certain whether this effect is due to saturation (and therefore, ultimately, to limited motivation) or more to an already studied decrease in the perception of threat and risk. An extra reason is that, in their opinion, the importance of the perceived threat implies that the lack of more drastic instruments undermines, by the underlying negative signalling, the softer actions that citizens should, in any case, accept, as the respiratory etiquette or hand washing.[33] After all, if the Government does not take other (stronger) measures, why should citizens be concerned about hygiene or not hug friends. Finally, it is argued that there may be fatigue in the fulfilment of command-and-control solutions with impositions, prohibitions, and sanctions, but most of all, there would be tiredness of nudges, which would be the first to be disrespected because there are no penalties associated with the non-compliance. This is, however, a fallacious argument, since the soft nature of nudges (some of which rely on the automatic cognitive system) may be the reason for their greater acceptability, stickiness, and even effectiveness in certain contexts, thus generating less exhaustion also because of the perceived idea that they may be removed at any time.

---

[31] https://sites.google.com/view/covidopenletter/home (last access 09 September 2021).

[32] Cowling et al. (2010), pp. 867–876. Reynolds et al. (2008), pp. 997–1007, reveal the difficulty of individual compliance with self-isolation measures, especially the longer and less understood they are, although a slight improvement was observed when the reasons for the quarantine are well comprehended, concluding the authors with concerns about the ineffectiveness of lockdowns as public health tools, especially when there is contagion by asymptomatic patients.

[33] Pandemic Influenza Preparedness Team (2011).

Strictly speaking, all arguments, on the one hand and on the other, are criticisable and susceptible to the phenomenon of "cherry-picking", insofar as there is no sufficient and specific knowledge, research, and literature on behaviour in the context of perception of high pandemic danger and over long and generalized confinements (although there is topical investigation in specific and very contextualized cases, of trapped miners or people temporarily arrested for weather or natural disasters[34] or more or less short lockdowns in some health outbreaks[35]). In this way, on the one hand, nothing substantially proves behavioural fatigue. On the other hand, nothing shows that it does not exist, although the long confinements and restrictive measures taken to manage Covid-19 seem, after 1 year, to bring new light on this issue, with outbursts, riots, evidence of degradation of mental health, uprisings of tiredness symptoms, numbing, and decrease in risk aversion and perception.[36] However, in general, a limited motivation of the "real man" (as opposed to the "econs") is widely recognized and acknowledged, even if we do not fully understand the circumstances and reasons that explain some variations.

One of the main lessons, here, is the need for caution in the use of experimental and empirical insights based on behavioural sciences and behavioural economics, in particular, to architect public strategies and policies, especially under a lot of pressure. Ultimately, the choices will depend more on ideological options[37] and on the perception of what citizens will approve or desire, in a phenomenon close to the herd effect, due to the loss aversion of political decision-makers and their interest, in the end, in being re-elected.

3 Response to the Pandemic by Governments and Citizens

The passions generated by the climate of special ignorance and uncertainty surrounding the new coronavirus have caused a very marked cleavage, with extreme positions between two opposite sides of the barricade, in a polarization phenomenon (with the direction of the polarization depending on the group's starting point) known in Social Psychology and in in-group and out-group relations, caused by normative influence (social comparison), informative influence (persuasion) and self-categorization, leaving little room for intermediate positions due to processes

---

[34] For example, Weems et al. (2007), pp. 2295–2306; Reynolds et al. (2008), pp. 997–1007.

[35] See the references in Cowling et al. (2010); Reynolds et al. (2008); and Pandemic Influenza Preparedness Team, (2011). See also the literature review in Webster et al. (2020).

[36] For all, see the recognition by the WHO of a pandemic fatigue: World Health Organization. Regional Office for Europe (2020). Demystifying pandemic fatigue as a cause for non-adherence and compliance with covidian restrictions, Reicher and Drury (2021).

[37] For all, with surprising results, van Holm et al. (2020).

of social validation and homogenization of the characteristics of group processes:[38] on the one hand, "deniers", on the other true "sanitary Nostradamus".

The former, as the name implies, or in a conspiracy theory reasoning, deny the existence of a pandemic, or recognizing it, they minimize the risk, comparing it with colds or the flu. In this line, they defend a "business as usual" logic, that is, non-change, or minimal changes in daily life and public policies, aiming to ensure the full functioning of the economy, since they believe that the "cure"—by way of prolonged and repeated lockdown strategies as long as there is no vaccine/group immunity or proven medical and pharmacological protocols for critically ill patients—will be more costly than the disease, namely due to the increase in poverty and consequent health degradation. Put in a simplistic way, when in doubt, privilege the economy. In international terms, this position has been assumed, albeit with some ups and downs, by the American (Trump) and Brazilian (Bolsonaro) presidents who have been heavily attacked and even ridiculed in the international and domestic press.[39] Their bombastic, controversial, and provocative statements, in which sometimes both political leaders cyclically substitute themselves for scientists in a phenomenon of bandwagon effect—as in the recommendation of hydroxychloroquine or to not comply with the established law (e.g., not wearing a mask on the street, in Brasilia)–, and the incoordination of public strategies and policies taken, aggravated by being federal states with different levels of decision, have been, at least in the first months of the pandemic, undermining the "denier" position and contaminating the appreciation of soft, but not denier, strategies like the Swedish or British solution (in an early stage).

On the other side, in a position that gains more popularity and international adherence and media salience and ubiquity are those who consider the threat to be very high, both for individual health and public health, i.e., with the fear of collapse of the health system because of overcrowding peaks and, in particular, having to determine priority criteria in the patients to be treated and, therefore, with an aversion to decisions about who should be saved or die. Thus, for this group, the priority is health (and life) even if it means stopping economic activity, thus revealing zero risk tolerance and a purpose of total eradication of the coronavirus, which uncovers, attending to the current knowledge of community and global transmission of SARS-CoV-2, a bias of illusion of control. In sum: *in dubio pro health* (immediate Covid 19). Thus, this faction supports very interfering and restrictive measures which include mandatory quarantines, prohibitions on visits

---

[38] For all, Sunstein (2001), p. 14.

[39] For example, Weible et al. (2000). See also, Gibney's film, Totally Under Control (codirected with Suzanne Hillinger and Ophelia Harutyunyan), documents the Trump administration's disastrous early response to the coronavirus pandemic; https://www.theatlantic.com/politics/archive/2020/11/trumps-lies-about-coronavirus/608647/ (last access 09 September 2021); https://www.theatlantic.com/politics/archive/2020/03/bolsonaro-coronavirus-denial-brazil-trump/608926/ (last access 09 September 2021. For the Brazilian case, see also: Schaefer et al. (2020); Cepedisa / Conectas (2020); https://www.dw.com/pt-br/em-pronunciamento-bolsonaro-minimiza-novo-coronav%C3%ADrus/a-52906298 (last access 09 September 2021).

between different households, closing borders, restrictions for all kinds of social events, stopping all non-essential economic activity, enhancing, by the intrusive dimension of the proposed solutions, a slippery slope for authoritarianism, and more or less in disguise police states in democratically weakened countries.

On both sides of the barricade, from the perspective of Behavioural Economics, the presence of several limitations (of rationality, motivation, and self-interest), the use of heuristics, the interference of emotions and biases, and the choice of scientific and technical support to the extent of convenience (confirmation bias) can be seen. In fact, the comprehensive and exponential opposition between Economy and Health is quite illustrative, as if both were antonyms and not two sides of the same coin, repeating here the Economy-Environment dichotomy that persisted (although it sometimes resurfaces) up until the construction and (un)happy trivialization of the concept of Sustainable Development.

Due to the prevalence of the "sanitary Nostradamus" group, with the politically correct discourse of "health and human lives first, economics later", we will try to explain, keeping the behavioural approach, its rapid success (at least in this first semester of 2020[40]) and, despite some nuances in its concrete implementation and communication, its transversal adoption in the four corners of the world, with implications for the design of current public policies.

First of all, this positioning feeds on social alarm and pedagogy of fear,[41] benefiting from the heuristic of availability with the daily and mediatic salience regarding the counting of the dead and infected[42] or impacting images from overcrowded hospitals or mass graves. The discourse is eminently pessimistic, reaching situations of manipulation of the facts with unproven causal links (e.g., youth parties or a greater number of tests as an explanation of the increase in confirmed cases in the Lisbon area, or that family gatherings are the major cause for contagion in Portugal),[43] partial view of reality (namely forgetting the economy,

---

[40] In Portugal, the mobility data collected show that even if the third wave was much worse than the first, the second national lockdown (also with the use of the pedagogy of fear) presented higher levels of mobility (+9.3% and increasing), suggesting fatigue and/or "immunity" and/or numbing to the level of risk and fear. https://expresso.pt/coronavirus/2021-02-25-Confinamento-desce-ha-tres-semanas-e-mobilidade-esta-70-acima-do-normal-nos-dias-uteis (last access 09 September 2021).

[41] This does not mean, at all, that on the "deniers" side the same strategy is not used, although it is not focused on the "health tragedy" but on the "economic tragedy".

[42] For the purposes of this article, no distinction will be made between infected, confirmed case or positive test with Covid or SARS-CoV-2.

[43] The Portuguese Health Authorities (and the Government) blamed families for infections, presenting data that 67% of the cases were due to family gatherings. A month later, the official data showed that more than 80% of the infections had unknown origins. So the 67% only counted for less than 20% of the whole cases, that is around 10%. https://covid19.min-saude.pt/convivios-familiares-responsaveis-por-67-das-infecoes/ (last access 09 September 2021); https://observador.pt/especiais/afinal-so-10-dos-casos-ocorrem-comprovadamente-nas-familias-mais-de-80-dos-casos-de-covid-em-portugal-sao-de-origem-desconhecida/ (last access 09 September 2021). As for most testing and therefore more cases, for example: https://rr.sapo.pt/2020/05/09/pais/covid-19-dgs-aponta-duas-razoes-para-aumento-do-numero-de-casos-em-lisboa/noticia/192178/ (last access

post-Covid and non-Covid patients) and misrepresentation of scientific explanations [e.g., exponential growth in cases of infection, forgetting that, in a pandemic (with a respiratory virus), after a peak, its number declines abruptly, in an inverted V curve, therefore not eternally ascending], overlooking, for example, that if people may die from (or with) Covid, others may die from fear of going to hospitals, the postponement of their consultations and treatments, or because of the diversion of funds due to covidian "monotheism"[44] or because of more negative or less direct effects from the economic and financial crisis that is already affecting most countries (with estimated falls of 6.8% of GDP in the Eurozone, comparing to 2019),[45] pushing millions into poverty and, consequently, reducing their access to health care, and emptying public coffers, leaving less money for health investment. The catastrophe reigns, even when the reality is not catastrophic, and the collapse of the health services did not generally happen across the globe (independently of the discussion about the role of confinement in the responsiveness of the hospitals). Although, for instance, in Portugal, we had the worse numbers during the so called third wave and there was a very critical saturation of health services, never did they fail or leave Covid patients (or any other urgent patient) without adequate medical care, even though, every single day during January the press would emphasize the catastrophic situation in hospitals a little bit more, for instance filming queues of ambulances at the door of medical facilities.[46] In short, there is an omnipresent narrative of

---

09 September 2021), forgetting that more important than the number of tests is the proportion of tests for each confirmed case; blaming young people gatherings: https://www1.folha.uol.com.br/mundo/2020/08/europa-limita-festas-dos-jovens-com-medo-de-rebote-de-coronavirus.shtml (last access 09 September 2021) and considerations of the Portuguese Decree-Law no. 28-B / 2020, of 26 June; against: https://www.publico.pt/2020/06/26/p3/noticia/escolher-grupo-manter-distancia-jovens-podem-sair-noite-seguranca-1921911.

[44] See in this regard the discussions on the excess of unjustified deaths (not Covid) during the confinement or the estimated 1.4 million deaths from tuberculosis by 2025 and a 5 to 8-year setback in terms of fighting this disease due to restrictive measures imposed by SARS-Cov-2 and to the displacement of funds to Covid-19. See, respectively, Cardoso et al. (2020), with some possible explanations; Vieira et al. (2020); Nogueira et al. (2020), with some explanations that include de decrease in access to health services during the lockdown; Stop TB Partnership in collaboration with Imperial College, Avenir Health, Johns Hopkins University and USAID (2020). For instance, in Portugal, by November 2020, there were less 121 thousand surgeries and 12 million consultations in hospitals than in 2019. https://observador.pt/2021/01/09/menos-121-mil-cirurgias-e-12-milhoes-de-consultas-nos-hospitais-ate-novembro/ (last access 09 September 2021). For all, Vos (2021), Table 2.2., p. 11.

[45] https://www.publico.pt/2021/02/16/economia/noticia/economia-zona-euro-caiu-68-2020-1950875 (last access 09 September 2021) The Portuguese GDP decreased 7.6% comparing to 2019.

[46] In Portugal, despite the high level of infections and mortality, most of the mediatic pictures of enormous queues of ambulances at the door of the main hospitals were misleading since they were due more to disorganization and wrong emergency medical protocols than real medical emergencies. For instance, the Administration of the central Hospital of Santa Maria, in Lisbon, recognized that only 15% of the patients in ambulances needed hospitalization. https://observador.pt/especiais/porque-ha-tantas-ambulancias-a-porta-do-hospital-de-santa-maria/ (last access 09 September 2021).

exaggeration that amplifies the perception of danger and explores informational asymmetries, emotions and affection.[47]

Now, the instrumentalization of fear, one of the most profound emotions that refers even to human animality and primitiveness, constitutes a very risky and potentially uncontrollable strategy, which may lead to uncoordinated and uncontrolled behaviours, which sustain a tragic race to the bottom.[48] Its main intention is to produce a greater and faster impact on the awareness of the need to change behaviours and decision-making, appealing to the survival instinct and, thus, speeding up and increasing responses, maintaining the incentives through a continued recall of the presence of the sword of Damocles hanging over our head. The heuristic of fear proves to be particularly galvanizing, and therefore dangerous, in matters of infectious diseases due to the invisible nature of the coronavirus, its somewhat uncontrollable dimension (science has not yet answered all the questions), more personal aspects (the contagion of oneself or family members, loved ones and acquaintances), and to its global presence and proximity (physical and timely).

The change in the perception of the threat level through the pedagogy of the catastrophe has repercussions in terms of moving away from the rational understanding of mathematical probabilities and, most of all, subjective probabilities, consequently conditioning the choices. This is all the more true when scientists do not agree on their objective probability assessments,[49] which can happen, namely due to reasoning with an underlying margin of uncertainty and the influence of predisposition, in a mix of heuristics of availability and anchoring, or when their predictions suffer from an "insensitivity to prior probability of outcomes",[50] i.e., an indifference to the frequency with which a result is expected to occur in the absence of any information, or when they suffer from an illusion of validity, that is an increased confidence without guarantee resulting from the favourable relationship between the expected result and the informative input, especially when it presents a high correlation. Indeed, as written elsewhere,[51] "working with probabilities, one is influenced by two factors: prior information and knowledge (which determine the predisposition in the treatment of data) and subjective sensitivity (in particular in view of the magnitude of the effects, the possibility of control and time proximity). In other words, the risk assessment prior to the decision derives from the sum of the danger (hazard) and the alarm or salience[52] (outrage) and the multiplication of mathematical probabilities by the magnitude of the event. Now, the danger and the alarm do not have the same weight, such as the probabilities and the dimension of the

---

[47] Weible et al. (2000).

[48] van Bavel et al. (2020), p. 462.

[49] It is also interesting to note a gap between the objective assessment of risk by the instruments and models developed by scientists and their perception by laypeople, generating a cognitive and understanding gap.

[50] Kahneman and Tversky (1974).

[51] Saraiva (2009), pp. 172–173.

[52] Sunstein (2006), p. 32; Alberton (2004), p. 12.

effects produced, prevailing, as a rule, the second element of the equation.[53] (...) In other words, there is a difference between the mathematical probability and the perceived probability. A low-risk and high-magnitude scenario (...) suggests taking action, not because the probabilities are frightening, but because of the unsustainable nature of its size,[54] in a true aversion to catastrophe and irreversibility.[55] Prospective Theory has verified, namely, that low probabilities are, as a rule, overestimated and very low probabilities either overestimated in an excessive or grossly neglected way. On the other hand, there is a tendency to underestimate high risks and overestimate low risks"[56,57] and, in association with the availability heuristic, to increase the perception of the magnitude of the effects, to the detriment of their probabilities. This can also be explained by the difference in the expected duration of the loss of life and in the reference point taken for the assessment, so that the risk of a prolonged future loss of life stands out in comparison with a short future loss in terms of time but in which, paradoxically, the number of deaths may even be higher.[58] Likewise, due to the discount rate, especially hyperbolic, and the consequent biased preference for the present, the present losses (e.g., number of Covid deaths) are excessively valued in comparison with future losses that may be (taking into account the correction of the discount rate) more significant (e.g.,—hypothetical[59]—non-Covid deaths due to restrictive measures in Covid or suffering caused).

The low probabilities and the magnitude of the effects encourage ambivalent psychological tendencies, drawing the former inertia and the latter action. The degree of alarm decides the weight of the scale, but, as mentioned above, it can cause paradoxical and contradictory effects such as scepticism, denial and apathy or impulsivity, mania, and motivation. From existing literature, the heuristic of fear works in the desired direction when there is a note of hope in its communication (light at the end of the tunnel) and some power and control over the situation are given, especially with the presentation of measures that can be imposed, such as

---

[53] Levitt and Dubner (2006), pp. 170–175; Sandman (2004).

[54] The scenario can also be thought of in an optimistic perspective. Just think of the EuroMillions or the Lottery: very low chances of winning but prospects of enormous wealth motivate millions of gamblers, especially in jackpot situations.

[55] Sunstein (2005), p. 33.

[56] Viscusi (1999), p. 31. On an (ir)rational consumption behaviour in a scenario of small-probabilities events in the context of Covid-19, Eichenbaum et al. (2020).

[57] Saraiva (2009), p. 173.

[58] Viscusi (1999), p. 31.

[59] It is still a hypothetical example at this stage, due to the lack of data, because there are yet no cross-sectional studies (using models and much less with empirical data, since the pandemic is not over). Most investigations focus on projections of what would happen in terms of non-confinement in terms of Covid deaths, or as seen in the case of tuberculosis, in terms of a specific pathology, or in terms of economic impacts, with no integrated treatment of the various health and/or non-health impacts. Nevertheless, see, Bayley and West (2020); Binlei et al. (2020), pp. 249–268. Looking at the impact on suicide, Carrion et al. (2020). Concerning more partial approaches, Flaxman et al. (2020); Peixoto et al. (2020); European Commission (2020); Eichenbaum et al. (2020a, b).

hand washing, surface disinfection, physical distancing, or respiratory etiquette.[60] In the case of perceived lack of control or useless action, catastrophic alarmism (for example, adopting a speech, although apparently well-intentioned, that even an "irritating optimist"[61] does not see the light at the end of the tunnel in order to convince the citizens of the need for maintaining hard confinement measures[62]) can ricochet, either causing paralysis and total discouragement (which in the covidian hypothesis may end up contributing to the politically desired quarantine), or inciting incoordination, boycott, and even violent behaviours such as riots or the growth of extreme and populist political forces and parties.

On the other hand, in the heuristic of fear, it is important not to minimize the potential effect of "Peter and the Wolf", i.e., the devaluation of catastrophic warnings of events that end up not occurring at all or in only part, and that discredits the emissary and may decrease, as a consequence, the perception of risk and, therefore, have an impact on behaviours, enhancing negligence, inertia, or provocation, reducing risk aversion. In the case of SARS-CoV-2, this may, to some extent, help to explain some disregard for WHO warnings, in the face of previous false alarms such as with influenza A (which even led, in Portugal, to the placement of disinfecting gel dispensers in public buildings and the purchase of two million vaccines, with about three quarters unused and discarded) or with the rhetoric that has been recurring for months that the present moment is a critical and dangerous point in the evolution of the pandemic. Regardless of the merit (or not) of this prediction, which we do not intend to discuss here, in an environment of acute stress and in an accelerated digital world, the time of its verification may be too long for the time of evidence that citizens and policy makers prefer and accept, thus causing this asynchrony: frustration, bewilderment, and/or loss of confidence in the authorities. The same is true, for example, in the Portuguese case, with the predictions of the peak of the first wave, which (understandably in terms of scientific uncertainty) varied greatly, pushing the date of its verification but which, for some, may have been perceived, after some time, as a "false" threat or unpreparedness of the scientific specialists. A similar episode happened during the third wave, not only concerning the peak, but also concerning the possible collapse of the national health system and, afterwards, the deadline for the deconfinement.

Furthermore, it is necessary to consider two other variables that influence the effectiveness of the alarm: the level of tolerance/aversion to risk (for genetic,[63] neurological,[64] contextual, and mental accounting[65] reasons) and the risk framework

---

[60] Lunn et al. (2020), p. 6.

[61] Reference to the nickname given to the Portuguese Prime-Minister António Costa.

[62] https://www.dnoticias.pt/pais/ainda-nao-e-momento-de-vermos-a-luz-ao-fundo-do-tunel-afirma-antonio-costa-DI6028621 (last access 09 September 2021).

[63] Think, for example, of the controversial thesis of Richard Dawkins' selfish gene.

[64] Camerer et al. (2005); Glimcher (2003); Loewenstein et al. (2003).

[65] Thaler (2000).

in terms of gains or losses (with a risk aversion to gains and tolerance or risk seeking to losses[66]).

In addition to the two main explanations hitherto advanced for the strengthening of the most sanitary thesis, namely the pedagogy of fear and the aversion to risk, in particular to losses, a third factor, correlated with the two others, is assumed to be as or more important: the herd effect.

This gregariousness, inherent to the very predominantly social condition of the human being, can be observed in the international political reaction, in particular in the taking of scientifically controversial measures such as the use of masks, closing of schools, or generalized quarantine, regardless of people being infected or not. Three major reasons can, plausibly, help to explain this mimetic phenomenon: the anchor set by the measures taken in the first affected countries; peer pressure; and the role of the media.

As for the first, we should recall that the first detected cases of Covid arose in the Chinese city of Wuhan,[67] with the authorities decreeing a mandatory confinement of the general population, the closure of almost all economic activities, the obsessive measurement of body temperature, and the use of a mask outside the home. This model of measures, with greater or lesser intensity, was extended to other areas of the country and to autonomous territories, such as Hong Kong and Macau, and then to most Asian countries, thus establishing a behavioural reference point for decision makers, politicians, and health authorities in other states. This behavioural anchoring phenomenon, well known to the behavioural sciences, has an impact on the definition of descriptive and later injunctive social norms,[68] framing the decisions taken, most often in a "sticky" way, and therefore making them difficult to overcome even when the heuristic is recognized.

Not pretending to make full judgments of adequacy, some doubts are raised as to the merit of (un)consciously setting a behavioural reference based on the Asian and, in particular, Chinese response. On the one hand, it is a culture that stands out for the predominance of the acceptance of duty and collective well-being over individual well-being, unlike the so-called Western civilizations. On the other hand, in the

---

[66] This situation is often illustrated by the example of the "Asian disease" presented by Kahneman and Tversky: Kahneman (2002), p. 457; Kahneman and Tversky (1981). Also, Kahneman and Tversky (2000a, b).

[67] We will assume that these were the first cases, although there are more and more studies corroborating the idea that SARS-CoV-2 was already circulating in China earlier than initially considered and even in Spain or Italy in March 2019. For example, Chavarria-Miró et al. (2020); Apolone et al. (2020).

[68] What is meant by social rule, in line with Ellickson, is the rule governing individual behaviour and which third parties, other than the State, impose diffusely through sanctions or social rewards for offenders and abiding respectively. Ellickson (2001), p. 3. Regarding the distinction between descriptive and injunctive norms, the former refer to beliefs regarding the concrete conduct of others, i.e., the behaviour itself, what it is; the latter regarding the belief about what others think should be done and therefore include the threat of a sanction, even if a large deviation from the perceived description may instill in the agent a fear of retaliation, indicating the importance of the anchor point. See also, Kinzig et al. (2013), p. 164.

Chinese case, despite the "one country two systems" policy, it is a manifestly authoritarian state, with little respect for rights, freedoms, and guarantees (as understood and conceptualized in Western democracies), controlling (and sanctioning) its citizens and information and with a strong, centralized and castrator inclination. In addition, in the situation of masks, their usage was already widespread, not so much for reasons of infectious diseases but for mitigating the effects of air pollution.

With regard to peer pressure, which is very much linked to anchors that fit social norms, contrary to what is often admitted, behavioural science is increasingly demonstrating the importance not only of judgement by others (especially about our behaviour) but also of the example they set for their actions, in other words, the importance of (present, imaginary, normative) others on our preferences, judgements, decisions, and behaviours. In this way, in a kind of contagion effect, with a multiplier potential, the conduct of others is replicated, either because we think we should behave like that (even in a context of cognitive dissonance), or because we perceive (wrongly or not, in a pluralistic ignorance[69]) that others consider that behaviour correct and normative. This may be owed, endogenously, to the social nature of human beings, to their need to feel belonging to a group and to be protected by it, in an evolutionary trace. In this way, there can even be a tendency towards conformity and living according to models of what is socially expected and defined as a role to play much when, at the outset, certain behaviours would be rejected due to the inherent values. Overwhelming examples can be found in the very controversial Stanford Prison Experience,[70] in which in a simulation of a prison in a University basement with students divided into prisoners and guards, they soon began to actually embody the roles that had been assigned to them, ending up with episodes of aggression and torture, or in Asch's conformity studies,[71] in which the individual's tendency to alter his/her answer to an objective and sensorially perceptible question (e.g., comparative line length) is observed in the presence of others, bringing it closer to that expressed by the majority of individuals within a group, albeit visibly wrong, as it contradicts the Theory of Social Comparison by demonstrating that uncertainty can arise as a result of social reality tests and that the theoretical distinction between social reality test and physical reality test is unsustainable.

Conformity may also be observed in the group thinking phenomenon, during the phase of preparation of decision making, leading to poor decisions. Several governments and health authorities suffered from this in different moments of the management of the pandemics. Small, cohere, homogeneous groups, led by partial leaders, like some minority governments, under tension, might make bad judgments and take

---

[69] Prentice (2012), p. 10. In pluralistic ignorance, individuals consider that the behaviour they observe on the part of others translates what they privately feel and think, concluding that they are not aligned when it may not be true, underestimating the behavioural limitations resulting from social impositions.

[70] Haney et al. (1973), pp. 4–17.

[71] Asch (1951), pp. 177–190; Asch (1956), pp. 1–70; Asch (1952), pp. 2–11.

wrong and even disastrous decisions, especially due to group pressure towards unanimity, which deteriorates the moral judgement, mental effectiveness, and skips a reality test. The symptoms include the illusion of invulnerability (overconfidence) and of unanimity, with mind-guards protecting the leader from opposed positioning; self-censorship; pressure against dissidents and opposition; collective rationalization of the decision taken, hence ignoring warnings, threats, and minority opinions; belief in the morality of the group and a stereotyping of the "enemies"/opposition. The group thinking will help the self-esteem and morale of the group, the mutual support between its members and decreases the perception of risk and therefore of guilt and regret. By not exploring all the alternatives, not widening the sources of information (with a self-confirmation bias), and not correctly assessing the risk of its decision, the group thinking promotes failure and lack of contingency plans. For instance, in the case of Covid-19, examples go from very hard confinements with high destructive economic and social impacts to uncontrolled lifting of restrictive measures, provoking new massive Covid waves.[72]

As was written elsewhere, "people tend to hide their normative behaviours which they deem divergent from the socially accepted ones and to reveal more the normative behaviours that go in the direction of being socially accepted, in the same way that they more easily express opinions that they find consistent with perceived social norms or that only deviate a little from the injunctive norm.[73] In short, public and social behaviour does not always coincide with private opinion, which raises a problem of illusion of choice,[74] especially, and paradoxically, in so-called democratic societies, since it is more easily assumed that social behaviour corresponds to private belief."[75]

Regardless of criticisms of the methodology used or conclusions reached, these studies indicate the power of conformity and normative social influence, even if with some resistance (namely, in situations of immorality and injustice),[76] which translates into public behaviour to obtain social rewards and/or avoid social punishments, in line with the theory of self-categorization of social influence (or referential informational influence), in which the observed conformity is reflected in a process of depersonalization, in which individuals expect to have the same positions as their peers (in group) and often adopt those opinions.[77]

This theoretical approach to social pressure and conformity also emphasizes the dynamics of the in-group and out-group relationship, which may lead to polarization and virulent attacks between "deniers" and "sanitary Nostradamus", and to those

---

[72] Vos (2021), Table 2.1., p. 10.

[73] Prentice (2012), pp. 8 et seq.

[74] Prentice (2012), p. 11.

[75] Saraiva (2016).

[76] Look at some of the disobediences in Milgram's experiments, Milgram (1963), pp. 371–378; Blass (1999), pp. 955–978.

[77] Turner (2010), pp. 243–272 (reprint of article from 1985); Turner et al. (1987).

who lie somewhere in the middle,[78] but also to redirection blame and the maintenance of a positive image of oneself and the group.[79] It also helps to explain a certain rhetoric of categorization and stereotyping, with serious and illustrative signs of xenophobia and of the power of fear, such as Chinese/Asians (including "Chinese" viruses) *vs* all others, especially in the first phase of the epidemic's arrival to other parts of the world,[80] inciting racist attacks and social exclusion but also the consequent phenomenon of incoordination in a typical problem of collective action (e.g., threats of compensation claims and commercial and economic retaliations), since the pandemic, by nature, must be managed through international collaboration. On the other hand, a similar trend is related to the Manichean dichotomy "risk group" *vs* "not at risk"; elderly people *vs* youth (with speeches that blame and/or segregate both of them over time and involving social and moral claims and complaints of their behaviours); or with the separation between "health professionals" *vs* others; or between "specialists/epidemiologists" *vs* lay people; or between those who "work" *vs* those who "telework" or who can stay at home and get paid; or between North *vs* South (or between different regions or states within a country).

The group dynamics is reflected in the behaviours, and there may be a tendency, under certain circumstances and contexts, to more vigorously disapprove of the conduct of foreign elements and, in others, to react more vehemently against the dissonant conduct of an element of the group. The viewing angle, that is, the (cognitive) perception of the actual behaviour is an important factor in the evaluation and imitation of behaviours. This could, for example, lead to a trial of the most "disapproving" alleged "festive" attitudes of young people on the part of risk groups that will better accept the breaking of the rules by their own or the conviction, by discord, of a government member for their peers as opposed to political opponents (from whom such conduct is expected). In other words, there is some ambiguity and plasticity in the interpretation and acceptance of behaviours, with asymmetric social and/or moral judgments, according to their author.[81]

This categorization discourse in groups has been extensively explored in the narrative of formal (Portuguese) social media,[82] making it easy to verify it just by reading the headlines that constantly refer to risk groups, specialists, health professionals, young people (in the Summer of 2020), in addition to the almost obsessive comparison with the pandemic situation elsewhere in terms of diagnosed

---

[78] This implies an effort to categorize what is meant by a group, in this specific case, and a social identification. Warning in general to this question, Ariely et al. (2009), p. 393. About group interaction in this pandemic, van Bavel et al. (2020), pp. 465–466.

[79] Douglas et al. (2019).

[80] The same phenomenon of stigmatization was witnessed in some Portuguese-speaking countries, but this time, in a distrust in relation to the Portuguese, due to the geographical evolution of the pandemic wave and also, in several countries, in relation to immigrant and emigrant communities (in the return to the country of origin).

[81] Shu et al. (2011), p. 10.

[82] We will not consider here the more informal and decentralized means of communication such as social networks, due to lack of data and we will only look at the Portuguese case that we know best.

and dead people but also, with the progressive reopening of the borders, with the distinction between countries that open their borders to direct flights from Portugal and those who forbid them, in a fight of "us against them".

However, the most important role of the media lies in its assumed contribution to the conditioning of individual and social behaviours during the pandemic, in the sense of prioritizing the protection of health, physical distancing, and confinement, in line with the compliance of the rules and guidelines defined by the authorities, in a mission of flattening the pandemic curve. In fact, in a very recent study, not yet published but whose results have been circulated to several institutional media, the preliminary data of a survey carried out by a group of researchers from the CECS of the University of Minho and CINTESIS, to 200 journalists, editors, coordinators, and directors of the Portuguese media (nationwide and general press, online titles, radio, and television), indicate that 92% of respondents expressly assume that they tried to guide citizens towards certain behaviours during the state of emergency, namely towards the lockdown, concluding that this action "may have contributed to the successful control of the Covid-19 pandemic in Portugal" (during the first wave).[83]

This "mission" was translated, on the one hand, in the simplification of information in order to make it more comprehensible across the various demographic strata, whether in pieces or news texts, as well as in infographics and explanatory boxes. In the same way, Covid information started to be highlighted in these media, for example, with headings on the online pages or as a reminder at the end of many news items. In addition, the televisions placed #FiqueEmCasa (#StayHome) in the corner of the screen and the news anchors repeated the message of confinement to exhaustion, using (moralistic) phrases such as "Your grandparents were asked to go to war. You are asked to stay on the sofa. Be aware!".[84] During the month of June 2020, the same happened in terms of gatherings, with recurring denunciations of these events and insistently urging, especially young people, not to congregate. On the other hand, teachings of behavioural sciences have also been explored to guide the message and push in the intended direction, namely, with the exploration of loss aversion, in particular through three main methods: the treatment of numbers, the heuristic of affection, and the saliency.

In the first case, just remember that the news (at least in Portugal for the last year) usually starts with the number of dead and infected, and then focuses on the number of hospitalized and intensive care patients and only in the end on the recovered. The number of people infected with SARS-CoV-2 or asymptomatic or Covid patients with mild symptoms hardly ever appears, thus enhancing drama and, therefore, contributing to a fear pedagogy. After all, 10 dead and 300 infected daily and

---

[83] http://www.cecs.uminho.pt/investigadores-do-cecs-estudam-mediatizacao-da-covid-19/ (last access 09 September 2021). It should be noted that we will not discuss here whether the Portuguese case, in the context of a state of emergency, was successful or not in terms of controlling effectively and efficiently the different waves of Covid-19.

[84] https://www.youtube.com/watch?v=44-Ztclq71w (last access 09 September 2021).

470 people accumulated in hospital have more impact than 300 recovered and 7000 without symptoms or with mild symptoms at home. In fact, national Portuguese health authorities have followed a similar model. It should be noted that, more often than not, data are presented in absolute terms and more rarely in relative terms (growth compared to the previous day) and even less in terms of demographic proportion (e.g., cases or deaths per million inhabitants). Anyway, 100 infected in Portugal is not equivalent to 100 cases in Brazil or China. The bombardment of comparative data from other states is also a constant while being symptomatic of the editorial line followed, taking into account the fact that, as a rule, only countries that present impressive absolute numbers are chosen. More striking is the fact that journalists know, because they are duly informed, that these comparisons are fallacious, not only due to demographic issues but because of the number of tests (and their quality) and counting methodologies, particularly in the case of deaths, in which there is no uniformity of criteria or transparency and access to real data. If this were true, North Korea would be the biggest success story in fighting the pandemic. Strangely enough (or not), all the discussions during the first wave around the quality of the raw numbers (e.g., levels of testing, counting methodologies, the veracity of governmental data) disappeared during the second and third waves, with numbers being presented by the media without any warning on their limitations. For example, the very low numbers in China or the data of developing countries (with their very scarce resources and fragile institutions) are assumed to be right.

On the other hand, the media explore, sometimes at the verge of morbidity, the emotional and affective connection (heuristic of affection)[85] with the infected, the sick, and the dead, saying their names, publishing their photographs, telling their stories, listening to their reports or their families, choosing preferably rare and/or extreme cases. Likewise, they try to do something similar with health professionals, showing pictures of their tiredness, the marks of the masks, or the new rooms where they had to move for fear of spreading Covid to their family. The proximity thus achieved promotes empathy through identification and reciprocity that feed altruism:[86] the subject manages to put him(her)self in the other's place and experience his/her drama, still hoping for reciprocity if (s)he ever finds him(her)self in the opposite scenario. Furthermore, the perceived non-impotence of the action (or the effect of the drop in the ocean) ends up functioning as encouraging feedback, as it is known that it can make a difference, and it reflects the good moral image that everyone likes to have of him(her)self and of one's mark in this life. Moreover, the heuristic of affection, due to the vivacity and emotionality that it instils, that is, the ability to more clearly record the memory of the facts and feelings experienced, allows, as a rule, to establish a direct correlation with the level of predisposition of help.

The salience and heuristic of availability are fundamental tools used in the conditioning of conducts by the media. The ubiquity of the covidian theme in the

---

[85] Slovic (2010), pp. 35–39.

[86] This effect is not always present. Castillo and Carter (2011).

media speaks for itself. Moreover, the use of shocking images, such as the famous photographs of ruptured Italian hospitals, mass graves in Manaus, or intubated and ventilated patients, or skinny recovered people, highlights the threat—as recurring reports about serious Covid damage in several (and increasingly more) organs or the lack of a curative medicine for the disease do, when, strictly speaking, almost 9 out of 10 infected cases (who are not usually interviewed, photographed or biographed) have no or only mild symptoms and need no stronger medication than an antipyretic and, in more severe cases, there are some solutions with good results today (although no overall incontrovertible full proof medicine protocol has yet been discovered).[87]

In short, believing in the conclusion that the contribution of Social Media helped in the desired flattening of the curve and, therefore, saved lives, makes the importance of how risk (and uncertainty) is communicated stand out—both for confinement or (responsible) deconfinement. Hence the importance of careful and appropriate framework of risk communication, considering the known cognitive, volitional, emotional, and altruistic biases and limitations has to be highlighted.[88]

Not wanting to discuss whether the option of "Staying at Home" is the most appropriate (and, therefore, the validity of the message), and even accepting that the pressure from the media was fundamental to pass on the main message from the health authorities and the one considered correct (after all they are known as the fourth power), one cannot fail to point out some concern with the fact that, in democracy, the media purposefully guide (and assume it without shame) behaviour, even if with "good intentions". There is a great risk of a slippery slope, to which ethical problems are added not only with the (perceived) truth and transparency but also with the use of (almost immoral and even illegal) nudges, such as shocking images or messages in the corner of the televisions, in a practice that approaches the subliminal (since the message is omnipresent and outside the central focus of vision). Furthermore, what if the heuristic of fear that underlies it (in the logic of the half-empty glass) generated social turmoil or, on the contrary, apathy and business as usual? Should the media legally be held responsible? Is the argument of their "good intentions" a factor of exclusion or of reduction of guilt?

However, there is a tendency for the prophecies of doom and inherent inaccuracy to be devalued, since it is accepted that exaggeration serves to help and protect. "After all, if the fire alarm goes off and there is no fire, that is a lesser evil. But if the fire spreads and the alarm does not go off, that is a serious problem."[89] In other words, as indicated by the lack of current debate on the CESC/CINTESI study, the media seems to have been forgiven by citizens for their decision to condition their conduct and for their paternalism. The same could happen to the health and

---

[87] We are not stating that there is a 100% cure, nor that there is no permanent and even serious sequelae in recovered patients. We just want to salient that attention is focused on one tenth of very serious cases, not showing that on the other side there are nine tenths or more without major concerns. In other words, the perspective is always that of a glass that is half empty and not half full or simply half.

[88] For all, Taylor (2019), pp. 79–86.

[89] Saraiva (2009), p. 52.

government authorities, if the aftermath of the fight against the pandemic is found to be inadequate (especially, by excess of its measures).

Indeed, from the point of view of the political decision-makers who are concerned with the retrospective judgment of voters (and with their re-election), it is perceived, for the reasons that have been pointed out, that they adopt more cautious and excessive measures.[90] This aversion to risk and loss on the part of decision-makers has legitimized the acceptance of a precautionary principle based on limited rationality, mainly considering the high magnitude of the estimated impacts,[91] and has motivated, in particular, the taking of collective decisions, despite the low level of objective probabilities of occurrence. At least in Portugal, the mantra from Government and health authorities has been that in precautionary measures, it is better to "sin in excess", devaluing the costs and inefficiency of this option. No politician wants to be held responsible for present deaths during his term because he did not know how to prevent, manage, and combat risk (unlike deaths and other future losses outside of his mandates that occur as a result of his present decisions).

In plain terms, the triad pedagogy of fear, aversion to risk and losses and gregariousness has an impact in terms of the biased preference for the present, efficiency, and the principle of precaution.

The preference for the present arises from a hyperbolic discount that misappropriately devalues the future, in which the present losses and benefits are disproportionately overvalued in terms of future losses and benefits. So, for example, saving a life (Covid) today, namely through restrictive measures of freedom of movement or private initiative to flatten the curve and/or attempt to eradicate SARS-CoV-2, will be worth much more than saving ten lives in the next 2 years (due to non-Covid, mental illness and/or increased poverty due to the freezing of the economy and the reallocation of scarce resources to fight the coronavirus).[92] Naturally, not only important ethical issues arise, particularly on the value of life, but also on efficiency, since a correct cost-benefit analysis (which may include ethical considerations) should take into account an intertemporal balance to assess merit, suitability, and efficiency of the choices made in the present and with future repercussions.

Indeed, the perception of risk influences the decisions to be taken and the call for regulation.[93] If this perception is biased, in an environment of scarcity of resources, its allocation for the satisfaction of certain needs inevitably means that these will be diverted, inefficiently,[94] from the satisfaction of others that were more justified, in an irreversible decision. Likewise, in a context of scarcity, the allocation of means to

---

[90] Bouglet et al. (2005), p. 19.

[91] Sandman (2004); Decanio (1997), p. 14.

[92] This example is hypothetical, since, as mentioned, it is too early to take stock of the pandemic management, just to illustrate what could happen, in terms of "irrationality" in a situation of hyperbolic discount.

[93] Sunstein and Kuran (1999), pp. 715–736; Shogren (1998), pp. 13–14.

[94] For all, Binlei Gong et al. (2020).

safeguard an option value leads to the non-satisfaction of another need, mainly present, which also constitutes an irreversible cost.[95] Irreversibility is, therefore, bilateral, which requires a case-by-case and correct consideration of intertemporal advantages and disadvantages. In other words, in a climate of risk and uncertainty, the perception of the risk of irreversibility (in particular, catastrophic) can greatly influence the assessment of decision making, namely between "acting and learning", "waiting and learning" or "acting slowly initially and then intensifying the action"[96] and the choice of whether or not to guarantee an option value to ensure some future flexibility as knowledge increases through the payment of an "irreversibility premium" (to avoid irrecoverable damage).[97] Thus, for "sanitary Nostradamus", in the balance between present lives irreversibly lost and an economic crisis, albeit a serious one, but reversible, the option for the present is clear and imperative. But for those who also equate the loss of future (irreversible) lives, mostly non-Covid or due to poverty, the intertemporal choice is much more complex.

The decision will be even more difficult for political decision-makers who are under pressure from citizens' anxieties, which often push them into a post-social state with paternalistic traits, into the arms of public power. Now, in democracy, the dependence of votes by the government promotes an alignment of interests between the concerns of voters and public policies.[98] Look at the closure of schools in Portugal during the first wave in a decision contrary to the advice of public health specialists or its delay, again against the scientists, during the second/third wave (with a change of direction precipitated by a sudden change of heart of the school community owed to a hasty panic with the heightening of Covid numbers). In the case of SARS-CoV-2, when immediate human life costs are incurred, and other costs are pushed into the future (e.g., with moratoriums postponed several times), adding the hope for financial support from the ECB and the European Union and promised flexibility of the budgetary stability rules, a tendency to act immediately and a preference for strong precautionary measures, even if excessive, seem evident to government authorities. After all, they will receive political retribution for the immediate benefits of lives saved and the unsaturation of hospital services, and will suffer little or no political loss due to long-term costs, all the more so as they can attribute them to an unexpected external cause that surpasses them, the pandemic, and to the associated economic recession, also due to an international, and European, incoordination in its management, taking no responsibility. In short, the pandemic will serve as a scapegoat for possible bad and inefficient present (and even future) political decisions, and it can be complicated, in an agency logic, for the political decision-maker (and the legislator) to manage to escape the social outcry when set on fire by the pre-mentioned triad. In other words, it is and will be difficult (and

---

[95] Sunstein (2008), pp. 10 et seq.; Sunstein (2005), pp. 21 et seq.
[96] Weitzman (2007).
[97] Sunstein (2008), pp. 9–10; Weiss (2003), p. 138; Fisher (2000), p. 9.
[98] Stavins (1995), p. 14.

unpopular) for governments not to comply with the (biased and passionate) expectations of their citizens in a context of perceived catastrophe and fear.

Thus, it is clear that, based on the precautionary principle, and with it on the principle of proportionality,[99] the interpretation and adoption of the former in this context will tolerate some excess, in an *in dubio pro* health application and, therefore, anti-economic understanding. That is, under uncertainty, excessive measures will be tolerated and even preferred, even if they prove their inefficiency and ineffectiveness, for example, to prohibit breastfeeding or body contact with an infected mother, or the availability of newspapers and magazines in cafes and hairdressers, or to impose the constant disinfection of surfaces, or the closure of economic activity at a certain time, or to impose the quarantine of uninfected people. In other words, the aversion to present losses and, more than an aversion, a high intolerance to uncertainty, ambiguity, and ignorance justify reducing the risk to almost zero, which seems to be a perversion of the principle of precaution. This radicality, as Pereira da Silva[100] rightly calls it, although in the context of the environmental issue, "or it is only a principle of consideration of the environmental dimension of the phenomena and, in this case, it is not only fully justified but also we cannot see why it will integrate the content of prevention; or it is a true presumption, which obliges anyone who intends to start any activity to prove that there is no danger of environmental damage and, then, assigning a legal dimension would represent an excessive burden, inhibiting any new reality, in any domain, since "zero risk" in environmental matters does not exist". Indeed, although praiseworthy, the health concern, in the case of the coronavirus, cannot be absolutist, promoting castrative interference by the State. In the words of Amado Gomes[101] (regarding the environment but extending to the health issue and the protection of present lives), "precaution is an unrealistic and dangerous idea (...). Unrealistic, because the zero risk it advocates is neither practicable nor desirable. Dangerous, because it presupposes an *ad infinitum* extension of decision-making powers in situations of uncertainty that unreasonably privileges security over freedom". In fact, quoting Demosthenes, "death is the end to which all men arrive and which cannot be avoided with the precaution of being closed at home."

In the end, by embarking on an overly comprehensive, and therefore inefficient, implementation of precaution, there is a risk of becoming, in a kind of path dependency phenomenon, stuck to public policies and indefinitely disproportionate intervening government decisions because of an aversion to regret and losses, resisting changing their choices and behaviours even if they should normatively do so, due to a feeling of personal and institutional commitment assumed with the design of those policies. In fact, the strategy may be aggravated by the possible interpretation that the deviation between the defined and observed objectives is owed

---

[99] About the close link between proportionality and precaution, Saraiva (2009), pp. 235–236.

[100] Pereira da Silva (2001), p. 19.

[101] Amado Gomes (2007), p. 361, developing her opinion on the precautionary principle in Amado Gomes (2000), pp. 28–39, 44 et seq. See also Amado Gomes (2001).

to a lack of resources or stronger measures, leading to their reinforcement.[102] See, for example, the approval of the recent diploma on administrative offenses in the context of the situation of calamity, contingency, and alert, Decree-Law no. 28-B/2020, of 26 June, which, starting from a consideration denied days before in a meeting between the Portuguese authorities and specialists, sanctions the violation of certain behaviours, removing the previously more pedagogical approach.[103] Likewise, the return to the "civic" duty of confinement (even with an endless list of exceptions) in several parishes in the metropolitan area of Lisbon, during the summer of 2020, can be read in this perspective of aversion to regret and anchoring measures previously taken. Another striking example is the second hard lockdown that began in January (as it also happened in other European countries) with the so-called third wave, where the Portuguese Government not only changed its rhetoric and communication strategy (refusing to present a set time and a deconfinement plan, even when asked by the President) but also aggravated the monitoring and sanction of non-compliant behaviours and applied a hard confinement policy after months of denying the return to this strategy for being too harmful. But how could the Government explain (and make it understood in a biased context) that it would not close schools and most non-essential economic activities and not send people home when the numbers were so many times higher than during the first wave? The anchor was too robust, especially when lighter measures during Christmas holidays seemed to be (one of the) reasons for the explosion of the third wave. Regrets attached to former (poor) decisions are also strong (and might lead to a longer lockdown than necessary and adequate).

4 Behavioural Economics as a Public Health Support

Understanding the real behaviours of individuals but also of institutions (in the aftermath of the new Behavioural Public Economics or Behavioural Political Economics) that seek to frame them is fundamental to the design of a more adequate, efficient, effective, and acceptable architecture of choice, in general, and in the context of a public health problem, in particular.

---

[102] Lobão (2013).

[103] "It appears that the new contagions are often the result of situations of non-compliance with the rules of physical distance, especially in events that imply the gathering of people." Regarding the administrative offense around gatherings, there may be a problem of unconstitutionality due to the restriction of the right of assembly. In fact, several measures taken to manage the pandemic, especially during the state of calamity (and, for the most part, contingency and alert) but also during the state of emergency, raise doubts about constitutionality, mainly because they are taken by Resolution of the Council of Ministers (with no intervention of the national Parliament), such as mandatory confinement for infected and non-infected, suspension and restriction of assembly rights or freedom of religion, interdiction of public places, like beaches, or a specific crime of disobedience. However, this is not the best place to discuss purely constitutional issues.

In line with the literature review by Lunn et al.,[104] we will look at what the empirical insights from Behavioural Economics reveal about individual behaviours[105] regarding the main measures imposed or recommended in most States to tackle Covid-19[106] and how this same knowledge can help align the behaviours with the desired conduct and greater acceptability and effectiveness of the measures. Thus, the washing and disinfection of hands will be addressed; respiratory etiquette, especially not touching the face; self-isolation in case of infection, quarantine and "social" distancing; altruistic and collaborative behaviours; and the importance of crisis communication. It should be stressed, however, that we do not intend to deify Behavioural Economics nor to suggest or affirm that its knowledge embodies absolute and indisputable truths. Here too, as has been pointed out, there are studies for all tastes, with contradictory and ambivalent results, in which methodological and contextual considerations must always be considered. Many are, in fact, the behavioural economists who start by warning about the risk of drawing normative conclusions from their research and results. This does not mean, however, similarly to what happens with other scientific approaches, that the information and knowledge developed should not be considered, especially since in certain subjects, such as hand washing (especially in a hospital environment), there is today a robust research work.[107]

Hand hygiene appeals have appeared since the beginning of the pandemic as one of the main (and theoretically easiest) measures to combat it. The purpose is to cement a habit and, therefore, make it an increasingly automatic gesture commanded by system 1, even if it is necessary to activate system 2 to promote it, particularly in the first adaptation phase, and to maintain it in a second phase of sustained maintenance. Its promotion, which has strong scientific support in behavioural literature, will have to take into account the context in which it is operated (e.g., health units, housing, workplace) and cultural environment. After all, there are demographic and geographic differences, with the data collected in 63 countries revealing that, if in Portugal and Greece 85% of respondents say they wash their hands after going to the bathroom, the same answer is given by 96% of Bosnians and 94% of Turks, against

---

[104] Lunn et al. (2020), pp. 1–15.

[105] We will not address here, with the exception of the issue of the crisis communication, questions of institutional and organizational behaviour, namely of the authorities, not only in the perspective of decisions (collective and institutional) taken or to be taken, but also in the perspective of reducing bureaucratic barriers (sludges) that hinder individual behaviour and that, in a perspective of management and mitigation of the economic and social crisis resulting from the pandemic, make it difficult to access means of support (e.g., lay-off processes, access to credit, and subventions).

[106] These measures varied, depending on the perception of risk, the call for regulation and/or the more or less democratic traditions and tools commonly used in different States, between nudges and commands, that is, between guidelines and impositions/prohibitions with harder or softer frameworks.

[107] For all, with a large literature review, Lunn et al. (2020).

75% of British, 62% of Spaniards and French, 57% of Italians and only 50% of Dutch.[108]

Different solutions have been tested, especially nudges of several types, from social norms (with a description of the behaviour of peers), information, educational campaigns, reminders and check lists, warnings, to other more ingenious ones of real re-architecture of the environment of choice such as colourful dispensers placed in very visible and passing places or water timers or songs with the duration that is considered adequate for proper hand washing. Some, especially related to system 2, such as educational campaigns and information provision, seem less effective than others more linked to system 1, like dispensers that stand out in central circulation areas.[109] The acronym EAST (easy, attractive, social, timely) used by behavioural economists to design effective nudges here seems to find empirical grounds.[110]

In the case of respiratory etiquette and not touching the face with the hands, the investigation is less robust, and it seems difficult to circumvent intuitive behaviours, such as touching the face, that individuals do not even notice and that usually happen many times per hour. Thus, and in view of these automatisms, the little existing literature seems to indicate the low effectiveness of mechanisms that activate system 2, like educational campaigns and information or even warnings, and it being apparently preferable to change the environment of choice with the ubiquitous, easy and close presence of materials for touching objects, mainly handkerchiefs and wipes.[111]

Concerning the use of masks, in line with hand hygiene, warnings, reminders, information, and education campaigns regarding their use, some with humour about their poor placement, or their availability and easy access at the entrance of spaces where its wear is more advisable or mandatory can help. For poorer populations, some lessons can be learned from experiences with vaccination or mosquito nets, in which it is observed that their free supply increases adherence, and this effect is enhanced when, on the one hand, material delivery is maintained, by ensuring the levels of availability and salience, and, on the other hand, when associated with basic necessities, such as a plate of food after the vaccine.[112] However, more studies are

---

[108] https://www.statista.com/chart/4111/do-europeans-wash-their-hands-after-using-the-toilet/ (last access 09 September 2021).

[109] Lunn et al. (2020), p. 2.

[110] Service et al. (2015).

[111] Lunn et al. (2020), p. 3.

[112] Glennerster and Kremer (2011); Vaccines, as merit goods and given their proven success, even with Covid (with a significant decrease of deaths and hospitalizations in the countries with higher rate of vaccination), should also be promoted as a fundamental tool in the war against the pandemics, together with masks, handwashing, physical distancing, and respiratory etiquette. This is even more important in a context of fear against vaccines, explored by anti-vaccination movements and conspiracy theories, especially when considering the record time in their development and the "reality show" of the pharmacological surveillance, mainly around the AstraZeneca and Janssen vaccines. An effective communication of cost-benefit and risk analysis is needed and also explaining the functioning of the vaccine, in educational campaigns. Some countries have adopted hard and intrusive measures, by making the inoculation mandatory (e.g., Brazil—art. 3, III,

lacking, especially outside the hospital environment, namely an understanding of whether continued use fosters, *per se*, a habit (and therefore an automatic mechanism) and whether non-infection during usage creates a kind of continuous feedback on the importance of that equipment and protective conduct or if, on the contrary, it promotes a false sense of security and, therefore, moral hazard, leading both to the misuse of the mask (e.g., misplaced or not washed or replaced) and to risky behaviours as for example reducing physical distancing and participating in gatherings.

The politicization of the use of masks in certain countries, for example in the United States, where the mask started to have an anti-Trump and paternalistic connotation, as well as the stigma associated with its use by black people (with the criminal stereotype),—which, in fact, has led some communities (namely in Oregon) to exclude African-Americans from wearing them—requires nudges to be more adequate in terms of the ideological, demographic, and cultural profiles of the nudgees. Research in this area is scarce.

With regard to physical distancing, self-isolation, and quarantine, there is now a set of solutions and empirical data, sometimes contradictory, that allow some insights for the construction of public policies and for the understanding of individual behaviours.

Regarding physical distancing, during the management of the pandemic, several instruments have been used, with solutions very similar to those related to hand hygiene, such as information, educational campaigns, warnings and reminders, use of social norms, rearrangement of spaces (e.g., with tabs, markers on the floor, longer tables and benches and/or with marking places not to be used with tape), and funny solutions have also been found for certain sectors of the population, children, and people who frequent bars (e.g., Mexican XL hats, helicopter hats, use of giant buoys), emphasizing the importance of targeting communication and measures and also the role that humour, or at least pleasantness, can play. Similarly, more research is lacking.

The imposition and sanction for non-compliance, namely for the crime of disobedience or the spread of disease, self-isolation of infected people and/or quarantine of the non-sick population are not a sufficient guarantee of behavioural

---

Law n.° 13.979/2020, although interpreted as not coercive). Others, despite considering it voluntary, found some "hoft" (i.e., hard & soft) solutions to "force" vaccination, like facilitating access to schools, jobs, public places, travels through vaccination "passports"/green ways, which may create, not only justice and fairness issues, but also perverse incentives, especially in a context of vaccines scarcity, leading to corruption, black market solutions, and delay in the risk groups immunization. See on this: Drury et al. (2021). Softer solutions, in line with real nudges and boosts, include health literacy to avoid an aversion to ambiguity with clear statistical data, free and easy vaccination (avoiding traditional bureaucratic sludges), reminders, culturally adapted incentives (e.g., food in poorer countries, cannabis and alcohol provision in New York), opt out solutions, social norms (e.g., information that more than 87% of Portuguese want to be vaccinated) leading to herd behaviour. On behavioural solutions and vaccination, see Corrêa and Cosentino (2021); Taylor (2019), pp. 87–98; Betsch et al. (2010, 2011); Cappelen et al. (2010); Saleska and Choi (2021); Buttenheim and Asch (2016).

adherence, whether or not the subjects are fully rational. A traditional cost-benefit analysis, in line with the Economic Analysis of the Law, can conclude net advantages in not fulfilling the confinement (and, therefore, the rationality of the decision), either by the low probability of inspection, or by the insufficient cost of the penalty, either by benefits enjoyed by breach of obligation (e.g., outdoors, socializing, feeling of normalcy, and freedom, acquisition of goods and services, income earning).[113] Also, errors and distortions, especially the probabilities of being infected or infecting someone else, of being caught or not infringing, as well as motivational limitations (the ability to remain continuously confined, day after day) and perceptions on future harder measures or on their "negatively surprised" length and scope[114] can hinder the conduct of self-isolation, all the more so since knowing yourself "stuck" can increase the feeling of "being stuck". For a completely rational agent, it should be indifferent, in behavioural terms, to be trapped in a "cage" with the door closed or with the door open, or, seen from another angle, being restricted by obligation or voluntarily.[115] However, for an agent that is not fully rational, the former may seem more claustrophobic than the latter and, consequently, more difficult to endure and fulfil. Furthermore, it should be noted that for certain individuals, non-compliance with the curfew may be perfectly rational from their point of view. In the case of the elderly, although some point out two irrationalities such as over-optimism or overconfidence regarding the contagion that would translate into feelings of invulnerability, even because they have reached a proven age, after several "scares" throughout life, it is necessary to consider the rationality of their decisions, in a less paternalistic, stereotyped and uniform interpretation of their cognitive abilities: due to their age, and the shorter number of expected years of life, the marginal utility of each day is much higher than the younger age groups. That is, each day has more value for them than for their children or grandchildren. Therefore, in the balance between the advantages and disadvantages of confinement, the costs may outweigh the benefits, namely by considering, within the scope of their free will and autonomy, that they prefer to take the risk of fewer days of life but with quality (e.g., visits from and to their family and friends, walking, playing cards and talking in the park) than more days with no quality. The same is true for family interaction, wanting to entertain guests, hug and kiss children and grandchildren, as opposed to wanting to follow recommendations from health authorities or to impose the suspension of exits

---

[113] Reicher and Drury (2021) salient the fact that non-adherence with lockdown measures has more to do with practicability than with psychological issues or personal traits. For instance, factors such as the availability of resources (and Government failures to provide the support necessary to follow the rules, especially in self-isolation cases), crowded housing, low habitability conditions, or impossibility of working from home in order to earn some income required to satisfy the family daily needs are the most prevalent explanations for not complying with quarantine measures.

[114] Van Holm et al. (2020), pp. 16–17; Briscese et al. (2020).

[115] van Bavel et al. (2020), p. 466, warn that it should be explained to the "confined", that this distancing is only physical and not social, because they may use telematic means to reduce this feeling of isolation and imprisonment.

and care home visits.[116] For young people in general, and for those who do not belong to the so-called risk groups, similarly, the decision to not self-isolate can, in a cost-benefit analysis, be rational, given their individual health and the low probability of severe symptoms or even lower death rate, although biases of overoptimism and confidence can be pointed out on the opposite side, both in terms of the effects on their health and the likelihood of being infected and infecting others. Furthermore, in their view, socialization can be, rationally or not, valued, especially since there are neurological and emotional reasons for such a need, and, in particular after a painful lockdown experience, with distanced learning, and carried out with zeal in most cases, the return to socialization will be perceived as a deserved prize and that their part in the global effort would be fulfilled, with the fear of a new suspension of their social life being painful and even understood as unfair.

In fact, and with some bibliographic support that has already been referenced, it seems clear that, in one condition or another, the fulfilment of a period of quarantine can have significant psychological and emotional impacts, such as pain, anguish, anxiety, sadness, depression, anger, obsessions, compulsions, saturation, and even post-traumatic stress processes, which naturally hinder the sustained compliance with its imposition/orientation. Three main strategies to minimize suffering, and, therefore, to support compliance with the confinement are based, on the one hand, on recognizing the difficulty of the same, on the other, on explaining the reason behind the decision or recommendation and, finally, on betting on a message that appeals to altruism.

Contrary to what might be anticipated, staying at home and being reduced to that space, especially being ill or living in a crowded place with poor conditions, is not necessarily idyllic, pleasant, or the opportunity to put the tidies and cleanings in order, the readings and films up to date or to discover meditation and yoga or have quality family time. The "house arrest" feeling and the potentiation of domestic conflicts, increased by a perception of external danger, can cause enormous emotional and psychological costs. Being informed, knowing and recognizing that the lockdown process is costly is a fundamental mindset for the correct grieving of the pre-quarantine experience and for finding strategies that help to overcome difficulties, such as maintaining old routines (e.g., hygiene, clothing, eating or sleeping times) and the construction of new ones (e.g., physical exercise, reading, meditation) that even serve as a "reward" for fulfilling another day of self-isolation. Transparency and truth regarding the conditions for sustained compliance of quarantines are therefore fundamental and will tend to allow greater acceptance.[117]

Communication, a topic to which will return a little later on in these pages, is a fundamental element for a successful public policy and for the greater or lesser effectiveness and acceptability of the toolbox used to manage and resolve a

---

[116] We are not taking into account problems of organization and internal circulation within homes that can generate contagions associated with an elderly person who rationally decides to go out for visits or who receives them at the institution.

[117] Webster et al. (2020), pp. 163–169; Lunn et al. (2020), pp. 3–4.

pandemic. A clear explanation to the citizens targeted by commands or lockdown recommendations about their reasons represents both a democratic requirement and an incentive to comply, facilitating, through their understanding, their acceptance. It is all the more important, in the case of Covid-19, for asymptomatic and non-infected or negatively tested. It should be noted, however, that in these last two cases the justification is, even from a technical-scientific point of view, complicated, just remembering the uncertainty (or even ignorance) that involves, at the time of writing, the role of asymptomatic people in the contagion and spread of the disease. Fortunately, the quarantine of negative cases of SARS-CoV-2 requires greater explanatory and justified care about its benefits and justifications,[118] including for constitutionality issues, namely for violating the tests of necessity and not excessiveness of the principle of proportionality for the suspension and restriction of rights, freedoms, and guarantees. Several arguments have been tested (although not always convincing for some sections of the population), such as not being able to test the entire population at all times, since the test result is a momentary photograph that does not invalidate the possibility that the disease has not yet manifested itself or that the tested person will not be infected immediately afterwards, giving a false sense of security. In other words, having no symptoms, even with a negative test, is no guarantee of not being or becoming infected, therefore being a potential propagator of the disease.

The main argument used, however, focuses on the issue of public health (and not so much an individual health problem) and the protection of others, that is, betting on a limited self-interest already identified by the behavioural sciences,[119] namely in various experiments concerning the dictator and the ultimatum games[120] and the prisoner's dilemma,[121] and by genetics.[122]

Indeed, the narrative, supported by psychologists, has been focusing, in particular on the first phase of response to the pandemic, on maintaining the response capacity of national health services and protecting groups at risk and, therefore, saving lives, reinforcing the message with the heuristic of affection, focusing the effort in the defence of grandparents and immunocompromised relatives. In other words, the message is that it is not so much an individual and private health problem as a public health problem and the importance of saving other lives or, by exploring loss aversion, not to (un)voluntarily cause death (irreversible) of others, thus appealing to a collaborative altruism.

---

[118] Webster et al. (2020).

[119] For all, Jolls et al. (2000), p. 16.

[120] Araújo (2007), pp. 322–326; Jolls (2007), p. 17; Frank and Sunstein (2000), pp. 13–14; Sunstein (1999), pp. 121–122, 125–129; (1997), pp. 12–13.

[121] Sunstein (1999), pp. 127, 134; (1997), p. 13; Carvalho (2009), p. 317.

[122] In research carried out at the Hebrew University of Jerusalem based on the dictators game, the existence of genes related to altruistic and selfish decisions is suggested. Subjects with a longer AVPR1 gene (linked to the vasopressin hormone associated with social behaviours such as affection) show more altruistic behaviours than those with the shorter version of the gene. Carvalho (2009), pp. 197–198. Some investigations with monkeys also reveal collaborative behaviour.

Now, in the face of an event perceived as serious enough that it, in order for it to be overcome or at least be managed, needs a collective and collaborative action, the eternal problem of (dis)coordination arises, that is, whether it will triumph, in a prevalence of self-interest, a race to the bottom, for example, with the hoarding of goods or the disregard of basic health norms (hand and respiratory hygiene and physical distancing), or if, on the contrary, cooperation will succeed.[123] Empirically, during this pandemic, there have been punctual phenomena of incoordination,[124] with the caricature of a shortage of toilet paper being paradigmatic, but also the hoarding of masks, alcohol-gel, canned food, or Remdesivir or price speculation, which, incidentally, in addition to being legally penalized, suffer from a strong social rejection.[125] Conversely, collaborative behaviours are observed, such as the confinement of healthy populations, even when only recommended and not imposed and with net costs for certain demographic fringes, in a manifestation of solidarity.

From the Behavioural Economics bibliography, especially around the dictator and ultimatum games and prisoner's dilemma, it stands out that individuals tend to sacrifice their material well-being to help those who are good for them but also to punish those who are not,[126] as these two motivations have a greater impact on behaviour when the material cost of sacrifice is reduced.[127] The result is evidence that reciprocity sustains and is apparently sustained by an evolutionary-cultural and even natural sense of justice.

As written elsewhere,[128] "human beings reveal themselves as *homo reciprocans*[129] who can sacrifice their own interests in order to be, or at least appear, fair, which seems to suggest, in addition to valuing a certain type of justice, the weight of constraints (see the contempt of others or the fear of bad reputation or the claim of maintaining a certain status)[130] and the internalization of social norms, *maxime* as a moral commitment.[131] Thus, when a decision is made, there is a tendency to consider the costs of violating social norms (...) especially in the

---

[123] Exploring this issue in relation to the current pandemic situation, Ling and Ho (2020), pp. 312–320.

[124] Seeming to argue that, in the case of panic, there tends to be more cases of cooperation than of incoordination, Lunn et al. (2020), p. 5.

[125] In the literature of Behavioural Economics, the repudiation of the violation of the social norms of the increase in the price of shovels after major snowstorms is known, even if this results from a normal game of demand and supply.; Sunstein (1999), p. 122; Sunstein (1997), pp. 1 (note 3), 13.

[126] Araújo (2007), pp. 322–326; Jolls (2007), p. 17; Frank and Sunstein (2000), pp. 13–14; Sunstein (1999), pp. 121–122, 125–129; Sunstein (1997), pp. 12–13.

[127] Based in Rabin, Jolls et al. (2000), p. 24.

[128] Saraiva (2009), p. 365.

[129] Sunstein (1999), p. 125; Sunstein (2000), p. 8.

[130] Brekke and Johansson-Stenman (2008), p. 3; Jolls et al. (2000), p. 25.

[131] This phenomenon is usually called Expressive Law. Van Aaken (2008), p. 11; Cooter (1998).

event of publicizing the behaviour."[132] Social norms, as Ostrom's works[133] well demonstrate, can be a powerful instrument for enhancing altruistic and collaborative action,[134] notably when they involve effective sanctions.[135]

Some studies show that the subjects are only available to cooperate when others do it or when they are informed about it. That is, they collaborate when perceiving similar behaviour on the part of the other, in conditioned cooperation.[136] Furthermore, there is a tendency to reciprocate when something is received beforehand, so the perception of bad intentions seems to remove the willingness to collaborate.[137] Thus, "if conditional co-operators (i.e., subjects who are willing to initiate cooperative action when they estimate that others will reciprocate and during the time that they consider that part of the others will collaborate) constitute a significant part of the population,[138] the potential of the social norms is great (...) for their expressive dimension and function,[139] especially in contexts of identification (in which the individual identifies himself by his characteristics with others) and iteratives that foster communication and in which free riders are punished. In other words, social norms (descriptive and injunctive) can be real drivers of change to align behaviour with the desired behavioural standards"[140] in the public health field. Therefore, they have a (de/re)constructive role,[141] although caution should be exercised to avoid harmful effects such as crowding out, single action,[142] conspicuous conservation,

---

[132] Sunstein (1999), p. 122; Sunstein (1997), pp. 1 (note 3), 13.

[133] Ostrom (1990, 2000a, b, 2002, 2009); Ostrom et al. (1993); Ostrom et al. (1994). It should be noted, however, that the polycentric and institutional approach proposed by Ostrom depends on a whole set of assumptions, starting with a logic of closed society (and, looking at the Nepalese and African examples studied, of small dimension) in which it is possible to exclude untitled external parties and through rules regarding the use, appropriation and provision of common resources that are appropriate and adapted to local conditions, that is, socially accepted or at least acceptable. At the same time, monitoring of use/appropriation and the settling of a sanctioning framework for offenders and an accessible and effective regime for resolving disputes (not necessarily legal) are required, mostly to reinforce the fundamental principles of reciprocity and trust within the group (attached, in the situations observed, to an identification principle).

[134] Posner (2004), pp. 303–304; Rachlinski (2000), pp. 1537 et seq.; Sunstein (1999), p. 127; Huang (2020), pp. 32–33, recalls that, in repeated games, subjects tend to rely more on informal social norms than on law to enforce property rights.

[135] Specifically regarding quarantines, Webster et al. (2020). Two studies also reveal the perceived importance of compliance with the law as a condition of compliance with confinement, Caleo et al. (2018); Cava et al. (2005), pp. 343–347.

[136] For all, Brekke and Johansson-Stenman (2008), p. 15.

[137] Brekke and Johansson-Stenman (2008), p. 16.

[138] Ostrom (2000b), p. 142; Goodman and Jinks (2012), p. 5.

[139] Green (2006), p. 429; Goodman and Jinks (2012) p. 8; Gopalan (2007), p. 811.

[140] Saraiva (2016).

[141] Saraiva (2015).

[142] Gertner (2009); Weber (2006), pp. 115–116.

warm-glow or Prius effect,[143] reputational cascades,[144] or alteration of the context that crowds out the intended conduct.[145] The danger of social punishments should also be noted, especially in contexts of high tension and social categorization, as it is linked to naming and shaming and the promotion of whistleblowing practices, verified in some countries with (even State) requests for private complaints of non-compliance with the imposed health rules, which in places like Portugal, still with memories of censorship and PIDE (political police of Salazar), raise high cultural reserves and feed potentially explosive cleavages, extremisms, polarization, and social pressure. In fact, one of the strategies that has, at first sight, achieved some success, applied particularly in New Zealand, is to promote the perception that everyone belongs to the same group and that the fight against the pandemic is a joint collaborative effort of all, for all and according to all New Zealanders, regardless of their ethnic, cultural, social, economic, demographic, political or religious characteristics and background.

This shows the importance not only of the message but of the way in which it is transmitted, therefore, the communication of the crisis is crucial for the success or failure, on the ground, of public policies. This has to be well thought out and, above all, intelligent.

In the first place, it is important to guarantee the truth and transparency of the information disclosed, notably when it regards uncertainties and ignorance, thus ensuring greater public confidence and less economic impact of the measures chosen and applied.[146]

Second, the message must be consistent, since coherence is appreciated by individuals, as a sign of knowledge and of a well-planned tactic and strategy. In the United States or Brazil, for example, where messages from different authorities vary widely, at the federal, federated and local levels, it becomes difficult not only to understand the message but also to understand what behaviour to adopt. Likewise, since the example acts as a behavioural reference, if the law stipulates the mandatory use of a mask and the government does not use it, or if there are recommendations for distancing and avoiding agglomerations and political or other gatherings are promoted, the signs are confused and instigate less adherence to the defined norms or guidelines.

Third, the communication must take into account its addressee. If it is true that, on the one hand, it may be important to cultivate a spirit of group and unity, namely by placing everyone, government and citizens, in the same boat, on the other, it is necessary to take into account different perceptions and aversions to risk, needs and preferences, which can vary demographically, professionally, and culturally.[147] It is

---

[143] Green (2006), p. 408; Sexton (2011).

[144] Sunstein (2002), pp. 87–88.

[145] Gneezy and Rustichini (2000), pp. 15–16.

[146] Binlei Gong et al. (2020).

[147] Caleo et al. (2018), for example, observed that some African communities did not comply with the confinement because culturally their duty is to support the ill and weak. Cava (2005);

important, then, to focus not only on cultural tuning, especially playing with local traditions, experiences, memories, and culture, but also on targeting and tailor-making of the message depending on the group with which one wants to communicate, since they have differentiated concerns, needs, and preferences. In other words, the message to stay (preferably) at home should not be the same for a Brazilian, Portuguese, North American, or Nordic,[148] just as it should not coincide in the format presented to a child, a young person, a family man, or an elderly. In Germany, on a paradigmatic basis, efforts have been made to fine-tune communication with addressees through the COSMO initiative, a weekly survey of citizens to ascertain and track their (declared) preferences and thus better design and tailor messages.

Fourth, and as a result of what has been written, communication in the case of the pandemic must be cautious in the use of the pedagogy of catastrophe and in over-dramatization, which does not, of course, prevent the provision of data on the dead, seriously ill, or injuries, or to seek empathy with the addressees and promote their characteristic solidarity of conditional reciprocators. In the end, however, a serious reflection on the media as a whole, formal and informal, generalist and specialized, must be made on their role, limits, regulation, and scrutiny, due to their power in shaping the narrative and consequently the public performance and the regulatory requests (or not) of the citizens.

For ordinary citizens, at this moment, the advice will be to reduce their sources and (obsessive) queries of information, to choose them according to credibility and trust, avoiding rumours, social networks and pseudo-specialists, keeping it simple but not simplistic, reliable, and reasoned.

5 Final Thoughts

In times of uncertainty and risk and also of some ignorance, scientific errors are expected, as well as in the definition of public policies and measures and in social and individual behaviour. However, truth, transparency, and accountability are required, although without falling into hindsight bias temptations, in order to allow their correction and the alignment of public and private, social and individual behaviours in the pursuit of effective, efficient, and proportional combat to the pandemic.

DiGiovanni et al. (2004), pp. 265–272, observed the power of a "civic duty" of citizenship in the compliance of the quarantine.

[148] Sunstein, recently, at a conference of the Inter-American Development Bank, on the pandemic, defended that for South American countries, for better communication and nudging, instead of the acronym EAST, FEAST should be considered, in which the F stands for fun, adapting itself better in cultural terms. https://vimeo.com/416031973 (last access 09 September 2021); See also, van Bavel et al. (2020), pp. 463–464; Lunn et al. (2020), p. 6.

Here the institutions' strengths or weaknesses are revealed, serving as an example, at both ends, the Swedish commitment already initiated to set up an independent committee for the evaluation of the public management of the pandemic and the Brazilian President's option to stop presenting data on deaths, infected and hospitalized by Covid. Now, the perception of national institutions, in particular of their inclusive or extractive characteristics,[149] influences confidence in their communications, strategies, and public policies and conditions the greater or lesser adherence to compliance with the rules and guidelines given to overcome the crisis, not to mention the issue of compliance dependence on the greater or lesser existence and/or provision of resources (e.g., Guiné-Bissau vs Germany).

Recently released studies have been warning about the "unexpected" and socio-political but also socio-economic side impacts of a health crisis with the dimension of Covid-19.

In fact, the investigations carried out by the Varieties of Democracy Network, linked to the University of Gothenburg,[150] reveal that the emergency and exceptional measures taken in response to the covidian pandemic have degraded democracy in at least 82 countries—34 at medium risk of decline and 48 at high risk, compared to 47 who, until mid-May 2020, did not show democratic corrosion—thus reinforcing autocracies globally.[151]

Furthermore, a study by the European Council on Foreign Relations[152] adds that the pandemic, contrary to what was perceived, did not increase the desire of European citizens[153] to have greater Government intervention, confidence in specialists or even support for nationalisms or, on the opposite, European federalism. On the contrary, there is some suspicion in relation to the capacity and adequacy of action by States, and also by the European Union, with only 29% of respondents advocating more public action and approving their performance in these months of health crisis. However, a closer look at this distrust makes it possible to foresee differences in terms of the strength of the respective institutions, thus alerting to the importance mentioned above of institutional quality. Thus, if in Denmark 60% of voters show more confidence in their Government and believe that it has performed well, at the other extreme, 61% of the French have lost confidence and have a

---

[149] Acemoglu and Robinson (2013).

[150] Lührmann and Rooney (2020); More uptated data: https://www.v-dem.net/media/filer_public/86/3c/863c20b1-05ca-4057-b78b-f3e96110afb5/clean_v2_us.csv (last access 09 September 2021) and https://www.v-dem.net/media/filer_public/72/20/7220f61e-b4fc-4399-8f12-bee59e1cfd14/pandem_codebook_v2.pdf (last access 09 September 2021).

[151] If Portugal, during the first wave did not seem to be affected democratically, at least in international assessments (internally several constitutionalists and courts raised doubts on a crisis management by Government decree with very low Parliament participation), recently it has seen a downgrade in the recent report "In Sickness or in Health" by The Economist Intelligence Unit.

[152] Krastev and Leonard (2020).

[153] Surveys were carried out in 9 European countries, including Portugal.

negative perception of the performance of their authorities.[154] However, if there is an electoral bias in most countries, due to voting preferences, in Sweden, a country that has been pointed out and criticized for a softer approach, based on a libertarian paternalism logic, despite the constant comparisons in their disadvantage regarding the number of deaths and infections, there is not only a high maintenance of confidence in their authorities and public health policy, but also an electoral transversality of this support. The choice of truth, transparency, accountability with acknowledgment, and accountability for the mistakes made supports the options taken and, consequently, is reflected in the sustained compliance with the Government guidelines.

As for confidence in the experts, the situation is similar. If it has not generally increased compared to before the pandemic, it remains high in countries like Denmark and Sweden and quite low in France, Spain, and Poland, with a perception in most countries of manipulation and instrumentalization of scientific information by government officials, although there are also significant differences in terms of political preferences. Still, countries known to have strong institutions, such as Denmark and Sweden, maintain confidence in specialists, and Portugal and Germany have the third and fourth best results, despite the fact that 43% of the Portuguese respondents think that there are hidden data and 25% of Germans have little confidence in experts.

Hence, we find a correlation between the teachings of behavioural sciences and their application in public policies with institutional quality, which deserves to be further investigated and deepened. Going further, it will be interesting to ascertain to what extent the perception of legal security and quality of law, in short, the solidity or fragility of the rule of law, influence the effectiveness and acceptability of a libertarian paternalism approach, based on the insights of Behavioural Economics.

Finally, we hope to have been able to demonstrate the importance of a behavioural approach to deal with the pandemic crisis. Decisions about public policies, especially in health, in a climate of risk and uncertainty, although they must consider the knowledge of science and health experts, should not be decided by them but by democratically elected leaders and with a broader view of the problem, weighing, beyond health reasons, economic, financial, social, cultural, environmental or other impacts that arise.[155] However, the consulted experts should, therefore,

---

[154] In the Portuguese case, quite possibly because the surveys were carried out during the first response phase, which includes the confinement and narrative of the "Portuguese miracle" during the first wave with the flattening of the curve and not overloading the health system, 41% of the respondents trust more authorities and think that they performed well and 43% did not suffer changes in their confidence and approve the intervention made. Only 11% saw their confidence decline and negatively appreciate the Government's strategy.

[155] As for Climate Change with the IPCC, an institutional and systemized structure that allows a bilateral dialectic communication between Science/Experts/Academia and Policy-Makers is fundamental in the adequate management (and crisis communication) of a pandemic. Some countries, like Sweden or the UK, found similar structures. In Portugal, a poor solution of scientific meetings with a very reduced and non-diverse number of experts, was put in place (and suspended and retaken), with the Government asking for scientific consensus without understanding the essence of science

not reduce themselves to epidemiologists, virologists, health professionals or epidemiological mathematicians, due to their tunnel vision. Because of the dimension of the problem and the transversal nature of its effects, scientists from other areas, including the social sciences and humanities must be heard: managers, economists, lawyers (namely constitutionalists due to the suspensive and restrictive measures to be considered), psychologists, sociologists, and philosophers (for example, from ethics), among others. Behavioural economists should also have a say.

References

Acemoglu and Robinson (2013) Porque Falham as Nações: As Origens do Poder, da Prosperidade e da Pobreza. Temas e Debates
Alberton M (2004) Comparing alternative regulation policies: an environmental law and economic approach. EAERE, FEEM & VIU
Amado Gomes C (2000) A Prevenção à Prova no Direito do Ambiente em Especial. Os Actos Autorizativos Ambientais. Coimbra Editora, Coimbra
Amado Gomes C (2001) Dar o Duvidoso pelo (In)Certo? Reflexões Sobre o Princípio da Precaução. RJUA, n. 15/16
Amado Gomes C (2007) Risco e Modificação do Acto Autorizativo Concretizador de Deveres de Protecção do Ambiente. Coimbra Editora, Coimbra
Apolone G et al (2020) Unexpected detection of SARS-CoV-2 antibodies in the prepandemic period in Italy. Trumori Journal, November. https://journals.sagepub.com/doi/full/10.1177/0300891620974755 (last access 09 September 2021)
Araújo F (2007) Introdução à Economia. Almedina, Coimbra
Ariely D (2011) O lado bom da irracionalidade. Lua de Papel
Ariely D, Ayal S, Gino F (2009) Contagion and differentiation in unethical behavior: the effect of one bad apple on the barrel. Psychol Sci
Asch SE (1951) Effects of group pressure on the modification and distortion of judgments. In: Guetzkow H (ed) Groups, leadership and men. Carnegie Press, Pittsburgh, pp 177–190
Asch SE (1952) Effects of group pressure on the modification and distortion of judgments. In: Swanson GE, Newcomb TM, Hartley EL (eds) Readings in social psychology. Holt, New York, pp 2–11
Asch SE (1956) Studies of independence and conformity. A minority of one against a unanimous majority. Psychol Monogr 70(9):1–70
Basol M et al (2020) Good news about bad news: gamified inoculation boosts confidence and cognitive immunity against fake news. J Cogn 3(1):9. https://doi.org/10.5334/joc.91. (last access 09 September 2021)
Bayley NW, West D (2020) Are the COVID19 restrictions really worth the cost? A comparison of estimated mortality in Australia from COVID19 and economic recession. Arxiv. https://arxiv.org/ftp/arxiv/papers/2005/2005.03491.pdf (last access 09 September 2021)
Betsch C et al (2010) The influence of vaccine-critical websites on perceiving vaccination risks. J Health Psychol 15(3):446–455
Betsch C et al (2011) The influence of narrative v. statistical information on perceiving vaccination risks. Med Decis Mak 31(5):742–753

---

itself. Nevertheless, this did not invalidate that some measures were taken with the scientific "legitimacy" and others refuted despite scientific consensus, creating some communication problems.

Binlei G et al (2020) A balance act: minimizing economic loss while controlling novel coronavirus pneumonia. J Chinese Gov 5(2)

Blass T (1999) The Milgram paradigm after 35 years: some things we now know about obedience to authority. J Appl Soc Psychol 29(5):955–978

Bouglet T, Lanzi T, Vergnaud J C (2005) Incertitude Scientifique et Décision Publique: Le Recours au Principe de Précaution. Recherches Economiques de Louvain

Brekke KA, Johansson-Stenman O (2008) The behavioural economics of climate change. University of Gothenburg. School of Business, Economics and Law, Working Paper in Economics n. 305

Briscese G et al (2020) Compliance with COVID-19 social distancing measures in Italy: the role of expectations and duration. Working Paper 26916, Paper Series. National Bureau of Economic Research. https://doi.org/10.3386/w26916 (last access 09 September 2021)

Buttenheim A, Asch D (2016) Leveraging Behavioral insights to promote vaccine acceptance: one year after Disneyland. JAMA Pediatr 170(7):635–636

Caleo G et al (2018) The factors affecting household transmission dynamics and community compliance with Ebola control measures: a mixed-methods study in a rural village in Sierra Leone. BMC Public Health 18(1)

Camerer CF, Loewenstein G, Prelec D (2005) Neuroeconomics: how neuroscience can inform economics. J Econ Liter, XLIII

Cameron L, Shah M (2011) Risk-taking behavior in the wake of natural disasters. Department of Economics, University of California-Irvine

Cappelen A, Mæstad O, Tungodden B (2010) Demand for childhood vaccination – insights from behavioral economics. Forum Dev Stud 37(3):349–364

Cardoso JF et al (2020) Mortalidade em tempos de COVID-19: a que contamos, mas também a que não contamos: Um olhar para o excesso de mortalidade em Espanha, Itália e Portugal. Universidade do Porto, CINTESIS. https://medium.com/@jfelixcardoso/mortalidade-em-tempos-de-covid-19-a-que-contamos-mas-tamb%C3%A9m-a-que-n%C3%A3o-contamos-a84a5e393f6d (last access 09 September 2021)

Carrion VG et al (2020) Increased Risk of Suicide Due to Economic and Social Impacts of Social Distancing Measures to Address the Covid-19 Pandemic: A Forecast. Preprint. http://med.stanford.edu/content/dam/sm/elspap/documents/MentalHealthForcastpaperpreprint4-7-2020-1-.pdf (last access 09 September 2021)

Carvalho JE (2009) Neuroeconomia – Ensaio sobre a Sociobiologia do Comportamento. Edições Sílabo

Castillo M, Carter M (2011) Behavioral responses to natural disasters. Discussion Paper, Interdisciplinary Center for Economic Science, George Mason University

Cava MA et al (2005) Risk perception and compliance with quarantine during the SARS outbreak. J Nurs Scholarsh 37:4

Cepedisa Conectas Human Rights (2020) Rights in the Pandemic – Mapping and Analysis of the Legal Rules in Response to Covid-19 in Brazil. https://cepedisa.org.br/publicacoes/ (last access 09 September 2021)

Chavarria-Miró G et al (2020) Sentinel surveillance of SARS-CoV-2 in wastewater anticipates the occurrence of COVID-19 cases. medRxiv preprint

Cooter RD (1998) Expressive law and economics. Berkeley Olin Program in Law & Economics, Working Paper n. 38, University of California at Berkeley

Corrêa H, Cosentino M (2021) Vacinação, compulsoriedade e mecanismos de convencimento Como a economia comportamental pode aumentar a efetividade das campanhas de vacinação?, Jota https://www.jota.info/opiniao-e-analise/artigos/vacinacao-compulsoriedade-e-mecanismos-de-convencimento-25012021 (last access 09 September 2021)

Cowling BJ et al (2010) Community psychological and behavioral responses through the first wave of the 2009 influenza A(H1N1) pandemic in Hong Kong. J Infect Dis 202(6)

Decanio SJ (1997) The economics of climate change. Redefining Progress, San Francisco, CA

DiGiovanni C et al (2004) Factors influencing compliance with quarantine in Toronto during the 2003 SARS outbreak. Biosecur Bioterrorism Biodefense Strategy. Pract Sci 2(4)

Douglas K et al (2019) Belief in conspiracy theories: looking beyond gullibility. In: Forgas JB, Baumeister RF (eds) The social psychology of gullibility: fake news, conspiracy theories, and irrational beliefs. Routledge Taylor & Francis Group, London, pp 61–76

Drury J et al (2021) Behavioural responses to Covid-19 health certification: A rapid review. MedRxiv. https://www.medrxiv.org/content/10.1101/2021.04.07.21255072v1 (last access 22 September 2021)

Eichenbaum MS et al (2020) How do People Respond to Small Probability Events with Large, Negative Consequences? NBER Working Paper n. 27988, Cambridge, MA. http://www.nber.org/papers/w27988 (last access 09 September 2021)

Eichenbaum MS, Rebelo S, Trabandt M (2020a) The macroeconomics of epidemics. NBER Working Paper n. 26882, Cambridge, MA

Eichenbaum MS, Rebelo S, Trabandt M (2020b) The macroeconomics of testing and quarantining. NBER Working Paper n. 27104, Cambridge, MA

Ellickson RC (2001) The market for social norms. Am Law Econ Rev, 3

Ester P, Mandemaker T (1994) Socialization of the environmental policy objectives: tools for environmental marketing. In: Dutch Committee for Long-Term Environmental Policy (ed) The environment: towards a sustainable future. Springer, pp 49–80

European Commission (2020) European Economic Forecast. Spring 2020. Institutional Paper 125

Fisher A (2000) Uncertainty, Irreversibility, and the Timing of Climate Policy. Paper

Flaxman S et al (2020) Estimating the effects of non-pharmaceutical interventions on COVID-19 in Europe. Nature

Forgas J, Baumeister RF (2019) Homo credulus: on the social psychology of gullibility. In: Forgas JP, Baumeister RF (eds) The social psychology of gullibility: fake news, conspiracy theories, and irrational beliefs. Routledge Taylor & Francis Group, London, pp 1–18

Frank RH, Sunstein CR (2000) Cost-benefit analysis and relative position. The University of Chicago, Working Paper n. 102

Gertner J (2009) The Green Issue: Why Isn't the Brain Green? The New York Times Magazine, 16/4

Glennerster R, Kremer M (2011) Small Changes, Big Results Behavioral Economics at Work in Poor Countries. Boston Review

Glimcher P (2003) Decisions, uncertainty, and the brain: the science of Neuroeconomics. MIT Press

Gneezy U, Rustichini A (2000) A fine is a price. J Legal Stud 29(1)

Goodman R, Jinks D (2012) Social mechanisms to promote international human rights: Complementary or contradictory? New York University Law School, Public Law Research Paper n. 11–74

Gopalan S (2007) Alternative sanctions and social norms in international law: the case of Abu Ghraib. Mich State Law Rev 785

Green A (2006) You can't pay them enough: subsidies, environmental law and social norms. Harv Law Rev 30

Haney C, Banks WC, Zimbardo PG (1973) A study of prisoners and guards in a simulated prison. Naval Res Rev 30:4–17

Huang PH (2020) Reasons within passions: emotions and intentions in property rights bargaining. Oregon Law Rev, 79, November

International Working Group on Financing Preparedness (2017) From Panic and Neglect to Investing in Health Security: Financing Pandemic Preparedness at a National Level, World Bank: Washington, DC. https://openknowledge.worldbank.org/handle/10986/26761 (last access 09 September 2021)

Jolls C (2007) Behavioral law and economics. NBER Working Paper n. 12879, Cambridge, MA

Jolls C, Sunstein CR, Thaler R (2000) A behavioral approach to law and economics. In: Sunstein CR (ed) Behavioral law and economics. Cambridge University Press, pp 13–58

Kahneman D (2002) Maps of bounded rationality: a perspective on intuitive judgement and choice. Prize Lecture, 2002

Kahneman D, Tversky A (1974) Judgement under Uncertainty: Heuristics and Biases. Science, 185

Kahneman D, Tversky A (1981) The framing of decisions and the psychology of choice. Science 211(4481)

Kahneman D, Tversky A (2000a) Prospect theory: an analysis of decision under risk. In Kahneman D and Tversky A (eds.) Choices, values, and frames, Cambridge University Press

Kahneman D, Tversky A (2000b) Advances in prospect theory: cumulative representation of uncertainty. In: Kahneman D, Tversky A (eds) Choices, values, and frames. Cambridge University Press

Kinzig AP et al (2013) Social norms and global environmental challenges: the complex interaction of behaviors, values, and policy. BioScience 63(3)

Krastev I, Leonard M (2020) Europe's pandemic politics: How the virus has changed the public's worldview. ECFR. https://www.ecfr.eu/publications/summary/europes_pandemic_politics_how_the_virus_has_changed_the_publics_worldview (last access 09 September 2021)

Levitt S, Dubner SJ (2006) Freakonomics: O Estranho Mundo da Economia. O Lado Escondido de Todas as Coisas. Editorial Presença

Ling GHT, Ho CMC (2020) Effects of the Coronavirus (COVID-19) pandemic on social behaviours: from a social dilemma perspective. Technium Soc Sci J 7

Lobão J (2013) O Factor Humano na Decisão Empresarial. Actual Editora

Loewenstein G, Read D, Baumeister RF (eds) (2003) Time and decision: economic and psychological perspectives on intertemporal choice, Russell Sage Foundation

Lührmann A, Rooney B (2020) Autocratization by Decree: States of Emergency and Democratic Decline. Working paper, V-Dem Institute/University of Gothenburg, Gothenburg, 2020. https://www.v-dem.net/media/filer_public/31/1d/311d5d45-8747-45a4-b46f-37aa7ad8a7e8/wp_85.pdf (last access 09 September 2021)

Lunn PD et al (2020) Using behavioural science to help fight the Coronavirus: a rapid, narrative review. J Behav Public Adm 3(1)

Mato H J (2018) A próxima pandemia: estamos preparados? Revista Pan-Amazônica de Saúde 9(3)

Meyer R (2010) Por que ainda não conseguimos aprender com os desastres? In Michel-Kerjan E, Slovic P (org.) Economia irracional. Elsevier-Campus

Milgram S (1963) Behavioral study of obedience. J Abnorm Soc Psychol 67(4):371–378

Myers DG (2019) Psychological science meets a gullible post-truth world. In: Forgas JP, Baumeister RF (eds) The social psychology of gullibility: fake news, conspiracy theories, and irrational beliefs. Routledge Taylor & Francis Group, London, pp 77–100

Nogueira PJ et al (2020) Excess mortality estimation during the COVID-19 pandemic: preliminary data from Portugal. Acta Médica Portuguesa 33(6)

Ostrom E (1990) Governing the commons: the evolution of institutions for collective action. Cambridge University, Cambridge

Ostrom E (2000a) A behavioral approach to the rational choice theory of collective action: presidential address. In: McGinnis MD (ed) Polycentric games and institutions: readings from the workshop in political theory and policy analysis, institutional analysis. University of Michigan

Ostrom E (2000b) Collective action and the evolution of social norms. J Econ Persp 14(3), Summer

Ostrom E (2002) The Drama of the commons. National Academy Press

Ostrom E (2009) A Polycentric Approach for Coping with Climate Change. World Bank Policy Research Working Paper n. WPS 5095

Ostrom E, Schroeder L, Wynne S (1993) Institutional incentives and sustainable development: infrastructure policies in perspective. Westview, Boulder, CO

Ostrom E, Walker J, Gardner R (1994) Rules, games, and common-Pool resources. University of Michigan, Ann Arbor

Pandemic Influenza Preparedness Team (2011) Demographic and attitudinal determinants of protective behaviours during a pandemic. UK Department of Health, London

Peixoto VR et al (2020) Rapid assessment of the impact of lockdown on the COVID-19 epidemic in Portugal. medRxiv
Pereira da Silva V (2001) Como a Constituição é Verde. AAFDL, Lisboa
Posner RA (2004) Frontiers of legal theory. Harvard University Press
Prentice DA (2012) The psychology of social norms and the promotion of human rights. Princeton University Press
Rachlinski JJ (2000) The limits of social norms. Chicago-Kent Law Rev 74
Reicher S, Drury J (2021) Pandemic fatigue? How adherence to covid-19 regulations has been misrepresented and why it matters. BMJ 372(137)
Reynolds D et al (2008) Understanding, compliance and psychological impact of the SARS quarantine experience. Epidemiol Inf 136(7)
Saleska J, Choi K (2021) A behavioral economics perspective on the COVID-19 vaccine amid public mistrust. Transl Behav Med 11(3):821–825
Sandman P (2004) Worst Case Scenarios
Saraiva R (2009) A Herança de Quioto em Clima de Incerteza, Análise Jurídico-Económica do Mercado de Emissões num Quadro de Desenvolvimento Sustentado. PhD Thesis, FDUL, Lisboa
Saraiva R (2013) A abordagem comportamental do Direito e da Economia das catástrofes naturais. In: Actas do Colóquio, Catástrofes Naturais: Uma realidade multidimensional. Instituto de Ciências Jurídico-Políticas, Lisboa
Saraiva R (2015) Protecção ambiental e normas sociais. In: Aragão A, Bester GM, Marques Alves Hilário EG (coord.) Direito e Ambiente para uma Democracia Sustentável – Diálogos multidisciplinares entre Portugal e Brasil, Instituto Memória, Curitiba
Saraiva R (2016) As normas sociais como instrumento de protecção dos direitos humanos. Revista ESMAT da Escola Superior da Magistratura Tocantinense 8(11)
Saunders-Hasting PR, Krewski D (2016) Reviewing the history of pandemic influenza: understanding patterns of emergence and transmission. Pathogens 5(4)
Schaefer BM et al (2020) Government actions against the new coronavirus: evidence from the Brazilian states. Revista da Administração Pública 54(5)
Service O et al (2015) EAST Four simple ways to apply behavioural insights. The Behavioural Insights Team, London. https://www.behaviouralinsights.co.uk/wp-content/uploads/2015/07/BIT-Publication-EAST_FA_WEB.pdf (last access 22 September 2021)
Sexton AL (2011) Conspicuous conservation: the Prius effect and willingness to pay for environmental Bona fides. University of California
Shogren J (1998) Benefits & costs of Kyoto. University of Wyoming
Shu LL, Gino F, Bazerman MH (2011) Ethical discrepancy: changing our attitudes to resolve moral dissonance. In: De Cremer D, Tenbrunsel AE (eds) Behavioral business ethics: ideas on an emerging field. Taylor and Francis
Slovic P (2010) Quanto mais pessoas morrem menos nos importamos. In: Michel-Kerjan E, Slovic P (org) Economia irracional. Elsevier-Campus
Sousa Mendes P (2000) Vale a Pena o Direito Penal do Ambiente?. AAFDL, Lisboa, 2000
Stavins R (1995) Environmental policy: better media coverage of risks. Nieman Reports 49(3)
Stop TB Partnership in collaboration with Imperial College, Avenir Health, Johns Hopkins University and USAID (2020) The potential impact of the Covid-19 response on tuberculosis in high-burden countries: a modelling analysis. http://www.stoptb.org/assets/documents/news/Modeling%20Report_1%20May%202020_FINAL.pdf (last access 09 September 2021)
Sunstein CR (1997) Behavioral analysis of law. Chicago University, Working Paper in Law & Economics n. 46, Chicago
Sunstein CR (1999) Behavioral law and economics: a progress report. Am Law Econ Rev I(1)
Sunstein CR (ed.) (2000) Behavioral law and economics. Cambridge University Press
Sunstein CR (2001) Laws of fear. The University of Chicago Law School, John M. Olin Law & Economics Working Paper Series, Working Paper n. 128
Sunstein CR (2002) Risk and reason: safety, law, and the environment. Cambridge University

Sunstein CR (2005) Irreversible or Catastrophic. AEI-Brookings Joint Center Working Paper n. 05–04, March

Sunstein CR (2006) On the Divergent American Reactions to Terrorism and Climate Change. AEI-Brookings Joint Center for Regulatory Studies, Working Paper n. 06–13

Sunstein CR (2008) Two conceptions of irreversible environmental harm. The University of Chicago, The Law School, John M. Olin Law & Economics Working Paper n. 407

Sunstein CR, Kuran T (1999) Availability cascades and risk regulation. Stanford Law Rev 51:715–736

Taylor S (2019) The psychology of pandemics: preparing for the next global outbreak of infectious disease. Cambridge Scholars Publishing, Cambridge

Taylor SE, Armor DA (1996) Positive illusions and coping with adversity. J Pers 64(4):873–898

Thaler RH (2000) Mental accounting matters. In: Kahneman D, Tversky EA (eds) Choices, values, and frames. Cambridge University Press

The Economist Intelligence Unit (2021) In Sickness or in Health. https://www.eiu.com/public/topical_report.aspx?campaignid=democracy2020 (last access 09 September 2021)

Turner JC (2010) Social categorization and the self-concept: a social cognitive theory of group behavior. In: Postmes T, Branscombe NR (eds) Key readings in social psychology. Rediscovering social identity. Psychology Press, pp 243–272. (reprint of article from 1985)

Turner JC et al (1987) Rediscovering the social group: a self-categorization theory. Blackwell, Oxford

van Aaken A (2008) Towards behavioral international law and economics? Comment on Kenneth W. Abbott. University of Illinois Law Review, 1

van Bavel JJ et al (2020) Using social and behavioural science to support COVID-19 pandemic response. Nat Human Behav, 4

van Holm EJ et al (2020) The impact of political ideology on concern and behavior during COVID-19. University of New Orleans. https://papers.ssrn.com/sol3/papers.cfm?abstract_id=3573224 (last access 22 September 2021)

Vieira A et al (2020) Excesso de Mortalidade, em Portugal, em Tempos de COVID-19. Centro de Investigação em Saúde Pública, Escola Nacional de Saúde Pública. Universidade Nova de Lisboa, Lisboa

Viscusi WK (1999) How do judges think about risk? Am Law Econ Rev 1(1)

Vos J (2021) The psychology of covid-19: building resilience for future pandemics. SAGE Publications

Vosoughi S et al (2018) The spread of true and false news online. Science 1151:1146–1151

Weber E (2006) Experience-based and description-based perceptions of long-term risk: why global warming does not scare us yet. Clim Chang 77

Webster RK et al (2020) How to improve adherence with quarantine: rapid review of the evidence. Public Health

Weems C et al (2007) The psychosocial impact of hurricane Katrina: contextual differences in psychological symptoms, social support, and discrimination. Behav Res Ther 45(10)

Weible C et al (2000) COVID-19 and the policy sciences: initial reactions and perspectives. Policy Science, pp 1–17. https://www.ncbi.nlm.nih.gov/pmc/articles/PMC7165254/ (last access 09 September 2021)

Weiss C (2003) Scientific uncertainty and science-based precaution. Int Environ Agreements Polit Law Econ, n. 3

Weitzman M (2007) Structural uncertainty and the value of statistical life in the economics of catastrophic climate change. NBER Working Paper n. W13490

World Health Organization. Regional Office for Europe (2020) Pandemic fatigue: reinvigorating the public to prevent COVID-19: policy considerations for Member States in the WHO European Region. World Health Organization. Regional Office for Europe

WWF (2020) Covid 19: Urgent call to protect people and nature. Gland. https://cdn2.hubspot.net/hubfs/4783129/WWF%20COVID19%20URGENT%20CALL%20TO%20PROTECT%20PEOPLE%20AND%20NATURE.pdf (last access 09 September 2021)

Contracts and the Coronavirus Crisis: Emergency Policy Responses Between Preservation and Disruption

A Legal Theory and Law and Economics Perspective

Valentin Jentsch

Abstract As of late spring 2021, three major Covid-19 waves have hit Europe. These waives were accompanied by three generations of emergency policy responses taken by national and supranational governments, consisting of containment and closure measures, economic measures, and health measures. Against this backdrop, the coronavirus crisis creates a wide variety of contract-specific problems. One key strategy to solve contract-specific problems during the coronavirus crisis is the preservation of a contract. The other key strategy to solve contract-specific problems during the coronavirus crisis is the disruption of a contract, in one way or another. Using a legal theory and law and economics approach, this article deals with the research question, whether emergency policy responses will pay off or cause even more harm in the long term. The article further aims to assess the impact of different generations of emergency policy responses on contract law in order to inform the ongoing debate in law and politics. This is important because any intervention in a functioning system increases complexity and creates a new equilibrium that may be inferior.

1 Introduction

"Was heute gilt, ist morgen vielleicht schon veraltet" (analogous translation: what counts today, may already be obsolete tomorrow), *Alain Berset*, Switzerland's Health Minister, proclaimed on the 1st of March 2020 in the popular boulevard newspaper *Blick*.[1] As simple as this statement might sound, it captures the nature of the coronavirus crisis quite well. Covid-19, the new coronavirus and its mutants, is a moving target, making it incredibly hard to come up with solid and sustainable

---
[1] See Blick (2020).

V. Jentsch (✉)
Max Planck Institute for Tax Law and Public Finance, Munich, Germany
e-mail: valentin.jentsch@tax.mpg.de

solutions to fix the underlying problem. Neither *Berset* nor anybody else on this planet dared to foresee at the time, what was actually in store for us in the months (and perhaps even years) to come.

As of late spring 2021, three major Covid-19 waves have hit Europe.[2] The first wave started in spring 2020, the second wave in fall 2020, and the third wave in spring 2021. These waives were accompanied by three generations of emergency policy responses taken by national and supranational governments, consisting of containment and closure measures, economic measures, and health measures.[3] Containment and closure measures aim at preventing or slowing down the spread of the coronavirus.[4] Economic measures and health measures during a lockdown, or after a reopening of the economy, aim at curing economic consequences caused by the coronavirus, but also serve the health of society.[5]

Against this backdrop, the coronavirus crisis creates a wide variety of contract-specific problems.[6] Business enterprises, customers, and other contracting parties may often ask themselves, whether existing contracts are still valid and binding and, as a result, must be adhered to, or whether performance may be suspended or its acceptance refused. The role of general legal institutions for risk allocation between both or all contracting parties has been examined on other occasions already.[7]

Using a legal theory and law and economics approach, this article deals with the research question, whether emergency policy responses will pay off or cause even more harm in the long term. The article further aims to assess the impact of different generations of emergency policy responses on contract law in order to inform the ongoing debate in law and politics. This is important because any intervention in a

---

[2] For new Covid-19 cases and deaths per 100,000 people, see The Economist (2021) (assembling data on Covid-19 cases and deaths for 39 countries and for 173 sub-national areas for which data are available, presenting the total number of deaths per 100,000 in the population and breaking down the infections and death rates for the past 7 days).

[3] For a rigorous and consistent tracking of various emergency policy responses around the world, see OxCGRT (2021) (tracking and comparing worldwide government responses to the coronavirus, using the COVID-19 Government Response Stringency Index, consisting of eight indicators on containment and closure policies, such as school closures and restrictions in movement, four indicators on economic policies, such as income support to citizens or provision of foreign aid, and eight indicators on health system policies, such as the Covid-19 testing regime, emergency investments into healthcare, and vaccination policies).

[4] For a comparison of lockdowns, see Financial Times (2021) (providing an ongoing visual representation of the worldwide imposition and relaxation of lockdown measures, using the COVID-19 Governement Response Stringency Index).

[5] For Europe, see Jentsch (2021a). See also Jentsch (2020b).

[6] From an international perspective, see Twigg-Flesner (2020); Wagner (2020). From a German perspective, see Lorenz (2020). For a first interpretative note under Austrian law, see Uitz and Parsché (2020). On the risk allocation in contracts under Swiss law, see Enz (2020); Enz and Mor (2020). On contract adaption under Swiss law, see Haefeli et al. (2020b). For a preliminary assessement under French law, see Landivaux (2020); Verroust-Valliot and Pelletier (2020). On the eternal conflict between the principles of pacta sunt servanda and rebus sic stantibus from an Italian perspective, see Roseti (2020).

[7] For Switzerland, see Jentsch (2020a). For Europe, see Jentsch (2021b). See also Jentsch (2021c).

functioning system increases complexity and creates a new equilibrium that may be inferior.

2 Emergency Policy Responses

In order to answer the critical question asked in this article, which basically relates to costs and benefits of emergency policy responses, a distinction can, and must, be drawn between commercial contracts, consumer contracts, employment contracts, and lease contracts. Against this backdrop, this section offers a discussion and analysis of various emergency policy responses taken by European (notably German, Austrian, Swiss, French, and Italian) governments and puts these responses into perspective.

2.1 Responses for Commercial Contracts

The emergency policy responses for commercial contracts include financial support and certain legislative changes.[8] The financial support mainly intends to ensure liquidity of funds, but partly also replace lost profits, for instance, in the form of tax deferrals. The Member States of the European Union (including Germany, Austria, France, and Italy) have themselves provided massive aid packages for their companies. In addition, the European Union itself has also adopted a temporary framework for State aid. This means that several pots with State aid are available to such companies not only in their respective countries, but also at the supranational level. As many companies are likely to meet the requirements of several aid packages and therefore can benefit from them in several ways, it might well be possible that some companies claim more State aid than they actually need, which is certainly not unproblematic. The legislative changes include temporary modifications or suspensions of certain provisions from insolvency law in order to avoid a major wave of bankruptcies because of illiquidity due to a lack of sales and profits, but also a standstill of procedural and/or substantive time limits. Italy even went a step further, enacting an overriding provision, according to which compliance with government-issued containment and closure measures shall always be considered when interpreting debtor's liability and contractual remedies for non-performance.

---

[8] For Germany, see Janssen and Wahnschaffe (2020); Mann et al. (2020); Otte-Gräbener (2020); Rehder and Schmidt (2020); Römermann (2020a, b); Thume (2020); Wagner et al. (2020); Wagner and Rarinato (2020). For Austria, see Angermair et al. (2020). For Switzerland, see Staehelin and Bopp (2020); Christ et al. (2020). For France, see Heinich (2020); Ziadé and Cavicchioli (2020). For Italy, see Gentili (2020).

An analysis and discussion of commercial contracts clearly reflect policy makers' main concern to preserve contractual relations in the near term.[9] In the longer term, however, legal systems should rather facilitate significant adjustment of contractual relations. For instance, a company's supply relations need to be changed in due course, if demand contracts for its production. Therefore, policy makers should also cope with this issue by codifying legal institutions on adaption or termination of contractual obligations. The main reason for a codification of such institutions is that adaption and termination of contracts will most likely become more important in the near future and the quality of judicial decisions would certainly benefit from clear requirements and consequences. Such a legislative intervention can provide transaction-cost efficiency and orderliness.

2.2 Responses for Consumer Contracts

The emergency policy responses for consumer contracts are largely contract-related.[10] Such measures include not only a moratorium for performance and termination of long-term contracts covering basic needs and contracts relating to consumer credits, but also voucher solutions for leisure events and facilities as well as travel tickets and packages. Other measures include the standstill of procedural and/or substantive time limits, the exclusion of contractual remedies, and a temporary standstill in debt collection for travel agencies, which—in fact, adversely—affect customers. Italy enacted an overriding provision, according to which compliance with government-issued containment and closure measures shall always be considered when interpreting debtor's liability and contractual remedies for non-performance.

An analysis and discussion of consumer contracts indicate that a distinction should be made between debt contracts, such as consumer credit, and other types of consumption, such as utilities.[11] As debt contracts can unduly restrict the economic progress of an individual, such contracts should not be enforced excessively in times of pandemic. Other types of consumption lack this systemic element and, therefore, such contracts should—as a rule of thumb—be performed as agreed. Therefore, contract law must address both of these issues through a combination of preservation and disruption strategies.

---

[9] On commercial contracts between preservation and disruption, see Jentsch (2020b, 2021a).

[10] For Germany, see Rüfner (2020); Schmidt-Kessel and Möllnitz (2020); Wolf et al. (2020). For Austria, see Haghofer (2020); Kellner and Liebel (2020); Mayr (2020). For France, see Deshayes (2020).

[11] On consumer contracts between preservation and disruption, see Jentsch (2020b, 2021a).

2.3 Responses for Employment Contracts

The emergency policy responses for employment contracts are numerous and concern various issues.[12] Interestingly, they not only vary considerably from one jurisdiction to the other, but also over time. The most important measure is arguably the facilitation and extension of state-sponsored short-time work programs. Under these schemes, employers reduce their employees' working hours instead of laying them off. Moreover, labour laws of many countries were amended during the early stages of the crisis, particularly with regard to the duty to pay wages, holiday arrangements, and time for childcare. Other measures, which were put in place since the reopening of the economies after a lockdown, concerned worker protection, including and in particular the protection of high-risk groups.

An analysis and discussion of responses for employment contracts suggest that pandemic-induced economic measures and health measures again aim for preservation against excessive disruption, but there would likely be longer-term changes to workplaces and work patterns.[13] In some sense, the coronavirus pandemic caused the future of work (new work), consisting of remote work, flexible hours, and technology-enabled tools, to arrive earlier than expected. Depending on how fast things develop over the coming months and years, it will probably be necessary to amend labour laws to these circumstances.

2.4 Responses for Lease Contracts

The emergency policy responses for lease contracts vary greatly from jurisdiction to jurisdiction.[14] The most common are rules and regulations concerning a moratorium prohibiting the termination of such contracts, if rent payments are delayed. The biggest bone of contention, which the countries have solved very differently so far,

---

[12] For Germany, see Bertram et al. (2020); Fischinger (2020); Fuhlrott and Fischer (2020); Geulen and Vogt (2020); Hohenstatt and Krois (2020); Hohenstatt and Sittard (2020); Kiesche and Kohte (2020); Müller and Becker (2020); Reifelsberger (2020); Sagan and Brockfeld (2020); Schmeisser and Fauth (2020); Schmidt (2020); Tödtmann and von Bockelmann (2020). For Austria, see Auer-Mayer (2020); Mazal (2020); Mosing (2020); Spitzl (2020). For Switzerland, see Blesi et al. (2020); Geiser (2020); Geiser et al. (2020); Schwaab (2020); Pietruszak (2020); Tschannen (2020); Wildhaber (2020). For France, see Duchange (2020); Leroy (2020); Radé (2020).

[13] On employment contracts between preservation and disruption, see Jentsch (2020b, 2021a).

[14] For Germany, see Artz and Steyl (2020), §3 paras 1–105; Häublein and Müller (2020); Hellmich (2020); Hellner (2020); Schall (2020); Schmid (2020); Sittner (2020); Warmuth (2020); Weidt and Schiewek (2020); Zehelein (2020). For Austria, see Hochleitner (2020); Krenn and Schüssler-Datler (2020); Laimer and Schickmair (2020), Ch. 11 paras 3–19; Ofner (2020). For Switzerland, see Haefeli et al. (2020a); Koller (2020); Lachat and Brutschin (2020a, b); Müller (2020); Wolf and Minnig (2020). For France, see Blatter (2020); Kendérian (2020); Regnault (2020). For Italy, see Pertot (2020).

concern rent for commercial premises, especially during a lockdown. This issue was long and particularly hard-fought in Switzerland, but ultimately abandoned.

An analysis and discussion of responses for lease contracts suggest that pandemic-induced economic measures and health measures aim for preservation against excessive disruption.[15] In the dispute over commercial leases, however, it is slowly but surely becoming apparent that most lessors and lessees have already found an agreement among themselves. This new situation makes any intervention by the legislator unnecessary.

3 Preservation, but Excuses and Remedies

One key strategy to solve contract-specific problems during the coronavirus crisis is the preservation of a contract. This strategy is relativized by excuses of contractual performance and remedies for breach of contract. From a public policy perspective, nobody should be legally committed to do or to refrain from doing something that is impossible. An important distinction to be made is whether an act or omission is permanently impossible or temporarily impossible. The first case concerns the legal institution of subsequent impossibility, the second that of delay, either by the debtor or by the creditor.

3.1 Subsequent Impossibility of Performance

The legal institution of subsequent impossibility generally applies to a situation where contractual performance becomes permanently impossible.[16] In such a situation, which may arise from a pandemic, all jurisdictions under examination (Germany, Austria, Switzerland, France, and Italy) excuse performance and counter-performance, at least if no party is responsible for the impediment, and provide for remedies such as damages, if a party is responsible for the impossibility. Switzerland and France are exceptions in this respect, not excusing parties from their duties, if they are at fault. In addition, impossibility is defined very broadly in Austria, for instance.

German courts have interpreted the rule on subsequent impossibility of performance to include objective impossibility, subjective impossibility, and legal impossibility.[17] Moreover, economic impossibility does not fall under this rule, and

---

[15] On lease contracts between preservation and disruption, see Jentsch (2020b, 2021a).

[16] On subsequent impossibility of performance from a functional and comparative perspective, see Jentsch (2021b, c).

[17] On objective impossibility, see BGH, 13 January 2011, III ZR 87/10, in BGHZ 188, 71; BGH, 8 May 2014, VII ZR 203/11, in Neue Juristische Wochenschrift 2014, 3365. On subjective

additional rules apply to practical impossibility and personal impossibility. In Austria, this concept includes not only factual impossibility, consisting of objective impossibility and personal impossibility, and legal impossibility, but also—and this is quite exceptional in international comparison—economic impossibility.[18] Under Swiss law, the provision on subsequent impossibility of performance includes factual impossibility and legal impossibility, but neither temporary impossibility nor economic impossibility. Although disputed in legal scholarship, the Swiss Federal Supreme Court does not subsume subjective impossibility under this provision.[19] In France, the concept of *force majeure* applies, requiring that the event preventing performance is external, it has not been reasonably foreseeable, and its effects on performance were unavoidable.[20] So far, French courts have been reluctant to accept an outbreak of an infectious disease as *force majeure*.[21] Government or administrative measures are more often recognized as *force majeure*, but courts are quite strict as well.[22] According to Italian legal doctrine, the provisions on subsequent impossibility of performance include only permanent impossibility and objective impossibility that is not attributable to the debtor, but not personal impossibility or subjective impossibility.[23]

Examples of permanently impossible performance in the context of the coronavirus pandemic include a birthday party or a wedding, concerts, and performing arts. In all five countries under examination, commercial and consumer contracts directly affected by an official order fall under these rules, but only in case of absolute

---

impossibility, see BGH, 25 October 2012, VII ZR 146/11, in BGHZ 195, 195. On legal impossibility, see BGH, 8 June 1983, VIII ZR 77/82, in Neue Juristische Wochenschrift 1983, 2873; BGH, 14 November 1991, III ZR 145/90, in Neue Juristische Wochenschrift 1992, 904; BGH, 11 December 1991, VIII ZR 4/91, in BGHZ 116, 268; BGH, 17 May 1995, VIII ZR 94/94, in Neue Juristische Wochenschrift 1995, 2026; BGH, 25 November 1998, XII ZR 12–97, in Neue Juristische Wochenschrift 1999, 635.

[18] See OGH, 21 November 1951, 3 Ob 589/51, in Evidenzblatt der Rechtsmittelentscheidungen 1952, no 103; OGH, 20 March 1963, 7 Ob 70/63, in SZ 36, no 44; OGH, 30 April 1963, 8 Ob 102/63, in Österreichische Immobilien-Zeitung 1963, 367. See also OGH, 14 February 2007, 7 Ob 255/06k, in SZ 82, no 25.

[19] See BGer, 15 January 2009, 4A_394/2008, in BGE 135 III 212, pp. 218–219. See also Schwenzer (2016), p. 465; Koller (2017), pp. 901–902; Emmenegger et al. (2014), p. 90 and pp. 93–99.

[20] See Cass. 1re civ., 9 March 1994, 91-17459, 91-17464, in I Bulletin, no 91; Com., 1 October 1997, 95-12435, in IV Bulletin, no 240; Cass. 2e civ., 18 March 1998, 95-22014, in II Bulletin, no 97; Cass. 1re civ., 16 November 2002, 99-21203, in I Bulletin, no 258; Cass. 1re civ., 30 October 2008, 07-17134, in I Bulletin, no 243.

[21] See Cour d'appel, Nancy, 22 November 2010, 09-00003; Cour d'appel, Basse-Terre, 17 December 2018, 17-00739; Cour d'appel, Besançon, 8 January 2014, 12-02291; Cour d'appel, Paris, 17 March 2016, 15-04263; Cour d'appel, Paris, 29 March 2016, 15-05607. See also Guiomard (2020).

[22] See Cass. 3e civ., 11 October 1989, 87-19490; Cour d'appel, Nancy, 6 November 2001, 2001-184443; Cass. 1re civ., 18 May 2005, 01-16243; Com., 31 January 2006, 04-15164; Cass. 3e civ., 28 November 2007, 06-17758, in III Bulletin, no 213; Cass. 3e civ., 1 June 2011, 09-70502, in III Bulletin, no 89.

[23] See Osti (1962), p. 287; Galgano (2010), para. 16, p. 115.

fixed-date obligations to be performed during a lockdown. Contracts only indirectly affected by the pandemic are generally not covered by these rules. Contracts that are still possible, but no longer make economic sense, are not governed by these rules, except in Austria.

3.2 Debtor's Delay of Performance

The legal institution of delay of debtor is applicable to situations, where contractual performance is only temporarily impossible due to a default of the debtor.[24] In general, no prevention, but only a suspension of contractual performance may result from such situations. Damages are in some cases owed regardless of the debtor's fault, in other cases only if the debtor is at fault. In addition, creditors have various remedies at their disposal, which indeed vary from one jurisdiction to another. In all jurisdictions examined (Germany, Austria, Switzerland, France, and Italy), this institution is important during a pandemic as it provides debtors with an incentive to perform a contract.

The requirements and consequences of delay of debtor are more or less the same in Germany, Austria, Switzerland, France, and Italy. Austrian law differs in one respect, however, namely by distinguishing between objective delay and subjective delay of debtor.[25] This distinction is important because the debtor is only liable for damages, if he or she is at fault.

A debtor may be affected either directly or indirectly by the coronavirus pandemic. Debtors directly affected by an official order are not permitted to sell goods or provide services during a lockdown, which concerns in most countries restaurants, at least for some time, but also gyms. Debtors indirectly affected by the consequences of the pandemic cannot fulfil the contract as promised, in particular, because of insufficient staff at the workplace or delays in global supply chains. With regard to the application of all these rules in each jurisdiction examined, this distinction, however, is not relevant.

3.3 Creditor's Delay of Performance

The legal institution of delay of creditor is also applicable to situations, where contractual performance is only temporarily impossible, but in this case, the

---

[24] On debtor's delay of performance from a functional and comparative perspective, see Jentsch (2021b, c).

[25] See Reischauer (2018), §918 para. 7; Gruber (2019), §918 paras 4–62.

impossibility of performance is due to a default of the creditor.[26] Under certain conditions, the debtor may excuse contractual performance, while the creditor remains bound by the contract. As a delay of creditor does not lead to a breach of contract, but to specific negative consequences, creditors are generally not liable for damages. In all jurisdictions examined (Germany, Austria, Switzerland, France, and Italy), this institution is important during a pandemic as it makes creditors accept performance and cooperate.

The requirements and consequences of delay of creditor are largely identical in Germany, Austria, Switzerland, France, and Italy. Therefore, there is no need to highlight a particular feature from one regime or the other.

A generic example of delay of creditor is a customer, who does no longer need goods or services ordered, and paid in advance, due to changed buying behaviour induced by the coronavirus pandemic. To give a few concrete examples, a diving set ordered from an internet dealer is no longer needed, users of public transportation are inclined to stop using trains and busses, and to cancel their subscription immediately, or large amounts of respiratory equipment purchased are (fortunately) no longer needed. For all of these cases in each jurisdiction examined, customers cannot step back from such contracts.

4 Disruption, Either Adaption or Termination

The other key strategy to solve contract-specific problems during the coronavirus crisis is the disruption of a contract, in one way or another. In the mild form, this strategy represents the adaption of a contract, in the strict form, it represents the termination of a contract. Under various institutions of civil law, contracts may be adapted or terminated not only under changed circumstances, but also for cause.

4.1 Adaption and Termination Under Changed Circumstances

It is generally accepted in all five jurisdictions under examination (Germany, Austria, Switzerland, France, and Italy) that a change of circumstances, which renders contractual performance impossible, may release a party from his or her obligations to perform under a contract.[27] Those jurisdictions evaluate it differently, however, whether economic disadvantages or mere impracticability arising from a

---

[26] On creditor's delay of performance from a functional and comparative perspective, see Jentsch (2021b, c).

[27] On adaption and termination of contracts under changed circumstances from a functional and comparative perspective, see Jentsch (2021b, c).

pandemic also have an effect on releasing the party from his or her contractual obligations. Germany and France have such institutions already codified in their civil codes. Austria, Switzerland, and Italy have not, but similar institutions are widely recognized here.

In Germany, the concept of interference with the basis of the transaction, an emanation of the *clausula rebus sic stantibus*, was developed by legal doctrine[28] and case law[29] in the early nineteenth century and ultimately codified in 2002. Austrian legal scholars[30] and courts[31] accept and acknowledge the concept of a *clausula*, which operates as a last resort (*ultima ratio*), applying to exceptional cases only. Similarly, the *clausula* is accepted in both legal doctrine[32] and case law[33] in Switzerland. In France, the concept of *imprévision* was incorporated into French law by a reform in 2016, allowing contracting parties to request a renegotiation or termination of a contract, if certain requirements are met.[34] Other than the concept of *eccessiva onerosità* (see below), Italian law does not contain a positivized *clausula*. Italian courts[35] have so far been rather reluctant to accept such a concept, although it is already well developed in legal scholarship[36] in Italy.

In all jurisdictions under examination, relevant legal institutions aimed at adapting and terminating contracts under changed circumstances are particularly important for the delivery of goods and the provision of services, which, although still possible, no longer make sense from an economic point of view. Typical

---

[28] See Oertmann (1921). See also Windscheid (1850).

[29] See RG, 3 February 1922, II 640/21, in RGZ 103, 328, pp. 331–332; RG, 6 January 1923, V 246/22, in RGZ 106, 7, p. 10; RG, 30 October 1928, II 28/28, in RGZ 122, 200, p. 203; RG, 21 June 1933, I 54/33, in RGZ 141, 212, pp. 216–217; BGH, 23 May 1951, II ZR 71/50, in BGHZ 2, 176, pp. 188–189; BGH, 29 April 1982, III ZR 154/80, in BGHZ 84, 1, p. 9. See also RG, 2 December 1919, VII 303/19, in RGZ 98, 18, p. 20.

[30] For a general overview, see Riedler (2018), para 25/4; Kletecka et al. (2018), para 510.

[31] See OGH, 13 July 1955, 3 Ob 330/55; OGH, 12 February 1970, 1 Ob 24/70, in Evidenzblatt der Rechtsmittelentscheidungen 1970, no 203; OGH, 15 September 1970, 8 Ob 181/70; OGH, 12 May 1977, 7 Ob 564/77; OGH, 28 June 1979, 7 Ob 509/79; OGH, 23 October 1986, 6 Ob 650/86; OGH, 4 November 1986, 14 Ob 176/86; OGH, 5 March 1987, 7 Ob 522/87, in SZ 60, no 42; OGH, 1 March 2012, 1 Ob 22/12k; OGH, 17 June 2015, 3 Ob 104/15p.

[32] See Schmid et al. (2014), pp. 327–331; Schwenzer (2016), pp. 278–280; Koller (2017), pp. 507–519; Berger (2018), pp. 399–401; Huguenin (2018), pp. 100–105 and p. 257.

[33] See BGer, 29 May 1934 (Rogenmoser v. Tiefengrund AG), in BGE 60 II 205, pp. 209–210; BGer, 7 December 1971 (Neumühle AG v. Stadtgemeinde Chur), in BGE 97 II 390, pp. 398–399; BGer, 26 September 1974 (Incommerz AG v. X), in BGE 100 II 345, pp. 348–349; BGer, 18 September 1981 (Baumann v. Rohr), in BGE 107 II 343, pp. 347–348; BGer, 21 March 1996 (G v. B), in BGE 122 III 97, pp. 98–99; BGer, 24 April 2001 (A v. Migros-Genossenschafts-Bund), in BGE 127 III 300, pp. 302–309; BGer, 28 October 2008, 4A_299/2008, in BGE 135 III 1, pp. 9–10; BGer, 31 July 2012, 9C_88/2012, in BGE 138 V 366, pp. 371–372.

[34] See Chantepie and Latina (2016), paras 522–530; Ancel (2017), paras 55–119.

[35] See Cass., 6 July 1971, 2104, in I Giurisprudenza italiana 1973, 1; Cass., 9 May 1981, 3074, in I Giurisprudenza italiana 1983, 1; Cass., 11 November 1986, 6584, in I La nuova giurisprudenza civile commentata 1987, 683; Cass., 31 October 1989, 4554.

[36] See Osti (1959), p. 353; Galletto (1988), p. 383.

examples include the delivery of fresh food to a restaurant or an ongoing beer supply contracts for a bar. The rules in those jurisdictions differ considerably as French law has a differentiated, three-step problem-solving procedure, namely to renegotiate, adapt, and terminate a contract.

4.2 Termination for Cause

Different from the Roman civil codes (France and Italy), the extraordinary termination of permanent contracts for cause is firmly established in the German-speaking jurisdictions (Germany, Austria, and Switzerland).[37] This institution was codified in Germany, while legal doctrine and case law in Austria and Switzerland generally recognize it without being codified there. Termination for cause leads to the dissolution of a permanent contract for the future, whereas performance already rendered is not affected by such termination. The relevant institutions in France and Italy only lead to similar results in some cases but often not. These institutions, nevertheless, may serve as a last resort in a pandemic.

In Germany, the concept of extraordinary termination of permanent contracts, eventually leading to contract termination by a court, was codified back in 2002. Austrian law contains no general provision on the termination of permanent contracts for cause, but it is well accepted in Austrian legal doctrine[38] and case law[39] that long-term contracts can be terminated without any grace period, if there is a compelling reason. The Austrian Supreme Court emphasized, however, that termination of long-term contracts may only be invoked as a last resort (*ultima ratio*).[40] Switzerland does not contain general rules on termination of permanent contracts for

---

[37] On termination of permanent contracts for cause from a functional and comparative perspective, see Jentsch (2021b, c).

[38] See Reischauer (2018), Vor §§918 ff. paras 57–75; Gruber (2018), §918 paras 15–18.

[39] See OGH, 30 June 1987, 2 Ob 652/86, in SZ 60, no 125; OGH, 24 September 1987, 7 Ob 646/87, in Juristische Blätter 1988, 446; OGH, 15 December 1987, 5 Ob 591/87; OGH, 24 January 1989, 5 Ob 504/89; OGH, 30 October 1998, 1 Ob 252/98k; OGH, 6 October 2000, 1 Ob 101/00k; OGH, 25 June 2001, 8 Ob 311/00v; OGH, 8 June 2005, 7 Ob 40/05s; OGH, 31 May 2006, 7 Ob 77/06h; OGH, 22 February 2007, 3 Ob 13/07v; OGH, 28 August 2007, 5 Ob 166/07h; OGH, 28 July 2010, 9 Ob 36/10z; OGH, 27 March 2013, 7 Ob 15/13a; OGH, 22 May 2014, 2 Ob 163/13d, 2 Ob 163/13d; OGH, 23 October 2015, 6 Ob 196/15i; OGH, 22 March 2018, 4 Ob 34/18f; OGH, 26 September 2018, 1 Ob 155/18b.

[40] See OGH, 10 July 1986, 7 Ob 585/86, in Juristische Blätter 1987, 180; OGH, 26 November 1987, 6 Ob 671/87; OGH, 10 December 1987, 6 Ob 719/87; OGH, 15 June 1989, 7 Ob 719/87; OGH, 25 June 1996, 4 Ob 2142/96w; OGH, 25 February 1997, 4 Ob 44/97t; OGH, 14 October 1997, 1 Ob 210/97g; OGH, 15 October 1998, 8 Ob 171/98z; OGH, 28 May 1999, 6 Ob 42/99s; OGH, 25 July 2000, 1 Ob 24/00m; OGH, 22 April 2003, 9 Ob 24/03z; OGH, 21 May 2003, 6 Ob 93/03z; OGH, 23 October 2006, 7 Ob 235/06v; OGH, 29 August 2007, 7 Ob 158/07x; OGH, 24 June 2014, 4 Ob 81/14m; OGH, 25 February 2016, 2 Ob 20/15b, in SZ 91, no 22; OGH, 6 April 2016, 7 Ob 201/15g; OGH, 22 February 2017, 8 Ob 89/16w; OGH, 31 July 2019, 5 Ob 91/19x.

cause either, but it is likewise widely accepted in Swiss legal doctrine[41] and case law[42] that parties to long-term contracts are entitled to terminate such contracts with immediate effect, if there is a compelling reason. In France, the concept of *caducité* was incorporated into French law by a reform in 2016, eventually leading to the termination of a validly formed contract, if one of its essential elements disappears.[43] In lack of a statutory definition of essential elements, French courts understand this statutory term to refer to circumstances relating to both validity and content of a contract.[44] Essential elements will thus relate either to essential motives of the parties for entering into the agreement and the purpose that the agreement is designed to serve, or to the subject matter of the contract. In Italy, the concept of *eccessiva onerosità* provides that the party in charge of performance that has become overly burdensome due to the occurrence of extraordinary and unforeseeable events may request termination of a contract for continuous or periodic performance. Although a party can request a court to terminate a contract, the other party may avoid such termination by offering an adequate modification of the terms of the contract.

In the German-speaking jurisdictions and Roman civil codes examined, termination of permanent contracts, either with (ordinary termination) or without (extraordinary termination) notice, could become more important during and after the coronavirus pandemic, but is most probably of limited help to contracting parties. One practical example of this concept is subscriptions for public transportation, another example a gym membership. The fact of a pandemic alone, however, will hardly ever constitute a compelling reason for extraordinary termination in the absence of other aggravating circumstances.

5 Conclusions

In the context of the coronavirus crisis, the triangle between emergency policy responses, preservation, and disruption of contracts deserves our attention. This article deals with the research question, whether emergency policy responses will pay off or even cause more harm in the long term. More specifically, the article aims to assess the impact of different generations of emergency policy responses on contract law in order to inform the ongoing debate in law and politics. As already mentioned in the introduction, this is important because any intervention in a functioning system increases complexity and creates a new equilibrium that may

---

[41] See Schwenzer (2016), p. 278; Koller (2017), pp. 498–502; Berger (2018), p. 402; Huguenin (2018), pp. 255–256.

[42] See BGer, 3 April 2002, 4C.175/2001, in BGE 128 III 428, pp. 429–434; BGer, 6 March 2007, 4P.243/2006, in BGE 133 III 360, pp. 363–366; BGer, 5 April 2012, 4A_589/2011, in BGE 138 III 304, pp. 317–322; BGer, 27 June 2017, 4A_45/2017, in BGE 143 III 480, pp. 483–494.

[43] See Chantepie and Latina (2016), paras 493 and 498–499.

[44] See Com., 3 March 2004, 02-12905, in IV Bulletin, no 42; Cass. 1re civ., 7 November 2006, 05-11775, in I Bulletin, no 457; Com., 30 October 2008, 07-17646, in I Bulletin, no 241.

be inferior. Therefore, it is understood that emergency policy responses may adversely affect the *Pareto*-efficient balance between preservation and disruption of contracts. Two observations, which both relate to economic measures, taken by governments during a lockdown, or after a reopening of the economy, seem particularly important and interesting in this regard.

From a legal theory perspective, it can be concluded that economic measures have a certain spill-over effect on contract law. Business enterprises, customers, and other contracting parties, who directly or indirectly benefit from any economic measures, should arguably not be able to release themselves from their obligations under a contract as easily as if no such measures would have been put in place or contracting parties make no use of them. In other words, neither a business enterprise nor a customer should be able to discharge its contractual obligations after the government has already assumed most of its business risk. The existing architecture of economic measures for business enterprises, including, but not limited to, State aid, liquidity support, non-repayable grants, loan subsidies and guarantees, bridging credits as well as deferred payments of social security contributions and taxes, not only on the national, but also on the supranational level, adds many additional complications on an already complex system. Other measures, namely designed to protect employees, such as state-sponsored short-time work programs, indirectly also serve business enterprises, simply by transferring wage costs, which are at risk due to the pandemic, to the government. This manoeuvre is basically nothing else than delaying an inevitable structural change at the expense of future generations. Courts are therefore obligated to make a holistic assessment, when deciding contractual disputes, where one or both parties have benefited from economic measures that have shifted the statutory or contractually agreed upon risk allocation.

From a law and economics perspective, it can be concluded that economic measures have adverse effects. Recent experience in a variety of contexts has shown that many of these measures often do not serve their original purpose. For obvious reasons, rational business enterprises claimed financial support, which was mainly intended to ensure liquidity of funds, without being in liquidity distress, but because this is a favourable form of refinancing. Also, governments have granted large aid packaged to airlines, but in the end, these lump-sum payments did not serve their purpose at all, because restructurings and mass layoffs have been inevitable at many airlines. The same is true for state-sponsored short-time work programs: not only did highly profitable business enterprises—anecdotal evidence tells, even (leading) law firms—place themselves under the umbrella of such programs, but also many small and medium-sized enterprises were, allegedly or demonstrably, in a position to claim compensation for lack of sales through short-time work, which they would not have achieved even in normal operations. In short, all these programs and aid packages have led to enormous distortions of competition that cannot easily be reversed. At least, the legislator has restrained itself from also pouring additional money into tenants' coffers for a risk that normally lies in their own sphere and not in that of the landlord.

As a result, the research question posed in this article must be answered rather critically, at least for economic measures. It cannot possibly be the idea that, thanks to such measures, business enterprises, customers, and other contracting parties are better off during the coronavirus crisis than in normal times without crisis. However, one caveat must be made at this point: both containment and closure measures and health measures are not covered in this article, which focusses predominantly on economic measures. Frankly speaking, that is not tragic. Containment and closure measures will be the subject of expert disputes for a long time to come, to which a distinguished virologist can perhaps contribute more than a simple lawyer. Health measures cannot be judged in a reliable way at the moment, because vaccination campaigns have only just begun, but this should not obscure the fact that there is good reason to remain optimistic. After all, it does not look like that the coronavirus crisis is going to be over any time soon, uncertainty and rumours on the market will continue, but one thing is for sure: we have learned from our mistakes and contract law has evolved and emerged stronger from the crisis.

References

Ancel P (2017) Imprévision. In: Répertoire de droit civil. Dalloz, Paris

Angermair T et al (2020) COVID-19-Gesetze: ausgewählte für Unternehmen relevante Fragen. Österreichische Notariatszeitung 152:121–134

Artz M, Steyl E (2020) Mietrecht. In: Schmidt H (ed) COVID-19: Rechtsfragen zur Corona-Krise, 2nd edn. Beck, Munich, pp 55–94

Auer-Mayer S (2020) Ausgewählte Fragen zur Kurzarbeit. Zeitschrift für Arbeits- und Sozialrecht 55:220–229

Berger B (2018) Allgemeines Schuldrecht, 3rd edn. Stämpfli, Berne

Bertram A et al (2020) Arbeiten im Home Office in Zeiten von Corona – ein Leitfaden zu Home Office und mobilem Arbeiten. Beck, Munich

Blatter JP (2020) Le bail, le covid-19 et le schizophrène. Actualité Juridique Droit Immobilier 31:245–249

Blesi A et al (2020) Arbeitsrecht. In: COVID-19: ein Panorama der Rechtsfragen zur Corona-Krise. Helbing Lichtenhahn, Basel, pp 39–76

Blick (2020) SP-Bundesrat Berset über das Coronavirus "Was heute gilt, ist morgen vielleicht schon veraltet." https://www.blick.ch/politik/sp-bundesrat-berset-ueber-das-coronavirus-was-heute-gilt-ist-morgen-vielleicht-schon-veraltet-id15774773.html. (last access 25 May 2021)

Chantepie G, Latina M (2016) La réforme du droit des obligations: commentaire théorique et pratique dans l'ordre du Code civil. Dalloz, Paris

Christ BF et al (2020) Hilfsmassnahmen für Unternehmen. In: COVID-19: ein Panorama der Rechtsfragen zur Corona-Krise. Helbing Lichtenhahn, Basel, pp 539–566

Deshayes O (2020) La prorogation des délais en période de Covid-19: quels effets sur les contrats? Recueil Dalloz 196:831–836

Duchange G (2020) Coronavirus et contrat de travail. Actualité Juridique Contrat 7:191–192

Emmenegger S et al (2014) Schweizerisches Obligationenrecht: allgemeiner Teil II, 10th edn. Schulthess, Zurich

Enz BV (2020) Risikozuordnung in Verträgen und die COVID-19 Situation: Teil 1 – Anwendungsbereich der clausula rebus sic stantibus, der Unmöglichkeit nach Art. 119 OR und der Kündigung aus wichtigem Grund. Jusletter. https://jusletter.weblaw.ch/juslissues/2020/1024/risikozuordnung-in-v_2595201a74.html. (last access 25 May 2021)

Enz BV, Mor S (2020) Risikozuordnung in Verträgen und die COVID-19 Situation: Teil 2 – Problemstellungen der COVID-19 Situation im Werkvertragsrecht. Jusletter. https://jusletter.

weblaw.ch/juslissues/2020/1031/risikozuordnung-in-v_e59b887593.html. (last access 25 May 2021)

Financial Times (2021) Lockdowns compared: tracking governments' coronavirus responses. https://ig.ft.com/coronavirus-lockdowns. (last access 25 May 2021)

Fischinger P (2020) Arbeitsrechtliche Fragen in der Corona-Krise. Juristische Arbeitsblätter 52:561–568

Fuhlrott M, Fischer K (2020) Corona: virale Anpassungen des Arbeitsrechts. Neue Zeitschrift für Arbeitsrecht 37:345–350

Galgano F (2010) Trattato di diritto civile: le obbligazioni in generale, il contratto in generale, i songoli contratti. Antonio Milani, Padova

Galletto T (1988) La clausola "rebus sic stantibus". In: Sacco R (ed) Digesto delle discipline privatistiche: Sezione civile. Utet, Torino

Geiser T (2020) Arbeitsrechtliche Regelungen im Zusammenhang mit dem Coronavirus. Aktuelle Juristische Praxis 29:545–551

Geiser T et al (2020) Klärung arbeitsrechtlicher Fragen im Zusammenhang mit dem Coronavirus. Jusletter. https://jusletter.weblaw.ch/juslissues/2020/1016/klarung-arbeitsrecht_27d573e839.html. (last access 25 May 2021)

Gentili A (2020) Una proposta sui contratti d'impresa al tempo del coronavirus. Giustizia Civile. https://giustiziacivile.com/obbligazioni-e-contratti/approfondimenti/una-proposta-sui-contratti-dimpresa-al-tempo-del. (last access 25 May 2021)

Geulen F, Vogt V (2020) Kurzarbeit in der Corona Krise. Arbeitsrecht Aktuell 12:181–185

Gruber M (2019) In: Kletecka A, Schauer M (eds) Online-Kommentar zum Allgemeinen bürgerlichen Gesetzbuch. Vienna, Manz

Guiomard P (2020) La grippe, les épidémies et la force majeure en dix arrêts. Dalloz actualité. https://www.dalloz-actualite.fr/flash/grippe-epidemies-et-force-majeure-en-dix-arrets. (last access 25 May 2021)

Haefeli A et al (2020a) Coronavirus SARS-CoV-2: Klärung mietrechtlicher Fragen. Jusletter. https://jusletter.weblaw.ch/juslissues/2020/1019/coronavirus-sars-cov_4f217bb313.html. (last access 25 May 2021)

Haefeli A et al (2020b) Anpassung privatrechtlicher Verträge infolge von COVID-19. In: COVID-19: ein Panorama der Rechtsfragen zur Corona-Krise. Helbing Lichtenhahn, Basel, pp 1–38

Haghofer T (2020) COVID-19-Pandemie: Gesetzgeber schützt betroffene Kreditnehmer. Zeitschrift für Verbraucherrecht 8:84–88

Häublein M, Müller M (2020) Wer trägt das Pandemierisiko in der Geschäftsraummiete? Zur Mietzahlungspflicht bei pandemiebedingten Geschäftsschliessungen und anderen Betriebsbeeinträchtigungen. Neue Zeitschrift für Miet- und Wohnungsrecht 23:481–492

Heinich J (2020) L'incidence de l'épidémie de coronavirus sur les contrats d'affaires: de la force majeure à l'imprévision. Recueil Dalloz 196:611–617

Hellmich J (2020) Vollständige Miete bei vollständigem Verlust der Nutzbarkeit? Die Untersagung des Publikumsverkehrs als Mangel im Sinne von § 536 Abs. 1 S. 1 BGB. COVID-19 und Recht 1:189–191

Hellner J (2020) Pacta sunt servanda – gilt dieser Grundsatz auch für die Miete in Zeiten der COVID-Pandemie? Oder: Annäherung an den Begriff des mietvertraglichen Verwendungsrisikos. Neue Juristische Online-Zeitschrift 20:769–774

Hochleitner C (2020) Die Auswirkungen von COVID-19 auf Geschäftsraummieter und Pächter: ist die Rechtslage tatsächlich so eindeutig? Österreichische Juristen-Zeitung 75:533–541

Hohenstatt KS, Krois C (2020) Lohnrisiko und Entgeltfortzahlung während der Corona-Pandemie. Neue Zeitschrift für Arbeitsrecht 37:413–418

Hohenstatt KS, Sittard U (2020) Arbeitsrecht in Zeiten von Corona – ein Leitfaden für Betriebe und Beschäftigte. Beck, Munich

Huguenin C (2018) Obligationenrecht: allgemeiner und besonderer Teil, 3rd edn. Schulthess, Zurich

Janssen A, Wahnschaffe CJ (2020) Der internationale Warenkauf in Zeiten der Pandemie. Europäische Zeitschrift für Wirtschaftsrecht 31:410–416

Jentsch V (2020a) The law of contracts in the age of the coronavirus pandemic: is the statutory risk allocation pursuant to the Swiss Code of Obligations still adequate? Jusletter. https://jusletter.weblaw.ch/juslissues/2020/1035/the-law-ofcontracts_c7a14932a8.html. Last access 25 May 2021

Jentsch V (2020b) Contract law responses to the Covid-19 pandemic: a functional and comparative approach. Oxford Business Law Blog https://www.law.ox.ac.uk/business-law-blog/blog/2020/10/contract-law-responses-covid-19-pandemic-functional-andcomparative. Last access 25 May 2021

Jentsch V (2021a) Government responses on corona and contracts in Europe: a compilation of extraordinary measures in times of crisis. European Business Law Review 32:1067–1092

Jentsch V (2021b) Contractual performance, breach of contract and contractual obligations in times of crisis: on the need for unification and codification in European Contract Law. European Review of Private Law 29:853–884

Jentsch V (2021c) Corona and contracts: a functional and comparative approach. Max Weber Programme Newsletter 20. https://newsletter.mwpweb.eu/2021-February/newsletter-mwp.html#CoronaandContracts. Last access 25 May 2021

Kellner M, Liebel F (2020) Das gesetzliche COVID-19-Kreditmoratorium: eine Analyse der gesetzlichen Stundung von Krediten nach dem 2. COVID-19-JuBG. Österreichische Juristen-Zeitung 75:629–640

Kendérian F (2020) Le droit civil des contrats et le bail commercial en temps de crise: l'exemple de la Covid-19. Revue trimestrielle de droit commercial et de droit économique 41:265–282

Kiesche E, Kohte W (2020) Arbeits- und Gesundheitsschutz in Zeiten von Corona – der Leitfaden für Betriebe und Beschäftigte. Beck, Munich

Kletecka A et al (2018) Grundriss des bürgerlichen Rechts I: allgemeiner Teil, Sachenrecht, Familienrecht, 15th edn. Manz, Vienna

Koller A (2017) Schweizerisches Obligationenrecht: allgemeiner Teil, 4th edn. Stämpfli, Berne

Koller T (2020) Corona-Krise und Mietrecht – Rechtsöffnungsrichter in der Verantwortung. Jusletter. https://jusletter.weblaw.ch/juslissues/2020/1022/corona-krise-und-mie_14d602f348.html. (last access 25 May 2021)

Krenn M, Schüssler-Datler A (2020) Sonderregelungen für Mietverhältnisse in der Corona-Krise: Mietrechtsänderungen durch das 2. COVID-19-Justiz-Begleitgesetz. Österreichische Juristen-Zeitung 75:581–585

Lachat D, Brutschin S (2020a) Die Mieten in Zeiten des Coronavirus. Zeitschrift für schweizerisches Mietrecht 35:99–143

Lachat D, Brutschin S (2020b) Le bail aux temps du coronavirus. La Semaine Judicaire 142:111–151

Laimer S, Schickmair M (2020) Ausgewählte zivilrechtliche Probleme in der COVID-19-Krise. In: Resch R (ed) Das Corona-Handbuch: Österreichs Rechtspraxis zur aktuellen Lage. Manz, Vienna, pp 253–280

Landivaux L (2020) Contrats et coronavirus: un cas de force majeure? Ça dépend ... Dalloz actualité. https://www.dalloz-actualite.fr/node/contrats-et-coronavirus-un-cas-de-force-majeure-ca-depend. (last access 25 May 2021)

Leroy Y (2020) Le droit du travail face au Covid-19: adaptation ou menace? Droit social 31: 577–580

Lorenz S (2020) Allgemeines Leistungsstörungsrecht und Veranstaltungsrecht. In: Schmidt H (ed) COVID-19: Rechtsfragen zur Corona-Krise, 2nd edn. Beck, Munich, pp 1–28

Mann M et al (2020) Vertrieb von Waren und Dienstleistungen in Zeiten von Corona – ein Rechtsleitfaden zu COVID-19-bedingten Vertragsstörungen. Beck, Munich

Mayr G (2020) COVID-19: Steuerpakete in Österreich und für eine Krise. Betriebs-Berater 75: 1495–1499

Mazal W (2020) Entgeltfortzahlung bei pandemiebedingter Einschränkung des sozialen Lebens. Fachzeitschrift für Wirtschaftsrecht 31:280–283

Mosing F (2020) COVID-19-Kurzarbeit. Journal für Arbeitsrecht und Sozialrecht 4:141–159

Müller JP (2020) Der "Lockdown" als Herausforderung für die Vertragsparteien bei der Miete und Pacht von Wohn- und Geschäftsräumen – eine Auslegeordnung. In: COVID-19: ein Panorama der Rechtsfragen zur Corona-Krise. Helbing Lichtenhahn, Basel, pp 77–122

Müller S, Becker M (2020) Pandemiebedingte Leistungshindernisse in der Arbeitsrechtspraxis. COVID-19 und Recht 1:126–130

Oertmann P (1921) Die Geschäftsgrundlage: ein neuer Rechtsbegriff. Deichert, Leipzig

Ofner H (2020) Mietrecht und die COVID-19-Pandemie in Österreich: Kündigungsschutz, Mietzinsminderung, Fixkostenersatz. Zeitschrift für Europarecht, Internationales Privatrecht und Rechtsvergleichung 61:107–113

Osti G (1959) Clausola rebus sic stantibus. In: Azara A, Eula E (eds) Novissimo digesto italiano. Utet, Torino, pp 353–360

Osti G (1962) Impossibilità sopravveniente. In: Azara A, Eula E (eds) Novissimo digesto italiano. Utet, Torino, pp 287–300

Otte-Gräbener S (2020) Auswirkungen der COVID-19-Pandemie auf Lieferverträge. Gesellschafts- und Wirtschaftsrecht 12:147–152

OxCGRT (2021) Oxford COVID-19 government response tracker. https://covidtracker.bsg.ox.ac.uk. Last access 25 May 2021

Pertot T (2020) Mietrecht in Zeiten des Coronavirus: italienische Perspektive. Zeitschrift für Europarecht, Internationales Privatrecht und Rechtsvergleichung 61:131–140

Pietruszak T (2020) Lockdown und Lohnfortzahlung. Jusletter. https://jusletter.weblaw.ch/juslissues/2020/1019/lockdown-und-lohnfor_cee5a04395.html. (last access 25 May 2021)

Radé C (2020) Covid-19 et force majeure. Droit social 31:598–601

Regnault S (2020) Covid-19 et bail commercial. Actualité Juridique Contrat 7:193–197

Rehder J, Schmidt D (2020) Auswirkungen der COVID-19-Pandemie auf die Vertragsabwicklungen unter Betrachtung des deutschen und US-amerikanischen Leistungsstörungsrechts. COVID-19 und Recht 1:459–465

Reifelsberger C (2020) Arbeitsschutz und COVID-19 – Haftung des Arbeitgebers. COVID-19 und Recht 1:357–363

Reischauer R (2018) In: Rummel P, Lukas M (eds) Kommentar zum Allgemeinen bürgerlichen Gesetzbuch, 5th edn. Vienna, Manz

Riedler A (2018) Zivilrecht I: allgemeiner Teil. In: Riedler A (ed) Studienkonzept Zivilrecht, 7th edn. LexisNexis, Vienna

Römermann V (2020a) Leitfaden für Unternehmen in der Covid-19 Pandemie – Insolvenzrecht, Gesellschaftsrecht, Arbeitsrecht, Steuerrecht. Beck, Munich

Römermann V (2020b) Erste Hilfe für Selbständige und Unternehmer in Zeiten von Corona – mit allen relevanten Themen wie u.a.: Insolvenzantrag, Mietverhältnis, Darlehen. Beck, Munich

Roseti ASM (2020) Il COVID-19 riaccende l'eterno conflitto tra il principio pacta sunt servanda e il principio rebus sic stantibus. Diritto del Risparmio. https://www.dirittodelrisparmio.it/2020/08/17/il-covid-19-riaccende-leterno-conflitto-tra-il-principio-pacta-sunt-servanda-e-il-principio-rebus-sic-stantibus. (last access 25 May 2021)

Rüfner T (2020) Das Corona-moratorium nach Art. 240 EGBGB. JuristenZeitung 75:443–448

Sagan A, Brockfeld M (2020) Arbeitsrecht in Zeiten der Corona-Pandemie. Neue Juristische Wochenschrift 73:1112–1117

Schall A (2020) Corona-Krise: Unmöglichkeit und Wegfall der Geschäftsgrundlage bei gewerblichen Miet- und Pachtverträgen. JuristenZeitung 75:388–396

Schmeisser F, Fauth M (2020) Kurzarbeit in Zeiten der Corona-Krise. COVID-19 und Recht 1:363–370

Schmid CU (2020) Corona und Mietrecht in Deutschland: insbesondere zur Verpflichtung des Gewerberaummieters zur Zinszahlung nach behördlichen Schliessungsanordnungen. Zeitschrift für Europarecht, Internationales Privatrecht und Rechtsvergleichung 61:113–119

Schmid J et al (2014) Schweizerisches Obligationenrecht: allgemeiner Teil I, 14th edn. Schulthess, Zurich

Schmidt B (2020) Erste Hilfe bei Kurzarbeit in Zeiten von Corona – ein Leitfaden zu Kurzarbeit und Kurzarbeitergeld. Beck, Munich

Schmidt-Kessel M, Möllnitz C (2020) Coronavertragsrecht – Sonderregeln für Verbraucher und Kleinstunternehmen. Neue Juristische Wochenschrift 73:1103–1107

Schwaab JC (2020) Le travailleur en quarantaine. Jusletter. https://jusletter.weblaw.ch/juslissues/2020/1016/le-travailleur-en-qu_1e69bbcc13.html. (last access 25 May 2021)

Schwenzer I (2016) Schweizerisches Obligationenrecht: allgemeiner Teil, 7th edn. Stämpfli, Berne

Sittner S (2020) Mietrechtspraxis unter Covid-19. Neue Juristische Wochenschrift 73:1169–1174

Spitzl A (2020) Sind Kündigungen des AG im Zuge von Kurzarbeit nichtig? Fachzeitschrift für Wirtschaftsrecht 31:474–477

Staehelin D, Bopp L (2020) Insolvenzrechtliche Massnahmen zur Bewältigung der Coronakrise. In: COVID-19: ein Panorama der Rechtsfragen zur Corona-Krise. Helbing Lichtenhahn, Basel, pp 513–538

The Economist (2021) Tracking the coronavirus across Europe: how countries and regions are coping with the Covid-19 pandemic. https://www.economist.com/graphic-detail/tracking-coronavirus-across-europe. Last access 25 May 2021

Thume KH (2020) Auswirkungen der COVID-19-Pandemie auf nationale und grenzüberschreitende Vertriebsverträge. Betriebs-Berater 75:1419–1425

Tödtmann U, von Bockelmann E (2020) Arbeitsrecht in Not- und Krisenzeiten: die Corona-Pandemie und ähnliche Krisensituationen. Beck, Munich

Tschannen EG (2020) Das Corona-Massnahmenpaket des Bundesrats: eine Würdigung aus arbeitsrechtlicher Perspektive. Jusletter https://jusletter.weblaw.ch/juslissues/2020/1019/das-corona-massnahme_8c3080553c.html. Last access 25 May 2021

Twigg-Flesner C (2020) A comparative perspective on commercial contracts and the impact of COVID-19 – change of circumstances, force majeure, or what? In: Pistor K (ed) Law in the time of COVID-19. Columbia, New York, pp 155–165

Uitz M, Parsché H (2020) Vertragsverstösse aufgrund COVID-19. COVID-19 und Recht 1. https://rdb.manz.at/document/rdb.tso.LIcure20200001. (last access 25 May 2021)

Verroust-Valliot C, Pelletier S (2020) L'impact du covid-19 sur les contrats de droit privé. Dalloz actualité. https://www.dalloz-actualite.fr/node/l-impact-du-covid-19-sur-contrats-de-droit-prive. (last access 25 May 2021)

Wagner E et al (2020) Auswirkungen von COVID-19 auf Lieferverträge. Betriebs-Berater 75:845–851

Wagner G (2020) Corona Law. Zeitschrift für Europäisches Privatrecht 28:531–542

Wagner J, Rarinato E (2020) COVID-19 und Steuerrecht – die wichtigsten Entwicklungen für Unternehmen. COVID-19 und Recht 1:286–291

Warmuth C (2020) § 313 BGB in Zeiten der Corona-Krise – am Beispiel der Gewerberaummiete. COVID-19 und Recht 1:16–21

Weidt C, Schiewek AC (2020) Geschäftsschliessungen wegen Corona – mietrechtlich ein Fall des § 313 BGB? Neue Juristische Online-Zeitschrift 20:481–485

Wildhaber I (2020) Das Arbeitsrecht in Pandemiezeiten. Zeitschrift für Schweizerisches Recht 139 Sondernummer: pp 157–179

Windscheid B (1850) Die Lehre des römischen Rechts von der Voraussetzung. Buddeus, Düsseldorf

Wolf C et al (2020) Die zivilrechtlichen Auswirkungen des Covid-19-Gesetzes – ein erster Überblick. Juristische Arbeitsblätter 52:401–411

Wolf S, Minnig Y (2020) COVID-19 und Mietrecht: zur Rechtslage in der Schweiz. Zeitschrift für Europarecht, Internationales Privatrecht und Rechtsvergleichung 61:119–130

Zehelein K (2020) COVID-19: Miete in Zeiten von Corona. Beck, Munich

Ziadé R, Cavicchioli C (2020) L'impact du Covid-19 sur les contrats commerciaux. Actualité Juridique Contrat 7:176–182

The Giant Awakens

Law and Economics of Excessive Pricing During the COVID-19 Crisis

Behrang Kianzad

Abstract Price gouging of essential items, and the global debate on pricing of vaccines and treatments during the COVID-19 crisis, provide an optimal proxy to revisit the law and economics discourse on excessive pricing as an abuse of dominant position. Beyond a normative soul-searching of the efficiency v fairness debate, this chapter analyses excessive pricing cases during the COVID-19 pandemic in the EU, US, and South Africa. The assertion is made that neoclassical, marginalist, and welfarist law and economics schools will forever be in direct conflict with the black letter law of European Competition Law, which prohibits unfair, excessive pricing, and thus, other law and economics schools such as Keynesian, Behavioural, and Neuro-economics offer far better congruence with the legislative intent and history of Article 102a TFEU.

1 Introduction

One should never let a good crisis go to waste, as Rahm Emanuel, President Obama's former chief of staff famously put it. The COVID-19 crisis is no exception, with many fortune seekers trying to enrich themselves through the crisis by way of price gouging and excessive pricing. This provides an optimal proxy to revisit law and economics of unfair pricing as an anti-competitive practice, with an added focus on the fairness v efficiency debate.

The perceived unfairness in taking undue advantage of an economically dependent position, especially in times of crisis such as war and pandemic, constitutes the ratio legis informing the prohibition from its inception centuries ago and onwards. The charging of unfair, excessive prices has long been prohibited in European Competition Law per Article 102a TFEU, applicable throughout all Member States

B. Kianzad (✉)
Center for Advanced Studies in Biomedical Innovation Law, Faculty of Law, Copenhagen University, Copenhagen, Denmark
e-mail: behrang.kianzad@jur.ku.dk

© The Author(s), under exclusive license to Springer Nature Switzerland AG 2022
K. Mathis, A. Tor (eds.), *Law and Economics of the Coronavirus Crisis*, Economic Analysis of Law in European Legal Scholarship 13,
https://doi.org/10.1007/978-3-030-95876-3_5

by way of direct effect, provided the investigated firm is "dominant" in the internal market and the practices are capable of affecting trade between Member States.

The prohibition of excessive pricing, in general, belongs to one of the oldest legal constructs in human history dating back to the days of Hammurabi, Jewish Halacha, The Bible, Islamic Law, Roman Law, and all the way to our present days.[1] Virtually all OECD-jurisdictions around the world contain some form of prohibition of "unfair" or "excessive" pricing and price gouging as an abuse of competition law—minus US, Canada, Mexico, Australia, and New Zealand—further demonstrating the universality of the concept beyond its profound historical roots.[2]

Like a mythical giant, dormant but defiant, excessive pricing time and again captures the attention of policymakers, competition law practitioners, and scholars, breaking away with normative and empirical chains bestowed upon its enforcement by a certain strand of law and economics.

Where one side of the debate elevates supposed virtues of excessive prices,[3] self-correcting markets,[4] and possible chilling effects in face of vigilant enforcement,[5] the other side of the axis points to wealth transfers being the prima facie competition law concern[6] as well as to the erroneous assumptions by the antagonists of enforcement,[7] thus forwarding fairness and social policy concerns beyond a "purist" economic efficiency doctrine.[8]

The economic standard model, roughly simplified, dictates that when demand surges, so do prices and competition for markets and customers. This causes competitors, in the long run, to enter the lucrative market and compete for market shares through higher efficiency and lower prices, for the benefit of consumers, innovation, and competition in general. One can, however, invoke the famous Keynesian quote that "In the long run we are all dead", with rather grave connotations in our current crisis, with the tragic loss of human life already towering in the short run. The COVID-19 global pandemic thus elevated the matter of price gouging of essential medical supplies, with excessive pricing cases being investigated by competition authorities around the world.[9] There is further an ongoing global debate

---

[1] Watkins (1922).

[2] OECD, Policy Roundtables, Excessive Prices, DAF/COMP(2011)18, 2011, available at: http://www.oecd.org/competition/abuse/49604207.pdf, (last access 20 February 2020); Important to note in regard to US is the fact that although excessive pricing are not banned on the Federal level, some 36 states contain different statutes prohibiting excessive pricing and/or price gouging. In regard to Canada, the Canadian Patent Act explicitly prohibits excessive pricing of patented pharmaceuticals, Canadian Patent Act (R.S.C., 1985, c. P-4), Section 83–85.

[3] Kühn (2017).

[4] Jenny (2018).

[5] Evans and Padilla (2005).

[6] Lande (1982).

[7] Ezrachi and Gilo (2009a).

[8] Woodcock (2018).

[9] Competition Commission South Africa, Commission cracks down on excessive pricing, Press Release April 15 2020, available at: http://www.compcom.co.za/wp-content/uploads/2020/04/

on pricing and access regarding COVID-treatments and vaccines at WHO, WTO, and WIPO levels.[10]

Dramatic, sudden price hikes on essential supplies (a practice known as price gouging, or excessive pricing) are reported in many countries[11] affected by the crisis. The Competition Authorities in some jurisdictions received many complaints[12] in regard to excessive pricing/price gouging and some pursued investigations, others are closely monitoring the developments.[13]

As many other OECD-countries' competition laws on excessive pricing have been modelled after the prohibition in European Competition Law, this jurisdiction has been chosen as the main analytical frame for the present chapter, with some references to US Antitrust, as the US Federal Law does not prohibit excessive

---

Media-Statement-COMMISSION-CRACKS-DOWN-ON-EXCESSIVE-PRICING.pdf, (last access 20 April 2020); US Department of Justice, Department of Justice and Department of Health and Human Services Partner to Distribute More Than Half a Million Medical Supplies Confiscated from Price Gougers, Press Release April 2 2020, available at: https://www.justice.gov/opa/pr/department-justice-and-department-health-and-human-services-partner-distribute-more-half, (last access 20 April 2020); Hellenic Competition Commission, Actions for the implementation of the competition rules, Press Release April 15 2020, available at https://www.epant.gr/enimerosi/deltia-typou/item/885-deltio-typou-energeies-gia-tin-efarmogi-ton-kanonon-tou-antagonismoy.html (last access 20 April 2020).

[10] WHO, WIPO, WTO, "An integrated health, trade and IP approach to respond to the COVID-19 pandemic" in Promoting Access to Medical Technologies and Innovation – Intersections between public health, intellectual property and trade, 2nd edition, 2020, https://www.wipo.int/edocs/pubdocs/en/wipo_pub_628_2020.pdf, p. 7 ff, (last access 20 September 2020); WTO, Council for Trade-Related Aspects of Intellectual Property Rights, Waiver from certain provisions of the TRIPS agreement for the prevention, containment and treatment of COVID-19 – Communication from India and South Africa, IP/C/W/669, 2 October 2020, available at https://docs.wto.org/dol2fe/Pages/SS/directdoc.aspx?filename=q:/IP/C/W669.pdf&Open=True, (last access 20 May 2020); Nathaniel Weixel, Biden backs COVID-19 patent waivers, The Hill, 05/05/21, https://thehill.com/policy/healthcare/551992-biden-backs-covid-19-vaccine-patent-waivers, (last access 29 May 2021).

[11] US Department of Justice, Justice Department Cautions Business Community Against Violating Antitrust Laws in the Manufacturing, Distribution, and Sale of Public Health Products, https://www.justice.gov/opa/pr/justice-department-cautions-business-community-against-violating-anti trust-laws-manufacturing; The Guardian, Do not exploit coronavirus panic, watchdog warns retailers, https://www.theguardian.com/world/2020/mar/05/do-not-take-advantage-of-coronavirus-panic-cma-warns-retailers (last access 11 September 2021); Forbes.com, Amid The Coronavirus Outbreak, Retailers Try To Combat Price-Gouging Online, https://www.forbes.com/sites/joanverdon/2020/03/04/coronavirus-related-price-gouging-is-a-risky-business-for-retailers/ (last access 11 September 2021); iAfrica, Over 500 Complaints Received Of Excessive Price-Hikes Since Start Of Lockdown, https://iafrica.com/over-500-complaints-received-of-excessive-price-hikes-since-start-of-lockdown/ (last access 11 September 2021).

[12] See e.g. UK Competition Authority, which have received more than 9000 such complaints, https://www.gov.uk/government/publications/cma-coronavirus-taskforce-update-21-may-2020/protecting-consumers-during-the-coronavirus-covid-19-pandemic-update-on-the-work-of-the-cmas-taskforce#fn:3 (last access 11 September 2021).

[13] Kianzad (2021).

pricing.[14] Nevertheless, many US States include excessive pricing/price gouging prohibitions in their laws, and during the COVID-19 pandemic, hoarding and price gouging of some designated essential items was explicitly banned per Presidential Order on Federal level.[15] Some cases pursued in South Africa are also analysed in-depth as these cases were directly related to COVID-19 price gouging and displayed a rather different approach compared to the European one, despite the South African law being modelled after Article 102a TFEU.[16]

The focus of the present chapter rests mainly on the normative, legal-economic as well as legal-philosophical ratio legis of the prohibition, and on the division between fairness and efficiency approaches regarding the object of European Competition Law. The string of recent case law[17] emerging around the EU (Denmark (CD Pharma), Italy (Aspen Pharma) and UK (Pfizer/Flynn Pharma) as well as the European Commission pursuing a unique excessive pricing case[18] ending in a commitment decision) further seems to indicate a possible shift in policy and jurisprudence.

A point which was also noted by Advocate General (henceforth AG) Pitruzzella in the most recent excessive pricing cases considered by the Court of Justice of the European Union (henceforth CJEU). As noted by AG Pitruzzella, "For a long time, the Commission and the national competition authorities pursued that type of anticompetitive practice on a rather limited basis. In recent years, however, there has been a revival of the concept of "unfair prices", as evidenced by the growing number of cases handled by the national competition authorities and the Commission, and by the cases brought before the Court."[19]

Indeed, despite the re-occurring criticism in the neoclassical, marginalist, and welfarist law and economics literature, both the European Commission as well as Member States and their competition authorities have time and again demonstrated their commitments to apply the law against unfair pricing "as is". The COVID-19 crisis demonstrated this willingness to pursue excessive pricing and price gouging once again, re-affirming the ratio legis of the prohibition.[20] The ability of COVID-19 vaccines and treatments to adjust towards an equilibrium offers a bleak prospect for rapidly resolving a global pandemic, having devastating effects on the global

---

[14] Gal (2004).

[15] White House, President Donald J. Trump Will Not Tolerate the Price Gouging and Hoarding of Critical Supplies Needed to Combat the Coronavirus, March 23, available at: https://trumpwhitehouse.archives.gov/briefings-statements/president-donald-j-trump-will-not-tolerate-price-gouging-hoarding-critical-supplies-needed-combat-coronavirus/ (last access 20 September 2021).

[16] Boshoff (2020).

[17] Kianzad and Minssen (2018).

[18] Case at.40394 – Aspen – commitments to the European Commission – 28 January 2021.

[19] Opinion of Advocate General Pitruzzella in Case C-372/19 Belgische Vereniging van Auteurs, Componisten en Uitgevers CVBA (SABAM) v Weareone.World BVBA, Wecandance NV, No. ECLI:EU:C:2020:598 (July 16, 2020), para. 21.

[20] Cary et al. (2020).

economy at large. The COVID-19 crisis thus provides an optimal analytical framework regarding significantly diverging views in competition law and economics on excessive pricing enforcement.

The paper is structured as follows. Following the introductory section depicting the excessive pricing theme in general, Sect. 2 offers a critical assessment of the neoclassical and welfarist law and economics theories, informing much of the scholarly debate on excessive pricing as an anti-competitive practice. Section 3 presents an overview of the prohibition as well as recent, non COVID-19-related enforcement actions in European Competition Law. Section 4 recounts some examples of excessive pricing and price gouging during the COVID-19 pandemic in the US, UK, EU, and South Africa. Section 5 concludes with some law and policy reflections.

2 The Giant in Chains: Excessive Pricing in Law & Economics

Excessive Pricing categorizes a situation where a dominant undertaking, often a legal monopolist, is able to reap supra-competitive profits, not being sufficiently challenged by normal forces of competition. The supra-competitive profits are thought to produce deadweight losses and allocative in-efficiencies as well as harm to consumers in the form of undue wealth transfer, depending on what economic theory of harm one avails oneself of.[21]

Most OECD-jurisdictions prohibit excessive pricing and/or price gouging, minus the US, Canada, Australia, New Zealand, and Mexico, although excessive pricing is banned in many states in the US. The historical roots and the near-universal codification of the concept of excessive pricing have, however, not mitigated the rather antagonistic debate alongside the seemingly unreconcilable legal-economic positions, ranging from those denying the very existence of excessive pricing,[22] let alone endorsing enforcement[23] to others advocating energetic enforcement against excessive pricing as the prima facie core function of Competition Law.[24] This tension reflects the divide between different strands of thought regarding antitrust economics and a starkly divided debate on whether fairness or efficiency should guide antitrust enforcement and policy.[25]

According to marginal price theory and the law of supply and demand, the competitive price should equal the marginal cost of production. However, in real life and markets, prices are set above marginal cost and carry the potential to act as a

---

[21] Atkinson and Audretsch (2011).
[22] von Hayek (1993).
[23] Evans and Padilla (2005).
[24] Lande (1982).
[25] Page (1991).

signal for entry to competitors, where post-entry prices are brought down to more competitive levels, but many times still exceeding marginal costs, depending on the nature of the markets. Nor do the assumptions[26] regarding rationality and profit (utility) maximization hold up in closer scrutiny.[27]

Excessive pricing categorizes a situation where an undertaking is able to set prolonged supra-competitive prices, which either do not act as a signal to entry or are being maintained through some deficiencies in the competitive structure of the market, in-elastic demand on the part of consumers, and/or price insensitivity. Many times the dominance is created through past state monopolies, exclusive rights or legal monopoly by way of intellectual property rights such as patents—or, in the case of a pandemic, temporary dominance and "market capture" resulting from a surge in demand.[28]

There is wide disagreement in the law and economics literature on the matter of excessive pricing, where both normative and empirical elements related to assessment and finding of proper competitive price and profit benchmarks are elevated.[29] Nevertheless, one might note a certain monolithic and circular character in the debate, relying on dubious neoclassical and marginalist assumptions,[30] exposing the normative tensions between the legal and economic disciplines,[31] especially so when regarding the Economic Analysis of Law in the Posnerian tradition and the European legal tradition.[32]

One such assumption is the supposed "rarity" of excessive price cases,[33] when in fact, the number of cases is oftentimes comparable with Margin Squeeze and Predatory Price cases.[34]

A second assumption asserts the supposed "lack of competence" of Competition Authorities and the "Impossibility Theorem" in regard to the assessment of competitive price and profit benchmarks, which is, as asserted by many directors and councils at Competition Authorities around the world,[35] a rather routine exercise in many other competition law cases at the Authorities. The same holds true in regard to courts having to deal with complex FRAND and Royalty-calculations, which are

---

[26] Korobokin and Ulen (2000).

[27] Akerlof and Yellen (1985).

[28] Jenny (2018).

[29] O'Donoghue and Padilla (2019).

[30] Kahneman et al. (1986a).

[31] Salzberger (2007).

[32] Posner (1979); For the criticism of the Posnerian and its inherent incompatibility with European Competition Law, see Mestmäcker (2007). Regarding Posnerian approach and its conflict with the legal science overall, see Sery (2017); Fortsont (2001); Also Dworkin (1980).

[33] Motta and de Streel (2006).

[34] This author has located no less 27 cases decided by the European Commission and CJEU between 1970–2021, and a further non-exhaustive list of 95 cases on Member State level between 2000–2021.

[35] Gilo (2018), Hoekstra and Sauter (2018) and Saavedra and Tapia (2017).

routinely done without meeting objections of the sort meeting excessive pricing cases.

A third assumption regards the supposed risk of false positives and the associated costs, the relative risk of false negatives, inaction, and the associated costs, i.e., a trade-off between Type I and Type II, albeit in-depth calculations of such risks and costs along empirical lines are few and far between, if ever undertaken on a formal basis.[36]

A fourth assumption regards the supposed self-correcting nature of excessive pricing, where excessive prices are held to act as signals to entry, although settled, centuries-old wisdom about markets should reveal that it is not mainly ex-ante prices but ex-post prices that are relevant for a potential competitor, and, more importantly, information about the incumbent efficiencies and the market structure overall that ultimately inform the decision of entry.[37]

A fifth assumption forwards the supposed harm to innovation,[38] asserting that if risky and costly innovations are not able to be rewarded with manifestly excessive pricing, which should be excluded from competition law scrutiny, long-term innovation and thus consumer welfare would be harmed. An assertion which still needs to be qualified along empirical lines,[39] let alone be normatively substantiated,[40] as empirical evidence that enforcing the legal prohibition against excessive pricing would harm innovation per se is lacking.

There is indeed some evidence demonstrating that more vigorous enforcement actually induces innovation,[41] which is coherent with the theory that more competition and competitive pressure, and not less, spurs innovation, especially in fields where competition is driven not by static price competition but first and foremost through dynamic, innovation-based competition.[42]

There are further exceptions to be taken with this quasi-Schumpeterian position[43] in equating monopoly profits as the necessary and most focal element behind innovation[44] as well as insulating abuses of intellectual property rights from competition law scrutiny,[45] but this is outside of the present context of the chapter.[46]

---

[36] Jenny (2018).
[37] Ezrachi and Gilo (2009b).
[38] Fletcher and Jardine (2008).
[39] Manne and Wright (2010).
[40] Brennan (2007).
[41] Levine et al. (2020).
[42] Canoy and Tichem (2018).
[43] Gilbert (2006).
[44] Diamond (2006).
[45] Lianos (2006).
[46] Baker (2007).

It suffices to point out that according to the settled case law of the CJEU,[47] perfectly legal life cycle management strategies under intellectual property law can come in conflict with prohibitions laid down in Article 101 and 102 TFEU—such as the imposition of unfair, excessive pricing, regardless if the goods in question are protected by any intellectual property rights or not.[48]

The empirical assessment and screening tests employed in the jurisprudence of the European Commission, Member States, and suggested in the literature will not be commented on in-depth, as this chapter grapples mainly with the normative assumptions and underlying arguments for and against enforcement, with a special view to COVID-19. The empirical objections to excessive pricing enforcement, in turn, rely on the normative scaffolding informed by assumptions regarding rationality, utility and wealth maximization, and exclusion of externalities such as fairness preferences.[49]

The present work will thus approach the matter of excessive pricing by way of a normative soul-searching of certain strands of economics (neoclassical, welfarist, Chicagoan) in regard to Competition Law analysis and enforcement, elevating the inherent tension between these strands of economics and the legal discipline, as well as the question why some other strands of economics (Keynesian, Behavioural, Neuro-economics) are much more suited and capable to appreciate the ratio legis of the prohibition against excessive pricing.

2.1 Legal-Economics of Price, Value, and Profit

As a normative starting point, a conceptual distinction between value, price, and profit must be made, a matter which has been the foundational cornerstone of political economy ever since its inception. Where Smith, Ricardo, Marx et alia advanced different notions of labour theory of value, Hayek, Walras, Pareto et alia of the neoclassical, marginal utility school focused more on exchange and market value as such. The latter is, however, incapable of properly accounting for the inherent value of a good beyond what it will fetch in a free and competitive market, making the notions of value and profit circular, with price being a function of competitive pressure, marginal cost, and cost of fixed capital.

Profit, however, is a function not of fixed capital, but of variable capital, where the price reflects marginal cost-plus profit as a function of variable capital. This is the main reason why marginal and neoclassical economics is at odds with profits being a function of an inherent value reflecting the cost of production, fixed and variable capital, and associated opportunity costs, but instead attempts to de-couple profit

---

[47] Case C-457/10 P, AstraZeneca AB and AstraZeneca plc v European Commission, Judgment of the Court (First Chamber), 6 December 2012, ECLI:EU:C:2012:770.
[48] Salzberger (2013).
[49] Holler and Leroch (2010).

from value, and thus price, making it impossible for the theory to come to terms with an "excessive profit", since no profit ever is excessive, as the profit is neither a function of value nor of price, but merely reflecting what the good can fetch in a (supposedly) free and competitive market populated with utility-maximizing, rational agents.

This is the main reason why the welfarist, marginalist, and neoclassical schools tend to focus on exclusionary elements regarding excessive pricing, and not on excessiveness in and of itself. Hence the theory is nearly incapable of answering the question of when a price is excessive relative to its economic value, since the economic value is defined only around exchange value, and not use-value, inherent value, cost of production, or comparing products etc., where profit only reflects demand-side dynamics, partly de-coupled from supply-side dynamics, cost of capital and so on. Profits thus can rise dramatically without having any relation to the "economic value", as seen from empirical research on historical mark-ups being increased through market power.[50]

Neoclassical economics, which has come to dominate much of the antitrust debate during the past decades, is characterized by five core assumptions, those being (1) the assumption of scarcity of resources, (2) the belief in Homo Oeconomicus, presupposing that all economic agents are self-interested and act based on perfect and complete information and that the human good consists in nothing more than economic welfare, (3) the idea of Utilitarianism, meaning that human behaviour can be reduced to rational calculation and maximization of welfare, (4) that the value of any given thing originates from the value individuals consider it to have, and (5) the belief in availability and readiness of multiple possibilities guiding the individuals in their search for the optimal choice.[51]

As noted by Mestmäcker:

> Cost-benefit analysis is end-neutral. It can be applied to any given purpose. Constitutions, statutes and precedents, however, are as a rule not end-neutral. The question then is how to accommodate the normative implications of economic analysis with diverse non-economic legal purposes.[52]

Mounting a powerful attack on the philosophical foundations of the Posnerian position and contrasting it to Hayek views, but also drawing on Kant and Nietzsche, he seeks to re-connect the core function of the law with legal and moral philosophy, which is and ought to be the DNA of the laws—although supplemented by sound economic analyses of laws where applicable. As further aptly summarized by Klaus Mathis:

> In people's minds, justice – however it is defined – has an immanent value, which is very difficult to weigh up against an increase in economic efficiency.[53]

---

[50] De Loecker et al. (2020).
[51] Maggiolino (2011).
[52] Mestmäcker (2007).
[53] Mathis (2009).

What harm is associated with excessive pricing is hence dependent on the chosen theory of harm informing the analysis, the core assumptions informing the theories, and what trade-offs on the policy-level are chosen. If the competition law rationale is to increase overall efficiency and total welfare, or instead to focus on consumer welfare and thus protect consumers from undue wealth transfer to the monopolist—naturally impact the normative ratio legis of the prohibition and concomitant enforcement priorities. This re-connects with the debate on efficiency or fairness as competition law objective(s),[54] where the mainstream, neoclassical economics put the emphasis on the former,[55] and the behavioural and neuroeconomics schools allow for more fairness considerations in pricing beyond economic efficiency.[56]

Evidently, there is a manifest tension between certain strands of economics and legal science, where the legal science by tradition and the letter of the law focuses on the administration of fairness and justice, and not on maximizing efficiency.[57] As noted by Mark Blaug in regard to Richard Posner, "What he argues, when criticized, is simply that users of distributive justice will have to be addressed outside the framework of standard economic analysis ... But this is exactly what Pareto, Kaldor and Hicks said years ago. Orthodox welfare economics, including the "efficiency of the common law hypothesis" upheld by Posner, has simply stood still ever since the 1930s."[58]

Nevertheless, even a Chicagoan such as Richard Posner, reflecting over the tectonic shocks of the Financial Crisis of 2008/9 and the crisis of capitalism, notes this deficiency in certain strands of economics, stating:

> Although they rested on unrealistic assumptions about people's capacity to acquire and process information, the tendency in economics was to assume (however unrealistically) that people are 'rational' in a very strong sense, and to seek to test the adequacy of economic theory by accuracy of its predictions rather than by the realism of its assumptions. The predictions have turned out to be inaccurate – both the predictions of rational-expectations theory and those of the efficient markets hypothesis in the strong form in which stock prices are assumed to discount future corporate profits accurately and 'noise' trading, 'momentum' trading, stock bubbles and other anomalies are assumed away.[59]

The Chicago School and its firm belief in market perfection thus lost some of its influence and appeal since the emergence of behavioural economics,[60] challenging and refuting some of the core assumptions of the former school.[61] Also, the recent findings by Neuro-economics invariably demonstrate a neural encoding[62] and an

---

[54] Mathis (2009).

[55] Kaplow and Shavell (2001).

[56] Kahneman et al. (1986b).

[57] Ulen (2015).

[58] Blaug (2001).

[59] Posner (2010).

[60] Sunstein et al. (1998).

[61] Piraino (2007).

[62] Hsu et al. (2008).

inherent human bias towards fairness in pricing and transactions,[63] therefore rebutting the utilitarian assumptions.[64]

However, many of the core assumptions and assertions are still repeated in both textbooks and policy comments as they would be as valid as when formulated some 80 years ago by the likes of Marshall and Jevons, leading some scholars to dub this strand of economics somewhat derogatorily to "Zombie Economics",[65] due to its astoundingly re-occurring character despite some of the core assumptions being invalidated time and again.

Recent years have seen the rise of The New Progressive Antitrust School (also called New Brandeis School or more derogatorily dubbed by neoclassical economists, Hipster Antitrust),[66] which calls for a re-thinking of (or return to) the soul of Antitrust law in line with Keynesian economics to incorporate some societal perspectives in respect to equality, fairness, and justice.[67] The COVID-19 crisis provided an apt example of revisiting centuries-old legal-economic debates such as the tension between efficiency and fairness. It is by no way accidental nor anecdotal that in times of global crisis (financial crisis, health pandemic etc.) we all become Kantian, and Keynesian, even antagonists such as Milton Friedman.[68]

2.2 The Gigantic Debate: Arguments Pro and Contra Excessive Pricing Enforcement

Notably, there are three main non-interventionist arguments elevated in the neoclassical law and economics literature against excessive pricing enforcement by competition authorities and courts, relying on some of the assumptions accounted for above.

Firstly, high, supra-competitive, or excessive prices are not seen as harmful in and of themselves, as high prices are presumed to entail a signalling effect to competitors to enter the market and bring the prices down in the long run.[69]

Secondly, excessive pricing cases are asserted to comprise complex and costly endeavours due to the difficulties of finding a proper competitive benchmark.

---

[63] Fehr and Camerer (2007).
[64] Berns et al. (2012).
[65] Krugman (2020).
[66] Wright et al. (2018).
[67] Lianos (2020).
[68] Milton Friedman, We are All Keynesians now, Time Magazine, December 31 1965, http://content.time.com/time/magazine/article/0,9171,842353,00.html, (last access 10 October 2020).
[69] See the oft-quoted passage by Justice Scalia in Verizon Communications, Inc v Law Offices of Curtis v Trinko, LLP 157 L Ed 2d 823, 836 (2004). Trinko did however not concern excessive pricing, and there is ample criticism against the judgement by leading US scholars, see Waller (2006), Fox (2004) and First (2019). On the irrelevance of the excessive quoting of Trinko, see Monti (2019).

Further, the number of cases is asserted to be rather limited, and vigorous enforcement would risk turning competition authorities into de-facto price regulators.[70]

Thirdly, excessive pricing enforcement is asserted to carry the risk of a chilling effect on dynamic sectors with costly and risky sunk costs, and thereby harming innovation and thus consumer welfare in the long run.[71]

These arguments are countered by the interventionist school. Firstly, high prices do not always act as a signalling effect and markets are not self-correcting, even in cases with lower barriers to entry, as it is the post-entry price that would be of interest for potential entrants and not the ex-ante price.[72] Secondly, the number of cases of excessive pricing is not all that limited, and the complexity of the cases and the reluctance of competition authorities to pursue such cases are rather exaggerated, as complex price-cost calculations are also done in predatory pricing and margin squeeze cases.[73] Thirdly, the valid law, legislative intent, and competition policy in regard to the protection of consumers against monopolists compels competition authorities to apply the law as is,[74] and substituting a theoretical long-term potential gain with a short-term manifest illegal conduct is not a workable standard for competition law, especially in cases of "captured" markets and consumer segments due to in-elasticity of demand.[75]

One of the main troubles plaguing the debate on excessive pricing in European Competition Law is the somewhat circular and monolithic references by the antagonists of the enforcement to a certain "common wisdom", "consensus", or "economic theory". This positing of one strand of economics as the only strand, or the most rational, all-encompassing and superior, risks being nothing more than a self-fulfilling prophecy, devoid of empirical content. Indeed, as with any other sciences, economics is comprised of many, in some instances opposing, schools of thought, which also holds true regarding law and economics of competition law.[76]

Furthermore, what would constitute "economic sense" is wholly irrelevant from the perspective of a European legal order,[77] which is not conditioned towards "economic sanity" or "welfare maximizing" attributes of a certain legal code, for the code to be applied in a coherent and uniform fashion. This is also where the main contribution of economic analysis of law is to be found, to complement the legal analysis (as with other social sciences such as psychology), where the elevated matters such as ex ante legal certainty regarding "fair" price levels and what competitive benchmarks would be most suitable are of relevance. Whereas the neoclassical economics find their root in the Utilitarian and Welfarist perspectives,

---

[70] Evans and Padilla (2005).
[71] Fletcher and Jardine (2008).
[72] Ezrachi and Gilo (2009b).
[73] Gilo (2018).
[74] Kirkwood and Lande (2008).
[75] van der Woude (2008).
[76] Ezrachi (2016).
[77] Wils (2014).

focusing on economic efficiency and total welfare, the Keynesian, neo-Keynesian, and the Behavioural schools allow more room for other public policy rationales beyond economic efficiency.[78]

It suffices to state that neoclassical, marginalist, and welfarist law and economics schools do not recognize the position expressed in European Law per Article 102 TFE, nor the settled case law,[79] neither normatively nor empirically. They thus point to what they perceive as normative and empirical fallacies of the legal prohibition, in turn forwarding excessive pricing as being ". . . not only not unlawful, but it is also an important element of the free market system."[80]

2.3 Efficiency v Fairness

Perhaps the most obvious contradiction in neoclassical, marginalist, and welfarist opposition to enforcement against excessive pricing is to be derived internally from the discourse's own positing of excessive prices as the ultimate form of abuse of dominance, creating deadweight loss and in-efficiencies, while at the same time advocating against enforcement on the normative level, no matter if proper competitive benchmarks can be found or not on the empirical level.

As somewhat rhetorically asked by Bruce Lyons, joining Ariel Ezrachi, David Gilo et alia mentioned above:

> If exclusionary abuses are bad because they ultimately exploit consumers, why should the policy emphasis not be on directly exploitative abuses?[81]

As per the legal tradition, it is the object and not only the effect that is of interest, due to the "unfairness" excessive pricing is perceived to entail. The reason for this per se illegality approach is made more clear through behavioural economics research[82] on the subject and insights into bounded rationality as well as context-specific preferences, demonstrating the human bias towards fairness in transactions[83]—we do care

---

[78] Atkinson and Audretsch (2011).

[79] Case 27/76 United Brands Company and United Brands Continentaal BV v Commission of the European Communities, ECLI:EU:C:1978:22; Case Case 26–75, General Motors Continental NV v Commission of the European Communities, Judgment of the Court of 13 November 1975, ECLI:EU:C:1975:150; Case 226/84, British Leyland Public Limited Company v Commission of the European Communities, Judgment of the Court (Fifth Chamber) of 11 November 1986, ECLI:EU:C:1986:421; Case C–177/16 – Biedrība Autortiesību Un Komunicēšanās Konsultāciju Aģentūra – Latvijas Autoru Apvienība Konkurences Padome, ECLI:EU:C:2017:689.

[80] Justice Antonin Scalia in Verizon Communications, Inc v Law Offices of Curtis v Trinko, LLP 157 L Ed 2d 823, 836 (2004).

[81] Lyons (2007).

[82] Sunstein et al. (1998).

[83] Kahneman et al. (1986b).

about fairness, sometimes more than we care about utility and efficiency[84]—thus it would be counter-intuitive to human nature and our legal history to deviate from this point in public policy expressed in laws governing human behaviour, society, and markets.

This contrasts to the marginalist and welfarist view, where at the height of the pandemic, one could note some economists cautioning against price gouging actions, stating, "The choice is between low prices with no availability and nothing to buy, or high prices where the supply is going to be available ... Price gouging laws won't do anything to address the panic buying because if prices stay low, then the toilet paper is going to get bought up by the people who get there first."[85]

The statement is an apt example of the hyper-formalist approach advancing overall economic efficiency as the sole value to be pursued, even during a pandemic, as this would be the most efficient allocation of scarce resources. As counter-intuitive as this would be to the ratio legis of the prohibition of price gouging and profiteering, during a pandemic or beyond, the argument deserves scrutiny.

In order for the argument to survive scrutiny, first, we must entertain the possibility of disproportionate death tolls as a direct result of excessive pricing of essential items, where only the wealthy and able can afford the price and the wait early in line to satisfy their "utility function".

Secondly, this position does not properly account for initial endowments, unfair distribution, nor the manifest possibility of bringing prices down and ensuring efficient and equitable allocation of resources when market forces and dynamics fail. The rich and benevolent are most plausibly able to buy their way through the line as well by paying agents.

Thirdly, the theory does not properly engage with an actual economic assessment of whether a price increase is justified as a function of rising costs, how much markup should be allowed during a pandemic, and how to distinguish between justified high prices, and unfair, excessive prices. This is deemed superfluous, near-impossible, and if possible harmful to a range of market and innovation dynamics. Not because it is intellectually unimaginable to do so, but because the theory rests upon a set of values and a narrow interpretation of the functionality and appropriateness of including such values into the analysis, matters which have been addressed by some Nobel Prize Laureates such as Paul Krugman.[86]

The notion that tasking competition law with anything but economic efficiency, since all other notions would be "political" or "moral" is a moral-political statement in itself, reflecting the consequentialist nature of welfarist school of law and economics, same with the notion that "fairness" is not an "economic concept", as both

---

[84] Konow (2003).

[85] Mark J. Perry in Washington Post, Economists: Federal crackdown on price gouging may do more harm than good, available at: https://www.washingtontimes.com/news/2020/mar/24/coronavirus-related-price-gouging-federal-crackdow/, (last access 25 September 2020).

[86] Paul Krugman, How Did Economists Get It So Wrong?, The New York Times, September 2 2009, https://www.nytimes.com/2009/09/06/magazine/06Economic-t.html, (last access 25 September 2020).

these assertions are rooted in a meta-subjective perspective on what (political) economic theory is or ought to be, and actually ignoring the economic inefficiency of excessive prices, let alone its "fairness" element as a matter of law.

The sheer number of Nobel Prizes in Economics awarded to economists dealing with the concept of "fairness" in one way or other as well as the vast numbers of journal articles and books dealing with "economics" and "fairness" demonstrate that the statements are not given by any natural order of things, as both concepts and reasoning in economics as well as in other areas of science are constantly evolving due to the growing understanding of the human nature and society in general.

The list of Nobel Laureates in Economics who have engaged themselves with the matter of fairness in one way or another can be extended to Richard Thaler (2017), Daniel Kahneman (2002), Amartaya Sen (1998), Robert Solow (1987), and Joseph Stiglitz (2001). To this list, and highly relevant in the context of a public health crisis, we shall add the seminal work by fellow Nobel Laureate in Economics, Kenneth J Arrow (1972), on the inherent deficiencies in the healthcare markets overall and the need for public intervention.

The excessive pricing debate thus exposes some of the most intricate issues in law and economics, price theory, and core assumptions in regard to utility, rational choice, collective preferences, fairness, and so on. The standard price theory does not fulfil its function in markets with in-elastic demand, price-insensitivity, bounded rationality, and inherent human bias towards fairness[87] in transactions as established by recent decades of research in Behavioural[88] and Neuro-economics.[89] The marginal price theory is further at odds with the sector where the marginal cost of production is negligible or close to zero (the case of tech-giants, multi-sided platforms, digital products and so on) and the competition is structured along dynamic, innovation-based discourse and not alongside traditional competition via prices and outputs.

Summing up, regarding the arguments against excessive pricing enforcement relying on crucial assumptions enabling the arguments, as articulated by Nobel Laureate Robert Solow, "All theory depends on assumptions which are not quite true. That is what makes it theory. The art of successful theorizing is to make the inevitable simplifying assumptions in such a way that the final results are not very sensitive. A "crucial" assumption is one on which the conclusions do depend sensitively, and it is important that crucial assumptions be reasonably realistic. When the results of a theory seem to flow specifically from a special crucial assumption, then if the assumption is dubious, the results are suspect."[90]

---

[87] Malc et al. (2016).

[88] Xia et al. (2004).

[89] Mendez (2009).

[90] Solow R (2010) Prepared Statement – Building a Science of Economics for the Real World.

3 A Familiar Giant: Excessive Pricing in European Competition Law & Policy

European Competition Law prohibits imposition of unfair pricing as per Treaty on the Functioning of the European Union, thereby imposing a special responsibility on dominant undertakings not to misuse their position of economic strength to reap trading benefits they otherwise would not. Article 102a TFEU thus states:

> Any abuse by one or more undertakings of a dominant position within the internal market or in a substantial part of it shall be prohibited as incompatible with the internal market in so far as it may affect trade between Member States. Such abuse may, in particular, consist in:
> (a) directly or indirectly imposing unfair purchase or selling prices or other unfair trading conditions

The statute does not define where the boundary between a high, competitive price, and an unfair, excessive price is to be drawn, but this question has been addressed by the jurisprudence of the Commission and the Court of Justice of the European Union. In its seminal United Brands decision,[91] the court created a two-step assessment which today still is the gold standard in regard to the assessment of excessive pricing, although developed and completed through subsequent jurisprudence and economic research. The Court in United Brands held that the alleged excessive nature of a price by a dominant undertaking could be determined "inter alia" based on a two-limb test:

The price must be "excessive", targeting the difference between the cost of production and the selling price of the product (excessive limb); and The price must be "unfair" either (i) in itself or (ii) when compared to competing products (unfairness limb)

Excessive prices per Article 102a TFEU were in this case—which concerned the pricing of Chiquita bananas within the European community—defined as prices having no reasonable relation to the economic value of the product. The excess, in turn, could be determined objectively if it would be possible to calculate it through a comparison between the selling price of the product and its cost of production, which would disclose the "profit margin". Thereafter the question to be determined would consist in answering the question if the disclosed difference between cost and price is "excessive", and whether this excessive price would be "either unfair in itself or when compared with competing products".[92]

Recently the decades-old test in United Brands was updated in the AKKA/LAA case,[93] concerning allegedly excessive rates set by a royalty collecting society in

---

[91] Case 27/76 United Brands Company and United Brands Continentaal BV v Commission of the European Communities, No. Case 27/76, ECLI:EU:C:1978:22.

[92] Judgment of the Court of 14 February 1978 in Case 27/76, United Brands Company and United Brands Continentaal BV v Commission of the European Communities, ECLI:EU:C:1978:22; See paras 250–253 regarding the test for excessive pricing.

[93] Case AKKA/LAA C-177/16 – Biedrība Autortiesību Un Komunicēšanās Konsultāciju Aģentūra – Latvijas Autoru Apvienība Konkurences Padome, EU:C:2017:286.

Latvia. The Latvian court had asked the CJEU to provide guidance on the United Brands test in regard to geographic comparisons of prices charged by similar undertakings in other member states. The court held that the comparator must be "selected in accordance with objective, appropriate and verifiable criteria", and done on a "consistent" basis, leading to an observance of a "significant and persistent" difference is "appreciable", in itself "indicative of an abuse".

Dominance has been defined as, inter alia, possessing more than 40 percent of the relevant market shares. Concerning the dominance issue, the CJEU clarified this matter in its United Brands judgement as being "a position of economic strength enjoyed by an undertaking which enables it to hinder the maintenance of elective competition on the relevant market by allowing it to behave to an appreciable extent independently of its competitors and customers."[94] This definition of dominance was later re-affirmed in the Hoffmann-La Roche case.[95]

The court once again re-iterated the above in the Michelin case with the addition of "… independently of its competitors and customers and ultimately of consumers."[96] The above is of importance when reflecting upon the matters of "temporary dominance" during a pandemic and economic dependence, a matter which was also addressed in the ABG Oil case,[97] where a temporary dominance during times of crisis would, given certain conditions, be sufficient to create liability.

Regarding the dominance criteria in order for the prohibition to be triggered, although the "rule of thumb" points to market shares of 40 percent and above, both the jurisprudence of CJEU as well as the Guidance by the Commission allow for alternative approaches to dominance. This is structured mainly around four themes, these being (a) defining the relevant market narrowly (b) temporary dominance along the lines of ABG Oil case (c) analysis of collective dominance if several undertakings are collectively dominant (d) considering the substantial difference in price relative to competitive level as an indicator of dominance.[98]

As envisaged by the Commission in its Guidance on Enforcement Priorities on Article 102 TFEU, "The Commission considers that an undertaking which is capable of profitably increasing prices above the competitive level for a significant period of

---

[94] Case 27/76 United Brands Company and United Brands Continentaal BV v Commission of the European Communities, No. Case 27/76, ECLI:EU:C:1978:22 (1978), para. 65; See also Case Case 26–75, General Motors Continental NV v Commission of the European Communities, Judgment of the Court of 13 November 1975, ECLI:EU:C:1975:150.

[95] Case 85/76, Hoffmann-La Roche & Co. AG v Commission of the European Communities, Judgment of the Court of 13 February 1979, ECLI:EU:C:1979:36, para. 70.

[96] Case 322/81, NV Nederlandsche Banden Industrie Michelin v Commission of the European Communities, Judgment of the Court of 9 November 1983, ECLI:EU:C:1983:313, para. 6.

[97] 77/327/EEC, Commission Decision of 19 April 1977 relating to a proceeding under Article 86 of the EEC Treaty (IV/28.841 – ABG/Oil companies operating in the Netherlands), OJ L 117, 9.5.1977, pp. 1–16.

[98] Cary et al. (2020).

time does not face sufficiently effective competitive constraints and can thus generally be regarded as dominant."[99]

The Sherman Act does indeed prohibit "unfair competition", without defining it further, in the same vein as the European Competition Law. As noted by Johannes Laitenberger, then director of DG Competition, in 2017, "Fairness" is as old as competition law itself. Standing on the floor of the U.S. Senate in 1890, Senator Sherman explained that his bill was about ensuring "free and fair competition ... Likewise, the Spaak Report of 1956 – when the EU competition rules were first discussed – stressed the importance of 'fair' competition."[100]

Moving on to distinguish "competition law" from "unfair trading" laws as per the German legal tradition, he pointed to the fact that although competition law is primarily more concerned with restriction of competition than inequitable behaviour among competitors, the matter of fairness belongs firmly to the realm of competition law, as well. He stated that, "The term 'fair' appears in Article 101(3) TFEU. The term 'unfair' appears in Article 102 TFEU. The preamble of the TFEU calls for concerted action in order to guarantee 'fair' competition. It is a rationale that underpins the EU competition rules."[101]

Margarethe Vesterager, then European Commissioner for Competition, on her part raised the matter of fairness to become the front and centre of the EU Competition policy, speaking on the matter of digital markets and fairness in 2018, she stated that:

> I don't think that we should be shy to admit that competition policy also reflects an idea of what society should be like. It reflects the idea of a Europe that works fairly for everyone ... So competition policy helps build a fair society. And it's been doing that since the start, sixty years ago ... We don't need a new rule of fairness in our system. Because fair markets are just what competition is about.[102]

She revisited the theme of fairness in yet another speech in 2018, this time at a conference titled "Fairness and Competition", stating, "The Code of Hammurabi sets out to make sure the market works fairly by regulating the prices for things like hiring a ferryboat. Those regulations, of course, could produce mixed results. But today, we have a more refined answer to that question of how to make markets fair – an answer that includes the competition rules."

In regard to the matter of exploitative, unfair, and excessive pricing by dominant undertakings and detailing the latest actions by the Commission in regard to exploitative pricing practices, in a speech in 2016, Vesterager stated that

---

[99] European Commission, Guidance on the Commission's Enforcement Priorities in Applying Article 82 EC Treaty of the EC Treaty to Abusive Exclusionary Conduct by Dominant Undertakings' COM (2008) 832 Final – OJ C 45, 24.2.2009, pp. 7–20 (Brussels, May 12, 2008), para. 11.

[100] Johannes Laitenberger, EU Competition Law in Innovation and Digital Markets: Fairness and the Consumer Welfare Perspective (Brussels, October 10, 2017), https://ec.europa.eu/competition/speeches/text/sp2017_15_en.pdf, (last access 20 April 2020).

[101] Laitenberger (2017).

[102] Vesterager (2018).

... We're still bound to come across cases where competition hasn't been enough to provide a real choice. Where dominant businesses are exploiting their customers, by charging excessive prices or imposing unfair terms ... But we also need to be careful that we don't end up with competition authorities taking the place of the market. The last thing we should be doing is to set ourselves up as a regulator, deciding on the right price. But there can still be times when we need to intervene. We need to act carefully when we deal with excessive prices. The best defence against exploitation remains the ability to walk away. So we can often protect consumers just by stopping powerful companies from driving their rivals out of the market. But we still have the option of acting directly against excessive prices. Because we have a responsibility to the public. And we should be willing to use every means we have to fulfil that responsibility.[103]

Going further back in time, Neelie Kroes, then Member of the European Commission in charge of Competition Policy in 2005, stated, "My own philosophy on this is fairly simple. First, it is competition, and not competitors, that is to be protected. Second, ultimately the aim is to avoid consumer harm. I like aggressive competition – including by dominant companies – and I don't care if it may hurt competitors – as long as it ultimately benefits consumers. That is because the main and ultimate objective of Article 82 is to protect consumers, and this does, of course, require the protection of an undistorted competitive process on the market."[104]

This particular legal-policy focus on fairness towards consumers as being a central tenet of European Competition Law is also self-evident in a range of other Commission statements and documents in regard to fairness and European Competition Law. One such legal-policy expression of the European focus on "excessive pricing" as something inherently evil and harmful to consumers warranting enforcement beyond market dynamics is the work of the Commission on combatting excessive mobile roaming surcharges. A legislative saga that begun in 2007 and ended some ten years later with the abolishing of all roaming charges within the European Union, therefore since 15 June 2017, European consumers have been able to use their mobile devices when travelling in the EU, paying the same prices as they would do at home, the so-called "Roam like at Home" principle.[105]

Others, such as Simon Bishop and Mike Walker, contest the economic sanity of the actions, labelling the cases as "an example of a regulator "knowing an abuse

---

[103] Margarethe Vesterager, Protecting Consumers from Exploitation (Chillin' Competition Conference, Brussels, November 21, 2016), https://ec.europa.eu/commission/commissioners/2014-2019/vestager/announcements/protecting-consumers-exploitation_en, (last access 20 April 2020).

[104] Kroes (2005), Preliminary Thoughts on Policy Review of Art. 82.

[105] European Commission, Roaming charges – What has the European Commission done so far?, https://ec.europa.eu/digital-single-market/en/roaming-charges-what-has-european-commission-done-so-far, (last access 20 April 2020); See also REGULATION (EC) No 717/2007 OF THE EUROPEAN PARLIAMENT AND OF THE COUNCIL of 27 June 2007 on roaming on public mobile telephone networks within the Community and amending Directive 2002/21/EC; and REGULATION (EU) No. 531/2012 OF THE EUROPEAN PARLIAMENT AND OF THE COUNCIL of 13 June 2012 on roaming on public mobile communications networks within the Union, OJ: JOL_2012_172_R_0010_01.

when I see One" even though they were unable to show it analytically (and hence dropped the Article 82 case). It was probably not the Commission's finest hour."[106]

The statement is somewhat surprising, since both investigations were supported by a detailed audit of the cost structure of the undertakings and competitive structure of the market, conducted by an external expert audit company. The affected companies are still in business, profitably so, and both the consumers and the competitive structure are much better off. One could probably argue that this was indeed one of the Commission's finest hours in regard to enforcing European Competition Law with a focus on Consumer Welfare. The Commission investigation and subsequent Commitment Decisions in both Gazprom[107] and Aspen Pharma[108] cases also document some recent Commission approaches in applying the legal content of Article 102a TFEU.

As formulated by Ioannis Lianos, "The normative conundrum that follows is not clarified by positive EU competition law, as the EU courts have embraced different goals and the drafting of the EU Treaties requires that EU competition law provisions should be interpreted in accordance with the rest of the EU Treaties' provisions, hence leading to the emergence a more holistic EU competition law",[109] albeit he also asserts that "the quest for the goals of competition law may prove in the end a meaningless exercise. Indeed, social goals affecting the interpretation and implementation of EU competition law are evolving and are highly dependent on the institutional and political context." It has also been asserted that competition law should not be viewed as rigidly and "purely" as one area of law governed wholly by economic reasoning, thereby ignoring legal concepts and reasonings that might be "alien" to economic thought, so Ezrachi, "the sponge-like characteristics of competition law make it inherently pre-disposed to a wide range of values and considerations. Its true scope and nature are not "pure" nor a "given" of a consistent objective reality, but rather a complex and, at times, inconsistent expression of many values."[110]

As further noted by Reto M Hilty in regard to the normative nature of competition law and justification for intervention in the market dynamics alongside other than economic elements, "It should be added that in a constitutional state ("Rechtsstaat"), committed not only to liberal values, but which also seeks to realise other sociopolitically consolidated values, the stated target values need not only be of an economic nature. The law of market behaviour may, in fact, find its justification also in, for example, social justice, cultural diversity or ecological sustainability."[111] Although much of the law and economics literature on the subject of excessive

---

[106] Bishop and Walker (2010).

[107] CASE AT.39816 – Upstream gas supplies in Central and Eastern Europe (Gazprom) – Final Commitment Decision, 24/05/2018.

[108] Case at.40394 – Aspen – Commitments to the European Commission – 28 January 2021.

[109] Lianos (2013).

[110] Ezrachi (2016).

[111] Hilty (2007).

pricing have elevated the scarcity of cases on the Commission level,[112] there have, in fact, consistently been many excessive pricing cases on the Member State level, with cases on Commission level being rather on pair with margin squeeze and predatory price cases.

The recent decade has noted a surge in excessive pricing cases in Italy, Denmark, the UK in the pharmaceutical sector, and also at the European Commission level, which is pursuing a historically unique excessive pricing case of off-patent pharmaceuticals.[113] Most cases thus were concerning a price hike of several thousand percent to older, off-patent essential medicines, where the competition authorities in different Member States applied different versions of the United Brands test (cost-plus approach, comparison with other markets, comparison with other products etc.). The European Commission investigated pricing practices by a South African pharmaceutical company across the Member States, assessing both cost-price elements but also profits prevailing in the sector and among competitors, leading the undertaking to offer commitments to lower prices by 70 percent across the EU.[114]

This development seems to coincide with a shift in policy towards emphasizing fairness and consumerist protection positions in European Competition Law in general.[115] The resolute commitment by the European Commission to enforce antitrust laws as a matter of statutory duty and not only as an effects-based approach was again voiced by Commissioner Margarethe Vesterager as recent as during the Enforcers Roundtable at the American Bar Association Spring meeting of 2020, delivered online due to the COVID-19 crisis.[116] As will be detailed in the next section, the COVID-19 crisis has also noted many instances of complaints in regard to excessive pricing and price gouging.

---

[112] Motta and de Streel (2007).

[113] European Commission, Press Release Commission Opens Formal Investigation into Aspen Pharma's Pricing Practices for Cancer Medicines – IP/17/1323, May 15, 2017, available at: https://ec.europa.eu/commission/presscorner/detail/en/IP_17_1323 (last access 11 September 2021).

[114] Case at.40394 – Aspen – commitments to the European Commission – 28 January 2021.

[115] European Commission, Impact Assessment for a possible New Competition Tool, available at: https://ec.europa.eu/competition/consultations/2020_new_comp_tool/index_en.html, (last access 01 July 2020); See also UK Competiton and Markets Authority Press-Release, New regime needed to take on tech giants, 1 July 2020, available at https://www.gov.uk/government/news/new-regime-needed-to-take-on-tech-giants, (last access 01 July 2020).

[116] Hazemi-Jebelli (July 7, 2020), p. 5; Margarethe Vesterager speech during ABA Spring meeting 2020 available at: https://www.youtube.com/watch?v=RM8ZGeHPHMI&feature=youtu.be&t=3413 (last access 11 September 2021).

4 The Giant Awakens: Excessive Pricing and Price Gouging During the COVID-19 Crisis

Extraordinary times create extraordinary situations. As noted by Motta, the ability of even small local shops to raise prices during the COVID-19 pandemic increased considerably, "In cases of excess demand, even a small firm may have considerable market power. Under normal demand conditions, if any firm tried to set a high price, its rivals would use their spare capacity to undercut it and sell more. But, if at that high price, each firm's demand is higher than its capacity, there would be no incentive to cut prices. When firms already sell at capacity, by lowering their price they would sell the same amount, but make less profit. In other words, when demand is much higher than capacity, even 'small' firms may be endowed with significant market power, that is, they may be dominant."[117]

The COVID-19 crisis amounting to a public health and economic crisis alike with demands surging for items such as facemasks, hand-sanitizers, funereal services, food items, and so on propelled the matter of price gouging and excessive pricing further to the centre stage. Despite many Competition Authorities at an early stage of pandemic warning against such practices,[118] there are many reports globally of occurrences of such price gouging episodes, with some authorities opening investigations.[119]

During a pandemic, war, or natural disaster, the normal forces of supply and demand might temporarily cease to function as demand surges for certain items and supply chains will be strained, thus resulting in higher prices which in many instances are justified by the higher costs incurred. Nevertheless, such an extraordinary situation invariably opens the possibility to price gouging and excessive pricing of items for which there is a surge in demand, which, according to some views, are a manifestation of economic laws of supply and demand, and thus should not constitute a concern for the legislature. If items are scarce and demanded by many, the "efficient" allocation would be that those who have the highest utility of the item, and thus prioritize to pay most for the item, would also come in possession of the desired items, whether that be COVID-19 treatment, facemasks or toilet paper.

This formalistic view is thus devoid of any "justice and fairness" considerations or otherwise distributional and public health elements and focuses solely on

---

[117] Massimo Motta, Price regulation in times of crisis can be tricky, April 22 2020, https://www.dailymaverick.co.za/opinionista/2020-04-22-price-regulation-in-times-of-crisis-can-be-tricky/ (last access 20 September 2020).

[118] UK Competition and Market Authority, CMA approach to business cooperation in response to coronavirus (COVID-19), https://www.gov.uk/government/publications/cma-approach-to-business-cooperation-in-response-to-covid-19, (last access 20 September 2020); European Competition Network (ECN), Antitrust: Joint statement by the European Competition Network (ECN) on application of competition law during the Corona crisis, 23 March 2020, https://ec.europa.eu/competition/ecn/202003_joint-statement_ecn_corona-crisis.pdf (last access 11 September 2021).

[119] Some part of this section on excessive pricing in European Union during COVID-19 has previously been published in Kianzad (2021).

"efficient allocation". Therefore, along with Utilitarian perspectives, Pareto Optimality,[120] and the Hands-Off approach, the formalistic view defers to market dynamics and the questions of distribution and access. The matter of initial endowments, which invariably affect the possibility of utility satisfaction of individuals, is deemed irrelevant in the strict positive economic analysis of law. Most jurisdictions nevertheless prohibit price gouging and "unfair" profiteering, especially during extraordinary circumstances, as a matter of public policy grounded on collective notions. This can indeed be seen as a manifestation of collective preferences[121] in regard to "justice and fairness", where there is an expectation that the public authority would act as unbiased arbiter and allocator during such an extraordinary situation. This can be compared to the hypothesis that if an economist is subject to a robbery, the robbery is castigated in a legal discipline not because it is deemed economically in-efficient, but because it is contrary to public morale and legality.

During a crisis or pandemic such as COVID-19, the surging demand and shortage of supply are capable of creating temporary but powerful dominance situations, also for undertakings that do not possess sizeable market power, but through the market deficiencies resultant from the pandemic are enabled to exercise market power vastly exceeding their actual market share. The risk of excessive pricing behaviour thus increases relative to the indispensable character of the products, the surge in demand, and the barriers to entry. At the same time, the legal requirement of a "dominant position" if defined as narrowly as market shares in percentages of the total relevant market might not be sufficient to properly take stock of the dynamics of excessive pricing during a pandemic, where temporary dominance can be levied albeit lacking legally established market shares.

In many instances, such temporary dominance and surge in prices will subside as a multitude of competitors enter the market, efficiently bringing the prices down to competitive levels. However, the increase in price during the dominance period still might constitute an undue wealth transfer in and of itself, and thereby an anti-competitive practice, if not properly explained by increases in production and distribution costs. As will be shown, some competition authorities opened investigations in regard to complaints received regarding sharp price hikes, but ultimately closed the investigations as prices had decreased to competitive pre-pandemic prices. From an economic point of view, this dynamic might be satisfactory and pointing to the self-correcting nature of excessive pricing. On the other hand, many emergency laws, as well as price gouging laws, define a pre-crisis benchmark regarding prices,

---

[120] Encyclopaedia Britannica defines Pareto Optimality as A state of affairs is Pareto-optimal (or Pareto-efficient) if and only if there is no alternative state that would make some people better off without making anyone worse off. More precisely, a state of affairs x is said to be Pareto-inefficient (or suboptimal) if and only if there is some state of affairs y such that no one strictly prefers x to y and at least one person strictly prefers y to x. The concept of Pareto-optimality thus assumes that anyone would prefer an option that is cheaper, more efficient, or more reliable or that otherwise comparatively improves one's condition., available at https://www.britannica.com/topic/Pareto-optimality; (last access 20 April 2020).

[121] Gilbert (2001).

allowing for some cost-based defences, thereby creating a benchmark many times lacking in a normal setting.

Nevertheless, from a legal standpoint, granting a carte-blanche to an abuse, simply owning to the fact that the abuse has ceased during the investigation, is not always satisfactory, although it might be argued that pursuing the case would be more costly and ultimately meritless since the abuse has ceased. Those final consumers who had been subjugated to the price hike might indeed not find justice being served in their case, thereby diminishing public confidence in the protective shield competition law professes to confer.

The OECD-note on exploitative pricing practices during the COVID-19 pandemic assumes a rather cautious position, albeit elevating some merits to excessive pricing enforcement, stating:

> Bringing excessive pricing cases in a crisis also comes with risks. Intervention against price increases can lead to products being diverted to places where prices are not regulated, and hence allowed to increase. Further, prices act as signals, and seeking to limit price increases can reduce incentives to increase production, thereby delaying market entry or production increases that would lower prices faster in the medium-term. Other risks include the consumption of agency resources to prepare very demanding excessive pricing investigations; and the possibility that bringing excessive pricing cases during a short-term crisis runs the risk of being untimely, given the time it may take to successfully bring such cases ... At the same time, bringing excessive pricing cases may well be justified, and the best available alternative to address the challenges caused by significant price increases of essential goods during a crisis. It has even been suggested that there may be a role for competition authorities to act as temporary price regulators in circumstances that allow for price gouging.[122]

There are further many and forceful objections to what would constitute a competitive price and profit margin, how this should be monitored, what effects on innovation and investments such a "cap" on profits would entail, if any, and so on. The value of a product, when not determined alongside the cost-plus approach, would, in turn, be given by what it would fetch in an open market.

However, this does not disclose the actual economic value of the product, which might be inflated, as a result of "capture" of a consumer segment by the dominant undertaking or the monopolist and/or as a result of competition deficiencies in the market, either via exploitative or exclusionary practices.

As noted by the OECD-note on excessive pricing during the COVID-19 crisis:

> Even as competition authorities feel public or political pressure to bring such cases, it is possible that the likelihood of success of such cases, and the deterrent effect of bringing them, is low. It is also important to bear in mind that intervention against high prices can reduce incentives to increase production and delay the achievement of a lower price equilibrium. Furthermore, intervention against high prices can lead to products being diverted to and ending-up in places where prices are not subject to constraints, leading to local consumers being worse off.[123]

---

[122] OECD, Exploitative Pricing in the Time of COVID, 2020, 15, available at: http://www.oecd.org/competition/Exploitative-pricing-in-the-time-of-COVID-19.pdf, (last access 01 October 2020).

[123] OECD, Exploitative Pricing in the Time of COVID, 2020, 15, available at: http://www.oecd.org/competition/Exploitative-pricing-in-the-time-of-COVID-19.pdf, (last access 01 October 2020).

The gist of the arguments above target uncertain outcomes, asserted (many times rather exaggerated) risk of errors, and a subtle value trade-off alongside mainly welfarist economic discourse. It also risks conflating competition law enforcement with other parallel price regulating actions, which serve different objectives, as the prohibition against excessive pricing is a legal matter regarding the unfairness in undue wealth transfer, and abuse of a dominant, albeit temporary, position.

As the South African cases demonstrate in this section, investigations can indeed take place during a short period of time (May–July) and be construed alongside sound legal-economic benchmarks comprised of prices prior to the crisis, taking into account justified defences in regard to increasing production and distribution costs.

As further stated by the OECD-note, "One option that could preclude the need to start formal proceedings consists of competition authorities making it clear that they are closely monitoring the market and ready to intervene promptly ... Another option is to bring interim measures. Such measures are appropriate in cases of urgency where there is a risk that competition will be seriously damaged ... A third alternative is to take into account the role that other regulatory tools, and regulators, can play in addressing exploitative pricing practices – e.g. consumer protection, public tender rules or price gouging laws."[124]

This overt cautious approach risks creating a false duopoly between, on the one hand enforcing the law "as is", and issuing warnings, interim measures, engaging in price monitoring activities, etc. on the other hand. As seen in this section in the cases of both the UK and South Africa, the authorities have been able to avail themselves of both sets of tools. If competition authorities would balk at availing themselves of the most important tool at their disposal, having centuries-old roots and a solid legal-economic framework (non-welfarist, that is), this would naturally erode the confidence of the public in the competition law, especially during a pandemic where abuses might be rather manifest and wide-ranging.

The lack of competence is raised next in the OECD-note, stating, "In most cases, the decision of whether to bring excessive pricing cases hinges not only on the legal framework, but also on the institutional capacity of regulators. Thus, an important preliminary question is whether competition authorities or other regulatory authorities have the most appropriate combination of tools and expertise to address excessive prices."[125]

This argument, albeit certainly of merit in some instances regarding very young competition authorities, is perhaps one of the frailest arguments of the antagonists of excessive pricing enforcement, as such arguments in regard to "institutional capacities" are not raised as fervently and frequently in regard to other rather complex areas of competition law and economics, such as mergers, predatory pricing, margin

---

[124] OECD, Exploitative Pricing in the Time of COVID, 2020, 15, available at: http://www.oecd.org/competition/Exploitative-pricing-in-the-time-of-COVID-19.pdf, (last access 01 October 2020).

[125] OECD, Exploitative Pricing in the Time of COVID, 2020, 15, available at: http://www.oecd.org/competition/Exploitative-pricing-in-the-time-of-COVID-19.pdf, (last access 01 October 2020).

squeeze etc. It might be of merit to ponder over why the regulation of excessive profits suddenly raises such objections.

Nevertheless, the OECD-note correctly elevates the importance of other areas of law which can be utilized to deal with excessive pricing. "It is true that neither consumer protection nor price gouging require the detailed effects analysis that competition law relies on to ensure that intervention leads to increased consumer welfare. This also means that enforcing these rules is less burdensome on agencies and can be achieved in a more timely manner. Further, consumer protection and price gouging rules do not apply only to dominant firms, since this is not the focus of their concerns."[126]

Below, some instances of law and policy in regard to excessive pricing and price gouging cases from the US, European Union, and the UK are depicted in order to demonstrate the similarities and differences in the global approaches.

4.1 United States

As excessive pricing in and out of itself does not constitute a Federal antitrust liability, or so goes the dominant US interpretation by the Federal Trade Commission and Department of Justice (with others contesting this interpretation),[127] price gouging was the focal point for US policy.

As many states already had price gouging statutes in place,[128] most complaints were voiced to State AGs. State laws prohibit price gouging along the lines of the sale of an "essential commodity" at an "unconscionable" price, some requiring a "triggering event", such as war, pandemic, natural disaster etc., while others do not raise such requirements, some (like California, District of Colombia, and New Jersey)[129] capping the price increase at 10 percent during a pandemic or an emergency. Some states opted to introduce emergency legislation and executive orders, such as the case of Michigan introducing enhanced restrictions on price gouging.[130]

---

[126] OECD, Exploitative Pricing in the Time of COVID, 2020, 15, available at: http://www.oecd.org/competition/Exploitative-pricing-in-the-time-of-COVID-19.pdf, (last access 01 October 2020).

[127] First (2019), Waller (2006), Woodcock (2018) and Fox (2004).

[128] The Food Industry Association, FMI, State Price Gouging Laws, https://www.fmi.org/docs/default-source/gr-state/price-gouging-state-law-chart.pdf?sfvrsn=9058b75c_2, (last access 20 September 2020).

[129] NBC News, States push price-gouging measures as coronavirus fuels consumer fears, March 20 2020, https://www.nbcnews.com/politics/politics-news/states-push-price-gouging-measures-coronavirus-fuels-consumer-fears-n1163846, (last access 20 September 2020).

[130] State of Michigan, Office of the Governor, EXECUTIVE ORDER No. 2020-8, Enhanced restrictions on price gouging, available at: https://content.govdelivery.com/attachments/MIEOG/2020/03/15/file_attachments/1401335/EO%202020_8%20Emergency%20Order%20.pdf, (last access 20 September 2020).

In a letter to all United States Attorneys as well as heads of departments and law enforcement agencies, Attorney General Barr voiced concerns about the possibility of price gouging and the need to be vigilant. "We will not tolerate bad actors who treat the crisis as an opportunity to get rich quick. We are beginning to receive reports of individuals using the crisis to hoard vital medical items and then make inappropriate, windfall profits at the expense of public safety and the health and welfare of our fellow citizens. Hoarding and price gouging activities inhibit the government, health care professionals, and the public from implementing critical measures to save lives and mitigate the spread of the virus."[131] The Department of Justice's National Center for Disaster Fraud (NCDF) complaint website offered the possibility to bring instances of price gouging and hoarding to the attention of the authorities.[132]

The Secretary of Health and Human Services issued a notice designating some essential items as exempt from hoarding or being sold at exorbitant prices, including Personal protective equipment (PPE), such as masks, shields and gloves, respirators, ventilators, drug products with the active ingredient chloroquine phosphate or hydroxychloroquine, sterilization services, disinfecting devices, and medical gowns or apparel.[133]

These actions relied on the Presidential Executive Order in regard to price gouging and hoarding, which was issued by President Donald J. Trump on 26 March 2020.[134] Thus making hoarding or price gouging of some designated essentials a misdemeanour, punishable by up to one year in prison and a fine of up to USD 10,000.[135] The Department of Justice (DOJ) further announced its commitment to pursue fraudulent activity and price gouging of items such as personal protective equipment (PPE) and ventilators.[136]

---

[131] Office of the Attorney General, MEMORANDUM FOR ALL HEADS OF DEPARTMENT COMPONENTS AND LAW ENFORCEMENT AGENCIES ALL UNITED STATES ATTORNEYS, March 24, https://www.justice.gov/file/1262776/download, (last access 20 September 2020).

[132] Department of Justice's National Center for Disaster Fraud (NCDF) complaint website, https://www.justice.gov/disaster-fraud/ncdf-disaster-complaint-form, (last access 20 September 2020).

[133] Department of Health and Human Services, Notice of Designation of Scarce Materials or Threatened Materials, Subject to COVID-19 Hoarding Prevention Measures Under Executive Order 13910 and Section 102 of the Defense Production Act of 1950, https://www.justice.gov/file/1264276/download, (last access 20 September 2020).

[134] Executive Order 13910 of March 23, 2020, Preventing Hoarding of Health and Medical Resources To Respond to the Spread of COVID-19, https://www.federalregister.gov/documents/2020/03/26/2020-06478/preventing-hoarding-of-health-and-medical-resources-to-respond-to-the-spread-of-covid-19, (last access 20 September 2020).

[135] OECD, 2020, Box 5; 50 U.S.C. §4513.

[136] OECD, 2020, Box 5; https://www.justice.gov/opa/pr/justice-department-cautions-business-community-against-violating-antitrust-laws-manufacturing, (last access 20 September 2020).

Indeed, there were many thousand instances[137] of both hoarding and price gouging reported to the authorities already in March 2020, regarding both online and retail trade, where Amazon on its part issued a statement in regard to removing 500,000 items off its marketplace and banning 3900 sellers for price-gouging.[138]

Nevertheless, as per a recent report by Public Citizen, numerous examples of price increases were found on the e-commerce platform regarding essential products, some as much as 1000 percent over the expected price, as Amazon publicly blamed so-called third-party sellers for price increases while continuing to allow third-party sellers to increase their prices.[139] In New York, a retailer accused of hoarding and price gouging of essential protective equipment like masks and hand-sanitizers settled a price-gouging case by donating more than $450,000 worth of personal protective equipment.[140] There are many reports of fines being awarded to some of those found liable for breaching State price gouging laws, such as in the case of New Jersey.[141]

As there now exists a Federal route by way of the Executive Order, one might foresee cases being pursued at the Federal level as well, depending on the willingness of the agencies to pursue such cases.

4.2 United Kingdom

The UK CMA belong to one of the most active authorities during the pandemic, using both "soft" instruments such as direct calls on certain sectors not to raise prices, combined with setting up a mechanism for complaints in regard to perceived excessive pricing and price gouging, and ultimately availing itself of investigative powers.

At the beginning of the pandemic, the UK CMA, as part of the European Competition Network, issued a joint declaration, where the principal commitment

---

[137] Politico, State AGs join DOJ, FTC, Congress to fight price-gouging, March 26 2020, https://www.politico.com/newsletters/morning-tech/2020/03/26/state-ags-join-doj-ftc-congress-to-fight-price-gouging-786404, (last access 20 September 2020).

[138] Amazon, Price gouging has no place in our stores, March 23 2020, https://blog.aboutamazon.com/company-news/price-gouging-has-no-place-in-our-stores, (last access 20 September 2020).

[139] Alex Harman/Public Citizen, Prime Gouging – How Amazon Raised Prices to Profit from the Pandemic, September 9 2020, https://www.citizen.org/article/prime-gouging/, (last access 20 September 2020).

[140] Pix11.com, LI retailer to donate $450,000 worth of PPE to settle price gouging case: officials, September 26 2020, (last access 30 September 2020).

[141] South Jersey Times, N.J. businesses fined for price gouging during coronavirus pandemic and lying about antibody tests, Sep 22, 2020, https://www.nj.com/coronavirus/2020/09/nj-businesses-fined-for-price-gouging-during-coronavirus-pandemic-and-lying-about-antibody-tests.html, (last access 25 September 2020).

to pursuing excessive pricing and price gouging cases was re-affirmed.[142] In June and July 2020 the CMA again cautioned against price gouging in certain sectors.[143]

In March 2020, the CMA established a dedicated COVID-19 taskforce to identify, monitor, and respond to competition and consumer problems arising from COVID-19 and the measures taken to contain it. On 21 May 2020, the CMA published a report[144] which contains an analysis of complaints received by the Covid-19 taskforce. According to the report, as of 17 May 2020, the CMA had received over 9000 complaints relating to potential excessive prices with reference to COVID-19. Taken together, these businesses account for over 3100 complaints, amounting to a third of the total number of actionable complaints received about price rises.

On 3 July 2020, the CMA published a further report,[145] showing that the number of price-related complaints had decreased from 76 per day in April to 11 per day in June. As per the report, the CMA had investigated complaints of unjustifiable price rises, and taken a number of steps to prevent and address such practices. These include writing to 277 traders that have collectively been the subject of over 4600 complaints—over 40 percent of the total number of actionable complaints received about price rises; which led to opening investigations into suspected breaches of competition law by four pharmacies and convenience stores.

The investigations related to suspected charging of excessive and unfair prices for hand sanitizer were tackled by working with trade associations, regulators, and other bodies to clarify expectations and warn about the potential consequences of charging unjustifiably high prices. Most recently, the CMA has published a joint letter with the General Pharmaceutical Council; and it has issued a joint statement with trade associations in the retail, wholesale, and pharmacy sectors.

As detailed per the report:

---

[142] UK Competition and Market Authority, CMA approach to business cooperation in response to coronavirus (COVID-19), https://www.gov.uk/government/publications/cma-approach-to-business-cooperation-in-response-to-covid-19, (last access 20 September 2020); European Competition Network (ECN), Antitrust: Joint statement by the European Competition Network (ECN) on application of competition law during the Corona crisis, 23 March 2020.

[143] UK Competition and Market Authority, CMA and trade bodies' joint statement against price gouging, 3 July 2020, https://www.gov.uk/government/publications/cma-and-trade-bodies-joint-statement-against-price-gouging, (last access 20 September 2020); UK Competition and Market Authority, "Joint letter from the CMA and the General Pharmaceutical Council: pricing during the COVID-19 pandemic", 29 June 2020, https://www.gov.uk/government/publications/joint-letter-from-the-cma-and-the-general-pharmaceutical-council-pricing-during-the-covid-19-pandemic, (last access 20 September 2020).

[144] UK CMA, Protecting consumers during the coronavirus (COVID-19) pandemic: update on the work of the CMA's Taskforce, Published 21 May 2020, https://www.gov.uk/government/publications/cma-coronavirus-taskforce-update-21-may-2020/protecting-consumers-during-the-coronavirus-covid-19-pandemic-update-on-the-work-of-the-cmas-taskforce#fn:9, (last access 20 September 2020).

[145] UK CMA, Update on the work of the CMA's Taskforce, Published 3 July 2020, https://www.gov.uk/government/publications/cma-coronavirus-taskforce-update-3-july-2020/update-on-the-work-of-the-cmas-taskforce, (last access 20 September 2020).

Between 20 March and 28 June, the proportion of complaints relating to food and drink vs hygiene and personal care has flipped, with the former going from around 70% to 25% and the latter doing the opposite. The medication category has grown somewhat over time, from around 4% in March to a little over 10% in June. Overall, the most complained about product is hand sanitiser, followed by toilet paper, chicken, rice and other meats.[146]

On 18 June 2020, the CMA launched four investigations into suspected charging of excessive and unfair prices for hand sanitiser products.[147] However, three of the investigations were closed in July, where the CMA explained its decision in two cases as follows:

Having carefully reviewed the evidence that it has gathered, the CMA considers that it is unlikely that the retailers' prices infringe competition law and that further investigation to reach a definitive view in these two cases would deliver limited, if any, consumer benefits. The decision to close the two cases does not amount to a definitive statement or finding as to whether the respective parties to the investigations have infringed competition law, nor should any inference be made to that effect.[148]

One case was closed due to the CMA not considering the price cited to be excessive under competition law. Finally, on 3 September 2020, the CMA closed the last investigation citing the same reason, however as in the case of the previous decision adding, "The decision to close the case does not amount to a definitive statement or finding as to whether the party to the investigation has infringed competition law, nor should any inference be made to that effect. The CMA's decision to close this case does not prevent the CMA from opening an investigation in the future if it were to receive new evidence which changed the assessment."[149] The CMA is, however, pursuing multiple excessive pricing cases within the pharmaceutical sector, unrelated to the COVID-19 pandemic.[150]

---

[146] UK CMA, Update on the work of the CMA's Taskforce, Published 3 July 2020, https://www.gov.uk/government/publications/cma-coronavirus-taskforce-update-3-july-2020/update-on-the-work-of-the-cmas-taskforce, (last access 20 September 2020), Section 3, Complaint Analysis.

[147] UK CMA, Hand sanitiser products: suspected excessive and unfair pricing, 19 June 2020, https://www.gov.uk/cma-cases/hand-sanitiser-products-suspected-excessive-and-unfair-pricing, (last access 20 September 2020).

[148] UK CMA, Statement regarding the CMA's decision to close certain investigations into suspected charging of excessive and unfair prices for hand sanitiser products during the coronavirus (COVID-19) pandemic, Case reference: Case 50924, Case closed: 13 July 2020, https://assets.publishing.service.gov.uk/media/5f0c5a7d3a6f40037ed4848c/Closure_Statement_.pdf, (last access 20 September 2020).

[149] UK CMA, 1 Statement regarding the CMA's decision to close aninvestigation into suspected charging of excessive and unfair prices for hand sanitiser products during the coronavirus (COVID-19) pandemic, Case reference: Case 50924, Case closed: 3 September 2020, https://assets.publishing.service.gov.uk/media/5f50df3f8fa8f535b650435c/3_September_2020_case_closure_statement.pdf, (last access 20 September 2020).

[150] UK CMA, Phenytoin sodium capsules: suspected unfair pricing, https://www.gov.uk/cma-cases/investigation-into-the-supply-of-pharmaceutical-products, (last access 20 September 2020); UK CMA, Hydrocortisone tablets: alleged excessive and unfair pricing (50277-1), https://www.gov.uk/cma-cases/pharmaceutical-sector-anti-competitive-practices, (last access 20 September 2020);

4.3 European Union

Competition Authorities around the EU (such as Greece,[151] France,[152] Luxembourg,[153] Portugal,[154] Spain,[155] and the UK[156]) at an early stage of the pandemic through public announcements made their intention know that they would closely monitor pricing behaviour regarding the supply of some essential goods in high demand due to COVID-19.[157]

This was part of a joint effort by the European Competition Network (ECN), which issued a joint statement in regard to the applicability of competition rules during the pandemic, noting:

> At the same time, it is of utmost importance to ensure that products considered essential to protect the health of consumers in the current situation (e.g. face masks and sanitising gel) remain available at competitive prices. The ECN will therefore not hesitate to take action against companies taking advantage of the current situation by cartelising or abusing their dominant position.[158]

Some of the Member States opted to introduce some price regulations, beyond issuing warnings at the onset of the crisis. This was the case in France, where the price of hydro-alcoholic sanitisers was regulated—50 ml bottles are priced at EUR

UK CMA, Liothyronine tablets: suspected excessive and unfair pricing, https://www.gov.uk/cma-cases/pharmaceutical-sector-anti-competitive-conduct, (last access 20 September 2020).

[151] Hellenic Competition Authority, https://www.epant.gr/enimerosi/deltia-typou/item/831-deltio-typou-antiantagonistikes-praktikes-se-eidikes-koinonikes-kai-oikonomikes-synthikes.html, (last access 20 September 2020).

[152] French Competition Authority, https://www.lefigaro.fr/flash-eco/coronavirus-l-autorite-de-la-concurrence-surveille-les-eventuels-prix-abusifs-20200316, (last access 20 September 2020).

[153] Luxemburg Competition Authority, https://concurrence.public.lu/fr/actualites/2020/coronavirus-responsabilite-entreprises.html, (last access 20 September 2020).

[154] Portuguese Competition Authority, http://www.concorrencia.pt/vEN/News_Events/Comunicados/Pages/PressRelease_202003.aspx, (last access 20 September 2020).

[155] Spanish Competition Authority, https://www.cnmc.es/sites/default/files/editor_contenidos/Notas%20de%20prensa/2020/20200312_NP_medidas_excepcionales_eng.pdf, (last access 20 September 2020).

[156] UK Competition and Market Authority, CMA approach to business cooperation in response to coronavirus (COVID-19), https://www.gov.uk/government/publications/cma-approach-to-business-cooperation-in-response-to-covid-19, (last access 20 September 2020).

[157] Christopher Thomas, Raphael Fleischer, Christian Ritz & Stefan Kirwitzke (Hogan Lovells), COVID-19 and Competition Law – Companies Must Not Quarantine Competition Law Compliance, April 2, 2020, Competition Policy International, https://www.competitionpolicyinternational.com/covid-19-and-competition-law-companies-must-not-quarantine-competition-law-compliance/, (last access 20 September 2020).

[158] European Competition Network, "Antitrust: Joint statement by the European Competition Network (ECN) on application of competition law during the Corona crisis".

2, 100 ml bottles are priced at EUR 3, 300 ml bottles are priced at EUR 5, and a litre of sanitiser costs EUR 15. It also fixed the price of surgical masks at EUR 0.95.[159]

This was the case also in Romania, where the Romanian competition authority announced that, should actions under its competences prove insufficient to limit price increases to acceptable levels, additional measures foreseen in a statute—including introducing price caps—might be necessary.[160] Other countries such as Malta also introduced such pricing regulations, as, during the peak of the crisis, there were complaints regarding the prices of masks, particularly disposable masks, which from inspections carried out in retail pharmacies by Officers from the Consumer Affairs Office were being sold in the range of €1.25 to €2.25. A price order was issued establishing the maximum price at which these masks could be sold.[161] Similar measures were introduced in Croatia.

In Italy, facing numerous complaints in regard to price gouging, the Italian Competition Authority (ICA) commenced investigations into the pricing of a private health and laboratory group for serological tests to identify COVID-19 antibodies.[162] The ICA also initiated proceedings against eBay and Amazon for misleading claims and price increases in the sale of masks, hand sanitisers, and other pharmaceutical products.[163] There is further a range of investigations ongoing at ICA.

In Spain, the CNMC, as of 2 June 2020, had received more than 500 complaints during the two months the mailbox for complaints was set up, which led them to further announce investigations into certain sectors such as funeral services, hydro-alcoholic gels, and financial lending.[164]

In Greece, the Hellenic Competition Council (HCC) launched an inquiry into possible price increases and output restrictions of healthcare materials and other products by way of requests for information to a large number of companies active in the production, import, and marketing of healthcare products, in particular surgical masks and disposable gloves, as well as other products such as antiseptic wipes and

---

[159] OECD, Exploitative Pricing in the Time of COVID, 2020, 15, available at: http://www.oecd.org/competition/Exploitative-pricing-in-the-time-of-COVID-19.pdf, (last access 01 October 2020), Box 6.

[160] OECD, Exploitative Pricing in the Time of COVID, 2020, 15, available at: http://www.oecd.org/competition/Exploitative-pricing-in-the-time-of-COVID-19.pdf, (last access 01 October 2020), Box 6; Romanian National News Agency, https://www.agerpres.ro/economic-intern/2020/03/25/chritoiu-daca-produsele-sanitare-nu-se-ieftinesc-vom-lua-masuri-de-urgenta-precum-rechizitionarea-sau-plafonarea-preturilor%2D%2D473985 (last access 11 September 2021).

[161] Times of Malta, Price of disposable masks, face shields, capped, May 3 2020, https://timesofmalta.com/articles/view/price-of-disposable-masks-face-shields-capped.789815, (last access 20 September 2020).

[162] OECD, 2020, Box 3; https://www.agcm.it/media/comunicati-stampa/2020/4/DC9877, (last access 20 September 2020).

[163] OECD, 2020, Box 5: https://www.agcm.it/media/comunicati-stampa/2020/3/PS11716-PS11717, (last access 20 September 2020).

[164] Spanish Market and Competition Authority, CNMC, https://www.cnmc.es/novedades/2020-06-02-la-cnmc-recibe-mas-de-500-quejas-y-consultas-traves-del-buzon-habilitado, (last access 20 September 2020).

antiseptic solutions.[165] The HCC employed an algorithmic approach in regard to the analysis of the data, finding some prices as outliers. The HCC made its intention known to further investigate any anti-competitive practices by imposing severe fines in case of any infringements of competition law, stating, "The development of algorithms that enable the automated analysis of Big Data derived from publicly available procurement databases is a primary goal and priority for HCC."[166]

Similarly, in Sweden, the Swedish Competition Agency (SCA), upon receiving news of price hikes, although no formal complaints, sent requests to a range of providers. The news concerned a spike of 900 percent[167] in the pricing of filtering half masks, protective suits, certain protective goggles and visors, as well as surface- and hand-sanitizers by one of the Government's major suppliers who cited force majeure as a reason for the price increase within the framework agreement. Both the Governmental Purchasing Center, which coordinates the government framework agreements, and the SKL Kommentus Purchasing Center, which coordinates Sweden's municipalities and regions, had approved the price increase.

The SCA conducted a study throughout the spring of 2020 regarding the pricing of hand sanitization products due to media reports of significantly raised prices within a central framework agreement. The preliminary findings of the study showed an initial spike in demand, in combination with increased production costs, resulting in a significant but temporary rise in prices. Production of hand sanitization products increased throughout most of the month of April, after which the curve had flattened. Prices thus returned to a normal level within the framework agreement in May, and there were no indications of continued concerns regarding excessive pricing of such products either within the framework agreement or in a more general sense.[168]

4.4 South Africa

South Africa belongs to one of the jurisdictions where some excessive pricing and price gouging cases were swiftly brought and adjudicated by the authorities, ending

---

[165] OECD 2020, Box 3; Hellenic Competition Council, Investigation in healthcare materials, Press Release, March 21 2020, https://epant.gr/en/enimerosi/press-releases/item/840-press-release-investigation-in-healthcare-materials.html, (last access 20 September 2020).

[166] Hellenic Competition Council, The interim results of HCC's investigations on health and hospital equipment during covid-19 pandemic, Press Release, September 11 2020, https://www.epant.gr/en/enimerosi/press-releases/item/1083-press-release-the-interim-results-of-hcc-s-investigations-on-health-and-hospital-equipment-during-covid-19-pandemic.html, (last access 20 September 2020).

[167] Dagens Nyheter, Increases the price of vital products by over 900 percent, April 3 2020, https://www.dn.se/nyheter/sverige/hojer-priset-pa-livsviktiga-produkter-med-914-procent/, (last access 20 September 2020).

[168] Swedish Competition Agency, Communication to Author on file, dated 2020-06-18.

in fines, settlements, and commitments.[169] The cases brought by the Competition Commission relied on the state of emergency declared on 15 March 2020, and the subsequent Consumer Protection Regulations issued by the Government in regard to the pandemic,[170] as well as existing competition rules on excessive pricing.[171]

In the two weeks following the declaration of the State of National Disaster, the Competition Commission received 559 complaints whereof 250 related to other matters, and the Commission opted for an expedited process, with companies given 48 h to respond to allegations.[172] The Minister for Trade and Industry on 3 April 2020 further laid down procedural rules regarding the Competition Tribunal, allowing 72 h for the respondent to file its response, including factual or expert testimony to be incorporated in the same time frame, with the Tribunal to hear the matter within 48 h from the close of pleadings.

As part of the issued consumer protection regulations, excessive pricing as per the Competition Act as well as "unconscionable, unfair, unreasonable, unjust or improper commercial practices"[173] as per the Consumer Protection Act were prohibited. As per Regulation 4, dominant firms are regulated regarding excessive pricing, stating that during any period of the national disaster, a material price increase of certain good or service which (a) does not correspond to or is not equivalent to the increase in the cost of providing that good or service; or (b) increases the net margin or mark-up on that good or service above the average margin or mark-up for that good or service in the three-month period prior to 1 March 2020, is a relevant and critical factor for determining whether the price is excessive or unfair and indicates prima facie that the price is excessive or unfair.[174]

The consumer protection regulations also proffer a definition of "price increase" meaning "a direct increase or an increase as a result of unfair conduct such as, amongst others, false or misleading pricing practices, covert manipulation of prices, manipulation through raising or reducing grade levels of goods and services."[175]

---

[169] The Centre for Competition Law and Economics (CCLE), Excessive Pricing COVID-19, https://ccle.sun.ac.za/excessive-pricing-covid-19/, (last access 01 October 2020).

[170] South Africa Disaster Management Regulation of March 18 2020, published in Government Notice 318 of Government Gazette no 43107, where para. 10(6) authorized the minister of Trade and Industry to, inter alia, issue directions to protect consumers from excessive, unfair, unreasonable or unjust pricing of goods and services during the the state of national emergency; The subsequent Consumer Protection Regulations issued by the Minister of Trade and Industry were published on March 19 2020, The Consumer and Customer Protection and National Disaster Management Regulations and Directions GN R350 GG 43116, 19 March 2020 (consumer protection regulations).

[171] South African Competition Act No. 89 of 1998, section 8(1)(a).

[172] Ratshisusu and Mncube (2020).

[173] Consumer protection regulations at 3.1.

[174] Consumer protection regulations at 4.

[175] Consumer protection regulations at 1.5.

Regarding the excessive pricing prohibition in the Competition Act, Sections 8(1)(a), 8(2), and 8(3) of the amended Act[176] prohibit a dominant firm from charging an excessive price to the detriment of consumers or customers, where if there is a prima facie case of abuse of dominance because the dominant firm charged an excessive price, the dominant firm must show that the price was reasonable.

Furthermore, any person determining whether a price is an excessive price must determine if that price is higher than a competitive price and whether such difference is unreasonable, determined by taking into account all relevant factors, which may include:

(a) the respondent's price cost margin, internal rate of return, return on capital invested or profit history;
(b) the respondent's prices for the goods or services—(i) in markets in which there are competing products; (ii) to customers in other geographic markets; (iii) for similar products in other markets; and (iv) historically;
(c) relevant comparator firm's prices and level of profits for the goods or services in a competitive market for those goods or services;
(d) the length of time the prices have been charged at that level;
(e) the structural characteristics of the relevant market, including the extent of the respondent's market share, the degree of contestability of the market, barriers to entry and past or current advantage that is not due to the respondent's own commercial efficiency or investment, such as direct or indirect state support for a firm or firms in the market; and
(f) any regulations made by the Minister ... regarding the calculation and determination of an excessive price.[177]

The 2018 amendments to the Competition Act changed the removed the definition of an "excessive price" previously contained in section 1(1)(ix) of the Act. That provision had defined an excessive price as having "no reasonable relation to the economic value of the product". The 2018 amendment effectively replaced the benchmark of "economic value" with the notion of a "competitive price" in 8(3).[178] Furthermore, under 8(4) the undertaking faced with a prima facie establishment of excessive pricing by the competent authority has the possibility of rebutting this by demonstrating that the price was reasonable after all.

The provisions, and the change in 2018, do indeed reflect the gist of some of the central works on the theme of excessive pricing. The transition from "economic value" to "competitive price" might indicate the increased emphasis on the formalistic rather than the legal-philosophical approach to finding of abuse alongside

---

[176] Competition Amendment Act 18 of 2018. (Amendment Act), into law on 14 February 2019, effective from 12 July 2019.
[177] Competition Commission South Africa v Dis Chem Pharmacies Limited, Case No: CR008Apr20, para. 60.
[178] Competition Commission South Africa v Dis Chem Pharmacies Limited, Case No: CR008Apr20, para. 61.

competitive markets, which is why the focus is on it being "price excessive when compared" rather than "price excessive in and out of itself."

However, there are valid objections to turning competition authorities into de facto price-regulators. Motta re-iterates some of the arguments in regard to asserted challenges and costs associated with excessive pricing enforcement, commenting on the South African context: "Excessive price actions may also create legal uncertainty: It is difficult to establish what price is excessive. For good or for bad, though, the government regulations clearly define as excessive any price above the pre-crisis price (unless justified by higher costs of production). Using the pre-crisis price as a benchmark is sensible because demand and supply conditions at that time were presumably 'normal'."[179]

Although seemingly agreeing with the actions by the South Africa Competition Authority to pursue a case regarding a sharp increase in mark-ups for face-masks, Motta remains sceptical of the general wisdom of excessive pricing, along economic lines, pointing to the establishment of dominance and competitive price as fundamental. This is naturally correct, however, the challenges with finding dominance as well as competitive benchmarks are rather exaggerated and are highly dependent on the specifics of the case, which Motta agrees with, in the case of pandemic and the mark-up cited. It should be noted that in the meantime, the company investigated for alleged excessive pricing of facial masks has been found liable and subsequently fined for breach of excessive pricing prohibition as detailed in this section.[180] Furthermore, Motta elevates the point that the physical restriction of movement of people due to lockdown naturally increases the demand-side restrictions, thereby somewhat increasing the validity of enforcement.

The demand-side dynamics are an important element in regard to price increases, and the cost-plus approach might not be particularly useful, since as noted by Ratshisusu and Mncube, "... the economic value of hand sanitizers and face masks in the COVID-19 crisis period cannot be measured by any reliable cost-price formula. Prices for hand sanitizers and face masks may increase in this immediate period of the COVID-19 crisis because demand has risen relative to the immediately available supply."[181] This re-connects with the circularity of defining economic value solely as a market exchange function addressed in the next section on normative assumptions of welfarist and marginalist law and economics theory.

Regarding the choice between excessive pricing and price gouging and the different benchmarks, Boshoff notes, "The differences between price-gouging and excessive-pricing benchmarks depends on the type of disaster-period demand shock.

---

[179] Massimo Motta, "Price regulation in times of crisis can be tricky", April 22 2020, https://www.dailymaverick.co.za/opinionista/2020-04-22-price-regulation-in-times-of-crisis-can-be-tricky/, (last access 20 September 2020).

[180] South African Competition Tribunal, BABELEGI GUILTY OF EXCESSIVE PRICING DURING COVID-19 CRISIS, FINED R76K, 01 June 2020, https://www.comptrib.co.za/info-library/case-press-releases/babelegi-guilty-of-excessive-pricing-during-covid-19-crisis-fined-r76k, (last access 20 September 2020).

[181] Ratshisusu and Mncube (2020).

They are similar following a transitory demand spike, provided sufficient time is allowed for dynamic price behaviour, but differ markedly when demand is elevated for the duration of the disaster period. Applying simple cost-based comparisons in recently concluded cases against smaller retailers are consistent with excessive pricing, given the presence of a demand spike."[182]

Below, there is an account of two South African COVID-19 excessive price cases with a view to the above.

4.4.1 Babelegi Workwear

On 9 April 2020, the South African Competition Commission referred its first excessive pricing case as a result of the COVID-19 pandemic to the Competition Tribunal. The case concerned excessive pricing charged by Babelegi Workwear, regarding facial masks, with markups of 750–1100 percent during some periods in February and March 2020 as a direct result of the pandemic. The markups subsequently fell to a lower percentage (25 percent) post 18 March 2020, being rather on pair with the markups during December 2019 of 23 percent. Thus, the alleged infringing period was cited between 31 January 2020 and 5 March 2020 by the Commission.

As noted by the South African Competition Tribunal, "... one can reasonably infer that Babelegi had market power during the Complaint Period since it behaved to an appreciable extent independently of its competitors, customers or suppliers. Babelegi is, therefore, a dominant firm during the Complaint Period in terms of section 7(c) of the Act." Notably, and mimicking much of European jurisprudence on the matter, market power in the South African context is defined as "... the power of a firm to control prices, to exclude competition, or to behave to an appreciable extent independently of its competitors, customers, or suppliers."[183]

The Tribunal further accepted a prima facie case of an abuse of dominance established by the Competition Commission because the undertaking in question had charged excessive prices for FFP1 masks during the complaint period ranging between 31 January 2020 and 5 March 2020. Some of the procedural aspects of the case revolved around the issue of the time frame and whether price increases prior to the issuing of Regulation 4 could be caught, where the Tribunal stated that the case would be heard under Section 8(1)(a) of the Competition Act. The Tribunal further noted that this was the first excessive pricing case to be heard post the amendment of the Competition Act as of 12 July 2019. Relevant for the deciding of the case was the

---

[182] Boshoff (2020).

[183] South African Competition Act of 1998, Chapter 1, XIII, cited in Oxenham et al. (2020).

dominance rule as per Section 7(c) of the Competition Act, applicable to firms with less than 35 percent of the relevant market.[184]

The dominance issue was resolved by resorting to the wording of the Competition Act Section 7(b) and (c), targeting the power of the firm to "control prices, or to exclude competition or to behave to an appreciable extent independently of its competitors and customers."[185] Although it was agreed upon by the Competition Commission and Babelegi that the market share of Babelegi did not exceed five percent during the complaint period, the circumstances in the case demonstrating the ability of Babelegi to increase prices as submitted by the Commission constituted the basis for the finding of dominance by the Tribunal.

While Babelegi referred to its ability to raise prices to be seen as "temporary dominance" and further referring to points made in the literature that the dominance and market power should be understood as "the ability to raise prices consistently and profitably over competitive levels",[186] this was not accepted by the Tribunal. The Tribunal, on its part, noted that market power and dominance during a pandemic are to be judged contextually, and beyond the SSNIP-tests regularly employed,[187] where the price increases are to be seen more like instances of price gouging. Nevertheless, it was common ground between the Tribunal and Babelegi that such cases also constitute a form or species of excessive pricing.

The Tribunal cites support for its assessment of "abnormal times" in the UK Competition and Market Authority Guidance on the issue, in turn stating, "The CMA will not tolerate unscrupulous businesses exploiting the crisis as a 'cover' for non-essential collusion. This could include, for example...a business abusing its dominant position in a market (which might be a dominant position conferred by the particular circumstances of this crisis) to raise prices significantly above normal competitive levels."[188] Thus, Babelegi's ability to raise prices, and the ipso facto price increases in ranges of 750–1100 percent, serve, according to the Tribunal, as a proxy to assess its market power.[189]

---

[184] Case no: CR003Apr20, The Competition Commission v Babelegi Workwear and Industrial Supplies CC, available at: http://blogs.sun.ac.za/ccle/files/2020/07/Non-Confidential-Tribunal-Reasons_CR003Apr20-CC-v-Babelegi-01062020-1.pdf, (last access 01 October 2020).

[185] Case no: CR003Apr20, The Competition Commission v Babelegi Workwear and Industrial Supplies CC, para. 54.

[186] Case no: CR003Apr20, The Competition Commission v Babelegi Workwear and Industrial Supplies CC, para. 61; referring to UK OFT415 Assessment of Market Power, 1999 at para 1.2; and Bishop & Walker, Economic of EC Competition Law, 2002, p. 45.

[187] Case no: CR003Apr20, The Competition Commission v Babelegi Workwear and Industrial Supplies CC, para. 68.

[188] UK Competition and Market Authority, CMA approach to business cooperation in response to COVID-19, 25 March 2020, available at: https://assets.publishing.service.gov.uk/government/uploads/system/uploads/attachment_data/file/875468/COVID-19_guidance_-.pdf, (last access 01 October 2020).

[189] Case no: CR003Apr20, The Competition Commission v Babelegi Workwear and Industrial Supplies CC, para. 92.

Regarding the test for excessiveness, the conditions are found in Section 8(3) of the Competition Act, requiring an establishment of (i) whether the price charged is higher than a competitive price; and (ii) whether such difference is unreasonable. A wording which closely mimics the seminal United Brands test rather closely, where the Tribunal noted that the basic test would entail a comparison to the counterfactual world of normal and sufficiently effective competition to determine if the price charged exceeds this benchmark, and the second step would entail an assessment if the difference found is unreasonable.[190]

The Tribunal settled for a test with a view to prices and mark-ups prevailing in the period prior to the "abnormal situation", granting defences along the lines of increased costs. The Tribunal, in doing so, cites Motta, stating, "Using the pre-crisis price as a benchmark is sensible because demand and supply conditions at that time were presumably 'normal'."[191] The Tribunal further refers to US State legislation on price gouging, where a price increase of more than 10 percent compared to the "normal" situation pre-dating the crisis is viewed as sufficient.[192]

Contrasting the decision by the UK Competition Appeals Tribunal (CAT)[193] in regard to what relevant factors must be weighed in, the South African Competition Tribunal stated that if a functionary is entrusted with discretion to consider what factors are of relevance, the significance to be attached to a factor, or if and the extent to which a particular factor affects the actual determination of the issue is at the discretion of the functionary.[194]

The Tribunal further referred to the decision by the former Competition Appeals Court in the Sasol case, where the price would be prima facie excessive where a dominant undertaking substantially raised its prices without a corresponding increase in costs.[195] This contrasts, nevertheless, to the finding of the Tribunal in the Dis Chem case, as will be shown. The Tribunal found Babelegi thus contravening Section 8(1)(a) during the complaint period, issuing an administrative penalty of 76 040 Rand.

---

[190] Case no: CR003Apr20, The Competition Commission v Babelegi Workwear and Industrial Supplies CC, para. 45.

[191] Case no: CR003Apr20, The Competition Commission v Babelegi Workwear and Industrial Supplies CC, para. 99.

[192] Case no: CR003Apr20, The Competition Commission v Babelegi Workwear and Industrial Supplies CC, paras 102–103.

[193] Abbott (2018).

[194] Case no: CR003Apr20, The Competition Commission v Babelegi Workwear and Industrial Supplies CC, para. 46.2.

[195] Case no: CR003Apr20, The Competition Commission v Babelegi Workwear and Industrial Supplies CC, para. 100.

4.4.2 Dischem Pharmacies

On 23 April 2020, the Competition Commission referred another excessive pricing case[196] to the Tribunal, this time concerning pricing practices of facemasks by Dis Chem Pharmacies Limited, in the range of 261 percent, 43 percent, and 25 percent, respectively, occurring during the month of March 2020.

In regard to the definition of the relevant market, considered a formal pre-requisite in the excessive pricing cases in the European context, the Tribunal opted to cite an OECD paper on the matter, noting, "In some cases it may be preferable to look for direct evidence of exploitation of market power (for example, abnormally high prices or profits) rather than focus on market definition."[197]

As the Competition Commission had not qualified the dominance in the relevant market, this view by the Tribunal might be of utmost importance and interest also for other cases beyond the COVID-19 pandemic. The Commission had instead relied on the market power, defined as the ability to raise prices independently of competitors, customers, and suppliers, where the Tribunal noted that "... it cannot be refuted that market power can be inferred from a firm's economic behaviour."[198]

Regarding market power, the Tribunal cited David Lewis in stating:

> A competition authority may conceivably be called upon to act as a price regulator in instances that may be characterised a 'price gouging'. For example, were Section 8(a) to be invoked in the event of a natural disaster, which had given rise to a temporary monopoly in some or other unregulated product or service that was vital to the life of the affected community, say ambulance services or fuel for heating, and this was exploited to affect a significant temporary price rise, the competition authority could easily assume the role of temporary price setter.[199]

In regard to the relevant market, the Tribunal defined this to be surgical masks, as the public at the time of alleged abuse by Dis Chem was required to wear surgical masks, thereby not accepting the assertion by Dis Chem that cloth face masks should also be

---

[196] Case No: CR008Apr20, The Competition Commission v DIS-CHEM PHARMACIES LIMITED, available at: http://blogs.sun.ac.za/ccle/files/2020/07/Public-Reasons-CC-v-Dischem-CR008Apr20.pdf, (last access 01 October 2020).

[197] Anderson R et al. (2020), Abuse of Dominance in Khemani R. S et al. (2013) A Framework for the Design and Implementation of Competition Law and Policy (OECD, Paris) available at: http://www.oecd.org/regreform/sectors/aframeworkforthedesignandimplementationofcompetitionlawandpolicy.htm, accessed 2020-10-01; cited in Case No: CR008Apr20, COMPETITION COMMISSION OF SOUTH AFRICA v DIS-CHEM PHARMACIES LIMITED, para. 103.

[198] Case No: CR008Apr20, COMPETITION COMMISSION OF SOUTH AFRICA v DIS-CHEM PHARMACIES LIMITED, para. 106.

[199] Lewis D Exploitative Abuses – a Note on the Harmony Gold v. Mittal Steel Excessive Pricing Case, Annual Proceedings of the Fordham Competition Law Institute: International Antitrust Law & Policy, Juris Publishing, Huntington (Footnote 4); cited in Case No: CR008Apr20, COMPETITION COMMISSION OF SOUTH AFRICA v DIS-CHEM PHARMACIES LIMITED, para. 113.

considered as part of the relevant market, as the public was advised to use cloth masks only in mid-April.[200]

Regarding the geographical market, and while referring to the European Commission notice on Relevant Market, the Tribunal noted that "... the key question is whether competitors from other geographic areas will be able to exercise sufficient competitive pressure on the relevant companies. This question should be a consumer-focused exercise: it is all about finding out what alternative suppliers are available to customers in a given area."[201]

Noting the inherent difficulties in movement caused by the pandemic, the Tribunal thus moved to the hypothetical question of "how far would a consumer, wanting to purchase a surgical face mask, be willing and able to travel if a store increased its prices for such face masks price by 5% over the period February and March 2020? ... If customers expected or experienced a shortage of masks, they would have bought them at whatever price charged by the firm who could supply them."[202] The submission by Dis Chem that one of its rivals indeed prices its products at a higher price was countered by the Tribunal that Dis Chem was not constrained by competitors as it opted to increase and not decrease its price relative to the price of the competitor cited. Thus, the geographical market was defined rather narrowly by the Tribunal.

The increased costs cited by Dis Chem consisted of the re-packaging of facemasks from boxes of 50 units to single units, settled between Dis Chem and the Competition Commission at 15%,[203] and further the fact that Dis Chem had to procure from local suppliers at Cash-On-Delivery (COD) as opposed to pre-pandemic supply, and finally that "price increases were implemented to "prepare" customers for future higher prices."[204]

The Tribunal, in regard to the economic assessment of the price increases, used the pre-pandemic price and profit levels in December 2020 as a benchmark, refusing to entertain a distinction between net and gross margin, and further not accepting the price increase defences forwarded by Dis Chem. The Tribunal thus noted, "In our view, Dis-Chem's massive price increases of surgical masks during the complaint period, which constitute an essential component of life saving first line protection in

---

[200] Case No: CR008Apr20, COMPETITION COMMISSION OF SOUTH AFRICA v DIS-CHEM PHARMACIES LIMITED, para. 116.

[201] Case No: CR008Apr20, COMPETITION COMMISSION OF SOUTH AFRICA v DIS-CHEM PHARMACIES LIMITED, para. 123.

[202] Case No: CR008Apr20, COMPETITION COMMISSION OF SOUTH AFRICA v DIS-CHEM PHARMACIES LIMITED, paras 128–136.

[203] Case No: CR008Apr20, COMPETITION COMMISSION OF SOUTH AFRICA v DIS-CHEM PHARMACIES LIMITED, para. 187.

[204] Case No: CR008Apr20, COMPETITION COMMISSION OF SOUTH AFRICA v DIS-CHEM PHARMACIES LIMITED, para. 191.

a pandemic of seismic proportions, without any significant increases in costs, are utterly unreasonable and reprehensible."[205]

Thus, Dis Chem was found liable of contravening section 8(1)(a) of the Competition Act for the period 1–31 March 2020 in that it has charged excessive prices for surgical masks to the detriment of consumers, and thereby liable to pay an administrative penalty of 1 200 000 Rand.

4.4.3 Analysis of the Cases in Light of Normative Views on Excessive Pricing

As a departing point of analysis of competition law dynamics in times of pandemic, a surge in demand combined with shortages in supply invariably causes the prices to rise, sometimes dramatically so.

Nevertheless, due to pandemic specific conditions (lockdown nullifying mobility and choice of consumers, the necessity of facemasks, hand sanitizers, and disinfectants due to public orders and overall measures to combat pandemic) the legal "fairness" rules are much more in the focus of the attention of authorities, as opposed to normal times, where competitive market forces are presumed (at least in theory) to act as price arbiters. Several European authorities did indeed make use of price regulation measures introduced by governments (and in the South African cases, the price regulations were also used in the competition law context), others used pre-emptive measures such as sending letters to different sector players urging them to abstain from profiteering.

Where investigations were opened in the EU, they assumed the character of investigating and monitoring price levels, and as price levels subsequently had decreased, the authorities opted not to pursue the cases further, e.g., Sweden and UK respectively, among others.

The institutional divide between Competition Authority on the one hand, and consumer protection authority, on the other hand, complicates the analysis, as the kind of "price gouging" in question in some jurisdictions is seen as "unfair pricing practices" to be dealt with by consumer protection authority, sometimes as a result of the governmental decrees issued in relation to the pandemic.

The results further indicate that the Member States, where the competition authorities in the past had pursued high profile excessive pricing cases (notably the UK and Italy) and had participated early on in the setting up of different reporting mechanism in regard to alleged excessive pricing practices, were also among those who had received the most complaints. This correlation of past high-profile cases and increased reporting of such practices during the COVID-19 pandemic does not amount to a causal relationship based on the limited scope of the inquiry, but is one

---

[205] Case No: CR008Apr20, COMPETITION COMMISSION OF SOUTH AFRICA v DIS-CHEM PHARMACIES LIMITED, para. 222.

plausible explanation regarding the manifest divergence in the number of complaints.

Generally, most competition authorities re-affirmed their commitment to pursue excessive pricing cases both during the pandemic and beyond. Nevertheless, one authority seemed to suggest that pricing levels were outside of the "remit" of competition law; a position which, if interpreted broadly, might come into conflict with the letter of the law (Article 102a TFEU) which explicitly prohibiting "unfair pricing" as an anti-competitive practice in and of itself. How the "unfair" and "excessive" price is to be determined neither affects the validity nor the applicability of the law. The same holds true regarding the Competition Authorities' mandate and strict obligation to intervene, as the assessment is an entirely different empirical matter, to be separated from the normative de lege lata of the prohibition.

The string of excessive pricing cases in the pharmaceutical sector is but one example of the increased activities on the part of European Competition Authorities. The inter-twined regulation and competition law approach are also seen in the energy sector,[206] on both Commission and Member State levels.[207]

Some European Competition Authorities raised the legal requisite of dominant position, as per the letter of the law and the settled jurisprudence of CJEU, unfair and excessive pricing are attributable to a position of dominance. This is in line with some parts of the economic theory of harm[208] where high prices are not able to be maintained (at least in the long-term) due to competitive market forces, and thus are only able to be maintained by way of a quasi-monopolist position, many times in markets protected by some barriers to entry, or other manifest market deficiencies.

The in-elasticity of the demand-side, captured consumer segments, and indispensable products, especially during a pandemic, complicate this general analysis. The European Competition Law approach to excessive pricing during a pandemic lacks the "price gouging" tool available in the US on state levels[209] (and on the Federal level by way of presidential order during the COVID-19 crisis[210]), and as

---

[206] See also the EU Commission Gazprom decision: European Commission, C(2018) 3106 final, Upstream gas supplies in Central and Eastern Europe, 24/05/2018, paras 62–63, available at: https://ec.europa.eu/competition/antitrust/cases/dec_docs/39816/39816_10148_3.pdf, (last access 01 October 2020); Regarding enforcement on Member State level, see German Bundeskartellamt enforcement activities regarding water and energy prices, e.g.: https://www.bundeskartellamt.de/SharedDocs/Meldung/EN/Pressemitteilungen/2015/19_10_2015_WSW.html, (last access 29 October 2020).

[207] Botta and Karova (2017).

[208] Atkinson and Audretsch (2011).

[209] Price Gouging Laws per State, see: https://www.ncsl.org/research/financial-services-and-commerce/price-gouging-state-statutes.aspx, (last access 29 October 2020).

[210] Executive Order 13910 of March 23, 2020, Preventing Hoarding of Health and Medical Resources To Respond to the Spread of COVID-19, https://www.federalregister.gov/documents/2020/03/26/2020-06478/preventing-hoarding-of-health-and-medical-resources-to-respond-to-the-spread-of-covid-19, (last access 20 September 2020).

seen in the case of South Africa,[211] where the dominance is not required per se, and pre-crisis prices are used as a comparative benchmark. This is also the case in some US states where a 10 percent increase is seen as a prima facie presumption of creative liability.

Nevertheless, in the case of a pandemic, even a local shop is able to exercise dominance, due to the reasons above, let alone the main supplier to a governmental procurement central. Without a solid investigation alongside settled assessment metrics (cost-plus and pre-crisis prices being the preferred methods in this context), the risk that certain anti-competitive exploitative pricing practices are given an ex-post free-pass is evident.

Pre-crisis prices are as aforementioned utilized as a benchmark in both the US[212] and South Africa,[213] although the two most recent South African COVID-19 cases[214] demonstrate diverging interpretations of how the metes and bounds of "excessiveness" should be defined. South Africa introduced measures in regard to the declaration of national emergency and its consequences for pricing in March 2020, as aforementioned. The regulations targeted material price increases, which did not correspond to increases in the costs of supplies, or increased the net margins

---

[211] South Africa Disaster Management Regulation of March 18 2020, published in Government Notice 318 of Government Gazette no 43107, where para. 10(6) authorized the minister of Trade and Industry to, inter alia, issue directions to protect consumers from excessive, unfair, unreasonable or unjust pricing of goods and services during the the state of national emergency; The subsequent Consumer Protection Regulations issued by the Minister of Trade and Industry were published on March 19 2020, The Consumer and Customer Protection and National Disaster Management Regulations and Directions GN R350 GG 43116, 19 March 2020 (consumer protection regulations).

[212] Executive Order 13910 of March 23, 2020, Preventing Hoarding of Health and Medical Resources To Respond to the Spread of COVID-19, https://www.federalregister.gov/documents/2020/03/26/2020-06478/preventing-hoarding-of-health-and-medical-resources-to-respond-to-the-spread-of-covid-19, (last access 20 September 2020); Many states already had "price gouging" laws in place, where an increase of 10 percent of price during a crisis compared to pre-crisis prices are prohibited.

[213] South Africa Disaster Management Regulation of March 18 2020, published in Government Notice 318 of Government Gazette no 43107, where paragraph 10(6) authorized the minister of Trade and Industry to, inter alia, issue directions to protect consumers from excessive, unfair, unreasonable or unjust pricing of goods and services during the the state of national emergency; The subsequent Consumer Protection Regulations issued by the Minister of Trade and Industry were published on March 19 2020, The Consumer and Customer Protection and National Disaster Management Regulations and Directions GN R350 GG 43116, 19 March 2020 (consumer protection regulations).

[214] South African Competition Tribunal, BABELEGI GUILTY OF EXCESSIVE PRICING DURING COVID-19 CRISIS, FINED R76K, 01 June 2020, https://www.comptrib.co.za/info-library/case-press-releases/babelegi-guilty-of-excessive-pricing-during-covid-19-crisis-fined-r76k, (last access 20 September 2020); Case No: CR008Apr20, COMPETITION COMMISSION OF SOUTH AFRICA v DIS-CHEM PHARMACIES LIMITED, available at: http://blogs.sun.ac.za/ccle/files/2020/07/Public-Reasons-CC-v-Dischem-CR008Apr20.pdf, (last access 01 October 2020).

or mark-ups above average margin or mark-up prevailing in the three-month period prior to 1 March 2020.

As noted by Ratshisusu and Mncube, "The regulations are appropriate in this immediate period of the COVID-19 national disaster, where market conditions are such that very high prices are unable to stimulate effective entry allowing the market to properly self-correct in a reasonable time frame. The COVID-19 restrictions entrench entry and expansion barriers in the immediate period. This means that prices will not be competed down, meaning that firms alleged to be excessively pricing have a captive customer base."[215]

Regarding the "excessiveness" limb in the United Brands parlance, the South African context differs materially, since as noted by the Tribunal, "Section 8(3) only requires that the 'price is higher than a competitive price and whether such difference is unreasonable'. Thus, the legal test in section 8(3) is that the price must be higher than a competitive price, without qualifying the size of that difference."[216] This was a further deviation from the previous competition regime in South Africa, since it was stated that, "Although decided under the previous 'excessive pricing' regime, the Competition Appeal Court (CAC) held that a price which was not more than 20 per cent of the economic value of the product cannot be considered 'excessive'."[217]

Combined with the doing away of qualifying dominance in the relevant and geographical market, this comes close to qualifying any price increase by even a non-dominant undertaking as compared to the "competitive price" as excessive, given certain circumstances in the specific case. The South African cases further considered prices charged in December 2020 as the competitive price benchmark, and did not consider factors like net margin v gross margin or other relevant factors, thus using prices prevailing in December 2020 and the overall profitability of the firm as the competitive benchmark. This method risks exposing the approach, at least in non-pandemic times, to various criticism raised in parts of the literature.

The approach by the Tribunal—to treat manifest price gouging cases during a pandemic under the excessive pricing institute—is further problematic, which has already been highlighted by some authors, noting, "Although it is widely accepted that price gouging may constitute a form of excessive pricing, there is an important distinction between legislation aimed specifically at prohibiting price gouging in a time of crisis and price gouging cases assessed under traditional competition laws."[218]

Citing David Lewis in its Dis Chem judgement, the South African Competition Tribunal engaged further with the price regulation issue in the affirmative, given certain circumstances such as a pandemic. More importantly, the temporal issue of

---

[215] Ratshisusu and Mncube (2020).

[216] Case No: CR008Apr20, COMPETITION COMMISSION OF SOUTH AFRICA v DIS-CHEM PHARMACIES LIMITED, para. 70.

[217] Oxenham et al. (2020).

[218] Oxenham et al. (2020).

self-correcting prices was also addressed against the pandemic background. The South African cases thus demonstrate a three-tiered approach considering competition law, consumer protection, as well as price regulation during a pandemic, taking note of different policy objectives such as preventing undue wealth transfer and enabling of excessive pricing during a pandemic.

5 Conclusion and Ways Forward

The legal discipline has castigated excessive, exploitative pricing for many centuries as an inherent evil in and of itself. This contrasts to the analysis by a strand of law and economics discourse on the subject, as well as to some legal-historical arguments. The latter concerning (contested) arguments[219] advancing the Ordoliberal origins of European Competition Law and policy in regard to the prohibition of excessive pricing.

The ratio legis behind the prohibition and the operative legal-economic analysis rests on the notion that there can be instances where the competitive market forces are not able to produce fair, efficient, and competitive price levels. This can be due to anti-competitive practices, such as exploitative, unfair pricing practices, which are able to be maintained through structural deficiencies on both producer and consumer sides. Such structural deficiencies are not easy to curb in the long-run, let alone in the short-run, especially given circumstances such as a pandemic. Thus, the abusive behaviour, and not only its underlying conditions, are prohibited in European Competition Law, a prohibition with deep historical roots, resting on a solid foundation regarding human biases towards fairness in transactions.

The somewhat misguided focus on curbing exclusionary elements in order to deal with exploitative abuses, as the exclusionary elements enable the exploitative abuse in the first place, tends to bypass the objective of prohibition regarding undue rent transfer. The abuse of a precarious, economically dependent situation is tantamount to a legal evil (malum in se), not only the conditions enabling the abusive practice. As per the direct effect of Article 102 TFEU, the European Competition Authority not only has a mandate, but an obligation, to pursue excessive pricing cases. This re-connects with the debate on efficiency or fairness as competition law objective(s), where the mainstream, neoclassical economics put the emphasis on the former, the Keynesian, behavioural, and Neuro-economics school allow for more fairness considerations in pricing beyond economic efficiency.

Economic theory is not monolithic, and judges are increasingly aware of this fact. Although economic theories rightly influence a body of jurisprudence concerned with the economic behaviour of undertakings and its impact on society in general, as stated by the European Commission, "... it should be made clear that economic theory cannot be the only factor in the design of policy for several reasons. Firstly,

---

[219] Akman (2009).

strict economic theory is just one of the sources of policy. In practice, the application of economic theory must take place in the context of the existing legal texts and jurisprudence. Secondly, economic theories are necessarily based on simplifying assumptions often obtained in the context of stylised theoretical models that cannot take into account all the complexities of real-life cases."[220]

As summarized by Massimo Motta in the context of excessive pricing and COVID-19:

> Excessive price actions in antitrust are often criticised because (i) they interfere with the regular functioning of the market, and (ii) they may 'expropriate' firms of the fruits of their investment and innovation. However, under the current circumstances, objection (i) will not apply if supply is unlikely to respond in the short-run; as for (ii), price spikes are due to sudden increases in demand or captivity of consumers and bear little relation to firms' investment or effort.[221]

One might add that the arguments in the normal non-pandemic setting are conditioned firstly towards a reliance that markets do function somewhat properly, and how "properly" is defined and for whom. Secondly, excessive pricing and profits are supposed to be "fruits of innovation and investment" and any action to correct undue wealth transfer which would not have been possible under a competitive, functioning market is akin to "expropriation".

As rhetorically asked by the South African Competition Tribunal: "How long should a competition authority wait until the market 'settles' or reaches equilibrium before it intervenes to protect consumers against pricing abuses by the suppliers of fresh or bottled water?"[222]

The force of the arguments against excessive pricing enforcement, also in non-crisis times, is thus conditioned towards what theory of harm is relied upon and, prominently, what normative weight is attached to the values and the trade-offs manifested therebetween. As a matter of doctrinal legal science, this balancing of trade-offs and division of values invariably avails itself of the traditional legal method, while in the past decades being increasingly informed by way of the positive economic analysis of law. As stated by John B. Kirkwood and Robert H. Lande on US Antitrust:

> The conventional wisdom in the antitrust community today is that the antitrust laws were passed to promote economic efficiency. This view, held by most economists, conservative scholars, federal enforcers, and practicing lawyers, is incorrect. Neither the sole nor even the

---

[220] European Commission, "Green Paper on Vertical Restraints in EC Competition Policy – COM (96) 721 Final," January 22, 1997, https://europa.eu/documents/comm/green_papers/pdf/com96_721_en.pdf, p. 26 (last access 11 September 2021).

[221] Massimo Motta, "Price regulation in times of crisis can be tricky", April 22 2020, https://www.dailymaverick.co.za/opinionista/2020-04-22-price-regulation-in-times-of-crisis-can-be-tricky/, (last access 20 September 2020).

[222] Case No: CR008Apr20, COMPETITION COMMISSION OF SOUTH AFRICA v DIS-CHEM PHARMACIES LIMITED, para. 144.

primary purpose of these laws is, or ever has been, to enhance efficiency. Instead ... the fundamental goal of antitrust law is to protect consumers.[223]

Wordings such as "most economists agree" or "there is a consensus among economists" or "it is commonly held" are as frequent in the literature on this subject as they are dubious; and at times discordant to the legal practice, which is not bound by any "economic reasoning", be it conventional or not. The often-asserted "conventional wisdom" of neoclassical, marginalist, and welfarist schools of economics in regard to the assessment of excessive pricing is indeed neither "conventional" nor particularly "wise" nor—most importantly for legal scholars, judges, and practitioners—unequivocally recognized in European law, as the supposed "wisdom" stands in direct conflict with black letter law, legal history, and legal intent.

Interestingly, this supposed "conventional wisdom" has been referred to by legal councils, and firmly rejected by judges in excessive price cases.[224] The literature on excessive pricing is ripe with countless references of the kind, alluding to a supposed "general consensus" or "conventional wisdom". There are both normative and empirical exceptions to be taken with such a line of reasoning. Since, firstly, a strongly held position shared by many is in no way a testament to its correctness but only conditioned towards the progression of actual knowledge and science, which routinely upend "traditional wisdom"; and, secondly, the so-called "wisdom" has upon closer examination not shown itself to be particularly wise nor coherent within its own context and given its own premises;[225] one of such being the assertion regarding the self-correcting nature of markets and the ignorance of the signalling effect and corrective justice virtues of excessive pricing.[226]

The appeal courts in Europe have all confirmed the results in the recent pharmaceutical excessive pricing cases, with UK Appeal Courts remanding the case to the CMA in some parts but simultaneously striking down the CAT reasoning as being wrong in law and going beyond what settled case law demands of a competition authority regarding the burden of proof and assessment methods chosen.[227]

As noted by Johannes Laitenberger, then Director-General of DG Competition,

> ... the CAT appears to require a very thorough benchmarking at both stages of the test – that is, excessiveness and unfairness – and an extremely detailed explanation on why some bench-marks, which may appear to be potential candidates, are not used. This appears to go further than previous case law.[228]

---

[223] Kirkwood and Lande (2008).

[224] See UK Competition Appeals Tribunal Case No. 1274/1/12/16 (IR), transcript of hearing for application of interim relief, 17 January 2017, paras 17–26.

[225] Lianos (2020).

[226] Canoy and Tichem (2018).

[227] European Commission (2019).

[228] Johannes Laitenberger, Competition assessments and abuse of dominance: Remarks on the two themes of the EUI Competition Workshop (Florence EUI Competition Workshop, Florence, 22 June 2018), https://ec.europa.eu/competition/speeches/text/sp2018_11_en.pdf, (last access 20 November 2020); See also the European Commission Amicus Brief in the Pfizer/Flynn case to UK Appeal Court, Amicus brief in case no. c3/2018/1847 and c3/2018/1874, UK Court of

Nevertheless, the intuitive and inherent evil perceived in legal tradition corresponds well to the manifest economic harm in the form of undue wealth transfer that is associated with a fairness-paradigm. This is also true in regard to the deadweight losses and in-efficiencies that are associated with a welfarist-paradigm.

As seen in the South African cases, the "abnormal" context of price increases impacts the assessment in regard to the definition of the relevant market, dominance, market power, the price benchmark, and related economic tests. Although the conflation of high prices resulting from a surge in demand with excessive prices, and what type of price increases should be treated as "excessive" and "unreasonable" is not sufficiently answered by the reasoning in the South African cases, they offer many points to both sides of the debate to ponder upon.

One might nevertheless submit that the long-held beliefs in regard to rationality assumptions and a strict dichotomy between efficiency and fairness as goals and rationales of competition law simply "do not stand serious scrutiny",[229] and they are indeed at odds with modern research into behavioural Economics,[230] Neuro-economics[231] and Neuro-ethics, proving the inherent human bias towards fairness and equity.[232] The fact that fairness is not defined per se in the statutes, such as Article 102a TFEU, does not mean it does not exist or is incalculable—it only allows the concept and its application to develop dynamically by way of jurisprudence.

Many of the textbook assertions on how markets function and what the role of competition law ought to be in regard to excessive pricing are found not to pass a basic "smell test", especially so during a pandemic. They stand in conflict with how the law is being administered around Europe and globally as the string of cases in the recent decade demonstrate and, most importantly for legal discipline, they are at odds with the legislative intent and the normative soul of competition law, and are, in turn, reflecting the aforementioned inherent values and human biases. The economic analysis of law, no matter how relevant and enlightening, is and will forever be an afterthought seen from the onset of legal tradition.

The synthesis of this normative framing of excessive pricing alongside the fairness-welfare paradigm should inform the analytical framework in regard to the ratio legis and economic soundness of enforcement, given that certain screening conditions are fulfilled. Many previously held conceptions (markets will self-correct, excessive pricing enforcement would harm innovation, competition law should focus solely on economic efficiency etc.) do not possess the theoretical and empirical vigour they profess to.[233] Looking at the policy development at the European Commission level, one also notes a shift towards an increased emphasis on

---

Appeals; Flynn Pharma limited Flynn Pharma (holdings) limited and Pfizer inc. Pfizer limited v. the Competition and Markets Authority; 14 June 2019, for hearing on 26–28 November 2019.

[229] Lianos (2020).
[230] Fehr and Schmidt (2006).
[231] Hsu et al. (2008).
[232] Cappelen et al. (2014).
[233] Lianos (2020).

"fairness",[234] a clear step from the overt reliance on "efficiency" as the sole legal and public policy objective to be pursued in regard to Competition Law and Economics.

The empirical challenge regarding the legal prohibition of excessive pricing concerns the appropriate threshold of when a supra-competitive price, e.g., due to efficiencies and customer valuation etc., surpasses the legal ban on unfairly high and harmful prices and profit levels, and thus creates antitrust liability. The normative under-development of the excessive pricing concept contributes to this prolonged debate.[235] Recent years have nevertheless noted many innovative suggestions[236] in that regard, as well as a rising tide of excessive pricing enforcement. As expressed already in the United Brands case "Other ways may be devised – and economic theorists have not failed to think up several – of selecting the rules for determining whether the price of a product is unfair."

Recent decades have also shown that in many cases certain sectors have noted excessive pricing (Telecom, Pharma, Energy, Water, and so on), and there is a mix of regulatory and competition law interventions in many instances, which have ultimately brought the excessive pricing practices to an end. There is, however, room to reflect on where the boundaries of competition law/regulatory affairs should be drawn, whether efficiency or fairness or (preferably) a synthesis of both should guide competition policy; and what theory of value should prevail post marginalist and labour theories of value in the face of dynamic, data-driven, and digital-based industries.

Informed by this background, the question: "Should and could competition law be pursued in isolation alongside 'economic efficiency' or be part of achieving the overall goals?" seems to have been sufficiently and correctly answered by a statement by the European Commission "... competition policy cannot be pursued in isolation, as an end in itself, without reference to the legal, economic, political and social context."[237]

Summing up, the normative objections and overt-cautious approach of welfarist, marginalist schools of economics risk not only conflict with valid law and legislative intent, but are also unsubstantiated to a high degree, regarding some fundamental assumptions such as self-correcting features of excessive prices, the General Equilibrium theory, and regarding the vision to entrust manifestly imperfect markets with the efficient allocation of resources during a pandemic. The empirical difficulties and the lack of competence raised at each and every turn, while of merit in some instances, lack the persuasion in and of themselves to act as arguments not to

---

[234] Johannes Laitenberger, EU Competition Law in Innovation and Digital Markets: Fairness and the Consumer Welfare Perspective (Brussels, October 10, 2017), https://ec.europa.eu/competition/speeches/text/sp2017_15_en.pdf (last access 11 September 2021); Margarethe Vesterager, "Fairness and Competition" (GCLC Annual Conference, Brussels, January 25, 2018); Vesterager (2016).

[235] Akman and Garrod (2011).

[236] Gani (2020).

[237] Commission (EC), XXIInd Report on Competition Policy 1992, p. 13, cited in Ezrachi (2016), p. 52.

apply the law "as is". The confusion of de lege lata with de lege ferenda is one of the re-occurring facets of the excessive pricing literature.

As some strands of economics do not consider fairness to be "an economic concept", despite thousands of economic research papers on the matter of Fairness and a host of Nobel Prize Laurates awarded to scholars whose work, in one way or another, address fairness, an in-depth engagement between the two disciplines—law and economics—seem forever strained.

This is the main reason why the excessive pricing Giant has a tendency to awaken, despite the chains bestowed upon it by the welfarist and marginalist schools. The ratio legis of the prohibition is firmly grounded on innate human preferences towards fairness in pricing and condemnation of the abuse of dominant positions, even more so during times of crisis.

References

Abbott FM (2018) The UK competition appeal tribunal's misguided reprieve for Pfizer's excessive pricing abuse. IIC – Int Rev Intellect Prop Compet Law 49:845–853 https://doi.org/10.1007/s40319-018-0734-y (last access 22 Sept 2021)

Akerlof GA, Yellen JL (1985) Can small deviations from rationality make significant differences to economic equilibria? Am Econ Rev 75:708–720

Akman P (2009) Searching for the long-lost soul of Article 82EC. Oxford J Leg Stud 29:267–303. https://doi.org/10.1093/ojls/gqp011 (last access 12 Sept 2021)

Akman P, Garrod L (2011) When are excessive prices unfair? J Compet Law Econ 7:403–426. https://doi.org/10.1093/joclec/nhq024 (last access 12 Sept 2021)

Atkinson RD, Audretsch DB (2011) Economic doctrines and approaches to antitrust. Indiana University-Bloomington: School of Public & Environmental Affairs Research Paper Series No 2011–01–02

Baker JB (2007) Beyond Schumpeter vs. Arrow: how antitrust fosters innovation. Antitrust Law J 74:575–602

Berns GS et al (2012) The price of your soul: neural evidence for the non-utilitarian representation of sacred values. Philos Trans: Biol Sci 367:754–762. https://www.jstor.org/stable/41433551 (last access 12 Sept 2021)

Bishop S, Walker M (2010) The economics of EC competition law: concepts, application and measurement, 3. ed., univ. ed. Sweet & Maxwell [u.a.], London

Blaug M (2001) Is competition such a good thing? Static efficiency versus dynamic efficiency. Rev Ind Organ 19

Boshoff WH (2020) South African competition policy on excessive pricing and its relation to price gouging during the COVID-19 disaster period. S Afr J Econ. https://doi.org/10.1111/saje.12268 (last access 12 Sept 2021)

Botta M, Karova R (2017) Sanctioning excessive energy prices as abuse of dominance: are the EU commission and the national competition authorities on the same frequency? In: Parcu P, Monti G (eds) Abuse of dominance in EU competition law. Edward Elgar Publishing

Brennan TJ (2007) Should innovation rationalize supra-competitive prices? A skeptical speculation. In: The pros and cons of high prices. Swedish Competition Authority, pp 88–127

Canoy M, Tichem J (2018) Lower drug prices can improve innovation. Eur Compet J 14:278–304. https://doi.org/10.1080/17441056.2018.1512231 (last access 12 Sept 2021)

Cappelen AW et al (2014) Equity theory and fair inequality: a neuroeconomic study. Proc Natl Acad Sci 111:15368–15372. https://doi.org/10.1073/pnas.1414602111 (last access 12 Sept 2021)

Cary GS et al (30 April 2020) Exploitative abuses, price gouging & COVID-19: the cases pursued by EU and national competition authorities. Concurrences 10

De Loecker J, Eeckhout J, Unger G (2020) The rise of market power and the macroeconomic implications*. Q J Econ 135:561–644. https://doi.org/10.1093/qje/qjz041 (last access 12 Sept 2021)

Diamond AM Jr (2006) Schumpeter – creative destruction. J Private Enterp 22:120–146

Dworkin RM (1980) Is wealth a value? J Leg Stud 9:191–226

Evans DS, Padilla AJ (2005) Excessive prices: using economics to define administrable legal rules. J Compet Law Econ 1:97–122. https://doi.org/10.1093/joclec/nhi002 (last access 1 Sept 2021)

European Commission Amicus Brief in the Pfizer/Flynn case to UK Appeal Court, Amicus brief in case no. c3/2018/1847 and c3/2018/1874, UK Court of Appeals; Flynn Pharma limited Flynn Pharma (holdings) limited and Pfizer inc. Pfizer limited v. the Competition and Markets Authority; 14 June 2019, for hearing on 26–28 November 2019

Ezrachi A (2016) Sponge. J Antitrust Enforcement jnw011. https://doi.org/10.1093/jaenfo/jnw011 (last access 12 Sept 2021)

Ezrachi A, Gilo D (2009a) Are excessive prices really self-correcting? J Compet Law Econ 5:249–268. https://doi.org/10.1093/joclec/nhn033 (last access 12 Sept 2021)

Ezrachi A, Gilo D (2009b) The darker side of the moon: assessment of excessive pricing and proposal for a post-entry price-cut benchmark. In: Article 82 EC: reflections on its recent evolution. Hart Publishing, pp 169–184

Fehr E, Camerer CF (2007) Social neuroeconomics: the neural circuitry of social preferences. Trends Cogn Sci 11:419–427. https://doi.org/10.1016/j.tics.2007.09.002 (last access 12 Sept 2021)

Fehr E, Schmidt KM (2006) Chapter 8 The economics of fairness, reciprocity and altruism – experimental evidence and new theories. In: Handbook of the economics of giving, altruism and reciprocity. Elsevier, pp 615–691

First H (2019) Excessive drug pricing as an antitrust violation. Antitrust Law J 82:59

Fletcher A, Jardine A (2008) Towards an appropriate policy for excessive pricing. In: Ehlermann C-D, Marquis M (eds) European Competition Law Annual 2007: a reformed approach to Article 82 EC. Hart Publishing, pp 533–547

Fortsont R (2001) Problems with Richard Posner's the problematics of moral and legal theory. William Mitchell Law Rev 27

Fox EM (2004) The trouble with trinko. American Bar Association, Antitrust Section Spring Meeting

Gal MS (2004) Monopoly pricing as an antitrust offense in the U.S. and the EC: two systems of belief about monopoly? Antitrust Bull 49:343–384. https://doi.org/10.1177/0003603X0404900109 (last access 12 Sept 2021)

Gani W (2020) Can statistical methods help prove excessiveness of dominant firm's prices evidence from the Tunisian Competition Council. Int J Econ Bus Res 20:1. https://doi.org/10.1504/IJEBR.2020.10030419 (last access 12 Sept 2021)

Gilbert M (2001) Collective preferences, obligations, and rational choice. Econ Philos 17:109–119. https://doi.org/10.1017/S0266267101000177 (last access 12 Sept 2021)

Gilbert R (2006) Looking for Mr. Schumpeter: where are we in the competition innovation debate? In: Innovation policy and the economy. MIT Press, Cambridge, pp 159–215

Gilo D (2018) A coherent approach to the antitrust prohibition of excessive pricing by dominant firms. In: Katsoulacos Y, Jenny F (eds) Excessive pricing and competition law enforcement. Springer International Publishing, Cham, pp 99–126

Hazemi-Jebelli K (2020) The new antitrust revolution. Compet Policy Int 5

Hilty RM (2007) The law against unfair competition and its interfaces. In: Hilty RM, Henning-Bodewig F (eds) Law against unfair competition. Springer, Berlin, Heidelberg, pp 1–52

Hoekstra J, Sauter W (2018) What standard for excessive pricing in EU law? A discussion of the competition appeal tribunal's judgment in the Pfizer/Flynn v CMA case. Eur Pharm Law Rev 2:215–221. https://doi.org/10.21552/eplr/2018/4/9 (last access 12 Sept 2021)

Holler MJ, Leroch M (2010) Efficiency and justice revisited. Eur J Polit Econ 26:311–319. https://doi.org/10.1016/j.ejpoleco.2009.11.007 (last access 12 Sept 2021)

Hsu M, Anen C, Quartz SR (2008) The right and the good: distributive justice and neural encoding of equity and efficiency. Science 320:1092–1095. https://doi.org/10.1126/science.1153651 (last access 12 Sept 2021)

Jenny F (2018) Abuse of dominance by firms charging excessive or unfair prices: an assessment. In: Katsoulacos Y, Jenny F (eds) Excessive pricing and competition law enforcement. Springer International Publishing, Cham, pp 5–70

Kahneman D, Knetsch JL, Thaler RH (1986a) Fairness and the assumptions of economics. J Bus 59:285. https://doi.org/10.1086/296367 (last access 12 Sept 2021)

Kahneman D, Knetsch JL, Thaler RH (1986b) Fairness as a constraint on profit seeking: entitlements in the market. Am Econ Rev 76:728–774

Kaplow L, Shavell S (2001) Fairness versus welfare. Harv Law Rev 114:961–1388

Kianzad B (2021) Excessive pricing during the COVID-19 crisis in the EU: an empirical inquiry. Concurrences 2021

Kianzad B, Minssen T (2018) How much is too much? Defining the metes and bounds of excessive pricing in the pharmaceutical sector. Eur Pharm Law Rev 2:133–148. https://doi.org/10.21552/eplr/2018/3/5 (last access 12 Sept 2021)

Kirkwood JB, Lande RH (2008) The fundamental goal of antitrust: protecting consumers, not increasing efficiency. Notre Dame Law Rev 84:55

Konow J (2003) Which is the fairest one of all? A positive analysis of justice theories. J Econ Lit 41:1188–1239

Korobokin RB, Ulen TS (2000) Law and behavioral science: removing the rationality assumption from law and economics. Calif Law Rev 88:1053–1144

Krugman P (2020, January 28) Arguing with Zombies: economics, politics, and the fight for a better future, 1st edn. W. W. Norton & Company

Kühn K-U (2017) Exploitative abuse: when does enforcement make sense? Concurrences Concurrences N°2-2017, pp 1–3

Lande RH (1982) Wealth transfers as the original and primary concern of antitrust: the efficiency interpretation challenged. Hastings Law J 34

Levine R et al (2020) Competition laws and corporate innovation, w27253, May 2020

Lianos I (2006) Competition law and intellectual property rights: is the property rights' approach right? Camb Yearb Eur Leg Stud 8:153–186

Lianos I (2013) Some reflections on the question of the goals of EU competition law. In: Lianos I, Geradin D (eds) Handbook on European competition law. Edward Elgar, pp 1–84

Lianos I (2020) Competition law as a form of social regulation. Antitrust Bull 65:3–86. https://doi.org/10.1177/0003603X19898626 (last access 12 Sept 2021)

Lyons B (2007) The paradox of the exclusion of exploitative abuse. In: The pros and cons of high prices. Konkurrensverket (Swedish Competition Authority), Stockholm, pp 65–88

Maggiolino M (2011) Intellectual property and antitrust: a comparative economic analysis of U.S. and EU law. Edward Elgar Publishing

Malc D, Mumel D, Pisnik A (2016) Exploring price fairness perceptions and their influence on consumer behavior. J Bus Res 69:3693–3697. https://doi.org/10.1016/j.jbusres.2016.03.031 (last access 12 Sept 2021)

Manne GA and Wright JD (2010) Innovation and the limits of antitrust. J Compet Law Econ 6:153–202. https://doi.org/10.1093/joclec/nhp032 (last access 12 Sept 2021)

Mathis K (2009) Efficiency instead of justice? Searching for the philosophical foundations of the economic analysis of law. Springer, New York

Mendez MF (2009) The neurobiology of moral behavior: review and neuropsychiatric implications. CNS Spectrums 14:608–620. https://doi.org/10.1017/S1092852900023853 (last access 12 Sept 2021)

Mestmäcker E-J (2007) A legal theory without law. Mohr Siebeck

Monti G (2019) Excessive pricing: competition law in shared regulatory space. Tillburg University Working Paper

Motta M, de Streel A (2006) Excessive pricing and price squeeze under EU law. In: European Competition Law Annual 2003: what is an abuse of a dominant position? Hart Publishing, pp 91–127

Motta M, de Streel A (2007) Excessive pricing in competition law: never say never? In: The pros and cons of high prices. Swedish Competition Authority, Kalmar, pp 14–46

O'Donoghue R, Padilla J (2019) Excessive pricing. The law and economics of Article 102 TFEU, 3rd edn, Forthcoming. Available at SSRN: https://ssrn.com/abstract=3484155 (last access 12 Sept 2021)

Oxenham J, Currie M-J, van der Merwe C (2020) COVID-19 price gouging cases in South Africa: short-term market dynamics with long-term implications for excessive pricing cases. J Eur Compet Law Pract. https://doi.org/10.1093/jeclap/lpaa070 (last access 12 Sept 2021)

Page WH (1991) Ideological conflict and the origins of antitrust policy. Tulane Law Rev 66

Piraino TA (2007) Reconciling the Harvard and Chicago Schools: a new antitrust approach for the 21st century. Indiana Law J 82:67

Posner RA (1979) Utilitarianism, economics, and legal theory. J Leg Stud 8

Posner RA (2010) Crisis of the capitalist democracy. Harvard University Press, Cambridge

Ratshisusu H, Mncube L (2020) Addressing excessive pricing concerns in time of the COVID-19 pandemic—a view from South Africa. J Antitrust Enforcement 8:256–259. https://doi.org/10.1093/jaenfo/jnaa030 (last access 12 Sept 2021)

Regulation (2007)(EC) No 717/2007 OF THE EUROPEAN PARLIAMENT AND OF THE COUNCIL of 27 June 2007 on roaming on public mobile telephone networks within the Community and amending Directive 2002/21/EC (2007)

Saavedra E, Tapia J (2017) Excessive pricing: towards a workable and objective rule. Compet Policy Int: 9

Salzberger EM (2007) The economic analysis of law – the dominant methodology for legal research?! University of Haifa Faculty of Law Legal Studies Research Paper No 1044382. https://doi.org/10.2139/ssrn.1044382 (last access 12 Sept 2021)

Salzberger EM (2013) Law and economics – limits of analysis: the case of intellectual property. In: Metelska-Szaniawska K (ed) Polish yearbook of law & economics. Wydawnictwo C.H. Beck

Sery J (2017) Richard Posner and the rhetoric of (economic) common sense. Common Law Rev 16

Sunstein CR, Thaler RH, Jolls CM (1998) A behavioral approach to law and economics. Stanford Law Rev 50:81

Ulen TS (2015) Law and economics, the moral limits of the market, and threshold deontology. In: Hatzis AN, Mercuro N (eds) Law and economics: philosophical issues and fundamental questions, 1st edn. Routledge

van der Woude M (2008) Unfair and excessive prices in the energy sector. Eur Rev Energy Markets 2

von Hayek FA (1993) Law, legislation, and liberty: a new statement of the liberal principles of justice and political economy, Reprinted 1993. Routledge, London

Waller SW (2006) Microsoft and Trinko: a tale of two courts. Utah Law Rev 901:741–759

Watkins E (1922) The law and the profits. Yale Law J 32. https://doi.org/10.2307/789272 (last access 12 Sept 2021)

Wils WPJ (2014) The judgment of the EU General Court in Intel and the so-called "more economic approach" to abuse of dominance. World Compet 37:405–434

Woodcock R (2018) The antitrust duty to charge low prices. Cardozo Law Rev 39. https://doi.org/10.2139/ssrn.2924828 (last access 12 Sept 2021)

Woodcock R (2018) The antitrust duty to charge low prices. Cardozo Law Rev 39

Wright JD et al (2018) Requiem for a paradox: the dubious rise and inevitable fall of hipster antitrust. SSRN Electron J. https://doi.org/10.2139/ssrn.3249524 (last access 12 Sept 2021)

Xia L, Monroe KB, Cox JL (2004) The price is unfair! A conceptual framework of price fairness perceptions. J Market 68:1–15

Balancing Lives and Livelihoods

Informality of the Economy as a Challenge to Implementing the Obligation to Fulfil (Provide) the Right to Adequate Food During the COVID-19 Pandemic

Jean-Claude Misenga

Abstract The aim of this paper is to analyze how informality of the economy can constitute a challenge to implementing the States' obligation to fulfil (provide) the right to adequate food during the COVID-19 pandemic and reflect on how this could be addressed, including during similar crises in the future. The right to adequate food is recognized by several international and regional human rights instruments. Like all human rights, the right to adequate food imposes three types of obligations on States parties, namely the obligations to respect, protect, and fulfil. The latter, on which this paper focuses, requires States to provide the right to adequate food directly whenever an individual or group is unable, for reasons beyond their control, to enjoy that right by the means at their disposal. This paper argues that during the COVID-19 pandemic, States may face increased financial difficulties or challenges to implement the obligation to fulfil (provide) the right to adequate food in contexts where the informal economy is prevalent. These challenges could result from and/or be exacerbated by the magnitude of the informal economy and the duration of the COVID-19 pandemic or measures to contain it or from both factors. The two could affect the economic accessibility of the right to food for people working in the informal economy. This paper recommends that one of the ways in which States could overcome the challenges described above is by resorting to a more predictable and sustainable means to mobilize the resources needed to address the factors that prevent persons working in the informal economy from having access to food during the COVID-19 pandemic through, more specifically, social security or social protection. However, the informality of the economy can also constitute an impediment to financing social protection and/or extending it to informal workers. This paper recommends ways and means to overcome those challenges.

The views expressed herein are those of the author and do not necessarily represent the views of the United Nations.

J.-C. Misenga (✉)
UN Office of the High Commissioner for Human Rights (OHCHR), Geneva, Switzerland

© The Author(s), under exclusive license to Springer Nature Switzerland AG 2022
K. Mathis, A. Tor (eds.), *Law and Economics of the Coronavirus Crisis*, Economic Analysis of Law in European Legal Scholarship 13,
https://doi.org/10.1007/978-3-030-95876-3_6

1 Introduction

The aim of this paper is to analyze how informality of the economy can constitute a challenge to implementing the States' obligation to fulfil (provide) the right to adequate food during the COVID-19 pandemic and reflect on how this could be addressed, including during similar crises in the future. Before proceeding, it is therefore important to clarify the meaning of "informal economy" and the right to adequate food. This paper adopts the definition of the International Labour Organization (ILO), according to which the term informal economy refers to "all economic activities by workers and economic units that are, in law or in practice, not covered or insufficiently covered by formal arrangements".[1]

The right to adequate food is recognized by several international[2] and regional human rights instruments.[3] Moreover, many States have recognized or included the right to food in their constitutions.[4] As far as international human rights instruments are concerned, article 25 (1) of the Universal Declaration of Human Rights provides, "Everyone has the right to a standard of living adequate for the health and well-being of himself and of his family, including food (...)." In a similar vein, paragraph 1 of article 11 of the International Covenant on Economic, Social and Cultural Rights (CESCR) stipulates, "the States Parties to the present Covenant recognize the right of everyone to an adequate standard of living for himself and his family, including adequate food (...)." In its paragraph 2, article 11 adds that "the States Parties (...) recognize the fundamental right of everyone to be free from hunger (...)." However, despite this recognition, the true meaning of this human right is still misunderstood by many. One of the most common misconceptions about the right to adequate food is that this right is sometimes equated with "the right to be fed".[5] Another misconception is assuming that the human right to adequate food means that governments will be obligated to feed everyone directly.[6] However, as explained later in this paper, the right to be fed by the State applies only in exceptional circumstances. Illustrating this misconception, for instance, during the World Food Summit, held in Rome, Italy, from 10 to 13 June 2002, the United States attached a reservation to the Declaration of the Summit in which it stated:

---

[1] International Labour Organization (ILO) (01 June 2002), para. 3; ILO Conference (2015), para. 2 (a).

[2] These include the Universal Declaration of Human Rights (UDHR) [art. 25 (1)]; the CESCR Convention (art. 11); the UN Convention on the elimination of all forms of discrimination against women [art. 12(2))]; the UN convention on the rights of the child [articles art. 24 (2) (c) and (e) and art. 27 (3)]; the Convention on the rights of persons with disabilities [in art. 25 (f) and art. 28 (1)].

[3] These include the African charter on the rights and welfare of the child [arts 14 (2) (c), (d) and (h)]; the protocol to the African charter on human and peoples' rights on the rights of women in Africa [arts 14 (2) (b) and 15]; and the additional protocol to the American convention on human rights in the area of economic, social and cultural rights (arts 12 and 17).

[4] Vidar et al. (2014), pp. 2–5.

[5] Kent (2005), p. 103; OHCHR (2010), pp. 3–4.

[6] Kent (2005), p. 103.

> The United States believes that the issue of adequate food can only be viewed in the context of the right to a standard of living adequate for health and well-being, as set forth in the Universal Declaration of Human Rights, which includes the opportunity to secure food (...) Further, the United States believes that the attainment of the right to an adequate standard of living is a goal or aspiration to be realized progressively that does not give rise to any international obligation or any domestic legal entitlement (...). Additionally, the United States understands the right of access to food to mean the opportunity to secure food, and not guaranteed entitlement (...).[7]

One of the contributing factors to misconceptions around the right to adequate food could be the fact that the various instruments which recognize this right are not particularly explicit about its content. Alluding to this lack of clarity, the Rome Declaration on World Food Security and the World Food Summit Plan of Action, which was adopted following the World Food Summit of 1996, contained several objectives, including "to clarify the content of the right to adequate food and the fundamental right of everyone to be free from hunger, as stated in the International Covenant on Economic, Social and Cultural Rights and other relevant international and regional instruments."[8] (Objective 7.4)

In response to this need for clarity, the United Nations Committee on Economic, Social and Cultural Rights (CESCR Committee) adopted in 1999 its General Comment no 12 on the right to adequate food in which it provides the normative content of the right to food.[9] General Comments constitute authoritative explanations and interpretations of the nature, content, and scope of treaty provisions.[10] They are intended to assist States Parties in the implementation of those provisions at the domestic level.[11]

In its General Comment no 12, the CESCR Committee explained that "the right to adequate food is realized when every man, woman and child, alone or in community with others, have physical and economic access at all times to adequate food or means for its procurement".[12] The CESCR Committee stresses that the concept of "adequacy" serves to underline a number of factors, which must be taken into account in determining whether particular foods or diets that are accessible can be considered the most appropriate under given circumstances for the purposes of article 11 of the Covenant.[13]

According to the CESCR Committee, the core content of the right to adequate food implies two key elements, namely, first, the "availability" of food in a quantity and quality sufficient to satisfy the "dietary needs" of individuals, "free from adverse

---

[7] Annex II: explanatory notes/reservation in Report of the World Food Summit: five years later. Rome, 10–13 June 2002 (2002), http://www.fao.org/3/Y7106E/y7106e03.htm (last access 13 February 2021).

[8] World Food Summit (1996), para. 61.

[9] CESCR Committee (12 May 1999).

[10] Coomans (2009), p. 302.

[11] Coomans (2009), p. 302.

[12] CESCR Committee (12 May 1999), para. 6.

[13] CESCR Committee (12 May 1999), para. 7.

substances", and acceptable within a given culture; and, secondly, the "accessibility" of such food in ways that are "sustainable" and that do not interfere with the enjoyment of other human rights.[14] The CESCR Committee explains what it means by some of the key concepts that it uses in its definitions of "availability" and "accessibility" of food.

As far as the first element is concerned, "availability" refers to the possibilities either for feeding oneself directly from productive land or other natural resources, or for well-functioning distribution, processing, and market systems that can move food from the site of production to where it is needed in accordance with demand.[15] "Dietary needs" implies that the diet as a whole contains a mix of nutrients for physical and mental growth, development and maintenance, and physical activity that are in compliance with human physiological needs at all stages throughout the life cycle and according to gender and occupation.[16] "Free from adverse substances" sets requirements for food safety and for a range of protective measures by both public and private means to prevent contamination of foodstuffs through adulteration and/or through bad environmental hygiene or inappropriate handling at different stages throughout the food chain.[17] "Cultural or consumer acceptability" implies the need to also take into account, as far as possible, perceived non nutrient-based values attached to food and food consumption and informed consumer concerns regarding the nature of accessible food supplies.[18]

As regards the second element of the core content of the right to adequate food, namely, the accessibility of adequate food in ways that are "sustainable" and that do not interfere with the enjoyment of other human rights, the CESCR Committee explains that the concept of "accessibility" encompasses both economic and physical accessibility.[19] "Economic accessibility" implies that personal or household financial costs associated with the acquisition of food for an adequate diet should be at a level such that the attainment and satisfaction of other basic needs are not threatened or compromised.[20] "Physical accessibility" implies that adequate food must be accessible to everyone, including physically vulnerable individuals".[21] "Sustainability" implies food being accessible for both present and future generations.[22]

In a more detailed definition, the former UN Special Rapporteur on the right to food, Mr. Jean Ziegler, explains, "the right to food is the right to have regular, permanent and free access, either directly or by means of financial purchases, to quantitatively and qualitatively adequate and sufficient food corresponding to the

---

[14] CESCR Committee (12 May 1999), para. 8.
[15] CESCR Committee (12 May 1999), para. 12.
[16] CESCR Committee (12 May 1999), para. 9.
[17] CESCR Committee (12 May 1999), para. 10.
[18] CESCR Committee (12 May 1999), para. 11.
[19] CESCR Committee (12 May 1999), para. 13.
[20] CESCR Committee (12 May 1999), para. 13.
[21] CESCR Committee (12 May 1999), para. 13.
[22] CESCR Committee (12 May 1999), para. 7.

cultural traditions of the people to which the consumer belongs, and which ensures a physical and mental, individual and collective, fulfilling and dignified life free of fear".[23] Elsewhere, he uses a similar definition and simply replaces "free access" with "unobstructed access" and "life free of fear" with "life free from anxiety."[24] In summary, definitions of the right to food vary. However, they all focus on what right-holders are entitled to. It is therefore important to analyze the corresponding obligations of States, in their capacity as duty-bearers.

2 The Obligation to Fulfil (Provide) the Right to Adequate Food

As mentioned earlier, like all human rights, the right to adequate food imposes three types of obligations on States parties, namely the obligations to respect, to protect, and to fulfil. The obligation to respect existing access to adequate food requires States not to take any measures that result in preventing such access.[25] The obligation to protect the right to adequate food requires States to take measures to ensure that that third parties such as individuals, armed groups, enterprises or any other non-State actor do not deprive right-holders of their access to adequate food.[26] The obligation to fulfil the right to adequate food incorporates both an obligation "to facilitate" and an obligation "to provide".[27] The obligation to fulfil (facilitate) the right to adequate food requires States to proactively engage in activities intended to strengthen people's access to and utilization of resources and means to ensure their livelihood, including food security.[28] The obligation to fulfil (provide) the right to adequate food on which this paper focuses requires States to provide that right directly whenever an individual or group is unable, for reasons beyond their control, to enjoy that right by the means at their disposal.[29] In other words, as a last resort, direct assistance may have to be provided by States to ensure freedom from hunger,[30] whenever people are unable to access adequate food for reasons beyond

---

[23] Commission on Human Rights (7 February 2001), para. 14; Commission on Human Rights (16 March 2006), para. 2. See the same definition used in: Ziegler et al. (2011), p. 18.

[24] United Nations General Assembly (23 July 2001), para. 22.

[25] CESCR Committee (12 May 1999), para. 15; Commission on Human Rights (7 February 2001), para. 27; United Nations General Assembly (23 July 2001), para. 26; Commission on Human Rights (16 March 2006), para. 22.

[26] CESCR Committee (12 May 1999), para. 15; United Nations General Assembly (23 July 2001), para. 26; Commission on Human Rights (16 March 2006), para. 23; Cotula and Vidar (2002), p. 31.

[27] CESCR Committee (12 May 1999), para. 15.

[28] CESCR Committee (12 May 1999), para. 15.

[29] CESCR Committee (12 May 1999), para. 15.

[30] Commission on Human Rights (16 March 2006), para. 24.

their control.[31] States would violate that obligation if they let people starve when they were in desperate need and had no way of helping themselves.[32] Put simply, under International Human Rights Law (IHRL), whenever an individual or group is unable, for reasons beyond their control, to enjoy the right to adequate food by the means at their disposal, this gives rise to States' obligation to feed that individual or group or to provide them with the means to acquire food. Such circumstances also create, on the part of right-holders, a corresponding legal entitlement to be fed or to be provided with the means to acquire food.

As rightly underlined by many, in normal circumstances, most people realize the right to adequate food through their own efforts, for instance, by producing food themselves or by using their income to purchase food.[33] The obligation to fulfil (provide) is, therefore, an exception to this general rule. George Kent rightly refers to this obligation as "a residual category, becoming operational when "respect", "protect" and "facilitate" prove inadequate".[34]

Given that the implementation of the obligation to fulfil (provide) the right to adequate food entails directly providing right-holders with food or the means to acquire food, translating such an obligation into action might require the allocation and spending of extensive financial resources. Some authors even suggest that the obligation to fulfil (provide) is arguably the most costly part of the trilogy of the obligations to respect, protect, and fulfil.[35] This point is particularly important because, on the one hand, implementing the obligation to fulfil (provide) the right to adequate food is key to ensuring the enjoyment of the right to be free from hunger. On the other hand, the obligation to ensure the right to be free from hunger is part of the State's minimum core obligations.[36] Besides, one of the defining features of minimum core obligations is that they have to be realized immediately by all States and are not subject to the doctrine of progressive realization.[37] This doctrine latter recognizes that the full realization of all economic, social, and cultural rights will generally not be able to be achieved in a short period of time[38] and also takes into account the constraints resulting from the limits of available resources.[39] On the contrary, as stressed by Susan Randolph and Shareen Hertel, unlike the right to

---

[31] United Nations General Assembly (23 July 2001), para. 26; Commission on Human Rights (16 March 2006), para. 24.

[32] Commission on Human Rights (16 March 2006), para. 24.

[33] Cotula and Vidar (2002), p. 27; Kent (2005), p. 24, 104; Way (2005), p. 212; Food and Agriculture Organization of the United Nations (FAO) (2009), p. 51; Apodaca (2010), p. 57; Ziegler et al. (2011), p. 50.

[34] Kent (2005), p. 108.

[35] Chapman and Russell (2002), p. 12; Riedel et al. (2014), p. 20.

[36] CESCR Committee (12 May 1999), paras 6 and 14; See also CESCR Committee (1991), para. 10.

[37] Tasioulas (2017), pp. 10, 21, 27: See also Randolph and Hertel (2013), pp. 23–24.

[38] CESCR Committee (1991), para. 9.

[39] CESCR Committee (1991), para. 1; CESCR Committee (12 May 1999), paras 6 and 14; See also Brems (2009), pp. 354–355.

adequate food, which is a "relative standard", in that it is subject to progressive realization,[40] the right to be free from hunger is an absolute standard that must be fulfilled with immediate effect because freedom from hunger constitutes the minimum core content of the right to food.[41] In a similar vein, Destaw A. Yigzaw stresses that being a fundamental survival right, the right to be free from hunger entitles the right-holder to an immediate and unconditional provision of a minimum package of calories".[42] In summary, from an economic perspective, implementing the obligation to fulfil (provide) the right to food can be a costly undertaking. The fact that under IHRL, this is an obligation that requires immediate implementation to ensure freedom from hunger may make this economic challenge more daunting on the part of duty-bearers.

It is true that in its General Comment no 3 on the Nature of States Parties' Obligations, the CESCR Committee argues that any assessment as to whether a State has discharged its minimum core obligation must also take account of resource constraints applying within the country concerned.[43] However, this appears to be a departure from the view that minimum core obligations are to be given immediate effect by all States irrespective of their differences in levels of available resources.[44] This also seems to contradict the distinction that the CESCR Committee makes in the same General Comment when it stresses, "(...) while the Covenant provides for progressive realization and acknowledges the constraints due to the limits of available resources, it also imposes various obligations which are of immediate effect".[45] In any case, in its General Comment on the right to adequate food, the CESCR Committee stresses that violations of the Covenant occur when a State fails to ensure the satisfaction of, at the very least, the minimum essential level required to be free from hunger.[46] In other words, given that the right to be free from hunger is a survival right, all States, regardless of their resources, might have to implement the obligation to fulfil (provide) the right to food in order for freedom from hunger to have a true meaning. Failure to implement the obligation to fulfil (provide) may result in subjecting right-holders to starvation, particularly when they are unable, for reasons beyond their control, to enjoy that right by the means at their disposal, as has been the case for many individuals and families during the COVID-19 pandemic. Eventually, this might defeat the purpose of the right to be free from hunger. Implementing the obligation to fulfil (provide) and ensuring the realization of the related right to be free from hunger require finding ways and means of overcoming

---

[40] Randolph and Hertel (2013), p. 23.

[41] Randolph and Hertel (2013), pp. 23–24.

[42] Yigzaw (2014), p. 97.

[43] CESCR Committee (1991), para. 10.

[44] Maastricht Guidelines on Violations of Economic, Social and Cultural Rights (Maastricht, 22–26 January 1997), para. 9, http://hrlibrary.umn.edu/instree/Maastrichtguidelines_.html (last access 25 December 2020); Tasioulas (2017), pp. 21, 27.

[45] CESCR Committee (1991), para. 1.

[46] CESCR Committee (12 May 1999), para. 17.

some economic challenges (particularly, the cost of implementing this right) and some IHRL challenges (the immediate effects deriving from the right to be free from hunger). In light of the above, this paper, therefore, seeks to contribute to the scholarly discussion on the challenges that States can face in implementing a cost-intensive legal obligation, such as the obligation to fulfil (provide) the right to adequate food in a context of economic uncertainty such as the one created by the COVID-19 pandemic. Indeed, the latter has negatively affected the world economy (and reduced resources available to States) while at the same time putting millions of people in a situation where they require States to step in and provide them directly with food in order to realize their right to adequate food. Ultimately, this paper, therefore, contributes to the academic discussion on the cost of implementing human rights obligations.

Discussions of the costs of implementing human rights could be misconstrued as an attempt to use the lack of financial resources as an excuse or a justification for States' failure to implement or comply with their human rights obligations. As a result, such discussions could be met with suspicion. To be sure, this paper is not an attempt to provide a *legal justification* for the failure to implement the obligation to fulfil (provide) the right to adequate food during the COVID-19 pandemic. However, given that the law does not operate in a vacuum, this paper seeks to provide a *contextual explanation* of how extra-legal factors such as informality of the economy can constitute a challenge to implement the *legal obligation* to fulfil (provide) the right to food during the COVID-19 pandemic, the ultimate goal being to identify ways and means to overcome that challenge. To that end, in terms of theoretical framework, this paper mainly draws from the Chayeses' "Managerial Model" which is based on the assumption that one of the reasons behind States' failures to implement and/or comply with their obligations under international law is their limitations of capacity to do so.[47]

Understanding how informality of the economy can constitute a challenge to implement the legal obligation to fulfil (provide) the right to adequate food during the COVID-19 pandemic requires looking outside the law. That is why this paper adopts a sociolegal approach or "the use of concepts or methods taken from social sciences and humanities in the study of legal phenomena".[48]

This paper proceeds as follows. The next section presents the key argument put forward in the paper. Section 4 analyses the negative impact of COVID-19 on the right to adequate food and elaborates on why under IHRL, States have a legal obligation to step in through the obligation to fulfil (provide). Section 5 elaborates on the key argument put forward in this paper by examining challenges to implementing the obligation to fulfil (provide) the right to adequate food in a predominantly informal economy, namely those that could result from and/or be exacerbated by the magnitude of the informal economy and the duration of the COVID-19 pandemic or measures to contain it or from both factors. Section 6

---

[47] Chayes and Chayes (1995), pp. 13–15.
[48] Clark (2007), p. 1529.

discusses how social protection could constitute a long-term and more sustainable means to address the challenges identified in Sect. 5 and fulfil (provide) the right to adequate food during COVID-19 like situations. While stressing the potential of social protection, the section also examines how informality of the economy can constitute a challenge to financing and expanding the right to social protection. Section 7 explores some of the ways in which States can overcome challenges posed by the informality of the economy and create fiscal space to mobilize the resources that they need to implement the obligation to fulfil (provide) the right to adequate food. The last section concludes the paper.

3 Key Argument

Many have rightly underlined that all human rights, whether civil and political or economic, social and cultural, have a cost when it comes to their implementation.[49] The COVID-19 pandemic has arguably contributed to increasing this cost in many ways. First, as already documented by many, the pandemic has had a negative impact on the world economy, including on growth, GDP, trade, and exports.[50] Because of its economic impact, COVID-19 has therefore contributed to the reduction of financial resources available to the primary duty-bearers when it comes to implementing human rights obligations, namely States. This is likely to negatively affect States' capacity to shoulder the cost of implementing their human rights obligations.

Unfortunately, this increased cost of implementing human rights is likely to be exacerbated by an upsurge in human rights needs resulting from the COVID-19 pandemic. Indeed, as discussed by many, the pandemic has negatively affected various dimensions of human rights.[51] For instance, as a health crisis, the COVID-19 pandemic has increased the need for resources to implement the right to health (article 12 of the CESCR Convention). As rightly pointed out by Sharifah Sekalala et al., COVID-19 has illustrated to many countries that their health systems are unable to withstand a prolonged health crisis.[52] Indeed, several States have been faced with increasing numbers of people suffering from COVID-19 who have to be cared for by health services, sometimes for very long periods. This, in a context

---

[49] See for instance Holmes and Sunstein (1999), pp. 43–47; Sepúlveda (2003), pp. 126–128; Galligan and Sandler (2004), pp. 34–35; Koch (2009), pp. 70–72; Nolan (2011), pp. 27–29; Joseph and Castan (2013), pp. 39–40; Giacca (2014), p. 36.

[50] OECD (2 March 2020a), p. 1; World Trade Organization (WTO) (8 April 2020), p. 1; Maliszewska et al. (2020), pp. 2, 6–8, 17; World Food Programme (WFP) (14 April 2020); OECD (7 May 2020b); United Nations Conference on Trade and Development (UNCTAD) (2020), pp. 11–24.

[51] Studies that provide an overview of rights affected by the COVID-19 pandemic include Bennoune (2020), pp. 666–676; Spadaro (2020), pp. 317–325; and Sekalala et al. (2020), pp. 1–7.

[52] Sekalala et al. (2020), p. 3.

where several States did not have sufficient health infrastructures in terms of size and number to cope with the scale of the pandemic. Moreover, the duration of the pandemic, through its multiple waves and the emergence of new and more contagious or lethal variants of the coronavirus, could exacerbate the problem.

However, COVID-19 is more than just a public health crisis. The pandemic has affected the capacity of millions of individuals and households to realize the right to adequate food. As mentioned earlier, according to the CESCR Committee, the core content of the right to adequate food implies two key elements, namely, first, the "availability" of food in a quantity and quality sufficient to satisfy the "dietary needs" of individuals, "free from adverse substances", and acceptable within a given culture; and, secondly, the economic and physical "accessibility" of such food in ways that are "sustainable" and that do not interfere with the enjoyment of other human rights.[53] While all these aspects might have been affected by the COVID-19 pandemic, this paper concentrates on economic accessibility or food affordability for individuals or households. This is a component that has been particularly affected by the COVID-19 pandemic.

Indeed, by negatively affecting the economy, the COVID-19 pandemic has either directly or indirectly contributed to reducing the purchasing power of millions of individuals and households. Many individuals and families have lost their jobs and, therefore, their main sources of income, partly due to the measures put in place to combat COVID-19, such as curfews and other containment measures. The ability of these individuals and families to meet their daily needs, including food, has therefore been reduced. In legal terms, the COVID-19 pandemic has created conditions in which the right of many people to be free from hunger is under threat. The pandemic has therefore increased the number of rights-holders who may require States' intervention, in terms of direct provision, to realize their human rights to, for instance, health or food. This, in a context where, because of the economic impact of COVID-19, States have suffered from a reduction in their financial resources.

Discussing these issues is important on a theoretical level. Indeed, understanding how the COVID-19 pandemic has increased the cost of implementing human rights is particularly crucial in many respects. First, as mentioned earlier, the obligation to fulfil (provide) is arguably the most costly part of the trilogy of the obligations to respect, protect, and fulfil.[54] In addition to that, it is important to stress, as acknowledged explicitly[55] or implicitly[56] by some authors, that direct provision of food by the State can be a particularly costly undertaking for States.

In light of the above, this paper argues that during the COVID-19 pandemic, States may face increased financial difficulties or challenges to implement the obligation to fulfil (provide) the right to food in contexts where the informal economy is prevalent. These difficulties or challenges could result from and/or be

---

[53] CESCR Committee (12 May 1999), para. 8.

[54] Chapman and Russell (2002), p. 12; Riedel et al. (2014), p. 20.

[55] Nickel (1987), p. 164; Nickel (1985), p. 224.

[56] Kent (2005), p. 112.

exacerbated by the magnitude of the informal economy and the duration of the COVID-19 pandemic or measures to contain it or from both factors. The two could affect the economic accessibility of the right to food for people working in the informal economy. More specifically, as stressed by many, the obligation to fulfil (provide) the right to food is an obligation of last resort.[57] Put differently, States would normally be expected to implement this obligation during exceptional circumstances, having to directly feed a small number of right-holders who are unable to access the right to food by their own means. As such, States may face challenges to implement this obligation in a context where unlike the ideal situation described above, the informal economy is prevalent and where, as a consequence, States are legally required under IHRL to feed a much higher number of right-holders, who normally work in the informal economy. This could happen when these right-holders are unable to work, earn a living, and feed themselves because of the economic impact of the COVID-19 pandemic and/or of measures taken by States to contain the pandemic (such as lockdowns, curfews, stay-at-home orders). Related to this, States may face challenges to implement the obligation to fulfil (provide) the right to food in a context where, due to various reasons, including a prolonged/protracted COVID-19 pandemic, States have to enforce measures to contain the pandemic (such as lockdowns, curfews, stay-at-home orders) for an extended period of time. In so doing, States would continue to put individuals who normally work in the informal economy in a situation where they are unable to earn an income and feed themselves and have to continue to rely on the State to feed them as a matter of IHRL. This paper recommends that one of the ways in which States could overcome the challenges described above is by resorting to a more predictable and sustainable means to address the factors that prevent persons working in the informal economy from having access to food during the COVID-19 pandemic, more specifically, through social security or social protection. Indeed, the right to social security or social protection, which is recognized, *inter alia,* under article 9 of the CESCR, encompasses the right to access and maintain benefits, whether in cash or in kind, without discrimination, in order to secure protection, *inter alia,* from lack of work-related income caused by unemployment.[58] However, the informality of the economy can constitute an impediment to financing social protection and/or extending it to informal workers here as well. This paper recommends ways and means those challenges could be overcome.

---

[57] United Nations General Assembly (23 July 2001), para. 26; Kent (2005), p. 108; Commission on Human Rights (16 March 2006), para. 24; Food and Agriculture Organization of the United Nations (FAO) (2009), p. 51; Cotula and Vidar (2002), p. 34; Way (2005), p. 212; Kent (2005), p. 108.
[58] CESCR Committee (4 February 2008), para. 2.

4 The Negative Impact of COVID-19 on the Right to Food and the Legal Obligation for States to Step in Through the Obligation to Fulfil (Provide)

In normal circumstances, most people realize the right to adequate food through their own efforts, for instance, by producing food themselves or by using their income to purchase food. However, the COVID-19 pandemic has negatively affected employment and ultimately incomes both in the formal and the informal economy. This, in turn, has affected the purchasing power of individuals and households and their ability to realize the right to food by their own means, or, put simply, to feed themselves. In this respect, the most recent data from the ILO provide a rather grim picture. Indeed, according to the ILO, the share of workers living in countries with COVID-19-related restrictions has remained high, with 93% of the world's workers residing in countries with some form of workplace closure measures in place in early January 2021.[59] In 2020, 8.8% of global working hours were lost relative to the fourth quarter of 2019, equivalent to 255 million full-time jobs.[60] Global labor income in 2020 was estimated to have declined by 8.3%, which amounted to US$3.7 trillion, or 4.4% of global gross domestic product (GDP).[61] The latest projections indicated a persistent work deficit in 2021.[62] In summary, the COVID-19 pandemic has affected and is likely to continue to affect many people's ability to earn an income and realize the right to adequate food by their own means. Illustrating this trend, several studies published recently have addressed the multiple ways in which the COVID-19 pandemic has affected the enjoyment of the right to food, including by reducing people's purchasing power (through, for instance, business closures) or by affecting agricultural production or the food supply chain and contributing to price hikes (through, for example, movement restrictions or border closures in countries that rely on food imports) in a context where many suffered a reduction or absence of earnings/income.[63] For instance, in a study examining the impact of movement restrictions, border closures, social distancing, quarantine, and closure of non-essential services in Kenya and Uganda, Monica K. Kansiime et al., found that the proportion of food insecure respondents increased by 38% and 44% in Kenya and Uganda respectively.[64] In a study focusing on South Africa, Channing Arndt et al. found that one of the direct impacts of the lockdown policies was that wage earnings were down by about 30% in total and that earnings by lower-educated workers (with at most primary school education) fell by

---

[59] ILO (25 January 2021), p. 1.
[60] ILO (25 January 2021), p. 1.
[61] ILO (25 January 2021), p. 2.
[62] ILO (25 January 2021), p. 2.
[63] See for instance Ayanlade and Radeny (2020), pp. 1 and 3; Arndt et al. (2020), pp. 1–5; Abdul (2020), pp. 1 and 3–4; Harris et al. (2020), pp. 841–849; Mottaleb et al. (2020), pp. 2–7 and 9–17; Summerton (2020), pp. 333–336 and 338; Kansiime et al. (2021), pp. 1–10.
[64] Kansiime et al. (2021), p. 2.

more than 40%.[65] They concluded that for a household dependent on wage earnings from low-educated labor, these declines were clearly sufficient to threaten food security, particularly if the household was already vulnerable.[66]

One of the categories whose capacity to realize the right to adequate food has been the most affected during the COVID-19 pandemic consists of persons working in the informal economy. Indeed, many people working in the informal economy cannot earn a living unless they go out on a daily basis. In other words, some of the measures that States have put in place to prevent the spread of COVID-19, for example, lockdowns, curfews, and stay-at-home orders have made it impossible for many people working in the informal economy to earn a living and obtain financial means to feed themselves.

As stressed by ILO:

> Many women and men in the informal economy need to earn an income to feed themselves and their families, as most of them cannot rely on income replacement or savings. Not working and staying home means losing their jobs and their livelihoods. 'To die from hunger or from the virus' is the all-too-real dilemma faced by many informal economy workers.[67]

Under IHRL, the situation described above requires States to step in and provide food directly to right-holders. However, as explained in the next section, States may face several challenges to implement the obligation to fulfil (provide) the right to food in a context characterized by an economy that is predominantly informal.

5 Challenges to Implementing the Obligation to Fulfil (Provide) the Right to Adequate Food in a Predominantly Informal Economy

The next subsections first elaborate on challenges that could result from and/or be exacerbated by the magnitude of the informal economy, and then on the ones that could result from and/or be exacerbated by the duration of the COVID-19 pandemic or measures to contain it.

5.1 The Magnitude of the Informal Economy

In an economy that is predominantly informal, where people are unable to realize the right to adequate food by their own means due to the COVID-19 pandemic, the sheer number of right-holders who require direct intervention by States to realize their

---

[65] Arndt et al. (2020), p. 3.
[66] Arndt et al. (2020), p. 3.
[67] ILO (May 2020), p. 1.

right to adequate food could be overwhelming. In this respect, it is worth recalling that, for instance, according to the ILO, in 2020, over two billion workers were earning their livelihoods in the informal economy (62% of all those working worldwide).[68] Informal employment represented 90% of total employment in low-income countries, 67% in middle-income countries, and 18% in high-income countries.[69] Providing food or the means to acquire food to such a sizeable proportion of the population in low-income countries might constitute a daunting challenge for States. Related to the sheer number of right-holders is the financial cost of the direct provision of food by States or the provision of the means to procure it for these rights-holders in a context where the economy is predominantly informal.

In this regard, as pointed by many, some States appear to have been faced with a dilemma between protecting public health by taking restrictive measures to prevent the spread of the COVID-19 pandemic and ensuring the food security of millions of right-holders who would be affected by such restrictive measures.[70] This dilemma seems to have been exacerbated by the magnitude of the informal economy.[71] In this respect, an analysis of public statements made by various officials in a number of countries suggests that the decision not to impose COVID-19 lockdowns or to implement less stringent measures was influenced partly by economic concerns regarding the perceived or real limited capacity on the part of the State to feed a population that is largely composed of persons working in the informal economy. These decisions were partly informed by the livelihood concerns of persons working in the informal economy. For instance, in a recent study, Regina Birner et al. found that in Zambia, Ghana, and Benin, governments justified the absence of stricter measures to prevent the spread of COVID-19 largely with poverty and food security concerns".[72]

More specifically, in Benin, where according to recent data, the informal economy represented 90.6% of total employment,[73] President Patrice Talon explained on 29 March 2020 that "unlike the citizens of developed countries in America, Europe and Asia, the vast majority of Beninese do not earn a wage income".[74] He asked, "How many people in Benin earn a monthly salary and can spend two, three or four weeks even without working and live on a monthly income? (...) How can one decree without notice, a long-term country-wide lockdown in such a context where most of our fellow citizens rely on the previous day's income to buy groceries?"[75] While President Talon insisted on the need to fight the COVID-19 pandemic, he equally stressed that, in the Beninese socio-economic context, nationwide lockdown

---

[68] ILO (May 2020), p. 1.
[69] ILO (May 2020), p. 1.
[70] Daniel et al. (2020), p. 2; Birner et al. (2020), p. 1.
[71] Daniel et al. (2020), pp. 2 and 5.
[72] Birner et al. (2020), p. 8.
[73] ILO (2018), p. 86.
[74] Vidjingninou (30 March 2020).
[75] Vidjingninou (30 March 2020).

measures would be counterproductive; that they would have the consequence of "starving everyone at once and for too long" and would also be "challenged and flouted without achieving their goals".[76] In lieu of the lockdowns imposed in neighboring countries, Benin opted for the less restrictive "sanitary cordon".[77]

In Zambia, where according to recent data 88.7% of the employed population worked in the informal economy,[78] on 24 April 2020, President Edgar Lungu announced the easing of some measures put in place on 25 March 2020 and stressed, inter alia, "(...) countrymen and women, we have to choose life or livelihood or both."[79] Speaking about the impact of the COVID-19 on households and alluding to people who rely on a daily income, President Lungu noted, "I feel your pain. I do not need to mention you individually but I know that little outlet that has been closed brings nshima[80] to your table. That little outlet that has been closed pays your rent. That little outlet pays school fees."[81]

Similar concerns were expressed in Tanzania, where according to recent data, the informal economy represented 83.5% of total employment.[82] Here, the deputy minister of health, Mr. Faustine Ndugulile, noted that "when you go for a total lockdown it means some will instead die of hunger."[83] It is worth noting that in the case of Tanzania, the adoption of less restrictive measures appears to have also been influenced by the well-documented denial and/or downplaying of COVID-19 by some of the authorities.[84]

The concerns expressed by countries whose decisions were informed by food security concerns appear to be justified. Indeed, Jean-Philippe Bonardi et al. found a correlation between informality of the economy and the poor compliance with lockdowns.[85] In a similar vein, Leonard E.G. Mboera et al. found that lack of food assistance is an impediment to compliance with lockdown measures.[86] Several countries put in place restrictive measures such as lockdowns, curfews and stay-at-home orders without taking similar measures to ensure that their populations continued to enjoy their right to food. As a result, some people disregarded those measures and left their homes in an attempt to earn an income. As perfectly summarized by one Nigerian newspaper, "Hunger obeys no order".[87] For people faced with the risk of starvation, survival instinct overrode the fear of punishment.

---

[76] Vidjingninou (30 March 2020).

[77] Gouvernement de la République du Bénin (27 March 2020).

[78] ILO and OECD (2019), p. 7.

[79] Republic of Zambia, State House (24 April 2020).

[80] "Nshima" is a staple food in Zambia.

[81] Republic of Zambia, State House (24 April 2020).

[82] ILO (2018), p. 85.

[83] Kell (2020).

[84] News 24 (21 April 2020), Odula (2020), and Rédaction Africanews (2021).

[85] Bonardi et al. (2020).

[86] Mboera et al. (2020), p. 309.

[87] Diamond et al. (2020).

Some States responded to these violations of lockdown and other curfews by sending in the police and other security forces to enforce these measures and apprehend those who broke them. In the process, these forces committed multiple human rights violations such as arbitrary arrests and detentions, torture and ill-treatment, excessive use of force, including lethal, as documented in various human rights reports.[88] Thus, taking restrictive measures to contain the COVID-19 pandemic without taking corresponding measures to ensure that right-holders continued to enjoy their right to food has contributed to further human rights violations. This highlights the interdependence of human rights.

The current subsection has explained and provided illustrations of how the magnitude of the informal economy can constitute a challenge to implement the obligation to fulfil (provide) the right to food. The next section discusses how this challenge could be exacerbated by the duration of the pandemic.

5.2 The Duration of the COVID-19 Pandemic in an Economy That Is Predominantly Informal as an Exacerbating Factor

As a means of last resort and an exceptional measure, the obligation to fulfil (provide) the right to adequate food is *prima facie* intended to be implemented in a short period of time, the expectation being that the small number of right-holders, who receive assistance from the State, will be able to provide for themselves as quickly as possible. As rightly stressed by George Kent, the obligation to fulfil (provide) is "a residual category, becoming operational when "respect", "protect" and "facilitate" prove inadequate".[89] However, if the COVID-19 becomes a protracted pandemic, the obligation to fulfil (provide) may shift from being an obligation of last resort to becoming "a routine obligation". Indeed, as long as the right-holders cannot realize the right to food by their own means because of the COVID-19 pandemic, States are required under IHRL to feed them directly or to provide them with the resources that they need to feed themselves. Depending on the duration of the COVID-19 pandemic (combined with the magnitude of the informal economy), some States may therefore face economic challenges that may limit their ability to implement their legal obligation to feed their populations directly. Some States may have to discontinue food assistance programmes because they cannot afford the cost. Others may choose to lift measures aimed at preventing the spread of COVID-19, sometimes prematurely and/or against scientific advice, so that they no

---

[88] See for instance The Open Society Justice Initiative (2020); Namwaya (2020); CBS News (2020); Human Rights Watch (2020a, b); Wurth and Conde (2020), https://www.hrw.org/news/2020/04/03/philippine-children-face-abuse-violating-covid-19-curfew (last access 24 May 2020); Human Rights Watch (2020a, b); Amnesty International (2020) pp. 11–19.
[89] Kent (2005), p. 108.

longer have to bear the financial costs generated by such measures, including the financial costs generated by the obligation to feed their populations. Illustrating this, a review of public statements made by various officials indicates that in some countries, the decision to ease or lift COVID-19 lockdown measures, sometimes prematurely and/or against scientific advice, was also partly informed by economic concerns regarding the perceived or real limited capacity on the part of States to feed populations that are largely composed of persons working in the informal economy. In some of those countries, national authorities referred, either implicitly or explicitly, to food security concerns facing persons working in the overwhelmingly informal economy of their countries as one of the reasons for prematurely lifting or loosening the COVID-19 prevention measures. For instance, regarding Ghana, a country where according to recent data, the informal economy's share of employment was 84.8%,[90] Regina Birner et al. explain that the President of the country explicitly cited food security risks when easing the lockdown relatively quickly.[91] Similar concerns appear to have been at play in the case of countries such as Djibouti (where the most recent data indicates that informal enterprises were estimated at about 60% of business activity)[92] or Nigeria (where according to the most recent data, the informal economy represented 80.4% of the total employment).[93]

In Djibouti, on 10 May 2020, the country started easing lockdown measures put in place on 23 March 2020.[94] The Minister of Foreign Affairs, Mr. Mahmoud Ali Youssouf, explained, "(...) the stakes are high but there is no other option: people need to make their living and go to work (...)."[95] While making this announcement, he also acknowledged that "new epicenters of contamination could emerge in the capital city (...)."[96] Illustrating the premature nature of this decision, on the same 10 May 2020, the Minister backpedaled and announced that the country had reversed course on the plan to begin lifting lockdown measures.[97] He explained that the government had decided to extend the lockdown for another week until 17 May 2020 because "the pre-requisite conditions for lifting lockdown are not in place."[98]

In Nigeria, on 27 April 2020, President Buhari announced "a phased and gradual easing of lockdown measures" in Abuja, Ogun, and Lagos.[99] These measures had been put in place on 30 March 2020, then extended on 13 April 2020. In his address,

---

[90] ILO (2018), p. 86.
[91] Birner et al. (2020), p. 11.
[92] African Development Bank Group (2011), p. 9.
[93] ILO (2018), p. 86.
[94] Krippahl (2020).
[95] Radio France Internationale (RFI) (2020a, b) and Al Jazeera (2020).
[96] Al Jazeera (2020).
[97] Agence France Presse (AFP) (2020).
[98] Radio France Internationale (RFI) (2020a, b).
[99] Kazeem (2020).

Table 1 Percentage of respondents who would face barriers to a 14-day stay-at-home order [Partnership for Evidence-Based Response to COVID-19 (PERC) (undated), p. 12]

	Northern region (%)	Eastern region (%)	Southern region (%)	Western region (%)	Central region (%)
Running out of food, water	23	73	70	83	83
Running out of money	26	48	51	62	61
Losing your job	19	16	20	16	18

he acknowledged that "such lockdowns have also come at a very heavy economic cost."[100] He explained that "many of our citizens have lost their means of livelihood" and that "many businesses have shut down"[101] before stressing that "no country can afford the full impact of a sustained lockdown while awaiting the development of vaccines or cures."[102] He explained that "the Federal and State Governments have jointly and collaboratively worked hard on (...) how to balance the need to protect health while also preserving livelihoods (...)."[103]

The food security concerns expressed by countries that prematurely eased COVID-19 restrictions also appear to be justified. For instance, as shown in Table 1, in a survey conducted between 29 March and 17 April 2020 in 28 cities across 20 African Union Member States, a majority of the respondents feared that they would run out of food, water, and/or money during a 14-day stay-at-home order.

What transpires from the discussion above is that informality of the economy seems to have constituted a challenge for many States when faced with the decision to put in place restrictive measures to contain the COVID-19 pandemic. One of those challenges has been how to ensure that the millions of individuals and families who were unable to earn an income because of these restrictive measures did not starve. The next section analyses how social security or social protection could help address that challenge.

---

[100] France 24 (2020).

[101] France 24 (2020).

[102] Orjinmo (2020).

[103] Address by H.E. Muhammadu Buhari, President of the Federal Republic of Nigeria on the cumulative lockdown order of Lagos and Ogun states as well as the federal capital territory on COVID-19 pandemic at the State House, Abuja Monday (2020), para. 28, https://nairametrics.com/2020/04/27/fill-speech-of-president-buhari-on-covid-19-pandemic/ (last access 25 December 2020).

6 Social Protection as a Long-Term and More Sustainable Means to Implement the Obligation to Fulfil (Provide) the Right to Food

Article 22 of the UDHR provides, "Everyone, as a member of society, has the right to social security." Article 9 of the CESCR provides that "the States parties to the present covenant recognize the right of everyone to social security, including social insurance." Before going further, it is worth clarifying that "social security" and "social protection" are sometimes used interchangeably in the literature.[104]

So, what is "social security" (hereinafter "social protection")? Definitions of "social protection" vary. The International Labour Organization (ILO) defines it as "the set of policies and programs designed to reduce and prevent poverty, vulnerability and social exclusion throughout the life cycle".[105] The Statistical Office of the European Communities (EUROSTAT), on its part defines social protection as "encompass(ing) all interventions from public or private bodies intended to relieve households and individuals of the burden of a defined set of risks or needs, provided that there is neither a simultaneous reciprocal nor an individual arrangement involved".[106] In a nutshell, social protection refers to policies, programmes, or interventions from public or private bodies to address a defined set of risks, needs, vulnerabilities, or contingencies faced by individuals, households, or communities throughout their life cycle. While acknowledging the importance of "informal" social protection provided, for instance, by relatives and other informal sources, this paper focuses on formal social protection provided by the State in its capacity as the primary duty-bearer when it comes to the implementation of human rights obligations.

Regarding the risks, needs, vulnerabilities, or contingencies addressed by social protection, the ILO Social Security (Minimum Standards) Convention of 1952 (no 102) groups them under nine branches. These are: medical care;[107] sickness benefit;[108] unemployment benefit;[109] old-age benefit;[110] employment injury benefit;[111] family benefit;[112] maternity benefit;[113] invalidity benefit;[114] and survivors'

---

[104] ILO (2017), p. 195.

[105] ILO (2017), p. 194.

[106] Statistical Office of the European Communities (EUROSTAT) (1996), p. 12.

[107] ILO (1952), articles 7–12.

[108] ILO (1952), articles 13–18.

[109] ILO (1952), articles 19–24.

[110] ILO (1952), articles 25–30.

[111] ILO (1952), articles 31–38.

[112] ILO (1952), articles 39–45.

[113] ILO (1952), articles 46–52.

[114] ILO (1952), articles 53–58.

benefit.[115] These nine categories are also reaffirmed by the CESCR Committee in its General Comment no 19 on the right to social security.[116] However, taking into account that all the nine categories cannot be achieved immediately, the international community has agreed on "social protection floors" enshrined in the ILO Recommendation no 202 adopted in 2012.[117]

Social protection floors are nationally defined sets of basic social security guarantees which secure protection aimed at preventing or alleviating poverty, vulnerability, and social exclusion.[118] More specifically, according to Recommendation no 202, national social protection floors should comprise at least the following basic social security guarantees: (a) access to a nationally defined set of goods and services, constituting essential health care, including maternity care, that meets the criteria of availability, accessibility, acceptability, and quality; (b) basic income security for children, at least at a nationally defined minimum level, providing access to nutrition, education, care, and any other necessary goods and services; (c) basic income security, at least at a nationally defined minimum level, for persons in active age who are unable to earn sufficient income, in particular in cases of sickness, unemployment, maternity, and disability; and (d) basic income security, at least at a nationally defined minimum level, for older persons.[119]

In a context such as the COVID-19 pandemic, which is primarily a public health crisis, the importance of a basic social security guarantee constituting essential health care cannot be overstated. In addition, given the economic impact of COVID-19, it goes without saying that a basic income security for persons in active age who are unable to earn sufficient income, in particular in cases of sickness or unemployment, is crucial. Now that the meaning of social protection is clear, the next sub-section examines how social protection can constitute a long-term and more sustainable means to implement the obligation to fulfil (provide) the right to adequate food during a crisis such as the COVID-19 pandemic.

6.1 The Complementarity Between Social Protection and the Obligation to Fulfil (Provide) the Right to Food

Social protection is one of the key vehicles for implementing the obligation to fulfil (provide) the right to adequate food. Social protection, contributes, *inter alia,* to removing the financial barriers to access food.[120] Social safety nets and food safety nets serve as a method by which States may fulfil their obligation to provide for the

---

[115] ILO (1952), articles 59–64.
[116] CESCR Committee (2008), paragraphs 12–21.
[117] ILO (14 Jun 2012).
[118] ILO (14 Jun 2012), para. 2.
[119] ILO (14 Jun 2012), para. 5.
[120] FAO (2017), p. 10.

implementation of the right to adequate food of those that, for reasons beyond their control, cannot provide for it themselves.[121]

From an IHRL perspective, a well-funded and well-functioning social protection system or program that provides universal access to essential social transfers and services can enable States to be better prepared to fulfil the rights of people under their jurisdiction, including the right to adequate food, when unpredictable events such as the COVID-19 pandemic occur. In a context where millions of right-holders are unable to earn an income, a well-funded social protection system or program can provide the desperately needed income replacement. Social protection systems or programs, therefore, provide a framework through which States can regularly and progressively invest resources that can help them respond to shocks such as the COVID-19 pandemic in a more predictable manner. In summary, social protection is an investment for the future.

As far as the COVID-19 pandemic is concerned, empirical data shows that social protection measures have had a positive impact on people's compliance with measures such as lockdowns.[122] Unfortunately, while the benefits of social protection are undeniable, the prevalence of informality in a country's economy can constitute a challenge to financing and expanding social protection.

6.2 Informality of the Economy as a Challenge to Financing and Expanding the Right to Social Protection

Informality can constitute a barrier to financing and expanding this right, particularly in contexts where social protection is mainly funded through taxes, specifically income taxes. Indeed, while in such contexts people working in the informal economy may constitute the majority of workers and therefore of potential taxpayers when it comes to income tax, several studies have found that the size of the informal economy contributes to a reduction in government fiscal revenues[123] and limit governments' ability to fund public programs such as social protection.[124] One of the reasons behind the correlation between the prevalence of the informal economy

---

[121] FAO (2006), p. 152.

[122] See for instance Akim and Ayivodji (2020), pp. 3 and 18.

[123] See for instance Davoodi and Grigorian (2007), p. 35; Chaudhry and Munir (2010), pp. 439–452 and 449; Besley and Persson (2014), pp. 100 and 109–110; Ebifuro et al. (2016), pp. 1–13; Munjeyi et al. (2017), pp. 142–146.

[124] See for instance Devereux and Sabates-Wheeler (2004), pp. 7–8; Barrientos and Hulme (2008), p. 13; Kundt (2017), p. 4; World Bank (2019), pp. 76, 105, 113, 115, 131, 158; Kundt (2017), p. 4.

and low fiscal incomes is because, as explained by many, taxing the informal economy is a challenging task.[125]

As far as the correlation between, one the one hand, the size of the informal sector, and on the other hand, low-income taxation and government expenditures, a World Bank study finds that in emerging markets and developing economies with the most pervasive informality, government revenues are lower by 5–10 percentage points of GDP and expenditures lower by 4–10 percentage points of GDP than in those with the lowest levels of informality.[126] Speaking specifically about social protection, Stephen Devereux and Rachel Sabates-Wheeler stress, for instance, that, in poor countries, one of the varieties of constraints that restrict the range of social protection services offered by the welfare state is the limited resources for formal social protection measures, given low tax-generated revenue and competing demands on the national budget.[127] This point can be better understood by looking closely at the level of financing required to ensure a minimum level of social protection. In this respect, the ILO carried out simulations for twelve low-income countries in Africa and Asia[128] to assess the resources required in relation to GDP between 2008 and 2034. The study found that the total expenditure would range between 3.8% and 10.6% of GDP in 2008 to 4.3% to 9.4% of GDP in 2034.[129] Referring to these projections, Armando Barrientos and David Hulme acknowledge that financing this basic level of social assistance appears affordable for most developing countries, but it is bound to be more difficult to achieve for low-income countries with low revenue mobilization capacity.[130] Looking at the impact of COVID-19, one could anticipate that the level of expenditure could even be higher. To that end, one simply needs to look at one of the four social protection benefits that is arguably among the most needed during COVID-19 lockdowns, namely unemployment benefit or "social assistance/employment scheme". The cost of the latter appears low at face value. Indeed, according to ILO projections, the annual cost of providing this benefit is estimated at between 0.3% and 0.7% of annual GDP in 2020.[131] However, when put in a context characterized by a high level of informality, one can quickly see the challenge that could result from the discrepancy between the high number of right-holders who need unemployment benefits and the limited resources that could be available to States to ensure that right-holders actually receive unemployment benefits.

---

[125] See for instance Schneider and Klinglmair (2004); Kundt (2017), pp. 2, 5–6, 8–9, 11, 13; Joshi et al. (2012), pp. 6, 9–10, 12; Keen (2012); Pimhidzai and Fox (2012); Besley and Persson (2014), pp. 109–110.

[126] World Bank (2019), pp. 131 and 158.

[127] Devereux and Sabates-Wheeler (2004), pp. 7–8.

[128] Those countries were Burkina Faso, Cameroon, Ethiopia, Guinea, Kenya, Senegal, United Republic of Tanzania, Bangladesh, India, Nepal, Pakistan, and Viet Nam.

[129] ILO (2008), p. 23.

[130] Barrientos and Hulme (2008), p. 16.

[131] ILO (2008), p. 24.

To make matters worse, the ILO costing model is based on the assumption that unemployment benefit would be provided to 10% of the working-age population in each country.[132] Here as well, in a context where the economy is predominantly informal, the percentage of potential beneficiaries is likely to exceed 10%. As mentioned earlier, according to the ILO, in 2020, approximately 62% of all those working worldwide were earning their livelihoods in the informal economy.[133] Informal employment represented 90% of total employment in low-income countries, 67% in middle-income countries, and 18% in high-income countries.[134]

Moreover, ILO simulations were based on the assumption that the simulated employment scheme would provide a benefit of a maximum of one US dollar per day that would be paid for a total of 100 days in the year.[135] The duration of the COVID-19 pandemic has shown that right-holders might need unemployment benefits for more than 100 days to realize their right to adequate food and meet their other basic needs. Responding to the human rights needs created by a pandemic whose economic effects have been felt since April–March 2020 would require paying unemployment benefits for more than the 100 days envisioned in the ILO simulations.

In summary, given their vulnerability to unemployment or income losses, people working in the informal economy are arguably among the segments of the population that may be the most in need of social protection. However, the prevalence of the informal economy can make it difficult for States to fund social protection. This means that in an economy where informality is prevalent, States should not rely on income taxes as the main means to mobilize financial resources that are required to fund social protection and ultimately implement their obligation to fulfil(provide) the right to adequate food. States need to look beyond and find other resources. In IHRL language, States need to use their "maximum available resources" (not only income taxes) to fund social protection. In economic terms, the obligation to use maximum available resources relate to creating fiscal space.

7 Using "Maximum Available Resources" to Overcome Challenges Posed by the Prevalence of the Informality of the Economy

Under article 2(1) of the CESCR, "Each State Party undertakes to take steps (...) to *the maximum of its available resources*, with a view to achieving progressively the full realization of the rights recognized in the Covenant (...)." The CESCR Committee has emphasized this obligation to use maximum available resources also in

---

[132] ILO (2008), p. 9.
[133] ILO (May 2020), p. 1.
[134] ILO (May 2020), p. 1.
[135] ILO (2008), p. 9.

the context of the right to adequate food[136] and the right to social protection.[137] Speaking about the right to social protection in the context of informal economy, the CESCR Committee stresses, *inter alia,* that "States parties must take steps to the maximum of their available resources to ensure that the social security systems cover those persons working in the informal economy".[138] The CESCR Committee underlines that "this duty is particularly important where social security systems are based on a formal employment relationship, business unit or registered residence."[139] The obligation to use "maximum available resources" is, therefore, key to mobilizing and hopefully utilizing resources that are needed to fund social protection and to implementing the obligation to fulfil (provide) the right to food, particularly in contexts where the economy is predominantly informal.

Before going further, it is important to clarify the meaning of the phrase "maximum available resources". Indeed, as pointed by many, this phrase can be subject to misinterpretation.[140] One reason behind this could be the fact that "maximum" and "available" can mean opposite things. As rightly explained by Robert E. Robertson, the phrase "maximum available resources" is a difficult phrase that combines two warring adjectives describing an undefined noun.[141] "Maximum" stands for idealism; "available" stands for reality.[142] "Maximum" is the sword of human rights rhetoric; "available" is the wiggle room for the state".[143] Put differently, a "narrow" interpretation of the phrase "maximum available resources" may tend to focus on the word "available" while a more "ambitious" interpretation would tend to focus on the word "maximum".

An analysis of Concluding Observations issued by United Nations Human Rights Bodies can help gain a better understanding of the meaning of the phrase "maximum available resources". In this respect, in its Concluding Observations, the CESCR Committee has recommended specific measures that States can take to mobilize "maximum available resources" needed for the implementation of socio-economic rights such as the right to adequate food or the right to social protection. Without claiming to be exhaustive, this paper identifies four areas where the CESCR Committee provides such guidance.

The first one is related to the formulation and implementation of budgets. Indeed, as stressed by OHCHR, a carefully developed, implemented, and evaluated budget is central to the realization of all rights.[144] Regarding the formulation and implementation of budgets, the CESCR Committee recommends, for instance, that States take

---

[136] CESCR Committee (1999), para. 17.
[137] CESCR Committee (2008), para. 4.
[138] CESCR Committee (2008), para. 34.
[139] CESCR Committee (2008), para. 34.
[140] Robertson (1994), p. 694; Haugen (2007), p. 93.
[141] Robertson (1994), p. 694.
[142] Robertson (1994), p. 694.
[143] Robertson (1994), p. 694.
[144] OHCHR (2017), p. 11.

appropriate measures to ensure that all budget proposals are prepared in a transparent and participatory manner.[145] Indeed, as emphasized by Olivier De Schutter, how States mobilize resources and how they define their spending priorities is a human rights issue, and those decisions cannot be left to the arbitrary and capricious choices of States and need to be scrutinized.[146] Transparent and participatory budget processes can help ensure that the voices and needs of right-holders are better taken into account when deciding on budget allocations. Ultimately, this could help mitigate the risks of misallocations of funds. Right-holders and other stakeholders participating in budget processes can help ensure that human rights issues are appropriately budgeted for.

The CESCR Committee also recommends that States take appropriate measures to ensure adequate budget allocations for social spending, including reprioritizing the allocation of resources, increasing the level of funding allocated to social services,[147] or reducing security and military spending.[148] This reprioritization can also result from recommendations made during a participatory budget process. In addition, the CESCR Committee recommends that States put in place or strengthen monitoring and accountability mechanisms to ensure that adequate budgetary resources are allocated to efforts towards the realization of the rights contained in the CESCR and that those resources are spent in a timely, effective, and transparent manner.[149] Monitoring and accountability mechanisms are crucial to prevent misuse of funds or other forms of wastage. One of the tools that could help assess the extent to which States are using their budgetary processes to mobilize and use their "maximum available resources" to realize the right to food is the human

---

[145] CESCR Committee (6 November 2018), para. 13; CESCR Committee, Concluding observations on the fourth periodic report of Cameroon, UN doc no: E/C.12/CMR/CO/4 (25 March 2019), para. 15; CESCR Committee, Concluding observations on the third periodic report of Senegal, UN doc no: E/C.12/SEN/CO/3 (13 November 2019), para. 11.

[146] De Schutter (2019), p. 59.

[147] CESCR Committee, UN doc no: E/C.12/UGA/CO/1 (8 July 2015), para. 8; CESCR Committee, UN doc no: E/C.12/IRQ/CO/4 (27 October 2015), para. 16; CESCR Committee, UN doc no: E/C.12/SDN/CO/2 (27 October 2015), para. 16 (d); CESCR Committee, UN doc no: E/C.12/PAK/CO/1 (20 July 2017), para. 16; CESCR Committee, UN doc no: E/C.12/PAK/CO/1 (20 July 2017), para. 16; CESCR Committee, UN doc no: E/C.12/MDA/CO/3 (19 October 2017), para. 15; CESCR Committee, UN doc no: E/C.12/KOR/CO/4 (19 October 2017), para. 12 (a); CESCR Committee, UN doc no: E/C.12/BGD/CO/1 (18 April 2018), para. 20; CESCR Committee, UN doc no: E/C.12/NZL/CO/4 (1 May 2018), para. 15; CESCR Committee, UN doc no: E/C.12/NER/CO/1 (4 June 2018), para. 10 (b); CESCR Committee, UN doc no: E/C.12/CPV/CO/1 (27 November 2018), para. 13 (a); CESCR Committee, UN doc no: E/C.12/EST/CO/3 (27 March 2019), para. 9; CESCR Committee, UN doc no: E/C.12/KAZ/CO/2 (29 March 2019), para. 20; CESCR Committee, UN doc no: E/C.12/UKR/CO/7 (2 April 2020), para. 5 (b).

[148] CESCR Committee, UN doc no: E/C.12/SDN/CO/2 (27 October 2015), para. 16 (c).

[149] CESCR Committee, UN doc no: E/C.12/GMB/CO/1 (20 March 2015), para. 10; CESCR Committee, UN doc no: E/C.12/PAK/CO/1 (20 July 2017), para. 16; CESCR Committee, UN doc no: E/C.12/KOR/CO/4 (19 October 2017), para. 12 (c); CESCR Committee, UN doc no: E/C.12/NER/CO/1 (4 June 2018), para. 10 (a); CESCR Committee, UN doc no: E/C.12/CPV/CO/1 (27 November 2018), para. 13 (b).

rights-based budget analysis. This includes analyzing how governments manage the economy and development; how they generate resources; how they allocate financial and other resources; how they actually spend the resources; the outcomes achieved by those expenditures and the processes of government in making these decisions.[150]

The second area where the CESCR Committee recommends specific measures that States can take to mobilize and use the "maximum available resources" needed for the implementation of socio-economic rights, is the one related to fiscal policies. Speaking about the linkages between fiscal policies and human rights, Philip Alston and Nikki Reisch explain how taxation affects the realization of human rights in all countries, developed and developing alike, through its role in resource mobilization, redistribution, regulation, and representation.[151] Stressing specifically the importance of the fiscal policies in the realization of economic, social, and cultural rights, Olivier De Schutter lists three reasons why taxation policies are human rights policies.[152] One of the reasons stressed by De Schutter is that taxation allows States to mobilize resources in order to invest in various sectors, which are indispensable for the enjoyment of the rights of the Covenant of the ICESCR.[153] Another reason stressed by De Schutter that is relevant in the context of this paper is that taxation allows States to redistribute wealth from the richest parts of the population to the poorest.[154]

When it comes to fiscal policies as a means of mobilizing "maximum available resources", the CESCR Committee recommends, for instance, measures to increase the collection of taxes and/or to ensure the optimal collection of taxes, including by expanding the tax base;[155] improving tax collection;[156] and increasing the collection of tax arrears.[157] In an economy that is predominantly informal, this would require, for instance, identifying other sources of taxes beyond income tax. The Committee also recommends combating illicit financial flows, tax fraud, tax avoidance, tax evasion, and tax abuse schemes.[158] In addition, the Committee recommends that States increase the fees charged to foreign investors for the exploitation of natural

---

[150] O'Connell et al. (2014), pp. 19–20.

[151] Alston and Reisch (2019), pp. 4–6.

[152] De Schutter (2019), p. 59.

[153] De Schutter (2019), p. 59.

[154] De Schutter (2019), p. 59.

[155] CESCR Committee, UN doc no: E/C.12/BGD/CO/1 (18 April 2018), para. 20.

[156] CESCR Committee, UN doc no: E/C.12/BGD/CO/1 (18 April 2018), para. 20.

[157] CESCR Committee, UN doc no: E/C.12/MEX/CO/5-6 (17 April 2018), para. 15 (b).

[158] CESCR Committee, UN doc no: E/C.12/KEN/CO/2-5 (6 April 2016), para. 18; CESCR Committee, UN doc no: E/C.12/LIE/CO/2-3 (3 July 2017), para. 10; CESCR Committee, UN doc no: E/C.12/BGD/CO/1 (18 April 2018), para. 20; CESCR Committee, UN doc no: E/C.12/ESP/CO/6 (25 April 2018), para. 16 (e); CESCR Committee, UN doc no: E/C.12/ZAF/CO/1 (29 November 2018), para. 17 (d); CESCR Committee, UN doc no: E/C.12/CHE/CO/4 (18 November 2019), para. 13; CESCR Committee, UN doc no: E/C.12/BEL/CO/5 (26 March 2020), para. 17; CESCR Committee, UN doc no: E/C.12/UKR/CO/7 (2 April 2020), para. 5 (d).

resources such as forests, fisheries, or extractive resources[159] as well as to regularly review the concessions or tax exemptions granted to investors to attract them to the various countries; assess the resulting loss of revenue and take corrective action as required.[160] More generally, the CESCR Committee recommends that States take measures, including evaluations or reviews, to ensure that fiscal policies contribute to maximizing the mobilization of domestic resources, are socially just, and have a broad redistributive effect.[161]

The third area where the CESCR Committee recommends specific measures that States can take to mobilize the "maximum available resources" needed for the implementation of socio-economic rights, is the fight against corruption.[162] Several authors have addressed the multiple ways in which corruption affects States' capacity to mobilize financial resources that they need to uphold their human rights obligations.[163] Fighting corruption is, therefore, a key part of efforts to mobilize "maximum available resources".

Lastly, the CESCR Committee recommends that States seek international assistance and cooperation, where necessary, in their efforts to mobilize resources.[164] In this respect, it is worth stressing that in its General Comment no 3 on the nature of States parties' obligations, the CESCR Committee notes that the phrase "to the maximum of its available resources" was intended by the drafters of the covenant to refer to both the resources existing within a state and those available from the international community through international cooperation and assistance.[165]

In summary, an analysis of Concluding Observations issued by United Nations Human Rights Bodies can help uncover the multiple options that States can explore

---

[159] CESCR Committee, UN doc no: E/C.12/CMR/CO/4 (25 March 2019), para. 15; CESCR Committee, UN doc no: E/C.12/SEN/CO/3 (13 November 2019), para. 11.

[160] CESCR Committee, UN doc no: E/C.12/ESP/CO/6 (25 April 2018), para. 16 (d); CESCR Committee, UN doc no: E/C.12/BEN/CO/3 (27 March 2020), para. 12; CESCR Committee, UN doc no: E/C.12/MLI/CO/1 (6 November 2018), para. 13.

[161] CESCR Committee, UN doc no: E/C.12/PAK/CO/1 (20 July 2017), para. 16; CESCR Committee, UN doc no: E/C.12/LKA/CO/5 (4 August 2017), para. 22; CESCR Committee, UN doc no: E/C.12/RUS/CO/6 (16 October 2017), para. 17; CESCR Committee, UN doc no: E/C.12/COL/CO/6 (19 October 2017), para. 20; CESCR Committee, UN doc no: E/C.12/MEX/CO/5-6 (17 April 2018), para. 15 (a); CESCR Committee, UN doc no: E/C.12/BGD/CO/1 (18 April 2018), para. 20; CESCR Committee, UN doc no: E/C.12/ESP/CO/6 (25 April 2018), para. 16 (b); CESCR Committee, UN doc no: E/C.12/ESP/CO/6 (25 April 2018), para. 16 (a); CESCR Committee, UN doc no: E/C.12/CPV/CO/1 (27 November 2018), para. 13 (d); CESCR Committee, UN doc no: E/C.12/ZAF/CO/1 (29 November 2018), para. 17 (a) and 17 (c); CESCR Committee, UN doc no: E/C.12/EST/CO/3 (27 March 2019), para. 9; CESCR Committee, UN doc no: E/C.12/ECU/CO/4 (14 November 2019), para. 22; CESCR Committee, UN doc no: E/C.12/UKR/CO/7 (2 April 2020), para. 5 (c).

[162] CESCR Committee, UN doc no: E/C.12/SDN/CO/2 (27 October 2015), para. 16 (b); CESCR Committee, UN doc no: E/C.12/KEN/CO/2-5 (6 April 2016), para. 18.

[163] See for instance Gathii (2009), pp. 126 and 174; Ngugi (2010), p. 246.

[164] CESCR Committee, UN doc no: E/C.12/GIN/CO/1 (30 March 2020), para. 13; CESCR Committee, UN doc no: E/C.12/CPV/CO/1 (27 November 2018), para. 13 (e).

[165] CESCR Committee (1991), para. 13.

to mobilize resources and hopefully utilize to implement their human rights obligations, including to fulfil (provide) the right to adequate food.

As mentioned earlier, in economic terms, mobilizing (and hopefully utilizing) maximum available resources is almost the IHRL equivalent of the concept of creating fiscal space that economists are familiar with. In this respect, Isabel Ortiz, Matthew Cummins, and Kalaivani Karunanethy argue that fiscal space and national capacity to finance social protection exist worldwide, even in the poorest countries.[166] They present eight financing alternatives to that end. Of the eight options, six are aimed at increasing the overall size of a country's budget. These are first, increasing tax revenues;[167] second, expanding social security coverage and contributory revenues;[168] third, lobbying for increased aid and transfers;[169] fourth, eliminating illicit financial flows;[170] fifth, borrowing or restructuring debt,[171] and sixth, adopting a more accommodative macroeconomic framework.[172] The other two options are about redirecting existing resources from one area to another, in this case, social protection. These two options are first re-allocating public expenditures[173] and; second, tapping into fiscal and foreign exchange reserves.[174] Many of these options have also been invoked by the CESCR Committee in its recommendations on how States can mobilize maximum available resources.

What transpires from the discussion above is that while informality of the economy constitutes a challenge to funding and expanding social protection, this challenge is not insurmountable. In addition to income taxes, which are difficult to mobilize and rely on in an economy that is predominantly informal, States have several other options that they can explore to finance social protection and the right to adequate food.

8 Conclusion

The aim of this paper was to analyze how informality of the economy can constitute a challenge to implementing States' obligation to fulfil (provide) the right to adequate food during the COVID-19 pandemic and to reflect on how this could be addressed, including in similar global and domestic crises (in the future). Following a short introduction and a presentation of the key argument put forward, this paper

---

[166] Ortiz et al. (2017), pp. 2 and 52.
[167] Ortiz et al. (2017), pp. 1 and 5–7.
[168] Ortiz et al. (2017), pp. 1 and 19–21.
[169] Ortiz et al. (2017), pp. 1 and 22–27.
[170] Ortiz et al. (2017), pp. 1 and 28–30.
[171] Ortiz et al. (2017), pp. 1 and 38–45.
[172] Ortiz et al. (2017), pp. 1 and 46–51.
[173] Ortiz et al. (2017), pp. 1 and 5–7.
[174] Ortiz et al. (2017), pp. 1 and 31–37.

analyzed the negative impact of the COVID-19 pandemic on the right to adequate food and explained why under IHRL, the States have a legal obligation to step in and implement their obligation to fulfil (provide) this right directly. The paper then examined two key challenges to implementing the obligation to fulfil (provide) the right to adequate food in contexts where the economy is predominantly informal. More specifically, the paper, firstly, analyzed challenges that could result from and/or be exacerbated by the magnitude of the informal economy and, secondly, those that could result from and/or be exacerbated by the duration of the COVID-19 pandemic or measures to contain the pandemic. This was followed by a discussion on how social protection can constitute a long-term and more sustainable means to address the challenges to implementing the obligation to fulfil (provide) the right to adequate food in a predominantly informal economy. While highlighting the positive role of social protection, this paper also reflected on how informality of the economy can constitute an obstacle to financing and expanding the right to social protection. Before this concluding section, the paper explored some of the ways in which States can overcome challenges posed by the prevalence of the informal economy and create fiscal space to mobilize resources that they need to implement the obligation to fulfil (provide) the right to adequate food. A key conclusion that can be drawn from this paper is that challenges to implementing the obligation to fulfil (provide) the right to adequate food in a predominantly informal economy are not insurmountable.

Indeed, this paper shows that there is a broad array of measures that States can take to overcome the above-mentioned challenges. Put differently, there is a broad array of measures that States could have taken over the years to better prepare themselves to address some of the human rights challenges resulting from the COVID-19 pandemic, including those relating to the implementation of the obligation to fulfil (provide) the right to adequate food in contexts where the economy is predominantly informal. As the saying goes, "better late than never." The COVID-19 pandemic should therefore serve as a wake-up call for States. While the COVID-19 pandemic constitutes a challenge, it should also serve as an opportunity to reflect on how States can proactively take all the appropriate measures that could enable them to be in a position to better implement their human rights obligations, should similar circumstances arise in the future. Indeed, the COVID-19 pandemic constitutes an unprecedented challenge for States, households, and individuals. The pandemic has shown us how unprepared our societies were to address some of the most pressing issues, such as providing health care or food to all who needed them. However, the pandemic is also an opportunity to learn from and better prepare for the future. In summary, the COVID-19 pandemic offers States an opportunity to "build back better" or "recover better". This means, amongst other things, moving beyond short-term emergency response measures to the COVID-19 pandemic and taking all appropriate measures to identify and address the multiple factors, including socio-economic ones, which have contributed to exacerbating the impact of COVID-19.[175]

---

[175] United Nations (September 2020a), pp. 63–66.

It also means transforming economies and creating more equitable societies that allow everyone to enjoy the full range of their human rights, including the right to adequate food.[176]

References

Books, Book Chapters and Journal Articles

Abdul IM (2020) COVID-19, lockdown and transitory food insecurity in Nigeria. Food Agribus Manag (FABM) 1(1):26–30
Alston P, Reisch N (2019) Introduction. In: Alston P, Reisch N (eds) Tax, inequality, and human rights. Oxford University Press, New York, pp 1–30
Apodaca C (2010) Child hunger and human rights: international governance. Routledge, Oxon
Arndt C et al (2020) COVID-19 lockdowns, income distribution, and food security: an analysis for South Africa. Glob Food Secur 26:1–5
Ayanlade A, Radeny M (2020) COVID-19 and food security in sub-Saharan Africa: implications of lockdown during agricultural planting seasons. Sci Food 4(13):1–6
Bennoune K (2020) "Lest we should sleep": COVID-19 and human rights. Am J Int Law 114(4): 666–676
Besley T, Persson T (2014) Why do developing countries tax so little? J Econ Perspect 28(4): 99–120
Brems E (2009) Human rights: minimum and maximum perspectives. Hum Rights Law Rev 9(3): 349–372
Chapman AR, Russell S (2002) Introduction. In: Chapman A, Russel S (eds) Core obligations: building a framework for economic, social and cultural rights. Intersentia, Antwerp, pp 1–19
Chaudhry IS, Munir F (2010) Determinants of low tax revenue in Pakistan. Pakistan J Soc Sci (PJSS) 30(2):439–452
Chayes A, Chayes AH (1995) The new sovereignty: compliance with international regulatory agreements. Harvard University Press, Cambridge
Clark DS (ed) (2007) Encyclopedia of law and society: American and global perspectives. Sage, Thousand Oaks
Coomans F (2009) The International Covenant on Civil and Political Rights. In: Isa FG, de Feyter K (eds) International human rights law in a global context. University of Deusto, Bilbao, pp 293–318
De Schutter O (2019) Taxing for the realization of economic, social, and cultural rights. In: Alston P, Reisch N (eds) Tax, inequality, and human rights. Oxford University Press, New York, pp 59–79
Ebifuro O, Mienye E, Odubo TV (2016) Application of GIS in improving tax revenue from the informal sector in Bayelsa State, Nigeria. Int J Sci Res Publ 6(8):1–13
Galligan D, Sandler D (2004) Implementing human rights. In: Halliday S, Schmidt P (eds) Human rights brought home: socio-legal perspectives on human rights in the national context. Hart, Oxford, pp 23–55
Gathii JT (2009) Defining the relationship between human rights and corruption. Univ Pa J Int Law 31(1):125–202
Giacca G (2014) Economic, social, and cultural rights in armed conflict. Oxford University Press, Oxford

---

[176] United Nations (27 October 2020b), pp. 1 and 13–14.

Harris J et al (2020) Food system disruption: initial livelihood and dietary effects of COVID-19 on vegetable producers in India. Food Secur 12:841–851

Haugen HM (2007) The right to food and the TRIPS Agreement: with a particular emphasis on developing countries' measures for food production and distribution. Martinus Nijhoff, Leiden

Holmes S, Sunstein CR (1999) The cost of rights: why liberty depends on taxes. W. W. Norton & Company, New York

Joseph S, Castan M (2013) The International Covenant on Civil and Political Rights: cases, materials, and commentary, 3rd edn. Oxford University Press, Oxford

Kansiime MK et al (2021) COVID-19 implications on household income and food security in Kenya and Uganda: findings from a rapid assessment. World Dev 137:1–10

Kent G (2005) Freedom from want: the human right to adequate food. Georgetown University Press, Washington D.C.

Koch IE (2009) From invisibility to indivisibility: the International Convention on the Rights of Persons with Disabilities. In: Arnardóttir OM, Quinn G (eds) The UN Convention on the Rights of Persons with Disabilities: European and Scandinavian perspectives. Martinus Nijhoff, Leiden, pp 67–79

Mboera LEG et al (2020) Mitigating lockdown challenges in response to COVID-19 in sub-Saharan Africa. Int J Infect Dis 96:308–310

Mottaleb KA, Mainuddin M, Sonobe T (2020) COVID-19 induced economic loss and ensuring food security for vulnerable groups: policy implications from Bangladesh. PLoS One 15(10):1–20

Munjeyi E et al (2017) The informal sector tax revenue potential: a case of Zimbabwe. Res J Finance Account 8(8):142–146

Ngugi JM (2010) Making the link between corruption and human rights: promises and perils. Am Soc Int Law Proc 104:246–250

Nickel JW (1985) The feasibility of welfare rights in less developed countries. In: Kipnis K, Meyers DT (eds) Economic justice: private rights and public responsibilities. Rowman & Allanheld, New Jersey, pp 217–225

Nickel JW (1987) Making sense of human rights: philosophical reflections on the universal declaration of human rights. University of California Press, Berkeley

Nolan A (2011) Children's socio-economic rights, democracy and the courts. Hart, London

O'Connell R et al (2014) Applying an international human rights framework to state budget allocations: rights and resources. Routledge, Oxon

Randolph S, Hertel S (2013) The right to food: a global perspective. In: Minkler L (ed) The state of economic and social human rights: a global overview. Cambridge University Press, New York, pp 21–60

Riedel E, Giacca G, Golay C (2014) The development of economic, social, and cultural rights in international law. In: Riedel E, Giacca G, Golay C (eds) Economic, social and cultural rights in international law: contemporary issues and challenges. Oxford University Press, Oxford, pp 3–48

Robertson RE (1994) Measuring state compliance with the obligation to devote the "Maximum Available Resources" to realizing economic, social, and cultural rights. Hum Rights Q 16(4):693–714

Sekalala S et al (2020) Health and human rights are inextricably linked in the COVID-19 response. BMJ Glob Health 5:1–7

Sepúlveda MM (2003) The nature of the obligations under the International Covenant on Economic, Social and Cultural Rights. Intersentia, Antwerpen

Spadaro A (2020) COVID-19: testing the limits of human rights. Eur J Risk Regul 11(2):317–325

Summerton SA (2020) Implications of the COVID-19 pandemic for food security and social protection in India. Indian J Hum Dev 14(2):333–339

Way S-A (2005) The role of the UN Human Rights bodies in promoting and protecting the right to food. In: Eide WB, Kracht U (eds) Food and human rights in development: legal and institutional dimensions and selected topics, vol 1. Intersentia, Antwerp, pp 205–226

Yigzaw DA (2014) Hunger and the law: freedom from hunger as a freestanding right. Houst J Int Law 36(3):655–714

Ziegler J et al (2011) The fight for the right to food: lessons learned. Palgrave Macmillan, Basingstoke

Online Documents

Akim A-M, Ayivodji F (2020) Interaction effect of lockdown with economic and fiscal measures against COVID-19 on social-distancing compliance: evidence from Africa (7 June 2020). https://papers.ssrn.com/sol3/papers.cfm?abstract_id=3621693. Last accessed 06 Feb 2021

Address by H.E. Muhammadu Buhari, President of the Federal Republic of Nigeria on the cumulative lockdown order of Lagos and Ogun states as well as the federal capital territory on COVID-19 pandemic at the State House, Abuja Monday (27th April 2020) paragraph 28. https://nairametrics.com/2020/04/27/fill-speech-of-president-buhari-on-covid-19-pandemic/. Last accessed 25 Dec 2020

African Development Bank Group (2011) Djibouti country strategy paper 2011–2015 (August 2011). https://www.afdb.org/fileadmin/uploads/afdb/Documents/Project-and-Operations/Djibouti%20-%20CSP%202011-15.pdf. Last accessed 14 Feb 2021

Agence France Presse (AFP) (2020) Hard-hit Djibouti delays plan to ease virus lockdown measures (10 May 2020). https://news.yahoo.com/hard-hit-djibouti-ease-virus-lockdown-measures-064546163.html. Last accessed 26 Dec 2021

Al Jazeera (2020) People need to make a living: Djibouti eases COVID-19 lockdown (10 May 2020). https://www.aljazeera.com/news/2020/5/10/people-need-to-make-a-living-djibouti-eases-covid-19-lockdown. Last accessed 26 Dec 2021

Amnesty International (2020) COVID-19 crackdowns: police abuse and the global pandemic (Amnesty International 2020). https://www.amnesty.org/download/Documents/ACT3034432020ENGLISH.PDF. Last accessed 07 Mar 2021

Barrientos A, Hulme D (2008) Social protection for the poor and poorest in developing countries: reflections on a quiet revolution (Brooks World Poverty Institute Working Paper 30, March 2008). http://citeseerx.ist.psu.edu/viewdoc/download?doi=10.1.1.371.310&rep=rep1&type=pdf. Last accessed 13 Nov 2020

Birner R et al (2020) We would rather die from Covid-19 than from hunger – exploring lockdown stringencies in five African countries (Hohenheim Working Papers on Social and Institutional Change in Agricultural Development Working Paper 005-2020, December 2020). https://490c.uni-hohenheim.de/fileadmin/einrichtungen/490c/Publikationen/WP_005-2020_Covid-19_Lockdowns.pdf. Last accessed 06 Feb 2021

Bonardi JP et al (2020) Fast and local: how did lockdown policies affect the spread and severity of COVID-19 (8 June 2020). https://e4s.center/wp-content/uploads/2020/09/Fastandlocal_full_EN-1.pdf. Last access 06 Feb 2021

CBS News (2020) South Africa security forces fire rubber bullets at people defying coronavirus stay-at-home orders (1 April 2020). https://www.cbsnews.com/news/south-africa-coronavirus-security-forces-rubber-bullets-stay-at-home-orders/. Last accessed 24 May 2020

Cotula L, Vidar M (2002) The right to adequate food in emergencies (FAO legislative study 77, FAO 2002). http://www.fao.org/3/a-y4430e.pdf. Last accessed 30 July 2020

Daniel E et al (2020) Informality and COVID-19 in sub-Saharan Africa (Policy brief, October 2020). https://www.theigc.org/wp-content/uploads/2020/10/Informality-and-Covid-19-in-SSA_final.pdf. Last accessed 07 Feb 2021

Davoodi HR, Grigorian DA (2007) Tax Potential vs. Tax Effort: A cross-country analysis of Armenia's stubbornly low tax collection (IMF Working Paper, WP/07/106, 2007). https://www.imf.org/en/Publications/WP/Issues/2016/12/31/Tax-Potential-vs-20642. Last accessed 20 Dec 2020

Devereux S, Sabates-Wheeler R (2004) Transformative social protection (Institute of Development Studies Working Paper 232, October 2004). https://opendocs.ids.ac.uk/opendocs/bitstream/handle/20.500.12413/4071/Wp232.pdf?sequence=1. Last accessed 13 Nov 2020

Diamond M, Adeowo A, Ezeilo O (2020) COVID-19 lockdown: hunger obeys no order, say Nigerians defying stay-at-home directive (25 April 2020). https://guardian.ng/saturday-magazine/covid-19-lockdown-hunger-obeys-no-order-say-nigerians-defying-stay-at-home-directive/. Last accessed 19 May 2020

FAO (2017) FAO social protection framework promoting rural development for all (FAO 2017). http://www.fao.org/3/a-i7016e.pdf. Last accessed 23 Jan 2021

FAO (2006) The right to food guidelines: information papers and case studies (FAO, Roma 2006). http://www.fao.org/docs/eims/upload/214344/rtfg_eng_draft_03.pdf. Last accessed 7 Aug 2020

FAO (2009) Methods to monitor the human right to adequate food. Volume I: Making the case for rights-focused and rights-based monitoring (FAO 2009). http://www.fao.org/3/i0349e/i0349e.pdf. Last accessed 30 July 2020

France 24 (2020) Nigeria to ease Covid-19 lockdown for millions in key cities on 4 May (28 April 2020). https://www.france24.com/en/20200428-nigeria-to-ease-covid-19-lockdown-for-millions-in-key-cities-on-4-may. Last accessed 25 Dec 2020

Gouvernement de la République du Bénin (2020) Coronavirus – Communiqué du Ministre de l'intérieur au sujet du Cordon Sanitaire (27 March 2020). https://www.gouv.bj/actualite/571/coronavirus%2D%2D-communique-ministre-interieur-sujet-cordon-sanitaire/. Last accessed 16 Mar 2021

Human Rights Watch (2020a) DR Congo: respecting rights key amid COVID-19 (3 April 2020). https://www.hrw.org/news/2020/04/03/dr-congo-respecting-rights-key-amid-covid-19. Last accessed 24 May 2020

Human Rights Watch (2020b) Uganda: respect rights in COVID-19 response (2 April 2020). https://www.hrw.org/news/2020/04/02/uganda-respect-rights-covid-19-response. Last accessed 24 May 2020

ILO (1952) Convention No. 102 on Social Security (Minimum Standards) (1952). https://www.ilo.org/dyn/normlex/en/f?p=NORMLEXPUB:12100:0::NO::P12100_ILO_CODE:C102. Last accessed 13 Nov 2020

ILO (2002) Resolution and conclusions concerning decent work and the informal economy (01 June 2002) para. https://www.ilo.org/wcmsp5/groups/public/%2D%2D-ed_norm/%2D%2D-relconf/%2D%2D-reloff/documents/meetingdocument/wcms_080105.pdf. Last accessed 23 May 2020

ILO (2008) Can low-income countries afford basic social security? (Social Security Policy Briefings, Paper 3, ILO 2008). https://www.social-protection.org/gimi/RessourcePDF.action?id=5951. Last accessed 17 Sept 2020

ILO (2012) Social Protection Floors Recommendation, 2012 (No. 202) (14 June 2012). https://www.ilo.org/dyn/normlex/en/f?p=NORMLEXPUB:12100:0::NO::P12100_INSTRUMENT_ID:3065524. Last accessed 23 May 2020

ILO (2017) World Social Protection Report 2017–19: universal social protection to achieve the Sustainable Development Goals (ILO 2017). https://www.ilo.org/wcmsp5/groups/public/%2D%2D-dgreports/%2D%2D-dcomm/%2D%2D-publ/documents/publication/wcms_604882.pdf. Last accessed 23 May 2020

ILO (2018) Women and men in the informal economy: a statistical picture (Third Edition, 2018). https://www.ilo.org/wcmsp5/groups/public/%2D%2D-dgreports/%2D%2D-dcomm/documents/publication/wcms_626831.pdf. Last accessed 19 Dec 2020

ILO (2020) COVID-19 crisis and the informal economy: immediate responses and policy challenges (May 2020). https://www.ilo.org/wcmsp5/groups/public/%2D%2D-ed_protect/%2D%2D-protrav/%2D%2D-travail/documents/briefingnote/wcms_743623.pdf. Last accessed 23 May 2020

ILO (2021) COVID-19 and the world of work: updated estimates and analysis (ILO Monitor, Seventh edition, 25 January 2021). https://www.ilo.org/global/topics/coronavirus/impacts-and-responses/WCMS_767028/lang%2D%2Den/index.htm. Last accessed 25 Feb 2021

ILO, OECD (2019) Informality and Poverty in Zambia: findings from the 2015 Living Conditions and Monitoring Survey, October 2018 (ILO, 2019). https://www.ilo.org/wcmsp5/groups/public/%2D%2D-africa/%2D%2D-ro-abidjan/%2D%2D-ilo-lusaka/documents/publication/wcms_697953.pdf. Last accessed 13 Feb 2021

International Labour Conference (2015) Recommendation concerning the transition from the informal to the formal economy, adopted by the conference at its one hundred and fourth session (recommendation 204) (12 June 2015). https://www.ilo.org/wcmsp5/groups/public/%2D%2D-ed_norm/%2D%2D-relconf/documents/meetingdocument/wcms_377774.pdf. Last accessed 15 Aug 2020

Krippahl C (2020) Lifting Africa's COVID-19 lockdown poses problems (12 May 2020). https://www.dw.com/en/lifting-africas-covid-19-lockdown-poses-problems/a-53401241. Last accessed 07 Feb 2021

Kundt TC (2017) Opportunities and challenges for taxing the informal economy and subnational taxation (October 2017). https://assets.publishing.service.gov.uk/media/5b3b64a6e5274a6fe8b7048e/Opportunities_and_challenges_for_taxing_the_informal_economy_and_subnational_taxation.pdf. Last accessed 20 June 2020

Joshi A, Prichard W, Heady C (2012) Taxing the informal economy: challenges, possibilities and remaining questions (ICTD Working Paper 4, August 2012). https://opendocs.ids.ac.uk/opendocs/bitstream/handle/20.500.12413/2309/ICTD%20Working%20Paper%204.pdf. Last accessed 20 June 2020

Kazeem Y (2020) Nigeria is set to ease its coronavirus lockdown in major cities despite mounting cases (28 April 2020). https://qz.com/africa/1846758/nigeria-to-ease-coronavirus-lockdown-from-may-2-says-buhari/. Last accessed 25 Dec 2020

Keen M (2012) Taxation and Development—Again (International Monetary Fund (IMF) Working Paper, WP/12/220, September 2012). https://www.imf.org/external/pubs/ft/wp/2012/wp12220.pdf. Last accessed 05 Sept 2020

Kell F (2020) Tanzania evades COVID-19 lockdown, but restrictions persist (21 May 2020). https://www.chathamhouse.org/2020/05/tanzania-evades-covid-19-lockdown-restrictions-persist. Last accessed 07 Feb 2021

Maliszewska M, Mattoo A, van der Mensbrugghe D (2020) The potential impact of COVID-19 on GDP and trade: a preliminary assessment (Policy Research Working Paper 9211, World Bank Group, April 2020). http://documents.worldbank.org/curated/en/295991586526445673/pdf/The-Potential-Impact-of-COVID-19-on-GDP-and-Trade-A-Preliminary-Assessment.pdf. Last accessed 13 June 2020

Namwaya O (2020) Kenya police abuses could undermine coronavirus fight (31 March 2020). https://www.hrw.org/news/2020/03/31/kenya-police-abuses-could-undermine-coronavirus-fight. Last accessed 24 May 2020

OHCHR (2017) Realizing human rights through government budgets (New York and Geneva, 2017). https://www.ohchr.org/Documents/Publications/RealizingHRThroughGovernmentBudgets.pdf. Last accessed 21 Dec 2020

OHCHR (2010) The Right to Adequate Food: Fact Sheet No. 34 (April 2010). https://www.ohchr.org/Documents/Publications/FactSheet34en.pdf. Last accessed 30 Aug 2020

The Open Society Justice Initiative (2020) Amid COVID-19 lockdown, justice initiative calls for end to excessive police checks in France (27 March 2020). https://www.justiceinitiative.org/newsroom/amid-covid-19-lockdown-justice-initiative-calls-for-end-to-excessive-police-checks-in-france. Last accessed 24 May 2020

Orjinmo N (2020) Coronavirus lockdown: Nigerians cautious as restrictions eased in Lagos and Abuja (04 May 2020). https://www.bbc.com/news/world-52526923. Last accessed 25 Dec 2020

Partnership for Evidence-Based Response to COVID-19 (PERC) (undated) Responding to COVID-19 in Africa: using data to find a balance. https://africacdc.org/wp-content/uploads/2020/05/PERC_Regional_Final.pdf. Last accessed 30 May 2020

Pimhidzai O, Fox L (2012) Taking from the poor or local economic development: the dilemma of taxation of small informal enterprises in Uganda (CSAE Working Paper, Washington DC: The World Bank, 2012). https://editorialexpress.com/cgi-bin/conference/download.cgi?db_name=CSAE2012&paper_id=500. Last accessed 05 Sept 2020

RFI (2020a) Djibouti backtracks on decision to ease coronavirus lockdown measures (10 May 2020). https://www.rfi.fr/en/africa/20200510-djibouti-backtracks-on-decision-to-ease-coronavirus-lockdown-measures. Last accessed 26 Dec 2020

Report of the World Food Summit: five years later. Rome, 10–13 June 2002 (2002) Annex II: explanatory notes/reservation. http://www.fao.org/3/Y7106E/y7106e03.htm. Last accessed 13 Feb 2021

Maastricht Guidelines on Violations of Economic, Social and Cultural Rights (Maastricht, 22–26 January 1997) paragraph 9. http://hrlibrary.umn.edu/instree/Maastrichtguidelines_.html. Last accessed 25 Dec 2020

News 24 (2020) God, not masks: Magufuli's Tanzania is an outlier on virus response (21 April 2020). https://www.news24.com/news24/africa/news/god-not-masks-magufulis-tanzania-is-an-outlier-on-virus-response-20200420. Last accessed 07 Feb 2021

Odula T (2020) God has "removed" coronavirus, Tanzania's president claims (9 June 2020). https://apnews.com/article/fcaaa816cd9ba159c840b5366107da50. Last accessed 25 Dec 2020

OECD (2020a) Coronavirus: the world economy at risk. OECD Interim Economic Assessment (2 March 2020). https://www.oecd.org/berlin/publikationen/Interim-Economic-Assessment-2-March-2020.pdf. Last accessed 13 June 2020

OECD (2020b) COVID-19 in Africa: regional socio-economic implications and policy priorities (7 May 2020). https://read.oecd-ilibrary.org/view/?ref=132_132745-u5pt1rdb5x&title=COVID-19-in-Africa-Regional-socio-economic-implications-and-policy-priorities. Last accessed 13 Aug 2020

Ortiz I, Cummins M, Karunanethy K (2017) Fiscal Space for Social Protection and the SDGs: Options to Expand Social Investments in 187 Countries (Extension of Social Security (ESS) ESS Working Paper No. 48, Second edition, ILO 2017). https://papers.ssrn.com/sol3/papers.cfm?abstract_id=2603728. Last accessed 23 Jan 2021

RFI (2020b) Djibouti backtracks on decision to ease coronavirus lockdown measures (10 May 2020). https://www.rfi.fr/en/africa/20200510-djibouti-backtracks-on-decision-to-ease-coronavirus-lockdown-measures. Last accessed 26 Dec 2020

Rédaction Africanews (2021) Tanzania's COVID-denying leader urges prayer as cases climb (19 February 2021). https://www.africanews.com/2021/02/19/tanzania-s-covid-denying-leader-urges-prayer-as-cases-climb//. Last accessed 25 Feb 2021

Republic of Zambia, State House (2020) Third national address on covid-19 by His Excellency, Dr. Edgar Chagwa Lungu, President of the Republic of Zambia (24 April 2020). https://www.mohe.gov.zm/download/speeches/Presidential-Speech-24April2020.pdf. Last accessed 07 Feb 2021

Schneider F, Klinglmair R (2004) Shadow economies around the world: what do we know? (IZA Discussion Paper NO. 1043, CESifo Working Paper Series No. 1167, March 2004). http://ftp.iza.org/dp1043.pdf. Last accessed 05 Sept 2020

Statistical Office of the European Communities (EUROSTAT), European System of Integrated Social Protection Statistics (ESSPROS) Manual (EUROSTAT, Luxembourg, 1996). https://ec.

europa.eu/eurostat/documents/3859598/5825921/CA-99-96-641-EN.PDF/0798c4b9-6b32-42 b8-8047-fd65301bea53. Last accessed 13 Nov 2020

Tasioulas J (2017) Minimum core obligations: human rights in the here and now (Research Paper, the Nordic Trust Fund and The World Bank, October 2017). https://openknowledge.worldbank.org/bitstream/handle/10986/29144/122563-WP-Tasioulas2-PUBLIC.pdf?sequence=1&isAllowed=y. Last accessed 02 Dec 2021

UNCTAD (2020) Impact of the pandemic on trade and development: transitioning to a new normal (2020). https://unctad.org/system/files/official-document/osg2020d1_en.pdf. Last accessed 07 Feb 2021

United Nations (2020a) United Nations comprehensive response to COVID-19: saving lives, protecting societies, recovering better (September 2020). https://unsdg.un.org/sites/default/files/2020-09/un_comprehensive_response_to_covid-16_Sep_2020.pdf. Last accessed 28 May 2021

United Nations (2020b) COVID-19, inequalities and building back better: policy brief by the High-level Committee on Programmes (HLCP) inequalities Task Team (27 October 2020). https://www.un.org/development/desa/dspd/wp-content/uploads/sites/22/2020/10/HLCP-policy-brief-on-COVID-19-inequalities-and-building-back-better-1.pdf. Last accessed 28 May 2021

Vidar M, Kim YJ, Cruz L (2014) Legal developments in the progressive realization of the right to adequate food (thematic study 3, The Food and Agriculture Organization of the United Nations (FAO), Rome, 2014). http://www.fao.org/3/I3892E/i3892e.pdf. Last accessed 10 Mar 2021

Vidjingninou F (2020) Au Bénin, Patrice Talon assume l'impossibilité d'un confinement général (30 March 2020). https://www.jeuneafrique.com/918313/politique/au-benin-patrice-talon-assume-limpossibilite-dun-confinement-general/. Last accessed 19 May 2020

WFP (2020) Economic and food security implications of the COVID-19 outbreak: an update with insights from different regions (14 April 2020). https://reliefweb.int/sites/reliefweb.int/files/resources/WFP-0000115786.pdf. Last accessed 24 Oct 2020

World Bank (2019) Global economic prospects, January 2019: darkening skies (World Bank 2019). https://openknowledge.worldbank.org/bitstream/handle/10986/31066/9781464813863.pdf. Last accessed 20 June 2020

World Food Summit (1996) Rome Declaration on World Food Security and World Food Summit Plan of Action (13–17 November 1996). http://www.fao.org/3/w3613e/w3613e00.htm. Last accessed 09 Jan 2020

WTO (2020) Trade set to plunge as COVID-19 pandemic upends global economy (press release, 8 April 2020). https://www.wto.org/english/news_e/pres20_e/pr855_e.pdf. Last accessed 13 June 2020

Wurth M, Conde CH (2020) Philippine children face abuse for violating COVID-19 curfew (2 April 2020). https://www.hrw.org/news/2020/04/03/philippine-children-face-abuse-violating-covid-19-curfew. Last accessed 24 May 2020

Documents of United Nations Human Rights Mechanisms

CESCR Committee, General Comment No. 3: The Nature of States Parties' Obligations (Art. 2, Para. 1, of the Covenant) adopted on in 14 December 1990 in CESCR Committee, report on the fifth session (26 November-14 December 1990), UN doc no: E/1991/23 (1991)

CESCR Committee, General Comment No. 12: The Right to Adequate Food (Art. 11), UN doc no: E/C.12/1999/5 (12 May 1999)

CESCR Committee, General Comment No. 19: The right to social security (Art. 9 of the Covenant), UN doc no: E/C.12/GC/19 (4 February 2008)

CESCR Committee, Concluding observations on the initial report of the Gambia, UN doc no: E/C.12/GMB/CO/1 (20 March 2015)

CESCR Committee, Concluding observations on the initial report of Uganda, UN doc no: E/C.12/UGA/CO/1 (8 July 2015)
CESCR Committee, Concluding observations on the fourth periodic report of Iraq, UN doc no: E/C.12/IRQ/CO/4 (27 October 2015)
CESCR Committee, Concluding observations on the second periodic report of the Sudan, UN doc no: E/C.12/SDN/CO/2 (27 October 2015)
CESCR Committee, Concluding observations on the combined second to fifth periodic reports of Kenya, UN doc no: E/C.12/KEN/CO/2–5 (6 April 2016)
CESCR Committee, Concluding observations on the combined second and third periodic reports of Liechtenstein, UN doc no: E/C.12/LIE/CO/2-3 (3 July 2017)
CESCR Committee, Concluding observations on the initial report of Pakistan, UN doc no: E/C.12/PAK/CO/1 (20 July 2017)
CESCR Committee, Concluding observations on the fifth periodic report of Sri Lanka, UN doc no: E/C.12/LKA/CO/5 (4 August 2017)
CESCR Committee, Concluding observations on the sixth periodic report of the Russian Federation, UN doc no: E/C.12/RUS/CO/6 (16 October 2017)
CESCR Committee, Concluding observations on the sixth periodic report of Colombia, UN doc no: E/C.12/COL/CO/6 (19 October 2017)
CESCR Committee, Concluding observations on the fourth periodic report of the Republic of Korea, UN doc no: E/C.12/KOR/CO/4 (19 October 2017)
CESCR Committee, Concluding observations on the third periodic report of the Republic of Moldova, UN doc no: E/C.12/MDA/CO/3 (19 October 2017)
CESCR Committee, Concluding observations on the combined fifth and sixth periodic reports of Mexico, UN doc no: E/C.12/MEX/CO/5–6 (17 April 2018)
CESCR Committee, Concluding observations on the initial report of Bangladesh, UN doc no: E/C.12/BGD/CO/1 (18 April 2018)
CESCR Committee, Concluding observations on the sixth periodic report of Spain, UN doc no: E/C.12/ESP/CO/6 (25 April 2018)
CESCR Committee, Concluding observations on the fourth periodic report of New Zealand, UN doc no: E/C.12/NZL/CO/4 (1 May 2018)
CESCR Committee, Concluding observations on the initial report of the Niger, UN doc no: E/C.12/NER/CO/1 (4 June 2018)
CESCR Committee, Concluding observations on the initial report of Mali, UN doc no: E/C.12/MLI/CO/1 (6 November 2018)
CESCR Committee, Concluding observations on the initial report of Cabo Verde, UN doc no: E/C.12/CPV/CO/1 (27 November 2018)
CESCR Committee, Concluding observations on the initial report of South Africa, UN doc no: E/C.12/ZAF/CO/1 (29 November 2018)
CESCR Committee, Concluding observations on the fourth periodic report of Cameroon, UN doc no: E/C.12/CMR/CO/4 (25 March 2019)
CESCR Committee, Concluding observations on the third periodic report of Estonia, UN doc no: E/C.12/EST/CO/3 (27 March 2019)
CESCR Committee, Concluding observations on the second periodic report of Kazakhstan, UN doc no: E/C.12/KAZ/CO/2 (29 March 2019)
CESCR Committee, Concluding observations on the third periodic report of Senegal, UN doc no: E/C.12/SEN/CO/3 (13 November 2019)
CESCR Committee, Concluding observations on the fourth periodic report of Ecuador, UN doc no: E/C.12/ECU/CO/4 (14 November 2019)
CESCR Committee, Concluding observations on the fourth periodic report of Switzerland, UN doc no: E/C.12/CHE/CO/4 (18 November 2019)
CESCR Committee, Concluding observations on the fifth periodic report of Belgium, UN doc no: E/C.12/BEL/CO/5 (26 March 2020)

CESCR Committee, Concluding observations on the third periodic report of Benin, UN doc no: E/C.12/BEN/CO/3 (27 March 2020)

CESCR Committee, Concluding observations on the initial report of Guinea, UN doc no: E/C.12/GIN/CO/1 (30 March 2020)

CESCR Committee, Concluding observations on the seventh periodic report of Ukraine, UN doc no: E/C.12/UKR/CO/7 (2 April 2020)

Commission on Human Rights, The right to food: Report by the Special Rapporteur on the right to food, Mr. Jean Ziegler, submitted in accordance with Commission on Human Rights resolution 2000/10, UN doc no: E/CN.4/2001/53 (7 February 2001)

Commission on Human Rights, The right to food: Report of the Special Rapporteur on the right to food, Jean Ziegler, UN doc no: E/CN.4/2006/44 (16 March 2006)

United Nations General Assembly, Preliminary report of the Special Rapporteur of the Commission on Human Rights on the right to food, Jean Ziegler, UN doc no: A/56/210 (23 July 2001)

Business Interruption Insurance and Covid-19: Between Embracing Risk and Spreading Loss

Piotr Tereszkiewicz

Abstract This paper seeks to demonstrate one of several ways in which insurance contract law may approach the allocation of pandemic-related risks and losses. Specifically, the paper shows how business interruption insurance policies turn out to be a private-market tool of loss spreading. The recent judgment of the UK Supreme Court, Financial Conduct Authority v. Arch Insurance (UK) Ltd [2021] UKSC 1, is discussed as an example of how courts weigh different considerations in determining whether cover under business interruption policies should be granted. The paper puts the judicial analysis of business insurance policies against the background of the theoretical discussion on the limits of embracing risks by those harmed as opposed to spreading risk in society by means of insurance contracts.

1 Introduction

"Insurance state" is an approach to governing in which the main objective of government is protecting citizens from risk. This school of thought has featured particularly prominently in the writings of *François Ewald and Tom Baker*.[1] As *Ewald* posits, responsibility is based on the principle that one person cannot transfer to another the burden of what happens to him.[2] It is in direct opposition to the principle of assistance; one of its main instruments is *insurance*. Building upon *Ewald*, *Baker* emphasizes that the twentieth century insurance state's responsibility

---

This research was funded by Narodowe Centrum Nauki, (NCN) [The National Science Centre] in Poland, grant number 2018/29/B/HS5/01281.

[1] Ewald (1986, 2002), Baker (2002b). On different concepts of "insurance" see Abraham (2013).
[2] Ewald (2002), p. 274.

P. Tereszkiewicz (✉)
Jagiellonian University, Kraków, Poland
e-mail: piotr.tereszkiewicz@uj.edu.pl

towards risk has two components: the first component is preventing harm, which, together with compensation, derives from the same philosophical paradigm of solidarity. The second component is compensating those who suffer the harm that is not prevented. In other words, the two components can be described as preventing and spreading loss or minimizing and spreading risk.[3]

Whereas the above considerations lay the conceptual groundwork, a substantive judgment is called for to make choices about when and how the two components are applied in the risk governance processes in society. On *Baker*'s account, embracing risk can be beneficial when it provides manageable incentives to individuals in a position to control and prevent risk. Nevertheless, the approach of embracing risk may indeed be counterproductive when it becomes "an excuse for leaving expensive losses on powerless individuals". In an important contribution, written just after the September 11th terrorist attacks on the WTC, *Baker* claims that embracing risk would be a disreputable justification for terror exclusion in property and casualty insurance.[4]

It seems that similar considerations can be applied to the discussion of business interruption insurance as a measure of compensating losses resulting from the Covid-19 pandemic. A pandemic is an example of both a "difficult" and a "systemic" risk.[5] Difficult risks are so vast that it is hardly possible to distribute them in reliable insurance pools. They resist diversification. Further, difficult risks are ambiguous as regards frequency, consequence, or both. Some difficult risks are demonstrated in events that lack geographic boundaries and have long timelines between their occurrence and remediation. Given their immense character, such difficult risks overwhelm private risk spreading and distribution mechanisms and may even challenge the capacity of governments to efficiently act as an insurer. These difficult risks, which put enormous stress on all possible risk-spreading mechanisms, are called "systemic". Typical systemic risks are global warfare, climate change, terrorism directed at crucial infrastructure, natural disasters, and pandemics.[6]

Countless studies have analyzed the financial consequences of the Covid-19 pandemic. As far as the focus of this chapter is concerned, the OECD has estimated that one month of strict confinement measures leads to approximately USD 1.7 trillion in revenue losses for businesses across different sectors.[7] Yet, it has been estimated that Covid-19 had exposed massive protection gaps in the area of business continuity risk: only less than 1% of the estimated USD 4.5 trillion global pandemic-induced GDP loss for 2020 will be covered by business interruption insurance.[8] This

---

[3] Baker (2002a), p. 4. See also Lehtonen and Liukko (2011), pp. 35–36.
[4] Baker (2002a), p. 9.
[5] Jerry II (2020), p. 25. I rely on this author's account of pandemic as "difficult" and "systemic" risk.
[6] Jerry II (2020), pp. 27–28. Bernstein (1998) provides a fascinating account of how perceptions of risk evolved over the centuries.
[7] OECD (2021), p. 2. See also Richter and Wilson (2020), pp. 190–191.
[8] Schanz et al. (2020), p. 9.

sector of insurance is relatively small and generates an annual premium income of about USD 30 billion.[9]

I believe it is worthwhile to look at the effects of business interruption insurance on the distribution of losses in the light of Ewald's and Baker's conceptual framework. As will be shown below, the construction of clauses in the business interruption insurance contracts, adopted by the United Kingdom Supreme Court in its FCA Test Case judgment, seems to have the effect of spreading the risk of the Covid-19 pandemic, its outbreak, and the government measures taken to contain it.

What do I mean by "spreading risk" and "spreading loss" in this context? Imagine you are a business owner, unable to use your property to run your walk-in store due to lockdown measures. Luckily, you have some odd business interruption insurance, bought on your lawyer's advice some time ago when threats like Covid-19 appeared mostly in Hollywood productions. The pay-out under the policy, if and when it eventually comes, will bring you some financial relief. But nobody will take away all your business losses resulting from the Covid-19 pandemic and all its side-effects. Paraphrasing the late John Gardner's account of the duty to repair, an insurer's duty to compensate is "none other than a duty to mitigate" one's damage.[10] Insurers do this by paying money. This is what I describe as "spreading risk" and "spreading loss" in the aftermath of the UK Supreme Court judgment in Financial Conduct Authority v. Arch Insurance (UK) Ltd: spreading risk is associated with potential threats which have not yet materialized and could be mitigated by purchasing insurance policies, while spreading losses is related to insured perils which have already occurred and triggered insurance cover. By being forced to make payouts under business interruption policies, insurers will bear some of business owners' losses.

The chapter assumes a micro level analysis. It is concerned with the question of how the design and interpretation of business interruption insurance policy may contribute to spreading the losses of policyholders. To this aim, selected judicial and regulatory developments in two major jurisdictions, the UK and the US, are presented and evaluated. An analysis of government backstop programmes, necessary to close the protection gap in business interruption loss, is beyond the scope of this chapter.

---

[9] Schanz et al. (2020), p. 9.
[10] Gardner (2018), p. 100.

2 Business Interruption Insurance in the Context of Covid-19

2.1 Business Interruption Insurance in the UK

The UK provides an important example of a jurisdiction in which the applicability of business interruption insurance to pandemic-related losses was subject to judicial review with implications for all market operators subject to the jurisdiction.

Immediately after the outbreak of the Covid-19 pandemic, the Financial Conduct Authority (FCA), the conduct regulator of insurers in the UK, wrote to all insurance companies, outlining the expectation regarding the settlement of business interruption claims and the need to assess and settle claims quickly. In the light of the uncertainty over the details of business interruption policies, the FCA submitted a claim for the benefit of policyholders under the Financial Markets Test Case Scheme (Financial Conduct Authority v. Arch Insurance (UK) Ltd).[11] This is a scheme which enables a claim raising issues of general importance to financial markets to be determined in a test case without the need for a specific dispute between the parties where relevant and authoritative English law guidance is immediately needed. Hence the FCA Test Case judgment, which will be discussed in depth below, did not involve an examination of individualized policy language in the light of specific facts.

Twenty-one different policy wordings were selected as a representative sample of all wordings that gave rise to uncertainty.[12] The High Court, acting as a first instance court, delivered preliminary rulings on the meaning of the selected policy wordings on 15 September 2020. Under the "leapfrog" procedure, which enables an appeal in exceptional circumstances to bypass the Court of Appeal and proceed directly to the UK Supreme Court, the Supreme Court upheld and extended the first instance decision of the High Court.

Most importantly, the UK Supreme Court[13] (as the High Court before) held that clauses conferring business interruption cover for losses caused by infectious disease and government measures are applicable to the Covid-19 pandemic.

In the judicial analysis, the selected policy wordings were grouped under three different headings, containing the main types of clauses subject to judicial review:

(a) "Disease Clauses" providing cover for business interruption losses caused by notifiable diseases at or within a specific proximity to the insured business;

---

[11] [2020] EWHC 2448 (Comm); [2021] UKSC 1, further referred to as the FCA Test Case Judgment. The FCA was the named claimant in the Test Case.

[12] Sample policies are available under https://www.fca.org.uk/publication/corporate/bi-insurance-test-case-representative-sample-of-policy-wordings-9-june.pdf (last access 09 September 2021).

[13] Referred to also as "the UKSC" or the Supreme Court.

(b) "Loss of Access Clauses" providing cover for business interruption losses resulting from the inability to access an insured premises caused by emergency actions taken by the government or local authorities;
(c) "Hybrid Clauses" that contain both a Disease Clause and a Loss of Access Clause.

Below follows an analysis of how the Supreme Court ruled on selected aspects of business interruption insurance that determine whether business insurance policies fulfil their objective of transferring (parts of) the loss from the policyholder to the insurers.

2.1.1 Disease Clauses: What is an "Occurrence of Disease" That Triggers Business Interruption Cover?

An analysis of whether a business interruption insurance contract will respond to losses resulting from the Covid-19 pandemic necessarily begins with the "disease clauses" contained in such contracts. A disease clause provides insurance cover for business interruption loss caused by the occurrence of a "Notifiable Disease" at or within a specified distance of the policyholder's business premises. Such clauses do not cover the effects of cases of Covid-19 that occur outside that geographical area.[14]

What follows is one of the clauses analyzed by the Supreme Court:

> We shall indemnify You in respect of interruption or interference with the Business during the Indemnity Period following:
> a. any
>   i. occurrence of a Notifiable Disease (as defined below) at the Premises or attributable to food or drink supplied from the Premises;
>   ii. discovery of an organism at the Premises likely to result in the occurrence of a Notifiable Disease;
>   iii. occurrence of a Notifiable Disease within a radius of 25 miles of the Premises.[15]

Crucially, the UKSC had to define what constituted an "occurrence" of Covid-19 under the policy.[16] There were two main questions about how the disease clause should be interpreted. The first concerned what was meant by the following words of the insuring clause: "any ... occurrence of a Notifiable Disease within a radius of 25 miles of the Premises." Second, it was necessary to clarify what the scope of the peril insured against by this provision was. In hindsight, one could say that the value of the policy for the policyholder turned on that Supreme Court's interpretative decision. In their submissions, insurers claimed that a disease clause only covered the business interruption consequences of any cases of a Notifiable Disease which

---

[14] On how clauses in policies offered by various insurers differed see Gürses (2021), pp. 74–75.

[15] Para. 50 of the FCA Test Case judgment, quoting the clause RSA 3 (Royal & Sun Alliance Insurance Plc).

[16] Para. 54 of the FCA Test Case judgment.

occurs within a radius of 25 miles of the premises insured under the policy. This implied that losses would have only been covered to the extent that it was possible to show that they resulted from the occurrence of the disease within the radius of 25 miles. Accepting this interpretation would clearly make the cover illusory for policyholders, since in most cases it is impossible to show that losses resulted from the localized occurrence of the disease, as opposed to the wider pandemic and the nationwide government response.[17]

By contrast, the FCA asserted that the disease clause covered the business interruption consequences of a notifiable disease wherever the disease occurs, provided it occurred (at least one case of illness caused by the disease) within the 25-mile radius specified in the policy.[18]

The Supreme Court largely agreed with this position, but took a different position on how to construct the clauses in question. It held that it is only an occurrence within the specified area that is an insured peril under business interruption policy and not anything that occurs outside that area. Further, each case of illness sustained by an individual is a separate occurrence and a "Notifiable Disease" in the meaning used in the wording is not the outbreak (of Covid-19) nor the disease itself but rather the illness sustained by any person resulting from that disease.[19] Specifically, this means that if the policyholder could identify a single instance of Covid-19 in the specified vicinity and a consequent interruption to his or her business, an "occurrence" under the business interruption policy was fulfilled, and cover would be granted.

It is submitted that the above stated interpretation of a disease clause renders the private insurance a realistic mechanism of loss spreading and accords with the policyholders' expectations as to its function and value when the peril insured against materializes. The Supreme Court expressed no doubt that Covid-19 falls squarely within the types of diseases for which all relevant business interruption insurance clauses provided cover.

2.1.2 Prevention of Access Clauses: Are Recommendations Sufficient or do we Need Mandates?

Another piece of the complex architecture of business interruption policies is prevention of access clauses. A prevention of access clause in a business interruption policy usually provides insurance cover for business interruption losses resulting

---

[17] Cf. para. 86 of the FCA Test Case judgment.

[18] In the first instance, the High Court had accepted the FCA's case, ruling that (i) the words of the clause do not confine cover to a situation where the interruption to the business has resulted only from cases of a Notifiable Disease within the 25-mile radius, as opposed to other cases elsewhere; and (ii) the Notifiable Diseases covered by the policies included diseases which are capable of spreading rapidly and widely and it would not make sense for the cover to be confined to the effects only of the local occurrence of a Notifiable Disease. See para 61 of the FCA Test Case judgment.

[19] Para. 93 of the FCA Test Case judgment.

from public authority intervention preventing access to, or use of, an insured premises. Such clauses contain a series of requirements which must all be satisfied to trigger the insurer's obligation to indemnify the policyholder against loss: (a) need for interruption; (b) interference in the use of premises; (c) public authority action; (d) underlying emergency/disease.[20]

The first of the interpretative decisions faced by the Supreme Court concerned the question of what force of law is necessary to assume that access to a policyholder's premises has been prevented by the government. The UKSC held that "restrictions imposed" by a public authority would be understood as ordinarily meaning mandatory measures "imposed" by the authority pursuant to its statutory or other legal powers since "imposed" connotes compulsion and a public authority generally exercises compulsion through the use of such powers. Yet, the UKSC held that business interruption cover applied when from "the context of the instructions, compliance with it is required, and would be reasonably understood to be required, without the need for recourse to legal powers".[21] This amounts to the rejection of the insurers' argument that business interruption cover should only apply where a restriction has the force of law, i.e., is legally capable of being enforced.[22]

It must be emphasized that while the UK Prime Minister gave directions to the public on specific measures on national television in March 2020, one could have doubts as to their legal nature and immediate enforceability.[23] Were one to follow the insurers' argument, business insurance cover would clearly have commenced later, and the extent of indemnity might have been diminished.

2.1.3 The "Inability to Use" Clauses

During the Covid-19 pandemic many store owners and service providers reacted to lockdown orders by rapidly opening up or expanding takeaway services or online sales. This gives rise to the question of how the adaptation of the policyholder's business model may affect the scope of the indemnity. As a matter of principle, the "inability to use" the business premises, and the "prevention of access" to the business premises must be total. Yet, as the Supreme Court held, these requirements do not have to be fulfilled with respect to the entire business premises.[24] Business interruption cover can be triggered where the "policyholder is unable to use the premises for a discrete part of its business activities or if it is unable to use a discrete

---

[20] Para. 96 of the FCA Test Case judgment contains an overview of several different prevention of access clauses.

[21] Para. 121 of the FCA Test Case judgment.

[22] Paras 116 and 121 of the FCA Test Case judgment.

[23] Annex I to the FCA Test Case judgment contains a detailed overview of the public authority measures relevant for the case.

[24] Paras 136 and 137 of the FCA Test Case judgment.

part of its premises for its business activities."[25] The Supreme Court explained that in both those situations there is a complete inability of use, either relating to a discrete business activity (e.g., dining in), or to using a discrete part of the business premises (e.g., a high street showroom). To demonstrate the effects of this construction, the Supreme Court provided the following example: "if there was a travel agent whose business was 50% walk-in customers, 25% internet sales and 25% telephone sales, it could only claim in relation to the loss of walk-in business, even though all parts of the business may have been depressed by the effects of COVID-19 and the governmental measures taken."[26] This construction of business interruption clauses ensures that businesses that stayed open for takeaway services or mail orders may submit claims for the loss of in-person business.

It is submitted that in broadly constructing the inability to use clauses, the Supreme Court adopted a position clearly favourable to the interests of policyholders who may have struggled to quickly adapt their business model to the lockdown reality with a view to cutting losses.

2.1.4 The Question of Causation

The question of causation requires answering what the insured peril is and what effects on the policyholder's business are covered. In this light the question as to what connection must be shown between any cases of the Covid-19 disease and the business interruption loss for which an insurance claim is made is crucial. Referring to the *Orient Express*[27] case, the insurers claimed that due to the widespread nature of the pandemic, policyholders would have suffered the same or similar business interruption losses even if the insured risk or peril (whether it be an occurrence of the disease within the given radius, or a public authority action causing a prevention of access) had not occurred, and as such the business interruption cover should not be granted.

Establishing Causality of Covid-19 Outbreaks to Establish Insurance Cover

The Supreme Court rejected the above claim, holding that the "but for" test was inadequate for ascertaining whether the test for causation had been satisfied in the case under review.[28] The causal connection required had to consider the nature of the cover provided in the business insurance policies under review, and it may be

---

[25] Para. 137 of the FCA Test Case judgment.

[26] Para. 141 of the FCA Test Case judgment.

[27] Orient-Express Hotels Ltd v. Assicurazioni Generali SpA [2010] EWHC 1186 (Comm); [2010] Lloyd's Rep IR 531. On Orient Express and its rejection in the FCA Test Case judgment see Gürses (2021), pp. 79–80.

[28] The question of causation is discussed by Gürses (2021), pp. 78–80.

satisfied if the insured peril, in combination with other similar uninsured events, brings about a loss with a sufficient degree of inevitability, even if the occurrence of the insured peril is neither necessary nor sufficient to bring about the loss by itself.

The Supreme Court referred to well-established principles. The first is that where there are two proximate causes of loss, neither of which is excluded but only one of which is insured against, insurers are liable for the loss.[29] The second is that where there are two proximate causes of loss, of which one is an insured peril, but the other is expressly excluded, the exclusion will generally prevail (although it is always a question of interpretation).[30] The Supreme Court held that there is no reason why such an analysis cannot be applied to multiple causes which act in combination to bring about a loss, as in the case of business interruption losses due to the Covid-19 outbreak and restrictions. According to the Supreme Court, in the present case it obviously could not be said that any individual case of illness resulting from Covid-19, on its own, caused the UK Government to introduce restrictions which led directly to business interruption. None of the Covid-19 cases on its own could cause the loss, but their combination did. Each of the illness cases were not sufficient but were necessary to cause the interruption.[31] However, the Government measures were taken in response to information about all the cases of Covid-19 in the entire country. The Supreme Court thus found that it is realistic to analyze this situation as one in which "all the cases were equal causes of the imposition of national measures."[32]

In the Supreme Court's view, all that matters is what risks the insurers have agreed to cover. This is a question of contractual interpretation, which must accordingly be answered by (objectively) identifying the intended effect of the policy as applied to the relevant factual situation.[33] In this light, the Supreme Court concluded that "there is nothing in principle or in the concept of causation which precludes an insured peril that in combination with many other similar uninsured events brings about a loss with a sufficient degree of inevitability from being regarded as a cause – indeed as a proximate cause – of the loss, even if the occurrence of the insured peril is neither necessary nor sufficient to bring about the loss by itself."[34]

---

[29] Para. 173 of the FCA Test Case Judgment quoting JJ Lloyd Instruments Ltd v. Northern Star Insurance Co Ltd (The Miss Jay Jay) [1987] 1 Lloyd's Rep. 32.

[30] Para. 173 of the FCA Test Case Judgment quoting Wayne Tank and Pump Co Ltd v. Employers Liability Assurance Corp. Ltd [1974] QB 57.

[31] Gürses (2021), p. 80.

[32] Para. 176 of the FCA Test Case Judgment.

[33] Para. 190 of the FCA Test Case Judgment.

[34] Para. 191 of the FCA Test Case Judgment.

Disease Clauses: How Many Outbreaks of Covid-19 Are Necessary?

The Supreme Court found it obvious that an outbreak of an infectious disease may not be confined to a specific locality or to a circular area delineated by a radius of 25 miles around a policyholder's premises. No reasonable person, in the Supreme Court's view, would suppose that, if an outbreak of an infectious disease occurred, which included cases within the relevant radius in the disease clause and was sufficiently serious to interrupt the policyholder's business, all the cases of disease would necessarily occur within the radius. Having recognized that, the Supreme Court considered it inappropriate to inquire into whether, but for the cases of disease within the radius, the loss would have been suffered, since the answer may well typically be in the affirmative, thus depriving the insured of an indemnity for wide area diseases, such as Covid-19:

> We agree with the FCA's central argument in relation to the radius provisions that the parties could not reasonably be supposed to have intended that cases of disease outside the radius could be set up as a countervailing cause which displaces the causal impact of the disease inside the radius.[35]

This assumption paved the way for the Supreme Court's conclusion that, on the proper interpretation of the disease clauses, in order to show that loss from interruption of the insured business was proximately caused by one or more occurrences of illnesses resulting from Covid-19, it is sufficient to prove that the interruption was a result of Government action taken in response to cases of disease which included at least one case of Covid-19 within the geographical area covered by the clause. Each of the individual cases of illness resulting from Covid-19, which had occurred by the date of any Government action, was a separate and equally effective cause of that action (and of the response of the public to it).[36]

Further, the Supreme Court pointed out that the relevant business interruption policy wordings do not confine cover to a situation where the interruption of the business has resulted only from cases of a notifiable disease within the radius (as the insurers claimed), as opposed to other cases elsewhere. The Supreme Court approved the FCA's argument that, to apply the general "but for" test in a situation where cases of disease inside and outside the radius are concurrent causes of business interruption loss would give the insurer similar protection to that which it would have had if the loss caused by any occurrence of a notifiable disease outside the specified radius had been expressly excluded from the cover. If the insurers had wished to impose such an exclusion, it was incumbent on them to include it in the terms of the policy.[37]

---

[35] Para. 195 of the FCA Test Case judgment.

[36] Para. 212 of the FCA Test Case Judgment.

[37] Para. 196 of the FCA Test Case Judgment.

Prevention of Access Clauses: The Cover Should not be Illusory

The Supreme Court expressed a similar view with respect to the prevention of access/hybrid clauses as regards concurrent Covid-19-related causes. In the Supreme Court's view, where insurance is restricted to the particular consequences of an adverse event, the parties do not generally intend other consequences of that event, which are inherently likely to arise, or the "source" event, to restrict the scope of the indemnity.[38] Applying this principle to the prevention of access and hybrid clauses, the Supreme Court held that the elements of the insured peril are inextricably connected in that the elements and their effects on the policyholder's business all arise from the same original cause—in this case the Covid-19 pandemic. Even if the elements of the insured peril had not led ultimately to the closure of the insured premises, they would have had other potentially adverse effects on the turnover of the business. The Supreme Court considered that it would undermine the commercial purpose of the business interruption cover to treat such potential effects as ones diminishing the scope of the indemnity. Even though these other potentially adverse effects are not part of the insured peril, according to the Supreme Court, they are "not a separate and distinct risk".[39]

The Supreme Court held that the principle applies equally to an originating cause of loss covered by the policy, which is not expressly mentioned in the clause. In the case under review, the originating cause of any local occurrence of disease (and of public authority actions and public reactions to it) is the global Covid-19 pandemic. In circumstances where the policy does not exclude loss arising from such an event, other concurrent effects of the pandemic on an insured business should not reduce the indemnity under the public authority clause.[40]

According to the Supreme Court's ruling, the prevention of access/hybrid wordings indemnify the policyholder against the risk of all the elements of the insured peril acting in causal combination to cause business interruption loss. The business insurance cover applies regardless of whether the loss was concurrently caused by other (uninsured but non-excluded) consequences of the Covid-19 pandemic, which was the underlying or originating cause of the insured peril.[41]

Concurrent Effects of the Covid-19 Pandemic

From the perspective of business interruption insurance as a means of loss sharing, the Supreme Court's position regarding the concurrent effects of the Covid-19 pandemic is significant. The Supreme Court held that concurrent effects of the Covid-19 pandemic were not excluded from the business interruption cover. The

---

[38] Para. 239 of the FCA Test Case judgment.
[39] Para. 237 of the FCA Test Case judgment.
[40] Para. 240 of the FCA Test Case judgment.
[41] Para. 243 of the FCA Test Case judgment.

cover was triggered regardless of whether the loss was concurrently caused by other uninsured but non-excluded from the policy consequences of the underlying or originating cause of the insured peril. This means the fact that a loss of customers would have occurred without lockdown measures was not an event that broke the chain of causation.[42] The Supreme Court held that the effects of uninsured perils should not reduce the scope of indemnity, where they arise from the same event as the insured peril.[43]

2.1.5 The Construction of Trends Clauses: The Scope of Indemnification

In contrast to the insuring clauses, trends clauses in business interruption policies do not address or seek to delineate the scope of the indemnity. Such clauses, as the Supreme Court explained, call for an inquiry into what the financial results of the business would have been if the insured peril had not occurred.[44] Trends clauses ought to ensure that the indemnity reflects the cover afforded by the policy, and it is not reduced by factors unrelated to the cover. For instance, the inquiry into how lost profit under business insurance cover is calculated must include the question of "windfall profits" that a policyholder might gain. Windfall profits are profits that go beyond indemnification due under the insurance contracts and unjustly enrich the policyholder.[45]

The Supreme Court judgment contains an illustrative survey of US courts on the matter.[46] Specifically, the US Fifth Circuit Court of Appeals' judgment in *Catlin Syndicate Ltd v. Imperial Palace of Mississippi Inc*[47] was considered. In that case, the casino was damaged by Hurricane Katrina that also caused damage to the surrounding area. After the casino had reopened, its revenue was much higher than before the hurricane since many other casinos in the area remained closed. The business interruption insurer and the casino disagreed over how the business

---

[42] Gürses (2021), p. 81.

[43] Para. 295 of the FCA Test Case judgment "(...) to reduce the indemnity to reflect a downturn caused by other effects of the pandemic, whenever they began, would be to refuse to indemnify the policyholder for loss proximately caused by the insured peril on the basis that the loss was also proximately caused by uninsured (but non-excluded) perils with the same originating cause. As discussed earlier, that is not permissible."

[44] Para. 267 of the FCA Test Case judgment.

[45] Castellain v. Preston, 11 Q.B.D. 380, 386 (1883): "[T]his contract means that the assured, in case of a loss against which the policy has been made, shall be fully indemnified, but shall never be more than fully indemnified. That is the fundamental principle of insurance, and if ever a proposition is brought forward which is at variance with it, that is to say, which either will prevent the assured from obtaining a full indemnity, or which will give the assured more than a full indemnity, that proposition must certainly be wrong."; see also Bybee (1979) pp. 145–160.

[46] Para. 278–279 of the FCA Test Case judgment.

[47] 600 F 3d 511 (2010).

interruption loss should be calculated. In the casino's view, the legal requirement to consider what would have happened, had the loss not occurred, meant assuming that no damage to the casino had occurred, but not that the hurricane had not occurred. It will not come as a surprise, one should add, that casino owners usually have their own ways of cutting losses. Unsurprisingly, the Fifth Circuit rejected the casino's claim. The below excerpt from its judgment is instructive:

> Imperial Palace asserts that Catlin asks us to interpret the business interruption provision in such a way that the phrase 'had no loss occurred' morphs into 'had no occurrence occurred'. Imperial Palace argues that instead, we should disentangle the loss from the occurrence and determine loss based on a hypothetical in which Hurricane Katrina hit Mississippi, damaged all of Imperial Palace's competitors, but left Imperial Palace intact: the occurrence occurred, but the loss did not. While we agree with Imperial Palace that the loss is distinct from the occurrence – at least in theory – we also believe that the two are inextricably intertwined under the language of the business-interruption provision.[48]

Similarly, the Fourth Circuit Court of Appeals in *Prudential LMI Commercial Ins. Co. v. Colleton Enterprises Inc.*[49] held that under the general no-windfall principle an insured under a business interruption policy may not claim as "a probable source of expected earning a source that would not itself have come into being but for the interrupting peril's occurrence".

Both US federal appellate decisions reject the theory that the loss should be estimated by comparing the actual results of the business with what they would have been if there had been no damage to the business operation (e.g., a hotel, a casino), but that the event (a hurricane) had still occurred causing all the other damage which actually befell the surrounding area in which the business operation was located. The opposite view, one must admit, appears out of touch with commercial reality and a common perception of fairness.

In the FCA Test Case judgment, the Supreme Court recognized that adopting this theory as a basis for loss assessment would have resulted in the windfall profits accruing to the business operator resulting from the fact that they were the only (undamaged) operator of their kind in the relevant area.[50] It follows that one must clearly delineate the part of the policyholder's operations affected by the pandemic.

One should acknowledge that challenges resulting from business interruptions resulting from government measures responding to Covid-19 are similar to those adjudicated after natural disasters. In the case of many businesses, only certain activities were interrupted by the operation of the insured peril (the occurrence of the disease), whereas discrete parts of the business remained active. For instance, a business operator was obligated to close its premises for customers but allowed to continue selling through its website. Depending on the type of goods offered, the demand during a pandemic may have fallen, sometimes abruptly.[51]

---

[48] 600 F 3d 511 (2010) at pp. 515–516.
[49] 927 F.2d 727 (1992) at pp. 731–732.
[50] Para. 280 of the FCA Test Case judgment.
[51] This includes, for instance, sellers of formal clothing who as a sector suffered considerable losses.

According to the Supreme Court, the business interruption policies under consideration do not cover any effects of Covid-19 and the government restrictions on business conducted online, given that selling through the website was not interrupted.[52] In the Supreme Court's view, the standard turnover or gross profit derived from the previous trading is adjusted only to reflect circumstances which are unconnected with the insured peril, and not circumstances which are inextricably linked with the insured peril in the sense that they have the same underlying or originating cause.[53]

In a given case, this requires adjusting the turnover from sales in the shop during the equivalent period in the previous year only to "reflect trends or circumstances unrelated to the COVID-19 pandemic". The insurer will be liable to indemnify the policyholder for loss calculated by reference to the difference between the adjusted figure and the actual turnover from such sales during the period of interruption (which would be nil if the business was closed).[54]

The Supreme Court explained the effects of the construction:

> The result will be that the amount recoverable by the policyholder will not be reduced if, had the shop not been compelled to close, its turnover would have been lower in any event as a result of other consequences of the pandemic. Nor will it be increased if, had the shop been allowed to remain open in circumstances where all its competitors were forced to close, its turnover would have been higher. At the same time the policyholder will not be able to recover any loss caused by a fall in website orders as such loss is not covered.[55]

The court's position in this respect appears favourable to the policyholders, as business interruption insurers cannot reduce the indemnity due to them. The Covid-19 pandemic and its consequences cannot be considered "trends", which must be assumed to take place when determining what the insured would have earned had the insured peril not materialized.

2.1.6 Preliminary Assessment of the Supreme Court's Judgment

The Supreme Court's FCA Test Case judgment is a powerful picture of what is at stake in business interruption policies for both policyholders and insurers. I have attempted to show that most choices made by the Supreme Court in the process of constructing business interruption policies could be seen as "value judgments", the outcome of which immediately translates into whether the cover will be granted or to how far it will extend. As such, these decisions determine what losses resulting from business interruption due to the Covid-19 pandemic will be spread and shared in the society. Remarkably, the concern that business interruption cover may turn out to be illusory (worthless) for the policyholder just when it is most needed features

---

[52] Para. 283 of the FCA Test Case judgment.
[53] Para. 287 of the FCA Test Case judgment.
[54] Para. 283 of the FCA Test Case judgment.
[55] Para. 287 of the FCA Test Case judgment.

prominently throughout the judgment.[56] As was nicely summarized in the concurring speech of Lord Briggs, the majority verdict rescued the policyholders from the at first sight sombre consequences of a narrow definition of the insured peril by a principled application of the doctrine of concurrent cause, where the existence of one or more concurrent causes of loss, other than the insured peril itself, does not prevent cover provided that the concurrent causes are not themselves expressly excluded.[57]

The recognition that the Covid-19 pandemic was an insured peril under business interruption policies on the UK market opens the door for many thousands of individual inquiries into the extent of losses recoverable by policyholders. It would be premature to undertake any generalized assessments to what extent business interruption insurance has provided financial relief to struggling businesses on the UK market.

An important practical restriction is that the Supreme Court's judgment in the FCA Test Case has not concerned traditional "all-risk" property policies, under which cover for business interruption losses has to be triggered by "physical loss" or "physical damage" to the business property. Such damage clauses in business interruption insurance were left out of the scope of the FCA Test Case. One must note, however, that the High (Commercial) Court has ruled that those "all-risk" policies are not triggered by the Covid-19 pandemic.[58] It is unclear whether there will be any further judicial or regulatory developments in this regard.

2.2 Developments in the US

2.2.1 Insurance Product Design and Regulatory Measures

In the US, the reaction of what *Baker* calls "the insurance state"[59] to business interruption losses resulting from the Covid-19 pandemic escapes an easy description. The US property and casualty sector envisioned the potentially widespread commercial effects of a pandemic well enough to specifically exclude it from a portion of business insurance policy forms more than a decade ago.[60] Consequently,

---

[56] See paras 238, 316, 321, 325 of the FCA Test Case judgment.

[57] Para. 319 of the FCA Test Case judgment, per Lord Briggs.

[58] TKC London Limited v. Allianz Insurance plc [2020] EWHC 2710 (Comm.): Para. 128: "(...) the expression 'loss ... of ... property' in the definition of 'Event' cannot sensibly be interpreted as including mere temporary loss of use of property"; per R. Saler QC, sitting as a Deputy Judge of the High Court.

[59] Baker (2002a), pp. 4–5, defines "the insurance state" as "a set of practices and ideas about the goals and responsibilities of governing that are developed and acted out in a wide variety of institutional settings, many of which lie well outside the official 'government'."

[60] Trice and Woleben (20 August 2020), Government backstop likely to be key for insurance coverage of future pandemics, https://www.spglobal.com/marketintelligence/en/news-insights/latest-news-headlines/government-backstop-likely-to-be-key-for-insurance-coverage-of-future-pandemics-59963140 (last access 09 September 2021).

policies of some insurers contain exclusions for "communicable diseases and epidemics/pandemics".

Yet, it is the insurance product design that poses the major difficulty for the policyholders in the context of the Covid-19 losses. One of the most popular policy forms is the Businessowners Policy (BOP), which is a multi-risk package policy written by the Insurance Services Office (ISO) for the small business market. BOP usually contains business interruption cover unless the cover is specifically removed by endorsement.[61] The Business Income clause, quoted below, contains several elements of cover which the policyholder must prove.

> We will pay for the actual loss of Business Income you sustain due to the necessary suspension of your 'operations' during the 'period of restoration'. The suspension must be caused by direct physical loss of or damage to property at the described premises. The loss or damage must be caused by or result from a Covered Cause of Loss [...] We will pay only for loss of Business Income that you sustain during the 'period of restoration' and that occurs within 12 consecutive months after the date of direct physical loss or damage.[62]

In contrast to the clauses discussed in the FCA Test Case judgment by the UK Supreme Court, the policyholder must prove that the suspension was "caused by direct physical loss or damage to property" at the premises described in the policy. In the context of Covid-19, it is difficult to prove that this virus brings about that kind of damage to the property.[63]

Still, some scholars advocate a policyholder friendly interpretation of such clauses. The phrase "physical loss of or damage" to the policyholders' property is undefined, so there may be an argument for interpreting it broadly as a layperson would understand it.[64] It is thus conceivable that courts might become inclined towards an interpretation that the consequences of government lockdown orders fulfil the requirement of "physical damage" to the property. *French* shows that in the past, courts held that government orders to evacuate properties due to a potential threat, such as a hurricane, building collapse, or a riot, can trigger business interruption cover.[65] Extending this argument beyond the narrow confines of policy clauses, one could claim that policyholders reasonably expect cover under business interruption policies when their business operations are interrupted due to catastrophic events beyond their control.

This brings us beyond the scope of private insurance into the realm of government regulatory measures. Already during the first wave of the Covid-19 pandemic, several state legislators proposed legislation that would obligate insurers to cover business interruption losses regardless of whether specific claims were covered by

---

[61] Jerry II (2020), p. 12.

[62] Quoted after Jerry II (2020), p. 16.

[63] Jerry II (2020), p. 18. For a survey of case-law predating the Covid-19 pandemic see French (2020).

[64] French (2020), p. 20, quoting several cases adopting this position.

[65] French (2020), p. 23. See also Katofsky (1989), pp. 788–791.

the policies purchased.[66] By May 2020, approximately twenty bills were filed in at least seven states seeking to retroactively mandate cover for business interruption losses.[67] Most importantly, these draft bills included declaring the virus exclusion void as against public policy or declaring, as a matter of law, that Covid-19 constitutes direct physical loss or damage to property. Early in 2021, it was observed that given the intense industry lobbying against these bills, none of them would be enacted.[68] As *Jerry II* points out, these bill proposals should be understood as efforts to use insurance companies as a conduit to quickly bring recovery funds from the federal government into the hands of businesses, as insurance companies may be able to do this more promptly than federal mechanisms.[69]

Parallel regulatory proposals, e.g., the Pandemic Risk Insurance Act, sought to provide compensation to insurers if they incurred losses as a result of cover related to pandemics and outbreaks of disease, including business interruption insurance.[70] In particular, the proposed Pandemic Risk Insurance Act followed a reinsurance model with similarities to the federal Terrorism Risk Insurance Act enacted in 2002, under which the federal government provides a backstop to insurers' cover of the terrorism risk. To date, these measures have not been approved. This means that courts will have a decisive role to fulfil in setting the extent to which the insurance industry will cover business owners' losses under business interruption policies.

2.2.2 The Position of the US Courts

In the US, insurance disputes are governed by state law, and the law can vary considerably from state to state.

As of the time of writing, the stance of US courts on business interruption insurance does not yield itself to any general description.[71] The outcomes of the litigation by the end of 2020 suggest that the presence of a virus exclusion in the business interruption policies may be significant: insurers have won their motions in just over 85 percent of the cases where the policy has a virus exclusion (97 out of 112), but only about 67 percent of the cases where the policy has no such exclusion (34 out of 51).[72] As *Jerry II* observes, it is reasonable to predict that insurers will win

---

[66] French (2020), p. 5.

[67] Jerry II (2020), p. 23.

[68] Jerry II (2020), p. 23. Still, in the 2021 legislative session, eleven US states have pending legislation addressing business insurance policies, see National Conference of State Legislatures, Business Interruption Insurance 2021, available at https://www.ncsl.org/research/financial-services-and-commerce/business-interruption-insurance-2021-legislation.aspx (last access 09 September 2021).

[69] Jerry II (2020), p. 23.

[70] https://www.congress.gov/bill/116th-congress/house-bill/6983?s=1&r=1 (last access 09 September 2021).

[71] Jerry II (2020), pp. 24–25.

[72] Jerry II (2020), p. 24.

some number of these cases on summary judgment motions, and where those motions are denied, they will win trial on the merits.[73] Further, in dozens of disputes, policyholders were not able to prove that the suspension was "caused by direct physical loss or damage to property" at the premises described in the policy.[74] Yet, one still awaits judgments by state supreme courts on that matter.

In the scholarship, *French* submits that holders of business interruption policies may argue that public policy (fairness) justifies providing cover for Covid-19 losses, as this fulfils the basic purpose of insurance as a social safety net in the modern regulatory state.[75] Specifically, in the context of Covid-19 business interruption losses, it should not matter that a policyholder's business was shut down because it was demonstrably contaminated with the virus. As a matter of public policy, business interruption losses caused by prophylactic government lockdown orders should also be covered.[76] It remains to be seen whether US courts will be receptive to this argument.

3 Loss Spreading Under Business Interruption Cover

Following the outbreak of the Covid-19 pandemic, representatives of the insurance industry have been arguing that pandemic-related claims are not covered under business interruption policies because the losses associated with pandemics are uninsurable correlated risks.[77] It is the task of various regulatory bodies and research institutes to verify whether this statement is entirely true. Given the objective of this writing, it is useful to provide an example of how business interruption insurance may have contributed to spreading losses resulting from the pandemic.

The first months of the pandemic already delivered examples of business interruption insurers making payouts. It has been reported that the organizers of the Wimbledon tennis tournament had been paying a substantial premium (around USD 1.9 million a year) to cover the cancellation of the tournament due to a pandemic since the SARS outbreak in 2003.[78] The Wimbledon organizers received an

---

[73] Jerry II (2020), p. 25: Where there is no material dispute about an issue of fact, cases will be decided in summary judgments, as interpretation of contract language is typically a question of law for the court to decide.

[74] See Gorenberg and Godes, *Update on Business Interruption Insurance Claims for COVID-19 Losses,* National Law Review (29 October 2020).

[75] French (2020), p. 15.

[76] French (2020), p. 33.

[77] For instance, the position of the American Property Casualty Insurance Association (APCIA), "Pandemic outbreaks are uninsured because they are uninsurable": Press Release, APCIA Releases New Business Interruption Analysis (6 April 2020).

[78] Wimbledon Shows How Pandemic Insurance Could Become Vital for Sports, Other Events, Forbes, 13 April 2020, https://www.insurancejournal.com/news/international/2020/04/13/564598.htm (last access 09 September 2021).

insurance payout of USD 142 million due to the cancellation of the tournament in 2020, having paid out roughly USD 31.7 million in premiums over the 17-year period. In contrast to Wimbledon, the two other Grand Slam tennis tournaments scheduled for 2020 after the Covid-19 pandemic outbreak, the US Open and the French Open, were postponed and eventually took place. Apparently, neither the US Open nor the French Open had purchased pandemic cover, whereas the organizers of Wimbledon had to cancel their event in order to collect on insurance premiums.[79]

There seems to be a broad agreement that policyholders reasonably expect cover under business interruption policies when their business operations are interrupted due to catastrophic events beyond their control. In the UK Supreme Court's judgment, this idea has been powerfully expressed by Lord Briggs, who agreed with all the conclusions of the majority judgment:

> 316[. . .]on the insurers' case, the cover apparently provided for business interruption caused by the effects of a national pandemic type of notifiable disease was in reality illusory, just when it might have been supposed to have been most needed by policyholders. That outcome seemed to me to be clearly contrary to the spirit and intent of the relevant provisions of the policies in issue. It therefore comes as no surprise to me that all the judges who have considered these issues have been unanimous in rejecting that outcome, albeit that this court has done so, rightly in my view, more comprehensively than did the court below. This is not to mis-use the dubious benefit of hindsight when applying an insuring clause to events which could not have been contemplated by the parties at the time of their bargain.

Given the scale of pandemic losses, private business interruption insurance will cover only a limited portion of losses suffered by businesses at large. Conceptually, however, it remains an important component of the risk spreading system, embracing both private market arrangement and government funded programmes. The collaborative effort of Baker's insurance state to spread losses is nicely illustrated by a report from Germany. In some cases, insurers offered to pay out certain parts of business owners' lost income (10–15%) as a gesture of goodwill without recognizing the legal duty to pay out under the policy.[80] It is expected that government bail-out schemes may be sufficient to cover the bigger part of lost income. What remains will be the business owners' burden to carry. Loss spreading may be just about the right word to describe the collective efforts to reduce losses suffered by business operators.

4 Conclusion

This chapter had the modest aim to demonstrate that private business interruption insurance contracts can contribute to the spreading and sharing of loss resulting from the Covid-19 pandemic. To this goal, selected developments in the UK and the US

---

[79] Dunlap (2020).

[80] https://www.haufe.de/recht/weitere-rechtsgebiete/wirtschaftsrecht/zahlen-betriebliche-versicherungen-bei-corona-einnahmeausfaellen_210_513040.html (last accessed 09 September 2021).

have been surveyed. The chapter identified the judgment of the UK Supreme Court in the FCA Test Case as the major point of interest. Importantly, the UK Supreme Court identified the Covid-19 pandemic as an insured peril under business interruption insurance policies on the UK market. While Covid-19 was not a disease which anyone could have specifically had in mind when the business interruption policies were written and marketed, it fell within the types of disease for which the relevant clauses provided cover. This paves the way for a detailed analysis of the factual scope of losses recoverable under the policies in question. The high international reputation of the UK Supreme Court means that its judgment in the *FCA Test Case* will draw considerable attention worldwide. Given its outcome, it may contribute to a policyholder-friendly construction of business interruption policies.

In sum, building upon *Baker's* account of the role the "insurance state" as an approach to spreading losses should play, I claim that insurance institutions, i.e., private insurers, and insurance market regulators, should adapt to facing the business interruption losses resulting from the Covid-19 pandemic. This contribution has attempted to suggest that they should adapt by construing business interruption clauses in a way that does not make them a completely illusory form of cover for a pandemic type of disease.

Acknowledgement This research was funded by Narodowe Centrum Nauki, (NCN) [The National Science Centre] in Poland, grant number 2018/29/B/HS5/01281. I gratefully acknowledge the research assistance of Patryk Walczak LL.M., a doctoral researcher in the above-mentioned research grant.

References

Abraham KS (2013) Four conceptions of insurance. Univ Pa Law Rev 161:653–698
Baker T (2002a) liability and insurance after september 11: embracing risk meets the precautionary principle. University of Connecticut School of Law Working Paper No. 4, available at: https://ssrn.com/abstract=812926 (last access 09 September 2021)
Baker T (2002b) Risk, insurance, and the social construction of responsibility. In: Baker T, Simon J (eds) Embracing risk. The changing culture of insurance and responsibility. The University of Chicago Press, Chicago
Bernstein PL (1998) Against the gods. The remarkable story of risk. Wiley, New York
Bybee JS (1979) Profits in subrogation: an insurer's claim to be more than indemnified. Brigham Young Univ Law Rev 3:145–160
Dunlap K (2020) Why were Wimbledon, British Open canceled instead of postponed?, Available at https://www.ksat.com/sports/2020/07/20/why-were-wimbledon-british-open-canceled-instead-of-postponed/ (last access 09 September 2021)
Ewald F (1986) L'Etat providence. Bernard Grasset, Paris
Ewald F (2002) The return of descartes's malicious demon: an outline of a philosophy of precaution. In: Baker T, Simon J (eds) Embracing risk. The changing culture of insurance and responsibility. The University of Chicago Press, Chicago, pp 273–301
French CC (2020) COVID-19 business interruption insurance losses: the cases for and against coverage. Connecticut Insur Law J 27:1–35
Gardner J (2018) From personal life to private law. Oxford University Press, Oxford

Gorenberg KM, Godes SN (2020) Update on business interruption insurance claims for COVID-19 losses. Natl Law Rev (29 October 2020), https://www.natlawreview.com/article/update-business-interruption-insurance-claims-covid-19-losses (last access 09 September 2021)

Gürses Ö (2021) The Supreme Court on business interruption insurance and COVID-19: financial conduct authority v arch insurance (UK) Ltd [2021] UKSC 1. King's Law J 32:71–83

Jerry RH II (2020) Reflections on COVID-19, insurance, business interruption, systemic risk, and the future. Icade: Revista de la Facultad de Derecho 110:1–40

Katofsky J (1989) Subsiding away: can California homeowners recover from their insurer for subsidence damages to their homes. Pac Law J 20:783–813

Lehtonen T-K, Liukko J (2011) The forms and limits of insurance solidarity. J Bus Ethics 103:33–44

OECD (2021) Responding to the COVID-19 and Pandemic Protection Gap in Insurance

Richter A, Wilson TC (2020) Covid-19: implications for insurer risk management and the insurability of pandemic risk. Geneva Risk Insur Rev 45:171–199

Schanz K-U, Eling M, Schmeiser H, Braun A (2020) An investigation into the insurability of the pandemic risk. Geneva Association, Geneva. Retrieved from: https://www.genevaassociation.org/sites/default/files/research-topics-document-type/pdf_public/insurability_report_web.pdf (last access 09 September 2021)

Remote Teaching and Remote Exams Due to COVID-19: Some Evidence from Teaching Law and Economics

Ido Baum, Jarosław Bełdowski, and Łukasz Dąbroś

Abstract The COVID-19 pandemic imposed an immediate and sweeping transformation on higher education all over the world. The vast majority of higher education institutions in advanced economies shifted from traditional classroom-based teaching and learning to remote teaching via internet platforms, especially in the humanities and social sciences. Social distancing necessitated substituting methods of remote evaluation for classroom exams. We used a dataset of grades from the European Master in Law & Economics programme provided by the consortium of EU and non-EU universities to evaluate the implications of the shift to remote teaching and remote examinations. Consistent with the existing literature, we did not find that shifting to remote teaching and exams had a significant adverse effect on student achievement. However, our findings suggest that weaker students are adversely affected by remote teaching. Put differently, remote teaching increases inequality in higher education outputs.

1 Introduction

There is no doubt that the COVID-19 pandemic is one of the most transformative and consequential events of the twenty-first century. As of a count in March 2021, more than 110 million people in 192 countries had been infected, and more than 2.5 million human beings had perished due to this virus. The COVID-19 pandemic caused colossal changes in almost every aspect of human activity, as countries affected by COVID-19 implemented harsh measures to curtail its spread and limit the number of casualties, including several long periods of lockdown, university and

---

I. Baum
The Haim Striks School of Law at COLMAN, Rishon Le Zion, Israel
e-mail: baumi@colman.ac.il

J. Bełdowski (✉) · Ł. Dąbroś
Warsaw School of Economics, Warsaw, Poland
e-mail: jbeldo@sgh.waw.pl; ld50376@doktorant.sgh.waw.pl

© The Author(s), under exclusive license to Springer Nature Switzerland AG 2022
K. Mathis, A. Tor (eds.), *Law and Economics of the Coronavirus Crisis*, Economic Analysis of Law in European Legal Scholarship 13,
https://doi.org/10.1007/978-3-030-95876-3_8

school closures, travel bans, compulsory remote work, and so-called social distancing. Such measures became a part of ordinary life for millions of Europeans, forcing individuals, businesses, and other organizations to rapidly adjust their behaviour.

The COVID-19 pandemic left its mark on education. Schools and universities, unable to organize traditional classes and exams, had to rapidly introduce remote learning and examination procedures to continue educating students under pandemic conditions. Such steps were taken by the authorities in charge of the European Master of Law and Economics (EMLE) programme provided by a consortium of EU and non-EU universities, a leading master's programme in the European Union, which we use as a case study. During the period of February 2020–June 2020, all classes in the EMLE programme were taught online using external communication platforms such as Zoom and Teams. Exams were also given remotely.

In our study, we use an extensive exam score dataset covering the years 2015 through 2020 to investigate how the switch to remote learning and examinations affected the academic performance of EMLE students. We selected the EMLE programme for various reasons, but primarily because each cohort comprises students from various countries, various individual backgrounds, and different educational tracks (students with a bachelor's degree in law and students with a bachelor's degree in economics). The natural composition of the programme provides a diverse group of students.

This chapter is organized as follows. Firstly, we briefly summarize the existing literature examining the issue of remote learning and examinations and the educational consequences of the COVID-19 pandemic. Secondly, we characterize the EMLE programme, its curriculum, organization, and scoring rules, and describe how the programme has adjusted to pandemic conditions. Thirdly, we present the dataset, the estimation strategy, and the results. Lastly, we summarize our observations and draw our conclusions.

2 Higher Education in the Time of COVID-19

Education is an essential pillar of a modern society. In growth economics, it is considered one of the roots of human capital, fuelling long-term economic growth[1] and increasing human prosperity. Numerous studies have shown other positive social outcomes of education for society, such as less crime[2] and higher social trust.[3] The benefits to society at large of education in general, and higher education in particular, are undisputed.

Also quite intuitive is that attaining higher education benefits the person partaking in the activity. Numerous studies confirm a robust link between an individual's

---

[1] Romer (1990), pp. S71 et seq.; Barro (2013), pp. 277 et seq.
[2] Buonanno and Leonida (2006), pp. 709 et seq., Lochner and Moretti (2016), pp. 155 et seq.
[3] Huang et al. (2011), pp. 287 et seq.

education level and income;[4] this link is attributed both to the so-called *sheepskin effect* (a school certificate or diploma is perceived by potential employers as a signal of greater skills) and the greater productivity of an educated employee. Moreover, more highly educated individuals tend to live longer[5] and be more satisfied with their lives.[6]

These findings and observations explain why education became one of policy makers' main concerns during the COVID-19 pandemic.[7] Because schools and universities had to be shut down to slow the spread of the infectious virus (with the closures affecting 1.6 billion learners all over the world—more than 91% of the global student population, as estimated by UNICEF), concerns that suspending classes would have a long-lasting negative impact on the lives, job market prospects, and careers of the affected students grew.

To allow students to continue their education in spite of the pandemic, numerous schools and universities switched to remote learning channels (most developed countries used the internet, whereas poorer regions of the world relied on traditional media such as TV and radio, as well as take-home study material).

Because, as of the time of writing, only a short time has elapsed since the beginning of the pandemic and pandemic-induced remote learning, there are few studies measuring the impact of remote learning on students' performance. However, there are pre-pandemic studies comparing online and traditional learning. One of them showed (using a natural experiment) that students who attended a series of university lectures performed better than students who watched the lectures on the internet (students were randomly allocated to the "offline" and "online" groups).[8] Others examined a dataset covering 230,000 students of a large for-profit university to show that students taking online classes received lower grades than those studying on campus.[9]

To our knowledge, there are only two studies (in the working stage) analyzing the effects of COVID-19-induced school closure. The first one used data from three Chinese middle schools that adopted different remote learning policies (the first school completely ceased operations and told its student to study on their own, the second school provided students with remote classes given by its own teachers, and the third school had its students attend online classes taught by a team of the best teachers in the city).[10] All three groups took the same exam after the end of the lockdown period (the exam was written and given in a traditional, offline way). The authors observed that students from the schools offering online classes performed significantly better than those from the school that had left its students with no

---

[4] For instance Aakvik et al. (2010), pp. 483 et seq.

[5] Lleras-Muney (2005), pp. 189 et seq.

[6] For instance del Mar Salinas-Jiménez et al. (2011), pp. 409 et. seq.

[7] Di Pietro et al. (2020), pp. 1 et seq.

[8] Figlio et al. (2013), pp. 763 et seq.

[9] Bettinger et al. (2017), pp. 2855 et seq.

[10] Clark et al. (2020), pp. 1 et seq.

support. By contrast, they employed data from the Higher Technical School of Telecommunications Engineers (Universidad Politécnica de Madrid) to show that an emergency switch to remote teaching had a positive impact on students' results (the researchers used data from previous academic years to track individual students).[11]

It is important to note that a problem related to remote teaching is assessing students' performance. Due to the threat of COVID-19, in many cases, it was impossible to host traditional tests or exams taken by students who are supervised to prevent cheating and receiving support from outside the exam room. As a result, schools and universities switched to online testing crafted in a way that reduced cheating opportunities (e.g., using tight time constraints, random questions, or supervision through an online internet camera during the exam).

There exist only a few articles investigating online examination procedures in the time of COVID-19. Some studies concentrate on students' opinions of remote exams and show that (quite counterintuitively) traditional examination is preferred. Students find online examination to be more stressful because of concerns about insufficient time and technical problems.[12] Moreover, they perceive unsupervised exams as unfair (a dishonest student can be aided by another person or use the internet to find answers).

3 European Master in Law and Economics: The Programme and its Organization

The European Master in Law and Economics was established in 1990 by the University of Ghent, the University of Paris IX, the University of Oxford, and the Erasmus University of Rotterdam, with around twenty students from EU member states enrolled. Over the years, it has grown significantly, and the member universities have changed. The programme now attracts seventy to eighty students from all over the world with one half coming from the European Union. The EMLE programme vastly extended its academic consortium reach. At present, the consortium that leads the programme consists of ten universities, eight from the European Union (Aix-Marseille Université, Universitat Pompeu Fabra, Ghent University, Universität Hamburg, Università Lumsa, Erasmus University Rotterdam, Universität Wien, and Warsaw School of Economics) and two from outside the European Union (University of Haifa and Indira Gandhi Institute of Development Research). From the beginning, the EMLE programme has been recognized and, since 2004, supported by the Erasmus Mundus Programme of the European Union

---

[11] Santiago et al. (2021), pp. 1 et seq.
[12] Alsaady et al. (2020), pp. 33 seq; Elsalem et al. (2020), pp. 271 et seq.; Elsalem et al. (2021), pp. 326 et seq.

for the promotion of academic exchanges (currently Erasmus+ Programme of the European Union).

The EMLE programme is a one-year master's programme requiring students to take courses totalling sixty academic credits (ECTS points) over three trimesters. Students are encouraged to study at a different university during each trimester and studying in one institution during all three trimesters is barred. In the first two terms, students may choose to study in one of three different teaching institutions and in the last trimester, they may choose one of seven universities. The first term provides a uniform five-course curriculum. The second term follows the same approach of mandated courses but with an exception for two specialized courses for those students who choose to follow one of the specialized study tracks ("Economic Analysis of Markets, Corporations & Regulators", "Economic Analysis of Public & International Law" or "Economic Analysis of Innovation and Intellectual Property"). It is also possible to attend the EMLE programme without choosing any specialized track. The third trimester, which is attended in one of seven partner institutions, includes two unique courses that differ according to the chosen institution. In addition, the students are required to write a master's thesis on a topic authorized and supervised by a professor from one of the partner institutions, usually the one attended by the student in the third trimester. For more detailed course information, please refer to Table 1 below.

The COVID-19 pandemic resulted in various measures being imposed on and implemented by all EMLE academic partner institutions. First, online examinations were introduced in the second semester of 2020, which corresponded with the outbreak of COVID-19 in Europe and the ensuing lockdowns. The online method of teaching was imposed to the third semester of 2020. Exams were conducted remotely. The EMLE programme requires professors to grade the exams to approximate a mandatory mean grade between 7.3 and 7.7 for each class. In more detail, in accordance with internal EMLE rules, grades for the course exams are awarded on a scale from 0 to 10 points, in increments of half points. Final course exam grades of first and second term courses are adjusted to an average between 7.3 and 7.7 to account for grading differences across EMLE partners (we address this issue in the robustness check). This requirement has not changed through the years, and it persisted during the COVID-19 semesters. No requirements are imposed on professors regarding the distribution of grades.

4 Available Data

As indicated above, the EMLE is a one-year master's programme divided into three terms and consisting of twelve courses (5 + 5 + 2), each with its own exam. The set of courses was not constant over the period of interest; a change in the curriculum occurred in the academic year 2018/19. The distribution of classes is shown in the table below.

Table 1 Courses attended by EMLE students in academic years 2015/16–2019/20

Term	Course no.	Academic years 2015/16–2017/18	Academic years 2018/19–2019/20
I	1	Introduction to Law and Economics	Introduction to Law
	2	Concepts and Methods of Law and Economics	Introduction to Microeconomics
	3	Competition Law and Economics	Concepts and Methods of L&E
	4	Public Law and Economics	Economic Analysis of Public Law
	5	Tort Law and Economics	Economic Analysis of Private Law
II	6	Corporate Law and Economics	Corporate Governance and Finance
	7	Property Law and Economics	Competition Law and Economics
	8	Contract Law and Economics	Empirical Legal Studies
	9	Empirical Legal Studies	Economic Analysis of Intellectual Property orEconomic Analysis of International Law orMarkets, Corporations & Regulators Moot Court
	10	Environmental Law or L&E of Courts or Economics of Constitutional and Administrative Law	Advanced Contract L&E or Advanced Economics of Regulations or Economic Analysis of Constitutions
III	11	Depends on the university of choice	Depends on the university of choice
	12		

Source: www.emle.org (last access 30 September 2021)

Our dataset consists of EMLE exam results for 406 students who participated in the EMLE programme during the period of our study. We obtained 4845 observations (defined as a student–exam pair), as some students dropped out and did not write all the required exams. The distribution of marks obtained by EMLE students in the academic years 2015/16–2019/20 is shown below (Fig. 1).

High median and mean values demonstrate good preparation of EMLE students (not surprising given the programme's highly selective recruitment process), low level of difficulty of exams, lenient grading policies, cultural differences towards grading in various universities or some combination of those factors.

To tentatively investigate whether the COVID-19 pandemic and the switch to remote learning and exams affected the students' results, we first compared the distribution of grades in the second and third terms of the 2019/20 year (when exams were conducted online) with those in the same semester of the 2018/19 year (the same curriculum was in place in both years). The students in the 2 years were, of course, different (Table 2).

N	Mean	S.D.	Min	Q1	Median	Q3	Max
4845	7.60	1.33	0.00	7.00	7.50	8.50	10.00

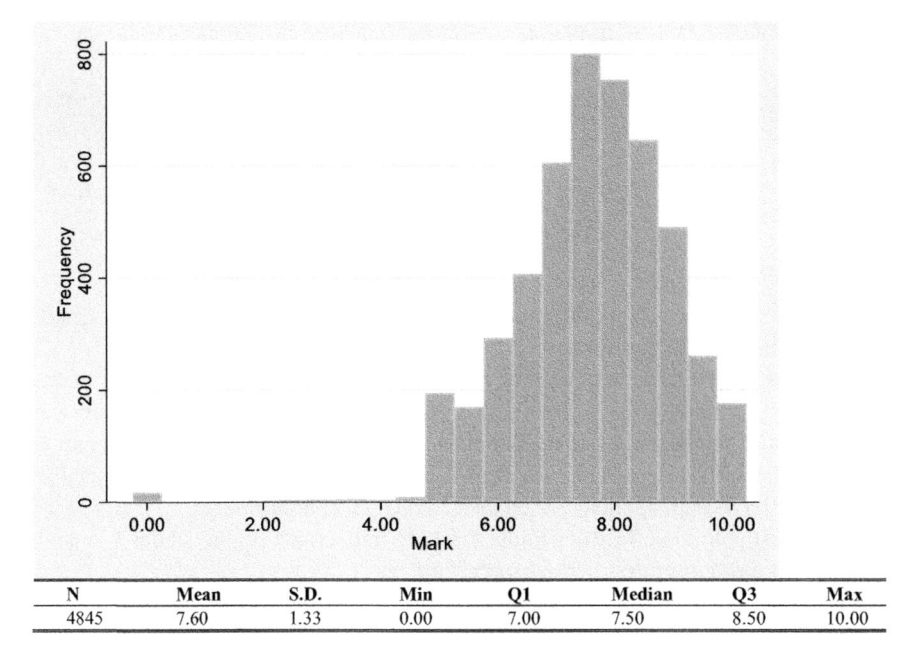

Fig. 1 Distribution of grades earned by EMLE students in academic years 2015/16–2019/20. Source: dataset provided by EMLE, own assessments

Table 2 Distribution of grades of EMLE students in the second and third terms of the academic years

Year [Terms]	N	Mean	S.D.	Min	Q1	Median	Q3	Max
2018/19 [2–3]	588	7.74	1.12	5	7	8	8.5	10
2019/20 [2–3]	497	7.43	1.63	0	6.5	7.5	8.5	10
2018/19 [2]	420	7.64	1.12	5	7	7.5	8.5	10
2019/20 [2]	355	7.46	1.38	0	6.5	7.5	8.5	10
2018/19 [3]	168	8.01	1.07	5	7.5	8	9	10
2019/20 [3]	142	7.36	2.14	0	7	8	8.5	10

Source: dataset provided by EMLE, own assessment

Comparing means and standard deviations across the two academic years, we observed that the students' results in the second and third terms in 2019/20 (remote teaching and exams) were worse and more widely dispersed than in the pre-COVID-19 academic year 2018/19. This comparison did not account for the hidden traits of

Table 3 Estimation results

Remote	(1)	(2)	(3)	(4)
Value	−0.047	−0.035	−0.153	−0.114
St. error	0.078	0.082	0.088	0.089
P-value	0.541	0.673	0.081	0.201
R2	0.521	0.530	0.537	0.54
N	4845	4845	4845	4845

Source: dataset provided by EMLE, own assessment

individual students, subject difficulty, or specifics of individual universities participating in the EMLE programme.

The EMLE programme's grading guidelines require professors to reach a mean grade of approximately 7.5 in grading the exams of their students in the second term. Regardless of that observation, mean grades, when teaching and exams were remote, were significantly lower than mean pre-COVID-19 grades. Additionally, standard deviations increased significantly under COVID-19 conditions.

To investigate the effect of remote teaching and exams on the students' results, we therefore proposed four model specifications:

$$mark_{ist} = \beta_0 + remote_{ist} * \beta_1 + \delta_{it} + \varepsilon_{ist} \quad (1)$$

$$mark_{ist} = \beta_0 + remote_{ist} * \beta_1 + univ_u + \delta_{it} + \varepsilon_{ist} \quad (2)$$

$$mark_{ist} = \beta_0 + remote_{ist} * \beta_1 + subj_s + \delta_{it} + \varepsilon_{ist} \quad (3)$$

$$mark_{ist} = \beta_0 + remote_{ist} * \beta_1 + subj_s + univ_u + \varepsilon_{ist} \quad (4)$$

In the first model, we assumed that a student's exam results depend on their individual skills (δ_{it}), and the dummy variable "remote" denotes whether an exam was given online (remote=1) or in a traditional way (remote=0). In the second model, we added the individual effect of the university where the exam was organized. In the third model, we added the individual effect of the subject of the exam. Finally, we combined the effects of the subject and the university in the fourth model. We used the OLS method and White standard errors to avoid difficulties that might be caused by heteroskedasticity.

The values of the *remote* parameter in a model comprising all five academic years (graduations in the years 2016–20) are as follows (Table 3).

The value of the remote parameter is negative but not significant for the conventional 5% significance level. Only in the third specification (accounting for the individual subjects' effects) is the parameter significant and negative at a more tolerant 10% level. Therefore, it can be stated that we see no statistically significant impact of remote examination on the EMLE students' performance. In order to check the robustness of our results, we also ran regressions only for the 1st and 2nd term (with grade mean adjustments) and only for the 3rd term (with grades distributed freely without alterations). However, this did not change the obtained results—the *remote* parameter remained insignificant.

5 Discussion

In this study, we used the dataset comprising exam results of the EMLE programme to calculate the effects of remote teaching and examinations on students' exam results in the academic year 2019/20 as compared to 2018/19. Although mean results in the second and third terms of the academic year 2019/20 were slightly worse than in the year 2018/19, and standard deviations were larger in the former, we do not find statistically significant evidence showing that remote teaching and examination negatively affected students' performance on the whole. However, this observation fails to capture the full story.

Attention should be given to the wider distribution of grades in the COVID-19 year as compared to the previous year. Although it is hard to disentangle the effects of remote exams from the effects of remote learning, this observation may indicate a reduction in the ability of weaker students to keep up with the class or to be identified by their teachers and brought up to speed. We find this phenomenon to be consistent with the fact that students who study using a remote platform tend to be less attentive and to refrain from asking questions that may expose their weak comprehension of the study material, and also consistent with the effects of the absence of group dynamics and peer learning of students.

Admittedly, it might be the case that EMLE teachers might have tried to keep the grade distribution similar to that of traditional pre-COVID-19 exams or even been more lenient so as to encourage students who were already upset by the COVID-19 crisis. Our observations do not change even if such a strategy was adopted. In fact, to the extent they did, the wider distribution of grades during the COVID-19 terms indicate that teachers were unable to fully correct the grades to erase the impact of remote learning and remote exams.

6 Conclusion

Higher education is important for economic growth. The COVID-19 pandemic had a significant and transformative influence on higher education. Almost the entire student population in developed countries shifted from classroom teaching and classroom examinations to remote teaching and learning and remote examinations. To date, the literature on the effectiveness of remote learning and remote examinations is scant. This chapter contributes to the literature by examining student grades in the European Master in Law and Economics programme and evaluating the effects of remote learning and remote examinations during the COVID-19 pandemic as compared with a pre-COVID-19 year.

Our findings indicate that shifting from classroom learning to remote learning did not have a significant impact on the grades of students participating in the EMLE programme. However, our findings do indicate that weaker students, from an academic perspective, may have done worse with distanced learning or remote examinations or both. This finding is congruent with the general effects of the COVID-19 pandemic, which are perceived as increasing national and global gaps in education and—in the long run—personal development. However, one shall be aware that this impact is limited as the database available is modest, and the students are highly selected in comparison to other master programmes in social sciences provided by universities around the world.

Further research is called for. In particular, our research does not answer the question of whether student achievement was affected predominantly by the shift from classroom to remote learning or by the shift from classroom exams to remote examinations.

References

Aakvik A, Salvanes KG, Vaage K (2010) Measuring heterogeneity in the returns to education using an education reform. Eur Econ Rev North-Holland 54(4):483–500. https://doi.org/10.1016/j.euroecorev.2009.09.001. (last access 22 September 2021)

Alsaady I et al (2020) Impact of COVID-19 crisis on exam anxiety levels among bachelor level university students. Mediterranean J Soc Sci 11(5):33–39

Barro RJ (2013) Education and economic growth. Annals Econ Finance 14(2):277–304

Bettinger EP et al (2017) Virtual classrooms: how online college courses affect student success'. Am Econ Rev 107(9):2855–2875. https://doi.org/10.1257/aer.20151193. (last access 22 September 2021)

Buonanno P, Leonida L (2006) Education and crime: evidence from Italian regions. Appl Econ Lett 13(11):709–713. https://doi.org/10.1080/13504850500407376. (last access 22 September 2021)

Clark AE et al (2020) Compensating for academic loss: online learning and student performance during the COVID-19 pandemic. J Edu 1(2):1–18. Available at: https://halshs.archives-ouvertes.fr/halshs-02901505 (last access 12 September 2021)

del Mar Salinas-Jiménez M, Artés J, Salinas-Jiménez J (2011) Education as a positional good: a life satisfaction approach. Soc Ind Res Springer, 103(3):409–426. https://doi.org/10.1007/s11205-010-9709-1. (last access 22 September 2021)

Di Pietro G et al (2020) The likely impact of COVID-19 on education: reflections based on the existing literature and recent international datasets. Publications Office of the European Union, Luxembourg. https://doi.org/10.2760/126686

Elsalem L et al (2020) Stress and behavioral changes with remote E-exams during the Covid-19 pandemic: a cross-sectional study among undergraduates of medical sciences. Annals Med Surg Elsevier Ltd 60(October):271–279. https://doi.org/10.1016/j.amsu.2020.10.058. (last access 22 September 2021)

Elsalem L et al (2021) Remote E-exams during Covid-19 pandemic: a cross-sectional study of students' preferences and academic dishonesty in faculties of medical sciences. Annals Med Surg. Elsevier Ltd, 62(January):326–333. https://doi.org/10.1016/j.amsu.2021.01.054. (last access 22 September 2021)

Figlio D, Rush M, Yin L (2013) Is it live or is it internet? experimental estimates of the effects of online instruction on student learning. J Labor Econ 31(4):763–784. https://doi.org/10.1086/669930. (last access 22 September 2021)

Huang J, van den Brink HM, Groot W (2011) College education and social trust: an evidence-based study on the causal mechanisms. Soc Ind Res 104(2):287–310. https://doi.org/10.1007/s11205-010-9744-y. (last access 22 September 2021)

Lleras-Muney A (2005) The relationship between education and adult mortality in the United States. Rev Econ Stud 72(1):189–221. https://doi.org/10.1111/j.1467-937X.2006.00398.x. (last access 22 September 2021)

Lochner BL, Moretti E (2016) American economic association the effect of education on crime: evidence from prison inmates, arrests, and self- reports author (s): Lance Lochner and Enrico Moretti Source. Am Econ Rev 94(1):(Mar. 2004):155–189

Romer PM (1990) Endogenous technological change. J Polit Econ 98(5):S71–S102. https://doi.org/10.1086/261725. (last access 22 September 2021)

Santiago I-P et al (2021) Emergency remote teaching and students, academic performance in higher education during the COVID-19 pandemic: a case study. Comput Human Behav 119(October 2020):106713. https://doi.org/10.1016/j.chb.2021.106713. (last access 22 September 2021)

Part II
Future Possibilities

Access and Development Rights in Pandemic Crises

Rolf H. Weber

Abstract The Internet offers many new data exchange possibilities, but the recent pandemic crisis has shown that members of civil society cannot always enjoy the appropriate data access rights around the globe. Therefore, data and infrastructure access rights must be broadened and understood as constitutional (human) rights. In addition, the right to development leading to an inclusive society should be strengthened. This contribution attempts to develop ideas on how these objectives could be realised.

1 Introduction

With the advent of the Internet for the whole society about three decades ago, the new information and communications (i.e., data exchange) possibilities were expected to lead to a knowledge-based community, allowing all members of civil society to enjoy a right to information and participation. But experience has shown that the realisation of the envisaged objectives is quite challenging. In situations of a pandemic environment such as COVID-19, the right to access and the right to development are particularly relevant but equally endangered.[1]

The following contribution attempts to develop ideas, which allow extending the notion of data access to a broader constitutional (human or fundamental) right.[2] Thereby, the individual should become empowered to control and dispose of his/her information. The existing international legal instruments are not very clear in this respect; however, interpretative room of manoeuvre exists, and recent developments appear encouraging.

---

[1] Weber (2020), pp. 75 et seqq.
[2] See also Weber (2020), p. 78.

R. H. Weber (✉)
University of Zurich, Zurich, Switzerland
e-mail: rolf.weber@rwi.uzh.ch

© The Author(s), under exclusive license to Springer Nature Switzerland AG 2022
K. Mathis, A. Tor (eds.), *Law and Economics of the Coronavirus Crisis*, Economic Analysis of Law in European Legal Scholarship 13,
https://doi.org/10.1007/978-3-030-95876-3_9

In addition, a future-oriented approach must also encompass efforts to strengthen the right to development leading to an inclusive society around the globe; a (geographical and social) extension of individual rights is particularly important in times of pandemic crises.

2 Broadening the Scope of Access Rights

2.1 Open Society and Fundamental Rights

In as early as 1945, Popper postulated the necessity of an "open society" evolving in a perpetual process.[3] Aims of this openness are the preservation of individual freedom as well as the ideal of a political-ideological pluralism.[4] This theory of an "open society" is particularly applicable in the case of the Internet; the "openness" presupposes that relevant data sources remain accessible and allow members of civil society to participate in public fora.[5]

The concept of an open society has been taken up by the two World Summits on the Information Society (WSIS) in Geneva (2003) and Tunis (2005). In particular, the Principles of the first Summit crystallised the main goal for an open society. Everyone should be able to acquire basic information and electronic education, and everyone should have access to infrastructure under adequate economic conditions.[6] Indeed, the freedom of information must be implemented by establishing access possibilities, not only to the technical infrastructure, but also to the content, that is, to the informational substance. The capacity of individuals to enjoy their rights in the social and political sphere can only be improved with better Internet and data access.[7]

Traditionally, fundamental rights (such as the freedom of information[8] in the context of the data access rights) are primarily shielded against State interventions into the protected spheres of individuals. But this traditional concept does not exclude that fundamental rights can also be invoked against non-state actors. States are obliged to dedicate the maximum of available resources to ensuring the realisation of human rights for everyone.[9]

---

[3] Popper (1945), p. 462.
[4] See also Sunstein (2001), pp. 105 et seqq.
[5] Weber (2016), pp. 208–209 with further references.
[6] World Summit on the Information Society (2003), Declaration of Principles, Building the Information Society, https://www.itu/int/net/wsis/outcome/booklet/declaration_C.html (last access 12 September 2021).
[7] Weber (2020), p. 76.
[8] Art. 19 of the United Nations' Universal Declaration of Human Rights (UDHR) of 10 December 1948 refers to the freedom of expression and the right to receive and impart information, https://www.ohchr.org/en/udhr/documents/udhr_translations/eng.pdf (last access 12 September 2021).
[9] Kaufmann (2018), p. 318.

The broadened scope of so-called indirect effects of fundamental rights gained importance since many businesses operate in multiple jurisdictions, with varying laws. Insofar it becomes decisive how resources are allocated in a fair way; only a global and wide fundamental rights understanding can enable an appropriate scope of individual protection.[10] In other words, a modern approach requires taking the horizontal and indirect effects of fundamental rights into consideration, which includes an obligation of non-state actors to comply with them.[11]

New technologies, facilitating a fuller realisation of communications exchanges, have the potential to support those persons who actively seek and impart information. Digital developments are empowering spaces for collaboration and participation. Internet access via manifold devices (including mobile devices) also enables (i) people to express themselves more directly in public arenas without having to go through the traditional media gatekeepers and (ii) activists to apply new tools in the application of fundamental rights.[12] Thereby, access must be available to the data as such and to the infrastructure used for the exchange of data.

2.2 Legal and Factual "Holding" of Data

During the last 20 years, civil society learned the ambivalent lesson that the technical access to the Internet or, more generally, to the data transmission infrastructure does not fully cover the needs of the individuals in the digital society, particularly not in times of crises. Such kind of access must be complemented with the access to specific and/or individual data being personal or non-personal (but relevant for the concerned person).

2.2.1 Limited Scope of Ownership Rules

The legal challenge for access rights consists in the fact that data ownership, to the extent such a concept is normatively accepted at all, does not play the most prominent role in reality; therefore, a "pure" L&E approach cannot sufficiently cope with the decisive issues at stake.

So far, data access rules exist in data protection laws, but the respective rights usually concern the "original" data delivered by the individual.[13] As soon as the data

---

[10] See also Weber (2013), p. 28.

[11] Kaufmann (2018), p. 322 with further references, particularly on the Guiding Principles on Business and Human Rights of the UN Human Rights Council; see also Besson (2015), pp. 244 et seqq.

[12] Weber (2020), p. 76.

[13] The right to data access is foreseen in Art. 15 of the EU General Data Protection Regulation and in Art. 25 of the new Swiss Data Protection Act.

is processed (for example, in big data analyses), the question arises whether the "new" data still is to be considered as personal data belonging to an "identifiable natural person" or whether the controller of the applied processes (i.e., the "owner" of the digital dossiers) has acquired an exclusive right of use.[14]

In most countries, the normative category of "property rights" encompasses objects with physical characteristics.[15] In contrast, the characteristics of data are different as data are non-rivalrous and generally non-exclusive.[16] Intellectual property rights, as well as neighbouring rights (or so-called ancillary rights), are equally unsuitable for establishing an exclusive ownership position in favour of the data holder.[17] Therefore, regulators usually are no longer building on the concept of property for data but on the concept of data access[18] as described hereinafter.

2.2.2 Factual Control of Data

Since legal ownership does not constitute a reliable foundation for the entitled person to claim individual rights, factual control becomes key, i.e., the person (or enterprise) holding or "controlling" the data and executing the data processing is in an "ownership-like position" and has the power to decide about the use of the data. As a consequence, for the individual being directly or indirectly concerned by the processing of data, the design of data access rules is crucial (particularly if health issues are at stake).[19] The interest balancing test in case of a contested access right claim must take into consideration at least three perspectives:[20] (i) From an economic angle, the question arises whether the holder of data, having invested efforts and money into the collection and processing of data, is entitled to an appropriate remuneration (L&E approach). (ii) From a strategic angle, the challenge occurs that a data access right to a computer could eventually distort competition. (iii) From a legal angle, data access rights are potentially conflicting with business secrecy and data protection rules.

Legal rules giving guidance in respect of this interest balancing test hardly exist. In particular, if data cannot be considered "personal", only limited data access rights of individuals are available in most legislations. Such access rights to non-personal data have only been introduced by the EU (not by the Swiss) legislator in the form of some sector-specific regulations (for example, in the automotive sector or in the

---

[14] See also Weber and Eggen (2020), p. 464.

[15] For a general overview see Heymann (2016), pp. 650 et seqq.; Hürlimann and Zech (2016), pp. 89 et seqq.

[16] Cooter and Ulen (2006), p. 40.

[17] See Weber and Eggen (2020), p. 462 with further references.

[18] Weber and Eggen (2020), p. 461; for the EU see European Commission, Communication "Building a European Data Economy" of January 2017, COM (2017) 9 final.

[19] Weber and Eggen (2020), p. 467.

[20] Thouvenin et al. (2019), pp. 107–108 with further references.

banking industry).[21] Furthermore, access to data can eventually be enforced based on competition (antitrust) law if the holder of the data has a market dominant position; however, the respective proceedings are time-consuming and costly.[22]

So far, health law rarely addresses data access and data sharing issues. Nevertheless, on the EU level (but not on the Swiss level), two limited exceptions are noteworthy: (i) In the REACH-Regulation governing the registration, evaluation, authorization, and restriction of chemical products, enterprises do have access rights in respect of general data of other enterprises (Art. 27b and 30).[23] (ii) Access to documents of other enterprises, if no business secrecies are concerned, can be achieved in connection with registration procedures at the European Medicines Agency (EMA).[24]

Access to data and an exchange of data can also be foreseen on a contractual basis. But as experience shows, the design of the respective bilateral provisions depends on the "market power" of the concerned contract parties. In the health sector, cooperatives ("Genossenschaften") can be a vehicle of data exchanges; in Switzerland, the "midata cooperative" is at least partly realising a model that allows data access even after data processing.[25]

2.3 Way Forward

The description of the given legal environment for access rights has shown that further initiatives are needed, and more measures must be implemented. In principle, a certain L&E impact is vested in the fact that access issues are often seen as elements of economic openness; this interrelation between fundamental freedoms and economic openness needs to be analysed in more detail. The analysis must be done in respect of access to data as such and of access to the appropriate infrastructure allowing the exchange of data.

2.3.1 International Legal Instruments (UNESCO, ICESCR)

(i) A certain "systematic" problem with access rights consists of the fact that the legal position of the individuals is often not considered as the expression of a

---

[21] For a recent overview describing the respective access rules in the European Union in detail, see Weber and Eggen (2020), pp. 468–469.

[22] For further details see Weber and Eggen (2020), pp. 469–471 with references to the relevant decisions of the European Court of Justice.

[23] Regulation 1907/2006 of 18 December 2006, OJ 2006 L 396/1; the reason for the respective rules is to be seen in the attempt of limiting animal tests in the context of registration procedures.

[24] Directive 2001/83 of 6 November 2001, OJ 2001 L 311/67.

[25] See https://www.midata.coop (last access 12 September 2021).

fundamental right, but as an element of economic openness (encompassing open standards, open access/architecture, net neutrality). A good example of such a two-tier approach can be seen in the Internet Universality (or R-O-A-M) Principles of United Nations Educational, Scientific, and Cultural Organization (UNESCO), adopted in 2014.[26] Obviously, linkages are existing between the two pillars; access and accessibility as a social dimension are intertwined with human rights,[27] but the overlap is not that clear at first instance. As a consequence, an artificial distinction between fundamental rights and economic openness does not seem to be future-oriented.

(ii) Similarly, the (often overlooked) International Convention on Economic, Social, and Cultural Rights (ICESCR[28]), having been adopted in 1966 together with the (simultaneously negotiated) International Covenant on Civil and Political Rights (CCPR[29]), shows the parallelism between human (civil, political) and economic/social rights. Both Covenants were negotiated in parallel and, therefore, they should be seen as a comprehensive, interrelated package. As far as the ICESCR is concerned, legal doctrine has clarified that economic constraints cannot dispense States from their obligation to dedicate all reasonably available resources to ensuring the progressive realisation of human rights in an effective manner.[30]

In particular, Article 2 of the ICESCR obliges States to create an environment, which enables civil society to make participative decisions and provide basic public services (including infrastructure) in order to support individuals in the realisation of their rights.[31] Access rights are an important element contributing to the widely accepted objective of promoting general welfare in a democratic society.[32]

Furthermore, Article 15 para. 1(a) of the ICESCR requires States to see to it that everyone has a right to take part in cultural life; a similar approach is applicable in the education context.[33] Finally, equal access to infrastructure and information is an area in which the principle of non-discrimination should apply. Indeed, digital means do have the potential for improving the capacity of individuals to exercise their rights in the given social and political sphere.

---

[26] https://en.unesco.org/internet-universality-indicators (last access 12 September 2021).
[27] See Weber (2015), pp. 18–19.
[28] https://www.ohchr.org/en/professionalinterest/pages/cescr.aspx (last access 12 September 2021).
[29] https://www.ohchr.org/en/porfessionalinterest/pages/ccpr.aspx (last access 12 September 2021).
[30] Kaufmann (2018), p. 318 with further references.
[31] See also Jørgensen (2006), pp. 53 et seqq.; Shiman (1999), pp. 2 et seqq.
[32] See Alston and Quinn (1987), pp. 192 et seqq.
[33] Weber (2013), p. 30.

2.3.2 Court Practice (ECOWAS)

The right of having access to the Internet (i.e., to the infrastructure, not to the data as such) was already subject to a decision of the Court of Justice of the Economic Community of West African States (ECOWAS-Court). The ECOWAS enshrines 15 West African States with more than 400 Mio. inhabitants; the ECOWAS Treaty was concluded in 1975 and substantially revised in 1993.[34] The judgments of the Court are immediately binding and not appealable (Article 15 para. 4 ECOWAS-Treaty). Since the adoption of the Additional Protocol of 2015 (A/SP.1/01/05), the Court is entitled to "determine cases of violations of human rights that occur in any Member State" (Article 9 para. 4).

In the hereinafter discussed proceedings, the plaintiffs complained that the blockage of the Internet in Togo had violated the freedom of expression and the freedom of information as enshrined in Article 9 of the African Charter on Human and Peoples' Rights (so-called Banjul-Charter) of 1 June 1981[35] and in Article 19 of the UDHR. Legally, the ECOWAS-Court is not bound by the interpretation and the application of a specific human rights declaration but can draw on all international legal instruments, including Article 38 of the Statute of the International Court of Justice (Article 19 para. 1 of the Protocol A/P1/7/91).[36]

The ECOWAS-Court published its judgment on 25 June 2020.[37] The question of whether access to the Internet can be derived from international human rights conventions has been answered in a quite clear way: "Access to Internet is not *stricto senso* a fundamental human right but since internet service provides a platform to enhance the exercise of freedom of expression, it then becomes a derivative right that is a component to the exercise of the right to freedom of expression. [...] It is necessary that access to internet and the right to freedom of expression be deemed an integral part of human right that requires protection by law and makes its violation actionable" (no. 38).

The main normative reference was Article 9 of the Banjul-Charter; the human rights quality of this provision has led the ECOWAS-Court to the following statement: "Access to internet should be seen as a right that requires protection of the law [...] just in the same way as the right to freedom of expression is protected [...] and any interference with it has to be provided for by the law specifying to grounds for such interference" (no. 38).

The government of Togo referred to national security interests as legitimation for the interference. However, according to the ECOWAS-Court, such far-reaching

---

[34] Revised Treaty: https://www.ecowas.int/wp-content/uploads/2015/01/Revised-treaty.pdf (last access 12 September 2021).

[35] See https://www.achpr.org/legalinstruments/detail?id=49 (last access 12 September 2021).

[36] See also Klimke (2020), p. 3.

[37] Amnesty International Togo et al. vs. Togolese Republic, ECW/CCJ/APP/61/18, https://africanlii.org/ecowas/judgment/ecowas-community-court-justice/2020/9 (last access 12 September 2021).

disobedience for human rights is not justified: "The fundamental basis of the exercise of this power of derogation is that it must be done in accordance with the law. In other words, there must exist a national legislation guaranteeing the exercise of this right whilst providing the conditions under which it can be derogated from" (no. 45). The government of Togo has been requested to establish all "necessary measures to guarantee non-occurrence of this situation in the future" (no. 47, v) and "to enact and implement laws, regulations and safeguards in order to meet its obligations with respect to the right of freedom of expression in accordance with international human rights instruments" (no. 47, vi).

Notwithstanding the fact that the judgment of the ECOWAS-Court is very welcome, some questions remained open, particularly in respect of the justified interference reasons. From the wording of the judgment, a limitation of the potential legitimate purposes of interferences cannot be drawn.[38] Insofar, reference could be made to the work of the UN Human Rights Council stating in its General Comment no. 34 what follows: "Restrictions [...] may only be imposed for one of the grounds set out... [content-specific reference]."[39] In particular, a total shutdown of the Internet is practically never compliant with the international human rights instruments.[40] Similarly, Principle 38 para. 2 of the 2019 revised Declaration of Principles on Freedom of Expression and Access to Information in Africa contains the following guarantee: "States shall not engage in or condone any disruption of access to the internet and other digital technologies for segments of the public or an entire population."[41]

2.3.3 Interim Conclusion

The right to have access to the own data is theoretically existing for many decades. Recently, combined with access to the network infrastructure in the digital environment, access possibilities gained importance and are decisive for the members of civil society. This appreciation corresponds to the more flexible interpretation of the existing legal instruments. Scholars are increasingly accepting the horizontal or indirect effects of fundamental rights leading to the consequence that not only States but also non-state actors have to comply with fundamental rights. Courts appear to be also more inclined to enforce access rights. Therefore, the existing paths seem to go in the right direction, and the access right might be more frequently applied, i.e. a

---

[38] See also Klimke (2020), p. 6.
[39] UN-Human Rights Committee, General Comment 34, CCPR/C/GC/34, no. 22.
[40] For further details see Klimke (2020), pp. 6–7.
[41] The new Declaration contains a whole chapter with rules specifying the access to the Internet and thereby going much further than international legal instruments influenced by Western countries; https://ijrcenter.org/2020/04/22/new.achpr-declaration-on-freedom-of-expression-access-to-infor mation/ (last access 12 September 2021).

3 Revitalising Development Rights

3.1 *International Legal Instruments*

The evolution of digital information is changing the ways in which opportunities and challenges need to be conceptualised and addressed. Better access to network infrastructures and to data can facilitate "control" over the person-oriented information and the flow of information, thereby improving the knowledge regarding the rights to free expression and information.[42] Individuals become empowered to apply the tools that they need in order to hold the third-party data "controllers" accountable for their behaviour.

3.1.1 Existing Covenants and Declarations

For the first time, the right to development was recognised in 1981 in Article 22 of the African Charter on Human and Peoples' Rights (Banjul-Charter) as an individual and a collective right as follows:[43] "All peoples shall have the right to their economic, social and cultural development with due regard to their freedom and identity and in equal enjoyment of the common heritage of mankind." On the international level, the mentioned ICESCR holds the States responsible for putting measures in place that will spur the realisation of economic and social rights to the maximum of their available resources.[44] According to Article 2 of the ICESCR, States are obliged to create an environment, which enables civil society to take advantage of basic public services and infrastructures that are able to support development.[45] More than 50 years ago, the ICESCR has laid the foundation for the realisation of a right to development, which needs to be further advanced under the given circumstances.

The notion of a right to development is also contained in the UN "Declaration on the Right to Development" of 1986.[46] Article 1 of this Declaration makes it clear that the right to development is a human right, and Article 4 reflects the commitment of the States to collaborate in formulating international development policies to facilitate the full realisation of the right to development. But despite being in place for

---

[42] Weber (2013), p. 26, 31.

[43] See above note 35.

[44] See above Chap. 2.3.1.

[45] Weber (2013), p. 29.

[46] Resolution 41/128 of 4 December 1986.

more than 30 years, the Declaration, not being a legally binding instrument, is suffering from a lack of implementation as well as of the political will required for international cooperation.[47]

On the occasion of the 30th anniversary of the Right to Development Declaration (2016), the UN Human Rights Office of the High Commissioner has put its activities under the heading "Moving Forward: The commitment to cooperate must be operationalized."[48] In line with Article 3 of the Declaration, States must cooperate to ensure an enabling environment for development that is sustainable and equitable; crises should be addressed in the spirit of solidarity and with the vision of acting in a fundamental rights-compliant way.[49] Indeed, the right to development merits more support from developed countries, based on a rights-based and people-oriented approach.[50] Legal policies should be reoriented toward promoting common values and be transformed from a set of rules preserving the present state of the existing environment into a regime enshrining social development objectives.[51]

Equally, such a perspective is of particular importance in connection with the UN Sustainable Development Goals (SDG); the objectives of most SDG are directly or indirectly linked to development issues. Mainly SDG 17 on the revitalisation of the global partnership on public health reflects the vision of cooperation for development as contained in Art. 3 of the Development Right Declaration.[52] Since the SDG are in an ongoing process of being implemented, more emphasis might be put on the right to development during the next few years.

3.1.2 New Initiatives

After the outbreak of COVID-19, international organisations were more intensively looking at the possibilities of revitalising the existing rules regarding the right to development. In particular, a detailed report of the United Nations Sustainable Development Group on "Shared responsibility, global solidarity: Responding to the socio-economic impacts of COVID-19" (March 2020) states that almost all the goals are affected by the present pandemic environment and that political leadership and cooperation is needed to combat COVID-19.[53]

---

[47] See also Weber (2013), p. 32; Sengupta (2001), pp. 2527 et seqq.: Schrijver (2020), pp. 84 et seqq.

[48] Information note, https://www.ohchr.org/Documents/Issues/RtD/RTD_InternationalCooperation.pdf (last access 12 September 2021), p. 2.

[49] For a general overview of the situation at that time see Arts and Tamo (2016), pp. 211 et seqq.

[50] See also Kaufmann (2018), p. 328.

[51] So also Wolfrum (2010), para. 10, in connection with the cooperation principle.

[52] Information note (supra note 48), p. 1.

[53] See https://unsdg.un.org/sights/default/files/2020-03/SG-Report-Socio-Economic-Impact-of-Covid19.pdf. (last access 12 September 2021), p. 11.

In a similar way, the OECD, in its report of spring 2020 with the title "COVID-19 and Responsible Business Conduct," particularly addresses resilience issues and calls for social dialogue as well as for stakeholder engagement in the context of the given pandemic crisis.[54] Thus, on the one hand, access to data and information through appropriate Internet connectivity and through third persons storing the data in digital dossiers must be secured; on the other, more personal and financial resources need to be invested in the advancement of economic and social development tasks, which are underpinned by an individual right to development.

In parallel, since 2016 (as some kind of "turning point"), the right to development has gained more attention. In its Resolution 33/14 of 29 September 2016, the Human Rights Council established the mandate of the Special Rapporteur on the right to development (Mr. Saad Alfarargi). In addition, the Human Rights Council appointed the Intergovernmental Open-ended Working Group on the Right to Development.[55] This Working Group holds yearly meetings in order (i) to review the implementation of the right to development around the globe and—since the adoption of the respective Human Rights Council Resolution 39/9 of May 2019—(ii) particularly to draft a new Convention in this field.

During its Session of May 2020, the Human Rights Council agreed to submit the "Draft Convention on the right to development" to interested persons and organisations.[56] The 16-pages document should be commented on and complemented by the public, bringing in its perceptions and regulatory wishes. In May 2021, the Human Rights Council has further discussed the implementation of the right to development around the globe and taken note of the comments to the Draft Convention without adopting it on this occasion.

In particular, Article 4 para. 1 of the Draft reads as follows: "Every human person and all peoples have the inalienable right to development by virtue of which they are entitled to participate in, contribute to and enjoy economic, social, cultural, civil and political development that is consistent with and based on all other human rights and fundamental freedoms". Furthermore, Article 3(b) states that the right to development should be realised in a manner that integrates the principles of accountability, empowerment, and participation. Article 13 para. 1(c) specifically refers to "health and related problems" in the context of the right to development, and Article 13 para 4(a) requires the promotion of a universal, rules-based, open, non-discriminatory, and equitable multilateral trading system.

---

[54] See https://mneguidelines.oecd.org/COVID-19-and-Responsible-Business-Conduct.pdf pp. 8–9 (last access 12 September 2021).

[55] See https://www.ohchr.org/en/issues/development/pages/wgrighttodevelopment.aspx (last access 12 September 2021).

[56] A/HRC/WG.2/21/2.

The Draft is quite comprehensive[57] and certainly leads to intensive and probably wide-ranging discussions.[58] A strategic question to be answered concerns the issue of having a completely new international legal instrument or rather a substantial amendment and strengthening of the existing 1986 Declaration.[59] However, whatever form is finally chosen, the right to development should have a broad-ranging stand:[60] (i) The right to development must function as a cluster right enshrining many facets of daily life of civil society. (ii) The right to development must play an integrative role encompassing political, economic, social, and cultural rights. (iii) The right to development must exercise a bridging function connecting the rights of individuals with those of groups and peoples. The enlargement of the previous concept is of particular importance in times of pandemic crises.

3.2 Need for a More Inclusive Approach

A formal adaptation of the existing international legal instruments in the area of a right to development is confronted with political "hurdles" since legislative processes in international organisations are usually quite slow. But the respective objectives can also be pursued in other ways. In particular, potential alternatives are self-regulatory measures or decisions taken by courts having an extraterritorial reach (as in the case of the discussed ECOWAS-Court).[61] Self-regulation and co-regulation need to be driven by industry or business associations as well as by civil society groups; in the Internet governance context, the multistakeholder approach has become known as a bottom-up and more inclusive model (indeed with some success as the NetMundial Conference held in 2014 in Brazil has shown).[62]

Looking from a general perspective, no standard way to form multistakeholder groups can be established. The actual dimensions of bottom-up processes must be designed differently, depending on the cultural and the contextual factors in shaping the functioning and the outcome of governance groups (for example, the pre-existing relationships between the stakeholders, the connection between the governance group and the governmental institution, the allocation of resources, and geopolitical factors); therefore, a broad spectrum of purposes can be listed, ranging from

---

[57] See also Schrijver (2020), pp. 90–91.

[58] For progress made in this process see the information on https://www.ohchr.org/en/issues/development/pages/wgrighttodevelopment.aspx (last access 12 September 2021).

[59] Schrijver (2020), p. 91.

[60] See also Schrijver (2020), p. 92.

[61] Weber (2020), p. 77.

[62] See https://netmundial.br/netmundial-multistakeholder-statement/ (last access 09 September 2021).

open-ended missions to issue-specific tasks.[63] Even if multistakeholderism is not a value as such, it should be considered as a possible approach for meeting salient public interest objectives by determining what types of policy-making are optimal in the given functional and political environment.

Court practice could also step in and interpret the present legal norms in a more extensive way. These ways forward might better meet L&E efficacy criteria and contain fewer limitations than the traditional legal and regulatory responses to new developments. Obviously, self-regulatory measures and court decisions, as well as forward-looking normative approaches based on more inclusive multistakeholder processes, need to materially convince a broad community across countries and cultures, but the COVID-19 crisis has shown that data access and sustainable development issues around the globe do have the potential of such a conviction.

4 Outlook

The recent pandemic crisis made it very clear that access to data (particularly to health data[64] as a key concern of individuals) is of utmost importance. Furthermore, from a global perspective, the right to development must also be strengthened. Some progress has been made during the last few years. The right to access to data is more widely accepted, and efforts on the international level exist that could lead to a better legal foundation for the right to development. Nevertheless, further initiatives are needed in this context. The partly negative experiences made with the tackling of the COVID-19 crisis in 2020 should be taken as an incentive to design an improved normative framework for the future.

References

Alston P, Quinn G (1987) The nature and scope of states parties' obligations under the international covenant on economic, social and cultural rights. Hum Rights Q 9(2):156–229
Arner DW et al (2021) Digital finance, COVID-19 and existential sustainability crises: setting the agenda for 2020s. AIIFL working paper No. 37, February
Arts K, Tamo A (2016) The Right to development in international law: new momentum thirty years down the line? Neth Int Law Rev 63:221–249
Besson S (2015) The Bearers of human rights' duties and responsibilities for human rights: a Quiet (R)Evolution? Soc Philosophy Policy 32(1):244–268
Cooter R, Ulen T (2006) Law and economics, 6th edn. Pearson, Boston
Heymann T (2016) Rechte und Daten, Warum Daten keiner eigentumsrechtlichen Logik folgen. Computer und Recht 32:650–657
Hürlimann D, Zech H (2016) Rechte an Daten, sui generis 3:89–95

---

[63] Weber (2016), p. 258.
[64] See also Arner et al. (2021), pp. 17–18.

Jørgensen RF (2006) The right to express oneself and to seek information. In: Jørgensen RF (ed) Human rights in the global information society. MIT Press, Cambridge MA, pp 53–72

Kaufmann C (2018) The covenants and financial crises. In: Moeckli D, Keller H (eds) The Human rights covenants at 50, their past, present, and future. Oxford University Press, Oxford, pp 303–333

Klimke R (2020) Ein Menschenrecht auf zugang zum internet? policy papers on transnational economic law, vol No. 56. Law School of Halle-Wittenberg University

Popper K (1945) The open society and its enemies. Routledge, London

Schrijver N (2020) A new convention on the human right to development: putting the cart before the horse? Neth Q Human Rights 38:84–93

Sengupta A (2001) Right to development as a human right. Econ Polit Wkly 36:2527–2536

Shiman DA (1999) Economic and social justice: a human rights perspective. University of Minnesota, Minneapolis, Human rights resource center

Sunstein C (2001) Republic.com. Princeton University Press, Princeton

Thouvenin F, Weber RH, Früh A (2019) Elemente einer Datenpolitik. Schulthess, Zürich

Weber RH (2013) ICT policies favoring human rights. In: Lannon J, Halpin EF (eds) Human Rights and Information Technologies: Trends and Consequences of Use. IGI Global Print, Hershey PA, pp 21–35

Weber RH (2015) Principles for governing the Internet. A comparative analysis, UNESCO Series on Internet Freedom. UNESCO Publishing, Paris

Weber RH (2016) Elements of a legal framework for cyberspace. Swiss Rev Int Eur Law 26:195–215

Weber RH (2020) Access as a human right. In: Belli, Pahwa, Manzar (eds) The value of internet openness in times of crisis, New Delhi. https://www.defindia.org/wp-content/uploads/2020/11/THE-VALUE-OF-INTERNET-OPENNESS-IN-TIMES-OFCRISIS.pdf. Accessed 22 Sep 2021

Weber RH, Eggen M (2020) Data ownership and data access in the internet of things (IoT). Eur J Consum Law 459–480

Wolfrum R (2010) Co-operation, international law of. In: Wolfrum R (ed) Max planck encyclopia of public international law. Oxford University Press, Oxford. (update December 2010)

COVID-19 and the Issue of Affordable Access to Innovative Health Technologies: An Analysis of Compulsory Licensing of Patents as a Policy Option

Muhammad Zaheer Abbas

Abstract The conflict between patents and public health has been a long-standing concern. The current COVID-19 crisis has further visualized the complexities of the global issue of availability, accessibility, and affordability of essential health technologies. Compulsory licensing is a policy option, provided under the World Trade Organization Agreement on Trade-Related Aspects of Intellectual Property Rights (TRIPS), to balance the conflicting interests of patent-holder brand-name pharmaceutical industry and low- and middle-income countries requiring access to the patented pharmaceutical drugs in a legal and sustainable way. The Doha Declaration on TRIPS and Public Health recognized the importance of compulsory licensing in addressing the issue of equitable access to medicines. Despite its established legitimacy, this regulatory tool has been the subject of immense controversy. This article evaluates the conflicting views on compulsory licensing to analyse the root causes of this controversy. It argues that compulsory licensing is not only politically sensitive but also procedurally cumbersome. It also considers empirical evidence on the actual use of compulsory licensing since Doha. Finally, it considers the recent compulsory licensing-related legislative measures adopted by different countries in response to COVID-19. It concludes that the compulsory licensing mechanism needs to be revisited and reformed to make it more responsive and practical. It proposes that the actual use of compulsory licensing safeguard should be backed by civil society mobilization to neutralize the pressures exerted by brand-name pharmaceutical corporations and their hosting countries.

A substantial part of an earlier draft of this article is derived from the author's Ph.D. thesis entitled "Community-Based Patent Opposition Model in India: Access to Medicines, Right to Health and Sustainable Development" submitted at QUT, Australia.

M. Z. Abbas (✉)
Faculty of Business and Law, Queensland University of Technology, Brisbane, QLD, Australia
e-mail: muhammadzaheer.abbas@connect.qut.edu.au

© The Author(s), under exclusive license to Springer Nature Switzerland AG 2022
K. Mathis, A. Tor (eds.), *Law and Economics of the Coronavirus Crisis*, Economic Analysis of Law in European Legal Scholarship 13,
https://doi.org/10.1007/978-3-030-95876-3_10

1 Introduction

In 1995, the World Trade Organization (WTO) linked intellectual property protection with trade.[1] To become a WTO member, signing the TRIPS Agreement is a prerequisite condition.[2] The TRIPS Agreement provided mandatory patent protection to inventions in all fields of technology for a period of 20 years.[3] It was anticipated at the time of drafting of the TRIPS Agreement that the exclusive rights granted under patent law may have serious practical implications for poorer countries in accessing affordable medicines.[4] Public health safeguards were therefore included in the original draft of the TRIPS.

Compulsory licensing is one of the most prominent public health safeguards provided under the TRIPS Agreement. A compulsory license is "an authorization given by a national authority to a person, without or against the consent of the titleholder, for the exploitation of a subject matter protected by a patent or other intellectual property rights."[5] It is a statutorily created license that allows certain people to pay a royalty or adequate remuneration to the patentee and use an invention without the patentee's permission. Though the term "compulsory licensing" has not been used in the TRIPS Agreement, a set of conditions have been stipulated under Art. 31 for grant of a non-voluntary license or "other use without authorization of the right holder".[6] A compulsory license can be issued for use by the government, by its agents, or by third parties, including corporate bodies and private individuals.[7]

Art. 31 does not provide a list of grounds for the issuance of compulsory licenses.[8] During the TRIPS negotiations, the U.S. sought to expressly limit the use of compulsory licensing to cases of national emergency and antitrust violation. Art. 27 of the Draft TRIPS Agreement (1990) stated: "Contracting Parties may limit the patent owner's exclusive rights solely through compulsory licenses and only to remedy an adjudicated violation of competition laws or to address, only during its

---

[1] Abbas and Riaz (2013a), p. 487; See more Abbas (2013), p. 256. The author would like to acknowledge his Ph.D. supervisors Professor Matthew Rimmer and Professor Richard Johnstone. The author would also like to acknowledge his wife, Dr. Shamreeza Riaz, for her unconditional support and valued cooperation. The views presented in this article and any mistakes are, however, the sole responsibility of the author.
[2] Ragavan (2012), p. 64; See Abbas and Riaz (2014), p. 111; See more Abbas and Riaz (2013b).
[3] TRIPS Agreement (1995), Arts 27 and 33, see p. 3838; See more Abbas (2020c).
[4] Abbas (2020b).
[5] Asok (2019), p. 125; See more Abbas and Riaz (2013a) pp. 482–483.
[6] TRIPS Agreement (1995), Art. 31.
[7] Owoeye (2019), p. 13.
[8] During the TRIPS negotiations, the U.S. sought to expressly limit the use of compulsory licensing to cases of national emergency and antitrust violation. Art. 27 of the Draft TRIPS Agreement stated: "Contracting Parties may limit the patent owner's exclusive rights solely through compulsory licenses and only to remedy an adjudicated violation of competition laws or to address, only during its existence a declared national emergency." See Draft Agreement on Trade Related Aspects of Intellectual Property (1990).

existence a declared national emergency." WTO Member States can issue compulsory licenses on any ground they deem fit. Possible grounds may include national emergency or circumstances of extreme urgency, anti-competitive practices, excessive pricing, failure to meet the demand for a patented product in a domestic market, abuses of patent rights, and lack of or insufficient working of the patent.[9] Non-working of patents locally has, however, remained a controversial ground for the issuance of a compulsory license. Art. 27 of the TRIPS Agreement states that patents shall be available "without discrimination as to the place of invention, the field of technology and whether products are imported or locally produced."[10] On the basis of this provision, which prohibits WTO Member States from refusing patents if patentees fail to manufacture locally, it has been argued that evidence of importation is enough to satisfy the working requirement.[11] Some commentators take a holistic approach and argue that Art. 5(A)(2) of the Paris Convention requires local working of patents.[12] The TRIPS Agreement preserves the rights and obligations of parties under the Paris Convention.[13] The use of lack of local working as ground for granting compulsory licenses is, therefore, consistent with the TRIPS Agreement.

By not specifying conditions or restricting the grounds on which compulsory licenses may be issued, the TRIPS Agreement provided flexibility for governments to authorize the use of a patent without the permission of the patent owner under their respective compulsory licensing or government/ crown use regime.[14] Because of this flexibility, national laws governing processes to apply for compulsory licenses and the grounds under which compulsory licenses may be granted vary from country to country.[15] This mechanism can be used even if the circumstances are not exceptional.[16] WTO Member States are, however, expected to make sure that this safeguard mechanism is not used on frivolous grounds.

The Doha Ministerial Declaration on the TRIPS Agreement and Public Health, unanimously concluded in November 2001, reaffirmed that 'each Member has the right to grant compulsory licenses and the freedom to determine the grounds upon which such licenses are granted'.[17] By using this flexibility, WTO Member States may authorize the production and sale of patented health technologies without the

---

[9] See Ranjan (2020), p. 136; See more Owoeye (2019), p. 13.

[10] TRIPS Agreement (1995), Art. 27.

[11] De Carvalho (2005), p. 196.

[12] Mercurio and Tyagi (2010), pp. 325–326.

[13] TRIPS Agreement (1995), Arts 2(1) and 2(2); See more Vienna Convention on the Law of Treaties, Art. 30(2).

[14] A compulsory license is issued upon a motion submitted by any interested party in cases of abuses of monopoly by a patentee while government use or crown use is invoked on grounds of national security or for the maintenance of essential supplies and services. See Khazin and Wu (2020).

[15] Correa (2020a), p. 19.

[16] Sundaram (2014).

[17] Doha Ministerial Declaration on TRIPS Agreement and Public Health 2001, para. 5(b); See Abbas and Riaz (2013a) p. 491; See more Abbas (2017), p. 443.

consent of the patent holders. WTO Member States reached a consensus that "public health crises, including those relating to HIV/AIDS, tuberculosis, malaria and other epidemics" can qualify as "a national emergency or circumstances of extreme urgency".[18] The Doha Declaration, therefore, reinforced the use of compulsory licensing to advance social policy goals and to protect the public interest.

Practical implementation of compulsory licensing safeguard has remained a controversial issue in international trade relations.[19] The true potential of compulsory licensing is largely unrealized because political and economic pressure exerted by developed countries prevents developing and least developed countries from exercising their rights under the TRIPS Agreement and the Doha Declaration.[20] Consequently, the issue of affordable and equitable access to innovative health technologies has been the subject of a long-standing global debate on intellectual property, trade, and public health. Stephen Lewis, a Canadian politician and UN Special Envoy on HIV/AIDS, noted that "access to medicines has become one of humankind's greatest crises, perhaps right behind climate change."[21] The United Nations Human Rights Council's resolution, adopted in June 2016, noted that "actual or potential conflicts exist" between the implementation of the TRIPS Agreement and the realization of the right to health.[22] Three months later, the UN High-Level Panel on Access to Medicines released its Report which echoed most of the sentiments expressed by the UN Human Rights Council in its resolution.[23]

The COVID-19 crisis has put this problem in the limelight because governments, even in economically advanced countries, have struggled to meet the health needs of their populations. Patent exclusive rights add to the cost of healthcare by allowing supra-competitive prices of protected technologies. On May 18–19, 2020, the annual meeting of the World Health Assembly (WHA) was held virtually to discuss the global response to COVID-19. The Resolution WHA73.1, titled COVID-19 Response, recognized that all countries should have timely and affordable access to COVID-related health technologies.[24] The resolution, however, failed to define any specific concrete actions or provide clear guidance on how to achieve this goal. WTO Member States are considering the available policy options to achieve this goal.

---

[18] Doha Ministerial Declaration on TRIPS Agreement and Public Health 2001, para. 5(c).

[19] Gibson (2010), p. 368.

[20] Abbas and Riaz (2014) pp. 3–10.

[21] Fran Quigley, Hope for the High-Level Panel on Access to Medicines (February 7, 2018) Health and Human Rights Journal, https://www.hhrjournal.org/2016/01/hope-for-the-high-level-panel-on-access-to-medicines/ (last access 24 December 2020).

[22] OHCHR (2016).

[23] UN Secretary-General and Co-Chairs of the High Level Panel, Report of the United Nations Secretary-General's High Level Panel on Access to Medicines: Promoting Innovation and Access to Health Technologies (2016) High Level Panel on Access to Medicines; See more Abbas (2020a) p. 26.

[24] World Health Organization, COVID-19 Response, Seventy-Third World Health Assembly, Doc. A73/CONF.Rev.1, May 2020.

In this context, this article evaluates the policy option of compulsory licensing and highlights its role in addressing this and future pandemics. This article has a six-part structure, including the introduction and the conclusion. Section 2 evaluates the "*privilege view*" and the "*maximalist view*" on patents—the conflicting views which provide an ideological basis to the controversy of compulsory licensing. It also draws upon real-world examples to argue that the actual use of compulsory licensing is coupled with the risk of damaging trade relations and diplomatic ties with high-income countries. Section 3 evaluates the procedural terms and conditions provided under the TRIPS Agreement for the use of compulsory licensing safeguards. It argues that this mechanism in its current form is less efficient in providing a quick solution in an emergency. Section 4 considers the empirical evidence on the actual use of compulsory licensing since Doha. It finds that although statistically, this flexibility seems to be used frequently, the number of high-profile compulsory licenses is relatively low. Section 5 considers the recent compulsory licensing-related legislative measures adopted by different countries in response to COVID-19. It supports these enabling measures as they send a clear signal to brand-name pharmaceutical corporations that governments will not put up with delays in accessing COVID-19 related health technologies. The conclusion in Sect. 6 calls for an uncomplicated, unambiguous, and more practical compulsory licensing mechanism with reduced transaction costs. It proposes that the actual use of this safeguard should be backed by civil society mobilization to neutralize the pressures exerted by brand-name pharmaceutical corporations and their hosting countries.

2 Compulsory Licensing: The Most Controversial Public Health Flexibility

Compulsory licensing has been one of the most controversial topics in the access to medicines debate, despite it clearly being permissible under the TRIPS Agreement.[25] The controversy or misunderstanding about compulsory licensing is caused by the following competing perspectives: the developing country perspective; and the patent owner perspective.[26] The polarized positions on the issue often result in quick dismissals of opposing views and even hostility.[27] Recognizing these seemingly irreconcilable perspectives is, therefore, critical to better understand not only the compulsory licensing controversy but also many other issues related to the access to drugs debate and to get beyond the deadlock. Cynthia M. Ho summarized these perspectives:

> One perspective of patents is that they are a mere privilege granted by a nation and thus inherently subject to limitations to accommodate other social goals, such as access to

---

[25] TRIPS Agreement (1995), Art. 31.
[26] Ho (2011), p. 157.
[27] Ho (2011), p. 158.

medicine. This view is referred to as the *privilege view* of patents. The alternative perspective views patents as a type of super-property right that should seldom, if ever, be subject to exception. This is referred to as an *uber-right view* in contrast to the traditional conception of property rights that necessarily include limitations and exceptions.[28]

It is important to note here that historically, patents were granted as a privilege by the Crown.[29] The *privilege view* sees patents as "a tool inherently subject to limitations".[30] According to this view, there are numerous competing societal goals that need to be balanced; promoting innovation is one of these societal goals, and it does not enjoy superiority over other goals.[31] Patents are seen as one of the tools to promote innovation.[32]

Brook K. Baker supports the *privilege view* as he noted that "patents are not 'property' in the traditional sense—they are government-granted rights that are intended to balance the interests of innovators and the public at large, and which are granted by governments with many express and implied conditions."[33] The view that patents must be "subject to limitations in the public interest" is also supported by the UN Commissioner of Human Rights.[34] Carlos Correa also maintains the view that "like other rights, patent rights are not absolute. There are situations in which their exercise can be limited to protect public interests. Such situations may arise, for instance, when access to needed pharmaceutical products must be ensured."[35]

Prior to the TRIPS Agreement, national approaches of countries, like India and China, suggest that they considered patents as a privilege as they sought to balance patent protection with other social interests by denying product patents for drugs.[36] Canada is another example as it has made broad use of drug patent compulsory licenses prior to signing up to the North American Free Trade Agreement (NAFTA).[37] An international agreement, like the TRIPS, that mandates patent protection for all technologies potentially conflicts with the *privilege view* because the Member States are no more allowed to decide whether or not to grant patents for certain technologies.

The alternative maximalist perspective—which views patents as a type of super-property right or a privileged property right—analogizes compulsory licensing to stealing.[38] The Big Pharma is the strongest supporter of this view. The Big Pharma is synonymous with around twenty-five innovative or research-based multinational

---

[28] Ho (2011), p. 159.
[29] Ho (2011), p. 159.
[30] Ho (2011), p. 161.
[31] Ho (2011), p. 161.
[32] Ho (2011), p. 161.
[33] Baker (2007).
[34] Office of the United Nations High Commissioner for Human Rights (2000).
[35] Correa (2020a), p. 13.
[36] Ho (2011), p. 162.
[37] Ho (2011), p. 162.
[38] Ho (2011), p. 163.

drug companies.[39] The United States represents around 50% of the global prescription drug market and the European Union a further 25%.[40] It has been estimated that the representation of the countries outside of North America, the European Union, and Japan in the global prescription drug market is only about 10%.[41] The Big Pharma is of the view that patents benefit all despite their implications for cost and affordability of patented drugs.[42] They contend that access to low-cost generic drugs[43] is possible because of patent protection. For instance, Fred Hassan, Chairman and CEO of Schering-Plough, noted that:

> IP protection for pharmaceutical innovation creates a wonderful cycle. It rewards and incentivizes the huge investments needed to create new medicines. Then, on the expiration of the patent, the innovation becomes freely available to all. Generic drugs are thus the direct result of IP-fuelled innovation. They would not exist without IP. And without IP, we would not see new advances in medicine that in turn would become generic drugs.[44]

Miles White, the Chairman and CEO of Abbott Laboratories, noted in a 2006 press release that:

> Generic manufacturers have an important role to play in lowering the cost of treatment over time, which offers value to society. But society cannot save its way to health with old treatments that gradually lose their effectiveness and offer no help against new diseases. By definition, generic manufacturers make nothing new. And AIDS is a disease that is always new – due to the constant evolution of the virus – and requires new solutions. Where will these come from if we hobble the patent system that drives innovation?[45]

Martin Adelman holds a similar view that "one cannot have access to something that does not exist."[46] Patents, in the *maximalist view*, are considered as a special right, and any exceptions to these special rights, like compulsory licensing, are allowed only in the narrowest of circumstances.[47] As noted by Christopher Gibson, who views compulsory licensing as inherently contentious, "the possibility of compulsory licenses [...] fundamentally undermines the stability of the patent regime and thereby makes unreasonable the reliance that an investor might otherwise place on its patent rights when making an investment."[48] Likewise, Brian Toohey, PhRMA Senior Vice President for International Advocacy, noted that compulsory licensing

---

[39] Löfgren (2017), p. 182.

[40] Löfgren (2017), p. 182.

[41] Löfgren (2017), p. 183.

[42] Ho (2011), p. 164.

[43] A generic drug can be defined as "a drug product that is comparable to brand-name drug product in dosage form, strength, route of administration, quality and performance characteristics, and intended use." See Brougher (2014), p. 135.

[44] Ho (2011), p. 164.

[45] White (2005); See further Flint and Payne (2013), p. 515.

[46] Ho (2011), p. 164.

[47] Ho (2011), p. 165.

[48] Gibson (2010), p. 388.

"creates significant uncertainty for biopharmaceutical innovators and harms patients by undermining incentives for future research."[49]

Some commentators even consider the curtailment of patent rights through compulsory licensing as a government-sanctioned theft.[50] Jamie Feldman argued that "if pharmaceutical companies are no longer able to have exclusive rights to control their products, they will essentially be robbed of the fruits of their labor."[51] Margo Bagley criticized the approach of characterizing compulsory licensing as theft or stealing. She rightly noted that:

> The drugs [produced under compulsory licensing] were going to poor people who would not be able to buy them at the price the originator pharmaceutical company was charging. These were not lost sales; these sales never would have been made by the patent owner [...]. Issuing a compulsory in accordance with TRIPS is not a morally culpable action and is far removed from theft. It is not even defined as stealing under international law and involves compensation to the patent owner. Yet it is too often characterized as theft in a way that appears to give pharmaceutical companies the moral high ground and allows them to play the victim in terms of public relations and inciting governmental action against offending countries [...]. The hard questions regarding who really is stealing from whom do not get asked.[52]

Margo Bagley rather views "the pharmaceutical companies trying to keep needed drugs from the poor as thieves."[53] She opposes the *maximalist view* of patents noting that "patent rights are limited property rights at best, and their contours and scope are constantly being adjusted through judicial, legislative, and administrative action. Every court or United States Patent and Trademark Office (USPTO) tribunal invalidation of a patent based on obviousness is an indictment of an absolute-rights stance."[54] She opined that "governments grant patents to meet utilitarian societal goals and governments decide the subject matter, scope, and duration of patents."[55] She further clarified that "allowing the public to absorb some beneficial spillovers without positively harming the property owner can be a virtuous policy choice."[56]

The patent system was not designed to uphold the *maximalist view* of patents. The U.S. Supreme Court noted in 1945:

> The possession and assertion of patent rights are 'issues of great moment to the public'. A patent by its very nature is affected with a public interest. As recognized by the Constitution, it is a special privilege designed to serve the public purpose of promoting the 'Progress of Science and useful Arts'. At the same time, a patent is an exception to the general rule against monopolies and to the right to access to a free and open market.[57]

---

[49] New (2019).

[50] See, for instance, Wright (2018); See more Cass (2007).

[51] Feldman (2009).

[52] Bagley (2018), pp. 2491, 2493 and 2494.

[53] Bagley (2018), p. 2493.

[54] Bagley (2018), p. 2479.

[55] Bagley (2018), p. 2479.

[56] Bagley (2018), p. 2480.

[57] Precision Instrument Mfg. Co. v. Automotive Maintenance Machinery Co. (1945).

Mandatory international patent protection standards, under the TRIPS Agreement, may seem to support the *maximalist view* of patents. There are, however, provisions in the TRIPS Agreement—like Art. 7 (which requires enforcement of IP rights in a manner conducive to social and economic welfare), Art. 8 (which allows members to adopt measures to protect public health), Art. 27.2 (which allows members to deny patent coverage to protect *ordre public* or morality, including to protect human, animal or plant life or health), Art. 30 (which authorizes general exceptions to patent protection), and Art. 31 (which authorizes compulsory licensing of patents)—that support the *privilege view* of patents. It is, however, challenging for countries to practically stick to the *privilege view* after becoming a party to the TRIPS Agreement. Patents are the backbone of the pharmaceutical corporations' business model as they create pricing power by conferring exclusive rights.[58] The actual use of compulsory licensing is not tolerated by the patent-holder pharmaceutical corporations and their home governments.

In 2000, the U.S. threatened Thailand with trade sanctions when the Thai government attempted to issue a compulsory license for Didanosine, an HIV/AIDS drug.[59] The Thai government succumbed to the U.S. pressure in this instance, but later, in 2006–2007, over a period of several months, Thailand issued three compulsory licenses.[60] The first was for Merck's HIV drug Efavirenz, the second was for Abbott's HIV drug Kaletra, and the third was for Sanofi-Aventis' heart disease medication Plavix.[61] With an aim to support Thailand's position, the Thai government issued an eighty-page brief in February 2007.[62] The Thai government tried to embrace the *privilege view* of patents as the brief stated that the compulsory licensing of three drug patents "allows the government to better achieve its commitment to universal access to medicines in the essential drug list and also is clear evidence of the government's commitment to put the right to life above the trade interest."[63] The Thai government's *privilege view* of patents was rejected outright by the Big Pharma and its home countries. Switzerland, for instance, handed in an "Aid memoir'" to the Thai government and emphasized that compulsory licenses, though permissible under the TRIPS, should be "used only as a last resort".[64]

The U.S. Department of State and the United States Trade Representative (USTR) asked Thailand to reconsider its compulsory licensing decision.[65] The Deputy USTR, Karan Bhatia, tried to exert pressure through diplomatic channels

---

[58] Durisch and Gajardo (2018) p. 8.

[59] Asok (2019), p. 129; See more Abbas and Riaz (2014) p. 8.

[60] The issuance of compulsory licenses in Thailand resulted in reduction of 350 million US dollars in government's health expenditure and allowed 85,000 additional patients to access lifesaving medicines. See Durisch and Gajardo (2018), p. 34.

[61] Thailand TM of PH and TNHSO (2007), p. iii.

[62] Thailand TM of PH and TNHSO (2007), p. iii.

[63] Thailand TM of PH and TNHSO (2007), p. 4.

[64] Public Eye (2008).

[65] Wetzler et al. (2009).

and delivered a message to the Thai Embassy in Washington DC.[66] Thai government officials described the message as "bullying".[67] The European Commissioner, Peter Mandelson, wrote a letter to the Thai government to warn about the pharmaceutical industry's reaction to the use of compulsory licensing.[68] In March 2007, Abbot Laboratories retaliated and withdrew the registration of several drugs from Thailand.[69] On March 20, the U.S. Chamber of Commerce released its survey report emphasizing that "issuance of compulsory licenses may jeopardize international investments".[70] On March 30, Thailand was elevated to the USTR Special 301 Report Priority Watch List as the issuance of compulsory licenses was seen as an indication of "a weakening of respect for patents".[71] The USTR's decision was supported by Pharmaceutical Research and Manufacturers of America (PhRMA).[72] In July 2007, the USTR, under the U.S. Generalized System of Preferences, withdrew duty-free access to the U.S. market for three Thai products.[73]

In May 2007, Brazil granted a compulsory license on Merck's HIV drug Efavirenz.[74] Merck reacted negatively and characterized the issuance of compulsory licenses as an expropriation. Merck issued a statement that "this expropriation of intellectual property sends a chilling signal to research-based companies about the attractiveness of undertaking risky research on diseases that affect the developing world, potentially hurting patients who may require new and innovative life-saving therapies."[75] The President of Merck's Latin American division warned that "the perception of Brazil will not be the same" and Merck will review its investment plan in the country.[76] The U.S. Chamber of Commerce responded to the issuance of the compulsory license by noting that the "government has made a major step backward. Breaking off discussions with Merck and seizing its intellectual property sends a

---

[66] Wetzler et al. (2009).

[67] Wetzler et al. (2009).

[68] Wetzler et al. (2009).

[69] Wetzler et al. (2009).

[70] Wetzler et al. (2009).

[71] Office of the US Trade Representative (2007), p. 27; The U.S Trade Representative's Special 301 Report is a Congressionally mandated annual report in which countries, depending on the gravity of intellectual property violations, are listed as "Priority Foreign Countries", "Priority Watch List" and "Watch List" countries. The unilateral Special 301 review mechanism, which is used as a weapon of intimidation as the U.S. government, conflicts with Art. 23.2(a) of the World Trade Organization's Agreement on Understanding on Rules and Procedures Governing the Settlement of Disputes; See Asok (2019), p. 126; See more Countries Under Section et al., Public Citizen Hearing Testimony for the 2015 Special 301 Review, 1.Public Citizen Hearing Testimony for the 2015 Special 301 Review 1.

[72] Wetzler (2009).

[73] Asok (2019), p. 129.

[74] Presidential Decree No. 6.108 (2007).

[75] Gibson (2010), p. 373.

[76] Correa (2013).

dangerous signal to the investment community."[77] The USTR raised concerns about Brazil's potential use of the compulsory licensing mechanism in its 2007 Special 301 Report, although the Report was finalized before Brazil issued the compulsory license.[78]

In 2010, Ecuador granted a compulsory license for an antiretroviral drug called Ritonavir. Abbott Laboratories, the owner of the compulsorily licensed patent, expressed its disappointment with the decision. According to Abbott, compulsory licenses "undermine the patent system and are a disincentive for research-based companies to invest in new treatments".[79] The U.S. Emergency Committee for American Trade argued that "Ecuador's decision appeared to be contrary to the TRIPS Agreement and qualified as an effort to nullify the protection of intellectual property."[80] Ecuador was listed in the Watch List on the USTR Special 301 Report. The Report also included a warning that the U.S. "will continue to monitor recent developments concerning compulsory licensing of pharmaceutical and agricultural chemical products in Ecuador".[81] In the 2011 USTR Special 301 Report, Ecuador remained on the Watch List with the same warning of the U.S. surveillance on Ecuador's compulsory licensing activity.[82]

In 2012, when India issued its first compulsory license to an Indian pharmaceutical company Natco Pharma for manufacture and sale of Bayer Corporation's patented drug Sorafenib,[83] it had to face serious retaliation from the U.S. and the EU, including threats of trade sanctions.[84] India was placed on the Priority Watch List by the USTR.[85] The USTR specifically cited the issuance of a compulsory license as a major patent deterioration.[86] India remained on the Priority Watch List in 2013 as well for the same reason.[87] In 2014, PhRMA cited the reason of compulsory licensing when it urged India's elevation into the "Priority Foreign Country List".[88] Although India was not labelled as a Priority Foreign Country, an out-of-Cycle Review was planned against India.[89] In 2016, the U.S.-India Business Council (USIBC) stated in its submission to the Office of the USTR that "the Government of India has privately reassured [. . .] (that) it would not use Compulsory Licenses for

---

[77] Correa (2013).

[78] Office of the US Trade Representative (2007), p. 30.

[79] Saez (2010).

[80] Saez (2010).

[81] Kirk et al. (2010), p. 31.

[82] Office of the US Trade Representative (2011), p. 34.

[83] Natco Pharma Ltd. v. Bayer corporation, CLA, no. 1, 2011 (9 March 2012).

[84] McMahon (2020), p. 339.

[85] Mathew Joe (2012).

[86] Kirk (2012), p. 35; See more Asok (2019), p. 127.

[87] Office of the US Trade Representative (2013), p. 38.

[88] Asok (2019), p. 127.

[89] Asok (2019), p. 127.

commercial purposes."[90] The Indian government, however, refuted any such reports.[91]

In 2016, when Colombia announced its intention to grant a compulsory license on the cancer drug Imatinib (Glivec), the patent-holder drug corporation Novartis asserted significant negative pressure on Colombia. To avoid the issuance of a compulsory license, the Swiss pharma giant threatened Colombia with international investment arbitration.[92] Novartis lodged two lawsuits at the Colombian Supreme Court to put additional pressure on Colombia.[93] The Colombian government was strongly intimidated by Switzerland (Novartis' hosting country) and the U.S.[94] The U.S. government officially threatened to withdraw financial support for the peace process in Colombia.[95] The U.S. "made Colombia choose between peace and public health".[96] Colombia stopped short of issuing a compulsory license despite the fact that "Glivec was marketed in Colombia at a price of approximately CHF 15,000 per patient per year, almost twice the average annual income in Colombia."[97]

It is clear that the use of compulsory licensing to override the exclusive patent rights is coupled with the risk of damaging trade relations and diplomatic ties with high-income countries.[98] Antony Taubman summed up the tensions between private interests and societal objectives, noting that:

> The grant of a compulsory license is inevitably a contested issue in trade relations, within or beyond the TRIPS regime, because it directly calibrates the boundary between legitimate expectations of patent holders and the public interest, in exceptional and egregious cases when the interests of producers and users of technology most closely approach a zero sum character: in these cases, the presumed systematic spur to technology diffusion created by an exclusive right in the hands of the technology developer gives way to a bare entitlement to adequate remuneration.[99]

Many low- and middle-income countries shy away from invoking this legitimate flexibility considering their bilateral relations with wealthy countries and the possibility of trade retaliation. Ellen 't Hoen expressed her concerns about public and diplomatic relations problems associated with the compulsory licensing option as it leads to "high profile political conflicts over IP rights involving the United States, the European Union, and patent-holding pharmaceutical companies".[100] Graham Dutfield also showed concerns about the pressure tactics of the U.S. and the

---

[90] Press Trust of India (2016).
[91] Press Trust of India (2016).
[92] Public Eye (2017).
[93] Public Eye (2017).
[94] Bagley (2018), p. 2484.
[95] Mathew Joe (2012).
[96] Durisch and Gajardo (2018), p. 35.
[97] New (2018).
[98] Abbas and Riaz (2013), pp. 3–10.
[99] Taubman (2008), pp. 942–943.
[100] 't Hoen and von Schoen-Angerer (2009), p. 30.

European Community as they "threaten to remove trade concessions" for developing countries.[101]

The effective use of compulsory licensing remains politically sensitive as political responses in high-income countries have been a substantial obstacle to the use of this safeguard. Despite the key significance of compulsory licensing in enabling the production and supply of cheaper generic medicines, the use of this flexibility by developing countries has been a bold and highly challenging step in the international arena because of the gross asymmetries in political and economic power. The use or threat of trade retaliations should be condemned at all appropriate forums as such pressure tactics are in violation of the human right to health and the agreed principles embodied in the TRIPS Agreement.

This analysis argues that sustained and strategic pressure applied by civil society, within the normative framework of human rights and sustainable development, can neutralize the massive pressure exerted by Big Pharma and high-income countries.[102] There must be visible and impactful public protests in response to every intolerable lack of access to essential health technologies. This argument is supported by evidence from history. For instance, when the Pharmaceutical Manufacturers Association of South Africa (PMA), a group of 39 pharmaceutical companies, challenged South Africa's legislative changes to enact patent flexibilities, it faced unprecedented public outcry and widespread condemnation by civil society organizations.[103] International NGOs like Oxfam and MSF joined hands with the South African civil society organization Treatment Action Campaign (TAC) to turn the case into a high public profile case at a global level.[104] MSF launched a petition against PMA and garnered around 250,000 signatures for the petition.[105] Adverse public opinion and intense media attention exerted formidable pressure on the group of multinational corporations.[106] Despite massive financial resources and legal firepower of 39 multinational companies, PMA had to withdraw the suit before judgment was reached.

3 Compulsory Licensing is Procedurally Cumbersome

The TRIPS Agreement allows the WTO Member States to grant compulsory licenses, on a case-by-case basis, after meeting certain procedural requirements. National laws determine the procedures for the processing of compulsory licensing

---

[101] Dutfield (2004), p. 52.
[102] Abbas (2021).
[103] Sundaram (2018), p. 176.
[104] Matthews (2011), p. 99.
[105] Matthews (2011), p. 99.
[106] Abbas and Riaz (2018), pp. 34–35.

applications. These procedures are required to be "fair and equitable".[107] Art. 31 of the TRIPS Agreement provides guidance on the process and procedures for the grant and review of a compulsory license and limits on its terms. It stipulates the following seven terms and conditions:

(1) Each authorization of a compulsory license "shall be considered on its individual merits".[108] The issuing authority is required to consider the peculiar facts of each case before making a decision. WTO Member States are not allowed to enact laws to automatically issue compulsory licenses as a matter of course.[109] The Compulsory licensing mechanism cannot be used in a blanket manner to address a specific disease or health issue like COVID-19. Individual compulsory licenses need to be granted for each patent covering each individual medicine or vaccine. This requirement not only adds to administrative burdens and transaction costs but also causes substantial delays in dealing with a health emergency.
(2) The party seeking a compulsory license must first make reasonable efforts to obtain a voluntary license from the right-holder on "reasonable commercial terms and conditions" within a "reasonable period of time".[110] It is within the purview of national laws and practices to determine what constitutes "reasonable commercial terms" and "reasonable period of time" as the TRIPS Agreement does not provide any details or standard in this regard. To address this ambiguity, WTO Member States should clearly stipulate the period during which the parties must negotiate in good faith. The period within which the patent-holder is bound to respond to a request for a voluntary license should be pre-determined. This condition of prior negotiation is, however, waived if a compulsory license is granted to remedy anti-competitive practices or in "circumstances of extreme urgency" or if there is "a national emergency".[111] This condition is also waived if the patented invention is used for "public non-commercial use" or "government use".[112] The government is required to inform the patent-holder promptly.[113]
(3) The scope and the duration of the license are limited to the purpose for which it was authorized.[114] This condition implies that a compulsory license can only be issued for a limited time and for a specific purpose. The condition of the limited duration of the license appears to be an unnecessary requirement because the issue of access to the needed drug will remain as long as the drug patent is in force. The unnecessary hassle of renewing the compulsory license for limited

---

[107] TRIPS Agreement (1995), Art. 62(4) and 41(2).
[108] TRIPS Agreement (1995), Art. 31(a).
[109] Owoeye (2019), p. 20.
[110] TRIPS Agreement (1995), Art. 31(b).
[111] Correa (2020a), p. 25.
[112] TRIPS Agreement (1995), Art. 31(b).
[113] TRIPS Agreement (1995), Art. 31(b).
[114] TRIPS Agreement (1995), Art. 31(c).

durations is an administrative burden. It is almost impossible, both practically and economically, to precisely determine the scope of the intended compulsory license, especially in the case of epidemics and pandemics when the on-ground situation changes abruptly and unforeseeably. Once a compulsory license granted in a health emergency ceases or terminates, the control on pricing and distribution will transfer back to the patent-holder. The issues of affordable and equitable access will re-emerge soon after.

(4) The grant of a compulsory license shall be non-exclusive,[115] and rights acquired under a compulsory license shall be non-assignable.[116] Non-exclusivity means that the patent-holder and/or other licensees may compete with the person or entity to whom a compulsory license is granted. As compulsory licensing targets "use" of the invention (without resulting in a transfer of legal title), the patent-holder retains ownership rights over the licensed patent.[117] By prohibiting sub-licensing or transfer of compulsory licenses, this condition enables patent holders to maintain a significant level of control over their invention to continue its commercial exploitation.

(5) Authorization of a compulsory license is predominantly for the supply of the domestic market of the state where the license is issued.[118] By restricting the export of pharmaceuticals manufactured under a compulsory licensing regime, this condition posed serious problems for countries having no or limited pharmaceutical manufacturing capacity. In 2003, the Implementation Decision adopted by the WTO General Council waived this condition for least-developed countries and developing countries with no manufacturing capacity of their own. It provides: "The obligations of an exporting Member under Article 31(f) of the TRIPS Agreement shall be waived with respect to the grant by it of a compulsory license to the extent necessary for the purpose of production of a Pharmaceutical Product(s) and its export to an eligible importing Member(s) [...]."[119] On January 23, 2017, the Protocol Amending TRIPS, based on the 2003 Implementation Decision, entered into force after receiving acceptance by two-thirds of WTO Member States.[120]

(6) The patent-holder shall be paid "adequate remuneration" in each case (except for anti-competitive reasons) considering the "economic value of the authorization".[121] Reasonable compensation is required so that compulsory licensing prevents abuse of the patent system without causing significant economic loss to patent-holders. The TRIPS Agreement, however, does not specify any transparent and easy-to-apply method of calculating remuneration or setting royalty

---

[115] TRIPS Agreement (1995), Art. 31(d).

[116] TRIPS Agreement (1995), Art. 31(e).

[117] Gibson (2010), p. 365.

[118] TRIPS Agreement (1995), Art. 31(f).

[119] The Implementation Decision of the WTO General Council (2003), para. 2.

[120] The World Trade Organization (2017).

[121] TRIPS Agreement (1995), Art. 31(h).

rates. The TRIPS Agreement is completely silent on what constitutes adequate remuneration and what should be the time, mode, and currency of payment. The national authorities issuing a compulsory license are expected to find a fair balance between private and public interests. They decide what level of remuneration is adequate on a case-by-case basis after considering the interests of the patent-holder, the government agency or third party to whom the compulsory license is issued, and the general public for whom the compulsory license is intended. The governments authorizing compulsory licenses face the risk of making contentious and fact-specific determinations in deciding adequate remuneration. This lack of clarity may pose a barrier as the decisions of WTO Member States on adequacy of the remuneration can be subjected to administrative or judicial review.[122] The execution of the license may be delayed frustrating the very purpose of granting the compulsory license.

(7) The compulsory license shall be liable to review and termination if and when the circumstances which led to it cease to exist and are unlikely to recur.[123] The issuing authority shall review the continued existence of circumstances upon motivated request. This condition implies that compulsory licenses are not only time-limited in nature but also subject to periodic review. The entire cumbersome procedure will need to be repeated all over again to alleviate access issues if the circumstances for the grant of a compulsory license reappear at a later stage.

A health emergency requires quick responsive action to save lives and relieve preventable suffering by providing access to urgently needed health technologies. The compulsory licensing safeguard in its current form is less efficient to provide a quick solution in an emergency. The ambiguities in compulsory licensing provisions cause tensions and delays. To speed up the process, national laws or regulations should provide more clarity on procedural requirements and specific time-periods within which decisions about the issuance of a compulsory license must be made by a competent authority. Carlos Correa quoted a relevant provision of the TRIPS Agreement to support less cumbersome compulsory licensing procedures. He noted that:

> Article 41.2 of the TRIPS Agreement requires that 'Procedures concerning the enforcement of intellectual property rights shall [...] not be unnecessarily complicated or costly, or entail unreasonable time-limits or unwarranted delays.' Although conceived to protect right holders, the same treatment should be accorded, in a non-discriminatory way, to all parties in procedures involving intellectual property rights.[124]

In order to be better prepared to deal with the current and future pandemics, WTO Member States—irrespective of their economic status—need to negotiate uncomplicated, unambiguous, and generous compulsory licensing mechanisms. Practical

---

[122] TRIPS Agreement (1995), Art. 31(j).
[123] TRIPS Agreement (1995), Art. 31(g) and 31(i).
[124] Correa (2020a), p. 27.

application of this safeguard is deterred if any ambiguities exist in compulsory licensing provisions. In order to reduce transaction costs and to promote predictability, WTO Member States need to develop a workable compulsory licensing scheme with clearer boundaries and simple and speedy processes. There is a serious need to develop adequate legal and administrative infrastructure with reduced bureaucratic formalities of this procedural safeguard in order to make it more practicable for responding to a health emergency.

4 The Uses of Compulsory Licensing Flexibility Since the Doha Declaration

Ellen 't Hoen and others have compiled a database covering instances of the use of the TRIPS flexibilities by 89 countries from 2001 onwards. According to this database, from 2001 to 2020, there were 110 instances that involved compulsory licenses or public non-commercial use[125] licenses. Compulsory licensing safeguard has been predominantly used to enable the production and supply of HIV/AIDS generic medicines.

Table 1 below provides the details of 110 instances that involved compulsory licenses or public non-commercial use licenses. Statistically, this flexibility seems to be used more frequently than is commonly assumed, but the number of high-profile compulsory licenses is relatively low. An instance, however, does not necessarily mean the actual use of a compulsory license or a public non-commercial use license. It refers to one of the following events: (a) a government's announcement of the intent to invoke this flexibility; (b) a third party's request or application to invoke

Table 1 Use of compulsory or public non-commercial licenses worldwide for access to medicines (2001–2020)[a]

Country classification	Disease		
	HIV	Cancer	Other
Developed Countries	2	3	11
Developing Countries	52	11	12
Least-Developed Countries	12	0	0
WTO Observer Countries	7	0	0
Total	73	14	23

[a]The data for Table 1 was derived from http://tripsflexibilities.medicineslawandpolicy.org (last access 31 December 2020)

---

[125] Public non-commercial use or government use is "an act by the government authorizing a government department to exploit by itself or through a contractor, public or private, a patented invention without the consent of the title-holder." This policy option provides a simpler and faster way of acquiring patented pharmaceutical drugs as it can be invoked by the government *ex officio* without prior negotiation and without a third party's request. See Correa (2020a), pp. 13 and 15.

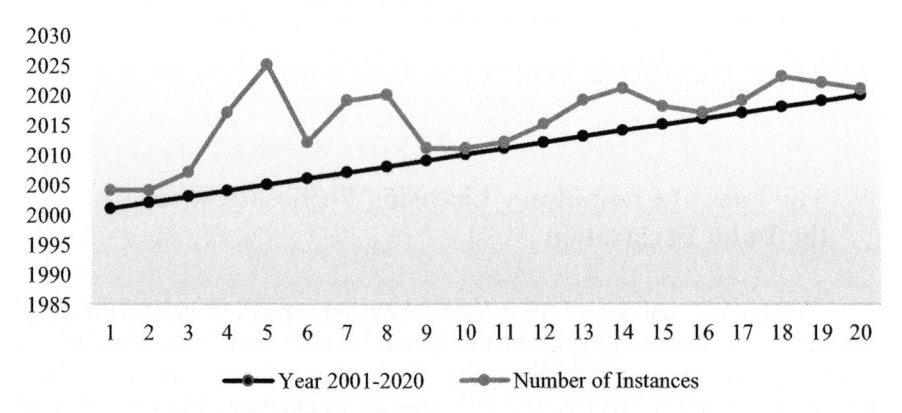

Fig. 1 Year-wise use of compulsory or public non-commercial licenses worldwide for access to medicines (2001–2020) (The data for Fig. 1 was derived from http://tripsflexibilities. medicineslawandpolicy.org (last access 31 December 2020))

this flexibility; (c) the actual use of this flexibility; and (d) a government's declaration that its territory has no relevant patents.[126]

It is clear from Fig. 1 that the use of compulsory licenses or public non-commercial use licenses has decreased significantly since 2008. It is unfortunate if WTO Member States forego one of the most important public health flexibilities because of economic and political pressures to accept the *maximalist view* of patent rights. It is critical for WTO Member States, especially low- and middle-income countries, to retain compulsory licensing as an active policy option in order to balance private and public interest in granting patents for health technologies.

As noted above, a compulsory licensing was not actually issued in all of the 110 instances. The actual use of a compulsory license or a public non-commercial use license is not required in every instance. An indication of potentially issuing a compulsory license or a mere public announcement can have a significant impact. Many times, in response to the threat of a compulsory license, the patent holder offers a price reduction or donation, or the patent holder agrees to a voluntary license.[127] The goal of negotiating price reduction can often be achieved by merely deploying the threat of using compulsory licensing.

---

[126] 't Hoen et al. (2018), p. 186.

[127] The data for Fig. 1 was derived from http://tripsflexibilities.medicineslawandpolicy.org (last access 31 December 2020).

Brazil, for instance, repeatedly negotiated pharmaceutical drug price reductions by using the threat of compulsory licensing to enhance its negotiating capacity.[128] In 2001, Brazil negotiated a significant price reduction for Roche's antiretroviral drug Viracept (Nelfinavir).[129] In 2005, Brazil negotiated with Abbott a steep price reduction for Kaletra, a top-selling drug for which Brazil was spending around 30% of its total budget for antiretrovirals.[130] According to the Economy and Brazilian National Institute of Industrial Property Directorate for Patents (2019) Brazilian government has decreed the public interest in the drug Kaletra through Ordinance No. 985. Through this Ordinance, the Brazilian government clearly signalled its intention to deploy the legal mechanism of compulsory licensing if the price negotiations with Abbott fail.[131] The actual grant of compulsory license was needless as Abbott decided to comply with the demand to reduce Kaletra's price.

In 2008, the Brazilian government again decreed the public interest in other drugs, like Tenofovir and Viread, through Ordinance No. 681.[132] Gilead decided to offer Tenofovir at a lower price resulting in significant cost-cutting to the Brazilian government.[133] By using the fairly credible threat of compulsory licensing, the Brazilian federal government also negotiated substantial price reductions for HIV/AIDS antiretroviral drugs like Indinavir (64.8%), Lopinavir (46%), and Nelfinavir (40%).[134] Brazil was, therefore, able to seek out affordable supplies of needed therapies by strategically using the credible threat of compulsory licensing.

In 2017, Malaysia announced its intention to issue a government use license to produce or import generic versions of Gilead's hepatitis C drug Sovaldi (Sofosbuvir).[135] A full course of three months treatment would cost MYR 300,000 (Approximately USD 74,300 at the current exchange rate) before this move to broaden access.[136] This price was too high to provide universal access to Sovaldi for Malaysia's around half a million people living with hepatitis C.[137] Arguably as a measure to avoid the government intervention, Gilead offered to include Malaysia in its voluntary license scheme soon after this announcement for a government use license.[138]

It is clear from these examples that the mere intention to grant a compulsory license has a significant positive impact on broadening access to patented health

---

[128] de Moura and Moura (2016), p. 35.
[129] Durisch and Gajardo (2018), p. 34.
[130] de Moura and Moura (2016), p. 35.
[131] de Moura and Moura (2016), p. 35.
[132] de Moura and Moura (2016), p. 5.
[133] de Moura and Moura (2016), p. 5.
[134] Yu (2008), p. 358; See more Matthews (2011), p. 132.
[135] Durisch and Gajardo (2018), p. 35.
[136] Durisch and Gajardo (2018), p. 35.
[137] Treatment Action Group (2017).
[138] Durisch and Gajardo (2018), p. 35.

technologies. These examples also confirm that brand-name pharmaceutical corporations have significant negotiation room because of their high-profit margins. Several commentators considered the importance of compulsory licensing as a powerful negotiation tool. Charles Lawson noted that compulsory licensing presents a "clear and present threat to patent holders to encourage them to voluntarily work their patents or license them [...] on reasonable terms and conditions".[139] Beall, Kuhn and Attaran acknowledged the empowering role of compulsory licensing in negotiating prices with the right-holder pharmaceutical corporations.[140] It is, therefore, important for low- and middle-income countries to incorporate compulsory licensing flexibility into their national laws to strengthen their bargaining power in negotiating drug prices with brand-name pharmaceutical corporations.

5 Recent Developments in Response to COVID-19

In response to the current pandemic, WTO Member States need to improve their legal capacity to use compulsory licensing as a policy option to override the existing or future patents on COVID-19 related health technologies. Domestic laws of Member States must have procedures in place to authorize compulsory licenses. Corporations are generally expected to understand that aggressive resistance to compulsory licensing is not the best business strategy amid a pandemic because of its public relations implications. Whilst some corporations may be expected to voluntarily license their patent rights to avoid reputational damage, many of them may not. Some brand-name pharmaceutical corporations may "fail to acknowledge their unique role in society as the providers of life-saving medicines".[141] Despite the existence of a global health emergency, it is entirely at the patent-holders' discretion to provide voluntary licenses, which results in a substantial reduction in profit because of loss of exclusivity.

Foreseeing the challenges posed by exclusive patent rights in response to the COVID-19 crisis, the South Centre called upon governments to "streamline and plan to make use of the legislative measures to permit the compulsory licensing or government use of products that are protected by patents".[142] Compulsory licensing acts as a safeguard against patent-holders' decision-making. The COVID-19 pandemic provides a valid justification for the use of this safeguard in case of non-cooperation of patent-holders. COVID-19 clearly falls in the ambit of compulsory licensing flexibility as the World Health Organization (WHO) has already declared it not only a pandemic but also a Public Health Emergency of International

---

[139] Lawson (2012), p. 1.
[140] Reed, Kuhn and Attaran (2015), pp. 493–501.
[141] Tanimoto et al. (2017), p. 455.
[142] See Correa and Seuba (2017), p. 1.

Concern.¹⁴³ This declaration by the WHO not only eases pressure on the Member States if they consider legitimate use of the compulsory licensing safeguard but also waives the condition of prior negotiation with the patent holder for a voluntary license.

Several countries are passing resolutions and reconsidering their national patent laws to prepare themselves for the foreseen uses of compulsory licensing in response to COVID-19 by improving their legislative mechanisms.¹⁴⁴ For instance, on March 17, 2020, Chile's legislature laid the legal groundwork to potentially use compulsory licensing safeguard.¹⁴⁵ The Chilean Chamber of Deputies—the lower house of Chile's bicameral Congress—passed Resolution No. 896.¹⁴⁶ The resolution declared that the current health crisis justifies the use of compulsory licenses, under Chile's Industrial Property Law, for the prevention and treatment of COVID-19.¹⁴⁷ The resolution asked the Chilean Minister of Health to declare the existence of public health reasons for compulsory licensing of patents on COVID-19 related technologies.¹⁴⁸

Similarly, on March 20, 2020, the Education, Culture, Science and Technology Commission of Ecuador's National Assembly passed a resolution in response to COVID-19.¹⁴⁹ The resolution asked Ecuador's President and Minister of Public Health to grant compulsory licenses on urgently needed COVID-related health technologies.¹⁵⁰ The Commission also requested the Minister of Health to authorize third parties to access clinical test data for the timely and affordable availability of COVID-19 vaccines and treatments in Ecuador.¹⁵¹

On March 23, 2020, France enacted Emergency Law No. 2020–290 in response to COVID-19.¹⁵² It introduced a new and wide provision, Art. L3131–15, into the French Public Health Code.¹⁵³ This new article empowers the French Prime Minister to take all measures for the availability of appropriate medicines to curb the pandemic "provided that such measures are strictly proportionate to the health risks at stake and appropriate to the circumstances of the time and place and are

---

[143] To date, the WHO has declared a Public Health Emergence of International Concern only in six occasions: H1N1 (2009), Polio (2014), Ebola in West Africa (2014), Zika (2016), Ebola in the Democratic Republic of Congo (2019), and most recently, COVID-19 in China (2020); See Lee (2020), p. 44.

[144] Kumar (2021), p. 1.

[145] World Trade Organization (2020), para. 5.8.

[146] Syam (2020), p. 2.

[147] Wong (2020), pp. 1–4; See more Khazin and Wu (2020) p. 16.

[148] Dani (2020), p. 872; See more Khazin and Wu (2020) p. 18.

[149] World Trade Organization (2020), para. 5.8.

[150] Dhar (2020), p. 10.

[151] Dani (2020), p. 872.

[152] Khazin and Wu (2020), p. 18.

[153] Dani (2020), p. 871.

terminated without delay when they are no longer necessary".[154] Compulsory licensing could fall within the scope of measures the French Prime Minister is allowed to take under Art. L3131–15.[155] The French Minister of Health noted in a parliamentary discussion, "I do not exclude the possibility of applying for compulsory licenses or price ceilings for drugs that would not be produced in France."[156]

On March 24, 2020, Canada, which already provided a compulsory licensing mechanism under its national patent laws, amended its Patent Act (Bill C–13) to make it faster for the government to utilize the compulsory licensing option in response to the current pandemic.[157] The amended law empowers the Commissioner of Patents to "authorize the Government of Canada and any person specified in the application to make, construct, use and sell a patented invention to the extent necessary to respond to a public health emergency that is a matter of national concern".[158] On a simple application to the patent office, the government or anyone it authorizes can obtain a compulsory license for 1 year.[159] The amended law allows the government to defer negotiations for remuneration or compensation. The new provision s.19.4 clarifies that the grant of a compulsory license—even when the patent-holder is capable of making, using, and selling the patented invention—is "not an infringement of the patent".[160]

On March 27, 2020, Germany enacted the "Prevention and Control of Infectious Diseases in Humans Act".[161] Section 5 of this legislation, effective from March 28, 2020, empowers the Federal Ministry of Health to take measures to ensure the supply of medicinal products if the German Federal Diet—the legislative body in Germany also known as Bundestag—finds that there is an "epidemic situation of national significance".[162] The additional powers granted to the Federal Ministry of Health, under this legislation, include the competence to order limitations on patents.[163] The Federal Ministry of Health is empowered to compulsorily authorize the use of an invention in the interest of public welfare.[164]

On March 29, 2020, the National Assembly of Hungary enacted Act XII of 2020 on the Containment of Coronavirus.[165] This Act, effective from March 31, 2020, authorizes the adoption of extraordinary measures to prevent COVID-19.[166] Under

---

[154] Khazin and Wu (2020), p. 18.
[155] Syam (2020), p. 3.
[156] Kluwer Patent Blog (2020).
[157] Ed Silverman (2020).
[158] House of Commons of Canada (2020).
[159] Flood et al. (2020), p. 582.
[160] Canadian Patent Act, s.19.4(7).
[161] Syam (2020), p. 3.
[162] Khazin and Wu (2020), p. 17.
[163] Dani (2020), p. 871.
[164] Dhar (2020), p. 9; See more Stothers and Morgan (2020), p. 590.
[165] Khazin and Wu (2020), p. 17.
[166] Fremer (2020).

this Act, on May 16, 2020, the Hungarian government adopted the Decree 212/2020 on Public Health Related Compulsory Licensing, which amended Art. 33/A of the Hungarian Patent Act.[167] Art. 33/B, a new article introduced by this Decree, empowers the Hungarian Intellectual Property Office to grant compulsory licenses for COVID-19 related health technologies.[168]

These resolutions and the enabling of legislative measures, not only in low- and middle-income countries but also in high-income countries, send a clear signal to brand-name pharmaceutical corporations that governments will not put up with delays in accessing COVID-19 related health technologies. It is critical for all governments, regardless of their economic status, to make sure that patents do not impede a rapid response to a health emergency. In order to prepare themselves to issue compulsory licenses if necessary, during this or a future pandemic, more WTO Member States need to review the compulsory licensing-related provisions in their national patent laws to ascertain whether their existing legal framework allows them the freedom to grant compulsory licenses in a time-efficient manner. If needed, they need to adopt appropriate enabling provisions on a priority basis or issue additional regulations to remove any potential roadblocks. It is important to avoid overly restrictive terms and conditions[169] to make the compulsory licensing mechanism economically feasible for generic manufacturing companies.

As the COVID-19 vaccine has been developed and approved, the issue of universal access to the vaccine is no more a hypothetical issue. Compulsory licensing is going to be relevant, as low- and middle-income countries are struggling to acquire doses of the COVID-19 vaccine. Pfizer allegedly bullied governments of Latin American countries during private and confidential negotiations to acquire the COVID-19 vaccine developed by the pharmaceutical giant.[170] Pfizer is pressuring certain governments to offer indemnity—exemption from legal liability—if vaccinated citizens suffer any adverse events.[171] It means the vaccine purchasing governments would be required to pay the compensation if a citizen files a claim against the vaccine manufacturer. Pfizer's demand for indemnity from civil cases is not justifiable. As noted by an Argentinian official:

> Argentina could compensate for the vaccine's adverse effects, but not if Pfizer makes a mistake [...]. For example, what would happen if Pfizer unintentionally interrupted the vaccine's cold chain [of -70 Celsius during transport and storage] and a citizen wants to sue them? It would not be fair for Argentina to pay for a Pfizer error.[172]

---

[167] Khazin and Wu (2020), p. 17.

[168] World Intellectual Property Organization (2020).

[169] For instance, Canada, under its COVID-19 Emergency Response Act, allows compulsory licenses to last for one year only. This time-limit makes the mechanism unattractive to manufacturers of generic drugs. See Flood et al. (2020), p. 582.

[170] Davies et al. (2021).

[171] Davies et al. (2021).

[172] Davies et al. (2021).

The use of compulsory licensing can be anticipated as governments are being denied access to available life-saving vaccines through abusive use of exclusive rights. However, in the case of COVID-19 vaccines, mere compulsory licensing of patents may not suffice. Unlike pharmaceutical drugs, which are fairly easy to copy, vaccines are complicated biological materials.[173] Generic manufacturers will not be able to do much unless brand-name companies openly share technology, know-how, and data. Corporations normally keep technology know-how and data information secret. In order to enhance the global production capacity, the technology and know-how should be shared with potential producers of vaccines. The use of compulsory licensing should be coupled with a binding arrangement for technology sharing and transfer by vaccine manufacturing corporations.

WTO Member States should not hesitate from actually using compulsory licensing safeguard to save lives in a health emergency. A compulsory license issued in one jurisdiction can have global knock-on effects as it can give rise to momentum for voluntary licensing of patent rights. For instance, in March 2020, Israel's Ministry of Health actually issued a compulsory license, under Sections 104 and 105 of Article 3 of the Israeli Patent Law 5727-1967, to secure access to AbbVie's Kaletra (Lopinavir/ Ritonavir).[174] The compulsory license was issued to boost supplies of Kaletra[175] by turning to generic alternatives from an Indian generic company.[176] Soon after Israel issued the compulsory license, the patent-holder expressed its voluntary commitment not to enforce its Kaletra patents globally for COVID-19.[177] By this move, AbbVie avoided a potential public relations disaster. Had AbbVie chosen to respond negatively to compulsory licensing, it would have faced greater opposition, political challenges, and public outcry. The legitimacy of the TRIPS system could be undermined if the patent-holder showed backlash against the compulsory licensing decision in the middle of a pandemic.[178] In a health emergency, the threat of compulsory licensing, backed by public pressure or civil society mobilization, can be used as an effective negotiation tool to achieve a substantial price-reduction or favourable terms in voluntary licensing.

Before proceeding to the conclusion, it is important to precisely debunk some myths related to compulsory licensing (Table 2).

---

[173] Vaccines Europe, "How are vaccines produced?", Vaccines Europe, https://www.vaccineseurope.eu/about-vaccines/how-are-vaccines-produced (last access 22 September 2021).

[174] Thiru (2020); See more Tellez (2020), p. 2.

[175] Kaletra is, otherwise, protected under patents until 2024 in Israel and until 2026 in some other countries like Georgia, Philippines, Serbia, South Africa. See https://www.medspal.org/?keywords=Kaletra&page=1 (last access 22 September 2021).

[176] Syam (2020), p. 3.

[177] McMahon (2020), p. 339.

[178] The brand-name pharmaceutical industry has a shared interest in preserving the legitimacy of the broader patent system. See Hein and Moon (2013), p. 169.

Table 2 Compulsory licensing myth-busting[a]

Myth	Reality
Compulsory licenses are only to be used in case of a national emergency or other extreme urgency circumstances.	An emergency situation may only have the potential to shorten the procedure.
Compulsory licensing is limited to a certain number of diseases, such as HIV/AIDS or communicable diseases with epidemic potential.	Compulsory licensing is not limited to one disease or to a category of diseases.
Compulsory licensing is limited to poor countries.	Each WTO Member State, regardless of its economic status, has the right to issue a compulsory license.
Compulsory licensing is a last resort tool.	Expropriation is the last resort tool.
Compulsory licensing equals expropriation.	The patent-holder remains the owner, and keeps the right to exploit the invention and receive adequate remuneration.
Compulsory licensing is an arbitrary tool.	The compulsory licensing mechanism is provided for by most national patent laws and by international law under the TRIPS.
Compulsory licensing deters incentives to innovate or to invest in R&D.	There is no evidence that compulsory licensing reduces investments in R&D.

[a]The information for Table 2 was derived from Durisch and Gajardo (2018), p. 32

6 Conclusion

The global community is faced with the challenge of universal and affordable access to treatments and vaccines to combat COVID-19. Compulsory licensing is one of the most important TRIPS flexibilities to not only address this challenge but also realize the right to health and global health equity objectives. The actual use of this powerful tool has, however, remained a controversial issue in international trade relations. This study proposes that the use of compulsory licensing as a safeguard should be backed by community support or civil society mobilization. Well-directed societal pressure can neutralize the massive pressure exerted by Big Pharma and high-income countries. If properly backed by community support, the use of compulsory licensing can be considered by low- and middle-income countries for the routine procurement of generic versions of novel but unaffordable essential medicines, subject to the provision of adequate remuneration to patent holders. This approach is important for resource-constrained countries in sustaining their public healthcare programs. If civil society organizations stand with the government and respond to political and economic pressures in a well-organized manner by framing the issue of access to medicines as a human rights issue, even the strongest countries and corporations will have to withdraw pressure.

The compulsory licensing safeguard in its current form is less efficient to provide a quick solution in a health emergency. In order to be better prepared to deal with the current and future pandemics, WTO Member States need to negotiate uncomplicated, unambiguous, and generous compulsory licensing mechanisms. Practical application of this safeguard is deterred if any ambiguities exist in compulsory licensing provisions. In order to reduce transaction costs and to promote predictability, WTO Member States need to develop a workable compulsory licensing scheme with clearer boundaries and simple and speedy processes—clearly stipulating the period during which the parties must negotiate in good faith. There is a serious need to simplify the procedures by reducing bureaucratic formalities of this safeguard in order to facilitate its implementation and make it more practicable for responding to urgent health problems in an emergency situation.

The condition to grant compulsory licenses on a case-by-case basis makes this safeguard inefficient to deal with an emergency. A single technology can be covered under several patents. Separate requests for compulsory licensing of each patent are considered on their individual merits. As patents are territorial in nature, compulsory licenses are issued at the national level. It will not be sufficient to remove patent barriers on one product in one jurisdiction. One can imagine the burdens of effective utilization of this safeguard in an emergency if a technology is protected under multiple patents in multiple jurisdictions and the legal avenues to obtain a compulsory license differ substantially in each country. The perplexing question of how adequate royalty should be set in each case in each jurisdiction is yet another obstacle as there is a complete lack of clarity on adequate remuneration. A case-by-case and country-by-country approach of compulsory licensing bars this safeguard from providing a global solution.

Compulsory licensing safeguard has serious limitations if the technology is protected by trade-secret protection. For effective utilization of this safeguard, WTO Member States need to negotiate an additional framework to mandate right-holders to disclose know-how and trade secret information once a compulsory license is issued. In order to have a more effective compulsory licensing system at the national level, to deal with a future pandemic, WTO Member States need to use the impetus of COVID-19 to address the key shortcomings of the global framework for compulsory licensing provided under the TRIPS. Compulsory licensing alone cannot provide an effective solution to ensure timely and universal access to health technologies even if its functioning is substantially improved. WTO Member States need to consider a range of complementary strategies to address the complex issue of global access to health technologies.

Acknowledgments The author would like to acknowledge his Ph.D. supervisors Professor Matthew Rimmer and Professor Richard Johnstone. The author would also like to acknowledge his wife, Dr. Shamreeza Riaz, for her unconditional support and valued cooperation. The views presented in this article and any mistakes are, however, the sole responsibility of the author.

References

Abbas MZ (2013) Pros and cons of compulsory licensing: an analysis of arguments. Int J Soc Sci Human 3(3):254–258. https://doi.org/10.7763/ijssh.2013.v3.239 (last access 21 September 2021)

Abbas MZ (2017) The issue of undeserving patent monopolies in innovation-based businesses and implications thereof for underprivileged consumers. Bus Manag Rev 9(1):3–4

Abbas MZ (2020a) Strategic use of patent opposition safeguard to improve equitable access to innovative health technologies: a case study of CAR T-cell therapy Kymriah. Global Public Health 0. https://doi.org/10.1080/17441692.2020.1825769 (last access 21 September 2021)

Abbas MZ (2020b) COVID-19 and the global public health: tiered pricing of pharmaceutical drugs as a price-reducing policy tool. J Generic Med Bus J Generic Med Sect 174113432096314. https://doi.org/10.1177/1741134320963146 (last access 21 September 2021)

Abbas MZ (2020c) Conflicting interests, competing perspectives and policy incoherence: COVID-19 highlights the significance of the United Nations high-level panel report on access to medicines. Aust Intell Prop J 31

Abbas MZ (2021) Parallel importation as a policy option to reduce price of patented health technologies. J Generic Med 4 https://doi.org/10.1177/1741134321999418 (last access 21 September 2021)

Abbas MZ, Riaz S (2013a) Evolution of the concept of compulsory licensing: a critical analysis of key developments before and after trips. Acad Res Int 4(2), https://eprints.qut.edu.au/90061 (last access 20 May 2021)

Abbas MZ and Riaz S (2013b) Flexibilities under trips: implementation gaps between theory and practice. Nordic J Commer Law 1:2

Abbas MZ, Riaz S (2014) Rationale of compulsory licensing of pharmaceutical patents in the light of human rights perspective. Pakistan Persp 19(1)

Abbas MZ, Riaz S (2018) WTO "Paragraph 6" system for affordable access to medicines: relief or regulatory ritualism? J World Intell Prop 21(1–2):34–35

Asok A (2019) Compulsory licensing for public health and usa's special 301 pressure: an indian experience. J Intellect Prop Rights 24(5–6):125–131

Bagley MA (2018) The morality of compulsory licensing as an access to medicines tool. Minn Law Rev 102(6)

Baker B (2007) Pharma's seven deadly lies about thai compulsory licenses (February 1, 2007) IP Disputes in Medicines, http://www.cptech.org/blogs/ipdisputesinmedicine/2007/02/pharmas-seven-deadly-lies-about-thai.html (last access 21 September 2021)

Brougher JT (2014) Intellectual property and health technologies: balancing innovation and the public's health. Intellect Prop Heal Technol Balanc Innov Public's Heal 9781461482:1–214. https://doi.org/10.1007/978-1-4614-8202-4 (last access 21 September 2021)

Cass RA (2007) Patent Remedy, Opinion https://www.wsj.com/articles/SB118824874547610202 (last access 21 September 2021)

Correa CM (2013) The use of compulsory licenses In Latin America. South Bull. https://www.southcentre.int/question/the-use-of-compulsory-licenses-in-latin-america/ (last access 21 September 2021)

Correa CM (2020a) Guide for the granting of compulsory licenses and government use of pharmaceutical patents. South Cent 27(32):2282–2283. https://doi.org/10.1021/cen-v027n032.p2282 (last access 21 September 2021)

Correa CM, Seuba X (2017) Intellectual property and trade measures to address the Covid-19 crisis. 74(February)

Dani M (2020) Public health comes first. J Intell Prop Law Pract 15(11)

Davies M, Ruiz I, Langlois J and Furneaux R (2021) Held to ransom: Pfizer plays hardball in Covid-19 vaccine negotiations with Latin American countries. StatNews, https://www.statnews.com/2021/02/23/pfizer-plays-hardball-in-covid19-vaccine-negotiations-in-latin-america/ (last access 21 September 2021)

Carvalho NP de (2005) The TRIPS regime of patent rights. Kluwer Law International

de Moura EP, Moura DP (2016) The challenges of providing affordable healthcare in emerging markets-the case of Brazil. J Manag Policy Pract 17(2):33–45

Dhar B (2020) Towards more affordable medicine: a proposal to waive certain obligations from the agreement on TRIPS 200 Asia-Pacific research and training network on trade

Draft Agreement on Trade Related Aspects of Intellectual Property (1990) Communication from the U.S., GATT Doc. No. MTN.GNG/NG11/W/70

Durisch P, Gajardo A (2018) Protect patients, not patents, (May). Public Eye 1(3)

Dutfield G (2004) Does one size fit all? Harv Int Rev 26(2):52

Feldman J (2009) Compulsory licenses: the dangers behind the current practice. J Int Bus Law 8(1): 137. <http://scholarlycommons.law.hofstra.edu/jibl/vol8/iss1/9>. 8 (last access 21 September 2021)

Flint A, Payne J (2013) Intellectual property rights and the potential for universal access to treatment: TRIPS, ACTA and HIV/AIDS medicines. Third World Q 34(3):500–515. https://doi.org/10.1080/01436597.2013.785344 (last access 21 September 2021)

Flood CM et al (2020) Vulnerable: the law, policy and ethics of COVID-19. http://hdl.handle.net/10393/40726%0A, https://press.uottawa.ca/vulnerable.html.html> (last access 21 September 2021)

Fremer I (2020) Hungary: national assembly adopts act giving government special powers during coronavirus pandemic. Global Legal Monitor, https://www.loc.gov/law/foreign-news/article/hungary-national-assembly-adopts-act-giving-government-special-powers-during-coronavirus-pandemic/ (last access 21 September 2021)

Gibson CS (2010) A look at the compulsory license in investment arbitration: the case of indirect expropriation. Transnatl Disput Manag 25(3):357–422 <http://digitalcommons.wcl.american.edu/auilr> (last access 21 September 2021)

Hein W, Moon S (2013) The impact of non-state actors on informal norms : nodal governance and global democracy in informal norms in global governance: human rights. Intellectual Property Rules and Access to Medicines

Ho CM (2011) Access to medicine in the global economy. Oxford University Press

House of Commons of Canada (2020) Bill C-13 An Act respecting certain measures in response to COVID-19 (2020) https://www.parl.ca/DocumentViewer/en/43-1/bill/C-13/third-reading (Part 12) (last access 21 September 2021)

Khazin BP, Wu X (2020) Patent-related actions taken in WTO members in response to the COVID-19 pandemic. World Trade Organ (WTO), Geneva

Kirk AR et al (2010) Office of the United States Trade Representative. 2010 Special 301 Report. p 54

Kirk AR et al (2012) Office of the United States Trade Representative, 2012 Special 301 Report, Intellectual Property Rights: Protection and Enforcement, pp 55–118

Kluwer Patent Blog (2020) Compulsory licenses granted by public authorities: an application in the Covid-19 crisis in France?, Kluwer Patent Blog, http://patentblog.kluweriplaw.com/2020/04/24/compulsory-licenses-granted-by-public-authorities-an-application-in-the-covid-19-crisis-in-france-part-2/?print=print (last access 21 September 2021)

Kumar S (2021) Compulsory licensing of patents during pandemics. University of Houston Law Center <https://papers.ssrn.com/sol3/papers.cfm?abstract_id=3636456> (last access 21 September 2021), p. 1

Lawson C (2012) Productivity Commission Locked Bag 2 Collins Street East Melbourne Victoria 8003 Dear Commissioner ' s, Re : Submission to the "Compulsory Licensing of Patents" Inquiry My concern is that if the Patents Act 1990 (Cth) is to have a compulsory licensin. (December): pp 1–7

Lee TS (2020) Global health in a turbulence time: a commentary. Asian J WTO Int Health Law Policy 15(1):44

Löfgren H (2017) The pharmaceutical industry and access to medicines in India. Polit Pharm Ind Access Med World Pharm India, pp 1–23. https://doi.org/10.4324/9781315136103 (last access 21 September 2021)

Mathew Joe C (2012) US to Keep an Eye on India's Compulsory Drug Licensing Move. https://www.business-standard.com/article/economy-policy/us-to-keep-an-eye-on-india-s-compulsory-drug-licensing-move-112050602001_1.html (last access 21 September 2021)

Matthews D (2011) Intellectual property, human rights and development: the role of NGOs and social movements. Edward Elgar Publishing, p 99

McMahon A (2020) The role of compulsory and government-use licensing in Ireland. Northern Ireland Legal Q 17(3):339

Mercurio B, Tyagi M (2010) Treaty interpretation in WTO dispute settlement: the outstanding question of the legality of local working requirements. Minnesota J Int Law 19(2):325–326

Natco Pharma Ltd. v. Bayer corporation, CLA, no 1, 2011 (9 March 2012)

New W (2018) Leaked letter shows pressure on Colombia not to issue compulsory licence for Glivec. Intellectual Property Watch. https://www.ip-watch.org/2018/02/06/leaked-letter-shows-pressure-colombia-not-issue-compulsory-licence-glivec/ (last access 21 September 2021)

New W (2019) Malaysia still under pressure to make Hepatitis C medicine more expensive. Intellectual Property Watch, https://www.ip-watch.org/2019/02/13/malaysia-still-pressure-make-hepatitis-c-medicine-expensive/ (last access 21 September 2021)

Office of the United Nations High Commissioner for Human Rights (2000) Intellectual Property Rights and Human Rights, Sub-Commission on Human Rights Resolution 2000/7

Office of the United States Trade Representative (2007), 2007 Special 301 Report

Office of the United States Trade Representative (2011), 2011 Special 301 Report

Office of the United States Trade Representative (2013), 2013 Special 301 Report

OHCHR (2016) Access to Medicines in the Context of the Right of Everyone to the Enjoyment of the Highest Attainable Standard of Physical and Mental Health, Doc. A/HRC/32/L.23/Rev.1, June 2016

Owoeye O (2019) The TRIPS compulsory licensing regime and access to medicines. Intell Prop Access Med Africa, pp 12–50

Precision Instrument Mfg. Co. v. Automotive Maintenance Machinery Co., 234 U.S. 806, pp. 815–816 (1945)

Press Trust of India (2016) India has right to grant compulsory licenses under WTO: Govt, Press Trust of India, https://www.business-standard.com/article/pti-stories/india-has-right-to-grant-compulsory-licences-under-wto-govt-116032201281_1.html (last access 21 September 2021)

Public Eye (2008) Switzerland Attacks Access to Medicines in Thailand, Public Eye, https://www.publiceye.ch/en/media-corner/press-releases/detail/switzerland-attacks-access-to-medicines-in-thailand/ (last access 21 September 2021)

Public Eye (2017) Compulsory licensing in Colombia: Leaked documents show aggressive lobbying by Novartis, Public Eye, https://bilaterals.org/?compulsory-licensing-in-colombia (last access 21 September 2021)

Ragavan S (2012) The international trade regime in perspective. In: Patent and trade disparities in developing countries. Oxford University Press, pp 63–102

Ranjan P (2020) Issuance of compulsory patent licences and expropriation in Asian BITs and FTA investment chapters: a study of India, China, Malaysia and Thailand. In: Liu K-C, Chaisse J (eds) The future of Asian Trade deals and IP. Hart Publishing, Oxford, pp 1–9

Saez C (2010) Ecuador Grants First Compulsory Licence, For HIV/AIDS Drug. Intellectual Property Watch, https://www.ip-watch.org/2010/04/22/ecuador-grants-first-compulsory-licence-for-hivaids-drug/ (last access 21 September 2021)

Silverman E (2020) A Canadian bill would make it easier to issue compulsory licenses for Covid-19 products (2020) Pharmalot, https://www.statnews.com/pharmalot/2020/03/25/canada-compulsory-license-coronavirus-covid19/ (last access 21 September 2021)

Stothers C, Morgan A (2020) IP and the supply of COVID-19-related drugs. J Intell Prop Law Pract 15(8)

Sundaram J (2014) India's trade-related aspects of Intellectual Property Rights compliant pharmaceutical patent laws: what lessons for India and other developing countries?

Sundaram J (2018) Pharmaceutical patent protection and World Trade Law: the unresolved problem of access to medicines, p. 176 <https://doi.org/10.1080/13600834.2014.891310> (last access 20 May 2021)

Syam N (2020) Intellectual property, innovation and access to health products for COVID-19: a review of measures taken. South Centre-Policy Brief 80:2

't Hoen E, von Schoen-Angerer T (2009) A patent pool for medicines: more medicines. The World Today 65(2)

't Hoen E, Veraldi J, Toebes B, Hogerzeil HV (2018) Medicine procurement and the use of flexibilities in the agreement on trade-related aspects of intellectual property rights, 2001–2016. Bull World Health Organ 96(3):185–193. https://doi.org/10.2471/BLT.17.199364 (last access 21 September 2021)

Tanimoto T et al (2017) Essential medicines for universal health coverage. The Lancet 389(10082): 1880 <https://doi.org/10.1016/S0140-6736(17)31211-4> (last access 21 September 2021)

Taubman A (2008) Rethinking TRIPS: adequate remuneration for non-voluntary patent licensing. J Int Econ Law 11(4)

Tellez VM (2020) The COVID-19 pandemic: R&D and intellectual property management for access to diagnostics, medicines and vaccines. Policy Brief 73

Thailand TM of PH and TNHSO (2007) Facts and Evidences on the 10 Burning Issues Related to The Government Use of Patents on Three Patented Essential Drugs in Thailand- Document to Support Strengthening of Social Wisdom on The Issue of Drug Patent. Thailand, Minist Public Heal Natl Heal Secur Off. https://doi.org/10.16194/j.cnki.31-1059/g4.2011.07.016 (last access 21 September 2021)

The Implementation Decision of the WTO General Council 2003, para. 2

Thiru B (2020) Israel issues compulsory license to allow the government to import generic versions of Kaletra. Knowledge Ecology International https://www.keionline.org/32503 (last access 21 September 2021)

Treatment Action Group, TAG Applauds Malaysian Government's Decision to Make Generic form of Life-Saving Hep C Cure (2017) Treatment Action Group https://www.treatmentactiongroup.org/statement/tag-applauds-malaysian-governments-decision-to-make-generic-form-of-life-saving-hep-c-cure/ (last access 21 September 2021)

Wetzler J, Burrowbridge A, Palmedo M (2009) Timeline for US-Thailand compulsory license dispute, Program on Information Justice and Intellectual Property

White M (2005) Drug patents are good for our health. Financial Times Nov. 29

Wong H (2020) The case for compulsory licensing during COVID-19. J Global Health 10(1)

World Intellectual Property Organization, Hungary: Government Decree No. 212/2020 on Public Health Compulsory Licenses for Exploitation Within Hungary (2020) World Intellectual Property Organization https://www.wipo.int/news/en/wipolex/2020/article_0009.html (last access 21 September 2021)

World Trade Organization (2017) WTO IP rules amended to ease poor countries' access to affordable medicines. The World Trade Organization https://www.wto.org/english/news_e/news17_e/trip_23jan17_e.htm (last access 21 September 2021)

World Trade Organization (2020) Report of the Trade Policy Review Body from the Director-General on Trade-Related Developments from mid-October 2019 to mid-May 2020 WT/TPR/OV/W/14, Para. 5.8

Wright E (2018) Compulsory pharmaceutical licensing is little more than government theft. The Hill, https://thehill.com/opinion/healthcare/400415-compulsory-pharmaceutical-licensing-is-little-more-than-government-theft (last access 21 September 2021)

Yu PK (2008) Access to medicines, BRICS alliances, and collective action. Am J Law Med 34(2–3)

Financial (In)Stability and the UN's Agenda 2030 on Sustainable Development in the Face of the Coronavirus Crisis

Giulio Peroni

Abstract The recent history of international economic relations has been marked by two crucial events: the financial crisis of 2008 (triggered by the subprime mortgages scandal occurring in the USA) and the economic crisis due to the Coronavirus pandemic in 2020. Both events led to a serious and dangerous economic-financial uncertainty that put great pressure on the financial stability at a global level as a result of the strong interconnection and interdependence existing between the various domestic and regional economic systems. The two crises show some significant differences, but one thing they have in common: the necessity for all international subjects and economic actors to ensure economic and financial stability. A global public good whose production and supply is essential for ensuring peace and security within the international community and above all for promoting the economic-social human rights, perfectly in line with the goals and targets of the UN Agenda 2030 on the Sustainable development.

1 The Rise of Economic and Financial Stability as a Driver of Contemporary International Economic Relations

The financial crisis of 2008 and, more recently, the economic crisis due to the Covid-19 pandemic have demonstrated the naïve simplicity of the view that, if the economic policies of individual economies are geared towards domestic economic and financial stability, and private actors are allowed to operate freely in such an environment, the global economy will work well.[1] On the contrary, those events

---

[1] This may, in a nutshell, be defined as the true leitmotiv that in recent years has characterized the international economic order of the neoliberal mould, for which market forces are always able to find "their" point of equilibrium in a "natural" way. On this aspect see Shirakawa (2012), in particular on p. 1 when it reports the position expressed by Padoa-Schioppa (2010).

G. Peroni (✉)
Department of Italian and Supranational Public Law, University of Milan, Milan, Italy
e-mail: giulio.peroni@unimi.it

© The Author(s), under exclusive license to Springer Nature Switzerland AG 2022
K. Mathis, A. Tor (eds.), *Law and Economics of the Coronavirus Crisis*, Economic Analysis of Law in European Legal Scholarship 13,
https://doi.org/10.1007/978-3-030-95876-3_11

have clearly demonstrated, on the one hand, how the market's self-correcting powers suffer from numerous limits and, on the other, how the search for stability within financial markets requires a joint effort by all subjects and actors that make up the wide community of economic and financial operators (states, international and supranational financial organizations like IMF, WB, OECD, EU-EMU) and by private operators (like international investment banks, multinational corporations, rating agencies, hedge funds et al.) since, due to the phenomenon of globalization, financial crises, just like epidemics, no longer know any borders.[2]

In this context,[3] it may be useful to recall how a specific event—precisely, the default of the US merchant bank Lehmann Brothers in September 2008[4]—gave rise to a chain of situations capable of producing, first of all, a true and proper wave of financial instability, and then political and social instability due to the particular impact of such financial turmoil on the real economy. Indeed, the crisis, fostered by that event, led to a global recession without precedent until the outbreak of the Covid-19 pandemic, which was followed by a sovereign debt crisis in the European Union, so serious that it threatened the survival of the Euro and the Economic and Monetary Union (EMU) underlying it.[5] The economic and financial instability that followed on a global scale then hit certain weaker nations, like those of North Africa and the Middle East, and, in turn, was the cause of the popular uprisings that characterized the well-known Arab Spring.[6]

Furthermore, in Europe, it caused a kind of migratory crisis, with tens of thousands of people, in search of asylum and better living conditions, starting to push against the borders of the European Union, generating new fears among European citizens and transforming the political structure of the Old Continent. Indeed, in the face of the threat of a future dominated by economic and political uncertainty, first British voters decided to throw themselves into the "void" of *Brexit*, and then US citizens chose a questionable businessman as their President (Trump). The French, on the other hand, when they elected Macron in 2017, decided to reject their country's entire political class, putting faith in a person who had become head of a party created for the occasion and practically out of nothing. Germany, too, in trusting in Angela Merkel for the fourth time, witnessed something that had not

---

[2] On the need for a global effort by all the major players in international economic life in order to realize an economic order as stable as possible over time see Peroni (2020), pp. 101–180.

[3] Here some of the considerations (with some additions) I made during the Financial Risk and Stability Conference 2018 held in Berlin with a speech entitled "Towards the financial stability: myth or reality?"

[4] To retrace the steps that led to the clamorous failure of Lehman brothers, the fourth largest investment bank in the United States, and examine the economic and financial effects that ensued on a global scale see Dosdall and Nichelmann (2018), pp. 312–324; De Grauwe (2014), pp. 105–109; Chorafas (2014), pp. 87–108; Mc Donald and Robinson (2009).

[5] See Peroni (2021) and Peroni (2012).

[6] This expression denotes a series of pro-democracy uprisings, begun in the spring of 2011 (hence the term), that engulfed several predominantly Muslim countries, especially Tunisia, Morocco, Syria, Libya, Egypt and Bahrain. See Bayat (2018), pp. 613–614.

happened since the end of the Second World War: the entry of an extreme right-wing party into Parliament with a number of representatives, which at the same time became the strongest opposition party. And lastly, in March 2018, Italian voters got rid of the old centre-left and centre-right parties, creating what some have designated the "Third Republic".

These circumstances, to which many others (such as the dramatic Venezuelan economic crisis connected to a hyperinflation which seems more and more reminiscent of the one that hit Germany during the Weimar Republic, or Argentina's new sovereign debt crisis) could be added, clearly show how economic and financial instability can lead to dangerous periods of political and social turmoil and, in the worst cases, can even put the rule of law in crisis.[7] Such events are also an expression of the desire of several large cross-sections of the population not only to do away with the "old" to make room for the "new" but, above all, to put an end to years of economic austerity, used excessively to restore faith in markets and, thus, market stability: a scenario that, at first glance, seems to have partially changed in 2020–2021, a period dominated by the Covid-19 health emergency. The reaction, in fact, especially at the European level, has seemed decidedly different compared with the recent past, since recourse has been had to various instruments both of a monetary nature (as in the case of the programme endorsed by the ECB, the so-called pandemic emergency purchase programme)[8] and of a more fiscal nature (as with the decision to temporarily suspend both the Stability and Growth Pact and the prohibition of state aid for national companies in difficulty),[9] which immediately seemed to go in another direction than that of the approach adopted during the previous crisis (2008).

Nonetheless, the aforementioned desire can certainly be shared with the wish to no longer be hostage to economic events, thus living in a constant state of precarious equilibrium. Indeed, one cannot help but observe how the economic, political, and social changes of the recent years have followed one on the other and continue to do so at an overwhelming pace, and that the responses that followed up to now, at national and supranational levels, have, unfortunately, not sufficed to satisfy people's natural need for greater economic and social security.

---

[7] Even the rule of law, which, as everyone knows, is at the basis of the protection and promotion of human rights and the correct functioning of a market economy, may, as has been seen, be compromised by phenomena of economic instability of particular intensity, along with the justice system in general. This occurs insofar as prolonged phases of instability can compromise the proper functioning of both the political and technocratic institutions in charge of regulating the economy. Locke (1967); Hayek (1960); Weingast (1997), pp. 245–263; Haggard et al. (2007), pp. 205–234; Koyoma and Johnson (2015), pp. 46–58; White (2010), pp. 451–463; Rockoff (1984); Gowder (2013), pp. 565–618; Fuller (1969); Cottier et al. (2014).

[8] It is a non-standard monetary policy measure initiated by ECB in March 2020 to counter the serious risks to the monetary policy transmission mechanism and the outlook for the euro area posed by the coronavirus (Covid-19) outbreak. See Demertzis and Dominguez-Jimenez (2020).

[9] On the fiscal action taken by European institutions during the pandemic crisis see Gros (2020), pp. 281–284.

Hence large cross-sections of the population have decided, as observed above, to support political movements that, in an attempt to offer new economic security to those who have voted for them, welcome the possibility of questioning several of the fundamental cornerstones of the current international legal-economic order, namely the rule *pacta sunt servanda*, the multilateral method, and the principle of non-discrimination.[10]

The failure to respect the aforesaid principles, as was the case, for example, with the former Trump administration regarding the application of duties against China or Mexico, or the wish to no longer to respect the criteria and parameters that inform the functioning of the European Monetary Union and the adoption of the Euro as the single currency, as was the case with Italy during the first year of its anomalous government (2018),[11] not only meant breaking WTO law in the former case and EU law in the latter, but also amounted to an attempt to destabilize economic and trade relations as we have known them thus far, in order to create an alleged new international economic system, which appeared, at first glance, to be based on economic nationalism and unilateralism and, therefore, on dangerous protectionist policies already witnessed in the past, i.e., those which characterized the first part of the last century.

2 The Success of the Neo-Liberal Economic Order and Its Subsequent Crisis

Thus, the international economic order that has seen the definitive emergence of the neo-liberal system—deeply inspired, since the late 1980s, by the *Washington consensus* theory[12] through the capitalist model underlying it, and which has conquered the greater part of the Planet by beating and even moving into Russia and China, ("bastions" of the economic systems inspired by communist ideology)—is in crisis today. As is also, first and foremost, the system of rules represented by the WTO,

---

[10] On these principles, at the basis of the International economic law, see Picone in Picone and Sacerdoti (1982), pp. 32–36; Carreau et al. (1999).

[11] Considered a mix of exponents of the populist and sovereigntist ideologies.

[12] The expression Washington consensus was used for the first time by John Williamson at the end of the 1980s, during a conference convened by the Institute for International Economics on the Latin American debt crisis. On that occasion, a group of economists and policy makers investigated the economic reforms in that area of the World and were in agreement on a common set of economic remedies to favour structural adjustments with the goal of substituting their traditional state economic system with a market based economic model. Precisely, ten reforms were elaborated as a summary of what most economists in Washington thought Latin America ought to be undertaking: (1) Fiscal discipline; (2) Reordering Public Expenditure Priorities; (3) Tax reform; (4) Liberalizing Interest Rates; (5) A competitive Exchange Rate; (6) Trade Liberalization; (7) Liberalization of Private Foreign Direct Investment; (8) Privatization; (9) Deregulation; (10) Protection of Property rights. On the expansion of the WC and its influence on the elaboration of the European Monetary Union during the negotiations of the Maastricht Treaty see Peroni (2017a), pp. 91–106.

thanks to which a single global market of goods and services has been progressively established since 1994, when the related constitutive agreement was signed.[13]

Nevertheless, that system has made no significant progress in regulating international trade for years, in particular since the 2003 Doha round. Indeed, no answer has been found to crucial questions such as those of social, environmental, and fiscal dumping, at the core of the profound asymmetry that has characterized trade relations between states over the last twenty years, inevitably favouring the relocation of companies from the western to the eastern hemisphere, thus radically transforming the economic and industrial fabric of many European countries, in particular France and Italy.

Downward competition between states with regard to environmental protection and the safeguarding of economic and social human rights, as well as to the taxation of income, inevitably results in the threatening of certain social entitlements, which in Western countries have long been taken for granted.

On the basis of the foregoing, it appears that the critical analysis of capitalism at the core of neo-liberalism, attributable to Marxist thought,[14] may still provide insight into why the profit-driven system has created and triggered forces with which it is unfamiliar and today can no longer dominate. Forces that, in this day and age, are no longer the rebellions of oppressed working classes of the past but increasingly of larger cross-sections of the population that are suffering a constant and progressive decline in their well-being and related economic and social rights as a result of the economic crisis; added to this are other irreparable injuries, like those inflicted on the environment in the name of profit and economic growth.

It is in this context that the contemporary nature of the fundamental practical message of Keynes's *General Theory*[15] can probably be added, according to which the capitalist economy based on a free market can or rather "needs to be stabilized", using appropriate monetary and fiscal policies to assure a fairer distribution of wealth, thus reducing inequality, without, moreover, renouncing the values in which the capitalist system is grounded: *freedom of initiative* and the protection of *private property*. All these aspects are clearly present in the United Nations' 2030 Agenda for Sustainable Development (see *infra*):[16] a legal and political document based on a soft law instrument (resolution) that, thanks to its ambitious 17 goals and 169 targets, has the power *to transform the World*,[17] in particular by inspiring actions

---

[13] See Petersmann (1997), Qureshi (1996) and Jackson (1997).

[14] See Marx (1890).

[15] See Keynes (1935–1936); For an analytical comment see Maglin (2018), pp. 1–11; La Malfa (2019).

[16] On 25 September, the United Nations General Assembly unanimously adopted the Resolution 70/1, Transforming our World: the 2030 Agenda for Sustainable Development. This historic document lays out the 17 Sustainable Development Goals, which aim to mobilize global efforts to end poverty, foster peace, safeguard the rights and dignity of all people, and protect the planet.

[17] See Kanie and Biermann (2017).

by states and international organizations in line with a human-based approach with the perspective of safeguarding the next generations.[18]

The need to modify the approach in economic policy choices, also with a view to providing greater protection for new generations, has become, above all, evident during this last year and a half dominated by the pandemic emergency which, as aforementioned, has seen the emergence of another approach than that taken in the first years of the 2008 financial crisis, when the national and supranational financial authorities' response was decidedly inspired by strict austerity. Today, in contrast, the action of economic policy seems to be grounded in logic and principles decidedly nearer to the Keynesian approach, according to which state action in the economy is not to be demonized but rather promoted, especially in times of crisis, so as to overcome market deficiencies and achieve those social and redistributive purposes, including those of a solidaristic character, which the market by its nature is unable to achieve.

Nonetheless, the use of economic and financial stabilization policies shared at the international level seems increasingly necessary if one considers the fact that there is no real alternative to the neo-liberal economic model and economic-trade globalization to date. The convergence of states towards a single economic and trade system has inevitably made their respective economies increasingly interdependent, meaning that the effects of any kind of crisis that hits a certain country or economic area, regardless of size, spread very quickly to other countries (spill-over effects), compromising regional or, in the worst-case scenario, global economic and financial stability, entailing the so-called contagious effect and systemic risk.

There is no doubt that the globalization of the economy and trade exchanges have caused a reduction in the fundamental prerogatives connected with and bound inextricably to state sovereignty. Nevertheless, the reconstruction of the changes sustained by states in the reduction of their economic and monetary powers,[19] with the exception of obvious cases like the adoption of a single currency at the European level, is by no means an easy task, not only because, on the one hand, the concept of sovereignty, in a broader sense, has changed over time (since the era of Jean Bodin's theory),[20] but also because, on the other, it suffers from the discord existing in international legal doctrine between those who consider that the competency of a state in a given matter exists only if it is regulated by international law and those who, conversely, deem that a state's competencies come before the international system, which only intervenes to limit them on the basis of the principle of peaceful co-existence among states within the international community. Nevertheless, beyond the debate on how the economic and monetary sovereignty of states has changed, the comments of the Permanent Court of Justice in the well-known Wimbledon case, in

---

[18] See McGoldrick (1996), p. 796 et seq.
[19] Burdeau (1988), p. 236; Mann (1992), p. 461.
[20] Bodin (1593), p. 157.

my opinion, hold true.[21] There, the Court highlighted that the limits to a state's economic and monetary sovereignty, which today may be those deriving from participation in the Single Currency, are still an expression of state sovereignty. The Court observed, indeed, that the conclusion of a treaty is not an abandonment of the sovereignty of the state through the mere fact of regulating the adoption of obligations, but rather an expression of one of its characteristic attributes.

The approach of those who try to link the subject of the construction of a new economic and monetary stability[22] to that of possible recovery of sovereignty by a given state is therefore wrong. The true focal point is the fact that states have not yet created a multilateral system capable of regulating the financial services sector from which, as is known, the crisis originated, and whose regulation at a global level is the responsibility of a number of supranational bodies (with inevitable potential conflicts of responsibility among them) which operate, mainly, with forms of soft law and, therefore, without any actual binding force.

Due to the widespread phenomenon of social, fiscal, and environmental dumping, as aforementioned, Western countries have witnessed progressive deindustrialization, which has led to the progressive conversion of their economies, with a particular strengthening of the services sector, in which, today, the financial sector seems to have prevailed.

Therefore, the more advanced economies, by focusing on the strategic sector of financial services and by relying, at an international level, on soft law as a regulatory tool and on a number of supranational bodies as guarantors of the sector's efficiency, have left the way open to major banking and insurance players in a legal framework characterized by a great lack of regulatory uniformity in the world's various economic areas. Otherwise, there would be no explanation as to why the sector lies outside the GATT-WTO system, as confirmed by the laconic content of the Annex dedicated to financial services stating that "A Member may recognize prudential measures of any other country in determining how the Member's measures relating to financial services shall be applied. Such recognition, which may be achieved through harmonization or otherwise, may be based upon an agreement or arrangement with the country concerned or may be accorded autonomously". This provision limits itself to recognizing the importance of financial stability, authorizing WTO member states to autonomously adopt the measures they unilaterally consider most effective to protect consumers.

On the contrary—by relying on the efficient jurisdictional system of the Dispute Settlement Body, which these days manages to ensure that treaty restrictions and the customary practices underlying international business law are respected—a shared legislative framework, or at least the essential factors of such a framework, could be created. But an actual will in said terms seems to have not yet affirmed itself,

---

[21] S.S."Wimbledon" Judgment of 17 August 1923 (Series A, No. 1) First Annual Report of the Permanent Court of International Justice (1 January 1922–15 June 1925), Series E, No. 1, pp. 163–168.
[22] Lastra (2006).

although important initiatives, even if not judicial in nature, have arisen in these recent years dominated by the crisis. I refer to the adoption of the Basel III accords[23] to make financial institutions more resilient to crises or to codes of conduct in the form of standards developed by the Financial Stability Board[24] or, even more recently, the proposal made at the 2021 Financial G7 to achieve a minimum global taxation of multinational companies,[25] which are all initiatives that seem to go in the direction described.

Indeed, attaining regulation, which is harmonized at a supranational level at the very least, could avoid scandals, such as that of the subprime loans, as well as the default of banks and insurance companies that led to the still ongoing financial crisis. In other words, the time has come for the law to take back the areas that the excesses of liberalism occupied in the years prior to the financial crisis in the name of solid liberalization, privatization, and deregulation policies, used as a basis of the aforementioned Washington consensus model which has been deeply inspired the IFIs' policies.[26]

3 The Advent of the Coronavirus Emergency and the Need for a Change of Approach to Achieve Economic and Financial Stability

In light of the impact of the Coronavirus emergency, to this author, it appears insufficient to use mere external economic restraints, fixed in agreements (see, for example, the EU Stability Growth Pact)[27] to which states voluntarily commit

---

[23] Visit the official website of Bank for International Settlement, where it is specified that "Basel III is an internationally agreed set of measures developed by the Basel Committee on Banking Supervision in response to the financial crisis of 2007-09. The measures aim to strengthen the regulation, supervision and risk management of banks. Like all Basel Committee standards, Basel III standards are minimum requirements which apply to internationally active banks. Members are committed to implementing and applying standards in their jurisdictions within the time frame established by the Committee."

[24] See The Compendium of Standards elaborated by the FSB that are internationally accepted as important for sound, stable and well-functioning financial systems, see https://www.fsb.org/work-of-the-fsb/about-the-compendium-of-standards/ (last access 09 September 2021).

[25] On this break event see the article of Giles, G7 strikes historic agreement on taxing multinational, in Financial Times, June 5, 2021.

[26] In these terms, the initiatives promoted by the Financial Stability Board and the so called standard setter bodies (like Basel Committee on Banking Supervision (BCBS), Committee on the Global Financial System (CGFS), Committee on Payments and Market Infrastructures (CPMI), Financial Action Task Force on Money Laundering (FATF), Financial Stability Board (FSB), International Association of Deposit Insurers (IADI)) in determining new set of rules in the form of code of conduct, are undoubtedly significant for realizing a new and more effective international legal framework also for financial services.

[27] See Buti et al. (2003), pp. 100–111.

themselves through internal adjustment procedures, in order to assure economic stability. Also, although it is internationally agreed that such stability is a global public good (see *infra*) that the entire international community must strive for, as we are taught by the economic and legal literature, there is no common vision on what is meant by this good and how it is to be achieved.[28]

This is the opposite of what happens in the case of internal monetary stability (price stability),[29] which, with the fixing of a 2% rate of inflation, bears witness to a numerical target agreed by the world's major central banks (European Central Bank, Federal Reserve, Bank of England, Bank of Japan).[30] An ability to more clearly define economic stability from a fiscal and financial point of view and with generally shared parameters, including quantitative parameters, would contribute to restricting the discretion of national and supranational players in the choosing of economic policies to be adopted in order to achieve said stability in more coordinated and shared terms.

In other words, the widespread recourse had by some governments, most often illegitimately (especially in recent years), to the justification clause of the "state of (economic) necessity",[31] so as to justify economic measures that in some cases have restricted individuals' access to essentials, like healthcare and education, as occurred during the Greek sovereign debt crisis,[32] could be reduced.

But an important example of change of this approach has been given by the Covid-19 pandemic emergency. All the IFIs (IMF and WB in particular) and the EU seem to have taken on a new vision, particularly regarding the use of the public debt to foster national economic recovery, while at the same time assessing the possibility of mutualizing sovereign debt in order to overcome the dramatic impact of the current economic crisis better and more rapidly. In other words, a clear reference to the aforementioned keynesian model.[33]

---

[28] See Camdessus (1999); Schinasi (2004); Dieter (2004), p. 28.

[29] In fact, it is one of the forms of stability which, together with fiscal and financial stability, constitute the broadest economic stability; see Peroni (2020), pp. 72–77.

[30] In Jackson Hole, dozens of central bankers, policymakers, academics, and economists from around the World are hosted by the Federal Reserve Bank of Kansas City for its annual economic policy symposiums that include prominent central bankers, finance ministers, academics, and financial market participants. Here, the central bankers convene to discuss the economic issues, implications, and policy options pertaining in particular to the level of inflation to purse during the years.

[31] On this point see Oraà (1992); Svensson-McCarthy (1998); Zagato (2006), pp. 137–156; Eboli (2010); Sommario (2018); Ouguergouz (1993), pp. 289–335; Draft Articles on Responsibility of States for Internationally Wrongful Acts (DARSIWA), in Yearbook of International Law Commission, 2001, Vol. II, Part Two, pp. 31 et seq.; Jimenez de Aréchaga and Tanzi (1991), pp. 347–380, in particular p. 355; Conforti (2007), p. 396; Heathcote (2007), pp. 53–91, in particular pp. 72 et seq.

[32] See Tsebelis (2016), pp. 25–41; Meegan et al. (2018), pp. 128–148.

[33] In said terms please read the different reports and proposals elaborated by IMF and WB during the pandemic crisis that seem to go in said direction, respectively at https://www.imf.org/en/Publications/SPROLLs/covid19-special-notes (last access 09 September 2021); https://www.

Not only would the human rights movements benefit from this, especially as concerns protection and promotion of social and economic rights, but so would international business and economic law as a whole, which could be made more efficient in creating stability through the action of international economic organizations, in particular, the International Monetary Fund and the Bank for International Settlements (monetary stability), the World Bank and the Organization for Economic Cooperation and Development (OECD) (fiscal stability) and the World Trade Organization (in the interest of a stable system of international trade).[34]

In this context, it is important to emphasize how, within the dimension of international law and especially of international economic law, the conceptual category of economic stability in its different forms (monetary, fiscal, and financial) is reconstructed within the regulatory framework of customary rules and treaty provisions. In said law sources, we find the legal basis (see, for example, UN Charter art. 1–2 and 55–56, IMF's art. I and IV) for financial and economic stability as a legal status of a global public good, for the provision of which a plurality of public and private entities and actors (states, international economic organizations, rating agencies, sovereign funds, multinational enterprises, hedge funds) are involved, operating in line with bases, perspectives, and aims that do not always coincide and, at times, are even in potential conflict.

This global public good, as observed above, is one whose pursuit and provision—because of its characteristic properties and the positive externalities it is able to produce—is in the common interest of all subjects of international law and of the various actors that make up the international economic community to commit themselves, in keeping with the traditional and multilateral approach that inspires international economic relations. This, therefore, ensures its widespread enjoyment for the benefit of all, while at the same time preventing dangerous opportunistic phenomena of free riding and moral hazard, which are at the root of many of the situations of economic instability that have occurred in the recent decades. This position was clearly expressed by the United Nations Development Program in 1999 with its Human Development Report,[35] in which it is highlighted how a "global public good" is a particular type of public good with two fundamental characteristics: non-excludability and non-rivalry, differentiating themselves from purely domestic characteristics by virtue of three criteria: geographic (their positive effects extend over more than one group of countries), socio-economic (the effects concern both "rich" and "poor" countries) and generational, since they concern the whole of humanity.

But the policies and stabilization mechanisms adopted at both the international and European level to overcome the serious economic uncertainty originating from

---

worldbank.org/en/about/what-we-do/brief/world-bank-group-operational-response-covid-19-coronavirus-projects-list (last access 09 September 2021).

[34] See Peroni (2020), pp. 64–100.

[35] See http://hdr.undp.org/en/content/human-development-report-1999 (last access 09 September 2021).

the financial crisis of 2008 and so to restore economic stability have essentially been inspired by a strict conditionality.[36] In other words, we have faced solutions that have entailed significant costs, if one considers the aforementioned social repercussions induced by them. Inevitably, many doubts and critical issues have been raised concerning not only the actual compatibility of those instruments as regards the protection of economic and social human rights but also the limitations they have imposed on states, especially those most in need of economic and financial support in terms of exercising their (economic) sovereignty, thus affecting one of the most characteristic aspects of state power: economic independence.

This has also raised the question of how to reconcile democratic methods and technocratic solutions, especially when certain choices that have a decisive impact on the lives of individuals and the various national communities have been made—partly because of the urgency of the moment—within fora and decision-making centres lacking in effective democratic legitimacy.[37]

The burden-sharing imposed by the production of the good that is stability would require, rather than recourse to the traditional international method based on multilateral or plurilateral cooperation, the adoption of the supranational method. Hereby, the member states of an organization, such as the EU, decide to limit their sovereignty, conferring the power to take binding decisions for all the states on the organization's institutions. But the European model represents a *unicum* on the international "panorama", although there are some legal entities like the International Tribunal for the Law of the Sea (see the UN Convention on the Law of the Sea, part XV), which, albeit with limitations, defines a system of mandatory jurisdiction, as is also the case with the WTO dispute settlement system.[38] The latter seems to go far enough in that direction to be considered a body expressing a form of transition from international law to supranational law, for it obliges countries that are not in agreement to reach a compromise on the basis of a defined mechanism.[39]

Thus, at the moment, with the significant exception of the EU, the "production" of GPG at a global level can essentially take place through cooperative and multilateral strategies based, above all, on the principle of differential treatment as regards developed countries on the one hand and underdeveloped countries on the other, a concept that strongly characterizes international economic law and international development law.[40] Indeed, this principle reflects the need to consider not only the different material conditions that characterize the numerous situations involved either through a "gradation" of the obligations incumbent on them or through a

---

[36] In accordance with what has always been IMF and World Bank practice, whereby economic aid for countries in financial difficulty is granted on condition that the beneficiaries conduct specific economic reform programmes serving to attain, within a certain lapse of time, specific quantitatively agreed economic targets.

[37] See Peroni (2017b), pp. 249–264.

[38] On the assessment described here, see Peroni (2020).

[39] See Helfer and Slaughter (1997), pp. 273–391.

[40] See Cullet (1999), pp. 549–582; Virally (1965), pp. 3–12; Feur and Cassan (1991).

better contextualization of those obligations, but also the intention to recognize the different levels of responsibility of the various countries and economic actors in determining the conditions of economic instability and the direct and consequential harm to the international economic order considered as a whole that may derive from the latter situation. A situation that could be resolved in part if states had the will to reform the International Monetary Fund or, even better, to introduce an international agency responsible for the solution of financial crises based on the model of the International Seabed Authority (ISA), which has introduced a mechanism for the management and control of activities related to the exploitation of mineral resources in maritime areas (outside national jurisdictions), which are considered a global public good whose protection is in the common interest of humankind.

Succeeding in implementing this aspect and, at the same time, combining economic reasons—especially those connected with the balancing of public accounts—with social aspects related to the defence of economic and social human rights is a very important challenge for states, for the international community and for the whole of humanity, above all in light of the dramatic economic impact of the Covid 19 pandemic, which has inevitably imposed important change at EU level, for the first time lending effectiveness to the principle of solidarity[41] among member states thanks to the recovery plan (Next Generation) adopted by the EU not only for the stabilization of each member state's economy but above all for the safeguarding of economic cohesion within the whole of Europe.[42]

The need to go beyond gross domestic product and other economic variables that work around the GDP figure to measure economic growth, development in general, and, above all, the well-being of a society is becoming increasingly great. Whereas chasing utopian models of happy de-growth, however, is out of the question. Indeed, the use of new indicators and the attainment of new goals and targets as set out in the UN's 2030 Agenda for Sustainable Development clearly move in this direction.

4 The Transformative Power of the UN's Agenda 2030 for a Better and More Stabilized International Economic Order

The 2030 Agenda represents a historic moment in the pursuit of the macro objective of sustainable development, since in the absence of an express and clear position on the legal qualification of the concept, the objectives that the Agenda sets, in the form of Sustainable Development Goals (SDGs), serve to prove the existence of an

---

[41] According to some, a structural principle of international law, whose essence would consist in the fact that "it links the factual and legal interdependence of states" see Fitzmaurice (2001), pp. 13 et seq.; on this topic see also Wolfrum (2006), pp. 1087 et seq.; Wellens (2005), p. 775 et seq., in particular, p. 802 et seq.

[42] See https://ec.europa.eu/info/strategy/recovery-plan-europe_en (last access 09 September 2021).

international practice designed to accord significance, from the international legal standpoint, to the principle under consideration, well summarized by the 1987 Bruntland report from which it originated. In particular, the SDGs draw on the experience acquired with the Millennium Development Goals (MDGs), from which, however, they differ in several respects, starting with the purely quantitative aspect. The MDGs, indeed, were structured in 8 objectives and 21 targets, while there are 17 SDGs covering as many as 169 targets. The most important differences are, however, two others, the first concerning the respective goals' scope of application, the second the different qualification of "development" set at their basis. As regards the first difference, it is noted that the MDGs essentially referred only to developing countries, substantiating themselves in a set of objectives functionally intended to defeat poverty. The new SDGs, while recognizing the central character of this issue, elevating it to the core of the complex action programme contained in the 2030 Agenda based on the "leave no one behind" principle, go beyond that fundamental goal, and are addressed to all countries, without distinction.

With regard to the second difference, it is noted that the MDGs were limited to promoting economic development in less developed countries alone, while the SDGs exhort all states to begin on programmes distinctly oriented towards sustainable development, grounded in specific national strategies and plans in implementation of the 2030 Agenda with the full participation of all stakeholders.[43] From this perspective, Resolution 70/1 adopts a holistic attitude, stating that the objectives specified are "integrated and indivisible", insisting in several points on the necessity of combining and balancing the three dimensions of sustainable development: economic, social, and environmental. For this reason, the SDGs, unlike the Millennium Development Goals, are universal, transversal, and interconnected.[44]

The SDGs thus represent an important innovation in the ambit of multilateralism and a strategic driver within the complex reform process underway at the United Nations, and with regard to the principal transformations of long-term political planning in many of the world's countries.[45] Their implementation constitutes an important moment for rethinking the regulations and the governance models used on both the international and national level with a view to pursuing sustainable development in its three dimensions.[46] With this purpose in mind, it is fitting to ask what

---

[43] In the first years of implementation of the 2030 Agenda, the issues regarding attainment of the Millennium Goals have gradually gained a position of primary importance in the political debate, involving also numerous stakeholders on both internal and international level to create paths of sustainable development that will be more equitable and broadly shared.

[44] These profiles have recently (22 January 2020) been reiterated by the United Nations Secretary General in his remarks to the General Assembly on priorities for 2020.

[45] The annual strategic report on implementation and reaching of the European Parliament's sustainable development goals puts it thus, cit., 24. See also Business and Sustainable Development Commission Report, Better Business, Better World, 2017, in https://sustainabledevelopment.un.org/index.php?page=view&type=400&nr=2399&menu=1515 (last access 14 September 2021).

[46] See United Nations General Assembly, Resolution 74/4 October 21, 2019, Political declaration of the high-level political forum on sustainable development convened under the auspices of the

their juridical nature is. On this subject, the majority position seems to be that of those authors who intend to accord a certain legal significance to the SDGs, mostly within the system of soft law regulations, albeit with various nuances,[47] notwithstanding the fact that their formulation is, in several points, generic and of political character.[48] Two particularly significant aspects favour this position: on the one hand, the legal instrument with which they have been adopted, such as that of resolution, a typical soft law measure, and on the other, the fact that the SDGs express values already contained, to a large extent, in other international rules of both customary and treaty nature, and would therefore constitute a subset of obligations, which, being already known in international law, could well be utilized to coordinate states' existing obligations.[49]

In the 2030 Agenda, particular attention is paid to the economic dimension of sustainable development, and in this respect the most significant goals are numbers eight, nine, and ten. The first two concern economic and industrial development;[50] the tenth addresses the issue of reduction of inequalities both among states and within each state. This last goal, a very ambitious one, indeed regards areas, which are different from one another; although income inequalities are the most obvious, it intends to eliminate all types of disparity, including those of "age, gender, disability, ethnicity, origin, religion or economic or other status". Thus, states are invited to take legislative measures and actions useful to ensure equality of opportunity and reduce income inequality, eliminating discriminatory rules and practices: all factors, which, if satisfied, are capable of improving social cohesion.[51]

In other terms, for the 2030 Agenda, focusing on GDP growth remains central for reducing internal inequality, especially in advanced countries, such as the United States and also in traditionally more egalitarian countries like Germany, Denmark, and Sweden.[52] In the terms described, the challenge that the 2030 Agenda outlines is a clear one: The resources produced must be utilized to design a new system of social protection, as occurred a century ago with the birth of the Welfare State, inspired by shared principles of distributive justice in order that the new model may be perceived and accepted by the various collectivities as fair and lawful in its foundations.

General Assembly. See also French and Kotzè (2018), in specie pp. 227–230; Pavoni and Piselli (2016), pp. 13–60; Schrijver (2007), p. 366.

[47] For a reconstruction of the various positions expressed see Montini (2019), pp. 2–21, in particular pp. 4–7.

[48] On the political nature of the SDGs see French (2017), pp. 151–178, in particular pp. 164–165.

[49] See Kim (2016), pp. 15–26.

[50] See Frey (2017), pp. 1164–1184; World Bank (2016).

[51] Implementation of the outcome of the World Summit for Social Development and of the twenty-fourth special session of the General Assembly: Report of the Secretary-General (A/74/205) July 22, 2019; UN General Assembly, Resolution 73/141 December 17, 2018, Implementation of the outcome of the World Summit for Social Development and of the twenty-fourth special session of the General Assembly.

[52] Berg and Ostry (2013) and Lakner and Milanovic (2013).

For the purposes stated, the 2030 Agenda vitally requires work not only on the strengthening of financing for development and of international trade but also on the sustainability of sovereign debt and, thus, on economic stability, above all on the fiscal side. In this regard, attention is fixed on external debt because of the impact that its ever-increasing size may have on the economic, social, and environmental development of the planet.[53] For the 2030 Agenda it is a matter of offering a solution to the present condition of fragmentation, both of the set of creditor entities (such as the Paris Club, the London Club, institutional creditors, and bondholders) and of the debt instruments: problematic and potentially harmful aspects for a possible orderly and efficient restructuring of sovereign debt once it has become unsustainable. An operation, which, according to the Agenda, should conform to the following principles: (1) respect for the macroeconomic policy choices of states, which should not be thwarted or impeded by abusive practices, all in keeping with the principles of good faith, (2) transparency and impartiality; (3) prohibition of discrimination between creditors, unless different treatment is justified on legal grounds; (4) respect for State immunity from jurisdiction with regard to debt restructuring processes, the efficiency of these processes depending on the reduction of the economic and social costs linked to them; (5) the principle according to which other states or an unrepresentative minority of creditors ought not to be able to obstruct the implementation of restructuring agreements approved by a majority of creditors.

On the whole, these are principles that can obviously be shared, but they at times suffer from being formulated in terms expressing mere wishes, too vague to be able effectively to guide the action of the states and other entities involved in the debt restructuring processes so as to render the debt actually sustainable. Hence the request addressed by the General Assembly in its 70th session, with the resolution on sustainability of foreign debt and development,[54] to the Economic and Social Council to consider new instruments to improve the processes of debt restructuring. A solicitation expressed by the General Assembly in subsequent resolutions nos. 71/215 (of 25 January 2017), 72/203 (of 24 July 2017) and 73/220, 74/202 (of 19 December 2019), in which, in addition to the emphasis on countercyclical economic policy measures avoiding the imposition of conditionality policies liable to depress the most fragile economies further, importance was placed on the lending, financing, and technical assistance of multilateral development banks and on the need to proceed with an even more thorough reform of the international economic system than that thus far effected by states and international financial institutions, so as to enable it to react more effectively to the constant risks to economic stability due to excessive financialization and to the existence of (essentially private) financial bodies too big to fail, to the still widespread presence of corruption and tax evasion

---

[53] On the need to continue with the processes of debt reduction and to review fiscal mechanisms for a better redistribution of resources see The Sustainable Development Goals, Report 2019, pp. 56–57, in https://unstats.un.org/sdgs/report/2019/ (last access 09 September 2021); in doctrine see Cecchetti et al. (2011); Kumar and Woo (2010).

[54] See Resolution n. 70/190.

and avoidance, and to excessive recourse to the valuations issued by the well-known rating agencies.

5 Conclusions

For the reason set forth above, the implementation of the *Principle of Sustainable Development*[55] can be an opportunity to define a new method to use to achieve an effective balance between political-economic interests and social interests, which, as noted, are in some cases opposed to one another.

Consequently, a solidaristic approach and vision in tackling common problems and satisfying common concerns derives from this principle. A new vision, in terms of behaviour and method of action, that can be the means of reaching a fair compromise at the international legal level between the need to ensure a stable economic and financial system and the defence of the economic and social rights of the person, at least of those rights considered essential, under massive pressure due to the Covid-19 pandemic's dramatic impact. This is a practicable solution to prevent new crises and, above all, safeguard the interests of future generations, as the EU Next Generation Plan aims to achieve and as the *Brundtland Report*—which gave impetus to the *Principle of Sustainable Development*—urges us to do.

---

[55] We are in front of a principle that has known a wide use in international law and that inevitably has generated considerable academic interest, as observed in the text. However, because of the evasive and flexible content of what has been termed by the International Court of Justice as a concept in the Gabcikovo-Nagymaros case (ICJ, Case Concerning the Gabcikovo-Nagymaros Project (Hungary vs. Slovakia) judgment of 25 September 1997), and more recently an objective in the Pulp Mills case (ICJ, Pulp Mills on the River Uruguay, Argentina v. Uruguay) Judgment of 20 April 2010, academics have often struggled to find out sustainable development's legal nature. One of the most interesting theses has been elaborated by Lowe's analysis. For Lowe, said principle expresses an interstitial or modifying norm, which exerts its normative influence as an interpretative tool in the hands of judges. Its interpretative function is certainly very important. In most cases, judges have had recourse to it to legitimize recourse to evolutive treaty interpretation, as a rule of conflict resolution, and even to redefine treaty obligations. However, beyond this particular function, sustainable development primarily purports to regulate state conduct. As an objective, it lays down not an absolute but a relative obligation to pursue sustainable development in its traditional dimensions (environmental, social, and economic). Such obligations are obligations of means or of best efforts and so all subjects and actors that compose the international community are under said obligation to pursue an effective sustainable development. For a detailed analysis of this principle see Barral (2012), pp. 377–400; Boyle and Freestone (1999), pp. 16 et seq.; French and Kotzè (2018), pp. 227–230.

References

Barral V (2012) Sustainable development in international law: nature and operation of an evolutive legal norm. Eur J Int Law:377–400
Bayat A (2018) Revolution without revolutionaries: making sense of the Arab Spring. Int J Middle East Stud 50(3):613–614
Berg AG, Ostry JD (2013) Inequality and sustainable growth: two sides of the same coin? In: IMF Staff Discussion Note
Bodin J (1593) Les six livres de la Republique. Paris, p 157
Boyle A, Freestone D (eds) (1999) International law and sustainable development. Past achievements and future challenges. Oxford, pp 16 et seq.
Burdeau G (1988) L'exercice des compétences monétaires par les états. Recueil des Cours, pp 236 et seq.
Buti M, Eijffinger S, Franco D (2003) Revisiting Emu's stability pact: a pragmatic way forward, i. Oxford Rev Econ Policy:100–111
Camdessus M (1999) International financial and monetary stability. A global public good? In: IMF Research Conference, Washington DC, 28 May
Carreau D, Flory T, Juillard P (1999) Droit international économique. Paris
Cecchetti SG, Mohanty MS, Zampolli F (2011) The real effects of debt. In: Bis Working Paper 352
Chorafas DN (2014) Banks, bankruptcies under crisis. Understanding failures and mergers during the great recession. New York, pp 87–108
Conforti B (2007) Diritto Internazionale. Napoli, p 396
Cottier T et al (eds) (2014) The rule of law in monetary affairs. Cambridge
Cullet P (1999) Differential treatment in international law: towards a new paradigm of inter-state relations. Eur J Int Law:549–582
De Grauwe P (2014) Ideology and economics in the failure of Lehman Brothers. In: Sanchis M, Marco I (eds) Economics of the Monetary Union and the eurozone crisis. Berlin, pp 105–109
Demertzis M, Dominguez-Jimenez M (2020) Monetary policy in the time of COVID-19, or how uncertainty is here to stay. In: Monetary Dialogue Papers, November
Dieter H (2004) The stability of international financial markets: a global public good? In: Schirm SA (ed) New rules for global markets. Public and private governance in the world economy. New York, p 28
Dosdall H, Nichelmann R (2018) The risk of financial risk management: the case of Lehman Brothers. In: Gephart RP Jr, Miller CC, Helgesson KS (eds) The Routledge companion to risk, crisis and emergency management. London, pp 312–324
Eboli V (2010) La tutela dei diritti umani negli stati d'emergenza. Milano
Feur G, Cassan H (1991) Droit International du développement. Paris
Fitzmaurice M (2001) International protection of the environment. In: Recueil des Cours de l'Academie de l'HAYE, pp 13 et seq.
French D (2017) The global goals: formalism foregone, contested legality and "re-imagining of international law". Ethiop Yearb Int Law:151–178
French D, Kotzè LJ (2018) Sustainable development goals: law, theory and implementation. Cheltenham, pp 227–230
Frey DF (2017) Economic growth, full employment and decent work: the means and ends in SDG 8. Int J Hum Rights:1164–1184
Fuller LL (1969) The morality of law. New Haven
Gowder P (2013) The rule of law and equality. Law Philos:565–618
Gros D (2020) Lesson from the Covid-19. Crisis for euro area fiscal rules. Intereconomics:281–284
Haggard S, MacIntyre A, Tiede L (2007) The rule of law and economic development. Annu Rev Polit Sci:205–234
Hayek F (1960) The constitution of liberty. London
Heathcote S (2007) Est-ce que l'état de nécessité est un principe de droit international coutumier? In Revue Belge de Droit Internationale, pp 53–91

Helfer LR, Slaughter AM (1997) Toward a theory of effective supranational adjudication. Yale Law J:273–391
Jackson J (1997) The world trading system: law and policy of international economic relations. London
Jimenez de Aréchaga E, Tanzi A (1991) International state responsibility. In: Bedjaoui M (ed) International law achievement and prospects. Dordrecht, pp 347–380
Kanie N, Biermann F (2017) Governing through goals: sustainable development goals as governance innovation. Cambridge
Keynes JM (1935–1936) General theory of employment, interest and money
Kim RE (2016) The nexus between international law and the sustainable developments goals. Rev Eur Comp Int Law:15–26
Koyoma M, Johnson B (2015) Monetary stability and the rule of law. J Financ Stab:46–58
Kumar MS, Woo J (2010) Public debt and growth. In: IMF Working paper, WP/10/174
La Malfa G (ed) (2019) J. M Keynes, Teoria generale dell'occupazione, dell'interesse e della moneta e altri scritti, in I Meridiani Mondadori, Milano
Lakner C, Milanovic B (2013) Global income distribution: from the fall of the Berlin Wall to the Great Recession, Policy Research Working Paper, No. 6719, Washington
Lastra MR (2006) Legal foundations of international monetary stability. Oxford
Locke J (1967) Two treatises of government. Cambridge
Maglin S (2018) Raising Keynes: a general theory for the 21st century. Economia:1–11
Mann FA (1992) The legal aspect of money. Oxford, p 461
Marx K (1890) Capital. A critique of political economy. London
Mc Donald LG, Robinson P (2009) A colossal failure of common sense: the inside story of the collapse of Lehman Brothers. New York
McGoldrick D (1996) Sustainable development and human rights: an integrated conception. Int Comp Law Q, pp 796 et seq.
Meegan A et al (2018) Financial market spill overs during the quantitative easing programmes of the global financial crisis (2007–2009) and the European debt crisis. J Int Financ Mark Inst Money 56:128–148
Montini M (2019) L'interazione tra gli SDGs ed il principio dello sviluppo sostenibile per l'attuazione del diritto internazionale dell'ambiente, in federalismi.it, pp 2–21
Oraà J (1992) Human rights in states of emergency in international law. Oxford
Ouguergouz F (1993) L'absence de clause de dérogation dans certain Traités relatifs aux droits de l'homme: les réponses du droit international général. In: Revue Générale de Droit International Public, pp 289–335
Padoa-Schioppa T (2010) Markets and government before, during, and after the 2007–20XX crisis, the Per Jacobsson Lecture in Basel, Switzerland, 27 June
Pavoni R, Piselli D (2016) The sustainable development goals and international environmental law. Normative value and challenges for implementation. In: Veredas Do Direito, pp 13–60
Peroni G (2012) La crisi dell'Euro: limiti e rimedi dell'Unione economico e monetaria. Milano
Peroni G (2017a) The constitutionalization of the Washington consensus in the European Union: like giving up the social market economy. In: Sciso E (ed) Transparency and democracy in The Bretton Woods Institutions. Springer, Giappichelli, Torino, pp 91–106
Peroni G (2017b) The European Central Bank and the European Democracy: a technocratic institution to rule all European states? In: Daniele L (ed) The democratic principle and the economic Monetary Union. Springer, Torino, pp 249–264
Peroni G (2020) Stabilità economica e sostenibilità nel diritto internazionale. Milano, pp 101–180
Peroni G (2021) Which future for the euro and the economic and Monetary Union after the European elections? Contributions of the Lecturers at the European Monetary and Economic Law (EMEL) – Jean Monnet Conference, held on 24th May 2019 at the University of Milan, Bari
Petersmann EU (1997) The GATT/WTO dispute settlement system: international law, international organizations and dispute settlement. London

Picone P (1982) Diritto internazionale dell'economia e costituzione economica dell'ordinamento internazionale. In: Picone P, Sacerdoti G (eds) Diritto internazionale dell'economia. Milano, pp 32–36

Qureshi AH (1996) The World Trade Organization. Implementing international trade norms. Manchester & New York

Rockoff H (1984) Drastic measures: a history of wage and price controls in the United States. Cambridge

Schinasi GJ (2004) Defining financial stability. IMF working paper WP/04/187

Schrijver N (2007) The evolution of sustainable development in international law: inception, meaning and status. In: Recueil des Cours. The Hague, p 366

Shirakawa M (2012) International financial stability as a public good, Keynote address by Mr Masaaki Shirakawa, Governor of the Bank of Japan, at a high-level seminar, co-hosted by the Bank of Japan and the International Monetary Fund, Tokyo, 14 October

Sommario E (2018) Stati d'emergenza e trattati a tutela dei diritti umani. Torino

Svensson-McCarthy A (1998) The international law of human rights and states of exception. The Hague

Tsebelis G (2016) Lessons from the Greek crisis. J Eur Public Policy, 01–02, 23(1):25–41

Virally M (1965) Vers un droit international du développement, in Annuaire Français de Droit International, pp 3–12

Weingast B (1997) Political foundations of democracy and the rule of law. Am Polit Sci Rev:245–263

Wellens K (2005) Solidarity as a constitutional principle: its expanding role and inherent limitations. In: Mac Donald RSJ, Johnston DM (eds) Towards world constitutionalism. Leiden, pp 775 et seq.

White LH (2010) The rule of law or the rue of central bankers. Cato J:451–463

Wolfrum R (2006) Solidarity among states: an emerging structural principle of international law. In: Dupuy MP et al (eds) Common values in international law, essays in honour of Christian Tomutschat. Kehl, pp 1087 et seq.

World Bank (2016) Poverty and shared prosperity 2016: taking on inequality. Washington

Zagato L (2006) L'eccezione per motivi di emergenza nel diritto internazionale dei diritti umani, in Deportate, esuli, profughe. Rivista telematica di studi sulla memoria femminile:137–156

Innovative Foods with Transparent Labels That Will Have the Next Pandemic for Breakfast

Danny Friedmann

Abstract Continued factory farming makes a new viral pandemic ineluctable. Plant-based and cell-cultured food (together "innovative food") producers use animal-based food names to signal a similar function, use, and taste, but without the negative externalities of the animal-based foods in regard to health, sustainability and ethicality. In the US and EU, the market share of animal-based products is shrinking. The animal-based food producers in the US have insisted on "Truth in Labeling" measures to exclude innovative foods from using animal-based food names, even though empirical research demonstrates that it does not lead to consumer confusion. The European Parliament has approved Amendment 171 to Regulation (EU) No. 1308/2013 to extend the dairy ban, even though it conflicts with the policy goals in the Farm to Fork Strategy to transition to a system of health, sustainability, clear information, and the implied goal of ethicality. Only after a massive public outcry, the European Parliament, European Council and European Commission rejected Amendment 171.

1 Introduction

One can argue that the pandemic outbreak of the SARS-CoV-2 virus that causes the COVID-19 disease, despite its enormous impact, is not a black swan event.[1] This is so because it lies in the realm of regular expectations: many epidemiologists and

---

[1] Black Swan event is defined by Taleb: "First, it is an outlier, as it lies outside the realm of regular expectations, because nothing in the past can convincingly point to its possibility. Second, it carries an extreme "impact". Third, in spite of its outlier status, human nature makes us concoct explanations for its occurrence after the fact, making it explainable and predictable." Taleb (2007), pp. 376–377.

D. Friedmann (✉)
Peking University School of Transnational Law, Shenzhen, China

© The Author(s), under exclusive license to Springer Nature Switzerland AG 2022
K. Mathis, A. Tor (eds.), *Law and Economics of the Coronavirus Crisis*, Economic Analysis of Law in European Legal Scholarship 13,
https://doi.org/10.1007/978-3-030-95876-3_12

experts have expected it and have warned about it for years.[2] Pandemics are predominantly interspecies contagions.[3] They start when a disease spreads from a non-human animal to a human animal. There is, for example, a high probability that the Spanish flu came from birds and horses (1918);[4] Marburg from bats (1967);[5] Ebola from bats or non-human primates (1976);[6] HIV AIDS from monkeys (1981);[7] Nipah virus from bats (1998)[8] and pigs (1999);[9] SARS from bats to civet cats (2002);[10] Swine flu from pigs (2009);[11] MERC from camels (2012);[12] and COVID-19 from bats (2019).[13] There are also zoonotic diseases that spread via bacteria: Bovine tuberculosis from cows to humans,[14] or prions: Bovine spongiform encephalopathy (BSE) that causes Creutzfeldt-Jakob ("mad cow" disease).[15] In a recent letter to the US Congress, 100 wildlife and environmental groups estimate that zoonotic diseases have quadrupled over the past 50 years.[16] There are two main

---

[2] Greger (2006); Benatar (2006), pp. 1545–1546; Morose et al. (2012), pp. 1956–1965; Quammen (2012); Felbab-Brown (2017), pp. 1, 6 and 30. Q-Koorts, een Kwestie van Erkenning, Nationale Ombudsman, 7 maart 2017, 11. Available at: https://www.nationaleombudsman.nl/system/files/onderzoek/2017030%20Rapport%20Q-koorts%20def.pdf (last access 12 September 2021).

[3] According to the Centers for Disease Control and Prevention, 3 out of every 4 new or emerging infectious diseases in people come from animals. Zoonotic Diseases, Centers for Disease Control and Prevention. Available at: https://bit.ly/3rmerjr (last access 12 September 2021).

[4] Hoag (2014); Barry (2004), pp. 2–3.

[5] Marburg virus disease, WHO, 15 February 2018. Available at: https://bit.ly/2MVenbo (last access 12 September 2021).

[6] Rajewski (2019).

[7] Lovgren (2003).

[8] Fruits Are Healthy, But Contamination With Nipah Virus Can Be Deadly! Centre for Food Safety, Government of the Hong Kong S.A.R. Available at: https://www.cfs.gov.hk/english/multimedia/multimedia_pub/multimedia_pub_fsf_144_03.html (last access 12 September 2021).

[9] Pigs were buried alive in Sungai Nipah, Malaysia, 22 March 1999. Tom Levitt, Farm animals and pandemics: nine diseases that changed the world, The Guardian, 15 September 2020. Available at: https://bit.ly/3bmnqeR (last access 12 September 2021).

[10] Chen et al. (2013), pp. 163–167; Sample and Gittings (2003); Out of the Shadows: The Origin of SARS, Economist, 1 November 2013.

[11] Gibbs et al. (2009).

[12] Middle East respiratory syndrome coronavirus (MERS-CoV), WHO, 11 March 2019. Available at: https://bit.ly/2O4LDxE (last access 12 September 2021).

[13] Hayes (2020).

[14] In 2018, based on the most recent Global Tuberculosis Report, an estimated 142,000 new cases of zoonotic tuberculosis, and 12,500 deaths due to the disease occurred. Global tuberculosis reports 1997–2020, WHO. Available at: https://www.who.int/teams/global-tuberculosis-programme/tb-reports (last access 12 September 2021); Levitt (2020).

[15] The use of meat, bone, cooked leftovers of the slaughtering process, as well as from the carcasses of sick and injured animals such as cattle or sheep, as a protein supplement in cattle feed was widespread in Europe prior to about 1987. Budkaa and Will (2015).

[16] "Coronavirus Wildlife Letter: Stimulus Package", 24 March 2020. Available at: https://www.documentcloud.org/documents/6819003-CoronavirusWildlifeLetterStimulusPackage.html (last access 12 September 2021).

causes for zoonotic spillover: on the one hand, human-animals are making ever deeper incursions in the habitat of non-human animals;[17] on the other hand, the animal-industrial complex[18] is a viral time bomb waiting to explode.

1.1 Incursions Into Nature

The habitat of non-human animals is shrinking. This leads to more interaction between non-human animals and human animals, which facilitates zoonotic spillover. This situation is exacerbated by bushmeat, trade of exotic animals, trade of live animals for Traditional Chinese Medicine, and wet markets.[19] At least 80 percent of the direct deforestation is due to clearance for cattle rearing.[20] It turns out that eating meat is also the leading driver of species extinction.[21] Quammen notices that "humanity is a kind of animal, inextricably connected with other animals: in origin and in descent, in sickness and in health."[22]

> We invade tropical forests and other wild landscapes, which harbor so many species of animals and plants – and within those creatures, so many unknown viruses. We cut the trees; we kill the animals or cage them and send them to markets. We disrupt ecosystems, and we shake viruses loose from their natural hosts. When that happens, they need a new host. Often, we are it.[23]

1.2 Animal-Industrial Complex

Greger calls factory farming a "perfect storm environment" for infectious diseases.[24] In the factory farming industry,[25] where each year 77 billion animals are

---

[17] Felbab-Brown (2017), pp. 1, 6 and 30.

[18] The animal-industrial complex coined by Noske. Noske (1989); Twine describes the concept as the "partly opaque and multiple set of networks and relationships between the corporate (agricultural) sector, governments, and public and private science. With economic, cultural, social and affective dimensions it encompasses an extensive range of practices, technologies, images, identities and markets." Twine (2012), pp. 12–39; Arcari describes it as the systemic exploitation of all animals commodified under the animal industrial complex—as food, entertainment, fashion, research, and companionship. Arcari (2020).

[19] Webster (2004), pp. 234–236.

[20] Lima et al. (2011); See also Unsustainable Cattle Ranching, WWF. Available at: https://bit.ly/3cfcZcc (last access 12 September 2021).

[21] Machovina et al. (2015), pp. 419–431.

[22] Quammen (2012), p. 1.

[23] Quammen (2020).

[24] Greger (2006).

[25] Brown describes the development from small scale, via Green Revolution, Livestock Revolution and Blue Revolution to factory farming. Brown (2020a); See also Wadiwel (2018), pp. 527–549.

slaughtered,[26] animals cannot express their natural behaviour (no social or family life, or natural reproduction), the integrity of their body is broken (castration and cutting the tails of pigs; dehorning cows; burning the beaks of poultry; ear tagging pig, goats, and cows; all without anesthesia); pigs, highly intelligent animals, are getting mentally disturbed by the impossibility to move and the absence of external incentives.[27] The insanitary conditions make things worse: "A pig is a clean animal. This means that she prefers not to fertilize or urinate where she has to lie or eat."[28] Chickens, pigs, and cows suffer in great numbers from lameness, respiratory problems, and inflammation partly as a result of standing in their own poo (air).[29] Between 10 and 20 percent of all pigs show a disease that is clearly visible.[30] People experience respiratory problems at ammonia concentrations around 7 ppm. However, concentrations between 5 and 18 ppm—and according to the European Scientific Panel for Animal Health and Welfare (EFSA) 40 ppm—are considered normal in pigsties. Pigsties in, for example, the Netherlands have minimum ventilation to save costs: in winter, the ammonia concentrations are between 35–45 ppm for fattening pigs and 50–60 ppm for piglets.[31] Ventilation is not only important to avoid bacterial infections such as *Mycoplasma hyopneumoniae*,[32] but also to prevent viral infections via aerosols. When ventilation systems of sealed stables broke down, the animals suffocated.[33] Since these stables have no windows, the animals do not get any day light, and their hormonal circadian rhythms are being manipulated to let them eat more feed.[34] Animals in factory farms are standardly fed antibiotics used as

---

[26]FAO Statistics, available at: http://www.fao.org/faostat/en/#search/Producing%20Animals%2 FSlaughtered (last access 12 September 2021); "An estimated 50 billion chickens are slaughtered for food every year – a figure that excludes male chicks and unproductive hens killed in egg production." Thornton (2019).

[27]120 Misstanden in de Nederlandse Varkenshouderij Anno 2015, Varkens in Nood 2015. Available at: https://bit.ly/3rsgaDX (last access 12 September 2021).

[28]De Lauwere (2003).

[29]Kiloknaller mestmarinade, Wakker Dier. Available at: https://files.wakkerdier.nl/app/uploads/2017/10/18172320/WD-2013-Kiloknaller-mestmarinade.pdf (last access 12 September 2021).

[30]120 Misstanden in de Nederlandse Varkenshouderij Anno 2015, Varkens in Nood 2015, 12. Available at: https://bit.ly/3cf1cuD (last access 12 September 2021).

[31]Dusseldorp (2008). Opinion of the Scientific Panel on Animal Health and Welfare on a request from the Commission related to animal health and welfare in fattening pigs in relation to housing and husbandry (18 October 2007) European Food Safety Authority (EFSA) Journal (2007) 564, pp. 1–14. Available at: https://doi.org/10.2903/j.efsa.2007.564 (last access 12 September 2021); Varkens.nl (15 March 2012): Slechte luchtkwaliteit verhoogt antibioticagebruik. Available at: https://www.varkens.nl/nieuws/2012/03/15/slechte-luchtkwaliteit-verhoogt-antibioticagebruik (last access 12 September 2021).

[32]Sierens (2011).

[33]Schriftelijke vragen, Tweede Kamer der Staten-Generaal, 21 Juni 2013. Available at: https://www.tweedekamer.nl/kamerstukken/kamervragen/detail?id=2013Z12951&did=2013D26544 (last access 12 September 2021).

[34]Boumans et al. (2017), pp. 82–93.

additives in feedingstuffs as growth promoters[35] and antiviral drugs, which cause drug resistance. In addition, a bacterium resistant to one member of a class of antibiotics may also become resistant to other antibiotics of the same class, in a process called "cross-resistance".[36] And where live animals are transported by boats,[37] trains, and trucks, sometimes during several days,[38] without sufficient water, food, or ventilation, in unhygienic circumstances, the resistance of the animals against diseases is very low. The torture of force-feeding great amounts of grains and fats to ducks and geese and subsequently binding their beaks to prevent them from vomiting to fatten their livers in the case of *foie gras*,[39] further degrades these animals' mental and physical health. This non-exhaustive list demonstrates how factory farming is imposing intense suffering and stress on animals, which makes them susceptible to viral infections. The poorly developed waste management systems of slaughterhouses around the world make it possible that zoonotic diseases spread even after the life of an animal was taken.[40] In addition, monocultures are particularly vulnerable to new diseases;[41] animals within a factory farm are genetically very uniform, because factory farms want uniform "performance" in regard to the yearly egg production, milk yields, milk fat content, and growth rates.[42] In the

---

[35] T-13/99, Pfizer Animal Health SA v Council of the European Union, Judgment of the Court of First Instance (Third Chamber) of 11 September 2002, ECLI:EU:T:2002:209, para. 44.

[36] T-13/99, Pfizer Animal Health SA v Council of the European Union, Judgment of the Court of First Instance (Third Chamber) of 11 September 2002, ECLI:EU:T:2002:209, para. 31.

[37] After leaving Spain in December 2020 and spending two months at sea being rejected by several ports, due to bluetongue disease suspects, the Karim Allah vessels finally docked on Thursday 26 February in Cartagena (Spain). Stubley (2021); All animals of the Karim Allah ship are to be killed. Live transport: Karim Allah's cattle about to be killed, Eurogroup for Animals, 27 February 2021. Available at: https://bit.ly/3c9YZ3v (last access 12 September 2021).

[38] In Canada, farmed animals aged eight days or younger, and for "compromised" animals the maximum time is 12 h. For cows, goats and sheep, the maximum time is 36 h without food, rest, or water. For horses and pigs, the maximum is 28 h. Hatchling birds may be transported for a maximum of 72 h from the time they are hatched. For "broiler chickens", "spent hens" and rabbits, the maximum is 24 h without water and 28 h without food. The regulations do not contain any concrete requirements with respect to temperature and weather conditions—a serious omission given the extreme temperatures experienced in Canada, in both summer and winter. Lazare (2020), p. 94.

[39] Foie Gras: Cruelty to Ducks and Geese, PETA. Available at: https://bit.ly/3kT2U8V (last access 12 September 2021); On the one hand force-feeding for foie gras is banned in Austria, Croatia, the Czech Republic, Denmark, Finland, Germany, Italy, Luxembourg, Norway, Poland, or following interpretation of general animal protection laws in Ireland, the Netherlands, Sweden, Switzerland, Turkey, and the United Kingdom.

On the other hand, France has stipulated in Article L654–27–1: "Foie gras is part of the cultural and gastronomic heritage protected in France. "Foie gras" is understood to mean the liver of a duck or a goose specially fattened by force-feeding."

[40] World Bank Study – Contract 7142400 Global Study of Livestock Markets, Slaughterhouses and Related Waste Management Systems, Final Report February 2009. Available at: https://bit.ly/3rtkOkW (last access 12 September 2021).

[41] Wallace (2016), p. 195.

[42] Gura (2007), p. 6.

language of the pandemic, factory farms can be described as potential "superspreaders".

1.3 Fur Farms

These risks are, of course, not limited to animals that are used for food, but also in the case of animals exploited for their fur, such as minks that appear to be especially susceptible to COVID-19. At many mink farms in Denmark, minks were infected with SARS-CoV-2. At these mink farms, the virus mutated into the so-called Cluster 5 mutation, which changed the amino acids and shape of the spike protein. At least 12 people were infected with this mutation, and more than 200 other people have contracted other mink-related strains of the virus.[43] In response to these outbreaks, 17 million minks were killed.[44] After the animals were killed and buried, they were dug up again, to be incinerated to prevent further infections.[45] These massive mink farms in Denmark and in the Netherlands are mainly to produce fur for export, since wearing fur is frowned upon in Denmark and the Netherlands.

1.4 Quiet Assassins

The place of origin of COVID-19 is not clear. French researchers have determined that COVID-19 already occurred at the Albert-Schweitzer de Colmar hospital in France in November 2019.[46] However, since the outbreak at a wet market in Wuhan, Hubei Province, in January 2020, the attention has been focused on the dangers of wet markets where human-animals come into contact with exotic non-human animals. China issued a temporary ban on trade in wild animal products on 22 January 2020. In China, wet markets were banned in 2003 as a reaction to the SARS outbreak in 2002–2004. Then this ban was lifted, and reinstated after the COVID-19 pandemic,[47] and lifted again in April 2020.[48] Lynteris and Fearnley argue that a ban would drive wet markets underground. Instead, they advocate scientific and evidence-based regulation.[49] However, the magnitude of danger of zoonotic spillover at factory farms is arguably 15 times higher. This is highlighted by the

---

[43] Murray (2020).

[44] Murray (2020).

[45] Covid: Denmark to dig up millions of mink culled over virus, BBC News, 21 December 2020. Available at: https://www.bbc.com/news/world-europe-55391272 (last access 12 September 2021).

[46] Foucart (2019).

[47] Greenfield (2020).

[48] Chen et al. (2020).

[49] Lynteris and Fearnley (2020).

distribution of wild mammal biomass to domesticated mammal biomass, where the wild ones are outnumbered by the domesticated ones by 15 to 1.[50] And this risk has repeatedly materialized. The Netherlands, the most animal-dense country in the world, where 640 million animals are slaughtered each year,[51] is a case in point.[52] Avian flu, a recurring phenomenon, killed a veterinarian in 2003.[53] In 2006, a Dutch goat dairy infected thousands of people with Q-fever (which is not a virus but the bacterium *Coxiella burnetii*), killing 74 people between 2007–2010 and then another 11 people; and it is understood that 519 people will never fully recover.[54] During the outbreaks between 2006 and 2009, the Dutch Ministry of Agriculture, Nature, and Food Quality did not want to point out which goat dairy farms were infected, to protect the interests of the goat dairy industry, and the Ministry of Health, Welfare, and Sport was taking a wait-and-see attitude. The implication of this silence is that unsuspecting people passed these farms and got infected as well. The main recommendations of the evaluation of this disaster were that the government should use the principle of precaution and that the Ministry of Health, Welfare, and Sport should have the highest competency to make decisions in cases of viral outbreaks.[55]

In case of an outbreak, animals are gassed, and one might think that is the end of it. However, virologists have shown, especially in the case of the avian flu,[56] that it is only a matter of time before the virus mutates so that it can jump from a wild bird to a farm chicken to a human etc. Even though in the Netherlands, the demand for animal-based products decreases, it is exporting more animal-based products and factory farming technology. For example, the Netherlands is exporting hatching eggs to Russia, which frequently has cases of avid flu.

---

[50] Bar-On et al. (2018), pp. 6506–6511.

[51] 2.5 million animals are slaughtered on a working day: 1200 per minute.

[52] In the Netherlands, there is the same number of livestock as 20 years ago, but 50 percent less farmers. In other words: factory farming has become even more concentrated.

[53] The reflex is to keep all the animals in the factory farms inside, which decreases the animals' natural resistance. The outbreaks have taken place in these farms where they animals were kept inside.

[54] Sterfte aan Q-koorts naar boven bijgesteld: 95 mensen overleden: Nieuwe cijfers uit Nationale Chronische Q-koorts Database, Radboud UMC, 2 November 2018. Available at: https://www.radboudumc.nl/nieuws/2018/sterfte-aan-q-koorts-naar-boven-bijgesteld (last access 12 September 2021).

[55] The State did not act unlawfully towards the plaintiffs, victims of the Q-fever, according to the Court of Justice The Hague, C/09/499740/HA ZA 15-1271, 25 January 2017, ECLI:NL:RBDHA:2017:587. Available at: https://uitspraken.rechtspraak.nl/inziendocument?id=ECLI:NL:RBDHA:2017:587 (last access 12 September 2021). According to the decision, at that time Q-fever was insufficiently known as a dangerous disease for people, in contrast to foot and mouth disease, swine fever and avian fever and was not an animal disease specified in an EU directive, for which mandatory (control) measures applied.

[56] "An Ounce of Prevention", Economist, March 19, 2016.

Arcari points to the 2009 strain of swine flu, that killed around 280,000 people,[57] which demonstrated that viruses can evolve in complex, non-linear ways.[58] It involved the "quadruple reassortment" of North American and Eurasian virus strains circulating between pigs, humans, and birds, and was especially facilitated by the concentration of farm animals, especially concentrated animal feeding operations (CAFOs).[59] In addition, the people working at abattoirs and meatpacking facilities are particularly prone to be infected with the SARS-CoV-2 virus.[60]

There is also a perverse connection between the lack of ecological habitats and the animal-industrial complex. Substantial patches of rainforest are burned down for the growing of palm oil and soy. The latter is predominantly used as animal feed. Both causes are likely to increase the risk that a zoonotic disease will develop in a pandemic. Another perverse connection is that obesity is predominantly caused by animal-based diets,[61] and that there is a strong correlation between the contraction of COVID-19 by obese people and mortality.[62] More generally, there is overwhelming evidence that a diet dominated by animal-based food can lead to health problems.[63] In addition, especially wild fish, but also farmed fish[64] can have arsenic, cadmium, lead, mercury, persistent organic pollutants (POPs) and toxic organic micropollutants (TOMPs),[65] pathogens, parasites,[66] viruses,[67] micro-particles of plastics due to plastic pollution in the ocean[68] and other pollutants. Especially farmed fish, but also wild fish can have antibiotics and animal drugs.[69] Instead of manifesting themselves after an incubation time, these health risks are quiet assassins that can lead to cardiovascular diseases, cancer, and other illnesses.

---

[57] Roos (2012).

[58] Gibbs et al. (2009) and Mena et al. (2016).

[59] Hospital, TMS 2016, 2009 swine flu pandemic originated in Mexico, researchers discover, ScienceDaily. Available at: https://www.sciencedaily.com/releases/2016/06/160627160935.htm (last access 12 September 2021); Mena et al. (2016); Schmidt (2009), pp. A394–A401.

[60] Southey (2020); Slaughterhouses: a major target for Covid-19 prevention, Press release from the French National Academy of Medicine and the Veterinary Academy of France, 24 June 2020. Available at: https://bit.ly/2RvsgPt (last access 12 September 2021).

[61] Wang and Beydoun (2009), pp. 621–628.

[62] People with obesity who contracted SARS-CoV-2 were 113 percent more likely than people of healthy weight to land in the hospital, 74 percent more likely to be admitted to an ICU, and 48 percent more likely to die. Popkin et al. (2020) and Wadman (2020).

[63] Keevican (2020) and Brown (2020b).

[64] Lundebye (2017).

[65] Olsen and Crichton-Stuart (2018).

[66] Lawton (2021), p. 39.

[67] Morton et al. (2017).

[68] Smith et al. (2018).

[69] Olsen and Crichton-Stuart (2018).

1.5 Inefficient Meat Production

Moreover, the production of meat is very inefficient. One needs about 7 kilos of grain to produce one kilo of meat. Factory farming uses 70 percent of all fresh water, occupies 40 percent of the earth's land surface, degrades the soil, and emits 25 percent of all greenhouse gases,[70] especially methane, which is 28 times as warming, and nitrous oxide, which is 265 times as warming per molecule than carbon dioxide. Animal-based farming is accompanied by enormous leakage of the nutrients nitrogen and phosphorus. Their compounds cause serious water pollution, eutrophication (enrichment with minerals and nutrients), and air pollution.[71] Per kilocalorie of food produced, wild-caught fish has a bigger global warming footprint than pork, chicken or dairy, because of the required long-distance travel and energy costs of cooling and freezing of fish.[72] It is said that some fish stocks are no longer depleted. However, if one compares their level to that of the 1950s, one can determine that their alleged sustainability is accurate only if you take a very low level as a benchmark.[73]

Aquaculture provides 52 percent of all the fish consumed, and this percentage is growing.[74] For example, salmon farming has problems with parasites, overuse of antibiotics, escaped fish breeding with wild ones, potentially diluting the gene pool of wild fish and leading to sterile offspring, and pollution of the sea floor underneath the pens.[75] Since salmon, tuna, sea bass, and many other farmed species are top predators that eat other fish, around 22 million tons of wild fish are caught to feed them.[76] "Aquaculture is not a producer of fish, it's a consumer of fish."[77] In regard to sea food: the environmental cost of feeding the shrimp and freighting them to Western markets makes that their calorie-for-calorie carbon footprint sometimes exceeds that of beef.[78]

1.6 Negative Externalities

Climate change will lead to a whole cascade of disasters in the future and in places that have the least means to cope with them. However, our brains seem best equipped to estimate direct risks of causal relationships (a lion attacking a member of the tribe) but are less inclined to take the risks related to unhealthy food, climate change, and

---

[70] Springmann et al. (2016).
[71] Buckwell and Nadeu (2018).
[72] Lawton (2021), p. 39.
[73] Lawton (2021), p. 39.
[74] Lawton (2021), p. 39.
[75] Lawton (2021), p. 39.
[76] Lawton (2021), p. 39.
[77] Lawton (2021), p. 40.
[78] Lawton (2021), p. 39.

pandemics seriously. These negative externalities of animal-based products have never been fully discounted in the price of meat.

In light of the growing world population that needs to be fed,[79] to increase a rational allocation of resources, mitigate the abovementioned risks and for ethical reasons,[80] governments and the public at large should stimulate plant-based analogues or cell-cultured food. Once the innovative food industry is able to scale-up its production, it is expected that the incumbent meat and dairy industry eventually cannot keep up and will have to transform into an innovative incarnation to survive. According to RethinkX, an independent think tank that focuses on the impact of disrupting technology, production volumes of the US beef and dairy industries and their suppliers will decline by more than 50 percent by 2030, and by nearly 90 percent by 2035.[81] An increasing percentage of consumers are enjoying the taste of meat, dairy, and seafood, but are opting for plant-based analogues or look forward to cell-cultured meat[82] that was already approved for consumption in Singapore in 2020.[83] Despite enormous pushback, which will be explored in this article, an explosion of disruptive food innovation is taking place in Silicon Valley, Tel Aviv, Wageningen, and other places. The Initial Public Offering of Beyond Meat Inc., a poster child of plant-based food producers at the Nasdaq Stock Market, introduced at USD 25 and USD 143.18 on 14 September 2020, was a case in point. Grocery sales of plant-based substitutes for meat and dairy grew by 29 percent from 2018 to 2020 to an amount of USD 5 billion.[84]

1.7 Pushback

For all their beneficial aspects, one would expect governments, especially those known for subsidizing their agricultural sector, to embrace and stimulate the development of plant-based[85] and cell-cultured animal-based products, help the stakeholders in the animal-industrial complex switch to these innovative food products which impose less negative externalities on the public at large and the animals. But so far, in the US, many states known for their animal-based agriculture have imposed

---

[79] Food for 3.5 billion people is consumed as animal feed. Poore and Nemecek (2018).

[80] Singer (1990), Reagan (1983) and DeGrazia (1996).

[81] Tubb and Seba (2019).

[82] Bryant is exploring the issues related to cultured meat as a technology with a diverse set of societal consideration. Bryant (2020).

[83] Oi (2020).

[84] SPINS retail sales data released March 3, 2020, shows that grocery sales of plant-based foods that directly replace animal products have grown 29% in the past two years to $5 billion. Plant-Based Market Overview 2020, GFI. Available at: https://bit.ly/35HXI7P (last access 12 September 2021).

[85] Plant based meats: foods that mimic the taste, texture and nutritional qualities of meat, without a single animal in sight. The Economist, Plant-based meat could create a radically different food chain, 12 October 2019. Available at: https://econ.st/3mpEP9S (last access 12 September 2021).

or are in the process of imposing so called Truth in Labelling (TiL) regulation, which is banning that plant-based or cell-cultured food is named after meat or dairy products in the name of preventing consumer confusion and deception.[86] The biggest exporter of agricultural products in the world, the EU, is also considering banning certain generic names for innovative foods, in addition to ag-gag laws (laws prohibiting debate or free expression of opinion in regard to agricultural aspects) against transparency of how animals are kept, transported and slaughtered, and food libel laws that make it more difficult to criticize a certain food product.

The TiL initiatives are based on the claim that innovative foods, by using names that are related to meat or dairy, misrepresent and deceive consumers about the taste, nutritional value, origin, and perpetuate gastronomical appropriation, even though a description of the origin is clarified on the label. The demand for transparency is easy to defend. However, the TiL movement and governments have interpreted this transparency narrowly. Consumers are not only interested in the origin and nutritional value of a product, but often also in the long-term health effects, environmental footprint of the food production, ethicality, and concomitant negative externalities. Of course, governments should be interested in lowering future health care costs and reducing greenhouse gases as well. In a previous article, this author has called for transparency of products' ethicality.[87] Many consumers would be interested to know where and how, for example, a cow was raised,[88] from where to where she was transported, and where and at what age she was slaughtered. Many US states' statutes include a TiL provision that provides a definition of meat. "Meat" must have originated "from a slaughtered animal". This is a restrictive etymological interpretation, which is as silly as when the traditional automobile industry would insist on the definition of "car" as "fossil fuelled", just to exclude electric car manufacturers from using this name for their functionally identical product. The TiL movement in regard to meat but also in regard to dairy can be partly explained by regulatory capture, a term coined by Stigler,[89] where the government operates in favour of special interest groups, rather than the public at large.[90] However, it seems

---

[86] When the New Zealand-based pizza chain Hell Pizza offered a new plant-based burger, it did not inform its customers that they were served a plant-based burger. Most customers did not notice the difference. Becher and Lai point out that customers sometimes do not mind to be deceived if it teaches them a lesson, while others do not appreciate it. Becher and Lai (2019).

[87] Friedmann (2020).

[88] For example, in Switzerland there are labels to describe the degree of animal friendliness of the stables. "Besonders tierfreundliche Stallhaltung" (BTS): particularly animal-friendly stables. In case of pigs, this means: The provisions of the Animal Welfare Ordinance are observed; the pigs have access to a littered lying area without perforations; daylight is mandatory; but the pigs do not have to be allowed outside.

[89] "We propose the general hypothesis: every industry or occupation that has enough political power to utilize the state will seek to control entry. In addition, the regulatory policy will often be so fashioned as to retard the rate of growth of new firm." Stigler (1971), p. 5.

[90] In addition, the National Cattlemen's Beef Association is also asking the Food and Drug Administration (FDA), the federal regulator, to outlaw what it sees as misleading labelling of plant-based meat.

to be a rear-guard fight, since many companies within the animal-industrial complex have also started to invest in or develop their own plant-based or cell-cultured alternatives.[91] One can argue that the average consumer is reasonably well-informed, observant, and circumspect, a norm used in trademark law. Courts have repeatedly rejected food class actions, because they do not take a completely infantile but a reasonable consumer as starting point.[92] However, the rationality of the consumer is flawed by behaviour that is sometimes inconsistent with or misaligned to her own chosen values. In addition, food labelling can sometimes make it more confusing for consumers: an example are the multiple "organic" labels in China, which tend to perpetuate a lack of consumer trust.[93]

While the attention in regard to the COVID-19 pandemic has been mostly focused on curative measures such as medicines and vaccines, this article focuses on possible preventative measures, such as replacing animal-based products with innovative foods.

Section 2 gives a non-exhaustive overview of some of these innovative foods; i.e., plant-based and cell-cultured foods that are analogues to animal-based products and the often oxymoronic names under which they are marketed;

Section 3 provides an overview of the regulation of innovative food, in regard to quality and labelling. This is followed by an exposé of the standard of identity of food which is used as a baseline for some amendments of Regulation (EU) No. 1308/2013 that aimed for banning the use of animal-based products for plant-based products and the extension of the dairy ban. An analysis will be made of the implication of this reform and whether it is conducive for the transition of the EU towards an agricultural sector that is increasing health, sustainability, and ethics.

Section 4 covers the concept of TiL, the DAIRY PRIDE Act, and whether the use of animal-based designations that are accompanied by clarifying or descriptive terms indicating the plant origin of the product lead to confusion. Two empirical studies research this question. One of the surveys is also looking into the mirror scenario of an animal-based product that is piggybacking on plant-based popularity to see if this leads to confusion. TiL initiatives are proposed in the name of transparency. However, the last part of this Section will demonstrate that at the same time, ag-gag legislation is stifling transparency and that food disparagement laws are chilling freedom of commercial speech.

Section 5 deals with labelling and whether it is the government's role to stimulate or stifle the consumption of certain food. The Section observes contradictory campaigns and uneven subsidies to the animal-based industry, caused by regulatory capture. How can the market mechanism be restored in the food industry, taking into

---

[91] The biggest US producer of animal meat by sales, Tyson Foods, Inc. introduced a vegan burger from pea protein. Polansek (2021); Another example is Danone, which has set the goal of increasing plant-based sales from 2.2 billion euro to 5 billion euro by 2025; Watson (2021).
[92] Silverman (2018).
[93] Snyder (2020).

account the negative externalities that outweigh the efficiency gains; in other words, what is the true price of animal-based and innovative food products?

Section 6 concludes that oxymoronic names for innovative foods should be allowed to stimulate their ascent, so that human-animals can relate in a more healthy, sustainable, and ethical way to non-human animals, plants, and the planet.

2 Innovative Foods and Their Names

> We shall escape the absurdity of growing a whole chicken in order to eat the breast or wing, by growing these parts separately under a suitable medium. – Winston Churchill, 1932[94]

Even if genetics and genomics are "aggressively applied",[95] via selective breeding, genetic modification to improve their physical or metabolic characteristics along the yardstick of exchange value,[96] or if a porthole is installed in the stomach of a cow,[97] so that the farmer can check her stomach at any time, animals are limited by their inherent biological design. Mammalian animals still need to be conceived, born, develop organs to maintain their bodies, breathe, eat, sleep, etc. With cell-cultured food, enormous efficiency gains can be achieved, since the cells can be fed directly, without a complex mammalian body or stomach. Plant-based and cell-cultured foods are much more open to innovation. Animal-based food could be characterized as hardware, plant-based and cell-cultured food as software. Therefore, investors and companies from Silicon Valley and other innovation centers around the world are strongly drawn to innovative foods. The Edison Group, an investment research and advisory company, gave an overview of the projections of the revenue for the global plant-based meat market: Kearney, a management consulting company, estimates it to grow from USD 46 billion to USD 120 billion between 2018 and 2025, representing a 15 percent Compound Annual Growth Rate. Longer-term growth projections vary greatly, with revenue estimates for the global market in 2030 ranging from USD 140 billion by Barclays to USD 252 billion by Kearney.[98] The global plant-based milk industry is expected to have a market revue of USD 21 billion by 2026 and is set to register an 11 percent Compound Annual Growth

---

[94] Churchill (1932), p. 397.

[95] Goodwin (2020).

[96] The use of hormones and selective breeding to accelerate growth and production resulting in chickens and pigs whose legs are unable to support their weight, turkeys too big to procreate naturally, "dairy" cows unable to walk due to excessive milk production, and chickens who lay so many eggs that they are "spent" after just two years. Taylor (2017).

[97] Dyer (2019).

[98] The lean, green money-making machine, Meat alternatives: An investment analysis, Edison October 2020, 5. Available at: https://www.edisongroup.com/wp-content/uploads/2020/10/Edison-Plant-based-report-v6-1.pdf (last access 12 September 2021).

Rate between 2020 and 2026, propelled by an increasing vegan population and the growing awareness of the health benefits of plant-based food.[99]

By 2025, Edison expects the cell-cultured food market to produce on an industrial scale and generate substantial revenues, which in turn will lead to substantial investments.[100] SoftBank Group, Temasek, Norwest, and Threshold Ventures, Bill Gates, Richard Branson, and animal-based food companies such as Tyson Foods and Cargill have invested more than USD 160 million in Memphis Meats.[101] Bill Gates, who is also an investor in plant-based meat companies (Beyond Meat and Impossible Foods), articulated the pushback that these innovative foods are getting: "There are all these bills that say it's got to be called, basically, lab garbage to be sold. They don't want us to use the beef label."[102]

Terms such as "veggie burger" and "veggie dog" are combinations of opposing terms; called *contradictio in adiecto*.[103] According to Professor Neuwirth, such oxymoronic concepts induce the need for holistic and dynamic thinking.[104] Thus, by combining "veggie" with "burger", each of these terms are transcended and form a new product category that symbolizes the ethical, environmental, and health benefits of plant-based products, and the taste, cultural and social function of animal-based products.

2.1 Plant-Based Food

In Asia, especially China, there is a long tradition of Buddhist or "temple" plant-based analogues for animal-based products. It was intended, on the one hand, to help people in their transition to vegetarianism, and on the other hand, to allow Chinese Buddhists or Taoists that also subscribe to a system of thought and behaviour, such as Confucianism, to substitute animal sacrifices and blood offerings for mock meat.[105] Wheat gluten was known as *miànjīn*, which means literally "wheat meat" in the Song dynasty (960–1279). George Ohsawa, the founder of the macrobiotic diet, coined the term "seitan" for the same food in 1961. Tofu, a food that dates back to prehistoric times in China, was known as "small mutton" in the tenth century,

---

[99] Plant Milk Market Revenue to Hit $21 Billion by 2026, Says Global Market Insights, Inc., Global Market Insights, Inc., 1 November 2020. Available at: https://prn.to/3rqs94Y (last access 12 September 2021).

[100] The lean, green money-making machine, Meat alternatives: An investment analysis, Edison October 2020, 6. Available at: https://bit.ly/3v1HR8J (last access 12 September 2021).

[101] Rowland (2020).

[102] Temple and Gates (2021); Gates (2021), pp. 112, 115, 16, 117, 126, 129, 222 and 241.

[103] Neuwirth (2018), p. 12.

[104] Neuwirth (2018), p. 253.

[105] Wei (2021); Louis Komjathy, Animals and Daoism, Brittanica. Available at: https://www.britannica.com/explore/savingearth/daoism-and-animals (last access 12 September 2021).

according to records.[106] In Japan and India, this is much less the case, "since meat was never a reference point to begin with."[107] Although there is an abundance of complete vegetarian and vegan dishes without meat analogues, a part of the vegetarians and vegans like the taste[108] of meat based on wholesome, ethical ingredients without or with much less negative externalities than meat. Since the market segment was modest and not growing so fast, not too many plant-based meat, fish, seafood, egg, and dairy analogues were introduced. Since the awareness of climate change went mainstream, which arguably happened after "An Inconvenient Truth" aired in 2006, the documentary in which the former vice-president of the US Al Gore educated the public about the dangers of global warming, the demand for plant-based food started to take off.[109]

WhiteWave's development demonstrates the evolution of plant-based food. Steve Demos founded WhiteWave Foods in Boulder, Colorado, in 1977. His mission was "creative integration of soy into the average American diet".[110] By using a classic gable-topped milk carton and insisting on being stocked next to regular milk, "Silk" (Silk = Soy Milk) broke out of the health-food category and went mainstream in two decades. Silk spent USD 10 million on a campaign that used slogans such as "Think globally, spoon locally", and "Have a nice life span", linking the product to sustainability and health.[111] In 2017, Danone, a multinational known for its dairy products, acquired WhiteWave for USD 12.5 billion.[112]

The number of vegans, vegetarians, and especially flexitarians, people who consume less meat, has risen significantly. In 2019, the retail sales of plant-based food reached USD 5 billion in the US.[113] This led to the supply of more plant-based meat analogues.[114] A virtuous cycle has started, where demand and supply amplify each other. Progressively, besides some shelves reserved for plant-based products, supermarkets put plant-based products on the shelves next to animal-based products.[115] This increases their visibility and accessibility; and ultimately their sales. Consumers were more likely to try out plant-based varieties and compare them to

---

[106] Erway (2018).

[107] Erway (2018).

[108] Miyoko Schinner: "Why do people want to eat meat? They want it because of the texture and the flavor, not because it's a dead animal." Erway (2018).

[109] Interestingly, as the documentary Cowspiracy made clear that the focus of most NGOs, such as Greenpeace, Oceana, Rainforest Action Network that promote environmental sustainability was not on the main emitter of greenhouse gases: animal-based agriculture. Cowspiracy: The Sustainability Secret 2014. Available at: https://www.cowspiracy.com/ (last access 12 September 2021).

[110] Mclean (2001).

[111] Mclean (2001).

[112] Watrous (2017).

[113] Redman (2020).

[114] Manufacturers include: "Beyond Meat", "Impossible Burger", "Gardeins", "Tofurky", etc.

[115] This also happens online. On the website of the Swiss supermarket Migros, one can find within the category "Milk and Egg products" for example also the vegan products Migros Bio V-Love Vegurt Soja Birchermüesli, Genuss am Stück Vegan, and Violife Greek white block.

their animal-based varieties. As long as the package, especially the label, preferably the front-of-pack label, of the product makes it sufficiently clear that the product is plant-based, chances for confusion are slim if consumers actually read the label.

It is true that non-animal-based products do not have the same level of negative externalities in regard to ethicality, health, and sustainability as animal-based products. However, not all non-animal-based alternatives are created equally. For example, oat milk uses 80 percent less water than almond milk; some have added sugar; others do not; etc.

2.2 Cell-Cultured Meat

According to the bible book of Genesis, after the flood, God made the concession to the children of Noah, that eating of meat was allowed under the condition of a sixth commandment as part of the Seven Laws of the Sons of Noah: to refrain from eating flesh torn from a living animal.[116]

This commandment was supposed to be applicable to the children of Noah, *i.e.*, the whole of humanity. It seems that the transgression of this commandment in the case of cell-cultured meat can have positive societal effects. Since 2000, there are different ongoing projects in regard to cell-cultured animal-based products to make them from product concept, develop them further, and scale them up to a commercially feasible production. Mark Post, the Dutch scientist responsible for the first cell-cultured hamburger, sees the cow as an inefficient intermediary:

> We feed the cow [vegetables] and then the cow feeds us. The intermediary, a cow is a very inefficient animal in terms of converting the vegetable proteins that they eat into the animal edible proteins to such an extent that we are already using 70 percent of all arable land to produce meat.[117]

The procedure of cell-cultured meat is that after a biopsy of an animal, the stem cells are isolated. In principle, the animal does not need to be slaughtered, stem cells can be harvested even from a feather. However, the question is whether these biopsies are still done from slaughtered animals in practice, which would raise ethical questions.[118] After a biopsy the harvested cells are replicated in a cell culture and

---

Milchprodukte & Eier, Migros. Available at: https://produkte.migros.ch/sortiment/supermarkt/lebensmittel/milchprodukte-eier (last access 12 September 2021).

[116] Genesis 9:4.

[117] The Meat Revolution | Mark Post, World Economic Forum, YouTube 21 October 2015, at 0.40 seconds. Available at: https://www.youtube.com/watch?v=1II9AwxKfTY (last access 12 September 2021).

[118] Lin fears that after immortal cell lines have become a possibility, that the experiments will continue with "cells from different types and species of animals, and those animals will be bred, kept, confined, used and killed in the never-ending search for a better product." Lin (2019).

fed with fetal bovine serum (FBS), which represents a serious ethical problem.[119] However, there are efforts made to replace FBS with a serum that is derived from algae and other plants.[120] An alternative route is chosen by Bond Pet Foods. This company from Boulder, Colorado, is inserting genes for chicken proteins into cells of brewer's yeast that reproduce faster than chicken cells do. Nurturing them is well-understood.[121]

The next step is that cells merge naturally and arrange themselves into myotubes (small fibers), which are grown in bioreactors around gel hubs (scaffoldings), contracting and bulking up as they grow into a small ring of tissue, to mimic muscular movement. In contrast to animal-based meat, germs, parasites, antibiotics, and other contaminants can be avoided in the production process of cell-cultured meat.

In 2013, Post presented the first cell-cultured hamburger for Mosa Meat that was produced for Euro 250,000 in London. By 2021, the price was expected to have dropped to Euro 9.[122] However, on 2 December 2020, the Californian start-up Eat Just's cultured chicken produced in Singapore was approved as a safe novel food and labelled "cultured meat" by the Singapore Food Agency (SFA) and is being sold for SGD 50 in Singapore (which is around Euro 31 on 8 March 2021). "No antibiotics were used in the process, and the chicken had lower microbiological content than conventional chicken", according to Eat Just.[123]

All kinds of cell-based foods are being developed. For example, for meat: Mosa Meat,[124] Memphis Meat,[125] SuperMeat,[126] Aleph Farms,[127] Future Meat

---

[119] Fetal bovine serum (FBS) is a common component of animal cell culture media. It is harvested from bovine fetuses taken from pregnant cows during slaughter. FBS is commonly harvested by means of a cardiac puncture without any form of anaesthesia. Jochems et al. (2002).

[120] Japan's IntegriCulture, plant-based serum. IntegriCulture, available at: https://integriculture.jp (last access 12 September 2021).

[121] Pets may soon be fed laboratory-grown meat, Economist 30 January 2021. Available at: https://tinyurl.com/97c849f9 (last access 12 September 2021).

[122] González and Koltrowitz (2021).

[123] Oi (2020).

[124] Mosa Meat, founded in the Netherlands in 2013 available at: https://mosameat.com/ (last access 12 September 2021).

[125] Memphis Meats, founded in 2015, Berkeley, California. Available at: https://www.memphismeats.com/ (last access 12 September 2021).

[126] SuperMeat, founded in Israel in 2015, available at: https://supermeat.com/ (last access 12 September 2021).

[127] Aleph Farms, founded in Israel in 2017, available at: https://aleph-farms.com (last access 12 September 2021).

Technologies;[128] for fish: BlueNalu,[129] for crustaceans: Shiok Meats;[130] for *foie gras*: Gourmey,[131] for mice (to be consumed by cats): Because Animals;[132] for dairy: Perfect Day.[133] The influential animal rights organization, People for the Ethical Treatment of Animals (PETA) has endorsed cell-cultured food,[134] as long as no animal has died for it.

3 Regulation for Innovative Food

Regulation can form a barrier to entry for food,[135] including innovative food. This Section will first shortly deal with the quality regulation of novel foods, whereby the Singapore Food Administration (SFA) is used as a case study, since this administration has already approved the manufacturing and sales of cell-cultured food.

3.1 Quality Regulation

According to the SFA:

> Novel foods are foods and food ingredients that do not have a history of safe use. A history of safe use is defined as substances that have been consumed as an ongoing part of the diet by a significant human population, for a period of at least 20 years and without reported adverse human health effects.[136]

---

[128] Future Meat Technologies, founded in Israel in 2018, available at: https://future-meat.com/ (last access 12 September 2021).

[129] BlueNalu, cell-cultured fish, San Diego founded in 2018, available at: https://www.bluenalu.com/ (last access 12 September 2021).

[130] Singapore's Shiok Meats; crustacean meats. Available at: https://shiokmeats.com. How artificial shrimps could change the world, Economist, 8 February 2020. Available at: https://www.economist.com/asia/2020/02/08/how-artificial-shrimps-could-change-the-world (last access 12 September 2021).

[131] Gourmey, available at: https://gourmey.com. (last access 12 September 2021). An ethical foie gras, without force-feeding and slaughter by 2023 or 2024.

[132] Pets may soon be fed laboratory-grown meat, Economist 30 January 2021. Available at: https://tinyurl.com/97c849f9 (last access 12 September 2021).

[133] Von Massow and Gingerich (2019).

[134] Yes, This Is Actual Meat, but No Animal Died for It, PETA, 21 March 2017. Available at: https://www.peta.org/living/food/memphis-meats-debuts-lab-grown-chicken-clean-meat/ (last access 12 September 2021).

[135] Snyder (2016, forthcoming).

[136] Requirements for the Safety Assessment of Novel Foods, version dated 23 November 2020. Available at: https://tinyurl.com/9xxyyxex (last access 12 September 2021).

Therefore, most plant-based products are not considered novel foods according to that definition. Unsurprisingly, those plant-based product companies that would like to use genetically modified organisms (GMO) will not be able to export to regions with tighter GMO regulation. However, most relevant to cell-cultured animal-based products is that "novel foods may also include compounds that are chemically identical to naturally-occurring substances, but produced through advances in technology."[137] Food businesses that intend to use novel foods for cell-cultured meat are required to submit an application to SFA by providing the information about the nutritional composition, identity, and source of cell lines, a description of methods used for selection and screening of cells; information on how the cell lines are prepared and banked following their extraction from animals; description of the modifications and adaptations made to the cell lines, and how these relate to the expression of substances that may result in food safety risk; information related to the culture media used, including the composition of media, identities, and purity of all added substances. The SFA must study the safety of all individual media substances, conduct tests to ascertain if the level of residual substances of the scaffoldings are safe, or if the components that are not absorbed have been completely removed from the cells. The types of tests used to determine the safety of media components are the same as those applied to any new food ingredient being introduced into the market, and include both chemical and toxicological characterization.[138]

In the US, the United States Department of Agriculture (USDA) and Food and Drug Administration (FDA) together will regulate cell-cultured food products from cell lines of livestock and poultry.[139]

In the EU, Article 3(2)(a)(vi) of Regulation (EU) 2015/2283 on novel foods stipulates that "food consisting of, isolated from, or produced from a cell culture or tissue culture from animals, plants, micro-organisms, fungi or algae"[140] is considered one of the novel food categories listed in the regulation. According to Vytenis Andriukaitis, at the time European Commissioner for Health and Food Safety: "Cultured meat may fall in this category. In such case, it would require a pre-market authorisation which would include a safety assessment performed by the European Food Safety Authority (EFSA)."[141]

---

[137] Requirements for the Safety Assessment of Novel Foods, version dated 23 November 2020. Available at: https://tinyurl.com/9xxyyxex (last access 12 September 2021).

[138] Requirements for the Safety Assessment of Novel Foods, version dated 23 November 2020. Available at: https://tinyurl.com/9xxyyxex, (last access 12 September 2021) paras 12 and 13.

[139] USDA and FDA Announce a Formal Agreement to Regulate Cell-Cultured Food Products from Cell Lines of Livestock and Poultry, USDA 7 March 2019. Available at: https://tinyurl.com/4sscpa9d (last access 12 September 2021).

[140] Regulation (EU) 2015/2283 of the European Parliament and of the Council of 25 November 2015 on novel foods, OJ L 327, 11.12.2015, pp. 1–22. Available at: https://eur-lex.europa.eu/eli/reg/2015/2283/oj (last access 12 September 2021).

[141] Parliamentary question: Mara Bizzotto, E-004200-18, 30 July 2018. Available at: https://www.europarl.europa.eu/doceo/document/E-8-2018-004200_EN.html (last access 12 September 2021).

3.2 Standard of Identity of Food; the Checkpoint for TiL Legislation

In 2015, in *Davis v Hampton Creek, Inc.*,[142] Unilever sued Just Mayo (Hampton Creek, Inc.), a manufacturer of egg-free mayonnaise for its "pervasive pattern of fraudulent, deceptive, false, and otherwise improper advertising, sales, and marketing practices" by selling a sandwich spread named "Just Mayo" that does not contain eggs. Unilever tried to stop Just Mayo from taking market share away from its own mayonnaise brand "Hellman's" that used eggs. The court ordered Unilever to demonstrate why this case should not be dismissed for lack of subject matter jurisdiction. After Hampton Creek, Inc. announced that it raised USD 90 million of investments, it learned that Unilever had dropped its lawsuit against it and even praised it for its "commitment to innovation and its inspired corporate purpose."[143] In 2018, Unilever launched its own egg-free mayonnaise: "Hellmann's Vegan Mayo".[144]

3.2.1 Standard of Identity for Food

Standard of identity for food: mandatory requirements which are set by a governing body that determine what a food product must contain to be marketed under a certain name in allowable commerce. In the US, the Code of Federal Regulations, Title 9 Animal and Animal Products, Part 319, provides definitions and standards of identity or composition of several meat names, for example, "Hamburger".[145] The USDA Food Standards and Labeling Policy Book is intended to be a guide to help manufacturers and prepare product labels that are truthful and not misleading. Examples: "Taco" must include at least 15 percent meat; "Samosa", which, traditionally is a vegetarian product, must include at least 25 percent meat. Inconsistencies include: "turkey ham" which is described as not pork, but "cured turkey thigh meat".

The dairy sector has a specific tradition of regulating production and trade through identity standards, and identity standards for milk and milk products are still important as legislative references for local and international trade. It is

---

Answer from Andriukaitis on behalf of the European Commission, E-004200/2018(ASW) 8 October 2018. Available at: https://www.europarl.europa.eu/doceo/document/E-8-2018-004200-ASW_EN.html (last access 12 September 2021).

[142] Davis v Hampton Creek, Inc., 2015 WL 13652723 (S.D. Florida 2015) Not Reported in Fed. Supp.

[143] Mac (2014).

[144] Selwood and O'Mahony (2018).

[145] Code of Federal Regulations, Title 9 Animal and Animal Products, Part 319, Subpart B—Raw Meat Products, §319.15(b). Available at: https://tinyurl.com/5nuwna66 (last access 12 September 2021).

interesting to notice that the word "milk" is defined in the Code of Federal Regulations, in Title 21, Part 131 Milk and Cream:

> Milk means the lacteal secretion, practically free from colostrum, obtained by the complete milking of one or more healthy cows [...].[146]

If this definition were taken seriously, that milk is only coming from healthy cows, this would mean that if the cows are not healthy that the milk could not be called as such.[147]

For example, results showed that 89.0 percent of U.S. dairy operations in 2007 had cattle seropositive for Bovine Leukosis Virus.[148] "Intramammary infections [mastitis or udder infections], as defined by positive milk cultures, were present in 48.5% of all cows,"[149] and causes pus to leak into the milk.[150] Bovine Respiratory Diseases come back every year in cattle and humans.[151]

In the EU, Regulation (EU) No. 1308/2013, Part III of Annex VII, provides a definition of milk:

> 1. 'Milk' means exclusively the normal mammary secretion obtained from one or more milkings without either addition thereto or extraction therefrom.[152]

In October 2016, two Italian MEPs, Paolo de Castro from the Socialists and Democrats party and Giovanni La Via from the European People's Party, urged the European Commission to intervene and regulate vegan and vegetarian products that use meat names, and introduce EU legislation to safeguard certain names relating to meat products, as was the case for dairy products.[153] At the end of 2016, Christian Schmidt, at the time German Federal Minister of Food and Agriculture, also advocated for a ban in the EU on meat names for plant-based products,[154]

---

[146] CFR, Title 21, Part 131, § 131.110 Milk. Available at: https://tinyurl.com/3kvddnws (last access 12 September 2021).

[147] Vegan Product Labeling Wars, Mic the Vegan, 16 April 2017. Available at: https://www.youtube.com/watch?v=iUyJpHVNXAY (last access 12 September 2021).

[148] Bovine Leukosis Virus (BLV) on US Dairy Operations, 2007, APHIS, Info Sheet, October 2008. Available at: https://tinyurl.com/yjbjk75y (last access 12 September 2021).

[149] Wilson et al. (1997).

[150] A litre of milk can have up to 400,000,000 somatic cells (pus cells) before it is considered unfit for people to drink. Ten things you should know about dairy [...], Animal Aid, 1 June 2017. Available at: https://tinyurl.com/3ev8fm42 (last access 12 September 2021).

[151] Van der Poel (1994).

[152] Regulation (EU) No 1308/2013 of the European Parliament and of the Council of 17 December 2013 establishing a common organisation of the markets in agricultural products, OJ L 347, 20.12.2013, pp. 671–854. Available at: https://eur-lex.europa.eu/eli/reg/2013/1308/oj (last access 12 September 2021).

[153] Question for written answer E-008161-16 to the Commission Rule 130, Paolo De Castro (S&D), Giovanni La Via (PPE) 28 October 2016. Available at: https://www.europarl.europa.eu/doceo/document/E-8-2016-008161_EN.html?redirect (last access 12 September 2021); Michail (2016).

[154] Schmidt will Verbot von Fleischnamen für Veggie-Produkte, Bild 28 December 2016. Available at: https://tinyurl.com/3pwamm9x (last access 12 September 2021).

because according to Schmidt: designations such as "vegetarian schnitzel" and "vegan curry sausage" are "completely misleading and are unsettling the consumer".[155] In the case of the German word "Schnitzel", one should know that it means "slice", so therefore "Papierschnitzel", is a slice of paper. This makes Smidt's assertion that "schnitzel" should be reserved for animal-based food dubious. At the time, the European Commission decided that there was no need for new regulation in this regard. In Germany, the Deutsche Lebensmittelbuch-Kommission (German Food Code Commission)[156] provided national guidelines, that are not binding. According to this commission, the designations for vegan/vegetarian foods are usually based on designations for cut pieces of meat, e.g., "vegan schnitzel", as far as there is a sufficient sensory similarity to the referred food of animal origin, especially in appearance and mouthfeel.[157] In contrast, designations for specific sausage products (e.g., "salami") are not common for vegan and vegetarian foods, according to the German Food Code Commission, and should be called "vegan tofu-sausage in salami-style".[158] These heuristics are not entirely convincing. "Consumers nor producers are happy with the rules."[159]

In France,[160] you could no longer use the name "fromage vegan" ("vegan cheese"), since a decree of 2007.[161] On 19 April 2018, a bill was adopted in France, to prohibit certain deceptive marketing practices for consumers, which associate terms such as "steak", "tenderloin", "bacon", and "sausage", with products which are not only, or not at all, composed of meat. More generally concerned are names referring to products of animal origin, in particular milk, cream, or cheese.[162]

---

[155] Schmidt will Verbot von Fleischnamen für Veggie-Produkte, Bild 28 December 2016. Available at: https://tinyurl.com/3pwamm9x (last access 12 September 2021).

[156] Deutsche Lebensmittelbuch-Kommission, Leitsätze für vegane und vegetarische Lebensmittel mit Ähnlichkeit zu Lebensmitteln tierischen Ursprungs Neufassung vom 04. Dezember 2018 (BAnz AT 20.12.2018 B1, GMBl 2018 S. 1174). Available at: https://tinyurl.com/yj5h47yz (last access 12 September 2021).

[157] Deutsche Lebensmittelbuch-Kommission, Leitsätze für vegane und vegetarische Lebensmittel mit Ähnlichkeit zu Lebensmitteln tierischen Ursprungs Neufassung vom 04. Dezember 2018 (BAnz AT 20.12.2018 B1, GMBl 2018 S. 1174). Available at: https://tinyurl.com/yj5h47yz (last access 12 September 2021), p. 5.

[158] Deutsche Lebensmittelbuch-Kommission, Leitsätze für vegane und vegetarische Lebensmittel mit Ähnlichkeit zu Lebensmitteln tierischen Ursprungs Neufassung vom 04. Dezember 2018 (BAnz AT 20.12.2018 B1, GMBl 2018 S. 1174). Available at: https://tinyurl.com/yj5h47yz (last access 12 September 2021), pp. 5–6.

[159] Labelling on plant-based products—Felix Domke and Julia Schneider at the New Food Conference 2019, ProVeg International 15 August 2019. Available at: https://www.youtube.com/watch?v=HljNlViHYk8 (last access 12 September 2021).

[160] Henriques (2020).

[161] Decree n°2007–628 of 27 April 2007 relating to cheeses and cheese specialties. Available at: https://www.legifrance.gouv.fr/loda/id/LEGITEXT000006056036/ (last access 12 September 2021); See also Poussard (2017).

[162] Bill n°627 for the balance of commercial relations in the agricultural and food sector and healthy and sustainable food, 19 April 2018. Available at: https://tinyurl.com/4y6k37eu (last access 12 September 2021).

However, on 25 October 2018, the Constitutional Council of France held the decree to be unconstitutional because it was unrelated to the initial object of the bill.[163] On 4 December 2019, the bill was successfully reintroduced.[164]

In 2017, the Court of Justice of the European Union (CJEU) in *TofuTown.com* confirmed that milk, as pointed out in Part III of Annex VII of Regulation (EU) No. 1308/2013, exclusively relates to the normal mammary secretion.[165] "Milk" and other dairy-related names could no longer be used as the designation of a plant-based beverage in the EU: the so called "dairy ban". The addition of descriptive or clarifying additions that indicate the plant origin of the product concerned has no influence on that prohibition, except if it is on a list of exceptions of the European Commission from 2010, which includes "products the exact nature of which is clear from traditional usage and/or when the designations are clearly used to describe a characteristic quality of the product," such as coconut milk, cacao butter, and peanut butter.[166] Thus, plant-based dairy products had to rebrand,[167] which can be costly for producers and confusing for consumers.

3.2.2 Reform of Regulation (EU) No. 1308/2013

On 7 May 2019, the Committee on Agriculture and Rural Development adopted the AGRI Report prepared by rapporteur Éric Andrieu, which included the Amendments 165 ("veggie burger ban") and 171 (extension of the existing "dairy ban") as part of a proposal for the regulation of the European Parliament and of the Council amending Regulations (EU) No. 1308/2013, establishing a common organisation of the markets in agricultural products.[168]

---

[163] Decision n°2018–771 DC of 25 October 2018, Constitutional Court. Available at: https://tinyurl.com/5hebw5jv (last access 12 September 2021).

[164] Bill 362, law on the transparency of the information on agricultural products and food. Available at: https://www.assemblee-nationale.fr/dyn/15/textes/l15t0362_texte-adopte-seance (last access 12 September 2021).

[165] C-422/16 Verband Sozialer Wettbewerb eV v TofuTown.com GmbH, Judgment of the Court (Seventh Chamber) of 14 June 2017, ECLI:EU:C:2017:458.

[166] The list of exceptions appears in Commission Decision 2010/791/EU of 20 December 2010 listing the products referred to in the second subparagraph of point III(1) of Annex XII to Council Regulation (EC) No 1234/2007 (OJ 2010 L 336, p. 55).

[167] "Oatly Milk" became "Oatly Drink".

[168] Report on the proposal for a regulation of the European Parliament and of the Council amending Regulations (EU) No 1308/2013 establishing a common organisation of the markets in agricultural products, (EU) No 1151/2012 on quality schemes for agricultural products and foodstuffs, (EU) No 251/2014 on the definition, description, presentation, labelling and the protection of geographical indications of aromatised wine products, (EU) No 228/2013 laying down specific measures for agriculture in the outermost regions of the Union and (EU) No 229/2013 laying down specific measures for agriculture in favour of the smaller Aegean islands (COM(2018)0394 – C8-0246/2018 – 2018/0218(COD)). Available at: https://www.europarl.europa.eu/doceo/document/A-8-2019-0198_EN.html (last access 12 September 2021).

Amendment 165 "Veggie Burger Ban"

"Meat" would mean the edible parts of the animals, including blood. The meat-related terms and names that fall under Article 17 of Regulation (EU) No. 1169/2011 and that are currently used for meat and meat cuts shall be reserved exclusively for edible parts of the animals, or products containing meat. The amendment provided some examples of designations reserved for animal-based products: "steak"; "sausage"; "escalope"; "burger"; and "hamburger".

Poultry products and cuts defined in Regulation (EU) No. 543/2008 shall be reserved exclusively for edible parts of the animals and products containing poultry meat.[169] On 23 October 2020, the European Parliament voted against Amendment 165.[170] However, Amendment 72, which was adopted by the European Parliament,[171] states that Annex VII to Regulation (EU) No. 1308/2013[172] "may prescribe the conditions under which [certain product names] are protected [...] against unlawful commercial use, misuse, imitation or evocation." The Commission has the power to modify the annex, by adding or removing names of the list through a delegated act. This leads, on the one hand, to flexibility and, on the other hand, to legal uncertainty.

Amendment 171 Extension of the Existing "Dairy Ban"

Amendment 171 aimed to extend the prohibition for plant-based products to use dairy names.

Those dairy designations shall also be protected from:

---

[169] Report on the proposal for a regulation of the European Parliament and of the Council amending Regulations (EU) No 1308/2013 establishing a common organisation of the markets in agricultural products, (EU) No 1151/2012 on quality schemes for agricultural products and foodstuffs, (EU) No 251/2014 on the definition, description, presentation, labelling and the protection of geographical indications of aromatised wine products, (EU) No 228/2013 laying down specific measures for agriculture in the outermost regions of the Union and (EU) No 229/2013 laying down specific measures for agriculture in favour of the smaller Aegean islands (COM(2018)0394 – C8-0246/2018 – 2018/0218(COD)). Available at: https://www.europarl.europa.eu/doceo/document/A-8-2019-0198_EN.html (last access 12 September 2021).

[170] 283 MEPs were in favour, 379 were against, and 27 abstentions. Plenary vote on amendment 165 by European Parliament, 23 October 2020, 136–137. Available at: https://www.europarl.europa.eu/doceo/document/PV-9-2020-10-23-RCV_EN.pdf (last access 12 September 2021).

[171] 471 in favour, 182 were against, and 39 abstentions. Plenary vote on amendment 72 by European Parliament, 23 October 2020, pp. 66–67. Available at: https://tinyurl.com/2mfyjpf8 (last access 12 September 2021).

[172] Regulation 1308/2013, Annex VII. Available at: https://tinyurl.com/44p5zpjd (last access 12 September 2021).

(a) any direct or indirect commercial use of the designation;

  (i) for comparable products or products presented as capable of being substituted not complying with the corresponding definition;

This part of the provision makes comparisons of plant-based products with dairy products impossible, while these are important for consumers to make informed choices about health, sustainability, and ethicality. Information such as that the production of a plant-based product causes 75 percent less emission of greenhouse gases than an animal-based product becomes impossible.

  (ii) in so far as such use exploits the reputation associated with the designation;

This part of the provision is broad and opaque. The question is, for example, if a plant-based beverage can use the word "creamy", or is this exploiting the reputation associated with dairy products?

(b) any misuse, imitation or evocation, even if the composition or true nature of the product or service is indicated or accompanied by an expression such as "style", "type", "method", "as produced in", "imitation", "flavour", "substitute", "like" or similar;

A very similar provision against usurpation, imitation, and evocation, the EU is also applying for protected designations of origin and protected geographical indications.[173] In this case, it would prohibit informative texts such as "dairy free", "contains no milk", and "alternative to butter", which would clarify ingredients, use, and function of the plant-based product for consumers. However, when the European Union Intellectual Property Office (EUIPO) rejected the registration of the slogan "It's like milk but made for humans" as a trademark by plant-based beverage producer Oatly,[174] conform the CJEU's decision in *TofuTown.com* in June 2017,[175] the Board of Appeal to the General Court of the EU came with a surprising decision on 20 January 2021:

> The applicant adds that the initial perception of the relevant public will not be that cow's milk is food for calves, but that it is produced for human consumption. It argues that it follows that the phrase 'it's like milk but made for humans' calls into question the relevant public's perception of milk as a substance intended for human beings by evoking the controversial idea that milk is not appropriate for human consumption. It submits that, consequently, that phrase, taken as a whole, is original, imaginative, paradoxical, surprising,

---

[173] Article 13.1(b) Regulation (EU) No 1151/2012 of the European Parliament and of the Council of 21 November 2012 on quality schemes for agricultural products and foodstuffs, OJ L 343, 14.12.2012, pp. 1–29.

[174] Vanni (2019).

[175] "Purely plant-based products cannot, in principle, be marketed with designations, which are reserved by EU law for animal products. The same is true if those designations are accompanied by clarifying or descriptive terms indicating the plant origin of the product concerned." C-422/16 *Verband Sozialer Wettbewerb eV v TofuTown.com GmbH*, Judgment of the Court (Seventh Chamber) of 14 June 2017, ECLI:EU:C:2017:458.

thought provoking and unexpected and is therefore capable of performing the essential function of a trade mark.[176]

This seems to be a teleological interpretation of EU law that is more aligned with the policy as articulated in the Farm to Fork Strategy[177] than the *TofuTown.com* decision.[178] One might wonder whether it is still such a "controversial idea" to assert that milk is not healthy in the face of growing evidence.[179]

(c) any other commercial indication or practice likely to mislead the consumer as to the product's true nature or composition.

This part of the provision is uncontroversial. Deception and confusion of the consumer should and can be prevented by disclaimers and clarifications on the label and front-of-package label.[180]

However, this provision shall not apply to the designation of products the exact nature of which is clear from traditional usage and/or when the designations are clearly used to describe a characteristic quality of the product.[181]

This part of the provision allows leeway for the courts to make exceptions.

On 23 October 2020, the European Parliament voted in majority for the adoption of Amendment 171.[182] Trilogue negotiations involving the European Parliament, the EU Council of Ministers, and the European Commission could still change the wording of the provision or reject it altogether.[183] However, on 24 May 2021, after a massive outcry of 34 organizations and more than 457,000 petitions, the European Parliament, European Council and European Commission withdrew Amendment 171.[184]

---

[176] Case T-253/20, Oatly AB v. EUIPO, Judgment of the General Court (Second Chamber) 20 January 2021, ECLI:EU:T:2021:21, para. 38.

[177] A Farm to Fork Strategy for a fair, healthy and environmentally friendly food system Communication from the Commission to the European Parliament, the Council, the European Economic and Social Committee and the Committee of the Regions, Brussels, 20 May 2020 COM (2020) 381 final, 2 and 13. Available at: http://tiny.cc/0mbstz (last access 12 September 2021).

[178] Friedmann (2021a).

[179] Milk and other dairy products are the top source of saturated fat in the American diet, contributing to heart disease, type 2 diabetes, and Alzheimer's disease. Studies have also linked dairy to an increased risk of breast, ovarian, and prostate cancers. Physicians Committee for Responsible Medicine. Available at: https://www.pcrm.org/good-nutrition/nutrition-information/health-concerns-about-dairy (last access 12 September 2021).

[180] Similar provisions can be found in consumer protection law, unfair competition law, trademark law and protection of geographical indications.

[181] *Supra* footnote 168.

[182] 386 MEPs were in favour, 290 against, and 16 abstentions. Vote on amendment 171 by European Parliament, 23 October 2020, 30–31. Available at: http://tiny.cc/7l9stz (last access 12 September 2021).

[183] Southey (2021).

[184] Barry (2021) and Friedmann (2021b).

3.2.3 Mismatch of Amendment 171 with EU Policy Goals

Despite the goals of the EU to have "[f]ood information [which] shall be accurate, clear and easy to understand for the consumer",[185] the provision of Amendment 171 did not further these laudable goals. The European consumer organization BEUC characterized the adoption of Amendment 171 as a missed opportunity and that it had nothing to do with consumer protection.[186] In addition, it flies in the face of the EU policy goals, articulated clearly in the "Farm to Fork Strategy"[187] and "European Green Deal",[188] in regard to empowering consumers to make informed choices that make it easier for consumers to choose healthy and sustainable diets.

Health

The Farm to Fork Strategy makes clear that the EU is well aware that "the average intakes of energy, red meat,[189] sugars, salt and fats continue to exceed recommendations, consumption of whole-grain cereals, fruit and vegetables, legumes and nuts is insufficient."[190] The Farm to Fork Strategy promotes the transition to sustainability and sees this as a "first mover" opportunity for the food industry in the EU.[191] It determined that the healthy choice is not always the easiest for consumers to select so far; especially since many labels are not very informative about sugar, fat, and salt content, and do not provide consumers an incentive to read the labels. One can argue that Amendment 171 would not have been conducive in this respect. The Farm to Fork Strategy points out that moving to a more plant-based diet with less red and processed meat and with more fruits and vegetables will reduce not only the risks of life-threatening diseases, but also the environmental impact of the food system.[192] It is estimated that in the EU in 2017, over 950,000 deaths (one out of five people) and

---

[185] Article 7(2) Regulation (EU) No 1169/2011 of the European Parliament and of the Council of 25 October 2011 on the provision of food information to consumers, ELI: http://tiny.cc/y7bstz (last access 12 September 2021).

[186] Southey (2021).

[187] A Farm to Fork Strategy, supra footnotes 177, 2 and 13. Available at: http://tiny.cc/0mbstz (last access 12 September 2021).

[188] European Green Deal, sets out how to make Europe the first climate-neutral continent by 2050. It maps a new, sustainable and inclusive growth strategy to boost the economy, improve people's health and quality of life, care for nature, and leave no one behind. A European Green Deal. Available at: https://ec.europa.eu/info/strategy/priorities-2019-2024/european-green-deal_en (last access 12 September 2021).

[189] Red meat includes beef, pig meat, lamb, and goat meat and all processed meats.

[190] Willett et al. (2019).

[191] Farm to Fork Strategy, supra footnotes 177 and 3.

[192] FAO and WHO (2019), Sustainable healthy diets – guiding principles.

over 16 million lost healthy life years were attributable to unhealthy diets, mainly cardiovascular diseases and cancers.[193]

The EU also wants to reduce the dependency on antimicrobials that leads to an estimated 33,000 human deaths in the EU/European Economic Area every year,[194] improve animal welfare, and the labelling in this respect through the food chain.[195]

Sustainability

As mentioned above, a plant-based diet can contribute to reducing greenhouse gas emissions. On 11 December 2020, the European Council endorsed a new 2030 target for emission reduction.[196] On 17 December 2020, the European Council approved the updated and enhanced target of at least a 55 percent reduction in greenhouse gas emissions by 2030 compared to 1990, in regard to the Paris Agreement,[197] and achieving climate neutrality by 2050.[198]

> Agriculture is responsible for 10.3% of the EU's [Greenhouse Gas] GHG emissions and nearly 70% of those come from the animal sector. They consist of non-CO2 GHG (methane and nitrous oxide). In addition, 68% of the total agricultural land is used for animal production.[199]

The EU assesses any proposal for support in regard to meat from the perspective of the need for overall sustainability.[200] However, it has been reported that previous drafts of the Farm to Fork Strategy were tougher on meat.[201]

---

[193] EU Science Hub. Available at: https://ec.europa.eu/jrc/en/health-knowledge-gateway/societal-impacts/burden (last access 12 September 2021).

[194] "There is an urgent need to reduce dependency on pesticides and antimicrobials, reduce excess fertilisation, increase organic farming, improve animal welfare, and reverse biodiversity loss." Farm to Fork Strategy, supra footnotes 177, 3 and 8.

[195] Farm to Fork Strategy, supra footnotes 177, 7 and 8.

[196] EU leaders agreed on a binding EU target for a net domestic reduction of at least 55% in greenhouse gas emissions by 2030 compared to 1990. European Council, 10–11 December 2020. Available at: https://www.consilium.europa.eu/en/meetings/european-council/2020/12/10-11/ (last access 12 September 2021).

[197] Paris Agreement on climate change, Council of the EU. Available at: https://www.consilium.europa.eu/en/policies/climate-change/paris-agreement/ (last access 12 September 2021).

[198] Commission proposal for a Regulation of the European Parliament and of the Council establishing the framework for achieving climate neutrality and amending Regulation (EU) 2018/1999 (European Climate Law), COM (2020) 80 final, 2020/0036 (COD).

[199] Farm to Fork Strategy, supra footnotes 177 and 7.

[200] Farm to Fork Strategy, supra footnotes 177, 7 and 8.

[201] Foote (2020a).

Ethics

The Farm to Fork Strategy presents health and sustainability as the two pillars that justify a transition from animal-based to plant-based food production. However, one can argue that there is a third pillar: ethicality. To not apply the negative form of the golden rule, "do not treat others in ways that you would not like to be treated" to all sentient beings demonstrates speciesism.[202] In Rawls' thought-experiment of the "original position", a fair society can only be developed under a veil of ignorance.[203] The legislator would not know which position he will be assigned in this society: perhaps he will return as a man or woman, healthy or handicapped, *etc*. Although Rawls never explicitly included the possibility that someone returned to society as a non-human animal, one could argue that this would perfect Rawls' thought experiment to make society truly fair for all sentient beings.

> If there was a good possibility that you could be born a cow and bred in a factory farm (after all, cows outnumber humans), would you make it legal for factories to confine and kill cows for their milk, meat, and skin?[204]

Transition

The Farm to Fork Strategy proposes tax incentives that should drive the transition to a sustainable food system and encourage consumers to choose sustainable and healthy diets. Value-added tax (VAT) rates could allow Member States to support organic fruit and vegetables.[205] The EU also wants to avoid marketing campaigns advertising meat at very low prices.[206]

> EU tax systems should also aim to ensure that the price of different foods reflects their real costs in terms of use of finite natural resources, pollution, GHG emissions and other environmental externalities.[207]

Finally, it seems that the European Commission was willing to acknowledge that the market has gone awry in the case of animal-based products and correct this by internalizing the negative externalities of animal-based products in the price by

---

[202] "Racists violate the principle of equality by giving greater weight to the interests of members of their own race when there is a clash between their interests and the interests of those of another race. Sexists violate the principle of equality by favouring the interests of their own sex. Similarly, speciesists allow the interests of their own species to override the greater interests of members of other species. The pattern is identical in each case." Singer (1990), pp. 6, 9.

[203] Rawls (1971); See also Harsanyi (1955).

[204] Justice for all: what the veil of ignorance shows us about a just society, anonymous, undated. Available at: https://www.animal-ethics.org/justice-for-all-what-the-veil-of-ignorance-shows-us-about-a-just-society/ (last access 12 September 2021).

[205] Farm to Fork Strategy, supra footnotes 177 and 14.

[206] Farm to Fork Strategy, supra footnotes 177 and 12.

[207] Farm to Fork Strategy, supra footnotes 177 and 14.

adding a Pigouvian tax,[208] to the value of the negative externalities. In addition, the EU also wants to avoid the externalisation and export of unsustainable practices.[209] This makes a lot of sense in the case of global warming and the risk of another worldwide pandemic due to zoonotic diseases.

However, if one takes the Amendment 171 into account, it seems the EU was taking one step forward, two steps back, only corrected at the eleventh hour.

Clear Information

> The provision of clear information makes it easier for consumers to choose healthy and sustainable diets, will benefit their health and quality of life, and reduce health-related costs.[210]

To make this happen, the European Commission proposes harmonised mandatory front-of-pack nutrition labelling and examines ways to harmonise voluntary green claims and to create a sustainable labelling framework that covers the nutritional, climate, environmental, and social (but not the explicit ethical) aspects of food products. It seems that Amendment 171 would have been counterproductive for achieving these goals as well.[211]

3.3 Farm to Zoonotic Disease

The Farm to Fork Strategy asserts that there is no connection between the current COVID-19 pandemic to food safety in the EU.[212] However, it linked the wildlife trade and consumption to possible future diseases and pandemics,[213] but not the other arguably more important link between factory farming and the risk for zoonotic diseases.[214] It also does not link animal-based food production and the risk that workers at slaughterhouses in the EU run to be infected with COVID-19.[215]

---

[208] A Pigouvian tax is a tax assessed against private individuals or businesses for engaging in activities that create adverse side effects for society.

[209] Farm to Fork Strategy, supra footnotes 177 and 7.

[210] Farm to Fork Strategy, supra footnotes 177 and 13.

[211] Farm to Fork Strategy, supra footnotes 177 and 13.

[212] Farm to Fork Strategy, supra footnotes 177, 10 and 11.

[213] Farm to Fork Strategy, supra footnotes 177 and 17.

[214] Cowspiracy: The Sustainability Secret 2014. Available at: https://www.cowspiracy.com/ (last access 12 September 2021).

[215] Foote (2020b); Francis Snyder, Public Health, Food Safety and Global Standards, Six Lessons from COVID-19, PKU Global Open Talks, 21 August 2020. Available at: https://www.youtube.com/watch?v=K7gSeUJ1hpk (last access 12 September 2021).

"Horizon 2020", the research framework of the EU, will focus explicitly on increasing the availability and source of alternative proteins such as plant, microbial, marine, and insect-based proteins and meat substitutes,[216] and algae industry.[217] The EU examines rules to reduce the dependency on critical feed materials (especially soy grown on deforested land) by fostering EU-grown plant proteins as well as the abovementioned alternative feed materials and by-products from the bio-economy (e.g., fish waste).[218]

4 TiL, Transparency and Commercial Speech

The manufacturers of animal-based products use the TiL movement in the US to exclusively use animal-based terms for their products, and exclude plant-based and cell-cultured products from using them. In order to do so, they rely on definitions that are sometimes older than 50 years and do not take into account the "foodscape" and societal realities. In August 2018, Missouri passed legislation prohibiting the use of animal-based designations for plant-based products.[219] In 22 states, especially those with substantial interests in factory farming, similar legislation was proposed with varying degrees of success: Alabama,[220] Arkansas,[221] Arizona,[222] Colorado,[223] Georgia,[224]

---

[216] Farm to Fork Strategy, supra footnotes 177 and 15.

[217] Farm to Fork Strategy, supra footnotes 177 and 10.

[218] Communication from the Commission to the European Parliament, the Council, the European Economic and Social Committee and the Committee of the Regions – A sustainable Bioeconomy for Europe: Strengthening the connection between economy, society and the environment, COM/2018/673 final.

[219] MO. ANN. STAT. § 265.494(7) (West 2018), amended by 2018 Mo. Legis. Serv. S.B. 627 & 925. [Missouri Senate Bill 627, passage date 17 May 2018 and entry into force on 1 June 2018.]

[220] Alabama HB 518/Act No. 2019-310, passage date 23 May 2019 and entry into force on 1 August 2019. Available at: https://legiscan.com/AL/bill/HB518/2019 (last access 12 September 2021).

[221] Arkansas Act 501, Section 1, 2-1-302, passage date 18 March 2019. Available at: http://www.arkleg.state.ar.us/assembly/2019/2019R/Acts/Act501.pdf (last access 12 September 2021).

[222] Arizona House Bill 2604, introduction date 11 February 2019, dead on 4 March 2019. Available at: https://legiscan.com/AZ/text/HB2604/id/1936512/Arizona-2019-HB2604-Engrossed.html (last access 12 September 2021).

[223] Colorado HB 1102, introduction date 14 January 2019. Available at: https://legiscan.com/CO/text/HB1102/id/1848025/Colorado-2019-HB1102-Introduced.pdf (last access 12 September 2021).

[224] Georgia Senate Bill 211, introduction date 27 February 2019, pending the House Agriculture and Consumer Affairs Committee on 11 March 2019. Available at: http://tiny.cc/m2estz (last access 12 September 2021).

Illinois,[225] Indiana,[226] Iowa,[227] Kentucky,[228] Louisiana,[229] Maine,[230] Mississippi,[231] Montana,[232] Nebraska,[233] New Mexico,[234] North Dakota,[235] Oklahoma,[236] South Carolina,[237] Tennessee,[238] Texas,[239] Vermont,[240] and Virginia.[241]

---

[225] Illinois House Bill 2556, introduction date 13 February 2019, re-referred to Rules Committee on 29 March 2019. Available at: https://legiscan.com/IL/text/HB2556/id/1907380/Illinois-2019-HB2556-Introduced.html (last access 12 September 2021).

[226] Indiana HB 1414, introduction date 14 January 2019, was planned to become effective as of 1 July 2019, but died in the House Agriculture and Rural Development Committee. Available at: https://legiscan.com/IN/text/HB1414/id/1848501/Indiana-2019-HB1414-Introduced.pdf (last access 12 September 2021).

[227] Iowa Senate Bill 404, introduction date 27 February 2019, pending Senate Agriculture Committee. Available at: https://legiscan.com/IA/text/SF404/id/1934993/Iowa-2019-SF404-Introduced.html (last access 12 September 2021).

[228] Kentucky HB 311, introduced on 11 February 2019, passage date 21 March 2019 and entry into force 27 June 2019. Available at: http://tiny.cc/ujestz (last access 12 September 2021).

[229] Louisiana Act No. 273, passage date 11 June 2019 and entry into force on 1 October 2020. Available at: https://legiscan.com/LA/text/SB152/2019 (last access 12 September 2021).

[230] Maine HB 351, passage date 12 June 2019 and entry into force on 12 June 2019. Available at: https://legiscan.com/ME/text/LD351/id/2042774/Maine-2019-LD351-Chaptered.pdf (last access 12 September 2021).

[231] Mississippi HB 793, introduction date 1 January 2019. Available at: https://legiscan.com/MS/text/HB793/id/1869911/Mississippi-2019-HB793-Engrossed.html (last access 12 September 2021).

[232] Montana HB 327, passage date 18 April 2019 and entry into force 19 April 2019. Available at: https://legiscan.com/MT/text/HB327/id/1978370/Montana-2019-HB327-Enrolled.pdf (last access 12 September 2021).

[233] Nebraska Legislative Bill 14, introduction date 10 January 2019. Bill was withdrawn on 24 January 2019. Available at: https://legiscan.com/NE/text/LB14/id/1843274/Nebraska-2019-LB14-Introduced.pdf (last access 12 September 2021).

[234] New Mexico HB 222, introduction date 15 January 2019, action postponed indefinitely on 5 February 2019. Available at: https://legiscan.com/NM/text/HB222/id/1846760/New_Mexico-2019-HB222-Introduced.pdf (last access 12 September 2021).

[235] North Dakota House Concurrent Resolution 3024, introduced on 22 January 2019, passage date on 7 March 2019 and entry into force on 1 August 2019. Available at: https://legiscan.com/ND/text/3024/id/1949032/North_Dakota-2019-3024-Enrolled.pdf (last access 12 September 2021).

[236] Oklahoma Senate Bill 392, passage date 26 April 2019 and entry into effect on 26 July 2019, according to Article V, Section 58 Oklahoma Constitution. Available at: https://legiscan.com/OK/bill/SB392/2019 (last access 12 September 2021).

[237] South Carolina Act No. 79, introduced on 13 March 2019, passage date 16 May 2019 and entry into effect on 16 May 2019. Available at: https://legiscan.com/SC/text/H4245/2019 (last access 12 September 2021).

[238] Tennessee SB 0003, introduction date 5 December 2018. The proposal has been withdrawn on 29 January 2019. Available at: https://legiscan.com/TN/text/SB0003/id/1828128/Tennessee-2019-SB0003-Draft.pdf (last access 12 September 2021).

[239] Texas House Bill 2761, introduction date 28 February 2019, dead in committee on 23 April 2019. Available at: https://legiscan.com/TX/text/HB2761/id/1938584/Texas-2019-HB2761-Introduced.html (last access 12 September 2021).

[240] Vermont House Bill 233, introduction date 14 February 2019, pending House Agriculture and Forestry Committee on Available at: http://tiny.cc/72fstz (last access 12 September 2021).

[241] Virginia HB 2274, introduction 8 January 2019. This bill was dead on 5 February 2019. Available at: https://legiscan.com/VA/text/HB2 (last access 12 September 2021).

Section 265.494 of Missouri's TiL legislation provides:

> No person advertising, offering for sale or selling all or part of a carcass or food plan shall engage in any misleading or deceptive practices, including, but not limited to, any one or more of the following: (7) Misrepresenting the cut, grade, brand or trade name, or weight or measure of any product, or misrepresenting a product as meat that is not derived from harvested production livestock or poultry.[242]

Section 265.300 provides a definition of "meat", which now also includes any edible portion captive cervid (deer) carcass or part thereof, next to livestock and poultry,[243] and of "commercial plant" as a euphemistic term for slaughter house.[244]

Most states' statutes prohibit the sales and marketing of animal-based designations if the product does not derive from an animal, or if it derived from an animal as is the case in cell-cultured food, that it is "not slaughtered for harvest in the traditional manner",[245] to prevent consumer confusion. Some states also prohibit dairy designations, not derived from the milk of a cow, goat, or other mammal. However, Oklahoma states that plant-based items are not considered in violation of the provisions, so long as the packaging displays that the product is derived from plant-based sources. Virginia makes clear that names for meat food products can be used for non-animal products, to the extent that their labels bear a type of uniform size and prominence, the word "imitation" and, immediately thereafter, the name of the meat food product imitated.

Kentucky urges the USDA to promulgate administrative regulations requiring imitation meat product manufacturers to adopt labelling and marketing terminology that is fully distinct from those traditional terms connoting "real" meat products, so that consumers can readily distinguish "real" meat products from imitation meat products or plant-based alternatives.

South Carolina does not allow the use of the designations "meat" or "clean meat" that is cell-cultured meat/protein, but these can be used for plant-based meat substitutes.

North Dakota states that a cell cultured protein product may not be packaged in the same, or deceptively similar, packaging as a meat food product; and must be labelled as a cell-cultured protein food product. Texas prescribes that if a non-animal-based food's label includes a claim comparing the food's nutritional value to that of meat, it should do so by disclosing the human benefit of the food.[246]

---

[242] Missouri Senate Bill 627, Section A "Section 265.494". Available at: http://tiny.cc/rjfstz (last access 12 September 2021).

[243] Missouri Senate Bill 627, Section A "Section 265.300(7)".

[244] Missouri Senate Bill 627, Section A "Section 265.300(4)": "'Commercial plant', any establishment in which livestock [or], poultry, or captive cervids are slaughtered for transportation or sale as articles of commerce intended for or capable of use for human consumption, or in which meat or meat products are prepared for transportation or sale as articles of commerce, intended for or capable of use for human consumption."

[245] Nebraska.

[246] Texas House Bill 3799, Section 1, "433A.0003".

In the case of Louisiana, a person that violates the TiL provision shall be fined an amount not to exceed USD 500 and, in Arkansas and Texas, USD 1000 for each violation per day. In Nebraska and South Carolina, upon conviction, a person must be either imprisoned not more than one year, or fined not more than USD 1000 per day, or both.

In several states, including Arkansas, Louisiana, and Missouri, lawsuits were brought against state legislation and enforcement actions against plant-based products that use animal-based designations, violating their First Amendment that protects manufacturers' right of commercial speech.[247]

In September 2019, Turtle Island Foods, doing business as Tofurky, challenged the Missouri statute that prohibits it from using meat-related names for its plant-based products, via a preliminary injunction.[248] However, the District Court dismissed the motion for preliminary injunction, since the statute at issue does not prohibit their speech, according to the court. In 2020, Turtle Island and the Good Food Institute (GFI) appealed this decision at the 8th Cir.[249]

Turtle Island Foods, GFI, American Civil Liberties Union (ACLU), and Animal Legal Defense Fund (ALDF) also challenged the Arkansas statute. In December 2019, The Arkansas court granted its motion for preliminary injunction, finding that Arkansas's statute is likely unconstitutional on the merits.[250]

In 2020, the GFI, ACLU, and ALDF challenged the Louisiana law on behalf of Turtle Island Foods,[251] at the U.S. District Court for the Middle District of Louisiana.

Federal legislation for cell-cultured meat and poultry was introduced in April 2019 that would lead to further legislation:

> Not later than 18 months after the date of enactment of this Act, the Secretary, in consultation with the Commissioner, shall issue final regulations 1) that prescribe the type and frequency of inspection required for the manufacture and processing of food products; and (2) for the prevention of the adulteration and misbranding of food products.[252]

---

[247] U.S. Const. amend. I, XIV §2.

[248] Turtle Island Foods, SPC v. Richardson, 2019 WL 7546586, at *5 (W.D. Mo., 30 September 2019).

[249] Turtle Foods, SPC, v Thomson 2020 WL 767362 (C.A.8).

[250] Turtle Island Foods, SPC v. Soman, 2019 WL 7546141, at *10 (E.D. Ark., 11 December 2019); Hauss (2019); See also Owens (2019).

[251] Tofurky Files First Amendment Challenge Against Louisiana Label Censorship Law, Animal Legal Defense Fund 7 October 2020. https://aldf.org/article/tofurky-files-first-amendment-challenge-against-louisiana-label-censorship-law/ (last access 12 September 2021).

[252] US Congress Senate Bill 1056, introduced on 4 April 2019, read twice and referred to the Committee on Agriculture, Nutrition, and Forestry. HR 4881. Available at: http://tiny.cc/ahgstz (last access 12 September 2021).

4.1 "A Solution in Search of a Problem"[253]

In January 2017, Senator Tammy Baldwin of Wisconsin proposed the Defending Against Imitation and Replacement of Yogurt, Milk, and Cheese to Promote Regular Intake of Dairy Everyday (DAIRY PRIDE) Act,[254] which would "require enforcement against misbranded milk alternatives." It was rejected. In September 2018, the FDA requested comments about labelling plant-based alternatives of dairy foods. In a comment to the FDA, the Plant Based Foods Association has called the DAIRY PRIDE Act "a solution in search of a problem."[255] FDA Commissioner Scott Gottlieb resigned in March 2019 and the bill has been reintroduced in the Senate, and it was rejected again.

Tom Balmer of the National Milk Producers Federation (NMPF) testified before the congressional subcommittee about the bill:

> Allowing non-dairy products to use dairy terms to promote goods with wildly different nutritional values has undermined public health and directly flouts the FDA's own rules.[256]

The Gleckel survey, see below, has demonstrated that no consumer confusion could be observed in regard to the nutritional value differences between animal-based and plant-based products. The claim that the different nutritional values have undermined public health is not convincing. According to Vasanti Malik, professor of nutrition at the Harvard T.H. Chan School of Public Health, for humans, there is no nutritional requirement for dairy products specifically,[257] and the ingredients that are in dairy can be found in plant-based products as well. On the contrary, milk can have several health drawbacks related to pathogens,[258] antibiotics residues,[259] hormones, lactose-intolerance, and is linked to several cancers.[260] One can argue that if the NMPF is right about the violations of the FDA's standard of identity, which the FDA has never enforced, for dairy product labelling, this would point to the need to update that standard to the new "foodscape" and societal realities. Dairy sales decreased because of oversupply and decreased consumption. Each successive

---

[253] Josh Tetrick of Just Mayo: "We need to update our regulations to fit a modern world with modern problems [...] and some solutions that are being used to fix them. Especially in food." Linneken (2016), p. 88.

[254] Dairy Pride Act, S. 130, 115th Cong. (2017). Rejected.

[255] Watson (2019).

[256] Newhart (2020).

[257] Plant milk or cow's milk: Which is better for you?, Harvard Health Publishing, Harvard Medical School. Available at: http://tiny.cc/9vgstz (last access 12 September 2021).

[258] The presence of various pathogens like Bacillus spp, Listeria spp, Salmonella spp and Escherichia coli O157:H7 in milk and milk products, especially made from raw, unpasteurized milks have been known to be sources of foodborne illnesses and diarrhoeal diseases around the world; Vanga and Raghavan (2018).

[259] Sachi et al. (2019).

[260] Ganmaa and Sato (2005).

generation consumes less animal-based milk. In the US, due to trade conflicts, retaliatory tariffs also contributed to fewer dairy exports.

> Competition from non-dairy alternatives to cow's milk also plays a small role in the decrease in revenue for dairy farms. Nondairy alternatives account for about 1.8 billion dollars of the total milk market while cow's milk represents about 12 billion dollars of that market.[261]

4.2 The Knife Cuts Both Ways

Transparency is a great good. But the knife cuts both ways: if transparency should apply to non-animal-based products, so should it apply to animal-based products to avoid "greenwashing"[262] and "humane-washing".[263] Therefore, it should apply to all the ingredients of animal-based food; clarifying the hormones, antibiotics, and other medicines added. Also adding the circumstances under which the animals are kept; from birth to slaughter. The link between the animals and the animal-based products has been either effectively concealed or camouflaged, and the link between the animals and their suffering has also been covered.

4.2.1 Deceptive Advertisements

Advertisements such as "La vache qui rit" (The laughing cow); and packages depict idyllic, bucolic portraits of animals in the meadow, such as on the packs of milk. Melkunie, for example, depicts a head of a calf surrounded by green grass and meadow flowers.[264] The reality is that the calves are directly removed from their mother, that the male calves' movements will be confined to make the meat more tender; that the calves are fed an all-liquid milk-substitute, purposely deficient in iron and fiber to give white color to the meat,[265] is not shared. Melkunie's "meadow milk" is using the Qlib certified "outdoor grazing" label, which entails that cows can stay indoors for a maximum of 245 days. Melkunie articulated their communication goal very clearly: "All the good for our cows! Ever since 1872 we would like to

---

[261] Lucas (2019).

[262] "Greenwashing" is to make people believe that your company is doing more to protect the environment than it really is. Cambridge Dictionary. Available at: https://dictionary.cambridge.org/us/dictionary/english/greenwash (last access 12 September 2021).

[263] "Humane washing" is the practice of making a misleading claim about the treatment of animals or the conditions in which they are born, raised, or killed. How False Advertising Lawsuits Help Animals, Animal Legal Defense Fund. Available at: https://aldf.org/article/how-false-advertising-lawsuits-help-animals/ (last access 12 September 2021).

[264] Melkunie. Q&A. Available at: https://www.melkunie.nl/qa/ (last access 12 September 2021).

[265] Dairy, Vegan Peace. Available at: https://www.veganpeace.com/animal_cruelty/dairy.htm (last access 12 September 2021).

contribute to a good feeling every day."²⁶⁶ Quite apart from its effects on human animals, does "all the good" include the cows and their feelings? Cows have the potential to live over 20 years but are repeatedly artificially impregnated in the animal farms and are already slaughtered after 3 or 4 birth cycles when the milk production is levelling off. Cow milk from Dutch Lady, part of Friesland Campina, a Dutch multinational dairy cooperative, depicts cows in the meadows, but cows are increasingly kept in the stable the whole year round.²⁶⁷ The name Dutch Baby Milk Industries was replaced by Dutch Lady after complaints from the International Baby Food Action Network.²⁶⁸ Monitoring has highlighted evidence of continuous, systematic violations of the International Code from the Dutch baby food company Friesland Campina²⁶⁹ and other milk companies that promote milk from a cow as a healthy alternative for breastfeeding, which it is not.

Research by Good Fish, at the request of the Consumentenbond (Dutch Consumer Organization) has determined that:

> EU legislation, regarding consumer labelling, has been fully implemented by just 1 out of the 97 locations visited. The other 99% of fish stores and stalls did not meet the EU's demands for consumer labelling of fishery and aquaculture products. An inspection of the labels has determined that more than 50% of the fish stores and stalls place labels next to their products but that these are often lacking mandatory information.²⁷⁰

4.2.2 Ag-Gag Laws

Lazare describes ag-gag as:

> Animal rights activism – in the form of farm occupations, protests, undercover investigations, and the resulting exposes – produces information that is otherwise kept hidden and that is crucial to public discourse on society's treatment of animals and on the ethics and morality of meat consumption and food production methods.²⁷¹

By restraining the freedom of expression, the animal-industrial complex was not only partly successful in securing TiL regulation, but it was also partly successful in securing ag-gag laws, which forbid undercover filming, photography, or audio-recording of activity on farms and sometimes also prohibit interaction with animals

---

[266] Al het goede voor onze koeien, Melkunie! 7 March 2019. Available: https://www.melkunie.nl/melkunie-stories/2019/3/al-het-goeie-voor-onze-koeien/.

[267] Thieme (2014).

[268] Breaking the Rules, Stretching the Rules 2004, Friesland, pp. 22–24. Available at: http://ibfan.org/art/302-8.pdf (last access 12 September 2021).

[269] Report on the Situation of Infant and Young Child Feeding in the Netherlands, The Committee on the Rights of the Child, Session 69/May-June 2015, 15. Available at: https://www.etoconsortium.org/nc/en/main-navigation/library/documents/?tx_drblob_pi1%5BdownloadUid%5D=153 (last access 12 September 2021).

[270] Duurzame vis bij viswinkels en viskramen, Een duik in het diepe, Consumentenbond, February 2021. Available at: http://tiny.cc/hajstz (last access 12 September 2021).

[271] Lazare (2020), p. 89.

in transport trucks, without the consent of their owner.[272] For the sake of transparency and the avoidance of consumer deception, live streaming of the places where animals are kept, stables, and transport cars and abattoirs, would be recommendable. This would quickly correct misconceptions consumers might have about the bucolic fairy tale portrayed in advertisements and on packages.

4.2.3 Country-of-Origin

Mandatory country-of-origin-labelling (COOL),[273] labeling of food sold in the United States was characterized as protectionist,[274] because it does not fit well within the globalist vision where animals and animal-based products can be traded between countries. After Canada and Mexico prevailed at the WTO in regard to removing the mandatory COOL law,[275] the US repealed the law for beef and pork, as part of an omnibus budget bill in 2015.[276] For example, under the Comprehensive Economic and Trade Agreement (CETA) between Canada and the EU, and since Canada is a member of the U.S.–Mexico–Canada Trade Agreement, animals or animal-based products from Mexico and the US can be traded via Canada to the EU under the conditions of CETA.[277] It has been argued that the level of animal welfare in these countries is very unequal. The WTO ultimately decided that if consumers want a country-of-origin labelling scheme, the market could provide it on a voluntary basis.[278]

4.2.4 Food Libel Laws

Then there are food disparagement laws in 13 states in the US that make it easier for food producers to sue their critics: under the Texas False Disparagement of Perishable Food Products Act of 1995, the plaintiff does not need to prove that the

---

[272] Lazare (2020).

[273] 7 U.S.C. §1638a.

[274] Dalrymple (2019).

[275] Canada and Mexico challenged mandatory COOL law of the US, because it treated imported livestock less favorably than domestic livestock: which caused a trade-distorting impact by reducing the value and the number of cattle and swine that were shipped to the U.S.

[276] Found in Section 759 of US Bill 2029. Available at: http://tiny.cc/a6kstz (last access 12 September 2021).

[277] According to the Mandatory origin-label schemes in 8 member countries of the EU, a country not from the EU can simply described as non-EU. Available at: https://www.europarl.europa.eu/RegData/etudes/BRIE/2018/625182/EPRS_BRI(2018)625182_EN.pdf (last access 12 September 2021).

[278] World Trade Organization, United States: Certain Country of Origin Labelling (COOL) Requirements, WT/DS384/AB/R, 29 June 2012, 209, https://docs.wto.org/dol2fe/Pages/SS/directdoc.aspx?filename=Q:/WT/DS/386ABR.pdf (last access 12 September 2021).

defendant is deliberately and knowingly spreading false information, as is usual under a US libel suit, but has to convince a jury that the statements were not based on reasonable and reliable scientific inquiry, facts, or data. In 1998 in *Texas Beef Group v Ophrah Winfrey*, Texas cattlemen sued television talk show host, producer and a guest, alleging false disparagement of perishable food products, common law business disparagement, common law defamation, based on comments concerning the danger of contracting "Mad Cow Disease," from beef because cows had been fed cows. The District Court held that: cattlemen failed to prove a violation of Texas' statute; and Texas cattlemen could not maintain a defamation claim under Texas law due to the failure to show that statements about feeding practices of American cattlemen were "of and concerning" them.[279] The Texas cattlemen appealed, but in 2000, the 5th Cir. affirmed the decision of the District Court.[280] One can argue that these kinds of statutes violate commercial speech or at least have a chilling effect on the freedom of expression in regard to the (animal-based) food industry.

4.3 Consumer Confusion or Commercial Speech

In 2013, in a case against WhiteWave at the United States District Court, Northern District of California, for WhiteWave's use of the designation "milk" for plant-based alternatives, the Court agreed with WhiteWave that the names "soymilk", "almond milk", and "coconut milk" accurately describe the defendants' products. As set forth in the regulations, these names clearly convey the basic nature and content of the beverages, while clearly distinguishing them from milk that is derived from dairy cows. Judge Samuel Conti held:

> [...] it is simply implausible that a reasonable consumer would mistake a product like soymilk or almond milk with dairy milk from a cow. The first words in the products' names should be obvious enough to even the least discerning of consumers. And adopting Plaintiffs' position might lead to more confusion, not less, especially with respect to other non-dairy alternatives such as goat milk or sheep milk.[281]

4.3.1 Empirical Research

The advocates of the TiL regulation have argued that the protection of consumers against confusion is a substantial governmental interest, which legitimizes the government to prohibit commercial speech. In 1980, *Central Hudson Gas & Elec. Corp. v. Public Serv. Comm'n of N.Y.*, the Supreme Court of the US has developed

---

[279] Texas Beef Group v. Winfrey, 11 F.Supp.2d 858, (US District Court N.D. Texas, 1998).

[280] Texas Beef Group v. Winfrey, 201 F.3d 680 (5th Cir. 2000).

[281] Alex Ang v Whitewave, 2013 WL 6492353 not reported in Fed. Supp. (D.C., N.D. California 2013).

the intermediate scrutiny test for commercial speech,[282] that needs to be protected under the First Amendment to the US Constitution: As long as the speech in question does not concern unlawful activity and is not inherently misleading, *Central Hudson* requires that: (1) the government has a substantial interest in prohibiting the speech; (2) the government's regulation directly advances the asserted governmental interest; and (3) the regulation is "not more extensive than is necessary to serve that interest."

In September 2019, the National Cattlemen's Beef Association (NCBA), the lobby organization for factory farming in the US, commissioned a survey that was aimed at proving consumer confusion relative to plant-based meat.[283] However, Gleckel points out that their survey does not demonstrate any significant consumer confusion.[284] The respondents of the NCBA survey could answer 4 questions in regard to the question of what the meaning is of plant-based meat: 1. Is completely vegan, containing no meat or animal byproducts (eggs, dairy); 2. Does not contain meat but may contain animal byproducts; 3. Can contain small amounts of meat, but is primarily plant-based; and 4. Contains meat, and there are no restrictions on the amount. It is clear that the 45 percent who chose answer 1. was not confused, but arguably, neither were those who chose answers 2. and 3., representing 31 percent and 17 percent, respectively, since these answers can be interpreted to deal with cross-contamination. Just as in the case of a product that warns "may contain peanuts".[285] Only 7 percent chose question 4., which points to confusion. In other words: 45 + 31 + 17 = 93 percent that was not confused versus 7 percent that was confused. This survey corresponds to the one conducted by the Federation of German Consumer Organizations where only 4 percent of the participants said they were confused and unwittingly bought a plant-based product.[286]

Gleckel was curious to see whether confusion could be determined in the case of plant-based products, and if companies would not use animal-based words, whether consumers would more likely be confused about the taste and function of the plant-based products. He used a "between subjects" design: One group answered questions about animal products, including terms such as "beef," or "butter", the control group answered questions about products that omitted these terms and replaced them with terms such as "veggie" or "spread."[287] Finally, Gleckel also explored whether participants expected "plant-based" products to have any animal products. Gleckel's survey shows that consumers are no more likely to think that plant-based products

---

[282] Central Hudson Gas & Elec. Corp. v. Public Serv. Comm'n of N.Y., 447 U.S. 557, 566 (1980).

[283] Meat Substitute Brand Understanding, National Cattlemen's Beef Association 2019. Available at: https://www.ncba.org/Media/NCBAorg/Docs/Media/NCBA%20Meat%20Substitutes%20Survey.pdf (last access 13 September 2021).

[284] Gleckel (2020), pp. 9–10.

[285] Gleckel (2020), p. 10.

[286] Domke (2018), p. 105.

[287] The research took precautionary measures, such as distractor questions, to avoid biases. The limitation of research is the sample size of 155 participants that were for two-third female, so that female participants were over-represented. Gleckel (2020), p. 26.

come from an animal if the product names incorporate words traditionally associated with animal products than if they do not.[288] *A fortiori*, omitting words that are traditionally associated with animal products from the names of plant-based products, actually increases consumer confusion about the taste and uses of these products, although it does not impact consumers' understanding of the products' nutritional attributes. Gleckel's survey has demonstrated that the prohibitions against using the names for animal-based products for plant-based products are not directly advancing the asserted governmental interest, namely the protection of consumers against confusion. On the contrary, this leads to consumer confusion about the functions of these products. And even if one could prove that there is a substantial governmental interest to prohibit commercial speech, and if the prohibition of the commercial speech would directly advance the governmental interest of protecting consumers against confusion, then one can argue that there are more proportional measures possible, such as a clarification of the differentiation between animal-based and plant-based products on the label.

In addition, the Food Drugs & Cosmetics Act (FDCA) contains a broad preemption provision which prohibits states or other political subdivisions from imposing any requirements regarding standard of identity that is not identical to the federal requirements.[289] The FDCA requires a food to be identified by "the common or usual name of the food, if any there be."[290] FDA regulations require that a "statement of identity" must be in terms of: (1) the name prescribed by federal law or regulation, "(2) [t]he common or usual name of the food; or, in the absence thereof, (3) [a]n appropriately descriptive term, or when the nature of the food is obvious, a fanciful name commonly used by the public for such food."[291]

4.3.2 Piggybacking on the Plant-Based Popularity Diluting the Meaning of Plant-Based

Gleckel's study also provides preliminary evidence that consumers expect "plant-based" products to not contain any animal products. Therefore, one can argue that using chicken eggs in products labelled "plant-based", such as Tyson's "Raised and Rooted: Plant-Based Nuggets" is misleading to consumers.[292] Thus a prohibition of the word "plant-based" for this product could be justified, or at least a clarification on

---

[288] The vast majority of participants thought it was either very unlikely (66.1%) or unlikely (22%) that "Next Generation Meat: Plant-Based Beef Burger" came from a cow; Next Generation Vegetables: Plant-Based Veggie Patty."; The vast majority of participants thought it was either very unlikely (61.5%) or unlikely (29%) that this product was made from a cow. Gleckel (2020), supra footnote 283, p. 18.

[289] 21 U.S.C. § 343–1(a).

[290] 21 U.S.C. §343(i).

[291] 21. C.F.R. § 101.3(b).

[292] Gleckel (2020), p. 24.

the labelling: such as "not 100 percent plant-based" or "includes eggs" on the front-of-pack label.

5 Labelling and the Government's Role to Stimulate or Stifle Certain Food

Domke states that food labelling influences and guides consumers:

> Considering, for example, a 'meaty' schnitzel and a 'vegan schnitzel', the appearance of both is round and breaded, the taste is salty, both are prepared by frying and eaten in a sandwich or with chips as an accompaniment. All these pieces of information are transported simply by the use of the word 'schnitzel'.[293]

If there are no specific TiL prohibitions in place, the manufacturer of innovative food can decide what name to use for its products: names of products can be brought within the purview of trademark law. The names of products are generic if they point to a category or class of goods: for example, in case of the plant-based products: "veggie burger" or "veggie dog".

Every producer should be able to use that name and it cannot be registered as a trademark. If a name is descriptive, for example, "meatless meatballs", it cannot be registered as a trademark, for the same reason as generic marks, unless the mark has acquired distinctiveness, by educating the (potential) consumers that the name can also refer to the source of the goods, such as "Meatless Farm" often accompanied with a certain distinctive font, logo, or use of colours.[294]

If a name is pointing to the source of the goods; it can be either suggestive ("Happy Cow" for vegan ice-cream; "Gardein" for vegan products), arbitrary ("Impossible" for vegan burgers; "Silk" for soy milk) or fanciful ("Alpro" plant-based drinks). In these cases, the name is distinctive, and the name can be registered as a trademark.[295]

The producers of plant-based alternatives for meat products often use misspellings (Chik'n, Toona, Sheese), allusions and wordplays (Tofurky) and superlatives (Impossible, Incredible, Beyond), which some perceive to signal inferior quality and/or to be infantilizing to vegetarians.[296] One can argue that names should have intuitive clarity, since consumers often make a decision in a split second. Despite the EU law, consumers in the street still call margarine, which is plant-based, "butter", because its functionality is similar. "The language is already on the street."[297]

---

[293] Domke (2018), pp. 104–105.

[294] Smithers (2020).

[295] Abercrombie & Fitch Co. v. Hunting World, 537 F.2d 4 (2nd Cir. 1976).

[296] Lange (2019).

[297] Rogier Smeets of Upfield. Plant-based naming and labelling: How draft regulation fits into the Farm to Fork strategy, EURACTIV 15 October 2020. Available at: https://www.youtube.com/watch?v=brgJ1UNlg7g (last access 12 September 2021).

Manufacturers of animal-based products also would like to have the monopoly on some qualifiers such as "traditional, "natural" and "simple". However, it is often a false comparison to argue that animal-based products are "traditional", "natural", "simple" and plant-based products are "non-traditional", "artificial" and "complex".[298]

5.1 Contradictory Campaigns

The EU has committed to achieving ambitious goals in regard to the reduction of greenhouse gases, which should conclude in carbon neutrality by 2050. This policy goal can be reached if the livestock is reduced, since it is responsible for about a quarter of the greenhouse gases. A reduction of the livestock would also reduce the supply of animal-based food, which would help increase the price of animal-based food in relation to plant-based food. The other important policy goal of the EU is to reduce health costs which can also be realized by a reduction of consumers' animal-based food intake. Despite these policy goals, the EU spent Euro 60 million to promote eating meat from the EU, while the "Voedingscentrum" a centre that gives recommendations about food, fully owned by the Dutch government, has started a campaign for men to eat less meat,[299] since "there is a sufficient relation between eating red meat, especially processed meat, and stroke, diabetes 2 and cancer",[300] and men were overrepresented in eating meat.

The EU financed campaigns between 2016–2018 to promote the consumption of pork,[301] and between 2017–2019 to promote the consumption of fruit and vegetables.[302] As the campaigns of the EU and Dutch government demonstrate, these campaigns can be contradictory and confusing to the consumer. Is it the EU or national government's role to incentivize a certain food while disincentivizing other food, and what kind of information should a label convey to consumers? Global warming and the COVID-19 pandemic demonstrate that sustainability and health

---

[298] Camille Perrin. Plant-based naming and labelling: How draft regulation fits into the Farm to Fork strategy, EUACTIV, 15 October 2020. Available at: https://www.youtube.com/watch?v=brgJ1UNlg7g (last access 12 September 2021).

[299] Voedingscentrum lanceert mannencampagne "Er is meer dan vlees", November 2018, Voedingscentrum. Available at: http://tiny.cc/vnlstz (last access 12 September 2021).

[300] Vlees, Voedingscentrum. Available at: https://www.voedingscentrum.nl/encyclopedie/vlees.aspx (last access 12 September 2021).

[301] Pork lovers Europe €1,366,348.20, 2016–2018. Consumers, Health, Agriculture and Food Executive Agency, available at: https://ec.europa.eu/chafea/agri/en/campaigns/pork-lovers-europe (last access 12 September 2021); See also Daniel Boffey, EU spending tens of millions of euros a year to promote meat eating, The Guardian 14 February 2020. Available at: http://tiny.cc/13mstz (last access 12 September 2021).

[302] Information programme on healthy eating practices linked to fruit and vegetable consumption € 1,204,956,00, 2017–2019. Consumers, Health, Agriculture and Food Executive Agency, available at: http://tiny.cc/3hmstz (last access 12 September 2021).

can have a transnational dimension. The EU has a shared jurisdiction with the EU countries in regard to public health.[303] It could play a positive role on the one hand in creating a legal framework where labels can inform consumers about health, sustainability, and ethicality, so that citizens of the EU can make well-informed decisions; on the other hand, by not subsidizing the animal-based food industry, which is not fair to the plant-based food industry.

5.2 Subsidies to the Animal-Based Industry

On 21 October 2020, the European Parliament voted in favour of a proposal by the European Commission to reform the Common Agricultural Policy (CAP) for the years 2021–2027, and approved a budget of Euro 387 billion that includes the continuation of 60 percent of the current direct payments to factory farmers with weak or non-existent green conditions attached. 37 percent of funds will be directed to measures to reduce greenhouse gases, soil conservation, improving water resources, and animal welfare. There will be 20 percent of direct payments for mandatory eco-schemes, but countries can propose their own eco-schemes to be approved by the European Commission. Given that such eco-schemes will not kick in during the CAP transitional period (2021 and 2022)[304] and that the EU ministers agreed on a two-year pilot phase, they will not become binding until 2025.

In the Netherlands, livestock farmers can receive subsidies to emit fewer greenhouse gases, ammonia, odour, and particulate matter/endotoxins. From 2020 to 2030, Euro 172 million is available for the subsidy modules for source-oriented sustainability of stable and management measures.[305] So instead of letting farmers and ultimately the consumers pay for these measures that reduce some negative externalities in regard to sustainability, the government is paying that for them. These costs are thus passed on to all tax payers in the Netherlands, including to those consumers who do not buy animal-based products. Livestock farmers also do not have to pay for the negative health effects that are caused by the consumption of animal-based products, nor for the risk of another pandemic that their method of production is causing, nor for the costs if a new pandemic would manifest. Although it has been known for the last twenty years that factory farming has become unsustainable,[306] unhealthy, and unethical, and induces zoonotic diseases, due to

---

[303] Articles 4.1.k and 168 Treaty on the Functioning of the European Union (TFEU).

[304] EU farm policy 2021–2022: MEPs approve transitional rules and €8bn recovery aid, News European Parliament, 16 December 2020. Available at: http://tiny.cc/ywmstz (last access 12 September 2021).

[305] Kan ik subsidie krijgen om mijn veehouderij te verduurzamen? Rijksoverheid. Available at: http://tiny.cc/8cnstz (last access 12 September 2021).

[306] Steinfeld et al. (2006).

several subsidy programmes it remained lucrative for farmers to be active in this industry.

5.3 Regulatory Capture

The influence of lobbyists in democracies cannot be underestimated. In the US, the federal government and many state governments favor animal food producers for subsidies: they receive more than thirty times the financial aid that fruit and vegetable growers receive.[307]

The biggest part of the subsidies is allocated to corn and soybean, which are mostly used for livestock feed.[308] Livestock feed is an important part of the costs of raising animals (half the costs for hogs, two-thirds for poultry and eggs). Simon estimates that in the US a total of USD 38.4 billion is given to the animal-based food industry each year.[309] The rationalizations for these subsidies vary from assisting the income of small farmers, ameliorate rural development, stabilizing commodity markets, and promoting national food security. However, subsidies distort the market since products are produced below cost and lead to dumping:[310] the supply is made artificially, which leads to lower prices, and thus much higher demand than in a scenario in which the negative externalities were internalized into the price.

> Given the costs of election campaigns, the lack of public funding for them, and the resistance of Congress to reform campaign finance laws, it is no mystery why legislators might not want to make decisions that displease [Political Action Committee] PAC contributors.[311]

Lopez' empirical research demonstrates that every US dollar given as a campaign contribution by an agricultural donor would yield an investment return of about USD 2000 in subsidy payments.[312]

Regulatory capture seems to have touched institutes such as the USDA. In 2010, nine of the thirteen panellists on the Dietary Guidelines Advisory Committee were linked to the animal-based industry, having served as advisors or consultants to corporations such as Dannon, McDonald's, Kellogg's, Tropicana, and General Mills.[313] This has led to schizophrenic outcomes: the USDA has recommended in covert ways to cut down on animal-based foods for health reasons and replace them

---

[307] Simon (2013a), chapter 5; Barnard (2016).

[308] "[W]e can see that the real winners are not those who produce these commodities, but those who purchase them at a low cost." Starmer et al. (2006).

[309] Simon (2013a), chapter 5.

[310] Dumping: But these small farmers have an even harder time competing when subsidies permit the large business to consistently sell at prices below its own cost of production. Borders and Burnett (2006).

[311] Nestle (2007), p. 105.

[312] Lopez (2001).

[313] Herman (2010).

with plant-based food,[314] but at the same time, it promoted animal-based products.[315] In 2015, the USDA was proposing a program to allocate additional funds, potentially totalling USD 160 million, to promote beef.[316]

5.4 Market Mechanism

> [B]y keeping the system in a perpetual state of disequilibrium, or market failure, the forces of meatonomics create problems that affect almost everyone.[317]

Prices of animal-based products and non-animal-based products have moved in opposite directions. In the US, from 1980 to 2008, the inflation-adjusted prices of ground beef and cheddar cheese decreased by 53 and 27 percent, respectively.[318] While, in about the same period, the inflation-adjusted prices of fruits and vegetables increased by 46 and 41 percent, respectively.[319] Animal-based products have become much cheaper because of efficiency gains and substantial subsidies.

According to Simon, the animal-based industry's total annual retail sales are approximately USD 251 billion. But the total externalized costs of animal food production are USD 414 billion, which is paid by consumers and non-consumers of animal-based products.[320] Simon made an estimate in regard to the true cost of a Big Mac (USD 12), using the formula:

Retail price + (cruelty + environmental losses + subsidies + health care costs) divided by the number of Big Macs.[321] This would change a Big Mac from an impulse purchase to a purchase that requires a bit more consideration. The amount

---

[314] The USDA, its Dietary Guidelines for Americans recommends that less cholesterol and saturated fat is consumed, but it fails to provide examples of foods that contain these substances (namely meat, fish, eggs, and dairy), and to reduce "saturated fatty acids by replacing them with monounsaturated and polyunsaturated fatty acids", which should communicate to consumers that they replacing animal-based foods for plant-based foods. Simon (2013a), chapter 4.

[315] For example: Dairy Management, a checkoff-funded group created by USDA delegates in 1995 to promote dairy sales, has a budget of $136 million and 162 employees. The USDA appoints some of its board members, approves its marketing campaigns and major contracts, and reports to Congress on its work. Simon (2013a), chapter 4.

[316] 66684 Federal Register/Vol. 79, No. 217/Monday, November 10, 2014/Notices. Available at: https://www.govinfo.gov/content/pkg/FR-2014-11-10/pdf/2014-26552.pdf (last access 12 September 2021).

[317] Meatonomics, is economics of the animal food system that imposes huge externalized costs on animals, the environment and taxpayers. Simon (2013a), chapter 5.

[318] US Bureau of Labor Statistics, "Consumer Price Index Average Price Data. Available at: http://www.bls.gov (last access 12 September 2021); Brian W. Gould, "Understanding Dairy Markets. Available at: https://wisconsinidea.wisc.edu/projects/612 (last access 12 September 2021).

[319] Leonhardt (2009).

[320] Simon (2013a), chapter 5.

[321] Simon applied this formula: USD 4.56 for the retail price + USD 0.38 for cruelty (total USD 20.7 billion) + USD 0.67 in environmental losses (total USD 37.2 billion) + USD 0.70 in subsidies (total

for cruelty was extrapolated from a study in which auction participants bid to end cruel farming practices.[322]

There are two ways that negative externalities can be offset. In the case of a polluter, one can pay the polluter not to pollute, or one can demand that the polluter pays if he pollutes. In the case of animal-based food production, the first method seems to be preferred by governments. Animal-based food producers are, for example, generously compensated if they stop their activities ("warm remediation"), even though it is well known for decades that their activities cause substantial negative externalities. It seems not fair that animal-based producers have realized an exceptional position in regard to subsidies, compensation against risks, and tolerance for negative externalities, because of the *idée fixe* of food security, even though animal-based food is not necessary for sustenance. This is very different from entrepreneurs that have to bear their own risks.

The argument of animal-based farmers was often that they produce what the consumer wants. However, within a country such as the Netherlands the consumption of animal-based products is decreasing but the production of animal-based products is growing, since it is for export. This distorts the mechanism where a population can "vote" with their currency to buy certain products over other products. Another distortion can be induced by advertisements of products that are ill-aligned with the values of consumers.

5.5 Efficiency Gains

Animal farming started out to be extensive, where a large area of land was needed. But when animal farming started to follow the path of industrialization and rationalization, animals no longer could graze and find their food outside. Instead, animals were all confined in highly concentrated farms where the feed was brought to the animals and processes automatized to reduce labor costs. Smaller farms were outcompeted by bigger ones, because of the economies of scale, which lead to consolidation, specialization[323] and further concentration of farms, slaughterhouses and processing of meat.[324]

USD 38.4 billion) + USD 5.69 in health care costs (total USD 314 billion incurred by Americans) = USD 12. Simon (2013b).

[322] Simon applied this formula: USD 4.56 for the retail price + USD 0.38 for cruelty (total USD 20.7 billion) + USD 0.67 in environmental losses (total USD 37.2 billion) + USD 0.70 in subsidies (total USD 38.4 billion) + USD 5.69 in health care costs (total USD 314 billion incurred by Americans) = USD 12. Simon (2013b).

[323] In the case of cows: cow calves producers; stocker; feed log industry; slaughter; processing; distribution; retail.

[324] For example: 4 big meatpackers in the US: Tyson, JBS, Cargill, and National Beef, control 85 percent of all beef. In the beginning of 2015, the cattle inventories was at the lowest point in 70 years. Despite demand, R-CALF alleged that due to the anticompetitive practices and antitrust

Simon points out that "animal production" has become more efficient due to selective breeding techniques, feed, hormones, medicines, *etc.*[325] The egg production per chicken doubled in a century,[326] dairy production of cows tripled, the average weight of broiler chickens almost tripled, while their growth rate has more than doubled.[327] However, all of these efficiency gains, have a price: for the animals, for the consumers' health, for the environment, and ultimately for the taxpayer.

6 Conclusion

There is an explosion of the supply of innovative foods such as plant-based and cell-cultured foods that provide a host of benefits in regard to the way they are produced (fewer greenhouse gases, no danger of antimicrobial resistance, no zoonotic diseases, cruelty free) and for the consumer (healthier), while the function, use, and taste are similar to that of animal-based products. To signal this similar function, use, and taste of these innovative food products, their producers and marketeers have used animal-based names.

The animal-based food producers, who saw their market share shrink due to growing demand for plant-based food, were reasonably successful in introducing TiL provisions, especially in the US at the state level, but also in the EU, especially in regard to dairy products. Outdated and inconsistent definitions used in standard identities of food have been used as a checkpoint to decide what name is allowed for a product. In the EU there were two amendments to reform Regulation (EU) No. 1308/2013, which is establishing a common organisation of the markets in agricultural products; Amendment 165 to ban "meaty" names for plant-based food (which was rejected), and Amendment 171 to extend an existing ban to use dairy names for plant-based beverages (which was first accepted but only after a public outcry rejected at the last moment). The implication of Amendment 171 would have been detrimental to the goals set by the Farm to Fork Strategy and European Green Deal of stimulating healthy, more sustainable food, and more transparency for the consumer. Although the Farm to Fork Strategy mentions animal welfare, it has not made ethicality of food production one of the explicit policy goals next to health and sustainability. The application of the veil of ignorance to its legislative process should convince the EU to take the lives of sentient beings, including non-human animals, seriously. The extension of the dairy ban will prohibit any use of dairy-

---

conduct by the 4 big meat processors below, the U.S. cattle market collapsed through 2015 and 2016. Erica Shaffer, Major processors target of R-CALF antitrust lawsuit, Meat + Poultry 24 April 2019. Available at: https://www.meatpoultry.com/articles/21223-major-processors-target-of-r-calf-antitrust-lawsuit (last access 12 September 2021).

[325] Simon (2013a), chapter 5.
[326] Marcus (2005).
[327] Roberts (2000).

related words, even in comparative advertising, which is not conducive to transparency. However, at the eleventh hour, the EU withdrew Amendment 171. Another bright spot was the decision by the Board of Appeal to the General Court of the CJ-EU allowing the slogan for Oatly, which uses the word "milk".

Even though the TiL provisions are introduced under the guise of consumer protection against confusion and improvement of transparency; two surveys, one commissioned by the NCBA and one by an independent researcher, both clearly demonstrate that there was no confusion due to clarifications or descriptive terms indicating the plant origin. Conversely, the independent survey shows that animal-based products that use only the name plant-based without such clarifications or descriptive terms indicating the animal origin are confusing to the consumer. Animal-based food producers are advocating transparency selectively: they have successfully introduced ag-gag laws that should make it impossible to expose animal abuse in farms and animal transports and intimidating food libel laws that potentially could silence criticism. Companies engaged in trading animals or animal-based products globally are in favour of the abolition of laws that require country-of-origin labels, which is adding opacity to the consumer about where the animal or animal-based product was coming from and under what circumstances it was produced, especially in regard to animal welfare.

It does not make any sense that governments finance contradictory campaigns. This is confusing to consumers who might become indifferent to campaign messages. The excesses of regulatory capture of institutions could be prevented by avoiding situations where "a butcher inspects his own steak". Applying this adage, the USDA should focus on quality of agriculture and not on giving dietary health recommendations. Also, in the Netherlands, if there is an outbreak of a zoonotic disease, the Ministry of Health, Welfare, and Sport should take the lead and not the Ministry of Agriculture, Nature, and Food Quality.

If the population of a country, that experiences the most direct harm of negative externalities (directly after the animals, that is), votes with its currency by reducing the purchases of animal-based products, then it cannot be justified that the production, including the negative externalities continue or even increase, because the animal-based products are exported.

Instead of compensating the animal-based farmer for not causing negative externalities, his products should be taxed with a "Pigouvian tax", which is a tax on a market activity that generates negative externalities, to the value of the negative externalities. This would mean, according to Simon, that eggs from a carton that cost USD 5 will cost USD 13 with Pigouvian tax, and a Big Mac of USD 4, will cost 12 USD with Pigouvian tax.

The fight over labels is a sign that animal-based producers are on the defensive. Meat, fish, dairy, and egg analogues can smoothen the transition from animal-based to plant-based food or cell-cultured food. "Any attempt to set our culture against our nature costs us at least the time and energy required to inculcate and enforce a cultural standard which runs counter to our inherited tendencies."[328] Ultimately, this

---

[328] Singer (2011), p. 59.

article touches upon how man relates to nature, or more precisely, how human-animals relate to non-human animals and plants. At present, almost all humans can not only survive but thrive without consuming animal-based products. Those who persist in these practices neglect not only at their own peril their health, but knowingly and willingly contribute to bringing a new zoonotic disease and climate change closer, and maintaining systemic animal cruelty. In light of the available alternatives for a gastronomic experience, this seems a minor price to pay.

Acknowledgments The author likes to thank professors Francis Snyder (Peking University School of Transnational Law), Rostam Neuwirth (University of Macau) and Kai Purnhagen (University of Bayreuth) for participation in the online Workshop "Standards of Food Labels and Pandemics" on 20 January 2021, which was enlightening for this author. In addition, the author highly appreciates the constructive feedback of Professors Snyder and Neuwirth on a previous version of this article and linguistic suggestions of Lyanne Elsener (University of Lucerne).

References

Arcari P (2020) Disconnection & demonisation: COVID-19 shows why we need to stop commodifying all animals, 13 May 2020. Available at SSRN: https://ssrn.com/abstract=3599772 (last access 12 Sep 2021)

Barnard N (2016) Meat and dairy subsidies make America sick. Physicians Committee for Responsible Medicine, 22 July 2016. Available at: https://www.pcrm.org/news/blog/meat-and-dairy-subsidies-make-america-sick (last access 12 Sep 2021)

Bar-On Y, Phillips R, Milo R (2018) The biomass distribution on earth. Proc Natl Acad Sci 115(25). Available at: https://www.pnas.org/content/115/25/6506 (last access 12 Sep 2021)

Barry J (2004) The site of origin of the 1918 influenza pandemic and its health implications. J Transl Med (2004). Available at: https://doi.org/10.1186/1479-5876-2-3 (last access 12 Sep 2021)

Barry S (2021) Cheesed off? Controversial amendment 171 withdrawn from EU. Euronews, 28 May 2021. Available at: https://bit.ly/2XJTpBm (last access 25 Sep 2021)

Becher S, Lai J (2019) How plant-based meat is stretching New Zealand's cultural and legal boundaries. The Conversation 3 December 2019. Available at: https://bit.ly/2Ov299R (last access 12 Sep 2021)

Benatar D (2006) The chickens come home to roost, Editorial. Am J Public Health 97(9): 1545–1546. Available at: https://ajph.aphapublications.org/doi/full/10.2105/AJPH.2006.090431 (last access 22 Sep 2021)

Borders M, Burnett HS (2006) Farm subsidies: devastating the world's poor and the environment. National Center for Policy Analysis, 23 March 2006. Available at: http://tiny.cc/8cnstz (last access 12 Sep 2021)

Boumans et al (2017) The importance of hormonal circadian rhythms in daily feeding patterns: an illustration with simulated pigs. Horm Behav 93. Available at: https://europepmc.org/article/med/28514644 (last access 12 Sep 2021)

Brown K (2020a) The pandemic is not a natural disaster. The New Yorker, 13 April 2020. Available at: https://www.newyorker.com/culture/annals-of-inquiry/the-pandemic-is-not-a-natural-disaster# (last access 12 Sep 2021)

Brown L (2020b) Eating meat: links to chronic disease might be related to amino acids – new findings. Medical Xpress, 17 February 2020. Available at: https://bit.ly/2MW5Hl3 (last access 12 Sep 2021)

Bryant C (2020) Culture, meat, and cultured meat. J Anim Sci 98(8). Available at: https://academic.oup.com/jas/article/98/8/skaa172/5880017 (last access 12 Sep 2021)

Buckwell A, Nadeu E (2018) What is the safe operating space for EU livestock? 2018. Rise Foundation, 7. Available at: https://bit.ly/3brB8NA (last access 12 Sep 2021)

Budkaa H, Will RG (2015) The end of the BSE saga: do we still need surveillance for human prion diseases? Swiss Med Wkly 145; w14212. Available at: https://smw.ch/article/doi/smw.2015.14212 (last access 12 Sep 2021)

Chen F et al (2013) Ten years after SARS: where was the virus from? J Thorac Dis 5(Suppl 2). Available at: https://www.ncbi.nlm.nih.gov/pmc/articles/PMC3747529/ (last access 12 Sep 2021)

Chen S, Kan K, Che C (2020) Wuhan is returning to life. So are its disputed wet markets. Bloomberg News, 8 April 2020. Available at: https://www.bloomberg.com/news/articles/2020-04-08/wuhan-is-returning-to-life-so-are-its-disputed-wet-markets (last access 12 Sep 2021)

Churchill W (1932) Fifty years hence, March 1932. Pop Mech Mag 57(3):390. Available at: https://bit.ly/3c0bG0h (last access 12 Sep 2021)

Dalrymple J (2019) Mandatory COOL: costly and unnecessary. The Heritage Foundation 18 December 2019. Available at: https://www.heritage.org/trade/report/mandatory-cool-costly-and-unnecessary (last access 12 Sep 2021)

de Lauwere C (2003) Welzwijn in de toekomst. Over varkenswensen voor varkensstallen: varkensbehoeften centraal in comfort class: de afweging tussen gevoel en verstand: uitdagingen voor de toekomst. Wageningen: Wageningen UR, Projectgroep Diergericht Ontwerpen. Available at: https://agris.fao.org/agris-search/search.do?recordID=NL2003678863 (last access 12 Sep 2021)

DeGrazia D (1996) Taking animals seriously. Cambridge University Press, Cambridge, England

Domke F (2018) Vegetarian and vegan products – labelling and definitions. Eur Food Feed Law Rev 13:102

Dusseldorp A (2008) Intensieve veehouderij en gezondheid. Overzicht van kennis over werknemers en omwonenden. Rijksinstituut voor Volksgezondheid en Milieu (RIVM). Bilthoven (RIVM briefrapport). Available at: https://bit.ly/3f2V9Mi (last access 12 Sep 2021)

Dyer C (2019) Undercover footage shows cows fitted with "portholes" into their stomachs at a French research facility so scientists can study their digestion, as activists call for the practice to be banned. Daily Mail 21 June 2019. Available at: https://bit.ly/30t6Aod (last access 12 Sep 2021)

Erway C (2018) The Buddhist Mock-Meats Paradox. Taste Cooking, 25 April 2018. Available at: https://www.tastecooking.com/buddhist-mock-meats-paradox/ (last access 12 Sep 2021)

Felbab-Brown V (2017) The extinction market: wildlife trafficking and how to counter it. OUP

Foote N (2020a) Farm to Fork Strategy softens stance on meat but backs alternative proteins. EURACTIV 22 May 2020. Available at: http://tiny.cc/ijdstz (last access 12 Sep 2021)

Foote N (2020b) Working conditions in meat processing plants make them hotbed for COVID-19. EURACTIV 27 June 2020. Available at: http://tiny.cc/zjcstz (last access 12 Sep 2021)

Foucart S (2019) Pandémie de Covid-19: le virus circulait sans doute en France dès novembre 2019, Le Monde 10 February 2021. Available at: https://www.lemonde.fr/planete/article/2021/02/10/le-sars-cov-2-circulait-sans-doute-en-france-des-novembre-2019_6069431_3244.html (last access 12 Sep 2021)

Friedmann D (2020) Correcting information asymmetry via deep consumer information; compelling companies to let the sunshine. In: Mathis K, Tor A (eds) Consumer law and economics. Springer, Cham, Switzerland, pp 151–176. Available at SSRN: https://ssrn.com/abstract=3373012 (last access 12 Sep 2021)

Friedmann D (2021a) Food labels, trademarks and how to prevent the next pandemic. J Intellect Prop Law Pract (Oxford University Press) (March 2021). Available at: https://doi.org/10.1093/jiplp/jpab060 (last access 12 Sep 2021)

Friedmann D (2021b) Factory farming a greater pandemic risk than consumption of exotic animals. South China Morning Post, 18 July 2021. Available at: https://bit.ly/2XIKYGu (last access 25 Sep 2021)

Ganmaa D, Sato A (2005) The possible role of female sex hormones in milk from pregnant cows in the development of breast, ovarian and corpus uteri cancers. Med Hypotheses 65(6). Available at: https://pubmed.ncbi.nlm.nih.gov/16125328/ (last access 12 Sep 2021)

Gates B (2021) How to avoid a climate disaster. Alfred A. Knopf, New York/Toronto

Gibbs AJ, Armstrong JS, Downie JC (2009) From where did the 2009 "swine-origin" influenza A virus (H1N1) emerge? Virol J 6:207. Available at: https://doi.org/10.1186/1743-422X-6-207 (last access 12 Sep 2021)

Gleckel J (2020) Are consumers really confused by plant-based food labels? An empirical study. University of Louisville, Louis D. Brandeis School of Law. J Anim Environ Law (forthcoming). Available at: https://ssrn.com/abstract=3727710 (last access 12 Sep 2021)

González A, Koltrowitz S (2021) The $280,000 lab-grown burger could be a more palatable $10 in two years. Reuters 9 July 2021. Available at: https://www.reuters.com/article/us-food-tech-labmeat-idUSKCN1U41W8 (last access 12 Sep 2021)

Goodwin S (2020) Frankenstein food versus happy cattle: how will the cookie crumble? Farm Online, 28 September 2020. Available at: https://bit.ly/3c8LDoh (last access 12 Sep 2021)

Greenfield P (2020) Ban wildlife markets to avert pandemics, says UN biodiversity chief. The Guardian, 6 April 2020. Available at: https://bit.ly/2OaM4X6 (last access 12 Sep 2021)

Greger M (2006) Bird flu: a virus of our own hatching. Lantern Books, New York

Gura S (2007) Livestock genetics companies, concentration and proprietary strategies of an emerging power in the global food economy. League for Pastoral Peoples and Endogenous Livestock Development, Ober-Ramstadt, Germany

Harsanyi J (1955) Cardinal welfare, individualistic ethics, and interpersonal comparisons of utility. J Polit Econ:63

Hauss B (2019) Arkansas made it illegal to call a "Veggie Burger" A "Burger." We're Suing. ACLU 22 July 2019. Available at: http://tiny.cc/c3gstz (last access 12 Sep 2021)

Hayes P (2020) Here's how scientists know the coronavirus came from bats and wasn't made in a lab. The Conversation, 13 July 2020. Available at: https://bit.ly/3kT2gs1 (last access 12 Sep 2021)

Henriques J (2020) L'étiquetage des produits végétariens: un enjeu de société majeur. Vegactu 9 March 2020. Available at: https://tinyurl.com/wpxxex79 (last access 12 Sep 2021)

Herman J (2010) Saving U.S. dietary advice from conflicts of interest. Food Drug Law J 65:285–326

Hoag H (2014) Study revives bird origin for 1918 flu pandemic; Model also links avian influenza strains to deadly horse flu. Nature 16 February 2014. Available at: https://go.nature.com/3sXwtJ3 (last access 12 Sep 2021)

Jochems C et al (2002) The use of fetal bovine serum: ethical or scientific problem? Altern Lab Anim 30(2):219–227. https://doi.org/10.1177/026119290203000208 (last access 22 Sep 2021)

Keevican M (2020) Doctors group calls for more plants, less meat and dairy in 2020–2025 dietary guidelines. Physicians Committee for Responsible Medicine, 4 June 2020. Available at: https://bit.ly/3rrQlE0 (last access 12 Sep 2021)

Lange J (2019) Stop giving vegetarian meat substitutes stupid names. The Week 16 September 2019. Available at: https://theweek.com/articles/864778/stop-giving-vegetarian-meat-substitutes-stupid-names (last access 12 Sep 2021)

Lawton G (2021) Plenty more fish in the sea? New Scientist, 13–19 February 2021

Lazare J (2020) Ag-Gag laws, animal rights activism, and the constitution: what is protected speech? Alta Law Rev 58:83

Leonhardt D (2009) What's wrong with this chart? New York Times 20 May 2009

Levitt T (2020) Farm animals and pandemics: nine diseases that changed the world. The Guardian, 15 September 2020. Available at: https://bit.ly/3eixR4V (last access 12 Sep 2021)

Lima M, Skutsch M, de Medeiros Costa G (2011) Deforestation and the social impacts of soy for biodiesel: perspectives of farmers in the South Brazilian Amazon. Ecol Soc 16(4):4. Available at: https://doi.org/10.5751/ES-04366-160404 (last access 12 Sep 2021)

Lin D (2019) Why laboratory-grown meat is not vegan lab-grown meat is not a panacea, nor is it cruelty-free. Treehugger, 12 July 2019. Available at; https://www.treehugger.com/laboratory-grown-meat-is-not-vegan-127673 (last access 12 Sep 2021)

Linneken B (2016) Biting the hands that feeds us. Island Press

Lopez R (2001) Campaign contributions and agricultural subsidies. Food Marketing Policy Center Research Report No. 59. Available at: https://ideas.repec.org/p/zwi/fpcrep/059.html (last access 12 Sep 2021)

Lovgren S (2003) HIV originated with monkeys, not chimps, study finds. National Geographic, 12 June 2003. Available at: https://www.nationalgeographic.com/science/2003/06/news-hiv-aids-monkeys-chimps-origin/ (last access 12 Sep 2021)

Lucas A (2019) 5 Charts that show how milk sales changed and made it tough for dean foods to avert bankruptcy. CNBC 13 November 2019. Available at: http://tiny.cc/2phstz (last access 12 Sep 2021)

Lundebye A-K et al (2017) Lower levels of persistent organic pollutants, metals and the marine omega 3-fatty acid DHA in farmed compared to wild Atlantic salmon (Salmo salar). Environ Res 155:49–59. Available at: https://doi.org/10.1016/j.envres.2017.01.026 (last access 12 Sep 2021)

Lynteris C, Fearnley L (2020) Why shutting down Chinese "wet markets" could be a terrible mistake. The Conversation, 31 January 2020. Available at: https://bit.ly/3rqOwY1 (last access 12 Sep 2021)

Mac R (2014) Unilever drops Mayo Lawsuit against egg-replacing startup Hampton Creek. Forbes 18 December 2014. Available at: https://tinyurl.com/ybkwt5vm (last access 12 Sep 2021)

Machovina B, Kenneth F, Ripple W (2015) Biodiversity conversation: the key is reducing meat consumption. Sci Total Environ 536. Available at: https://pubmed.ncbi.nlm.nih.gov/26231772/ (last access 12 Sep 2021)

Marcus E (2005) Meat market: animals, ethics & money. Brio Press, Boston

Mclean B (2001) Profile in persistence in 1977 Steve Demos had an idea to sell soy-based foods to health-conscious Americans. Two Decades Later, It's Paying OFF, CNN Money, 1 May 2001. Available at: https://money.cnn.com/magazines/fsb/fsb_archive/2001/05/01/302536/index.htm (last access 12 Sep 2021)

Mena I et al (2016) Origins of the 2009 H1N1 influenza pandemic in swine in Mexico. eLife: Epidemiol Global Health Microbiol Infect Dis 5:e16777

Michail N (2016) MEPs oppose plant-based alternatives using meat terms. Foodnavigator.com 16 December 2016. Available at: https://tinyurl.com/29cmpsr5 (last access 12 Sep 2021)

Morose S et al (2012) Prediction and prevention of the next pandemic zoonosis. Lancet 380(9857). Available at: https://www.ncbi.nlm.nih.gov/pmc/articles/PMC3712877/ (last access 12 Sep 2021)

Morton A et al (2017) The effect of exposure to farmed salmon on piscine orthoreovirus infection and fitness in wild Pacific salmon in British Columbia, Canada. PLoS ONE 16(3):e0248912. Available at: https://journals.plos.org/plosone/article?id=10.1371/journal.pone.0188793 (last access 13 Sep 2021)

Murray A (2020) Coronavirus: Denmark shaken by cull of millions of mink. BBC News 11 November 2020. Available at: https://www.bbc.com/news/world-europe-54890229 (last access 12 Sep 2021)

Nestle M (2007) Food politics: how the food industry influences nutrition and health. University of California Press, Berkeley

Neuwirth R (2018) Law in the time of oxymora: a synaesthesia of language, logic and law. Routledge, Milton Park, Oxfordshire

Newhart B (2020) US dairy groups press Congress on Dairy Pride Act, Dairy Reporter 6 February 2020. Available at: https://www.dairyreporter.com/Article/2020/02/06/US-dairy-groups-press-Congress-on-Dairy-Pride-Act (last access 12 Sep 2021)

Noske B (1989) Humans and other animals: beyond the boundaries of anthropology. Pluto Press, London

Oi M (2020) Singapore approves lab-grown "chicken" meat. BBC News 2 December 2020. Available at: https://www.bbc.com/news/business-55155741 (last access 12 Sep 2021)

Olsen N, Crichton-Stuart C (2018) What is the difference between wild and farmed salmon? 22 August 2018. Available at: https://www.medicalnewstoday.com/articles/322847 (last access 12 Sep 2021)

Owens N (2019) Truth in labeling inked by Governor. Arkansas Democrat Gazette, 20 March 2019. Available at: https://bit.ly/2K6ck00 (last access 12 Sep 2021)

Polansek T (2021) Tyson foods, beyond meat face off with new plant-based burgers. Reuters 3 May 2021. Available at: https://www.reuters.com/business/retail-consumer/tyson-foods-beyond-meat-face-off-with-new-plant-based-burgers-2021-05-03/ (last access 12 Sep 2021)

Poore J, Nemecek T (2018) Reducing food's environmental impacts through producers and consumers. Science 360(6392):987–992

Popkin B et al (2020) Individuals with obesity and COVID-19: a global perspective on the epidemiology and biological relationships. Obesity Review 26 August 2020. Available at: https://onlinelibrary.wiley.com/doi/full/10.1111/obr.13128 (last access 12 Sep 2021)

Poussard B (2017) Moselle: Un camembert vegan français est né, mais il ne peut pas s'appeler fromage, 20 minutes 22 November 2017. Available at: https://tinyurl.com/839sze58 (last access 12 Sep 2021)

Quammen D (2012) Spillover: animal infections and the next human pandemic. W. W. Norton & Company

Quammen D (2020) We made the coronavirus epidemic. The New York Times, 28 January 2020, https://www.nytimes.com/2020/01/28/opinion/coronavirus-china.html (last access 12 Sep 2021)

Rajewski G (2019) Hunting Ebola's Origins. Tufts Now, 25 January 2019. Available at: https://now.tufts.edu/articles/hunting-ebola-s-origins (last access 12 Sep 2021)

Rawls J (1999 [1971]) A theory of justice, rev. ed. Harvard University Press, Cambridge

Reagan T (1983) The case for animal rights. University of California Press, Berkeley

Redman R (2020) Plant-based food retail sales reach $5 billion. Supermarket News, 3 March 2020. Available at: https://www.supermarketnews.com/consumer-trends/plant-based-food-retail-sales-reach-5-billion (last access 12 Sep 2021)

Roberts M (2000) U.S. animal agriculture: making the case for productivity. AgBioForum 3

Roos R (2012) CDC estimate of global H1N1 pandemic deaths: 284,000, CIDRAP. Available at: https://www.cidrap.umn.edu/news-perspective/2012/06/cdc-estimate-globalh1n1-pandemic-deaths-284000 (last access 12 Sep 2021)

Rowland MP (2020) Memphis meats raises $161 million in funding, aims to bring cell-based products to consumers. Forbes 22 January 2020. Available at: https://bit.ly/3caw2nZ (last access 12 Sep 2021)

Sachi S et al (2019) Antibiotic residues in milk: past, present, and future. J Adv Vet Anim Res 6(3): 315–332. Available at: https://www.ncbi.nlm.nih.gov/pmc/articles/PMC6760505/ (last access 12 Sep 2021)

Sample I, Gittings J (2003) In China, the civet is a delicacy – and may have caused SARS. Guardian, 23 May 23, 2003

Schmidt CW (2009) Swine CAFOs & Novel H1N1 Flu: separating facts from fears. Environ Health Perspect 117(9):A394–A401

Selwood D, O'Mahony A (2018) Hellmann's taps plant-based trend with Vegan Mayo. The Grocer 7 September 2018. Available at: https://tinyurl.com/4bfxa52f (last access 12 Sep 2021)

Sierens A (2011) Enzoötische pneumonie bij varkens, Landbouw & Techniek, 14 January 2011. Available at: https://edepot.wur.nl/301376 (last access 12 Sep 2021)

Silverman C (2018) In search of the reasonable consumer: when courts find food class action litigation goes too far. Univ Cin Law Rev 86:1. Available at: https://scholarship.law.uc.edu/uclr/vol86/iss1/1/ (last access 12 Sep 2021)

Simon DR (2013a) Each time McDonald's sells a Big Mac, We're Out $7, Meatonomics Blog, 15 August 2013. Available at: https://meatonomics.com/2013/08/15/each-time-mcdonalds-sells-a-big-mac-were-out-7/ (last access 12 Sep 2021)

Simon DR (2013b) Meatonomics. Conari Press, San Francisco

Singer P (1990) Animal liberation, 2nd edn. Random House Trade, New York, NY

Singer P (2011) The expanding circle: ethics, evolution, and moral progress. Princeton University Press

Smith M et al (2018) Microplastics in seafood and the implications for human health. Curr Environ Health Rep 5(3):375–386. https://doi.org/10.1007/s40572-018-0206-z (last access 12 Sep 2021)

Smithers R (2020) Vegan food company provokes with M*** F*** advertising campaign. The Guardian 3 August 2020. Available at: http://tiny.cc/vykstz (last access 12 Sep 2021)

Snyder F (2016) EU, China, and product standards. In: Wei S et al (eds) Routledge handbook of EU-China relations, forthcoming. Routledge. Available at: https://papers.ssrn.com/sol3/papers.cfm?abstract_id=2843008 (last access 12 Sep 2021)

Snyder F (2020) Understanding the regulation of ecological food in China: regulatory intermediation, path dependence and legal pluralism. In: Goh B, Price R (eds) Regulatory issues in organic food safety in the Asia Pacific. Springer, Singapore, pp 11–34. Available at: https://doi.org/10.1007/978-981-15-3580-2_2 (last access 12 Sep 2021)

Southey F (2020) Can coronavirus be transmitted via meat products? Foodnavigator.com 26 June 2020. Available at: https://bit.ly/3sZUgbk (last access 12 Sep 2021)

Southey F (2021) Plant-based dairy censorship: Oatly, Upfield and ProVeg petition to overthrow Amendment 171, Foodnavigator.com 14 January 2021. Available at: http://tiny.cc/peastz (last access 12 Sep 2021)

Springmann M et al (2016) Analysis and valuation of the health and climate change cobenefits of dietary change. Proc Natl Acad USA, 21 March 2016. Available at: https://www.pnas.org/content/early/2016/03/16/1523119113.abstract (last access 12 Sep 2021)

Starmer E, Witteman A, Wise TA (2006) Feeding the factory farm: implicit subsidies in the Broiler Chicken Industry working paper, 06-03, Global Development and Environment Institute 2006, 10. Available at: https://econpapers.repec.org/scripts/redir.pf?u=https%3A%2F%2Fageconsearch.umn.edu%2Frecord%2F37162%2Ffiles%2F06-03BroilerGains.pdf;h=repec:ags:tugdwp:37162 (last access 13 Sep 2021)

Steinfeld H et al (2006) Livestock's long shadow: environmental issues and options. Food and Agriculture Organization of the United Nations, Rome. Available at: http://www.fao.org/3/a0701e/a0701e00.htm (last access 12 Sep 2021)

Stigler G (1971) The theory of regulation (Spring 1971). Bell J Econ Manag Sci 2(1):3–21. Available at: https://www.jstor.org/stable/3003160?origin=JSTOR-pdf&seq=1 (last access 12 Sep 2021)

Stubley P (2021) Vets inspect hundreds of cows stuck on "hellish" ship for months over bluetongue virus fears. Independent 27 February 2021. Available at: https://bit.ly/3kWx3E4 (last access 12 Sep 2021)

Taleb NN (2007) The Black Swan: the impact of the highly improbable, 2nd edn. Penguin, London

Taylor S (2017) Beasts of burden: animal and disability liberation. The New Press, New York

Temple J, Gates B (2021) Rich nations should shift entirely to synthetic beef. MIT Technology Review 14 February 2021. Available at: http://shorturl.at/fjDH9 (last access 12 Sep 2021)

Thieme M (2014) Opinie: Melk. Niet goed voor elk. Partij voor de Dieren, 13 August 2014. Available at: https://www.partijvoordedieren.nl/nieuws/melk-niet-goed-voor-elk (last access 12 Sep 2021)

Thornton A (2019) This is how many animals we eat each year. World Economic Forum, 8 February 2019. Available at: https://bit.ly/3c8Kr4h (last access 12 Sep 2021)

Tubb C, Seba T (2019) Rethinking food and agriculture 2020-2030, the second domestication of plants and animals, the disruption of the cow, and the collapse of industrial livestock farming, RethinkX Sector Disruption Report, September 2019

Twine R (2012) Revealing the "animal-industrial complex" – a concept & method for Critical Animal Studies? J Crit Anim Stud 10(1)

van der Poel WH et al (1994) Respiratory syncytial virus infections in human beings and in cattle. J Infect 29(2):215–228. Available at: https://pubmed.ncbi.nlm.nih.gov/7806887/ (last access 12 Sep 2021)

Vanga SK, Raghavan V (2018) Nutritionally speaking, soy milk is best plant-based milk. McGill Newsroom, 29 January 2018. Available at: http://tiny.cc/y8hstz (last access 12 Sep 2021)

Vanni G (2019) Brand turnaround in plant based milk: oatly, business of plants, 14 January 2019. Available at: https://www.businessofplants.com/blog/oatlyturnaround (last access 12 Sep 2021)

von Massow M, Gingerich M (2019) Lab-grown dairy: the next food frontier. The Conversation 12 June 2019. Available at: https://theconversation.com/lab-grown-dairy-the-next-food-frontier-117963 (last access 12 Sep 2021)

Wadiwel D (2018) Chicken harvesting machine: animal labor, resistance, and the time of production. South Atl Q 117:3

Wadman M (2020) Why COVID-19 is more deadly in people with obesity – even if they're young. Science, 8 September 2020. Available at: https://bit.ly/3qs75JO (last access 12 Sep 2021)

Wallace R (2016) Big farms make big flu, dispatches on infectious diseases, agribusiness, and the nature of science. Monthly Review Press, New York

Wang Y, Beydoun MA (2009) Meat consumption is associated with obesity and central obesity among US adults. Int J Obes (Lond) 33(6):621–628

Watrous M (2017) Danone seals the deal with WhiteWave. Food Business News 14 April 2017. Available at: https://www.foodbusinessnews.net/articles/9197-danone-seals-the-deal-with-whitewave (last access 12 Sep 2021)

Watson E (2019) PBFA members to FDA: banning use of dairy terms on plant-based foods is a solution in search of a problem, Foodnavigator.com 3 January 2019. Available at: https://www.dairyreporter.com/Article/2020/02/06/US-dairy-groups-press-Congress-on-Dairy-Pride-Act (last access 12 Sep 2021)

Watson E (2021) Danone expands presence in plant-based segment with deal to acquire Vegenaise maker Follow Your Heart, Foodnavigator-usa.com 19 February 2021. Available at: https://bit.ly/30kqRMX (last access 12 Sep 2021)

Webster RG (2004) Wet markets – a continuing source of severe acute respiratory syndrome and influenza? Lancet 365

Wei C (2021) Plant-based meat has thrived in Asia for centuries – and it's still going strong. Food & Wine 16 February 2021. Available at: http://shorturl.at/gmnKX (last access 12 Sep 2021)

Willett W et al (2019) Food in the anthropocene: the EAT–Lancet Commission on healthy diets from sustainable food systems. Lancet 393:447–492

Wilson DJ, Gonzalez RN, Das HH (1997) Bovine mastitis pathogens in New York and Pennsylvania: prevalence and effects on somatic cell count and milk production. J Dairy Sci 80(10): 2592–2598. Available at: https://tinyurl.com/3hdn8wa9 (last access 12 Sep 2021)

The Coming of Age of Open Data

John M. Yun

Abstract In our increasingly digitized economy, a massive amount of data is generated every moment. While data has always been fundamental to innovation and decision making, the current scale, scope, and speed at which data is collected, organized, and analyzed is unprecedented. Yet, having more data is different from harnessing that data to power useful analytics. Can governments and organizations employ data in a manner that results in even greater value and insights to solve complex problems? This issue has come to the forefront with the Covid-19 outbreak and the attendant societal lockdowns. This Article focuses on one aspect of the data debate, that of "open data", that is, data that is widely available to the public without cost or restrictions. Led by the United States and Europe, there is a growing open data movement and the associated goal of more transparent and open governments. Yet, what incentivizes governments, businesses, and individuals to open data? This Article first approaches this question from an economic perspective focusing on the characteristics of data that distinguish it from other types of inputs. Next, this Article explores potential privacy concerns within a basic framework and details the concept of a data "life cycle". Further, the Article explicitly considers the incentives that governments, businesses, and individuals have to open data. These incentives fundamentally boil down to the ability to appropriate, to some degree, the value derived from subsequent use of the open data. Finally, perhaps in the same spirit as the open data movement, there have been increasing calls for competition authorities and governments to wield open data and interoperability as remedies within antitrust and competition laws. This Article highlights some concerns with these "open data antitrust" proposals.

J. M. Yun (✉)
Antonin Scalia Law School, George Mason University, Fairfax, VA, USA
e-mail: jyun9@gmu.edu

1 Introduction

Data is all around us and is collected on a nearly continuous basis.[1] The potential for novel uses of data is part of the reason there is optimism surrounding innovations such as the 5G cellular network, the Internet of Things, autonomous cars, cloud computing, machine learning, and artificial intelligence. While the use of data has always been fundamental to innovation and decision making, the current scale, scope, and speed at which data is collected, organized, and analyzed is unprecedented. Simply put, there is a massive amount of data generated every moment in an increasingly digitized economy. Perhaps no other example illustrates this point better than the Covid-19 outbreak, where vast amounts of data on the virus are being generated daily. Nonetheless, having more data is not the same as actually harnessing that data to power useful analytics, better decision making, and innovation. As society has seen with public policies related to Covid-19, these decisions can literally mean the difference between life and death.

One particular aspect of the data debate is that of "open data". Data can broadly be characterized as "closed" or "open". Closed, or "siloed", data is information that is not in the public domain.[2] For example, consider individual medical records. This type of data is held by the specific patient, as well as various other stakeholders, including doctors, hospitals, and insurance providers. While medical records are typically considered highly sensitive and private, privacy is not fundamentally about keeping things "secret"—but is rather about the ability to control relevant information.[3] Other examples of closed data include trade secrets; a company's transaction data; experimental results from a new product prototype; and individual employee data.

In contrast, data is "open" "if anyone can freely use, re-use and redistribute them, for any purpose, without restrictions."[4] An example of open data would be the number of patients admitted for the Covid-19 virus at the city, county, state, and

---

[1] See e.g. Data Never Sleeps 6.0, DOMO, https://www.domo.com/learn/data-never-sleeps-6 (last access 30 April 2021) ("By 2020, it's estimated that for every person on earth, 1.7 MB of data will be created every second.").

[2] In this Article, the words "data" and "information" are used interchangeably. In information science, some have made distinctions between data, information, knowledge, and wisdom (that is, the DIKW hierarchy or pyramid). See e.g. Ackoff (1989). In some respects, the DIKW categorization mirrors the concept of a data "life cycle", which is discussed in infra Sect. 3.

[3] See e.g. Acquisti et al. (2016). Naturally, there are other concepts of "privacy" based more on notions of autonomy and anonymity. See, e.g., Gavison (1980), p. 423 (defining privacy as "the extent to which we are known to others, the extent to which others have physical access to us, and the extent to which we are the subject of others' attention."); Hirshleifer (1980), p. 649 ("The central domain of what we mean by 'privacy' is, rather, a concept that might be described as autonomy within society.").

[4] The World Bank, Open Data in 60 Seconds, http://opendatatoolkit.worldbank.org/en/open-data-in-60-seconds.html (last access 30 April 2021).

national levels.[5] Another, perhaps less conventional, example is the set of expired patents. Given their expiration, these patents have entered the public domain and are discoverable through an online database.[6] One can even search for unexpired, yet inactive, patents using Michigan Technological University's database, which is part of their open source initiative.[7] These databases exist in order to facilitate the dissemination and use of these novel and nonobvious ideas, which is the ultimate purpose of the patent system, and the intellectual property system more generally.[8] Specifically, for a limited time, authors and inventors are given legal rights over their respective works and ideas in exchange for having those works and ideas ultimately available for societal use without restriction, that is, open data.[9]

While discussions regarding the value of open data have only begun to emerge in earnest in the past decade, it is certainly not a new concept.[10] For instance, the United States government conducted its first census in 1790 under the direction of President George Washington and published the results soon thereafter.[11] To this day, governments at all levels and various organizations routinely collect, organize, and publish data to the public domain. That information, such as the current and past U.S. census, is used in countless areas in society to inform decisionmakers and to

---

[5] See e.g. Johns Hopkins, University of Medicine, CORONAVIRUS RESOURCE CENTER, https://coronavirus.jhu.edu/us-map (last access 30 April 2021).

[6] U.S. Patent & Trademark Office, Search for Patents, https://www.uspto.gov/patents-application-process/search-patents (last access 30 April 2021).

[7] See Michigan Technological University, Free Inactive Patent Search, http://freeip.mtu.edu/home (last access 30 April 2021).

[8] See U.S. Constitution, Article I, Section 8, Clause 8 ("To promote the progress of science and useful arts, by securing for limited times to authors and inventors the exclusive right to their respective writings and discoveries.").

[9] To that end, a central requirement to obtain a U.S. patent is a full disclosure of the idea to the general public. This disclosure is immediately available and can potentially be used to gain insight into various innovation trends and even by rivals to design around the patent. Along the same lines, Professor Amanda Levendowski has conducted research showing how public trademark filings can be used to learn about developing surveillance technologies. See Levendowski (2021).

[10] See e.g. Open Data Handbook, Introduction, http://opendatahandbook.org/guide/en/introduction (last access 30 April 2021) ("The notion of open data and specifically open government data – information, public or otherwise, which anyone is free to access and re-use for any purpose – has been around for some years. In 2009 open data started to become visible in the mainstream, with various governments (such as the USA, UK, Canada and New Zealand) announcing new initiatives towards opening up their public information."). According to one source, the term "open data" was first introduced in the mid-1990s. See Simon Chignard, A Brief History of Open Data, Paris Innovation Review, Mar. 29, 2013, http://parisinnovationreview.com/articles-en/a-brief-history-of-open-data (last access 30 April 2021) ("The term open data appeared for the first time in 1995, in a document from an American scientific agency. It dealt about the disclosure of geophysical and environmental data.").

[11] See U.S. Census Bureau, Decennial Census Official Publications, https://www.census.gov/programs-surveys/decennial-census/decade/decennial-publications.1790.html (last access 30 April 2021).

contribute to research.[12] The recent Covid-19 outbreak and subsequent societal lockdowns perhaps represent the coming-of-age for open data initiatives given the unprecedented amount of shared data on the virus and subsequent tools built off that data.[13]

While the decision to "open" or "close" data is not unique to our current digital era, what has changed are a number of key economic factors. First, due to innovations such as modern computers, software, and the Internet, the amount of data generated and captured from economic and personal activities has grown exponentially.[14] Second, the costs involved in the various stages, or "life cycles", of data have changed dramatically.[15] This change has not only been in the ability to efficiently collect data but also in the ability to extract value from it. Finally, there is a recognition that, in the ever-increasing connected nature of our lives, there are tremendous gains from harnessing the power of analytics that can only emerge from combining different sets of data to solve complex problems. This has led to increased public initiatives to open data and make it readily accessible.[16]

This Article directly addresses the topic of open data from an economic perspective. The focus is on the incentives that governments and organizations have to "open" information and data rather than the larger societal benefits of open data per se, which are well documented.[17] Section 2 provides an overview of the

---

[12] See e.g. United States Census 2020, Importance of the Data, https://2020census.gov/en/census-data.html (last access 30 April 2021) ("Over the next decade, lawmakers, business owners, and many others will use 2020 Census data to make critical decisions. The results will show where communities need new schools, new clinics, new roads, and more services for families, older adults, and children.").

[13] See e.g. National Institute of Health, Open-Access Data and Computational Resources to Address COVID-19, https://datascience.nih.gov/covid-19-open-access-resources (last access 30 April 2021) ("COVID-19 open-access data and computational resources are being provided by federal agencies, including NIH, public consortia, and private entities. These resources are freely available to researchers, and this page will be updated as more information becomes available."). See also Larry Dignan, As COVID-19 Data Sets Become More Accessible, Novel Coronavirus Pandemic May Be Most Visualized Ever, ZDNet, Apr. 20, 2020, https://www.zdnet.com/article/as-covid-19-data-sets-become-more-accessible-novel-coronavirus-pandemic-may-be-most-visualized-ever (last access 30 April 2021).

[14] In 2018, the International Data Corporation (IDC) estimated the global volume of data to be 33 zettabytes, which is equivalent to 33 trillion gigabytes—forecasting it to grow to 175 zettabytes in 2025. See Reinsel et al. (2018), p. 6.

[15] See Sect. 3 for a fuller discussion of the life cycle of data.

[16] Examples include the U.S. federal government's Data.gov website, Europe's Open Data Europe Portal (ODP), and the European Data Portal (EDP). More local initiatives include New York City's Open Data project (https://opendata.cityofnewyork.us (last access 30 April 2021)). In the Netherlands, the Rijkswaterstaat, which is a division of the Department of Infrastructure and Environment, manages key areas of infrastructure and publishes data such water height and location of road signs. See Eckartz et al. (2014), pp. 256–257.

[17] See e.g. Berends et al. (2020), p. 3 ("Despite the method applied by the studies and the estimates they provide, there is one finding that is beyond dispute: when opened, data can become a force of growth and development for all countries, regardless of geography and level of economic development.").

characteristics of data that distinguishes it from other types of inputs. Intimately related to discussions of open data are privacy concerns, which are discussed within the context of a basic privacy framework. Section 3 details the "life cycle" of data and how innovations have changed the various costs and efficiencies at each specific stage. Section 4 more fully discusses the economic forces that incentivize open data at the government, organization, and household levels. These incentives are fundamentally related to the ability to appropriate, to some degree, the value derived from subsequent uses of the data.

Finally, Section 5 explores open data in the context of antitrust and competition policy. A likely spillover effect of the open data movement and the ease to which the digital entities can "plug into" various large multisided platforms is the notion that competition agencies and courts should consider the use of open data and interoperability remedies to solve competition issues and violations. A number of high-profile and influential reports have already made these proposals.[18] While well-intended, remedies mandating open data and interoperability in the digital sectors likely will result in unintended consequences that have the potential to disincentivize innovation and raise the cost of operations. Moreover, the benefits to competition from these proposals are likely minimal as there is little evidence that the lack of data prevents entry and is hampering startups.

2 Characteristics of Data & Privacy

In order to understand data policy, it is useful to identify the characteristics of data. Like all goods and services, data has certain economic properties which give us insights into how it is generated and used, including its supply and demand. Further, these characteristics allow us to better assess the normative aspects of data—namely, in terms of how the production and use of data impact economic efficiency.[19] Thus,

---

[18] See e.g. Australian Competition and Consumer Commission (2019), p. 11 ("The ACCC considers that opening up the data, or the routes to data, held by the major digital platforms may reduce the barriers to competition in existing markets and assist competitive innovation in future markets. This could be achieved by requiring leading digital platforms to share the data with potential rivals [...]. Another is to require the platforms to provide interoperability with other services."); Digital Competition Expert Panel (2019), p. 76 ("The digital markets unit should use data openness as a tool to promote competition, where it determines this is necessary and proportionate to achieve its aims [...]. One model would be to require a dataset to be shared in a controlled environment, with access granted to approved businesses.").

[19] In order to understand the concept of economic efficiency, it is useful to start with a description of inefficiency. Economic inefficiency results when achievable benefits are not fully realized. Under such a situation, it is possible to make someone better off without making someone worse off. It follows that allocative efficiency is achieved when you cannot make someone better off without making someone worse off, that is, Pareto Efficiency. See e.g. Lawrence B. Solum, Legal Theory Lexicon 060: Efficiency, Pareto, and Kaldor–Hicks, Legal Theory Lexicon, https://lsolum.typepad.com/legal_theory_lexicon/2006/10/legal_theory_le_1.html (last access 30 April 2021).

this section explicitly considers how data fits into the standard economic classification scheme used for various types of goods and services and how data interfaces with privacy considerations, which is a topic intimately related to policy discussions regarding open data, its value, and its potential misuse.

2.1 The Nature of Goods & Services

Data and information are scarce.[20] As a consequence, individuals in society operate with less than perfect information, which explains a great deal of economic conduct and phenomena.[21] Consequently, the individual choice to become more informed involves weighing the incremental benefits and costs of that choice. Having additional information allows for better decisionmaking and, therefore, more efficient markets. Consequently, it follows that there are unrealized potential gains from trade that could be achieved (or achieved at a lower cost) if market participants, governments, and organizations all had access to better data and information.

We can begin to assess data by understanding its underlying features, which influence how it is "consumed" and, in turn, how it is produced (Table 1). The nature of goods and services can be broadly characterized along two dimensions: Products are (1) either *rivalrous* or *nonrivalrous* and (2) either *excludable* or *nonexcludable*. Therefore, products fall into one of four categories: (i) rivalrous & excludable ("private goods"), (ii) rivalrous & nonexcludable ("common resources"), (iii) nonrivalrous & excludable ("club goods"), and (iv) nonrivalrous & nonexcludable ("public goods").[22] We will return to these four categories after discussing rivalry and excludability separately.

Table 1 Standard classification scheme for goods & services

	Excludable	Nonexcludable
Rivalrous	Private good	Common resource
Nonrivalrous	Club good	Public good

---

[20] This fundamental insight was brought to the forefront of economic research by Professor George Stigler in the context of market search costs. See Stigler (1961), p. 224 ("The identification of sellers and the discovery of their prices are only one sample of the vast role of the search for information in economic life.").

[21] Advertising, warranties, trademarks, value of signaling, brands, and reputations are just a few topics that cannot be fully analyzed without incorporating the idea of imperfect information. See, e.g., id.; Spence (1973).

[22] See e.g. Mankiw (2015), pp. 216–217.

2.1.1 Rivalrous or Nonrivalrous

The first dimension on which goods and services are classified is whether they are *rivalrous* or *nonrivalrous*. A rivalrous product is one where the consumption of a product by one individual reduces the ability of another to consume that same product. For example, if one museum displays an antique chair, then its use is rivalrous to other museums that would like to display the same chair for their particular exhibit. Rivalry holds for other durable goods such as homes, cars, and computers—as well as nondurable goods such as groceries and prescription drugs.

A nonrivalrous product, in contrast, is commonly defined as a product where one person's use does not diminish another person's ability to use the same product. The quintessential example, while not a "product" in the conventional sense, is an idea. Two companies that use the same business method to organize their production, for instance, are nonrivalrous in the use of that method or idea; although, they could be considered "rivalrous" in terms of their subsequent competition. Let us return to the museum example; while the antique chair is rivalrous between museums, once displayed, the chair is nonrivalrous among museum goers who can all enjoy seeing the chair without diminishing the utility of others.

More technically, a nonrivalrous product confers a benefit to an additional user at zero, or near zero, marginal cost.[23] Let us consider services such as national defense, broadcast television, or radio broadcasts. When an additional person uses these services, it comes at almost no cost.[24] Along similar lines, we can consider products such as music, movies, and software as nonrivalrous from the perspective that the expansion of these products to more consumers can be achieved at zero or near zero cost. Thus, when one user downloads software, for example, this does not diminish another user's ability to download and use the same software.

Importantly, products that are nonrivalrous in use or consumption can be rivalrous in terms of value. Examples that come to mind are trade secrets. A trade secret is nonrivalrous, in that multiple firms could use the same process or formula, yet this could diminish the economic value of the trade secret if multiple firms used it. The same holds for other areas of intellectual property rights, including patents, copyrights, and trademarks.

The fundamental feature of nonrivalry in consumption is that, since there is no cost to increasing output, it is economically efficient to expand output to everyone who has a positive valuation for the product. To the extent that this expansion does not occur, there is "too little" consumption from the normative perspective of economic efficiency.

Yet, that is not the full story. While distributing a nonrivalrous good to every consumer with a positive value maximizes efficiency—in a static sense—it can

---

[23] See Dorman (2014), p. 317.

[24] Note that these examples also highlight that there are degrees of nonexcludability. For instance, a radio station has reception limits based on the type of modulation used, that is, FM or AM. National defense becomes more costly with more people if they are at the outskirts of a nation's border.

create a disincentive to create the product in the first place. Economists call this idea the "free rider problem", which is the inability to exclude nonpayers. Yet, without the ability to exclude and charge for the good or service (at least for a period of time), this would dampen innovation incentives and could result in a sub-optimal level of provision of a good or service. One classic example is Napster, which was an early digital sharing platform that took copyrighted music and freely distributed it to all who wished to download it.[25] This distribution increased economic efficiency—in the sense that it spread music to everyone who had a positive valuation for the song or album, but it also severely dampened the incentive to create music in the first place.[26]

More specifically, without the ability to have some degree of exclusivity and to charge a price above marginal cost, then there are insufficient revenues to cover the fixed costs of creation and production. This fundamental idea is behind most countries' intellectual property system, which attempts to balance the potential inefficiency from limiting the use of ideas and expressions through the assignment of property rights with the dynamic incentive effects to create those ideas and expressions in the first place.[27] The same is also true with data. Once data is created, there is typically an efficiency gain from distributing the data widely to all parties who have a positive valuation for it. Yet, uncontrolled and indiscriminate sharing of that data can lead to dampened incentives to create that knowledge, idea, or data.[28] Consequently, without some ability to control data, then this can lead to an overall loss in welfare from reduced levels of innovation.[29]

That being said, control over data does not necessarily imply that firms will find it in their interest to completely close off access to that data. However, in order for there to be open data in the first place, there needs to be an incentive to create and organize the data. Consequently, without initial property rights over data, then there

---

[25] See e.g. Alex Winter, The Short History of Napster 1.0, Wired Magazine, Apr. 4, 2013, https://www.wired.com/2013/04/napster (last access 30 April 2021).

[26] See e.g. Hong (2013), p. 299 ("These results therefore suggest that file sharing is likely to explain about 20% of the total sales decline during the Napster period, mostly driven by downloading activities of households with children aged 6–17.").

[27] See e.g. Posner (2005), p. 57.

[28] Of course, there is a certain type and amount of data that is created from the mere use or provision of a product—that is, "data exhaust". See e.g. Terry (2012), pp. 389–390 ("[...] 'exhaust data', or data created unintentionally as a byproduct of social networks, web searches, smartphones, and other online behaviors."). Arguably, widespread use of such data, while perhaps undesirable from the perspective of the firm generating the data, would not impact economic efficiency if the widespread use does not change the ex ante incentives to provide the product. That does not mean that all data exhaust should be open and freely available, however, as there are other considerations including trade secrets, privacy, and incentives to change the nature of the exhaust, which can all impact innovation and efficiency.

[29] While some have called for "open innovation" in terms of not having an explicit intellectual property rights regime, there are problems with such a move. For a discussion of open innovation, see, e.g., Dreyfuss (2010), p. 1437.

is a potential "tragedy of the commons".[30] Thus, we must not conflate initiatives to facilitate the exchange and sharing of data voluntarily with the forced sharing of data through interoperability requirements and other regulatory protocols.[31] Such a conflation would mix the idea of efficiency in distribution (allocative efficiency) with that of the incentives to create data and information (dynamic efficiency).[32]

2.1.2 Excludable or Nonexcludable

The second dimension that differentiates the nature of products is whether goods and services are *excludable* or *nonexcludable*. A product is excludable when an owner can legally stop others from consuming a product. When a movie theater only admits theatergoers with a ticket, then it is imposing excludability even though the movie itself is nonrivalrous (although, the physical space of the theater is rivalrous). Similarly, data and information are nonrivalrous, but they can be either excludable or nonexcludable. This ability to exclude is somewhat based on technology.[33] For instance, if someone's personal data used on one digital platform is siloed and protected from outside access, then that data is not available for other platforms and is, thus, excluded; although, it is nonrivalrous.[34] The ability to silo or exclude data is therefore not based on anything fundamental about data itself. It is rather based on the ability to economically control access to the data. A central question about open data, which is addressed in *infra* Sect. 4, is to consider the incentives that individuals and firms have to keep data in silos.

Nonexcludable, however, "describes goods for which it is impractical to deny use or access to those who do not pay for them."[35] Again, what is practical or impractical will depend to an extent on technology and circumstances (e.g., it is impractical to deny the use of certain areas of a city during civil unrest). Classic examples of

---

[30] See Hardin (1968). See also Hsu (2005), p. 77 ("[A] tragedy of the commons involves resource users overexploiting a resource and imposing mutual externalities upon each other.").

[31] See, e.g., Hazlett and Caliskan (2008), p. 477 (2008) ("Cable modem services held nearly a two-to-one market share advantage when DSL carriers were most heavily obligated to provide 'open access' to competing ISPs. Once the FCC eliminated a key provision of that access regime . . . DSL subscribership increased dramatically [. . . and] was 65% higher – more than 9 million households – than it would have been under the linear trend established under 'open access' regulation.").

[32] See e.g. Easterbrook (1981).

[33] See e.g. Tucker (2020), p. 12 ("In general, though data is non-rivalrous, it is possible to exclude access to particular data if the data are not public. Sometimes, the legal treatment of data has focused on the idea of non-rivalry – which is indeed a key component of the definition of a public good – without also acknowledging that much of the time the same digital tools that allow the collection of vast datasets also permit control over who accesses it.").

[34] The term "platforms" (a.k.a. multisided or two-sided markets) describes firms that have developed a system or network where more than one group (e.g., users, merchants, advertisers) all participate in order to engage in mutually beneficial exchange. See e.g. Evans (2003); Hagiu and Wright (2015), p. 163.

[35] Dorman (2014), p. 316.

nonexcludable goods include national defense and clean air, where it is not practical to deny one household the benefits of national defense (e.g., if they refuse to pay income taxes) or deny a serial violator of environmental regulations the benefits of clean air.

A recent example of a business choosing to make something "open" and nonexcludable that was previously a trade secret is Ikea during the societal lockdowns over Covid-19. Ikea shared its recipe for its popular Swedish Meatballs with the general public.[36] Other firms also released their own recipes.[37] This is a particularly relevant episode because Ikea's decision is a microcosm of the possible decision of firms, organizations, and governments to "release" or "un-silo" information and data. What went behind Ikea's decision to release its long-held secret recipe—or at least its close cousin? We will explore this question in subsequent parts.

2.1.3 Four Classifications of Goods & Services

When we consider both dimensions jointly, that is, rivalrous-nonrivalrous with excludable-nonexcludable, then goods and services fall within one of four possible categories: private goods, common resources, club goods, and public goods.[38] While these discrete categories are useful to organize ideas, as has been previously discussed, there are different degrees of rivalry and excludability. Additionally, goods and services can flow from one category to another depending on

---

[36] See Bridie Pearson-Jones, Make Your Own IKEA Meatballs: Furniture Giant Shares Six-Step Recipe for Its Famous Swedish Dish So Fans Can Cook It in Lockdown, DAILY MAIL, Apr. 20, 2020, https://www.dailymail.co.uk/femail/food/article-8236433/IKEA-shares-recipe-famous-meat-balls-make-home.html (last access 30 April 2021). Although, the public version of the recipe does not appear to be the same as the original recipe. See Michelle Gant, Ikea Shares Recipe for Swedish Meatballs to Make During Quarantine, TODAY.COM, https://www.today.com/food/ikea-shares-recipe-swedish-meatballs-make-during-quarantine-t179469 (last access 30 April 2021) ("'Our 'real' meatballs and Swedish cream sauce recipe remains a closely guarded secret, known only to a select few. However, in good conscience we couldn't deprive the nation from missing out on their meatball fix, so we've made an almost-as-delicious alternative that can be easily made at home! We hope that it fills a gap until we can meet again. (...)' Lorena Lourido, country food manager at Ikea U.K. and Ireland.").

[37] See, e.g., Doubletree Hotel's chocolate chip cookies (Hilton, For the First Time, DoubleTree by Hilton Reveals Official Chocolate Chip Cookie Recipe so Bakers Can Create the Warm, Welcoming Treat at Home, Apr. 9, 2020, https://newsroom.hilton.com/static-doubletree-reveals-cookie-recipe.htm (last access 30 April 2021)); Canada's Wonderland's funnel cake (Canada's Wonderland, How to Make the Classic Canada's Wonderland Funnel Cake at Home, Apr. 17, 2020, https://www.canadaswonderland.com/blog/2020/april-2020/how-to-make-canadas-wonderland-classic-funnel-cake-at-home (last access 30 April 2021)); Wagamama's katsu curry chicken (Aoife Hanna, Wagamama Shared Its Katsu Curry Recipe on IG So You Can Enjoy the Signature Dish at Home, BUSTLE, Apr. 23, 2020, https://www.bustle.com/p/wagamama-shared-its-katsu-curry-recipe-on-ig-so-you-can-enjoy-the-signature-dish-at-home-22842002 (last access 30 April 2021)).

[38] See Sect. 2.1.

circumstances. For instance, if we drive on highways at 5 a.m. in the morning, then we would generally consider highways to be nonexcludable and nonrivalrous. Yet those same highways at 5 p.m., while still being nonexcludable, are generally highly rivalrous due to rush-hour traffic—that rivalry results in significantly longer commutes and a higher opportunity cost to drive.

The same idea is true for data. Data in the form of a new idea could be considered a public good—in the sense that its use by others would be nonexcludable and nonrivalrous. However, if a patent is granted by the U.S. Patent and Trademark Office, the idea moves from a public good (that is, nonrivalrous & nonexcludable) to a club good (that is, nonrivalrous & excludable) due to patent protection.

On the other hand, let us consider data collected on the operations of a local government, such as traffic patterns, education metrics, and crime statistics.[39] This data starts as a club good because it is excludable by virtue of the fact that the data is not accessible outside of the local government. Releasing this data to the public, in some form, would move the data from a club good to a public good. Thus, moving data from proprietary to open clearly changes the degree of excludability. Of course, the change does not have to be an all-or-nothing decision. It could involve releasing some, most, or all of the data, or forms of the data (e.g., aggregated), in various ways.

2.2 *Framework for Assessing Privacy*

Issues of privacy are intimately tied with the use of data. That being said, while data and privacy are often discussed together, it is not always clear what "privacy" means in this context. Does privacy refer to personal information? If so, what type of personal information? Or is it not really about a particular type of information per se (such as, medical records, web browsing history) but more about control of that information in terms of what an individual wishes to keep personal versus to make public? Not surprisingly, the topic of privacy and the law & economics of privacy is an increasingly important area of research.[40]

The goal of this section is certainly not to arrive at a universal definition of privacy, but rather to achieve the more modest goal of giving a frame of reference when discussing privacy in the context of open data. This framework is based on two core observations. First, "privacy sensitivities and attitudes are subjective and

---

[39] This type of data can be labeled public sector information (PSI). See, e.g., The National Archives UK, *About PSI*, https://www.nationalarchives.gov.uk/information-management/re-using-public-sector-information/about-psi ("Any information (content) whatever its medium (form) – including print, digital or electronic, and sound recordings – produced, held or disseminated by a public sector body is considered public sector information. This includes an enormous range: corporate information such as reports and financial data, codes of practice, public records, statistics, still and moving images, press releases, artefacts, publication schemes, and so on.").

[40] See e.g. Acquisti et al. (2016); Baye and Sappington (2020); Cooper (2013).

idiosyncratic."[41] One person might be perfectly willing to share his birthday, address, marital status, and employment history online, while another would consider one or more of these details to be private information. Second, what an individual considers private can change depending on the context, circumstance, and audience.[42]

Let us consider an individual, Jeannie Gray, who has various "spheres" in which she shares or withholds data, or information about herself. To simplify, let us suppose there are three primary areas of connections, or spheres, in her life: (1) Family & Friends, (2) Professional, and (3) Social Media.[43] For each sphere, suppose there is a total amount of information, I, which she can either reveal, R, or keep secret, S. Thus, for each sphere, total information is the sum of revealed and secret information, $I = R + S$. Consequently, across all spheres, the total amount of information about Jeannie is $I_T = \sum_{i=1}^{n} R_i + S_i$, where n is three spheres in this particular example—eliminating duplicates.[44] Further, let us assume that a key decision that individuals can make to maximize their utility is the choice to reveal information within a given sphere. This decision is made by weighing the relative benefits and costs of providing a given type (and amount) of information. For instance, revealing your location data via your mobile device can create disutility associated with the discomfort from being tracked but can also provide substantial benefits, e.g., navigation apps that provide driving directions.[45]

A number of possible implications emerge from this very simple framework. First, "privacy" can mean different things in different contexts.[46] Similarly, it could mean different things to different people in the same context (*e.g.*, some people are comfortable sharing salary and bonus information while others are not). Consequently, discussing "privacy" on the basis of specific types of data or information is likely a poor approach if this means the information should always be kept secret (*e.*

---

[41] Acquisti et al. (2016), p. 446.

[42] See e.g. Acquisti et al. (2016), p. 467 ("[O]ne of the major themes of this article: the consequences and implications of data sharing or data protection vary very much with context – such as what specific type of data is being shared, how, and when.").

[43] The idea is that each sphere involves fundamentally different considerations regarding what type of information Jeannie wishes to share with people. As a whimsical illustration of this idea that different spheres of our lives can involve different considerations of how we "present" ourselves, there recently was a "Dolly Parton Challenge" on social media where individuals posted different profile pictures based on the specific social network, e.g., LinkedIn v. Instagram. Of course, for some, the profile picture might be the same regardless of the network e.g. Chuck Norris (https://imgflip.com/i/3nhqa2 (last access 07 May 2021)).

[44] For instance, she could have the same information, such as, education history, in more than one sphere e.g. Family & Friends and Professional.

[45] Of course, this is not an "all or nothing" decision as consumers might be willing to share location data while actively using an app but not when the app is running in the background. This is evident by mobile operating systems giving this precise option to users. See e.g. Location Services & Privacy, APPLE, https://support.apple.com/en-us/HT207056 (last access 07 May 2021).

[46] Again, this is assuming that privacy is more about control rather than autonomy, anonymity, and freedom from outside stimuli.

g., always considering one's age or smartphone location history as private data).[47] Of course, some information is likely to be kept secret across the majority of spheres and across the majority of individuals (*e.g.*, Social Security number, medical history, criminal record). In contrast, some information is likely to be revealed across all or most spheres (e.g., marital status, academic degrees).

Second, individuals reveal and hide information based on considering the marginal benefit versus the marginal cost of revealing that information. Importantly, these benefits and costs could differ across spheres. Given that we live in a world with imperfect information, we often reveal information that is costly to fake—as a signal of our abilities or loyalties.[48] Thus, part of the calculus of what we reveal, and in what context, is based on considerations of these signals. For example, Jeannie might wish to reveal her political views to family and friends but keep those views private on social media and the workplace. In contrast, a political pundit would reveal all her political views on social media because it distributes her ideas more widely.

This gets to the third implication. While one can easily speak of modeling distinct spheres, the reality is that these "silos" are not airtight. Revealing and hiding information in one sphere or silo could "leak" to other spheres or silos. A common example of this is when someone reveals information on social media. This can negatively impact other spheres such as the workplace.[49] In contrast, we would not expect many positive spillovers from data leaks since, if it conferred a benefit to reveal certain information or data, then the person would have already revealed it. Thus, data spillovers from one sphere to another can cause significant harm. For example, Jeannie may be willing to share grades/transcript information with employers on a job application but would not want that posted on social media.[50]

The extent and likelihood of potentially negative spillovers also impact how much information is actually shared in the first place. This risk is incorporated into the benefits and costs of sharing or revealing information in a given sphere or silo. For instance, the more likely it is that employers search social media for information on applicants and employees, then the more likely people will seek to limit/alter what is revealed on their social media accounts.[51] As a corollary, the easier it is to

---

[47] See e.g. Baye and Sappington (2020).

[48] See e.g. Spence (1973).

[49] The employment, and legal, consequences from negative spillover effects of social media is an increasingly important area of scholarship. See e.g. Papandrea (2012); Ghoshray (2013); Mund (2017).

[50] She wishes to reveal grades to employers because *not* providing that information would be considered a negative signal of her "type," that is, it would give the impression that Jeannie's grades are worse than those applicants who did choose to reveal their grades. The result is an information unraveling where everybody—even those with less than stellar grades—would reveal this information.

[51] Another example of spillover effects from the use of social media data is its use by law enforcement agencies. See Ferguson (2015), p. 334 ("Social media sites, such as Twitter and Facebook, even disclose what we think. Currently, law enforcement officers may access many of

"silo" data and keep it from spilling over, the greater the likelihood that more information will be revealed in a particular silo. This creates a strong incentive, all else equal, for data stewards such as digital platforms and employers to properly silo information and limit spillovers if these spillovers lead to less usage or sharing of personal information within that silo.[52]

Ultimately, does this privacy framework help us to understand open data? In one respect, it seems that discussions of privacy have no real bearing on open data policy since open data is, well, "open". Yet, privacy does enter the debate in a number of ways. First, privacy considerations are involved if the opened data contains personally identifiable information—or creates a greater risk that creative methods could be used to form a probability-based profile of an individual.[53] Again, this risk will, in turn, impact the ex-ante incentives to reveal information within a given silo. For instance, if a business routinely shares salary information about its employees, then this would deter potential applicants who have a strong preference to keep financial information private. In a similar way, if governments open data without sufficient de-identification measures, then this will, in turn, raise public resistance to open data efforts and/or cause greater "opt outs" to the extent that option is available to citizens.

Second, if we consider "semi-open" data, i.e., data that is not strictly open to all but rather accessible to some, then the privacy policies of the collecting organization will again dictate the ex-ante incentive for participants to opt-in. An example would be a data collaborative where businesses and organizations across industry sectors exchange data in order to develop more effective medical treatments.[54] Without

---

these records without violating the Fourth Amendment, under the theory that there is no reasonable expectation of privacy in information knowingly revealed to third parties.").

[52] See e.g. Thomas C. Redman & Robert M. Waitman, Do You Care About Privacy as Much as Your Customers Do?, HARV. BUS. REV., Jan. 28, 2020, https://hbr.org/2020/01/do-you-care-about-privacy-as-much-as-your-customers-do (last access 07 May 2021) ("Privacy actives see respect for privacy as core to the brands of the companies with whom they do business: 90% believe the ways their data is treated reflects how they are treated as customers. Not surprisingly, they also say they will not buy from companies if they don't trust how their data is used."). Within the realm of privacy, however, there is a consistent finding that there is a wide gulf between what consumers say in surveys and consumers' actual behaviour, which is called the "privacy paradox." See e.g. Susan Athey, Christian Catalini, & Catherine Tucker, The Digital Privacy Paradox: Small Money, Small Costs, Small Talk, Stanford Institute for Economic Policy Research (SIEPR), Working Paper No. 17–032 (Sep. 17, 2017), https://siepr.stanford.edu/sites/default/files/publications/17-032.pdf (last access 07 May 2021).

[53] See e.g. Hardy and Maurushat (2017), p. 33 ("Even an agency's best efforts at de-identifying its data may not prevent that data from being combined with other sources of information to re-identify an individual."). Similarly, there are concerns regarding public access to court records based on privacy considerations along with First Amendment considerations. See Ardia (2017).

[54] An example is the Sentinel Initiative. See Sentinel Initiative, GovLab, https://datacollaboratives.org/cases/sentinel-initiative.html (last access 07 May 2021) ("The US Food and Drug Administration established the Sentinel Initiative with operations overseen by the Harvard Pilgrim Health Care Institute. It uses a distributed database through which the FDA can run analytical programs on local

adequate assurances that the data will be properly siloed, the data sharing initiative, which could bring significant social benefits, will be doomed to failure.

3 The Life Cycle of Data

We can consider the cost of data in terms of its "life cycle."[55] The basic idea is that there is a fundamental difference between having data and using data in a manner that provides value—hence, the need for data to go through a series of changes. We can depict the life cycle as a six-step process: (1) Generation, (2) Collection, (3) Storage, (4) Organization, (5) Analytics, and (6) Actionable Items (Fig. 1).

These steps are largely self-explanatory and, importantly, intimately linked. For instance, how data is stored can influence how it is collected and *vice versa*. Further, the efficiency to which the data is stored, and subsequently accessed, will influence the costs involved in the latter stages of the life cycle. Particularly in a digital economy, the accessibility of stored and organized data is paramount—examples include indexes such as the consumer product index (CPI) and the Dow Jones Industrial Average (DJIA).

The penultimate stage is to analyze the data.[56] This can include a plot of the data, simple statistics, multivariable regressions, and other machine learning techniques. This step is "at the heart of data science."[57] It is also the stage that can differentiate

| Generation | Collection | Storage | Organization | Analytics | Actionable Items |

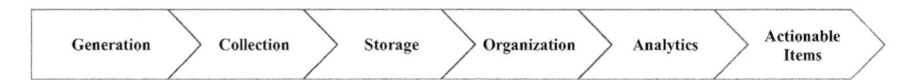

Fig. 1 Life cycle of data

---

databases of health providers, such as Humana, Inc. and Blue Cross Blue Shield [...] Sentinel intends to actively monitor adverse reactions of medical products after they are on the market.").

[55] This concept of a "life cycle" of data can be found in various forms in the area of data management and science. See e.g. Wing (2019); National Network of Libraries of Medicine, Data Lifecycle, https://nnlm.gov/data/thesaurus/data-lifecycle (last access 07 May 2021). See also Oliver Bethell & Alexander Waksman, Applying Economics to the Internet: Can Regulators and Competition Authorities Keep Pace?, Dec. 2019, https://papers.ssrn.com/sol3/papers.cfm?abstract_id=3492966 (last access 07 May 2021), p. 8 ("At Google, we tend to think of data in terms of four layers. At bottom, we have raw data...At the second layer, we can start analyzing the information [...] At the third layer, we obtain insights [...] And at the fourth layer, we can use those insights to develop our products."). Our focus is on data as an input into a larger production process rather than where data itself is the product—*e.g.*, services such as ACNielsen and IRI, but even these data products involve a life cycle.

[56] Again, these categorizations are not always so clear cut. Organization and analysis can overlap. Consider the process of cleaning a dataset where observations are dropped if they are missing or outliers.

[57] Wing (2019), p. 4.

firms in a competitive environment.[58] The final stage, and the ultimate point of collecting data in the first place, is to have actionable items from the data. This is just a broad term to capture the idea that data informs decisionmakers in all areas of society—from households all the way to governments.

As the life cycle framework illustrates, data is fundamentally a means to an end. Each stage is relevant, and the efficiency of each stage influences the value received in the last stage. For instance, starting with bad data, such as poor statistical sampling from public opinion polls, can lead to bad insights and decisions—irrespective of the quality and efficiency of each subsequent stage. Of course, good data is not enough either—as the mere possession of data confers no marketplace advantage.[59]

Segmenting data into a life cycle also highlights the fact that each phase involves costs. These costs will influence how much data is used, the manner in which it is used, and, ultimately, the quality of the actionable items. For instance, on digital platforms, data collection is achieved largely automatically. Additionally, it is not just sales data that is collected (assuming there is a transaction) but also associated user behaviours (*e.g.* what items were viewed, how long the shopper stayed on the site, which links were clicked). Previously, collecting this type of data on shopper behaviour took enormous resources for brick-and-mortar stores.[60] Yet now, tracking user behaviour on websites and platforms is routine and captured at a relatively low cost. This has increased the type of data that can be used and the quality of the actionable items.

Take, for instance, a local restaurant that is considering moving to online ordering along with the development of a mobile app. The restaurant will estimate the quantity of incremental sales from such a move as well as the expected costs to develop and maintain the ordering system and app. This benefit-cost calculus could change significantly depending on shifts in consumer preferences (e.g. increased use of smartphones to order on the go) as well as lower costs to implement (e.g. the app could be seamlessly integrated with the in-store ordering system and inventory management). Additional benefits from such a system could be that restaurants now have a distribution channel (the website and mobile app) to share open data, including real-time updates on wait times, specials, and inventory (e.g. "did the triple berry pie sell out?").

Another example is Harvard Law School's Caselaw Access Project (CAP), which involved the digitization of roughly 40 million pages of court decisions owned by the

---

[58] See e.g. Krzepicki et al. (2020); Yun (2019).

[59] See e.g. Martin Casado & Peter Lauten, The Empty Promise of Data Moats, Andreessen Horowitz, May 9, 2019, https://a16z.com/2019/05/09/data-network-effects-moats (last access 07 May 2021) ("The point of this is not to make a categorical statement about the utility of data as a defensive moat – our point is that defensibility is not inherent to data itself." [Emphasis original]).

[60] *However, this is changing for brick-and-mortar stores as well. For example, Amazon Go stores continually track the movements of shoppers while in they are in the store, which allows the shoppers to just walk out with their items without stopping at a cashier.* See https://www.amazon.com/b?ie=UTF8&node=16008589011 (last access 07 May 2021).

school going as far back as 1658.[61] CAP also offers a free browsable application program interface (API), which allows researchers to access the entire database more efficiently. While cases are technically in the public domain, commercial services such as Lexis and Westlaw have developed around organizing, structuring, and charging access to legal cases. While it is too early to predict how more innovative open data projects like CAP will change how legal data is made available,[62] it represents an opportunity to divert economic resources from commercializing, and hence limiting, access to data to focusing more on enabling value-add services that utilize legal data. In other words, projects like CAP can significantly reduce frictions within the life cycle of data, which, in turn, allow for more, and better, insights built off the data.

Ultimately, understanding the life cycle of data informs questions regarding open data.[63] Consider a local government that has limited resources and expertise to collect the data needed to forecast elementary school enrollment, recycling volume, park usage, et cetera. As technology develops to allow even governments with relatively limited financial resources to more seamlessly collect, store, and organize data (e.g. snowplow drivers using an app to track their routes), then we would expect there to be more structured data. With more structured data, then, holding the preference to share and open data constant, we would expect there to be more open data and associated services from that data.[64] More importantly, open data could be used in increasingly novel ways to provide society with valuable services and information.[65] Along these lines, there are clear initiatives to facilitate governments to open their data and lower their costs.[66] Yet, even with lower costs to collect,

---

[61] Caselaw Access Project, About, https://case.law/about (last access 07 May 2021) ("CAP includes all official, book-published United States case law [...] includes all state courts, federal courts, and territorial courts for American Samoa, Dakota Territory, Guam, Native American Courts, Navajo Nation, and the Northern Mariana Islands. Our earliest case is from 1658, and our most recent cases are from 2018.").

[62] There are currently a variety of sources that provide free access to various legal cases including FindLaw, Google Scholar, and Court Links.

[63] See e.g. Conradie and Choenni (2014), p. S10 ("We have found that important indicators for data release are how the data is stored (distributed/decentralized versus centralized), how the data is obtained, and the way data is used by the organization.").

[64] For example, the Iowa Department of Transportation's Track a Plow map allows residents to track the location and number of plows—including the ability to "view from the plow." See https://iowadot.maps.arcgis.com/apps/webappviewer/index.html?id=3d5bc4ec8c474870a19c7e8f44b39c9c (last access 07 May 2021).

[65] See e.g. Ben Miller, 7 Ways Local Governments Are Getting Creative with Data Mapping, Government Technology, Jan. 25, 2016, https://www.govtech.com/7-Ways-Local-Governments-Are-Getting-Creative-with-Data-Mapping.html (last access 07 May 2021) ("Boston's platform is open for users to submit their own maps. And submit they have. The city portal offers everything from maps of bus stops to traffic data pulled from the Waze app.").

[66] Examples of initiatives to reduce frictions and costs to open data is the Open Data Policy Lab. See https://opendatapolicylab.org (last access 07 May 2021).

store, and organize data, there must be some benefit for organizations to open data, which is addressed in the next section.

4 The Incentives to Open Data

What incentives do governments, businesses, organizations, and individuals have to "share" or open their data? There are both immediate, or "direct," benefits as well and "indirect" benefits—which are benefits that are primarily received by users of the data, but which can, in turn, create benefits to the original data provider. This distinction should not be overemphasized as the decision to open data ultimately boils down to the net benefit to the data provider—regardless of the classification as "direct" or "indirect". Nonetheless, this classification can serve as a useful distinction. In the following sections, we will separately discuss these incentives for governments, private entities, and households.

4.1 Benefits to Governments to Provide Open Data

Governments at all levels are leaders in providing open data.[67] In 2009, the U.S. government created Data.gov, which is a repository of open data, and is part of a larger U.S. federal government initiative to have an open data policy.[68] While containing predominantly federal agency data, Data.gov also includes data from states, counties, cities, universities, private entities, and non-profits.[69] Cities such as New York have their own open data portals.[70] The EU has both the Open Data Europe Portal (ODP) as well as the European Data Portal (EDP), which together provide datasets collected by various European institutions and countries.[71] The United Kingdom and Japan have their own respective Data.gov sites: Data.gov.uk

---

[67] See e.g. Takagi (2014), p. 121 ("Open data is not necessarily limited to government, but the open data movement has mainly evolved in the public sector.").

[68] See About Data.gov, Data.gov, https://www.data.gov/about (last access 07 May 2021) ("Under the terms of the 2013 Federal Open Data Policy, newly-generated government data is required to be made available in open, machine-readable formats, while continuing to ensure privacy and security."). See also Office of the Federal Chief Information Officer, M-13–13 – Memorandum for the Heads of Executive Departments and Agencies, May 13, 2013, https://policy.cio.gov/open-data/ (last access 07 May 2021) ("Making information resources accessible, discoverable, and usable by the public can help fuel entrepreneurship, innovation, and scientific discovery – all of which improve Americans' lives and contribute significantly to job creation.").

[69] See Data Catalog, Data.gov, https://catalog.data.gov/dataset#sec-organization_type (last access 07 May 2021).

[70] See NYC Open Data, https://opendata.cityofnewyork.us (last access 07 May 2021).

[71] See European Data Portal, Frequently Asked Questions, https://www.europeandataportal.eu/en/faq (last access 07 May 2021).

and Data.go.jp. It is fair to say that, in the past decade, there has been an explosion of government-lead open data sources and portals to access data in more convenient ways.

The benefits to the public from open data are clear—both conceptually and empirically. Numerous studies have estimated the value of open data to economic activity and innovation.[72] A specific example is the Covid-19 outbreak. Internationally, governments shared a tremendous amount of highly detailed data associated with the virus.[73] Organizations and individuals can then take the data, analyze it, and present it in a way to inform the public and decisionmakers.[74] Given the variety and volume of data on Covid-19, it is likely not hyperbole to predict that there will be an unprecedented amount of research performed over the coming years, which will result in associated spillover benefits for combating future viruses and social policies related to the efficacy of lockdowns.

Importantly, governments are often best positioned to collect a great deal of information and data about social and economic activities within their jurisdictions.[75] Further, the release and subsequent use of the data is significantly less "rivalrous" from the perspective of a government—as compared to private enterprises who compete in the marketplace where insights from data can represent a competitive advantage.

Ultimately, the reason why governments are at the forefront of opening data is that they receive a significant amount of both direct and indirect benefits from its provision.[76] The most obvious direct benefits include freeing resources and lowering

---

[72] See e.g. Berends et al. (2020). See also Vickery (2011); James Manyika, Michael Chui, Diana Farrell, Steve Van Kuiken, Peter Groves, & Elizabeth Almasi Doshi, Open Data: Unlocking Innovation and Performance with Liquid Information, MCKINSEY & Co., Oct. 2013, https://www.mckinsey.com/business-functions/mckinsey-digital/our-insights/open-data-unlocking-innovation-and-performance-with-liquid-information (last access 07 May 2021).

[73] See e.g. Centers for Disease Control and Prevention (CDC), Coronavirus Disease 2019 (COVID-19), Cases, Data, and Surveillance, https://www.cdc.gov/coronavirus/2019-ncov/cases-updates/index.html (last access 07 May 2021); EU Open Data Portal, COVID-19 Coronavirus Data, https://data.europa.eu/euodp/en/data/dataset/covid-19-coronavirus-data/resource/55e8f966-d5c8-438e-85bc-c7a5a26f4863 (last access 07 May 2021).

[74] See, e.g., Stanford University's Center for Artificial Intelligence in Medicine & Imaging, COVID-19 + Imaging AI Resources, https://aimi.stanford.edu/resources/covid19 (last access 07 May 2021); Centers for Disease Control and Prevention, Coronavirus Disease 2019 in Children – United States, February 12 – April 2, 2020, https://www.cdc.gov/mmwr/volumes/69/wr/mm6914e4.htm (last access 07 May 2021).

[75] See e.g. Open Data Handbook, Why Open Data?, http://opendatahandbook.org/guide/en/why-open-data (last access 07 May 2021) ("Many individuals and organizations collect a broad range of different types of data in order to perform their tasks. Government is particularly significant in this respect, both because of the quantity and centrality of the data it collects, but also because most of that government data is public data by law, and therefore could be made open and made available for others to use.").

[76] See e.g. Alan McQuinn, The Economics of "Opt-Out" Versus "Opt-In" Privacy, ITIF.com, Oct. 6, 2017, https://itif.org/publications/2017/10/06/economics-opt-out-versus-opt-in-privacy-rules (last access 07 May 2021) ("Many uses of data generate positive externalities, and these benefits

costs of operation.[77] One example is the increased efficiency in accessing its own data across different agencies or ministries.[78] Another example is the potential to lower the compliance costs associated with government transparency regulations such as the U.S. Freedom of Information Act (FOIA).[79]

More indirectly, these large datasets allow businesses, academia, and everyone else to "be able to draw new insights from that data and contribute innovative solutions to complex policy problems."[80] In effect, open data allows all activities within a government sphere to run more efficiently. For example, consider the real estate site Zillow.com, which is a digital platform that uses open data on real estate transactions.[81] A service such as Zillow can facilitate the matching of buyers and sellers as well as the provision of information to better assess home values. This can create benefits for local governments in the form of markets clearing more quickly and efficiently, which creates greater certainty for schooling and other local services that require demand forecasting. Another example of an indirect benefit is governments buying back data after it has been "aggregated and enriched by data-rich service providers."[82] There are also indirect benefits from the creation of entirely new services based on open data.[83] As the life cycle costs of data management as

---

grow as more parties share the data. For example, health researchers can use data to track diseases, research cures, and accelerate innovation in health care, and the opportunities for these benefits increase as the data becomes available to more parties.").

[77] See e.g. Berends et al. (2020), p. 22 (describing various examples of government efficiency gains from opening data including reduced number of service inquiries and freeing employee resources).

[78] See e.g. Stott (2014), para. 24 ("The amount of use of Open Data within government has been one of the unexpected and surprising observations of the last five years: for instance, one third of the data downloads from the Open Data portal of the province of British Columbia in Canada have been observed to be coming from the province's own internet addresses; and in the Catalonia Region of Spain the cost savings and efficiencies to public institutions themselves of open metadata on geospatial datasets mandated by the EU INSPIRE Directive recovered four years of development costs in just six months.").

[79] See e.g. Berliner et al. (2018), p. 867 ("FOI [Freedom of Information] is now just one good governance tool in an increasingly crowded field of transparency policy areas. Focus is increasingly shifting toward technology-enabled open data reforms.").

[80] Hardy and Maurushat (2017), pp. 30–31.

[81] See Zillow, Where does Zillow get information about my property?, https://zillow.zendesk.com/hc/en-us/articles/213218507-Where-does-Zillow-get-information-about-my-property- (last access 07 May 2021) ("Zillow receives information about property sales from the municipal office responsible for recording real estate transactions in your area.").

[82] See Stott (2014), para 24 ("Like other business consumers, public institutions are purchasers of data-rich services. Indeed, in some cases they buy back their own data after it has been aggregated or enriched by data-rich service providers.").

[83] See e.g. Open Data Handbook, Why Open Data?, http://opendatahandbook.org/guide/en/why-open-data (last access 07 May 2021) ("A woman in Denmark built findtoilet.dk, which showed all the Danish public toilets, so that people she knew with bladder problems can now trust themselves to go out more again. In the Netherlands a service, vervuilingsalarm.nl, is available which warns you with a message if the air-quality in your vicinity is going to reach a self-defined threshold tomorrow. In New York you can easily find out where you can walk your dog, as well as find other people who use the same parks. Services like 'mapumental' in the UK and 'mapnificent' in

well as increasing evidence that open data benefits the public in often unforeseeable ways, we would expect the open data initiatives to continue to grow along with the associated social benefits.[84]

Further, as experience with open data grows, governments can move beyond the role of "just putting it out there" to a model that involves a deeper relationship with those who use the data. Sieber and Johnson describe various open data "models" that governments can adopt ranging from a fairly narrow view of data as a downloadable commodity to a broader view of government actively participating and engaging with users of the data including exchanging contributions.[85] This level of involvement is not just a model for government but potentially for businesses and organizations.

Governments are not only a source of open data, but they can also influence the amount of open data provided by organizations and businesses through regulation. Take the Securities Act of 1933, which required the mandatory disclosure of detailed financial information for all publicly traded companies.[86] Holding aside the larger policy question of the economic welfare consequences of the regulation, there is little doubt that the widespread availability of such data, albeit in a somewhat unstructured form, has been beneficial to research and transparency. More recently, the DATA Act of 2014 and the OPEN Government Data Act of 2019 mandate that all federal agencies publish data and information to the public in an accessible and standardized manner.

4.2 Benefits to Private Enterprises to Provide Open Data

While governments hold monopoly power over certain services within their jurisdiction, the same is generally not true for private firms and organizations. Firms compete with each other in the marketplace, and the resulting competition benefits consumers. Yet, it can also create strong incentives to close data in order to maintain a competitive advantage.

Germany allow you to find places to live, taking into account the duration of your commute to work, housing prices, and how beautiful an area is. All these examples use open government data.").

[84] There is also a public choice aspect to opening data. To the extent that open data results in new and more efficiently provided government benefits, then this will result in more votes for incumbents providing these services.

[85] See Sieber and Johnson (2015), pp. 311–312 ("A participatory model presents open data as a formalized conduit between citizen and government, where citizen contributions are integrated into decision-making [...] This bi-directional linkage can also take the form of a co-management framework, with the end goals to encourage the stable provision of open data, improve quality and utility of datasets, and to highlight areas for expanded data collection to support community or private sector needs.").

[86] The Laws that Govern the Securities Industry, U.S. Securities and Exchange Commission, https://www.sec.gov/answers/about-lawsshtml.html#secact1933 (last access 07 May 2021).

The benefits to open data for private enterprise are generally more indirect. Yet, this does not mean they are zero. Like for governments, there are certain immediate benefits to businesses and organizations to making data and information available to the public, which can lower their costs including those associated with customer service. Examples include businesses posting information about their hours online as well as detailed information about store inventory (e.g. "two items left in stock"); SEC filings that provide detailed financial data for current and potential investors; and utility providers giving detailed information on service outages and estimated repair times.[87]

One type of benefit, whether categorized as direct or indirect, could come in the form of greater goodwill towards the company and its associated brand(s). Let us return to the prior examples of companies sharing their previously closely guarded recipes during the Covid-19 societal lockdown, such as, Ikea's Swedish meatballs, DoubleTree's chocolate chip cookies, and Wagamama's katsu curry chicken. Why did these companies release these trade secrets for the first time during the crisis? There is almost certainly a host of reasons—including a sense of contribution during a time of collective hardship. Yet, the recipes have to be, in a sense, costly to share, that is, have some commercial value, in order for the signal of contribution to be credible. Thus, whatever signal these companies were conveying, it must be credible in order to build the brand—even if the goal was not explicitly "to build the brand." The effect can be similar to other marketing activities (e.g. promotions, sales, and giveaways). As more firms gain experience and awareness of data sharing as a brand building activity, then we would expect to see more of it—all else equal.

Another example is Apple's Mobility Trends Reports, which were also released for the first time during the Covid-19 lockdown.[88] Apple provides downloadable data as well as a web interface that allows users to visualize mobility trends for specific locations. While this initiative by Apple is likely to be temporary, it illustrates how circumstances, which impacts the calculus of opening data, can change quickly. While it is hard to predict future conditions that would incentivize more episodes of open data, it seems clear that having more experience with open data will facilitate the opening of more data.

Another example is Tesla's policy of allowing the general public to use all of its patents without an explicit license.[89] This policy almost certainly improves Tesla's

---

[87] See e.g. Outages, Dominion Energy, https://www.dominionenergy.com/outages (last access 07 May 2021).

[88] See Apple, Mobility Trends Reports, https://www.apple.com/covid19/mobility (last access 07 May 2021) ("Learn about COVID-19 mobility trends. Reports are published daily and reflect requests for directions in Apple Maps. Privacy is one of our core values, so Maps doesn't associate your data with your Apple ID, and Apple doesn't keep a history of where you've been.").

[89] See Elon Musk, All Our Patent Are Belong to You [sic], Tesla.com, Jun. 12, 2014, https://www.tesla.com/blog/all-our-patent-are-belong-you (last access 07 May 2021).

branding and the public's perception of the brand.[90] Of course, providing open data could also generate benefits in the form of lowering the cost of innovation and the development of complementary products and infrastructure in the electric car industry. This, in turn, creates tangible benefits to Tesla given its market leading position.[91] In fact, all else equal, a market leading firm that faces less competition might have the strongest incentive to open various types of data—to the extent that the release of such data leads to complementary innovation by third-parties. The reason is that market leaders are in a position to more fully "internalize" the benefits of these innovations since they do not have as strong a fear that a competitor will free ride off of the innovations and insights gained from the open data.

One avenue that businesses can use to mitigate a potential free rider problem is to offer prizes for subsequent "add on" innovations that emerge from the use of open or semi-open data. Depending on how the prize is structured, it could involve assigning property rights to the subsequent innovation to the open data provider. Alternatively, even without a property right transfer, the use of a prize will attract resources to the specific firm's dataset, and the firm can steer the innovation efforts to solve a particular problem that the firm is interested in addressing. An example is the Yelp Dataset Challenge, which involved Yelp sharing "user data on restaurants across cities [...] for participating researchers to build tools and provide research on urban trends and behaviour."[92] While the use of prizes to spur innovation is a well-researched topic,[93] its intersection with the open data movement will be an interesting area to watch.

There are also potential benefits from open data to local businesses in the form of lower costs and increased demand for their goods and services. As mentioned earlier, businesses could post data such as hours of operation, menus & specials, wait times, seating capacity, and inventory on a common data-sharing platform. This would allow services such as search engines and local business apps to more easily plug into and access the data in real-time. By having local businesses directly control and release their information, this would maximize the dissemination of accurate information and potentially facilitate the development of new startups and entries—given that these entrants can access the data at zero cost rather than incur the expense of gathering the data on their own. Consequently, in this particular example, open data

---

[90] See e.g. Eric Loveday, Tesla Is Now Consumer Reports' Highest Ranked U.S. Automotive Brand, InsideEVs, Feb. 20, 2020, https://insideevs.com/news/399837/tesla-tops-consumer-reports-u-s (last access 07 May 2021).

[91] See e.g. Fred Lambert, Tesla Owns More Than Half the US Market, Keeps Electric Car Sales Growing, Electrek, Feb. 4, 2020, https://electrek.co/2020/02/04/tesla-electric-car-sales-us-market-share (last access 07 May 2021).

[92] Yelp Dataset Challenge, GovLab, https://datacollaboratives.org/cases/yelp-dataset-challenge.html (last access 07 May 2021). See also Past Winners, Yelp, https://www.yelp.com/dataset/challenge/winners (last access 07 May 2021).

[93] See e.g. Shavell and Van Ypersele (2001); William A. Masters & Benoit Delbecq, Accelerating Innovation with Prize Rewards, IFPRI Discussion Paper 00835, Dec. 2008, http://ebrary.ifpri.org/utils/getfile/collection/p15738coll2/id/15644/filename/15645.pdf (last access 07 May 2021).

could spur online search competition, increase demand for the goods and services of local businesses, and provide more valuable information to consumers. Therefore, tools that lower the costs for local businesses to provide their data seem a particularly fruitful channel for open data resources and investments.

Complementary to the discussion of open data is what is called data collaboratives, which "refers to a new form of collaboration, beyond the public-private partnership model, in which participants from different sectors – including private companies, research institutions, and government agencies – can exchange data to help solve public problems."[94] One way to consider data collaboratives is that they involve semi-open data—where, rather than having data open to all, the data is opened to all the participants within the particular data collaboration, or silo. These data collaborations could result in "learning by doing" and getting a better understanding of all the benefits, as well as costs and privacy considerations, with opening data. This could spill over into efforts to have fully open data.

4.3 Benefits to Households and Individuals to Provide Open Data

The final group, as a potential source of open data, is households and individuals. Of course, when data becomes more granular and at a household- or individual-level, privacy considerations come to the forefront. Yet, this does not mean that households cannot be a source of valuable open data.

Perhaps the most visible "open data" that households and individuals provide are social media posts—such as on Twitter, Facebook, and Instagram. Companies and services routinely scour social media to measure engagement levels on specific issues, topics, and brands.[95] The public sector is also increasingly monitoring social media to gain insights into service improvements.[96] This can create enormous insight into word-of-mouth type of data, which was previously extremely costly, if

---

[94] Stefaan Verhulst & David Sangokoya, Data Collaboratives: Exchanging Data to Improve People's Lives, Medium, Apr. 22, 2015, https://medium.com/@sverhulst/data-collaboratives-exchanging-data-to-improve-people-s-lives-d0fcfc1bdd9a (last access 07 May 2021). For instance, GovLab is an organization based out of New York University's Tandon School of Engineering that provides resources to encourage data collaboratives. See GovLab, https://www.thegovlab.org (last access 07 May 2021).

[95] See e.g. Edward Cherry, Top 17 Social Media Monitoring Vendors for Business, SocialMedia.biz (Jun. 8, 2018) ("Successful companies in the world make huge profits every year because they use the best social media monitoring tools to understand their markets, monitor reach, listen to their customers' needs, and track engagements."). See also Sutherland (2021).

[96] See e.g. Loukis et al. (2017), p. 99 ("Motivated by the multiple 'success stories' of the open innovation paradigm in the private sector, and also by the increasing complexity of social problems and needs, the public sector has started moving in this direction, attempting to exploit the extensive knowledge of citizens ('citizen-sourcing'), in order to develop innovations in public policies and services [...]").

not impossible, to obtain. It also points to the importance of distribution channels to share data and information. Before social media, a reasonable hypothesis is that individuals had the same desire to share their views on politics and cultural issues as they do today. Yet, social media simply gave them a platform. Thus, the incentivization of open data at the individual level seems principally about user-friendly tools to share the information.

Consider the potential to post medical records online in an open manner. Why would individuals do this given privacy concerns? Again, privacy can be more about control than specific content. There are a variety of reasons why an individual might be willing to share medical data online. One example is cancer treatment. When someone gets diagnosed with cancer, this can be a massively stressful life event for not only the patient but family, friends, and caregivers. As patients consider various treatment options and learn more about the cancer, there is tremendous value in studying the experiences of current patients and cancer survivors.

Given this benefit, current patients and cancer survivors likely gain some level of utility from sharing their information if they know this will help others—especially for less common cancers such as mesothelioma. What is needed is a catalyst to coordinate those who are willing to share the information with those who would value the information. This is precisely the role that multisided platforms play.[97] A platform could allow individuals to seamlessly post their medical records online to share with health care professionals and other patients who are looking for more information on treatment options. A platform with a user-friendly interface would lower the cost of information sharing and could feature the ability to scrub medical records of more detailed personal information (but would preserve other pertinent information about treatment). In fact, there seems to be initiatives starting along these lines.[98] Another example are individuals volunteering information during the Covid-19 lockdown.[99]

Thus, the sharing of data, whether within a specific silo or publicly online, involve weighing costs and benefits. Benefits are harder to quantify unless there is a well-functioning market—but they exist. For individuals and households, the amount of open data will be dictated less on the basis of the costs associated with

---

[97] While definitions can vary, platforms primarily serve as an intermediary that attracts and coordinates various groups who derive some value from interacting or transacting with each other. See e.g. Yun (2020).

[98] See e.g. Jonathan Shieber, Citizen Raises $17 Million to Give Cancer Patients Better Control Over Their Health Records, Tech Crunch, Jan. 17, 2019, https://techcrunch.com/2019/01/16/ciitizen-raises-17-million-to-give-cancer-patients-better-control-over-their-health-records (last access 07 May 2021) ("Ciitizen, like Gliimpse before it, is an attempt to break down the barriers that keep patients from being able to record, store and share their healthcare information with whomever they want in their quest for treatment.").

[99] For example, the Covid-19 Symptom Study App was developed by the company ZOE in collaboration with individuals at the King's College of London and the Massachusetts General Hospital. Individuals download the app and volunteer data related to Covid-19 based on a daily one-minute survey. The site reports that, as of April 20, 2021, 4.6 million people are contributors. See Covid Symptom Study, https://covid.joinzoe.com/us (last access 07 May 2021).

collecting, storing, and managing the data but more on the ability to seamlessly share the data (e.g., through transparent and clear "opt in" features for apps that collect data in the background or with a user-friendly interface to share data).

5 Open Data as an Antitrust Remedy

As the open data movement has continued to grow worldwide,[100] calls to incorporate open data and interoperability within antitrust and competition law have also grown.[101] This Part examines the wisdom of open data antitrust policies as it pertains to digital platforms.

The most basic proposal to alleviate the market leadership of various digital platforms is to allow digital platform participants, such as users and advertisers, to more easily and seamlessly port their data to rival platforms.[102] The idea is to lower switching costs and lock-in effects, which will facilitate the ability of platform participants to multi-home or switch altogether.[103] Of course, there is a major difference between using this proposal as a remedy to address demonstrable anti-competitive harms versus as a proactive regulatory intervention in an effort to improve market outcomes. As a remedy, the benefits of this proposal are that it can be targeted at specific practices, users, and platforms. These benefits, however,

---

[100] For instance, in Europe, the Open Data Directive (Directive (EU) 2019/1024) went into force in 2019, which replaced the earlier Public Sector Information Directive (Directive 2003/98/EC) from 2003. The goal of the Open Data Directive is to provide public access to dynamic data generated by member states for re-use through application programming interfaces (APIs) and other means. See European Commission, European Legislation on Open Data and the Re-Use of Public Sector Information, Mar. 8, 2020, https://ec.europa.eu/digital-single-market/en/european-legislation-reuse-public-sector-information (last access 07 May 2021). In the U.S., in January 2019, President Donald Trump signed the OPEN Government Data Act into law, which is part of the larger Foundations for Evidence-Based Policymaking Act of 2018. The act requires agencies to appoint chief data officers (CDOs) and to release all non-sensitive data to the public in a machine-readable format. Pub. L. No. 115–435, 132 Stat. 5529 (Jan. 14 2019).

[101] See e.g. Competition and Markets Authority (2020), p. 24 (recommending "[i]ncreasing consumer control over data, which includes providing choices over the use of data and facilitating consumer-led data mobility; Mandating interoperability to overcome network effects and coordination failures; Mandating third-party access to data where data is valuable in overcoming barriers to entry and expansion and privacy concerns can be effectively managed.").

[102] Data portability is already part of the EU's General Data Protection Regulation (GDPR). See Regulation (EU) 2016/679 of the European Parliament and of the Council of 27 April 2016 on the Protection of Natural Persons with Regard to the Processing of Personal Data and on the Free Movement of Such Data and Repealing Directive 95/46/EC, at 2016 O.J.L. 119, 4.5.2016, Article 20, https://eur-lex.europa.eu/legal-content/EN/TXT/PDF/?uri=CELEX:32016R0679&from=EN (last access 07 May 2021) (users "shall have the right to receive the personal data concerning him or her, which he or she has provided to a controller, in a structured, commonly used and machine-readable format and have the right to transmit those data to another controller without hindrance.").

[103] Multi-homing is the practice of concurrently using two or more competing platforms.

might not translate to a regulatory setting, where the statutory language will likely have to be broader. This potentially opens the door for creative means where a platform could adhere to a strict reading of the regulation but implement measures that undermine its effectiveness in actually lowering lock-in and switching costs. This concern is likely significantly mitigated when data portability is used as a remedy—again, as remedies are intended to solve a specific competition problem and, thus, attempts to undermine the stated objective will more likely be flagged as an order violation. Additionally, given that many digital markets have already moved towards data portability as a best practice,[104] the value of mandatory data mobility proposals are more limited. Of course, there are also complications involved with data portability including issues of privacy and data security.[105]

There are also calls for more aggressive remedies including data sharing and interoperability, which involves taking platforms' intellectual property and requiring them to share it with rivals. There are a number of concerns with these types of open data antitrust proposals. First, there are major questions whether data sharing would actually solve the problem at issue—given that advantages in data do not necessarily translate into advantages in innovation and quality.[106] It would seem that a necessary condition to impose such a remedy is a finding that data is an essential facility.[107] Further, even if data sharing achieves the objective of boosting the success of rivals, the question becomes the dynamic incentive effects. Will the dominant platform engage in inefficient "upgrades" and technology shifts in order to constantly have rivals adapting to their system? In other words, by tethering the cost of rivals to a dominant platform's product design decisions, the dominant platform now has an additional lever by which to raise rivals' costs.

Second, data sharing and interoperability inevitably bring rival platforms closer together and further their interdependence. This can result in consumer harm in a number of ways. For instance, while it is ostensibly appealing to have leading platforms coordinate on the design and infrastructure of their platforms, it also raises

---

[104] See About Us, Data Transfer Project, https://datatransferproject.dev (last access 07 May 2021) ("The Data Transfer Project was launched in 2018 to create an open-source, service-to-service data portability platform so that all individuals across the web could easily move their data between online service providers whenever they want." Apple, Facebook, Google, Microsoft, and Twitter have all committed to the project.).

[105] See e.g. Swire and Lagos (2013), pp. 373–375.

[106] See e.g. OECD, Big Data: Bringing Competition Policy to the Digital Era 3, No. DAF/COMP/M (2016)2/ANN4/FINAL (Apr. 2017), https://one.oecd.org/document/DAF/COMP/M(2016)2/ANN4/FINAL/en/pdf (last access 07 May 2021) ("The control over a large volume of data is a not sufficient factor to establish market power, as nowadays a variety of data can be easily and cheaply collected by small companies – for instance, through point of sale terminals, web logs and sensors – or acquired from the broker industry."); Tucker (2019), pp. 684–687.

[107] The essential facilities doctrine has a long history in U.S. antitrust jurisprudence and involves the recognition that, while firms normally have no duty to help their rivals, there are instances when a monopolist control over an input is so essential to a rival's ability to compete, that withholding or foreclosing that input is considered an illegal restraint of trade. See e.g. Pitofsky (2002). In Europe, the essential facilities doctrine developed from Article 82 of the EC Treaty. See e.g. Evrard (2004).

concerns about "bad" coordination, that is, agreements that soften competition rather than sharpen it.[108] Further, "standardization" could be implemented in an overly technical and complex manner, where the intent is to actually hinder, rather than facilitate, entry. This would serve only to entrench the incumbents.

Third, increased interdependence on a dominant platform could translate into less differentiated products where all competitors within a market converge to common features and methods to use data. This can result in free-rider concerns and a market becoming stagnant and increasingly homogenous in features. Further, by making rivals more dependent on the success of dominant platforms, this can create a cascading effect within a market. For instance, if a dominant platform is hit by some type of outage or, even, unravels altogether, the market would not be as robust to withstand these unpredictable events. As a consequence, this can increase uncertainty and reduce the resiliency of markets.

Finally, forced sharing has been demonstrated to dampen incentives and reduce innovation.[109] In Verizon Communications v. Trinko, Justice Antonin Scalia raised serious concerns regarding any type of duty to deal with one's rivals:

> Compelling such firms to share the source of their advantage is in some tension with the underlying purpose of antitrust law, since it may lessen the incentive for the monopolist, the rival, or both to invest in those economically beneficial facilities.[110]

In sum, the basic message is that remedies and regulations intended to fix the professed competitive deficiencies of a digital market are inevitably going to lead to unintended consequences, which can ultimately do more harm than good. Further, attempts to promote rival products through open data remedies such as data sharing and interoperability are likely to negatively impact dynamic incentives. Thus, these proposals, while well-intended, should only be seriously considered after a thorough analysis of the full benefits and costs. As a remedy, there certainly can be instances where these proposals could address the harm from proven anticompetitive conduct.[111] Yet, even in those cases, agencies and courts should be aware of their inherent weaknesses and, thus, they should be implemented in the narrowest manner possible.

---

[108] For details on the types of agreements between competitors that can result in anticompetitive harm, see U.S. Federal Trade Commission and Department of Justice (2000).

[109] See, e.g., Hazlett and Caliskan (2008).

[110] 540 U.S. 398, 407–408 (2004).

[111] Although, one burden that courts must face when it imposes a data sharing obligation is the potential administrative costs after the order. See Trinko, 540 U.S. at 414-15 ("Effective remediation of violations of regulatory sharing requirements will ordinarily require continuing supervision of a highly detailed decree."). See also Hurwitz (2020) (documenting that regulatory duty to deal imposed on AT&T's telephone network, known today as the Kingsbury Commitment, in the early twentieth century).

6 Conclusion

We are in an age where continued innovations in harnessing data will reap significant returns in terms of innovation and economic growth. Thomas Kuhn observed that innovation happens in leaps through paradigm shifts rather than through incremental progress along the same technological trajectory.[112] The same is perhaps true for the use of open data.

We are already seeing an unprecedented amount of open data based on initiatives by governments around the world including the U.S., Europe, Asia, and South America. The fruits of the open data movement have been especially highlighted with the Covid-19 outbreak and associated government responses and measures. Ultimately, the volume and quality of open data come down to the central maxim of weighing benefits and costs. As the frictions along a data's life cycle are further minimized, this opens immense possibility for open data and the combination of various data sets to reach even greater insights. Further, as the benefits of open data are realized and experience with open data increases, it is also likely that we will see even more open data, both absolutely and as a percentage of all forms of data. As it relates to competition policy, however, the use of open data remedies and regulations should be employed cautiously and narrowly—if at all.

Acknowledgments Support for this research from a research grant from Microsoft is gratefully acknowledged. I thank Seth Sacher, Lyanne Elsener, and Philipp Gisler for valuable comments and suggestions.

References

Ackoff R (1989) From data to wisdom. J Appl Syst Anal 16:3–9
Acquisti A, Taylor C, Wagman L (2016) The economics of privacy. J Econ Lit 54:442–492
Ardia D (2017) Privacy and court records: online access and the loss of practical obscurity. Univ Ill Law Rev 2017:1385–1454
Australian Competition and Consumer Commission (2019) Digital platforms inquiry final report. https://www.accc.gov.au/system/files/Digital%20platforms%20inquiry%20-%20final%20report.pdf (last access 07 May 2021)
Baye M, Sappington D (2020) Revealing transactions data to third parties: implications of privacy regimes for welfare in online markets. J Econ Manag Strategy 29:260–275
Berends J, Carrara W, Radu C (2020) Analytical Report 9: the economic benefits of open data. European Data Portal. https://www.europeandataportal.eu/sites/default/files/analytical_report_n9_economic_benefits_of_open_data.pdf (last access 07 May 2021)
Berliner D, Ingrams A, Piotrowski S (2018) The future of FOIA in an open government world: implications of the open government agenda for freedom of information policy and implementation. Vill Law Rev 63:867–894

---

[112] See Kuhn (1996).

Competition and Markets Authority (2020) Online platforms and digital advertising: market study final report. https://assets.publishing.service.gov.uk/media/5efc57ed3a6f4023d242ed56/Final_report_1_July_2020_.pdf (last access 07 May 2021)

Conradie P, Choenni S (2014) On the barriers for local government releasing open data. Gov Inf Q 31:10–17

Cooper J (2013) Privacy and antitrust: underpants gnomes, the first amendment, and subjectivity. Geo Mason Law Rev 20:1129–1146

Digital Competition Expert Panel (2019) Unlocking digital competition. https://assets.publishing.service.gov.uk/government/uploads/system/uploads/attachment_data/file/785547/unlocking_digital_competition_furman_review_web.pdf (last access 07 May 2021)

Dorman P (2014) Microeconomics a fresh start. Springer, New York

Dreyfuss R (2010) Does IP need IP? Accommodating intellectual production outside the intellectual property paradigm. Cardozo Law Rev 31:1437–1474

Easterbrook F (1981) Insider trading, secret agents, evidentiary privileges, and the production of information. Sup Court Rev 1981:309–365

Eckartz S, Hofman W, Van Veenstra A (2014) A decision model for data sharing. In: Lindgren I et al (eds) Electronic government. Springer, Switzerland, pp 253–264

Evans D (2003) The antitrust economics of multi-sided platform markets. Yale J Reg 20:325–382

Evrard S (2004) Essential facilities in the European Union: Bronner and beyond. Colum J Eur Law 10:491–526

Ferguson A (2015) Big data and predictive reasonable suspicion. Univ Pa Law Rev 163:327–410

Gavison R (1980) Privacy and the limits of law. Yale Law J 89:421–471

Ghoshray S (2013) Employer surveillance versus employee privacy: the new reality of social media and workplace privacy. North Ky Law Rev 40:593–626

Hagiu A, Wright J (2015) Multi-sided platforms. Intl J Indus Org 43:162–174

Hardin G (1968) The tragedy of the commons. Science 162:1243–1248

Hardy K, Maurushat A (2017) Opening up government data for big data analysis and public benefit. Comput Law Secur Rev 33:30–37

Hazlett T, Caliskan A (2008) Natural experiments in U.S. broadband regulation. Rev Netw Econ 7:460–480

Hirshleifer J (1980) Privacy: its origin, function, and future. J Leg Stud 9:649–664

Hong S (2013) Measuring the effect of napster on recorded music sales: difference-in-differences estimates under compositional changes. J Appl Econ 28:297–324

Hsu S (2005) What is a tragedy of the commons? Overfishing and the campaign spending problem. Albany Law Rev 69:75–138

Hurwitz J (2020) Digital duty to deal, data portability, and interoperability. In: Wright J, Ginsburg D (eds) The Global Antitrust Institute Report on the Digital Economy. https://gaidigitalreport.com (last access 07 May 2021)

Krzepicki A, Wright J, Yun J (2020) The impulse to condemn the strange: assessing big data in antitrust. CPI Antitrust Chron, https://papers.ssrn.com/sol3/papers.cfm?abstract_id=3544218 (last access 07 May 2021)

Kuhn T (1996) The structure of scientific revolutions, 3rd edn. University of Chicago Press, Chicago

Levendowski L (2021) Trademarks as surveillance transparency. Berkeley Technol Law J 38:101–130

Loukis E, Charalabidis Y, Androutsopoulou A (2017) Promoting open innovation in the public sector through social media monitoring. Gov Inf Q 34:99–109

Mankiw N (2015) Principles of economics, 7th edn. Cengage Learning, Samford

Mund B (2017) Social media searches and the reasonable expectation of privacy. Yale J Law Technol 19:238–273

Papandrea M (2012) Social media, public school teachers, and the first amendment. N C Law Rev 90:1597–1642

Pitofsky R (2002) The essential facilities doctrine under U.S. antitrust law. Antitrust Law J 70:443–462

Posner R (2005) Intellectual property: the law and economics approach. J Econ Perspect 19:57–73

Reinsel D, Gantz J, Rydning J (2018) The digitization of the world: from edge to core. https://www.seagate.com/files/www-content/our-story/trends/files/idc-seagate-dataage-whitepaper.pdf (last access 07 May 2021)

Shavell S, Van Ypersele T (2001) Rewards versus intellectual property rights. J Law Econ 44:525–547

Sieber R, Johnson P (2015) Civic open data at a crossroads: dominant models and current challenges. Gov Inf Q 32:308–315

Spence M (1973) Job market signaling. Q J Econ 87:355–374

Stigler G (1961) The economics of information. J Pol Econ 69:213–225

Stott A (2014) Open data for economic growth. The World Bank, https://www.worldbank.org/content/dam/Worldbank/document/Open-Data-for-Economic-Growth.pdf (last access 07 May 2021)

Sutherland K (2021) Social media monitoring, measurement, analysis and big data. In: Strategic social media management. Palgrave Macmillan, Singapore. https://doi.org/10.1007/978-981-15-4658-7_7 (last access 07 May 2021)

Swire P, Lagos Y (2013) Why the right to data portability likely reduces consumer welfare: antitrust and privacy critique. Md Law Rev 72:335–380

Takagi S (2014) Research note: an introduction to the economic analysis of open data. Rev Socionetwork Strat 8:119–128

Terry N (2012) Protecting patient privacy in the age of big data. UMKC Law Rev 81:385–416

Tucker C (2019) Digital data, platforms and the usual [antitrust] suspects: network effects, switching costs, essential facility. Rev Indus Org 54:683–694

Tucker C (2020) Digital data as an essential facility: control. CPI Antitrust Chron., https://www.competitionpolicyinternational.com/digital-data-as-an-essential-facility-control (last access 07 May 2021)

U.S. Federal Trade Commission and Department of Justice (2000) Antitrust guidelines for collaboration among competitors. https://www.ftc.gov/sites/default/files/attachments/dealings-competitors/ftcdojguidelines.pdf (last access 07 May 2021)

Vickery G (2011) Review of recent studies on PSI re-use and related market developments. https://ec.europa.eu/digital-single-market/en/news/review-recent-studies-psi-reuse-and-related-market-developments (last access 07 May 2021)

Wing J (2019) The data life cycle. Harv Data Sci Rev 1:1–6

Yun JM (2019) Antitrust after big data. Criterion J Innov 4:407–429

Yun JM (2020) Overview of network effects & platforms in digital markets. In: Wright J, Ginsburg D (eds) The Global Antitrust Institute Report on the Digital Economy. https://gaidigitalreport.com (last access 07 May 2021)

Index

A
Access rights, 252–255, 258
Adaption and termination under changed circumstances, 113–115
Antitrust, 34, 125, 127, 131, 143, 148, 149, 165, 169, 172, 255, 266, 375, 396–398

B
Behaviour, vii, 3–7, 9–11, 15, 18, 20, 21, 23, 48, 59, 66, 69, 74, 76–79, 82, 88, 89, 92–96, 113, 131, 136, 140, 142, 145, 153, 159, 162, 168, 238, 259, 310, 318, 326, 328, 384, 386, 393
Behavioural economics, vii, 4, 9, 22, 59–99, 132, 135
Big data, 155, 397
Business interruption insurance, 215–234

C
Cell-cultured food, 324, 325, 327, 328, 332, 333, 347, 363
Challenges, 18, 34, 146, 158, 184, 186, 189, 192, 194, 205, 227, 259, 284, 288
Compliance, 4, 8–20, 23, 68, 69, 80, 86, 89, 91, 94–98, 107, 108, 153, 180, 191, 197, 221, 390
Compulsory licensing, 266–290
Contracts, 105–118
Coronavirus diseases-19 (COVID-19) pandemic, vii, 3–8, 10–14, 16–19, 21–23, 32, 106, 110–112, 123–173, 177–205, 219, 222, 223, 228, 231, 232, 234, 237–246, 251, 260, 261, 263, 266–290, 295–310, 315, 316, 320, 322, 326, 344, 357, 373, 374, 389, 392
Crisis, 59–99, 123–173, 295–310

D
Data life cycle, 385
Delay of performance, 112, 113
Development, 35, 48, 65, 88, 143, 155, 171, 172, 180, 194, 202, 251, 252, 259–263, 277, 304–310, 317, 324, 329, 359, 374, 386, 390, 393

E
Embracing risk, 215–234
Emergency, 32, 72, 80, 97, 105–118, 145, 148, 156, 166, 205, 219, 221, 240, 266, 268, 269, 275, 278–281, 284–290, 297, 300, 302–306
Ethicality, 325, 330, 339, 343, 358, 362
European Competition Law, 123, 125–128, 134, 138–143, 165, 168
European Union (EU), 36, 38, 42–52, 84, 97, 107, 126, 127, 130, 135, 138–144, 148, 153–155, 164, 165, 172, 238, 240, 253–255, 271, 275, 276, 296, 298, 302, 303, 305, 306, 310, 319, 321, 325, 326, 333, 335, 337–345, 351, 352, 356–358, 362, 388–390, 396
Excessive pricing, 123–173

F

Fake News, 32–52
Financial stability, 295, 300, 301, 303
Free speech, 33, 34, 36–38, 40, 42, 45, 46

G

Global public good, 303, 304, 306

H

Health, 3–5, 8–12, 17–22, 32, 59–61, 65, 67–72, 74–77, 79–87, 89, 90, 92–94, 97, 98, 106, 109, 110, 118, 125, 133, 137, 144, 149, 153–155, 165, 166, 178, 179, 185, 186, 190, 191, 194, 196, 205, 254, 255, 259–261, 263, 266–290, 297, 317–319, 322, 325, 326, 328–330, 332, 339, 343, 344, 349, 357–360, 362–364, 385, 390, 395

I

Implementation, 37, 51, 71, 85, 125, 142, 179, 182, 185, 195, 196, 200, 202, 203, 205, 260, 261, 268, 290, 307, 309, 310
Impossibility of performance, 110–112
Infodemic, 32, 33, 49
Informal economy, 178, 184, 186, 188–192, 197, 199, 200, 205
Information platforms, 32–52
Innovative, 172, 266–290, 315–364, 387, 390
Intermediaries, 34, 35, 47
International economic order, 295, 298, 306
Interoperability, 375, 379, 396–398

L

Law and economics, 106, 117, 123–173
Liability, 34, 38, 40, 41, 44–47, 52, 107, 108, 139, 148, 166, 172, 287

M

Mandates, 4, 6–9, 20, 23, 83, 220–221, 270

N

Non-rivalrous, 254, 379
Nudges, 4–9, 13, 20, 23, 68, 82, 87–89
Nudging, 8, 96

O

Obligation to fulfil, 177–206

Open data, 372–399
Ownership rules, 253, 254

P

Pandemic, 3–14, 16, 18–23, 32, 59–65, 67–70, 72, 74, 75, 79–81, 83, 84, 86, 87, 89, 91–93, 95–98, 108–113, 115–117, 123–128, 133, 136, 139, 144–148, 150–153, 155, 156, 158–160, 162–169, 171, 172, 178, 183–186, 188–190, 192–194, 196, 197, 199, 204, 205, 216–222, 225–230, 232–234, 251, 252, 259–263, 284–288, 290, 295–297, 300, 303, 306, 310, 315, 320, 322, 326, 344, 357, 358, 374
Patents, 128, 267, 269, 270, 272–274, 282, 284–288, 290, 373, 377, 392
Plant-based food, 324, 328, 329, 343, 357, 358, 360, 362, 363
Platform regulation, 46, 52
The precautionary principle, 85
Price gouging, 136, 150
Privacy, 40, 43, 372, 375–384, 388, 394–397
Public health policy, 67, 98

R

Rational, 8, 10, 18, 63, 64, 73, 74, 90, 117, 131, 132, 134, 137, 324
React, 60, 79, 309
Reaction, 67, 76, 229, 274, 297, 320
Recommendations, 5, 62, 90, 92, 95, 201, 204, 220–221, 321, 341, 357, 363
Regulation, 4, 5, 7, 8, 11, 23, 39, 42, 47, 49, 52, 83, 87, 96, 144, 148, 158, 164, 165, 167, 169, 202, 262, 301, 302, 320, 325, 326, 332, 333, 336, 337, 351, 353, 355, 379, 391, 397
Remote, 109, 238–240, 242–246
Remote examination, 244
Remote learning, 238, 239, 242, 245, 246
Response, 4–10, 13, 14, 20, 22, 23, 32, 59, 60, 64, 70, 76, 92, 97, 98, 144, 151, 153, 156, 160, 179, 205, 220, 223, 224, 268, 269, 277, 282, 284–287, 300, 302, 304, 320
Right to adequate food, 177–205
Right to development, 259–263
Risk, 231
Risk spreading, 216, 233

S

Self-regulation, 38

Social norms, 4, 8, 10, 15–18, 22, 66, 76–78, 88, 89, 93, 94
Social protection, 185, 187, 194–200, 204, 205, 308
Solidarity, 93, 96, 216, 260, 306
Students' performance, 239, 240, 244, 245
Sustainability, 23, 68, 142, 309, 323, 326, 329, 330, 339, 341–343, 357, 358, 362
Sustainable development, 71, 260, 295–310

T
Termination for cause, 115–116
Trade-Related Aspects of Intellectual Property Rights (TRIPS), 125, 266–270, 272, 273, 275–281, 288–290

U
UN Agenda, 295–310
United States (US), 8, 17, 19, 21, 36–42, 45, 46, 52, 67, 89, 95, 106, 124, 125, 127, 133, 140, 148–150, 161, 165, 166, 169, 178, 179, 199, 217, 226, 227, 229–233, 266, 271–276, 296, 308, 316, 324–326, 329, 333–335, 345, 348, 350, 352–354, 359–362, 373, 374, 381, 384, 387–391, 393, 396–399

V
Vaccines, 3, 23, 63–65, 70, 75, 88, 125, 126, 194, 278, 285, 287–289, 326

W
World Health Organization (WHO), vii, 4–7, 10, 12, 13, 15, 17–19, 21, 22, 32, 33, 40, 59, 63, 69, 70, 75, 78, 80, 82–85, 87, 89, 91, 93, 94, 97, 113, 117, 125, 136, 137, 144, 146, 149, 155, 163, 164, 185–187, 189–192, 194, 196, 198, 205, 216, 222, 227, 233, 239–242, 245, 253, 271, 272, 274, 284, 285, 296, 298, 300, 301, 308, 316, 322, 327–329, 341, 354, 358, 359, 362–364, 377–379, 382–384, 389–391, 395
World Trade Organization (WTO), 125, 185, 266–268, 277–282, 284, 287–290, 298, 301, 305, 352

Printed by Printforce, the Netherlands